T0210529

Lecture Notes in Computer Science 8930

Commenced Publication in 1973
Founding and Former Series Editors:
Gerhard Goos, Juris Hartmanis, and Jan van Leeuwen

More information about this series at http://www.springer.com/series/7410

Frédéric Cuppens · Joaquin Garcia-Alfaro
Nur Zincir Heywood · Philip W.L. Fong (Eds.)

Foundations and Practice of Security

7th International Symposium, FPS 2014
Montreal, QC, Canada, November 3–5, 2014
Revised Selected Papers

 Springer

Editors
Frédéric Cuppens
TELECOM Bretagne
Cesson Sévigné
France

Nur Zincir Heywood
Dalhousie University
Halifax, NS
Canada

Joaquin Garcia-Alfaro
TELECOM SudParis
Evry
France

Philip W.L. Fong
University of Calgary
Calgary
Canada

ISSN 0302-9743   ISSN 1611-3349 (electronic)
Lecture Notes in Computer Science
ISBN 978-3-319-17039-8   ISBN 978-3-319-17040-4   (eBook)
DOI 10.1007/978-3-319-17040-4

Library of Congress Control Number: 2015935046

LNCS Sublibrary: SL4 – Security and Cryptology

Springer Cham Heidelberg New York Dordrecht London

Printed on acid-free paper

Springer International Publishing AG Switzerland is part of Springer Science+Business Media
(www.springer.com)

Preface

The 7th International Symposium on Foundations and Practice of Security (FPS 2014) was hosted by Concordia University, Montreal, Quebec, Canada, during November 3–5, 2014. FPS 2014 received 48 submissions, from countries all over the world. Each paper was reviewed by at least three committee members. The Program Committee selected 18 regular papers, 2 position papers and 5 short papers for presentation. The program was completed with two excellent invited talks given by Kui Ren (University of Buffalo) and Jean-Louis Lanet (University of Limoges and Inria Rennes).

Many people contributed to the success of FPS 2014. First, we would like to thank all the authors who submitted their research results. The selection was a challenging task and we sincerely thank all the Program Committee members, as well as the external reviewers, who volunteered to read and discuss the papers. We greatly thank the General Chair, Mourad Debbabi (Concordia University) and the Organization Chair Lingyu Wang (Concordia University) for their great efforts to organize and perfectly control the logistics during the Symposium. Finally, we also want to express our gratitude to the two Publication Chairs, Joaquin Garcia-Alfaro (Télécom SudParis) and Nur Zincir Heywood (Dalhousie University), and the webmaster Said Oulmakhzoune (Télécom Bretagne), for the huge work they provide for programming, editing the proceedings, and managing the website.

As security becomes an essential property in the Information and Communication Technologies, there is a growing need to develop efficient methods to analyze and design systems providing a high level of security and privacy. We hope the articles in this proceedings volume will be valuable for your professional activities in this area.

December 2014

Frédéric Cuppens
Philip W.L. Fong

Organization

General Chair

Mourad Debbabi   Concordia University, Canada

Program Chairs

Frédéric Cuppens   Télécom Bretagne, France
Philip W.L. Fong   University of Calgary, Canada

Organization Chair

Lingyu Wang   Concordia University, Canada

Publication Chairs

Joaquin Garcia-Alfaro   Télécom SudParis, France
Nur Zincir Heywood   Dalhousie University, Canada

Webmaster

Said Oulmakhzoune   Télécom Bretagne, France

Program Committee

Diala Abi Haidar	Dar Al-Hekma College, Saudi Arabia
Carlisle Adams	University of Ottawa, Canada
Esma Aïmeur	Université de Montréal, Canada
Gildas Avoine	INSA, Rennes, France
Guillaume Bonfante	Université de Lorraine, LORIA, France
Jordi Castellà-Roca	Rovira i Virgili University, Spain
Ana Cavalli	Télécom SudParis, France
Frédéric Cuppens	Télécom Bretagne, France
Nora Cuppens-Boulahia	Télécom Bretagne, France
Mila Dalla Preda	University of Bologna, Italy
Jean-Luc Danger	Télécom ParisTech, France
Mourad Debbabi	Concordia University, Canada
Nicola Dragoni	Technical University of Denmark, Denmark
Philip W.L. Fong	University of Calgary, Canada
Sara Foresti	Università degli Studi di Milano, Italy
Eric Freyssinet	Université Paris 6, France

Sebastien Gambs	Université de Rennes 1, France
Joaquin Garcia-Alfaro	Télécom SudParis, France
Ali Ghorbani	University of New Brunswick, Canada
Roberto Giacobazzi	University of Verona, Italy
Sylvain Guilley	Télécom ParisTech, France
Abdelwahab Hamou-Lhadj	Concordia University, Canada
Jordi Herrera	Universitat Autònoma de Barcelona, Spain
Bruce Kapron	University of Victoria, Canada
Hyoungshick Kim	SungKyunKwan University, South Korea
Evangelos Kranakis	Carleton University, Canada
Pascal Lafourcade	Université de Clermont 1, France
Yassine Lakhnech	Joseph Fourier University, France
Georgios Lioudakis	National Technical University of Athens, Greece
Luigi Logrippo	Université du Québec en Outaouais, Canada
Stefan Mangard	Infineon Technologies AG, Germany
Jean-Yves Marion	École Nationale Supérieure des Mines de Nancy, France
Joan Melia-Segui	Universitat Pomepu Fabra, Spain
Ali Miri	Ryerson University, Canada
Guillermo Navarro-Arribas	Universitat Autónoma de Barcelona, Spain
Jordi Nin	Universitat Politècnica de Catalunya, Spain
Andreas Pashalidis	Katholieke Universiteit Leuven, Belgium
Emmanuel Prouff	Agence Nationale de la Sécurité des Systèmes d'Information, France
Silvio Ranise	FBK-Irst, Italy
Jean-Marc Robert	École de technologie supérieure, Montreal, Canada
Alessandro Sorniotti	SAP Research, France
Anna Squicciarini	Pennsylvania State University, USA
Chamseddine Talhi	École de technologie supérieure, Montreal, Canada
Nadia Tawbi	Université Laval, Canada
Alexandre Viejo	Rovira i Virgili University, Spain
Lena Wiese	Georg-August-Universität Göttingen, Germany
Nicola Zannone	Eindhoven University of Technology, The Netherlands
Mohammad Zulkernine	Queen's University, Canada

Additional Reviewers

Shivam Bhasin
Sofiene Boulares
Jordi Casas-Roma
Elisa Costante
Jannik Dreier
Raul Armando Fuentes Samaniego
Samuel Paul Kaluvuri
Thomas Korak
Amrit Kumar
Vinh Hoa La
Aouadi Mohamed
Huu Nghia Nguyen

Florian Praden
Sujoy Ray
Diego Rivera
Thomas Roche
Giada Sciarretta
Mouna Selmi
Hari Siswantoro
Bernard Stepien
Fatih Turkmen
Mario Werner
Thomas Zefferer

Contents

Short Papers

Attacks and Vulnerabilities

On Acoustic Covert Channels Between Air-Gapped Systems

Brent Carrara$^{(\boxtimes)}$ and Carlisle Adams

School of Electrical Engineering and Computer Science,
University of Ottawa, Ottawa, ON, Canada
{bcarr092,cadams}@uottawa.ca

Abstract. In this work, we study the ability for malware to leak sensitive information from an air-gapped high-security system to systems on a low-security network, using ultrasonic and audible audio covert channels in two different environments: an open-concept office and a closed-door office. Our results show that malware installed on unmodified commodity hardware can leak data from an air-gapped system using the ultrasonic frequency range from 20 kHz to 20.5 kHz at a rate of 140 bps and at a rate of 6.7 kbps using the audible spectrum from 500 Hz to 18 kHz. Additionally, we show that data can be communicated using ultrasonic communication at distances up to 11 m with bit rates over 230 bps and a bit error rate of 2 %. Given our results, our attacks are able to leak captured keystrokes in real-time using ultrasonic signals and, using audible signals when nobody is present in the environment - the **overnight attack**, both keystrokes and recorded audio.

Keywords: Malware communication · Audio communication · Ultrasonic · Jumping air-gaps · Out-of-band covert channels

1 Introduction

Physically separating computers on a high-security network from computers on a low-security network is a security practice that is commonly employed in high and medium security environments to protect sensitive information from unauthorized access [12,22]. This security practice prevents malware on the low-security network from attacking computers on the high-security network by means of traditional virus and worm network propagation vectors (e.g. e-mail, network shares, web servers, and web clients). The physical separation between the two networks is commonly referred to as an **air-gap**, a term that predates wireless networks, because of the literal physical air-gap separation between the two networks.

Air-gapped networks are employed in many industrial and government settings, including military [12], financial [12], nuclear power [22], and aviation [27] environments. In addition to being used in high-security environments, the practice of using air-gapped machines is recommended by security researchers (see Schneier [23], for example) and even Osama bin Laden was reported to have used

© Springer International Publishing Switzerland 2015
F. Cuppens et al. (Eds.): FPS 2014, LNCS 8930, pp. 3–16, 2015.
DOI: 10.1007/978-3-319-17040-4_1

one to protect his communications while in seclusion [6]. Given Schneier's setup in [23], once the air-gapped machine is configured and disconnected from the network there is no risk that a machine connected to the Internet (low-security machine) could access the air-gapped system via the network. Even so, there are still a number of ways that malware could be installed on the air-gapped system including a malicious insider [19], trojan horse executable [25], malicious payload in a trusted file format [24], or a malicious actor in the supply chain [4]. Once the malware is installed on the air-gapped system, the software requires a covert channel to propagate data to and from the low-security network. A covert channel can be characterized as a channel that has a low probability of intercept (LPI) and when evaluating a covert channel, the adversary and the adversary's capabilities must be assumed so that the effectiveness of the adversary's ability to detect the presence of the covert channel can be evaluated.

In our study, we analyzed the ability for malware introduced onto an air-gapped system, using any of the methods described above, to communicate sensitive information to a remote system on a low-security network using an *out-of-band covert channel*, the audio channel, in real-world settings. We studied both ultrasonic audio communication in the range of 20 kHz to 22 kHz (20 kHz is understood to be the cutoff frequency that can be heard by a young person, which decreases with age [9]) and audible audio communication in the range of 0 Hz to 20.5 kHz. Our results demonstrate that, in general, captured keystrokes, encryption key material (e.g. private keys, shared keys), credentials (e.g. passwords), documents, and even recorded audio can effectively be leaked from compromised air-gapped systems. Furthermore, our attack requires no hardware modifications to the air-gapped system or any system on the low-security network. Our attack requires only that the air-gapped system be equipped with a speaker and that a system on the low-security network be equipped with a microphone. Additionally, we consider our victim as unaware and unassuming of our attack and therefore measure the covertness of our channel by a human's natural ability to hear the communication.

In our study, we analyzed the effectiveness of our attack, i.e. the malware's ability to leak data using audio communications, in two traditional office environments: a closed-door office containing a single desk and multiple computers (approximately 3 m × 3 m × 2.8 m in dimension) and an open-concept office containing four desks, each holding multiple computers (approximately 4.27 m × 4.27 m × 2.8 m in dimension). Furthermore, we evaluated the ability for malware to covertly communicate within both of these environments in two different scenarios: the malware on the air-gapped system leaks data from the air-gapped machine when humans are present in the room (i.e. during regular business hours) and the malware leaks data from the compromised air-gapped machine after hours when no humans are present (i.e. after regular business hours), an attack we call the **overnight attack**.

As a result of our study, we make the following novel contributions:

1. We demonstrate that, in general, unmodified commodity hardware from major hardware vendors is capable of the following:

    (a) communication using the ultrasonic spectrum (i.e. 20 kHz to 20.5 kHz) at bit rates greater than 140 bps and bit error rates (BERs) below 10 %.

    (b) communication using the audible spectrum (i.e. 0 Hz to 20 kHz) at bit rates greater than 6.7 kbps and BERs below 15 %.

2. We introduce the concept of the **overnight attack** and demonstrate that, given our achievable bit and BERs, the threat of the overnight attack challenges the traditional threat model that is based on the assumption that covert audio communication is strictly low-bandwidth [7,8].

3. We demonstrate that covert ultrasonic audio communication is an effective mechanism for leaking data, including captured keystrokes in real-time, from air-gapped systems in real-world environments (e.g. open-concept and closed-door offices) under real-world settings (e.g. people talking and a radio playing nearby).

4. We demonstrate that ultrasonic communication can leak data from compromised systems at distances up to 11 m at bit rates of over 230 bps and a BER of 2 %.

Our paper is organized as follows. In Sect. 2, we review the related literature. In Sect. 3, we introduce the acoustic channel, its effects on audio communication, and the physical environments we studied in this work. In Sect. 4, we present our experiments in detail as well as our results. Furthermore, in Sect. 5, we present protection mechanisms that can be employed to detect our attack and, finally, in Sect. 6, we conclude.

2   Related Work

Utilizing audio signals for the purpose of covert communication and leaking information from an air-gapped system has previously been discussed in [7,8,19]. In [7], Hanspach, et al., built a proof-of-concept network using five identical Lenovo laptops to demonstrate that audio communication between the computers can be achieved in the near-ultrasonic range from 17 kHz to 20 kHz. Their research demonstrates that frequency-hopping spread spectrum (FHSS) with 48 sub-channels can be used effectively to establish a covert channel capable of transmitting data at a rate of 20 bps up to a distance of 19.7 m. While novel, their research demonstrates extremely low bit rates and their paper provides no in-depth BER analysis. Furthermore, their study only examines the ability of five identical model laptops, Lenovo T400, running Debian Linux to communicate with one another. In contrast to their study, we demonstrate our attack on multiple systems from various manufacturers running both Mac OS X and Windows. Furthermore, we demonstrate that orthogonal frequency-division multiplexing (OFDM) is a much more appropriate modulation scheme given the nature of the audio channel and that as a result of using OFDM we are able to effectively demonstrate bit rates over 25x faster than those previously reported using the near-ultrasonic and ultrasonic bandwidths. In [8], Hanspach, et al., documented the ability to communicate using the same Lenovo T400 model laptops, over the ultrasonic range from 20.5 kHz to 21.5 kHz at a speed of 20 bps up to a range of 8.2 m. In our study, we found that, in general, commodity hardware has difficulty reliably communicating above 20.5 kHz, but that bit rates above 200 bps can be achieved, in general, in the 20 kHz to 20.5 kHz bandwidth. In [7,8], Hanspach, et al., also proposed filtering out near-ultrasonic and ultrasonic frequencies from all audio being sent to the speakers as a defensive mechanism. This technique would be ineffective against our **overnight attack**. In [19], O'Malley, et al., established a covert channel between a MacBook Pro and a Lenovo Tablet using Frequency Shift Keying (FSK) in the ultrasonic range between 20 kHz and 23 kHz using an external speaker. The bit rates they achieved using external hardware, in the ultrasonic range, are comparable to ours; however, in our attack no additional hardware is required.

The use of audio has also been researched as an alternative to traditional wireless communication (e.g. infrared (IR), Bluetooth, radio frequency (RF), Wi-Fi, and near-field communications (NFC)); however, due to the relatively low bandwidth available in the channel when compared to IR and RF as well as the negative impacts of audio on humans and animals, this alternative solution has been primarily only studied in academic circles [5,10]. In [5], Gerasimov, et al., studied the use of audio communication over-the-air for the purposes of device-to-device communication and were able to achieve bit rates of 3.4 kbps, about half the bit rate we were able to achieve using the spectrum from 0 Hz to 20 kHz. In [13–15], researchers examined the ability to communicate using audio signals that are pleasant to humans to exchange pre-authorization information required for wireless networks as well as uniform resource locators (URLs). The researchers synthesized audio signals using frequencies from musical scales, chords, and lullabies as well as from fictional characters (e.g. R2D2 from Star Wars) and insects. Similarly, in [3], Domingues, et al., studied the ability to communicate using audio signals that sound like musical instruments (e.g. piano, clarinet, and bells). In [16,17], Madhavapeddy, et al., examined audio communication as an alternative to Bluetooth wireless communication through the use of dual-tone multi-frequency (DTMF) signalling, on-off keying and melodic sounds. Of relevance to our study, Madhavapeddy, et al., studied ultrasonic communication between two laptops with third-party speakers. Lastly, in [18], Nandakumar, et al., experimented with audio communication as an alternative to NFC.

3   Acoustic Channel

In this section, we take an in-depth look at the characteristics of the acoustic channel and demonstrate, by way of measurement, that the over-the-air channel causes multipath delays and has a non-ideal frequency response.

3.1   Environments Studied and System Requirements

The main goal of our study was to challenge the existing threat model posed by unauthorized audio communication between air-gapped systems. Previous researchers have demonstrated the ability to use audio signals to bridge the

Table 1. Machines and parameters of our study

ID	Make	Model	Distance, ∠ in closed environment	Distance, ∠ in open environment
Audio1	Lenovo	IdeaPad S10	1.19 m, 50 °	3.89 m, 4 °
Audio2	Lenovo	ThinkPad X120e	1.55 m, 10 °	N/A, N/A
Audio3	Dell	Precision T3500	1.88 m, 33 °	3.68 m, 21 °
Audio4	HP	HP Mini	1.50 m, 38 °	1.47 m, 90 °
Audio5	Acer	Aspire One	1.91 m, 355 °	3.33 m, 335 °
Audio6	Alienware	M15X	2.36 m, 330 °	1.45 m, 305 °
Audio7	Sony	Vaio	2.11 m, 340 °	3.84 m, 47 °
Audio8	Apple	MacBook Pro	N/A, N/A	N/A, N/A

air-gap; however, they have only demonstrated very limited bit rates on very specific hardware in constrained environments [7,8,19]. Our study shows that not only is audio communication possible using unmodified commodity hardware but that the achievable bit rates in both the ultrasonic and audible ranges are well above what has previously been reported. Our work demonstrates that audio provides an effective covert channel to communicate low volumes of data, such as captured keystrokes and cryptographic key material, as well as more substantial data streams, such as captured audio.

In our study, we placed a desktop with a USB headset as well as seven laptops in two real-world office environments. In all our experiments, the MacBook Pro, **Audio8**, was used as the air-gapped system and the remaining seven systems were connected to the low-security network. The distances and angles between **Audio8** and the other machines can be seen in Table 1 for both our environments, where an angle of 0° can be taken to be directly in front of **Audio8** and positive offset angles are measured clockwise. The systems in our study were all configured with Windows 7, aside from the MacBook Pro, which was configured with OS X 10.9. Additionally, none of the machines in our study had any hardware added or modified with the exception of the Dell desktop, **Audio3**, which had a USB headset with a microphone and speaker added because it had none built in. Unfortunately, our Lenovo ThinkPad, **Audio2**, suffered from a hardware failure following our closed-door office tests and was unavailable for testing during our open-concept office tests.

The detailed hardware and configuration requirements for the systems in our study are summarized here:

- **Air-Gapped System:**
  1. An audio speaker
  2. No network connections to the low-security machines
  3. Configured according to the steps outlined in [23]
- **Low-Security System:**
  1. A microphone

Given the uniform manner in which the systems were configured we feel that our study's environmental model closely mimics a real-world corporate office where the same version of Windows is installed on every machine. It should be noted that, for the sake of brevity, we only show detailed bit rate and BER results with the MacBook Pro as the air-gapped system using uni-directional communication. In Sect. 4, we provide the combined microphone and speaker frequency responses of each of the other machines' speakers and the MacBook Pro's microphone in order to assure the reader that all the machines tested are capable of transmitting audio signals in the audible and ultrasonic ranges in addition to receiving them.

3.2 Measured Channel Characteristics in Our Environments

To properly engineer our attack, we measured the noise and the reverberations caused by objects in the environment as well as the frequency response of the microphones and speakers built into the systems used in our study. In this section, we present the experiments we used to measure each of these quantities.

It has previously been reported that audible background noise drops off exponentially with frequency [26]. For the purposes of our study, we noted that the noise levels in our environment, in general, are quite low. Particularly at frequencies above 5 kHz and especially so for frequencies above 10 kHz. This is due to a combination of factors: equipment in our environment is generating very little audible background noise at frequencies above 5 kHz and the frequency response of the microphones in the systems we studied are not as sensitive to frequencies above 10 kHz as they are to frequencies between 0 Hz and 10 kHz. Furthermore, ultrasonic communication is not subject to the same degree of background noise that audible communication is subject to. This manifests itself in our results through the fact that the error rates for ultrasonic communication are lower than the error rates for audible communication.

We quantified the *multipath spread* of the channel in our environments by performing two experiments. In the first, we transmitted a 100 ms signal from **Audio8** consisting of pure-tone frequencies between 5 kHz and 10 kHz at 500 Hz intervals and, in the second, we transmitted a 100 ms signal from **Audio8** consisting of pure-tone frequencies between 20 kHz and 22 kHz also at 500 Hz intervals. To measure the *multipath spread* of the channel, we took the two received waveforms, filtered out all frequencies outside of the passbands (e.g. 5 kHz to 10 kHz and 20 kHz to 22 kHz, respectively), then cross-correlated them with the original signal according to the algorithm in [20]. We then plotted the normalized magnitude of the cross-correlated signals over time to determine the *multipath spread* for two dB thresholds, −10 dB and −15 dB. Our experiment showed that copies of our original signal were received for 175 ms at the −10 dB threshold after the line-of-sight signal was received and 200 ms at the −15 dB threshold in the closed-door environment using audible signals. The observed reverberations varied from system to system due to their location in the room. Given the results of our experiments in the closed office setting, we performed experiments using delays of 125 ms for our tests using ultrasonic frequencies and

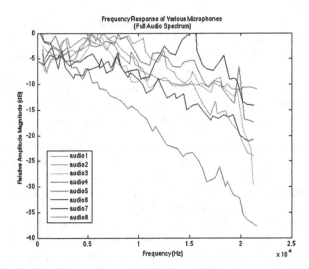

Fig. 1. The combined normalized frequency response of the audio channel. From the diagram it is clear that, over the $W = 0\,\mathrm{Hz}$ to $22.05\,\mathrm{kHz}$ bandwidth, the channel does not have an ideal frequency response.

delays of 175 ms and 225 ms for our tests using audible frequencies. For our tests in the open-concept office environment, we performed experiments using 80 ms for our ultrasonic tests and 125 ms and 150 ms for our audible tests as there were much fewer echoes to deal with in the open-concept environment.

The frequency responses of the systems are shown in Fig. 1. All quantities are in dB and are normalized to the highest amplitude received by each of the speakers for any frequency component. An ideal frequency response would show as a horizontal line at the 0 dB level across all frequencies. From the figure it can be seen that the audio channel used in our study does not have an ideal frequency response. Furthermore, the majority of the frequency responses demonstrate a near-ideal response up to around 5 or 6 kHz. This is to be expected as the human voice consists primarily of frequencies between 300 Hz and 3.4 kHz [2] and it would be expected that the manufacturers of the microphones would design a device that has an ideal frequency response in this range. Given the non-ideal frequency response of the audio channel, we used OFDM as our modulation scheme. We divided the available channel bandwidth, W, into a number of equal-bandwidth sub-channels, N, such that each of the sub-channels has an ideal frequency response. We then modulated symbols using FSK on each sub-channel.

4   Experiments and Results

We performed a number of experiments in both the open-concept and closed-door office environments to determine the achievable bit rates and corresponding BERs using audio communication in the ultrasonic and audible frequency ranges. We measured the achievable bit rates to better model the threat posed by malware using an audio covert channel to leak sensitive data from an air-gapped machine. By quantifying the achievable bit rates we are able to determine the type of sensitive data that can be leaked by malware in real-world scenarios. We tested our attack in real-world environments (e.g. open-concept office, closed-door office) under real-world conditions (e.g. radio playing, people talking) in real-world scenarios (e.g. when humans are present, when they are not). In this section, we present the results of the following experiments:

1. In both the open-concept and closed-door office environments, we varied the channel bandwidth, W, the delay or *settle time*, k, and the number of sub-channels, N, to determine the maximum bit rate at which we could communicate with the lowest BER (note that increasing W, increasing N, and decreasing k all increase our effective bit rate).
2. Given the optimal bandwidth, *settle time*, and number of sub-channels, we attempted to communicate in the ultrasonic spectrum while a clock radio was playing a local radio station in the closed-door office environment.
3. Given the optimal bandwidth, *settle time*, and number of sub-channels, we attempted to communicate in the ultrasonic spectrum while conversations were taking place in the closed-door office environment.
4. We used **Audio7** to determine the maximum distance that we could communicate over using our ultrasonic attack.
5. Lastly, we tested **Audio8**'s ability to receive ultrasonic communication from each of the other machines in our study.

In Fig. 2, we show the BER for our ultrasonic tests using the $W = 20\,\text{kHz}$ to 20.5 kHz bandwidth. From the figure it can be seen that as we increased the number of channels in the ultrasonic experiments, our BER increased dramatically.

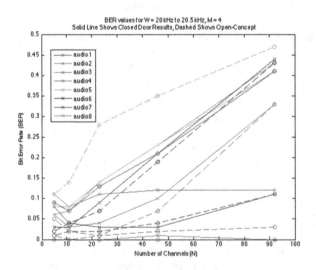

Fig. 2. BER for our ultrasonic tests in both the open-concept and closed-door environments.

Table 2. Average time (s) to leak popular document types

Document type	Average size (kb) per page [1]	Leak time using **overnight attack**
Microsoft Word	15	3.27
Microsoft Excel	6	1.31
Microsoft PowerPoint	57	12.42
Portable Document Format	100	21.79
Text	1.5	0.33
Email	10	2.18
Tagged Image File Format	65	14.16

In the closed-door office environment we achieved a BER of approximately 10 % or less for all machines with $N = 5$ and $N = 11$ and in the open-concept environment we also achieved a BER of 10 % with $N = 5$. With $N = 11$ all machines had a BER below 10 % except our Acer machine, **Audio5**, in the open-concept environment. This was due to the increased distance between **Audio8** and **Audio5** in our two environments, i.e. 1.91 m in the closed-door environment versus 3.33 m in the open-concept environment. The corresponding bit rates for $N = 5$ and $N = 11$ were 140 bps and 189 bps respectively. The results of our tests using the $W = 20 \,\text{kHz}$ to $21 \,\text{kHz}$ bandwidth produced BERs above 20 % and 25 % for all machines in the closed-door and open-concept environments, respectively. This leads us to conclude that receiving ultrasonic signals above 20.5 kHz is not generally well supported in commodity hardware at the distances we tested.

Although not shown, we were able to communicate using the combined near-ultrasonic and ultrasonic ranges (i.e. 18 kHz and above) using $N = 17$ subchannels for an effective bit rate of over 500 bps and BERs of 10 % and 15 % in the closed-door office and the open-concept office environments, respectively. As a comparison, previous researchers were only able to achieve a bit rate of 20 bps with a BER of 0 % using the same bandwidth. Furthermore, in our tests using the audible spectrum (i.e. $W = 0 \,\text{Hz}$ to $20.5 \,\text{kHz}$), we achieved BERs below 10 % and 15 % for the closed-door and open-concept environments respectively, with the exception again being **Audio5**, which achieved a BER of 19 % in the open-concept tests. We used $N = 812$ to achieve these results, which gave us a bit rate of over 6.7 kbps. We were also able to transmit data at a rate over 8.7 kbps using $W = 500 \,\text{Hz}$ to $20.5 \,\text{kHz}$ and $N = 1857$ to achieve BERs below 25 % and 30 % for all machines in the closed-door and open-concept office experiments, respectively.

In order to reduce our error rates to acceptable levels, an $[n, k, d]$ block code (where n is the block length, k is the message length, and d is the distance), capable of correcting $\lfloor \frac{d-1}{2} \rfloor$ random errors, such as $[n, k, n - k + 1]$ Reed-Solomon Codes [21], could be used. To correct up to 10 % and 15 % bit errors using Reed-Solomon codes, an overheard of approximately 20 % and 30 %

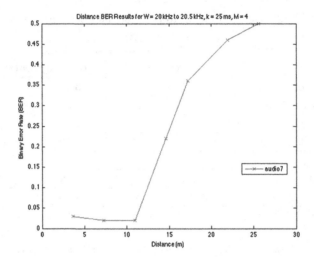

Fig. 3. BER for our distance experiment. We tested **Audio8**'s ability to communicate with **Audio7** over increasing distances. The parameters for the distance tests were $W = 20$ kHz to 20.5 kHz, $k = 25$ ms, $M = 4$, and $N = 46$.

is respectively required. Given our results, our bit rates after error correcting would then be reduced to 112 bps and 4.7 kbps using the ultrasonic and audible frequency ranges, respectively. To put these data rates into perspective, an individual typing 7-bit ASCII text at 80 words per minute and an average word length of 5.1 characters would produce data at an average rate of 47.6 bps. Similarly, voice can be streamed using the LPC-10 codec at 2.4 kbps [11]. Given these bit rates, our **overnight attack** can effectively leak both keystrokes and recorded audio data. Additionally, Table 2 provides average document sizes in kilobits (kb) and the amount of time that would be required to leak the document using our **overnight attack**. Lastly, both our attacks are effectively able to leak cryptographic key material such as a 256-bit shared key within seconds.

Using the parameters $W = 20$ kHz to 20.5 kHz, $k = 25$ ms, $M = 4$, and $N = 11$, we tested our ultrasonic attack with both a clock radio playing in the background as well as conversations taking place in the room while data was being leaked. We saw our resulting BER only increase marginally. This was due to the fact that while the human voice is predominantly composed of frequencies below 4 kHz there are still some near-ultrasonic and ultrasonic frequencies present which interfered with our data symbols. We noted that the majority of the energy in the clock radio and the conversations was in the 0 Hz to 15 kHz bandwidth and, in general, did not adversely affect our ultrasonic communication. Additionally, in order for our test to be performed in true ultrasonic fashion our pilot signal needed to be set to an ultrasonic frequency. In our experiments we used a pure-tone pilot signal at 20 kHz. Although this did work in most cases, some of the equipment, namely **Audio4**, **Audio5**, and **Audio6** had issues reliably picking up a 20 kHz pilot tone.

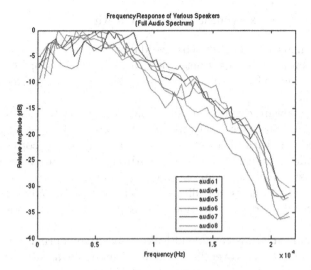

Fig. 4. The combined normalized frequency response of the audio channel. Each curve represents the frequency response of the channel with each of the machines in the study as the transmitter and **Audio8** as the receiver. Although the received signal strength in the ultrasonic range from 20 kHz to 20.5 kHz is relatively low, ultrasonic frequencies are still present.

Additionally, we performed a distance experiment to determine the maximum distance over which we could transmit ultrasonic signals as a means to compare our results to previous work. To determine our maximum transmission range we set up **Audio8** to transmit to our Sony laptop, **Audio7**, over increasing distances in 3.66 m (12') increments from 3.66 m to 25.60 m (84'). The results of our experiment are shown in Fig. 3. Our attack using ultrasonic communication is able to effectively communicate up to distances of 11 m with BERs under 2 % and up to a distance of 15 m with BERs around 20 %. With $W = 20$ kHz to 20.5 kHz, $k = 25$ ms and $N = 46$, we are able to communicate at over 230 bps. With error correcting we are therefore able to communicate at a distance of 15 m with an effective bit rate of 138 bps. As a comparison, the researchers in [8] were only able to communicate 20 bps up to a maximum distance of 8.2 m with a BER of 0 %.

Lastly, we performed an experiment to measure **Audio8**'s ability to receive ultrasonic communication from all the other machines in our study. In our experiment we placed each of the other systems, with the exception of **Audio2** and **Audio3**, 1 m in front of **Audio8** and played the same broadband white noise sample that we used to determine the frequency response of the channel in our previous experiment. We then plotted the combined frequency response of the other systems' speakers and **Audio8**'s microphone. The results are shown in Fig. 4. From the figure it is clear that the frequency response of the channel as observed by the microphone in **Audio8** is similar to the frequency response curves shown in Fig. 1. For the sake of brevity, we present this as evidence that the other systems in our study are capable of transmitting ultrasonic signals.

The results of our experiments show the following:

1. In general, malware can leak sensitive data using ultrasonic communication to systems on a low-security network at a bit rate of 140 bps (112 bps after error correction) with all machines observing a pre-error corrected BER of 10 % or under.
2. In general, malware can leak sensitive data using our **overnight attack** to systems on a low-security network at a bit rate of 6.7 kbps (4.7 kbps after error correction) with all machines observing a pre-error corrected BER of 15 % or under (the exception being **Audio5**, which experienced a BER of 19 %, at least 4 % higher than all other machines).
3. Our ultrasonic attack is not affected by either a clock radio playing music in the environment or conversations taking place while the communication is taking place.
4. Our ultrasonic attack is capable of leaking sensitive information at distances up to 11 m and bit rates over 230 bps. Furthermore, ultrasonic communication can be used to leak sensitive information at a distance of 15 m and a bit rate of 138 bps.
5. In general, all the systems in our study can produce ultrasonic signals in the $W = 20$ kHz to 22 kHz range.

5   Protection Mechanisms

Our attack can be eliminated by physically removing any speakers from the high security machine. If removal is not possible, disabling the speaker in software is the next best option; however, disabling the speaker in software could be overwritten by malware installed on the machine and could therefore provide a false sense of assurance to users of high security machines that our attack is not possible. The most effective way to detect our attack is to passively monitor the audio channel for abnormally high peaks of energy, especially in areas of the spectrum where there are typically none (e.g. the ultrasonic frequency range above 20 kHz). An effective way to detect our attack would be to periodically perform the fast Fourier transform (FFT) of the ambient audio in the environment and examine the resulting frequency components for abnormally high peaks. By calculating the FFT and comparing the resulting energy levels in a given bandwidth to some baseline or by checking if the resulting energy is above a certain threshold, our attack could be detected. With this method however, the distance from the transmitter is of utmost importance. If the device scanning the ultrasonic spectrum is too far from the transmitter, these approaches will not work. Furthermore, while we have discussed this countermeasure for our ultrasonic attack, this methodology works similarly for our **overnight attack** with the spectrum analysis simply shifted down into the audible range. Lastly, we feel it is imperative that this analysis be done by a specialized hardware device that is less likely to be attacked by malware that could render it ineffective.

6 Conclusion

In this work, we studied the ability for malware to leak sensitive information to low-security machines using ultrasonic and audible audio communication. We measured the achievable bit rate and BERs when transmitting signals in the 20 kHz to 20.5 kHz range as well as the 0 Hz to 20.5 kHz range using commodity hardware from a number of major laptop and desktop vendors. Our study showed that, in general, data can be communicated using ultrasonic communication at a bit rate of 140 bps with BERs below 10 %. Furthermore, we showed that malware can leak information when nobody is around to hear it, using an attack we call the **overnight attack**, at a rate of 6.7 kbps with a BER below 15 %. Additionally, we showed that our ultrasonic attack is not affected by ambient conversations taking place at the same time as the communication, nor by a radio playing a local radio station. Lastly, we showed that data can be communicated using ultrasonic communication across distances up to 11 m and at bit rates over 230 bps and a BER of 2 %. Given the achievable bit rates, our attack is able to leak captured keystrokes in real-time using the ultrasonic attack and both keystrokes and recorded audio using the **overnight attack**. A passive detection strategy was also presented.

References

1. File sizes and types (2014). http://help.netdocuments.com/file-sizes/
2. Baken, R.J., Orlikoff, R.F.: Clinical Measurement of Speech and Voice. Cengage Learning, Clifton Park (2000)
3. Domingues, N., Lacerda, J., Aguiar, P.M., Lopes, C.V.: Aerial communications using piano, clarinet, and bells. In: 2002 IEEE Workshop on Multimedia Signal Processing, pp. 460–463. IEEE (2002)
4. Ellison, R.J., Goodenough, J.B., Weinstock, C.B., Woody, C.: Evaluating and mitigating software supply chain security risks. Technical report, DTIC Document (2010)
5. Gerasimov, V., Bender, W.: Things that talk: using sound for device-to-device and device-to-human communication. IBM Syst. J. **39**(3.4), 530–546 (2000)
6. Goldman, A., Apuzzo, M.: How bin Laden emailed without being detected (2011). http://www.nbcnews.com/id/43011358/
7. Hanspach, M., Goetz, M.: On covert acoustical mesh networks in air. J. Commun. **8**(11), 758–767 (2013)
8. Hanspach, M., Goetz, M.: Recent developments in covert acoustical communications. In: Sicherheit, pp. 243–254 (2014)
9. Kinsler, L.E., Frey, A.R., Coppens, A.B., Sanders, J.V.: Fundamentals of Acoustics, 4th edn., p. 560. Wiley-VCH, December 1999. ISBN: 0-471-84789-5
10. Landström, U.: Noise and fatigue in working environments. Environ. Int. **16**(4), 471–476 (1990)
11. Lee, K.S., Cox, R.V.: A very low bit rate speech coder based on a recognition/synthesis paradigm. IEEE Trans. Speech Audio Process. **9**(5), 482–491 (2001)
12. Lindqvist, U., Jonsson, E.: A map of security risks associated with using COTS. Computer **31**(6), 60–66 (1998)

13. Lopes, C.V., Aguiar, P.M.: Aerial acoustic communications. In: 2001 IEEE Workshop on the Applications of Signal Processing to Audio and Acoustics, pp. 219–222. IEEE (2001)
14. Lopes, C.V., Aguiar, P.M.: Acoustic modems for ubiquitous computing. IEEE Pervasive Comput. **2**(3), 62–71 (2003)
15. Lopes, C.V., Aguiar, P.M.: Alternatives to speech in low bit rate communication systems. arXiv preprint. arXiv:1010.3951 (2010)
16. Madhavapeddy, A., Scott, D., Sharp, R.: Context-aware computing with sound. In: Dey, A.K., Schmidt, A., McCarthy, J.F. (eds.) UbiComp 2003. LNCS, vol. 2864, pp. 315–332. Springer, Heidelberg (2003)
17. Madhavapeddy, A., Sharp, R., Scott, D., Tse, A.: Audio networking: the forgotten wireless technology. IEEE Pervasive Comput. **4**(3), 55–60 (2005)
18. Nandakumar, R., Chintalapudi, K.K., Padmanabhan, V., Venkatesan, R.: Dhwani: secure peer-to-peer acoustic NFC. In: Proceedings of the ACM SIGCOMM 2013 Conference on SIGCOMM, pp. 63–74. ACM (2013)
19. O'Malley, S.J., Choo, K.K.R.: Bridging the air gap: inaudible data exfiltration by insiders. In: 20th Americas Conference on Information Systems (AMCIS 2014), pp. 7–10 (2014)
20. Proakis, J.G.: Digital Communications. McGraw-Hill, New York (2008)
21. Reed, I.S., Solomon, G.: Polynomial codes over certain finite fields. J. Soc. Ind. Appl. Math. **8**(2), 300–304 (1960)
22. Sanger, D.E.: Obama order sped up wave of cyberattacks against Iran. The New York Times 1, 2012 (2012)
23. Schneier, B.: Air Gaps (2013). http://aiweb.techfak.uni-bielefeld.de/content/ bworld-robot-control-software://www.schneier.com/blog/archives/2013/ 10/air_gaps.html?utm_source=feedburner&utm_medium=feed&utm_ campaign=Feed%3A+feedburner%2FbDnSB+(Schneier+on+Security)
24. Stallings, W.: Network Security Essentials: Applications and Standards. Pearson Education, India (2007)
25. Szor, P.: The Art of Computer Virus Research and Defense. Pearson Education, Indianapolis (2005)
26. Tempest, W.: The Noise Handbook. Academic Press, New York (1985)
27. Zetter, K.: FAA: Boeings new 787 may be vulnerable to hacker attack (2008). http://www.wired.com/politics/security/news/2008/01/dreamlinersecurity

Location-Dependent EM Leakage
of the ATxmega Microcontroller

Thomas Korak[✉]

Institute for Applied Information Processing and Communications (IAIK),
Graz University of Technology, Inffeldgasse 16a, 8010 Graz, Austria
thomas.korak@iaik.tugraz.at

Abstract. Nowadays, low power microcontrollers are widely deployed
in wireless sensor networks, also implementing cryptographic algorithms.
These implementations are potential targets of so-called side-channel
analysis (SCA) attacks which aim to reveal secret information, e.g. a
secret key. In this work we evaluate the resistance of AES implementations on an *Atmel AVR XMEGA* microcontroller against SCA attacks
using the electromagnetic (EM) emanation measured at different locations on the chip surface from the front side and the rear side. Results
show that the exploitable leakage for correlation attacks of a software
implementation is higher compared to the leakage of the AES crypto
engine, a hardware accelerator implemented on the microcontroller. Further investigations show that front-side EM measurements lead to better
results and the measurement location is crucial if the number of measurements is limited.

Keywords: Microcontroller · CEMA · Wireless sensor networks ·
Wireless sensor nodes · AES

1 Introduction

Microcontrollers are widely used in all kinds of applications nowadays. One reason for the exhaustive usage is the great amount of functionalities they provide
as well as their flexibility compared to application-specific integrated circuits
(ASICs). One popular field of application is that of wireless sensor networks
(WSN). WSNs consist of several sensor nodes which communicate with each
other over a wireless channel. Each WSN typically has one base station which
acts as the master in the network and forwards the received data from the sensor nodes to a backend system. The data transmitted by the sensor nodes varies
depending on the field of application. WSNs are employed e.g. in healthcare
systems, for environmental monitoring, energy monitoring or building administration. In order to make attacks like eavesdropping or data alteration infeasible
the data is encrypted before transmission. Due to the data encryption additional
computational costs are introduced. The additional computational costs need to
be minimized because sensor nodes are typically battery powered and the battery lifetime needs to be maximized. In order to achieve a long battery lifetime,

© Springer International Publishing Switzerland 2015
F. Cuppens et al. (Eds.): FPS 2014, LNCS 8930, pp. 17–32, 2015.
DOI: 10.1007/978-3-319-17040-4_2

efficient cryptographic primitives need to be used and implemented in an efficient way. Besides energy, code size and RAM size are also limited resources on sensor nodes.

One popular cryptographic primitive is the Advanced Encryption Standard (AES), a standardized block cipher. AES supports three key lengths (128 bits, 192 bits, or 256 bits) depending on the required security level. Software implementations of AES exist for nearly every microcontroller platform. Some microcontrollers (e.g. ATxmega, TI MSP430) also have an integrated AES hardware accelerator (AES crypto engine). The usage of an AES hardware accelerator allows faster data encryption/decryption and also parallel execution of other tasks during encryption/decryption. Besides the efficiency of the data encryption/decryption, the leakage of secret information (e.g., the secret key) caused by side channels has to be analysed. Typical side channels with a correlation with secret information are the runtime of the algorithm, the power consumption or the electromagnetic (EM) emanation of the device.

1.1 Related Work

The Rijndael algorithm [6] was standardized by the US National Institute of Standards and Technology (NIST) as the Advanced Encryption Standard (AES) in 2001. Today, AES is among the most frequently used block ciphers. In wireless sensor networks, AES is used to encrypt the transmitted data in order to prevent eavesdropping or data alteration, meaning that the block cipher is used in a special operation mode [15].

AES is proven to be mathematically secure, but side-channel analysis (SCA) attacks are still feasible due to implementation-specific properties. These type of attacks use some key-dependent leakage in the power consumption (e.g., by Kocher et al. [13]), the EM emanation (e.g., by Gandolfi et al. [8]) or the runtime (e.g., by Kocher et al. [12]) of the cryptographic algorithm.

There have been several SCA attacks on implementations of the AES on various platforms in the past. In [18] the authors show an AES key extraction of an FPGA implementation in less than 0.01 s. In this work the authors point out that the signal-to-noise ratio on the attacked device is 30 dB to 40 dB lower than an implementation on an ATxmega microcontroller. Kizhvatov et al. [11] have performed a power-analysis attack on the hardware accelerator included in ATxmega microcontrollers. This article serves as the basis for our work.

The AES implementation is often also a building block for higher-layer cryptographic protocols. In [9] the authors use an AES hardware accelerator for an authenticated encryption algorithm. In [20], the authors take advantage of an AES hardware accelerator in order to create hash-based signatures.

Several works also deal with the implementation issues for cryptographic primitives, which arise because of the existing constraints for sensor nodes used in WSNs. In [4], the authors focus on the energy efficiency of security algorithms for WSN devices. They also compare software implementations with hardware accelerators from the point of view of energy efficiency. Rehman et al. [16] compare different encryption techniques for message authentication codes (MACs) in WSNs. In [21] a security mechanism for WSNs, called *MoteSec-Aware*, is presented. *MoteSec-Aware* is based on the AES.

1.2   Our Contribution

When studying the related work above, it is clearly observable that the AES is the most popular encryption algorithm for sensor nodes, so this algorithm is the target for our attacks. Atmel's ATxmega microcontroller is frequently used for sensor-node applications as the list of sensor nodes [22] shows. It also has a AES crypto engine integrated, which makes it the perfect device for our evaluations. In contrast to [11] we use the EM emanation of the device for the SCA attacks on the ATxmega microcontroller. One advantage of the EM side channel when compared to the power-consumption side channel is that no modification of the attacked circuit is required (e.g. inserting a resistor in order to enable power consumption measurements).

The contributions of this work can be summarized the following:

- We compare the EM leakage of a software AES implementation with the EM leakage of the AES crypto engine of the ATxmega microcontroller. Results show very similar leakage patterns for both implementations.
- EM signals are measured at different locations on the chip to find out at which point the maximum leakage appears. This information is helpful in scenarios where only a limited number of measurements is available and the approach can be applied on any device.
- We further compare two different power models for attacking the AES crypto engine, one based on the Hamming weight of an intermediate value and the other one based on the Hamming distance between two register values. The second power model has been used in [11].
- EM signals are measured from the front side and the rear side of the chip in order to compare the amount of exploitable leakage. Results show that front-side measurements lead to better results.
- We practically show that the number of required encryptions for a successful attack can be decreased by combining the EM signal in specific points.

1.3   Outlook

In Sect. 2 we introduce the microcontroller used in the experiments. A short introduction to the Advanced Encryption Standard as well as information about the software and hardware implementation is provided in Sect. 3. Section 4 explains the experimental setup as well as the results of the practical experiments. A discussion of the results can be found in Sect. 5. Some conclusions as well as future work are given in Sect. 6.

2   Used Microcontroller

In this section we introduce the microcontroller which was used for the evaluations. We decided to use an AVR XMEGA microcontroller, the ATxmega 256A3 to be exact. Due to the low power consumption, the high integration as well as the real-time performance this microcontroller is frequently used on wireless sensor nodes. Furthermore it has an AES hardware accelerator (in the following named as *AES crypto engine*) implemented.

In the following section we provide some more detailed facts about the ATxmega 256A3 microcontroller. The ATxmega 256A3 has 256 kB in-system self-programmable flash memory, 8 kB of boot-code section, 4 kB EEPROM, and 16 kB SRAM. The CPU is based on the AVR enhanced RISC architecture equipped with 32 general purpose working registers. The microcontroller can be operated with voltages between 1.6 V and 3.6 V and the maximum clock frequency is 32 MHz. Additional features are: One 16 bit Real-time counter, 16 bit timer/counter for PWM and compare modes, serial interface, ADCs, one DAC, 50 general-purpose I/O lines, and several other microprocessor-specific features. In addition to the AES crypto engine a DES accelerator is also included. The DES accelerator is out of the scope of this work, so no detailed description about this feature is provided. For more detailed information about the ATxmega 256A3 we refer to the datasheet [3]. Typical applications for this microcontroller are industrial control, factory automation, metering, and medical applications, to mention only a few. Although it is not explicitly noted as a high-security device we are sure that the cryptographic features the microcontroller provides are used frequently. So it makes sense to analyze possible weaknesses of these features.

3   AES Implementations

In this section, a short description of the AES algorithm in general is given followed by an introduction to the software AES implementation for the ATxmega microcontroller. The AES crypto engine is also introduced in this section.

3.1   Description of AES

The Advanced Encryption Standard (AES) is a symmetric block cipher. It supports a block size of 128 bits (equals state size) and key sizes of 128 bits, 192 bits and 256 bits. The cipher is round-based and generates one block of cipher text in 10, 12 or 14 rounds, depending on the used key length. Four transformations are performed on the state in each round: round-key addition (*add round-key*), byte substitution (*Sbox lookup*), byte permutation (*shift rows*), and a matrix operation (*mix column*). Further information about the AES can be found in [5,6].

For correlation attacks, which are performed in this work, an intermediate value (IV) of the attacked implementation has to be found which depends on a known input (e.g. plain text) and the secret key. In the case of AES the IV after the *Sbox lookup* in the first AES round is a popular choice. This value is calculated using $IV_i = Sbox(p_i \oplus k_i)$ where p_i is one byte of the known plain text and k_i is one byte of the secret key. For AES-128, both the plain text and the secret key have a length of 128 bits ($i = 1 \ldots 16$). The resulting cipher text also has a length of 128 bits. The Hamming weight of IV_i, written as $HW(IV_i)$, serves as the power model. The Hamming weight of a value equals the sum of ones of its binary representation [14]. In the following we denote the key guesses for byte position i as $k_{g,i}$ and the correct key at byte position i as $k_{c,i}$.

3.2   Software AES Implementation

The software AES implementation is written in assembler. The implementation is optimized for fast encryption/decryption and no countermeasures against SCA attacks or fault attacks are implemented. The round key is calculated after each round and the byte substitution is implemented as a table lookup. It takes 4 054 clock cycles to encrypt one block of plain text. This is close to the 3 766 clock cycles given in [17].

3.3   AES Crypto Engine

The AES crypto engine requires 375 clock cycles to encrypt one block of plain text and it supports a key length of 128 bits. Comparing the run time of the AES crypto engine with the figures given for the software implementation it can be said that the AES crypto engine is approximately ten times faster. The usage of the AES crypto engine allows to perform other tasks in parallel to the encryption process.

Detailed information about the crypto engine can be found in [2]. In order to perform an encryption the plain text must be loaded into the AES State Register and the key into the AES Key Register. In the AES Control Register the decrypt bit has to be cleared and the encryption process is then started by setting the start bit. An interrupt as well as the status bit in the AES Control Register indicate when the encryption is finished. The cipher text equals the content of the AES State Register. The hardware crypto engine also supports the cipher block chaining (CBC) mode of operation in order to increase the efficiency when using CBC. For this purpose, it is necessary to set the XOR bit in the AES Control Register.

4   Practical SCA Experiments

In this section, the measurement setup used to record the EM traces is introduced. Then, a description of the performed experiments is given, followed by the results achieved for the software implementation and for the AES crypto engine, respectively.

4.1   Measurement Setup

In order to perform the measurements we have implemented a simple program on the microcontroller. After setting the AES key with an initial command, the plain text followed by a single control byte is sent to the microcontroller using the serial interface. This control byte is used to select which implementation should be used for the encryption. The value $00h$ indicates that the software implementation should be used and $01h$ indicates that the AES crypto engine should be used. Just before the encryption process starts, one output pin (trigger pin) of the microcontroller is set to high. Setting the pin to low again indicates that the encryption is finished. In a last step the result is sent back to the control computer. This setup clearly indicates that we know the key of the attacked device. This fact simplifies the creation of two-dimensional EM-leakage landscapes.

A probe manufactured by *Langer EMV Technik* (model: *LF B 3*) has been used to measure the EM emanation of the chip. The signal of the probe was amplified with a 30 dB amplifier. The amplified signal was digitized using a *LeCroy WavePro 725Zi* oscilloscope. The sampling rate on the oscilloscope was set to 1 GS/s and the microcontroller was clocked with a frequency of 13.56 MHz.

Figure 1(a) shows the grid on the chip, where the probe has been placed in order to measure the EM signal, from the front side. The grid has a size of 9×9 points, leading to a total of 81 points. The distance between the points is 1 mm. Figure 1(b) shows the grid on the chip for the measurements from the rear side. Here, we have removed the package material in order to measure directly on the chip die. The chip die has a size of 5 mm × 5 mm. For the rear-side measurements, the focus was put on the die area, so a step size of 0.55 mm was used leading to a grid of 9×9 points again. In both cases, the probe has been moved using a stepper table. This allowed us to automate the measurement process up to a high degree. The amplitude of the measured EM signal varied for different points. Because of this observation, a calibration step in each point was performed before the traces were recorded. This calibration step ensures the same resolution of the voltage values in each point.

Figure 1(c) shows the board where the microcontroller is mounted on. Using this board it is hardly possible to perform power measurements without irreversible modifications. This is true for most real-world devices. Therefore, EM measurements are the best choice for measuring side-channel information. However, in order to perform the rear-side measurements, we had to develop a custom board which allows to mount the chip inverted.

4.2   Experiment Descriptions

Location-Dependent EM Leakage: For verification of the location-dependent EM leakage N EM traces were recorded in every point P ($P = 1 \ldots 81$). The measurement interval covered the first AES round and the same set of N random plain texts was used in each point. In total $81 \cdot N$ traces were recorded. A correlation EM analysis (CEMA) attack was performed for each of the points separately. In order to validate the success of the location-dependent correlation attacks the absolute value of the factor ρ_{border} (Eq. 1) was subtracted from the absolute maximum correlation coefficient of the correct key ($\rho_{c,P}$). ρ_{border} is a function of the number of used traces N and the derivation of ρ_{border} can be found in [14]. 99.99 % of all the correlation values are in this border. If $|\rho_{c,P}| > |\rho_{border}|$, the correct key can be distinguished from the remaining key guesses. The resulting vector $\bar{\rho}_{margin}$ has a

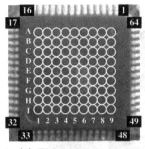 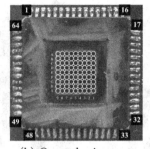 

(a) EM measurement points, front side. (b) Opened microcontroller, rearside. (c) Microcontroller board, front side.

Fig. 1. The attacked microcontroller.

length of 81 (Eq. 2). Positive values indicate that the attack is successful and negative values indicate that the attack fails in the specific point. For visualization reasons all negative values of $\bar{\rho}_{margin}$ were set to zero. In order to map the vector $\bar{\rho}_{margin}$ to the locations, the vector is transformed into a 9 x 9 matrix M according to Eq. 3. The 1st entry in the 1st row corresponds to point $A1$, and the 9th entry in the last row corresponds to point $I9$.

$$\rho_{border} = \pm\frac{4}{\sqrt{N}} \tag{1}$$

$$\bar{\rho}_{margin} = [|\rho_{c,1}|, |\rho_{c,2}|, \ldots, |\rho_{c,81}|] - |\rho_{border}| \tag{2}$$

$$M = \begin{bmatrix} \rho_{margin,1} & \rho_{margin,2} & \cdots & \rho_{margin,9} \\ \rho_{margin,10} & \rho_{margin,11} & \cdots & \rho_{margin,18} \\ \vdots & \vdots & \ddots & \vdots \\ \rho_{margin,73} & \rho_{margin,74} & \cdots & \rho_{margin,81} \end{bmatrix} \tag{3}$$

Relation Between EM Leakage and Number of Traces: In the next experiment the number of traces used for the correlation attacks was gradually reduced during several iteration. For each iteration the matrix M was visualized in a two-dimensional plot. The resulting plots visualize the leakage locations for different numbers of traces.

4.3 Results for Software Implementation

Location-Dependent EM Leakage: The first experiments targeted the AES software implementation. $N = 2000$ traces were recorded in each point, which leads to a total of $2000 \cdot 81 = 162\,000$ traces. This number was sufficient for the location-dependent EM leakage verification. For the correlation attack the Hamming weight of the output of the first substitution box, $HW(Sbox(p_i \oplus k_{g,i}))$, served as power model. Figure 2 shows the EM leakage landscape. The brighter the point is, the higher $\bar{\rho}_{margin}$ in that point. Black points indicate regions where

24   T. Korak

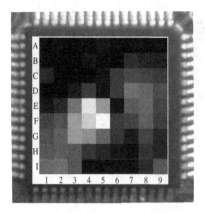

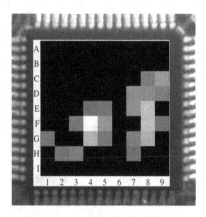

Fig. 2. Landscape of the leakage of the AES software implementation using 2000 traces.

Fig. 3. Landscape of the leakage of the AES crypto engine using 10 000 traces and the Hamming weight power model.

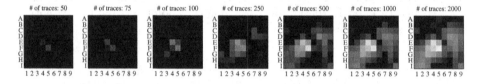

Fig. 4. EM-leakage landscape for different numbers of traces used for the CEMA attacks on the software AES implementation.

the attack yields a wrong key byte. The results discussed in this paragraph were achieved for key byte 1, the attacks targeting key bytes 2 to 16 lead to similar results. Due to the clear results, we did not further evaluate rear-side measurements for the software implementation.

Relation Between EM Leakage and Number of Traces: Figure 4 depicts the relation between CEMA success expressed by $\bar{\rho}_{margin}$ and the number of measurements used for the CEMA attack. With 50 measurements, the correct key can be extracted in two points. The fewer measurements are available, the more critical the location where the EM side-channel signal is measured.

4.4   Results for AES Crypto Engine

For the CEMA attacks targeting the AES crypto engine, two different power models were used. The first power model, which will be referred to as Hamming distance model in the rest of this paper, is the model used in [11]. This model takes into account two subsequent bytes of the plain text (p_i, p_{i+1}) and two bytes of the key $(k_{g,i}, k_{g,i+1})$: $HW((p_i \oplus k_{g,i}) \oplus (p_{i+1} \oplus k_{g,i+1}))$. The second model, named Hamming weight model, is the same model as is used for attacking

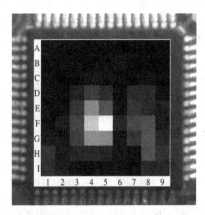

Fig. 5. Landscape of the leakage of the AES crypto engine using 10 000 traces, the Hamming distance power model and front-side measurements.

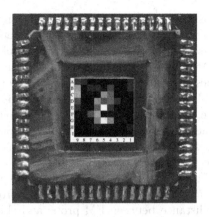

Fig. 6. Landscape of the leakage of the AES crypto engine using 10 000 traces, the Hamming distance power model and rear-side measurements.

the software implementation: $HW(Sbox(p_i \oplus k_{g,i}))$. The disadvantage of the Hamming distance model is that two 8 bit values $k_{g,i}, k_{g,i+1}$ are unknown and as a result the complexity of the attack increases. Instead of 2^8 key hypotheses, 2^{16} key hypotheses are required in theory. In [11] the authors show that the complexity can be decreased. To achieve this, they perform a full key recovery for all the 256 key values for the first key byte. Applying an exhaustive search, the correct key can be extracted from the 256 candidates in a final step. If the value of only one key byte is known (e.g., by using the Hamming weight model in a first step) all the other values can be revealed iteratively and the exhaustive search can be prevented. Furthermore, measurements captured from the front side and the rear side of the chip are analyzed.

Location-Dependent EM Leakage: For the CEMA attacks targeting the AES crypto engine, 10 000 EM traces were recorded in each point, once from the front side and once from the rear side. As mentioned in [11], 3 000 traces are sufficient to reveal the correct key bytes when using power measurements. Taking this as a reference point, 10 000 traces seemed to be a realistic value in order to achieve meaningful results.

First, CEMA attacks were performed in each point using the Hamming weight model. The landscape of the EM leakage in each point is plotted in Fig. 3 for front side measurements. It is clearly visible that there are several locations where the attack reveals the correct key byte value. With the Hamming weight model and rear-side measurements, no successful attacks could be performed.

Second, the experiments above were repeated using the Hamming distance model. Figure 5 shows the landscape of the EM leakage for front-side measurements and Fig. 6 shows the landscape of the EM leakage for rear-side measurements. Here, several locations can be detected where the attacks reveal the correct key byte for measurements from both sides of the chip. For these attacks we assume that one key byte is known, resulting again in 2^8 key hypotheses. By comparing the results for the attacks using front-side measurements and rear-side measurements, the following observations can be made:

Attacks using the measurements from the front side lead to higher correlation values. Wires from the metal layers on top of the chip produce the exploitable EM signals. Therefore, front-side measurements seem to be better suited to capture these signals, although there is some package material between probe and chip surface. The fact, that measurements from the front side contain more exploitable leakage than rear-side measurements has also been observed by Heyszl et al. [10]. Here the authors target an FPGA.

Correlation values for the wrong key hypotheses are smaller when using rear-side measurements. Opening the chip from the rear side allowed us to minimize the distance between EM probe and chip die. This smaller distance minimizes the measurement noise leading to smaller correlation values for the wrong key hypotheses.

Relation Between EM Leakage and Number of Traces: Figure 7 depicts the relation between CEMA success expressed by $\bar{\rho}_{margin}$ and the number of measurements used for the CEMA attack. Bright points indicate a location yielding a successful attack ($\rho_{margin} > 0$). Black points indicate a location where the attack fails ($\rho_{margin} = 0$).

Plot (a) depicts the evolution when using the Hamming weight model. 4 000 traces are necessary in order to reveal the correct key byte. When less than 4 000 traces are used the attacks do not succeed, i.e. the correct key byte cannot be distinguished from the wrong key guesses. The more traces are used the more points leak key-dependent information. Plot (b) depicts the evolution when using the Hamming distance model together with front-side measurements. When applying this model, 1 000 traces are necessary in order to reveal the correct key byte. The more traces are used the more points leak key-dependent information. Plot (c) depicts the evolution when using the Hamming distance model together with rear-side measurements. Here, 1 000 traces are necessary in order to reveal the correct key byte. Increasing the number of traces decreases the influence of the location.

5   Discussion of the Results

The results presented in Sect. 4 show that a software AES implementation on a microcontroller which is not secured against SCA attacks, can be successfully attacked within seconds even without modifying the device. Measuring the EM emanation does not require any modification. The attack reveals the correct key byte with only 50 traces. For attacks with this low number of traces, the location where the EM side-channel signal is measured is critical. From Fig. 8, it can be seen that attacks lead to correct results in only two points. The higher the number of traces, the less critical the influence of the location is. When using 2 000 traces, attacks at 62 of the 81 locations lead to correct results.

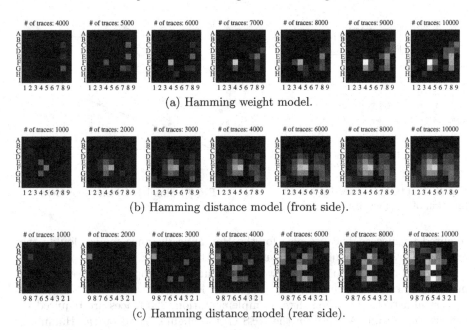

(a) Hamming weight model.

(b) Hamming distance model (front side).

(c) Hamming distance model (rear side).

Fig. 7. EM-leakage landscape for different numbers of traces used for the CEMA attacks on the AES crypto engine. Note that for (a) and (b) the covered area is 9×9 mm, while for (c) the covered area equals 5×5 mm.

The results achieved for the AES crypto engine clearly show that this hardware part is also not secured against SCA attacks. The leakage of the key-dependent signal is smaller, so more traces for a successful attack are required compared to the software implementation. Nevertheless, the factors of $\frac{1000}{50} = 20$ (Hamming distance model) and $\frac{4000}{50} = 80$ (Hamming weight model) do not indicate a security improvement compared to the software implementation. The additional measurement effort is negligible when keeping in mind the power of today's measurement equipment. As Fig. 8 shows, when using only 1 000 traces for the Hamming distance model, the attack only succeeds in six locations. The situation for the Hamming weight model is similar; here at least 4 000 traces are required and with this minimum number only the measurements at four out of 81 locations lead to successful attacks.

There are two important observations when comparing the results achieved for front-side and rear-side experiments. First, less measurements are required for a successful key recovery when front-side measurements are used although the chip for the rear-side measurements was opened to minimize the distance between probe and chip die. Interconnects in the metal layers on top of the chip create the EM signals and it seems that the silicon between probe and wires attenuates these signals stronger (rear-side measurements) than the package material (front-side). Second, the Hamming weight power model does not yield any successful attack when applied on the rear-side measurements for the AES crypto engine. Here, the assumption is that more than 10 000 traces are

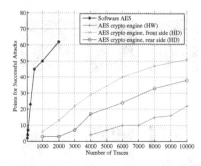
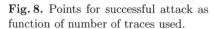
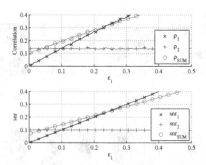

Fig. 8. Points for successful attack as function of number of traces used.

Fig. 9. Simulated leakage model.

required to succeed because also for the Hamming distance model double the amount of traces is required for a successful attack.

To draw a fair comparison between the four attack approaches, we give the number of traces, where at least 20 of the 81 locations (equals 24.7%) lead to successful attacks. For the software implementation, 220 traces are required to achieve this result. Attacks on the AES crypto engine, based on the Hamming distance model, required 2 780 traces (4 800 traces for rear-side measurements, respectively) to succeed in at least 20 locations. When using the Hamming weight model, attacks in at least 20 locations succeed when more than 9 700 traces are used. Table 1 summarizes the depicted results from Fig. 8.

In order to further improve the attacks (i.e., reduce the number of traces required for a successful attack) we present an approach where the EM signals of two measurement points are combined. A comparable multi-channel SCA attack is presented in [1]. In this work the authors show how to combine power and EM measurements attacking a DES implementation. As a result the number of measurements can be significantly reduced. Elaabit *et al.* [7] present two combined attacks: In the first attack, a four-bit model and a mono-bit model are combined resulting in a higher success rate. The second attack uses a combination of samples at different time instances to improve the success rate for

Table 1. The minimum number of traces required in order to reveal the correct key byte value in at least *Nr. of locations* locations.

Nr. of locations	Percentage %	SW AES	AES crypto engine		
			HW	HD,fs	HD,rs
10	12.3	125	6 000	1 570	3 300
20	**24.7**	**220**	**9 700**	**2 780**	**4 800**
30	37.0	330		4 180	7 400
40	49.4	440		6 000	
50	61.7	1 000		9 500	
60	74.1	1 830			

correlation power-analysis attacks. Souissi et al. [19] propose two methodologies for combined attacks. In the first approach commonly used side-channel distinguishers are combined. In the second approach EM signals caused by two specific decoupling capacitors are combined. Both approaches lead to a significant improvement of the attacks. In our attack the assumption is that the attacker has two similar EM probes measuring the EM emanation on the chip surface. This fact enables the attacker to measure the EM emanation at two different points in parallel. This assumption is realistic as most modern oscilloscopes provide four independent channels which allow for the recording of up to four signals in parallel. If the traces of two points with a high leakage are combined, the result of the attack can be improved. The sum of the two traces has been used as combination function. The traces participating to the sum were recorded at two different locations during the encryption process of the same plain text.

Before we present the practical results, we want to give a theoretical explanation. The leakage in two points can be expressed mathematically as L_1 and L_2, according to Eq. 4. The values c_1 and c_2 are constants, V_1 and V_2 are functions of the correct key byte k_c and the known plain-text byte p ($V = f(p, k_c)$). r_1 and r_2 are normal distributed random values with zero mean and standard deviation one ($r \sim \mathcal{N}(0,1)$, $\sigma \cdot r = \mathcal{N}(0,\sigma^2)$), representing the noise. We further assume that the leakage functions in the two points are similar ($V_1 = V_2 = V$). The signal-to-noise ratio (SNR) is calculated as given in Eq. 5.

$$L_1 = c_1 + \epsilon_1 \cdot V_1 + \sigma_1 \cdot r_1 \qquad L_2 = c_2 + \epsilon_2 \cdot V_2 + \sigma_2 \cdot r_2 \qquad (4)$$

$$snr_i = \frac{\epsilon_i}{\sigma_i}; \quad i = 1,2 \qquad (5)$$

Adding two traces in order to improve the attack, equals adding L_1 and L_2. The result of this summation is given in Eqs. 7 and 8, respectively. Equation 6 shows how to calculate the sum of two normal distributions with different values for the standard deviations. Equation 8 allows us to calculate the SNR for L_{SUM}, snr_{SUM} (Eq. 9). This result allows us to come to the conclusion, that the attack can only be improved by adding the leakage in two different points, if Eq. 9 holds.

$$\mathcal{N}(0,\sigma_1^2) + \mathcal{N}(0,\sigma_2^2) = \mathcal{N}(0,\sigma_1^2 + \sigma_2^2) = \sqrt{(\sigma_1^2 + \sigma_2^2)} \cdot \mathcal{N}(0,1) \qquad (6)$$

$$L_{SUM} = L_1 + L_2 = (c_1 + c_2) + (\epsilon_1 + \epsilon_2) \cdot V + \sigma_1 \cdot r_1 + \sigma_2 \cdot r_2 \qquad (7)$$

$$L_{SUM} = c_{SUM} + \epsilon_{SUM} \cdot V + \sqrt{(\sigma_1^2 + \sigma_2^2)} \cdot r_{SUM} \qquad (8)$$

$$snr_{SUM} = \frac{\epsilon_{SUM}}{\sqrt{(\sigma_1^2 + \sigma_2^2)}}; \qquad snr_{SUM} > max(snr_1, snr_2) \qquad (9)$$

In order to visualize the relation given in Eq. 9, we have performed a simulation using MATLAB. We have varied ϵ_1, which influences snr_1, while snr_2 has been kept constant for the whole simulation run. Figure 9 depicts the results of the simulation. The lower plot shows the SNR and the upper plot shows the evolution of the correlation coefficients for the two points and the sum, respectively. In the range where Eq. 9 holds, the summation leads to an improvement.

Table 2. Results of the CEMA attacks before and after the combination of traces recorded at two different locations.

Software AES, (Hamming weight, front side)				Gain / %
Location	E4	F5	E4 and F5	
N_{min}	43	40	29	27.5
AES crypto engine, (Hamming weight, front side)				**Gain / %**
Location	F4	F8	F4 and F8	
N_{min}	3086	4444	2215	28.2
AES crypto engine, (Hamming distance, front side)				**Gain / %**
Location	F5	G4	F5 and G4	
N_{min}	396	683	295	25.5
AES crypto engine, (Hamming distance, rear side)				**Gain / %**
Location	E5	G5	E5 and G5	
N_{min}	1890	1850	1093	40.9

By improvement, we mean $\rho_{SUM} > max(\rho_1, \rho_2)$. In practice, the SNR values are typically not known. To circumvent this, we recommend the combination of only two points where the single attacks yield to similar correlation coefficients ρ_1 and ρ_2, respectively. From Fig. 9, it can be seen that the combination yields the best result if $\rho_1 = \rho_2$.

In order to prove that the theoretical assumptions also hold true in practice, we have combined points with similar correlation coefficients from the experiments above and analysed the results. For the attack targeting the software implementation $\rho_{c,P}$ could be increased from 0.630 to 0.740. For the attacks targeting the AES crypto engine, $\rho_{c,P}$ could be increased from 0.072 to 0.085 (Hamming weight power model). For the Hamming distance power model, $\rho_{c,P}$ could be increased from from 0.201 to 0.233 (front-side measurements) and from 0.093 to 0.121 (rear-side measurements) respectively. Table 2 lists the achieved results for the combination of measurements at two different locations. Furthermore the value N_{min} is given. This value equals the minimum number of traces required for a successful attack when the correlation value $\rho_{c,P}$ is given. N_{min} is calculated according to Eq. 10 and the deviation can be found in [14].

$$N_{min} = (\frac{4}{\rho_{c,P}})^2 \tag{10}$$

6   Conclusion

In this work we have shown the location-dependent EM leakage of the ATxmega microcontroller. We have compared the leakage of a software AES implementation with the leakage of the AES crypto engine, a hardware accelerator for AES encryptions. For the software implementation, less than 50 traces are sufficient to reveal the AES key if the EM signal is measured at an appropriate position. Attacks targeting the AES crypto engine require about 700 EM measurements if captured from the front side and about 1 900 EM measurements if captured from the rear side. Again, an appropriate measurement position is a prerequisite. In all scenarios, the number of required measurements can be decreased if leakage information from two points are combined. Here, it is important that the signal-to-noise ratio (SNR) in the points which are combined is similar. This is shown in theory and verified in practical experiments.

The presented attacks pose a serious threat for sensor nodes, as the required number of EM measurements can be recorded in a few minutes and no modification of the circuit is required.

Acknowledgements. This work has been supported by the European Commission through the FP7 program under project number 610436 (project MATTHEW).

References

1. Agrawal, D., Rao, J.R., Rohatgi, P.: Multi-channel attacks. In: Walter, C.D., Koç, Ç.K., Paar, C. (eds.) CHES 2003. LNCS, vol. 2779, pp. 2–16. Springer, Heidelberg (2003)
2. Atmel. AVR1318: Using the XMEGA built-in AES accelerator (2008) (accessed 5 November 2013)
3. Atmel. 8/16-bit AVR XMEGA A3 Microcontroller (2013) (accessed 5 November 2013)
4. Botta, M., Simek, M., Mitton, N.: Comparison of hardware and software based encryption for secure communication in wireless sensor networks. In: Telecommunications and Signal Processing (TSP), pp. 6–10. IEEE (2013)
5. Paar, C., Pelzl, J.: Understanding Cryptography. Springer, Heidelberg (2010)
6. Daemen, J., Rijmen, V.: AES Proposal: Rijndael. NIST AES Algorithm Submission (September 1999). http://csrc.nist.gov/archive/aes/rijndael/Rijndael-ammended.pdf
7. Elaabid, M.A., Meynard, O., Guilley, S., Danger, J.-L.: Combined side-channel attacks. In: Chung, Y., Yung, M. (eds.) WISA 2010. LNCS, vol. 6513, pp. 175–190. Springer, Heidelberg (2011)
8. Gandolfi, K., Mourtel, C., Olivier, F.: Electromagnetic analysis: concrete results. In: Koç, Ç.K., Naccache, D., Paar, C. (eds.) CHES 2001. LNCS, vol. 2162, pp. 251–261. Springer, Heidelberg (2001)
9. Gouvêa, C.P.L., López, J.: High speed implementation of authenticated encryption for the MSP430X microcontroller. In: Hevia, A., Neven, G. (eds.) LatinCrypt 2012. LNCS, vol. 7533, pp. 288–304. Springer, Heidelberg (2012)
10. Heyszl, J., Merli, D., Heinz, B., De Santis, F., Sigl, G.: Strengths and limitations of high-resolution electromagnetic field measurements for side-channel analysis. In: Mangard, S. (ed.) CARDIS 2012. LNCS, vol. 7771, pp. 248–262. Springer, Heidelberg (2013)
11. Kizhvatov, I.:. Side-channel analysis of AVR XMEGA crypto engine. In: Proceedings of the 4th Workshop on Embedded Systems Security, p. 8. ACM (2009)

12. Kocher, P.C.: Timing attacks on implementations of diffie-hellman, RSA, DSS, and other systems. In: Koblitz, N. (ed.) CRYPTO 1996. LNCS, vol. 1109, pp. 104–113. Springer, Heidelberg (1996)
13. Kocher, P.C., Jaffe, J., Jun, B.: Differential power analysis. In: Wiener, M. (ed.) CRYPTO 1999. LNCS, vol. 1666, pp. 388–397. Springer, Heidelberg (1999)
14. Mangard, S., Oswald, E., Popp, T.: Power Analysis Attacks - Revealing the Secrets of Smart Cards. Springer (2007). ISBN 978-0-387-30857-9
15. National Institute of Standards and Technology (NIST). Special Publication 800–38A 2001 ED, Recommendation for Block Cipher Modes of Operation - Methods and Techniques (December 2001). http://csrc.nist.gov/publications/nistpubs/800-38a/sp800-38a.pdf
16. Rehman, S.U., Bilal, M., Ahmad, B., Yahya, K.M., Ullah, A., Rehman, O.U.: Comparison Based Analysis of Different Cryptographic and Encryption Techniques Using Message Authentication Code (MAC) in Wireless Sensor Networks (WSN) (2012). arXiv preprint arXiv:1203.3103
17. Rinne, S., Eisenbarth, T., Paar, C.: Performance Analysis of Contemporary Light-Weight Block Ciphers on 8-bit Microcontrollers (June 2007). http://www.crypto.ruhr-uni-bochum.de/imperia/md/content/texte/publications/conferences/lw_speed2007.pdf
18. Skorobogatov, S., Woods, C.: In the Blink of an Eye: There Goes your AES Key. IACR Cryptology ePrint Archive 2012:296 (2012)
19. Souissi, Y., Bhasin, S., Guilley, S., Nassar, M., Danger, J.-L.: Towards different flavors of combined side channel attacks. In: Dunkelman, O. (ed.) CT-RSA 2012. LNCS, vol. 7178, pp. 245–259. Springer, Heidelberg (2012)
20. Eisenbarth, T., von Maurich, I., Ye, X.: Faster hash-based signatures with bounded leakage. In: Lange, T., Lauter, K., Lisoněk, P. (eds.) SAC 2013. LNCS, vol. 8282, pp. 223–244. Springer, Heidelberg (2014)
21. Tsou, Y.-T., Lu, C.-S., Kuo, S.-Y.: MoteSec-Aware: a practical secure mechanism for wireless sensor networks. IEEE Trans. Wireless Commun. 12(6), 2817–2829 (2013)
22. Wikipedia. List of Wireless Sensor Nodes – Wikipedia, The Free Encyclopedia (2013) (accessed 4 November 2013)

Privacy

Privacy-Preserving Public Auditing in Cloud Computing with Data Deduplication

Naelah Alkhojandi$^{(\boxtimes)}$ and Ali Miri

Ryerson University, Toronto, Canada
{naelah.alkhojandi,ali.miri}@ryerson.ca

Abstract. Storage represents one of the most commonly used cloud services. Data integrity and storage efficiency are two key requirements when storing users' data. Public auditability, where users can employ a Third Party Audithor (TPA) to ensure data integrity, and efficient data deduplication which can be used to eliminate duplicate data and their corresponding authentication tags before sending the data to the cloud, offer possible solutions to address these requirements. In this paper, we propose a privacy-preserving public auditing scheme with data deduplication. We also present an extension of our proposed scheme that enables the TPA to perform multiple auditing tasks at the same time. Security and computational analyses for both cases are also presented.

Keywords: Cloud computing · Data deduplication · Public auditing · Third Party Auditor · Batch auditing · Privacy preservation

1 Introduction

One of the most important services in cloud computing is data storage, which allows users to store their data in the cloud. Although cloud storage offers many advantages, it also introduces new security challenges in data integrity and availability. To verify the integrity of data stored in the cloud and to save computational resources of cloud users, it is important to enable auditing services, including those done on behalf of users by a TPA that can check the integrity of their data. Some recent work in the literature has tried to tackle issues related to public auditing [1,6,7,11,12]. Some of this work considers protecting the privacy of user's data from the TPA, while others consider dynamic data. The authors of [1] propose a secure cloud storage system supporting privacy-preserving public auditing. Their work also includes an efficient scheme in which a TPA performs multiple auditing tasks in batch mode. In their proposed protocol, they utilize a public key scheme based on a Homomorphic Linear Authenticator (HLA) with random masking. Unlike previous auditing protocols, this scheme removes the need to download all the stored data, and it has improved communication and computation costs. The proposed protocol guarantees that the TPA cannot derive any knowledge from the stored data.

To increase storage efficiency, storage providers often identify and remove redundant data and keep only one copy of each file (file-level deduplication) or

© Springer International Publishing Switzerland 2015
F. Cuppens et al. (Eds.): FPS 2014, LNCS 8930, pp. 35–48, 2015.
DOI: 10.1007/978-3-319-17040-4_3

block (block-level deduplication). Data deduplication may occur before the data is transmitted to the cloud (client-side deduplication) or after it is transmitted (server-side deduplication) [2]. Standard server-side deduplication, in particular those associated with Cloud Service Providers (CSPs), require full access to the content of users' data, which may limit the types of information that can be stored by these types of services. In particular, storing sensitive organizational data may not be appropriate. Furthermore, although deduplication can be used with single user data, it has been reported [3] that an average of 60 % of data can be deduplicated for individual users by using a cross-user deduplication technique that identifies redundant data among different users.

The authors of [9] proposed the Public and Constant cost storage integrity Auditing scheme with secure Deduplication (PCAD). Although the paper considers public auditing with deduplication, it does not consider the privacy-preserving property. In addition, the deduplication is done on the cloud server at the file-level.

In the remainder of this paper, we use the results from [1,10] to propose a two-level privacy-preserving public auditing protocol, which enables cross-user data deduplication achieving both data integrity and storage efficiency. In our protocol, we only assume that the TPA and the CSP are semi-trusted, and we will prove that the TPA would not learn the content of users' data while performing its tasks. Our analytical and experimental results show the efficiency of our proposed protocol.

2   Problem Statement

Figure 1 depicts a typical setting for our proposed protocol. X-enterprise users' files are stored with a CSP. Any of these users should be able to use the services of a TPA to ensure the integrity of their data. To do so, prior to data upload, each user computes the signature of its data. To ensure publicly verifiable data deduplication, our protocol uses an enterprise level mediator. The mediator has two main tasks to perform. Its first task is to do a client-side deduplication to eliminate duplicated blocks before sending the data to the cloud, so the amount of uploaded data and the bandwidth used between the enterprise and the CSP are both reduced. Since users should have the ability to check the integrity of their own stored data, the mediator's second task helps with calculating aggregated signatures that can be used by the TPA to perform its task.

2.1   System Model:

We consider cloud storage services that involve four entities: *Cloud User (U):* who has large number of data files to be stored in the cloud; *Cloud Server (CS):* which is managed by the Cloud Service Provider (CSP) to provide data storage services and has significant storage space and computational resources; *Third Party Auditor (TPA):* who can verify the integrity of U's data upon request and on their behalf; and *Mediator:* who performs block-level deduplication on users'

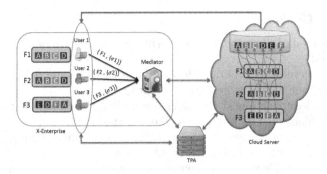

Fig. 1. The architecture of the proposed scheme

data before they are sent to the CSP, and also computes an aggregate signature for the duplicated blocks instead of sending multiple signatures with each block.

2.2 Threat Model:

The Mediator is trusted and allowed to see the content of the blocks and their signatures, but it is prohibited from knowing the private keys of the users, so it cannot generate a valid signature on behalf of any user. The TPA is semi-trusted and allowed to check the integrity of the blocks on behalf of the users/mediator, but it is prohibited from seeing the content of the blocks. The CS is semi-trusted and allowed to see the content of the blocks and their signatures, but it is required to follow the steps needed for the auditing process.

Protocol Overview:

Users have files that are to be sent to the cloud. Each user divides his file into n blocks and computes the signature of each block for integrity verification using his private key. Then the users send their files (blocks) with their signatures to the mediator. There is no interaction between the users during the signing process. The mediator calculates the hash value of each block and compares them to identify duplicated blocks. Then it calculates the aggregated signature of the duplicated blocks utilizing the multisignature scheme of [10]. Instead of sending one (identical) block with multiple signatures from multiple users, the mediator sends the aggregated signature with the block and deletes the local copy. The metadata of the deduplication process is stored locally and in the cloud. The TPA checks the data integrity on behalf of the users or the mediator upon request. To do so, it sends a challenge message to the cloud server to make sure that the cloud has retained the data properly. To generate that challenge, the TPA picks a random c-element subset of the set $[1, n]$. For each element, the TPA chooses a random value. The challenge message specifies the positions of the blocks required to be checked. The cloud server generates a proof of data storage correctness and sends it to the TPA. The TPA verifies the proof using a verification equation.

2.3 Design Goals:

1. Public audibility: allow the TPA to verify the correctness of the stored data in the cloud.
2. Storage correctness: ensure that the cloud cannot cheat and pass the auditing process without having stored the data intact.
3. Client-side deduplication at the block-level: allow the Mediator to eliminate duplicated blocks before sending the data to the cloud.
4. Privacy Preservation: ensure that the TPA cannot learn anything about content of the stored data during the audit process.
5. Lightweight: provide the scheme with low communication and computational overheads.
6. Batch auditing: allow the TPA to perform multiple auditing tasks at the same time.

We design two protocols that satisfy these goals. The first protocol provides the first five goals, whereas the second protocol described in Sect. 3.3 also provides support for batch auditing.

3 Proposed Protocols

For the sake of clarity, we begin with the case where two users have identical files. Then, we extend this case to where the two users have identical blocks of (possibly different) files.

Scheme Details. Let $\mathbb{G}_1$, $\mathbb{G}_2$, and $\mathbb{G}_T$ be multiplicative cyclic groups of prime order p, and $e : \mathbb{G}_1 \times \mathbb{G}_2 \to \mathbb{G}_T$ be a bilinear map. Let g be a generator of $\mathbb{G}_2$. $H(\cdot)$ is a secure map-to-point hash function $H:\{0,1\}^* \to \mathbb{G}_1$, and $h(\cdot)$ is a hash function $h: \mathbb{G}_T \to \mathbb{Z}_p$. We define the users as $U = \{u_1, \ldots, u_m\}$. User u_i has files F_i. The blocks are denoted by $m_{i,j}$ where $1 \le i \le k$ and $1 \le j \le n$, for some k and n.

3.1 Case 1: Two Users Have the Same File

Suppose we have two users who have the same file (same blocks) as described in Fig. 2. With no interaction, they send their files and signatures to the mediator who performs a block-level deduplication on the files and aggregates the signatures of the duplicate blocks. Then the mediator sends the files and the signatures after the deduplication process to the cloud. Assuming that user 1 asks the TPA to check the correctness of his files, we have the following:

Fig. 2. Case 1: Two users have the same file

- Setup phase: KeyGen: Each user u_i selects a random x_i in $\mathbb{Z}_p$, computes $y_i = g^{x_i}$, and selects a random u_i in $\mathbb{G}_1$. The user u_i's public and private keys (sk_i, pk_i) are set to be $(x_i, (y_i, g, u_i, e(u_i, y_i)))$. SigGen: Each user computes the signature of each block of his file as $\sigma_{i,j} = (H(m_{i,j}) \cdot u_i^{m_{i,j}})^{x_i} \in \mathbb{G}_1$. Then each user u_i sends $(F_i = \{m_{i,j}\}, \{\sigma_{i,j}\})$ to the Mediator. Dedup: The deduplication is done by the Mediator at the block-level. The mediator calculates the hash value of each block and compares them to identify the duplicates. Then it calculates the aggregated signatures of the duplicated blocks as $\sigma_j = \prod \sigma_{i,j}$. For example, $\sigma_A = \prod_{i \in L}(H(m_A) \cdot u_i^{m_A})^{x_i}$ and so on to the end of the file. After that, he sends $(F = \{m_j\}, \{\sigma_j\}, L)$ to the cloud, where L = the subgroup of users.
- Audit phase: the TPA can check the integrity of files/blocks on behalf of the users/mediator by sending $chal = \{(s, v_s)\}$ to the cloud server $s \in I = \{s_1, \ldots, s_c\}$ for the set of blocks $[1, n]$. GenProof: the cloud server selects $r \in \mathbb{Z}_p$, and computes $R_i = e(u_i, y_i)^r \in \mathbb{G}_T$. CS also computes $\mathcal{R} = R_1 \cdot \ldots \cdot R_m$, $\mathcal{L} = y_1 \| \ldots \| y_m$, and $\gamma = h(\mathcal{R}\|\mathcal{L})$. CS computes as well $\mu' = \sum_{s \in I} v_s \cdot m_s$, $\mu = r + \gamma \mu'$, and $\sigma = \prod_{s \in I} \sigma_s^{v_s}$. Then CS sends $\{\mu, \sigma, \{H(m_s)\}, \mathcal{R}, L\}$ to the TPA. VerifyProof: the TPA computes $\gamma = h(\mathcal{R}\|\mathcal{L})$, and verifies $\{\mu, \sigma, \{H(m_s)\}, \mathcal{R}, L\}$ via:

$$\mathcal{R} \cdot e(\sigma^\gamma, g) \stackrel{?}{=} \prod_{i \in L} e((\prod_{s \in I} (H(m_s)^{v_s})^\gamma \cdot u_i^\mu, y_i) \tag{1}$$

The correctness of the above verification equation is elaborated as follows:

$$\mathcal{R} \cdot e(\sigma^\gamma, g) = \prod_{i \in L} e(u_i, y_i)^r \cdot e((\prod_{s \in I} \sigma_s^{v_s})^\gamma, g)$$

$$= \prod_{i \in L} e(u_i, y_i)^r \cdot e(\prod_{s \in I} (\prod_{i \in L} ((H(m_s) \cdot u_i^{m_s})^{x_i})^{v_s})^\gamma, g)$$

$$= \prod_{i \in L} e(u_i, y_i)^r \cdot \prod_{i \in L} e(\prod_{s \in I} (H(m_s)^{v_s} \cdot u_i^{v_s \cdot m_s})^\gamma, y_i)$$

$$= \prod_{i \in L} e(\prod_{s \in I} (H(m_s)^{v_s})^\gamma \cdot u_i^{\mu'\gamma + r}, y_i)$$

$$= \prod_{i \in L} e((\prod_{s \in I} (H(m_s)^{v_s})^\gamma \cdot u_i^\mu, y_i)$$

3.2   Case 2: Two Users Have Identical Blocks

Suppose we have two users who have some identical blocks as described in Fig. 3. With no interaction, they send their files and signatures to the mediator. The latter performs a block-level deduplication on the files and aggregates the signatures of the duplicate blocks. Then, the mediator sends the files and the signatures after the deduplication process to the cloud. Assuming that user 1 asks the TPA to check the correctness of his file (e.g. F_1), we have the following:

- Setup phase: KeyGen, SigGen, and Dedup as in the previous case. The mediator calculates the aggregated signatures of the duplicated blocks as $\sigma_j = \prod \sigma_{i,j}$. For example, $\sigma_A = \prod_{i \in L}(H(m_A) \cdot u_i^{m_A})^{x_i}$, $\sigma_B = (H(m_B) \cdot u_1^{m_B})^{x_1}$ since this block is owned only by User 1, and $\sigma_C = \prod_{i \in L}(H(m_C) \cdot u_i^{m_C})^{x_i}$

Fig. 3. Case 2: Two users have some identical blocks

– Audit phase: the TPA can check the integrity of files/blocks on behave of the users/mediator by sending $chal = \{(s, v_s)\}$ to the cloud server $s \in I = \{s_1, \ldots, s_c\}$ for the set of blocks $[1, n]$. GenProof: the cloud server selects $r \in \mathbb{Z}_p$, and computes $R_i = e(u_i, y_i)^r \in \mathbb{G}_T$. CS also computes $\mathcal{R} = R_1 \cdot \ldots \cdot R_m$, $\mathcal{L} = y_1 \| \ldots \| y_m$, and $\gamma = h(\mathcal{R} \| \mathcal{L})$. CS computes $\mu_i' = \sum_{s \in I} v_s \cdot m_s$, $\mu_i = r + \gamma \mu_i'$ for each user u_i, and $\sigma = \prod_{s \in I} \sigma_s^{v_s}$. Then CS sends $\{\{\mu_i\}, \sigma, \{H(m_s)\}, \mathcal{R}, L\}$ to the TPA. VerifyProof: the TPA computes $\gamma = h(\mathcal{R} \| \mathcal{L})$, and verifies $\{\{\mu_i\}, \sigma, \{H(m_s)\}, \mathcal{R}, L\}$ via:

$$\mathcal{R} \cdot e(\sigma^\gamma, g) \stackrel{?}{=} \prod_{i \in L} e((\prod_{s \in I} (H(m_s)^{v_s})^\gamma \cdot u_i^{\mu_i}, y_i) \tag{2}$$

The correctness of the above verification equation is elaborated as follows:

$$\mathcal{R} \cdot e(\sigma^\gamma, g) = \prod_{i \in L} e(u_i, y_i)^r \cdot e((\prod_{s \in I} \sigma_s^{v_s})^\gamma, g)$$

$$= \prod_{i \in L} e(u_i, y_i)^r \cdot e((\prod_{s \in I} (H(m_s) \cdot u_i^{m_s})^{x_i})^{v_s})^\gamma, g)$$

$$= \prod_{i \in L} e(u_i, y_i)^r \cdot \prod_{i \in L} e(\prod_{s \in I} (H(m_s)^{v_s})^\gamma) \cdot u_i^{v_s \cdot m_s \cdot \gamma}, y_i)$$

$$= \prod_{i \in L} e(\prod_{s \in I} (H(m_s)^{v_s})^\gamma \cdot u_i^{\mu_i' \cdot \gamma + r}, y_i)$$

$$= \prod_{i \in L} e((\prod_{s \in I} (H(m_s)^{v_s})^\gamma \cdot u_i^{\mu_i}, y_i)$$

3.3   Support for Batch Auditing

The TPA may handle multiple auditing tasks from different users. It may be inefficient to treat them as individual tasks rather than batch them together

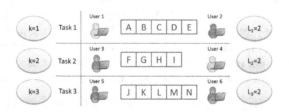

Fig. 4. Batch auditing of case 1

and audit at the same time. Suppose we have K auditing tasks on K distinct files from K different users. By modifying the protocols in the one user case, the aggregation of K verification equations is obtained.

Batch Auditing of Case 1: Two Users Have the Same File. Suppose there are L users who want to check K distinct files by delegating K auditing tasks. Each auditing task consists of two users who have the same file as described in Fig. 4. User 1 delegates auditing Task 1 ($k = 1$) of file $F1$, User 3 delegates auditing Task 2 ($k = 2$) of file $F2$, and User 5 delegates auditing Task 3 ($k = 3$) of file $F3$. Each auditing task has two users, so $L = 2$ for each task k. In general, each user k has a file $F_k = \{m_{k,1}, \ldots, m_{k,n}\}$, which is also owned by another user $u_{k,i}$, where $k \in \{1, \ldots, K\}$ and $i \in \{1, \ldots, L\}$.

Setup phase: Each user $u_{k,i}$ selects a random $x_{k,i} \to \mathbb{Z}_p$, computes $y_{k,i} = g^{x_{k,i}}$, and selects a random $u_{k,i} \to \mathbb{G}_1$. Denote the secret key and the public key of each user $u_{k,i}$ as $(sk_{k,i}, pk_{k,i}) = (x_{k,i}, (y_{k,i}, g, u_{k,i}, e(u_{k,i}, y_{k,i})))$. Then, each user computes the signature of each block of his file as $\sigma_{k,i,j} = (H(m_{k,i,j}) \cdot u_{k,i}^{m_{k,i,j}})^{x_{k,i}} \in \mathbb{G}_1$. Then it sends $(F_{k,i} = \{m_{k,i,j}\}, \{\sigma_{k,i,j}\})$ to the Mediator. The Mediator calculates the hash value of each block and compares them to identify the duplicates. Then it calculates the aggregated signatures of the duplicate blocks as $\sigma_{k,j} = \prod \sigma_{k,i,j}$. After that, the Mediator sends $(F_k = \{m_{k,j}\}, \{\sigma_{k,j}\}, L_k)$ to the cloud, where L is the subgroup of users.

Audit phase: the TPA sends the audit challenge $chal = \{(s, v_s)\}$ to the cloud server for auditing data files of all K users. Upon receiving $chal$, the cloud server selects $r \in \mathbb{Z}_p$ and computes $R_{k,i} = e(u_{k,i}, y_{k,i})^r \in \mathbb{G}_T$. The cloud server also computes $\mathcal{R} = R_{k,1} \cdot \ldots \cdot R_{K,m}$, and $\mathcal{L} = y_{k,1} \| \ldots \| y_{K,m}$. Then it computes $\gamma = h(\mathcal{R} \| \mathcal{L})$. The cloud generates the proof as follows: $\mu'_k = \sum_{s \in I} v_s \cdot m_{k,s}$, $\mu_k = r + \gamma \mu'_k$, and $\sigma_k = \prod_{s \in I} \sigma_{k,s}^{v_s}$. Then the cloud sends $\{\{\mu_k\}, \{\sigma_k\}, \{H(m_{k,s})\}, \mathcal{R}, \{L_k\}\}$ to the TPA. To verify the response, the TPA computes $\gamma = h(\mathcal{R} \| \mathcal{L})$ Next, he verifies $\{\{\mu_k\}, \{\sigma_k\}, \{H(m_{k,s})\}, \mathcal{R}, \{L_k\}\}$ via:

$$\mathcal{R} \cdot e(\prod_{k=1}^{K} \sigma_k^{\gamma}, g) \stackrel{?}{=} \prod_{k=1}^{K} (\prod_{i \in L} e((\prod_{s \in I} (H(m_{k,s})^{v_s})^{\gamma} \cdot u_{k,i}^{\mu_k}, y_{k,i})) \tag{3}$$

The correctness of the above verification equation is elaborated as follows:

$$\mathcal{R} \cdot e(\prod_{k=1}^{K} \sigma_k^{\gamma}, g) = R_{k,i} \cdot \ldots \cdot R_{K,m} \cdot \prod_{k=1}^{K} e(\sigma_k^{\gamma}, g)$$

$$= \prod_{k=1}^{K} (\prod_{i \in L} R_{k,i} \cdot e(\sigma_k^{\gamma}, g))$$

$$= \prod_{k=1}^{K} (\prod_{i \in L} e(u_{k,i}, y_{k,i})^r \cdot e(\sigma_k^{\gamma}, g))$$

$$= \prod_{k=1}^{K} (\prod_{i \in L} e((\prod_{s \in I} (H(m_{k,s})^{v_s})^{\gamma} \cdot u_{k,i}^{\mu_k}, y_{k,i}))$$

Batch Auditing of Case 2: Two Users Have Identical Blocks. Suppose there are L users who want to check K distinct files by delegating K auditing tasks. Each auditing task consists of two users who share some blocks as described in Fig. 5. User 1 delegates auditing Task 1 of file $F1$, User 2 delegates auditing Task 2 of file $F2$, and User 3 delegates auditing Task 3 of file $F3$. In general, each user k has a file $F_k = \{m_{k,1}, \ldots, m_{k,n}\}$, and some of these blocks are also owned by another user $u_{k,i}$, where $k \in \{1, \ldots, K\}$ and $i \in \{1, \ldots, L\}$.

Setup phase: As in the previous case.

Audit phase: the TPA sends the audit challenge $chal = \{(s, v_s)\}$ to the cloud server for auditing data files of all L users. Upon receiving $chal$, the cloud server selects $r \in \mathbb{Z}_p$ and computes $R_{k,i} = e(u_{k,i}, y_{k,i})^r \in \mathbb{G}_T$. The cloud server also computes $\mathcal{R} = R_{k,1} \cdot \ldots \cdot R_{K,m}$, and $\mathcal{L} = y_{k,1} \| \ldots \| y_{K,m}$. Then it computes $\gamma = h(\mathcal{R} \| \mathcal{L})$. The cloud generates the proof as follows: computes the linear combination of sampled blocks for each user in L in each task in K as $\mu'_{k,i} = \sum_{s \in I} v_s \cdot m_{k,s}$, $\mu_{k,i} = r + \gamma \mu'_{k,i}$. Then it computes $\sigma_k = \prod_{s \in I} \sigma_{k,s}^{v_s}$ for each task in K. Next, the cloud sends $\{\{\mu_{k,i}\}, \{\sigma_k\}, \{H(m_{k,s})\}, \mathcal{R}, \{L_k\}\}$ to the TPA. To verify the response, the TPA computes $\gamma = h(\mathcal{R} \| \mathcal{L})$ Next, it verifies $\{\{\mu_{k,i}\}, \{\sigma_k\}, \{H(m_{k,s})\}, \mathcal{R}, \{L_k\}\}$ via:

$$\mathcal{R} \cdot e(\prod_{k=1}^{K} \sigma_k^\gamma, g) \stackrel{?}{=} \prod_{k=1}^{K}(\prod_{i \in L} e((\prod_{s \in I}(H(m_{k,s})^{v_s})^\gamma \cdot u_{k,i}^{\mu_{k,i}}, y_{k,i})) \tag{4}$$

The correctness of the above verification equation is elaborated as follows:

$$\mathcal{R} \cdot e(\prod_{k=1}^{K} \sigma_k^\gamma, g) = R_{k,i} \cdot \ldots \cdot R_{K,m} \cdot \prod_{k=1}^{K} e(\sigma_k^\gamma, g)$$

$$= \prod_{k=1}^{K}(\prod_{i \in L} R_{k,i} \cdot e(\sigma_k^\gamma, g))$$

$$= \prod_{k=1}^{K}(\prod_{i \in L} e(u_{k,i}, y_{k,i})^r \cdot e(\sigma_k^\gamma, g))$$

$$= \prod_{k=1}^{K}(\prod_{i \in L} e((\prod_{s \in I}(H(m_{k,s})^{v_s})^\gamma \cdot u_{k,i}^{\mu_{k,i}}, y_{k,i}))$$

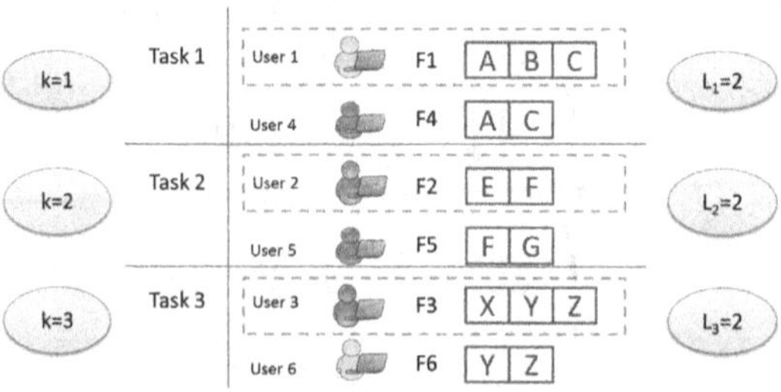

Fig. 5. Batch auditing of case 2

4 Evaluation

4.1 Security Analysis

The security guarantees of our proposed schemes are based on analyzing (a) the storage correctness and (b) the privacy preservation of these schemes.

For the storage correctness, we have to provide proofs that the cloud server can only compute the correct reply to the TPA inquiry if the integrity of the data stored on the cloud is preserved. Such computations will be based on file or block contents in cases 1 and 2. So, although duplicate blocks or files are removed in our scheme, the reliance on the content implies that the security proofs given in [1,4] are directly applicable. In particular, we refer the reader to Sect. 4 of [4] where different cases for the cloud server behaviour acting as an adversary are discussed.

Similar arguments for the proof of the privacy-preserving property of our schemes can be made. That is, the proof generated by the cloud server and sent to the TPA is based on the data content. Hence, if the TPA can learn about the user's data content based on the proof generated by the cloud server, it can also do the same for non-duplicated data violating the proof of theorems 2 and 3 in [1].

4.2 Performance Analysis

The experiment was conducted using C code on a Linux system with an Intel Core i3 processor running at 2.13 GHz, 4 GB of RAM, and a 5400 RPM Toshiba 320 GB Serial ATA drive with a 8 MB buffer. We also used the Pairing-Based Cryptography (PBC) library version 0.5.13, and MNT elliptic curve with base field size 159 bits and the embedding degree 6.

Cost Analysis. We estimated the computation cost in terms of basic cryptographic operations [1] (see Table 1 for notations).

Table 1. Notation of cryptographic operations

$Hash^t_{\mathbb{G}}$	Hash t takes values in group $\mathbb{G}$
$Add^t_{\mathbb{G}}$	t additions in group $\mathbb{G}$
$Mult^t_{\mathbb{G}}$	t multiplications in group $\mathbb{G}$
$Exp^t_{\mathbb{G}}(\ell)$	t exponentiations g^{a_i}, for $g \in \mathbb{G}, |a_i| = \ell$
$m\text{-}MultExp^1_{\mathbb{G}}(\ell)$	t m-term exponentiations $\prod^m_{i=1} g^{a_i}$
$Pair^t_{\mathbb{G}_1,\mathbb{G}_2}$	t pairings $e(u_i, g_i)$, where $u_i \in \mathbb{G}_1, g_i \in \mathbb{G}_2$
$m\text{-}MultPair^t_{\mathbb{G}_1,\mathbb{G}_2}$	t m-term pairings $\prod^m_{i=1} e(u_i, g_i)$

CS Computation:

- CS selects $r \in \mathbb{Z}_p$, $|p| = 160$ bits.
- For each user, CS computes $R_i = e(u_i, y_i)^r \in \mathbb{G}_T$, so the corresponding computation cost is $R_i = Exp^1_{\mathbb{G}_T}(|p|)$, and the size of R_i close to 960 bits.

- CS computes $\gamma = h(\mathcal{R}\|\mathcal{L})$, so the corresponding computation cost is $\gamma = Hash^1_{\mathbb{Z}_p}$
- In case 1, CS computes $\mu' = \sum_{s \in I} v_s \cdot m_s$ and $\mu = r + \gamma\mu'$, so the corresponding computation cost for μ' is $Mult^c_{\mathbb{Z}_p} + Add^c_{\mathbb{Z}_p}$ and for μ si $Add^1_{\mathbb{Z}_p} + Mult^1_{\mathbb{Z}_p}$. However, in Case 2, CS computes for each user: $\mu'_i = \sum_{s \in I} v_s \cdot m_s$ and $\mu_i = r + \gamma\mu'_i$, so the corresponding computation cost for μ'_i is $Mult^c_{\mathbb{Z}_p} + Add^c_{\mathbb{Z}_p}$ and for μ_i is $Add^1_{\mathbb{Z}_p} + Mult^1_{\mathbb{Z}_p}$.
- CS computes $\sigma = \prod_{s \in I} \sigma_s^{v_s}$, so the corresponding computation cost for σ is $-MultExp^1_{\mathbb{G}_1}(|v_i|)$

TPA Computation (Single Auditing):

- The TPA computes $\gamma = h(\mathcal{R}\|\mathcal{L})$, so the corresponding computation cost for γ is $Hash^1_{\mathbb{Z}_p}$.
- The TPA computes $\mathcal{R} \cdot e(\sigma^\gamma, g)$, so the corresponding computation cost is $Exp^1_{\mathbb{G}_1}(|p|) + Pair^1_{\mathbb{G}_1,\mathbb{G}_2} + Mult^1_{\mathbb{G}_T}$.
- In Case 1, the TPA computes $\prod_{i \in L} e((\prod_{s \in I}(H(m_s)^{v_s})^\gamma \cdot u_i^\mu, y_i)$, so the corresponding computation cost is $(c - MultExp^1_{\mathbb{G}_1}(|v_i|)) + Exp^{2L}_{\mathbb{G}_1} + Mult^L_{\mathbb{G}_1} + L - MultPair^1_{\mathbb{G}_1,\mathbb{G}_2}$. However, in Case 2 the TPA computes $\prod_{i \in L} e((\prod_{s \in I}(H(m_s)^{v_s})^\gamma \cdot u_i^{\mu_i}, y_i)$, so the corresponding computation cost is $L(c - MultExp^1_{\mathbb{G}_1}(|v_i|)) + Exp^{2L}_{\mathbb{G}_1} + Mult^L_{\mathbb{G}_1} + L - MultPair^1_{\mathbb{G}_1,\mathbb{G}_2}$

TPA Computation (Batch auditing):

- The TPA computes $\mathcal{R} \cdot e(\prod_{k=1}^K \sigma_k^\gamma, g)$, so the corresponding computation cost is $K - MultExp^1_{\mathbb{G}_1}(|p|) + Pair^1_{\mathbb{G}_1,\mathbb{G}_2} + Mult^1_{\mathbb{G}_T}$
- In Case 1, theTPA computes $\prod_{k=1}^K (\prod_{i \in L} e((\prod_{s \in I}(H(m_{k,s})^{v_s})^\gamma \cdot u_{k,i}^{\mu_k}, y_{k,i}))$, so the corresponding computation cost is $K(c - MultExp^1_{\mathbb{G}_1}(|v_i|)) + Exp^{2L}_{\mathbb{G}_1} + Mult^L_{\mathbb{G}_1} + L - MultPair^1_{\mathbb{G}_1,\mathbb{G}_2} + Mult^{K-1}_{\mathbb{G}_T}$. However, in Case 2 the TPA computes $\prod_{k=1}^K (\prod_{i \in L} e((\prod_{s \in I}(H(m_{k,s})^{v_s})^\gamma \cdot u_{k,i}^{\mu_{k,i}}, y_{k,i}))$, so the corresponding computation cost is $L(c - MultExp^1_{\mathbb{G}_1}(|v_i|)) + Exp^{2L}_{\mathbb{G}_1} + Mult^L_{\mathbb{G}_1} + L - MultPair^1_{\mathbb{G}_1,\mathbb{G}_2} + Mult^{K-1}_{\mathbb{G}_T}$

Experiment 1: Suppose we have two users who have the same files, case 1 for simplicity, and we want to check 100 blocks. Each auditing task consists of one file (e.g. "coding.pdf" with size of 513.4 KB and 125 blocks). This file is owned by two users. Table 2 shows the computation time of the Mediator, the CS, and the TPA in seconds when the TPA checks 100 blocks of the file. The CS computed time is the time of generating the proof, while the TPA time is the time of verifying the proof. In Fig. 6, the chart shows that the computation time of (the Mediator, the CS, and the TPA) are increased by increasing the number of blocks inthe file. However, the computation time of checking 100 blocks of the file consumed by the TPA is slightly larger than the CS computation time.

Table 2. The computation times of the mediator, the CS, and the TPA when 100 blocks are checked. Times in seconds

File name	Size	Number of blocks	Mediator computation time	CS computation time	TPA computation time
coding.pdf	513.4 KB	125	0.15	0.27	0.30
1.pdf	1.7 MB	415	1.61	0.47	0.49
4.pdf	4.8 MB	1181	12.76	0.91	0.99
6.pdf	6.3 MB	1536	21.76	1.13	1.22
7.ppt	7.1 MB	1725	26.69	1.27	1.37

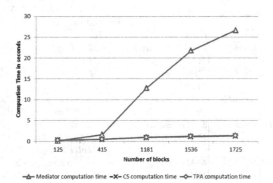

Fig. 6. Comparison of the time consumed by the mediator, the CS, and the TPA when 100 blocks are checked of each file in each auditing task. Each file is owned by two users

Batch Auditing Efficiency. Due to the batch auditing process, the TPA can perform multiple auditing tasks at the same time. First we compare the computation cost between the single auditing task and the batch auditing task in order to test whether the batch auditing process is more efficient than multiple processes of the single task. Table 3 shows the computational cost of the Audit Phase of the single and Batch auditing in Case 1, for simplicity. Precisely, we compare the computational cost of the verification equations of both methods (Eqs. 1 and 3). The $Hash_{Z_p}$ operation is computed more often in the single task than the batch task. However, it is negligible and we may ignore it. There are more pairing operations in the Right Hand Side (RHS) of the single verification equation than the in Batch auditing equation. Moreover, the Left Hand Side (LHS) of both ways is almost the same except that the batch auditing has $Mult_{G_T}$.

The author of [5] computed the time needed for the mathematical operations in pairing groups using the CHARM benchmarking suite. Table 4 shows the computation time in seconds of multiplication, exponentiation, and pairing over type D ellipt ic curve. We use the table to compute the computational cost of the

Table 3. Comparison of the computational cost between the single and batch auditing tasks in the audit phase. Where K = number of tasks, and L = consists of the number of subgroup of users in each task

		Single auditing task	
	γ	RHS	LHS
$K=1,L=2$	$Hash^1_{Z_p}$	$Exp^1_{G_1}$ + $Pair^1$ + $Mult^1_{G_T}$	$c\text{-}MultExp^1_{G_1}$ + $Exp^4_{G_1}$ + $Mult^2_{G_1}$ + $2\text{-}MultPair^1_{G_T}$
$K=1,L=3$	$Hash^1_{Z_p}$	$Exp^1_{G_1}$ + $Pair^1$ + $Mult^1_{G_T}$	$c\text{-}MultExp^1_{G_1}$ + $Exp^6_{G_1}$ + $Mult^3_{G_1}$ + $3\text{-}MultPair^1_{G_T}$
$K=2,L=(2,2)$	$Hash^2_{Z_p}$	$Exp^2_{G_1}$ + $Pair^2$ + $Mult^2_{G_T}$	$2(c\text{-}MultExp^1_{G_1})$ + $Exp^8_{G_1}$ + $Mult^4_{G_1}$ + $2\text{-}MultPair^1_{G_T}$
$K=3,L=(2,3,2)$	$Hash^3_{Z_p}$	$Exp^3_{G_1}$ + $Pair^3$ + $Mult^3_{G_T}$	$3(c\text{-}MultExp^1_{G_1})$ + $Exp^14_{G_1}$ + $Mult^7_{G_1}$ + $2\text{-}MultPair^2_{G_T}$ + $3\text{-}MultPair^1_{G_T}$
$K=4,L=(3,3,2,2)$	$Hash^4_{Z_p}$	$Exp^4_{G_1}$ + $Pair^4$ + $Mult^4_{G_T}$	$4(c\text{-}MultExp^1_{G_1})$ + $Exp^{20}_{G_1}$ + $Mult^{10}_{G_1}$ + $2\text{-}MultPair^2_{G_T}$ + $3\text{-}MultPair^2_{G_T}$
		Batch auditing task	
	γ	RHS	LHS
$K=1,L=2$	$Hash1^1_{Z_p}$	$Exp^1_{G_1}$ + $Pair^1_{G_T}$ + $Mult^1_{G_T}$	$c\text{-}MultExp^1_{G_1}$ + $Exp^4_{G_1}$ + $Mult^2_{G_1}$ + $2\text{-}MultPair^1_{G_T}$
$K=1,L=3$	$Hash1^1_{Z_p}$	$Exp^1_{G_1}$ + $Pair^1_{G_T}$ + $Mult^1_{G_T}$	$c\text{-}MultExp^1_{G_1}$ + $Exp^6_{G_1}$ + $Mult^3_{G_1}$ + $3\text{-}MultPair^1_{G_T}$
$K=2,L=(2,2)$	$Hash1^1_{Z_p}$	$2\text{-}MultExp^1_{G_1}$ + $Pair^1_{G_T}$ + $Mult^1_{G_T}$	$2(c\text{-}MultExp^1_{G_1})$ + $Exp^8_{G_1}$ + $Mult^4_{G_1}$ + $2\text{-}MultPair^1_{G_T}$ + $Mult^1_{G_T}$
$K=3,L=(2,3,2)$	$Hash1^1_{Z_p}$	$3\text{-}MultExp^1_{G_1}$ + $Pair^1_{G_T}$ + $Mult^1_{G_T}$	$3(Hash^1_{G_1}$ + $c\text{-}MultExp^1_{G_1})$ + $Exp^14_{G_1}$ + $Mult^7_{G_1}$ + $2\text{-}MultPair^2_{G_T}$ + $3\text{-}MultPair^1_{G_T}$ + $Mult^2_{G_T}$
$K=4,L=(3,3,2,2)$	$Hash1^1_{Z_p}$	$4\text{-}MultExp^1_{G_1}$ + $Pair^1_{G_T}$ + $Mult^1_{G_T}$	$4(c\text{-}MultExp^1_{G_1})$ + $Exp^{20}_{G_1}$ + $Mult^{10}_{G_1}$ + $2\text{-}MultPair^2_{G_T}$ + $3\text{-}MultPair^2_{G_T}$ + $Mult^3_{G_T}$

equations above and transfer Table 3 to computed times in Table 5. The latter table shows that the computation time of the LHS of both methods is almost the same. On the other hand, the computation time of the RHS of the batch auditing when $K > 1$ is less than computation time of the single task, see Fig. 7.

In summary, the batch auditing process reduces the computational cost of the TPA side by decreasing the pairing operations, which is the most expensive

Table 4. Computation time for mathematical operations in pairing groups (in seconds)

$MultG_1$	2.558×10^{-6}
$MultG_2$	2.360×10^{-5}
$MultG_T$	6.992×10^{-6}
$ExpG_1$	5.895×10^{-5}
$ExpG_2$	5.314×10^{-3}
$ExpG_T$	1.100×10^{-3}
Pairing	3.798×10^{-3}

Table 5. Comparison of the computational time between the single and the batch auditing tasks in the audit phase, where K = number of tasks, and L = consists of the number of subgroups of users in each task. Times are in seconds.

	Single auditing task		Batch auditing task	
	RHS	LHS	RHS	LHS
K = 1, L = 2	3.864×10^{-3}	7.851×10^{-3}	3.864×10^{-3}	7.851×10^{-3}
K = 1, L = 3	3.864×10^{-3}	1.178×10^{-2}	3.864×10^{-3}	1.178×10^{-2}
K = 2, L = (2,2)	7.728×10^{-3}	1.570×10^{-2}	3.928×10^{-3}	1.571×10^{-2}
K = 3, L = (2,3,2)	1.159×10^{-2}	2.748×10^{-2}	3.990×10^{-3}	2.749×10^{-2}
K = 4, L = (3,3,2,2)	1.546×10^{-2}	3.925×10^{-2}	4.051×10^{-3}	3.928×10^{-2}

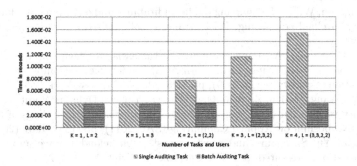

Fig. 7. Comparison of the computational time in the RHS of the verification equations between the single and the batch auditing tasks

operation according to Table 4, from $(L+1)$, as required in the single user cases, to $(L_k + \ldots + L_K + 1)$.

5 Conclusions

In this paper, we have proposed a privacy-preserving public auditing system with data deduplication that provides data integrity and storage efficiency in cloud computing. The proposed protocol uses a two-level architecture that utilizes a mediator to perform a client-side cross-user deduplication. The mediator also aggregated multi-user signatures for duplicate blocks of data. Our protocol is computationally lightweight, and is proven secure in a random oracle model. The construction of the protocol also allows for an extension to support a batch auditing process that can further improve overhead costs.

References

1. Wang, C., Chow, S., Wang, Q., Ren, K., Lou, W.: Privacy-preserving public auditing for secure cloud storage. IEEE Trans. Comput. **62**(2), 362–375 (2013)
2. Harnik, D., Pinkas, B., Shulman-Peleg, A.: Side channels in cloud services: deduplication in cloud storage. IEEE Secur. Priv. **8**(6), 40–47 (2010)
3. Soghoian, C.: How dropbox sacrifices user privay for cost savings, April 2011. http://paranoia.dubfire.net/2011/04/how-dropbox-sacrifices-user-privacy-for.html. Accessed 10 Aug 2014
4. Shacham, H., Waters, B.: Compact proofs of retrievability. In: Pieprzyk, J. (ed.) ASIACRYPT 2008. LNCS, vol. 5350, pp. 90–107. Springer, Heidelberg (2008)
5. Martin, R.: Group selection and key management strategies for ciphertext-policy attribute-based encryption. Master's thesis, Rochester Institute of Technology, New York, August 2013
6. Ren, K., Lou, W., Li, J.: Enabling public auditability and data dynamics for storage security in cloud computing. IEEE Trans. Parallel Distrib. Syst. **22**(5), 847–859 (2011)
7. Erway, C., Kupcu, A., Papamanthou, C., Tamassia, R.: Dynamic provable data possession. In: Proceedings of the 16th ACM Conference on Computer and Communications Security (CCS 2009), pp. 213–222. ACM, New York (2009)
8. Zhu, Y., Wang, H., Hu, Z., Ahn, G.-J., Hu, H., Yau, S.: Dynamic audit services for integrity verification of outsourced storages in clouds. In: Proceedings of the 2011 ACM Symposium on Applied Computing (SAC 2011), pp. 1550–1557 (2011)
9. Yuan, J., Yu, S.: Secure and constant cost public cloud storage auditing with deduplication. presented at IACR Cryptology ePrint Archive, 2013, pp. 149–149 (2013)
10. Boldyreva, A.: Threshold signatures, multisignatures and blind signatures based on the Gap-Diffie-Hellman-Group signature scheme. In: Desmedt, Y.G. (ed.) PKC 2003. LNCS, vol. 2567, pp. 31–46. Springer, Heidelberg (2003)
11. Ateniese, G., Di Pietro, R., Mancini, L., Tsudik, G.: Scalable and efficient provable data possession. In: Proceedings of the 4th International Conference on Security and Privacy in Communication Netowrks (SecureComm 2008), pp. 1–10 (2008)
12. Wang, C., Wang, Q., Ren, K., Cao, N., Lou, W.: Toward secure and dependable storage services in cloud computing. IEEE Trans. Serv. Comput. **5**(2), 220–232 (2012)

A Maximum Variance Approach for Graph Anonymization

Hiep H. Nguyen$^{(\boxtimes)}$, Abdessamad Imine, and Michaël Rusinowitch

LORIA/INRIA Nancy-Grand Est, Villers-lès-Nancy, France
{huu-hiep.nguyen,michael.rusinowitch}@inria.fr,
abdessamad.imine@loria.fr

Abstract. Uncertain graphs, a form of uncertain data, have recently attracted a lot of attention as they can represent inherent uncertainty in collected data. The uncertain graphs pose challenges to conventional data processing techniques and open new research directions. Going in the reserve direction, this paper focuses on the problem of anonymizing a deterministic graph by converting it into an uncertain form. The paper first analyzes drawbacks in a recent uncertainty-based anonymization scheme and then proposes *Maximum Variance*, a novel approach that provides better tradeoff between privacy and utility. Towards a fair comparison between the anonymization schemes on graphs, the second contribution of this paper is to describe a quantifying framework for graph anonymization by assessing privacy and utility scores of typical schemes in a unified space. The extensive experiments show the effectiveness and efficiency of Maximum Variance on three large real graphs.

1 Introduction

Graphs represent a rich class of data observed in daily life where entities are represented by vertices and their connections are characterized by edges. With the appearance of increasingly complex networks, the research community requires large and reliable graph data to conduct in-depth studies. However, this requirement usually conflicts with privacy protection of data contributing entities. Specifically in social networks, naive approaches like removing user ids from social graphs are not effective, leaving users open to privacy risks. Structural attacks to re-identify or de-anonymize users are shown feasible [1,10]. Recent surveys on security and privacy issues in OSNs (e.g. [9]) enumerate real-world breaches and possible defenses. Anonymization is such an effective countermeasure with many schemes proposed recently [4–6,12,20,22,25,26].

Given a social graph, the existing anonymization methods fall into four main categories. The first category includes *random* additions, deletions and switches of edges to prevent the re-identification of nodes or edges. The methods of second category provide k-anonymity [19] by *deterministic* node/edge additions or deletions, assuming attacker's background knowledge regarding some property of its target node. The methods falling in the third category assign probabilities to edges to add uncertainty to the true graph. Finally, the fourth class of

© Springer International Publishing Switzerland 2015
F. Cuppens et al. (Eds.): FPS 2014, LNCS 8930, pp. 49–64, 2015.
DOI: 10.1007/978-3-319-17040-4_4

techniques cluster nodes into super nodes of size at least k. Note that the last two classes of schemes induce *possible world* models, i.e., we can retrieve sample graphs that are consistent with the anonymized output graph.

The third category is the most recent class of methods which leverage the semantics of edge probability to inject uncertainty to a given deterministic graph, converting it into an uncertain one. In [2], Boldi et al. introduced the concept of *(k,ε)-obfuscation*, where $k \geq 1$ is a desired level of obfuscation and $\epsilon \geq 0$ is a tolerance parameter. However, this approach exposes several shortcomings in the selection of potential edges and the formulation of minimizing the standard deviation of the sampling distribution. We clarify these points in Sect. 3.2.

In this paper, we introduce *Maximum Variance* (MV) approach based on two crucial observations. First, we observe that nodes gain better privacy if their incident uncertain edges constitute large degree variance. To avoid the trivial solution of all edges having probabilities 0.5 and to keep the expected node degrees for utility, we formulate a quadratic program with constraints that the expected node degrees should be as in the true graph. Second observation emerges naturally from the formation of real networks that display community structure where new links are largely formed by *transitivity*. Therefore, we propose adding potential edges only by distance 2 (*friend-of-friend*). The extensive experiments show the elegance and effectiveness of MV over (k, ϵ)-obfuscation. We believe that the present work suggests an extensible approach for graph anonymization. Our contributions are summarized as follows:

- We analyze several disadvantages in the previous work [2], showing that their pursuit of minimum standard deviation σ has high impact on privacy (Sect. 3).
- We propose MV, a novel anonymization scheme also based on the semantics of uncertain graphs (Sects. 4 and 5). MV provides better privacy and utility by using two key observations. It proposes *nearby* potential edges and tries to maximize the *variance* of node degrees by a simple quadratic program.
- Towards a fair comparison between the anonymization schemes on graphs, this paper describes a generic quantifying framework by putting forward the distortion measure (Sect. 6). Rather than Shannon entropy-based or min entropy-based privacy scores with a parameter k as in previous work, the framework utilizes the *incorrectness* concept in [17] to quantify the re-identification risks of nodes. As for the utility score, we select typical graph metrics [2,23].
- We evaluate the MV approach on three large real graphs and show its outperformance over (k, ϵ)-obfuscation (Sect. 7).

2   Related Work

2.1   Anonymization of Deterministic Graphs

There is a vast literature on graph perturbation that deserves a survey. In this section, we enumerate only several groups of ideas that are related to our proposed scheme.

Anonymizing Unlabeled Vertices for Node Privacy. In unlabeled graphs, node identifiers are numbered in an arbitrary manner after removing their labels. The attacker aims at reidentifying nodes solely based on their structural information. For this line of graphs, node privacy protection implies the link privacy. Techniques of adding and removing edges, nodes can be done randomly or deterministically. Random perturbation is a naive approach and usually used as a baseline method. More guided approaches consist of *k-neighborhood* [25], *k-degree* [5,6,12], *k-automorphism* [26], *k-symmetry* [22], *k-isomorphism* [4] and k^2-*degree* [20]. These schemes provide k-anonymity [19] semantics and most of them rely on heuristics to avoid combinatorial intractability, except optimal solutions based on dynamic programming [5,6,12]. K-automorphism, k-symmetry, and k-isomorphism can resist *any* structural attacks by exploiting the inherent symmetry in graph. K-symmetry partitions a graph into automorphic orbits and duplicate subgraphs. k^2-degree addresses the friendship attacks, based on the vertex degree pair of an edge. Ying and Wu [23] propose a spectrum preserving approach which wisely chooses edge pairs to switch in order to keep the spectrum of the adjacency matrix not to vary too much. The clearest disadvantage of the above schemes is that they are inefficient, if not infeasible, on large graphs.

Apart from the two above categories, perturbation techniques have other categories that capitalize on *possible world* semantics. Hay et al. [10] generalize a network by clustering nodes and publish graph summarization of super nodes and super edges. The utility of this scheme is limited. In another direction, Boldi et al. [2] take the uncertain graph approach. With edge probabilities, the output graph can be used to generate sample graphs by independent edge sampling. Our approach belongs to this class of techniques with different formulation and better privacy/utility tradeoff. Note that in *k-symmetry* [4], the output sample graphs are also possible worlds of the intermediate symmetric graph.

Anonymizing Labeled Vertices for Link Privacy. If nodes are labeled, we are only concerned about the link disclosure risk. For example, Mittal et al. [13] employ an edge rewiring method based on random walks to keep the mixing time tunable and prevent link re-identification by Bayesian inference. This method is effective for social network based systems, e.g. Sybil defense, DHT routing. Link privacy is also described in [23] but only for Random Switch, Random Add/Del.

Min Entropy, Shannon Entropy and Incorrectness Measure. We now survey some commonly used notions of privacy metrics. *Min entropy,* [18] quantifies the largest probability gap between the posterior and the prior over all items in the input dataset. K-anonymity has the same semantics with the corresponding min entropy of $\log_2 k$. So k-anonymity based perturbation schemes in the previous subsection belong to min entropy. Shannon entropy argued in [3] and [2] is another choice of privacy metrics. The third metrics that we use in MV is the *incorrectness* measure from location privacy research [17]. Given the prior information (e.g. node degree in the true graph) and the posterior information harvested from the anonymized data, incorrectness measure is the number of incorrect guesses made by the attacker. This measure gauges the *distortion* caused by the anonymization algorithm.

Table 1. List of notations

Symbol	Definition
$G_0 = (V, E_{G_0})$	true graph
$\mathcal{G} = (V, E, p)$	uncertain graph constructed from G_0
$G = (V, E_G) \sqsubseteq \mathcal{G}$	sample graph from $\mathcal{G}$
$d_u(G)$	degree of node u in G
$d_u(\mathcal{G})$	expected degree of node u in $\mathcal{G}$
n_p	number of potential edges, i.e. $|E| = |E_{G_0}| + n_p$
$\mathcal{N}(u)$	neighbors of node u in $\mathcal{G}$
$\Delta(d)$	number of d-degree nodes in G
R_σ	truncated normal distribution on $[0,1]$
$r_e \leftarrow R_\sigma$	a sample from the distribution R_σ
p_i (p_{uv})	probability of edge e_i (e_{uv})
$Hi_G(u)$	signature Hi of node u in graph G

2.2 Mining Uncertain Graphs

Uncertain graphs pose big challenges to traditional mining techniques. Because of the exponential number of possible worlds, naive enumerations are intractable. Typical graph search operations like k-Nearest neighbor and pattern matching require new approaches [15,24,27]. Those methods answer threshold-based queries by using pruning strategies based on Apriori property of frequent patterns.

3   Preliminaries

This section starts with common definitions and assumptions on uncertain graphs. It then reveals several shortcomings in the main competitor [2]. Table 1 summarizes notations used in this paper.

3.1   Uncertain Graph

Let $\mathcal{G} = (V, E, p)$ be an uncertain undirected graph, where $p \colon E \to [0,1]$ is the function that gives an existence probability to each edge. The common assumption is on the *independence* of edge probabilities. Following the *possible-worlds* semantics in relational data [7], the uncertain graph $\mathcal{G}$ induces a set $\{G = (V, E_G)\}$ of $2^{|E|}$ deterministic graphs (worlds), each is defined by a subset of E. The probability of $G = (V, E_G) \sqsubseteq \mathcal{G}$ is:

$$Pr(G) = \prod_{e \in E_G} p(e) \prod_{e \in E \setminus E_G} (1 - p(e)) \tag{1}$$

Note that deterministic graphs are also uncertain graphs with all edges having probabilities 1.

3.2 (k, ϵ)-obfuscation and Its Limitations

In [2], Boldi et al. extend the concept of k-obfuscation developed in [3].

Definition 1. *(k,ϵ)-obfuscation [2]. Let P be a vertex property, $k \geq 1$ be a desired level of obfuscation, and $\epsilon \geq 0$ be a tolerance parameter. The uncertain graph $\mathcal{G}$ is said to k-obfuscate a given vertex $v \in G$ with respect to P if the entropy of the distribution $Y_{P(v)}$ over the vertices of $\mathcal{G}$ is greater than or equal to $\log_2 k$:*

$$H(Y_{P(v)}) \geq \log_2 k \qquad (2)$$

The uncertain graph $\mathcal{G}$ is a (k, ϵ)-obfuscation with respect to property P if it k-obfuscates at least $(1 - \epsilon)n$ vertices in $\mathcal{G}$ with respect to P.

Given the true graph G_0 (Fig. 1a), the basic idea of (k, ϵ)-*obf* (Fig. 1b) is to transfer the probabilities from existing edges to potential (non-existing) edges. The edge probability is sampled from the truncated normal distribution R_σ (Fig. 1c). For each existing sampled edge e, it is assigned a probability $1 - r_e$ where $r_e \leftarrow R_\sigma$ and for each non-existing sampled edge e', it is assigned a probability $r_{e'} \leftarrow R_\sigma$.

Table 2 gives an example of how to compute degree entropy for the uncertain graph in Fig. 1b. Here vertex property P is the node degree. Each row in the left table is the degree distribution for the corresponding node. For instance, $v1$ has degree 0 with probability $(1 - 0.8).(1 - 0.3).(1 - 0.9) = 0.014$. The right table normalizes values in each column (i.e. in each degree value) to get distributions $Y_{P(v)}$. The entropy $H(Y_{P(v)})$ for each degree value is shown in the bottom row. Given $k = 3, \log_2 k = 1.585$, then $v1, v3$ with true degree 2 and $v2, v4$ with degree true 1 satisfy (2). Therefore, $\epsilon = 0$.

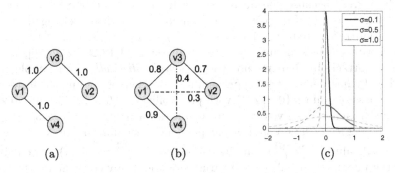

(a)   (b)   (c)

Fig. 1. (a) True graph (b) An obfuscation with potential edges (dashed) (c) Truncated normal distribution on $[0,1]$ (bold solid curves)

While the idea is quite interesting as a guideline of how to come up with an uncertain version of the graph, the specific approach in [2] has two drawbacks. First, it formulates the problem as the minimization of σ. With small values of σ, r_e highly concentrates around zero, so existing sampled edges have probabilities nearly 1 and non-existing sampled edges are assigned probabilities almost 0.

Table 2. The degree uncertainty for each node (left) and normalized values for each degree (right)

	deg=0	deg=1	deg=2	deg=3
v1	0.014	0.188	0.582	0.216
v2	0.210	0.580	0.210	0.000
v3	0.036	0.252	0.488	0.224
v4	0.060	0.580	0.360	0.000

$Y_{P(v)}$	deg=0	deg=1	deg=2	deg=3
v1	0.044	0.117	0.355	0.491
v2	0.656	0.362	0.128	0.000
v3	0.112	0.158	0.298	0.509
v4	0.187	0.362	0.220	0.000
$H(Y_{P(v)})$	1.404	1.844	1.911	0.999

By the simple rounding technique, the attacker can easily reveal the true graph. Even if the graph owner only publishes sample graphs, re-identification attacks are still effective. As we show in Sect. 7, the $H2_{open}$ risk in the uncertain graph produced by [2] may be up to 50 % of the true graph while it is only 2 % in our approach. Also note that in [2], the found values of σ vary in a wide range from 10^{-1} to 10^{-8}. Second, the approach in [2] does not consider the locality (subgraph) of nodes in selecting pairs of nodes for establishing potential edges. As shown in [8], *subgraph-wise perturbation* effectively reduces structural distortion.

4   Maximum Variance Approach

In this section, we present two key observations underpinning the MV approach.

4.1   Observation #1: Maximum Degree Variance

We argue that efficient countermeasures against structural attacks should hinge on node degrees because the degree is the fundamental property of nodes in unlabeled graphs and if a node and its neighbors have degree changed, the re-identification risk is reduced significantly. Consequently, instead of replicating local structures as in k-anonymity based approaches [4,12,20,22,25,26], we can deviate the attacks by changing node degrees *probabilistically*. For example, node $v1$ in Fig. 1a has degree 2 with probability 1.0 whereas in Fig. 1b, its degree gets four possible values $\{0, 1, 2, 3\}$ with probabilities $\{0.014, 0.188, 0.582, 0.216\}$ respectively. Generally, given edge probabilities incident to node u as $p_1, p_2, ..$ $p_{d_u(\mathcal{G})}$, the degree of u is a sum of independent Bernoulli random variables, so its expected value is $\sum_{i=1}^{d_u(\mathcal{G})} p_i$ and its variance is $\sum_{i=1}^{d_u(\mathcal{G})} p_i(1-p_i)$. If we naively target the maximum (local) degree variance without any constraints, the naive solution is at $p_i = 0.5$ for every incident edge i. However, such an assignment distorts graph structure severely and deteriorates the utility. Instead, we should use the constraint $\sum_{i=1}^{d_u(\mathcal{G})} p_i = d_u(G_0)$. Note that the *minimum variance* of an uncertain graph is 0 and corresponds to the case $\mathcal{G}$ has all edges being deterministic, e.g. when $\mathcal{G} = G_0$ and in edge-switching approaches. In the following section, we show an interesting result relating the *total* degree variance with graph edit distance.

4.2 Variance of Edit Distance

The *edit distance* between two deterministic graphs G, G' is defined as:

$$D(G, G') = |E_G \setminus E_{G'}| + |E_{G'} \setminus E_G| \tag{3}$$

A well-known result about the expected edit distance between the uncertain graph $\mathcal{G}$ and the deterministic graph $G \sqsubseteq \mathcal{G}$ is:

$$E[D(\mathcal{G}, G)] = \sum_{G' \sqsubseteq \mathcal{G}} Pr(G')D(G, G') = \sum_{e_i \in E_G} (1 - p_i) + \sum_{e_i \notin E_G} p_i \tag{4}$$

Correspondingly, the variance of edit distance is defined as

$$Var[D(\mathcal{G}, G)] = \sum_{G' \sqsubseteq \mathcal{G}} Pr(G')[D(G, G') - E[D(\mathcal{G}, G)]]^2 \tag{5}$$

We prove in the following Theorem that the variance of edit distance is the sum of edge variances and does not depend on the choice of G.

Theorem 1. *Assume that* $\mathcal{G}(V, E, p)$ *has* k *uncertain edges* $e_1, e_2, \ldots, e_k$ *and* $G \sqsubseteq \mathcal{G}$ *(i.e.* $E_G \subseteq E$*). The edit distance variance is* $Var[D(\mathcal{G}, G)] = \sum_{i=1}^{k} p_i(1 - p_i)$ *and does not depend on the choice of* G.

Proof. See Appendix A.1.

4.3 Observation #2: Nearby Potential Edges

As indicated by Leskovec et al. [11], real graphs reveal two temporal evolution properties: *densification power law* and *shrinking diameters*. Community Guided Attachment (CGA) model [11], which produces densifying graphs, is an example of a hierarchical graph generation model in which the linkage probability between nodes decreases as a function of their relative distance in the hierarchy. With regard to this observation, (k, ϵ)-obfuscation, by heuristically making potential edges solely based on node degree discrepancy, produces many inter-community edges. Shortest-path based statistics will be reduced due to these edges. MV, in contrast, tries to mitigate the structural distortion by proposing only *nearby* potential edges before assigning edge probabilities. Another evidence is from [21] where Vazquez analytically proved that the *Nearest Neighbor* can explains the power-law for degree distribution, clustering coefficient and average degree among the neighbors. Those properties are in very good agreement with the observations made for social graphs. Sala et al. [16] confirmed the consistency of Nearest Neighbor model in their comparative study on graph models for social networks.

5 Algorithms

This section describes steps of MV to convert the input deterministic graph into an uncertain one.

5.1 Overview

The intuition behind the new approach is to formulate the perturbation problem as a *quadratic programming* problem. Given the true graph G_0 and the number of potential edges allowed to be added n_p, the scheme has three phases. The first phase tries to partition G_0 into s subgraphs, each one with $n_s = n_p/s$ potential edges connecting nearby nodes (with default distance 2, i.e. *friend-of-friend*). The second phase formulates a quadratic program for each subgraph with the constraint of unchanged node degrees to produce the uncertain subgraphs sG with maximum edge variance. The third phase combines the uncertain subgraphs sG into $\mathcal{G}$ and publishes several sample graphs. The three phases are illustrated in Fig. 2.

By keeping the degree of nodes in the perturbed graph, our approach is similar to the *edge switching* approaches (e.g. [23]) but ours is more subtle as we do it implicitly and the switching occurs not necessarily on pairs of edges.

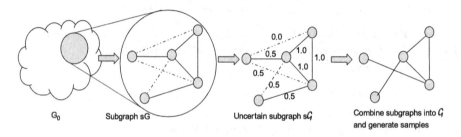

G_0 Subgraph sG   Uncertain subgraph s$\mathcal{G}$ Combine subgraphs into $\mathcal{G}$ and generate samples

Fig. 2. Maximum Variance approach

5.2 Graph Partitioning

Because of the complexity of exact quadratic programming (Sect. 5.3), we need a pre-processing phase to divide the true graph G_0 into subgraphs and run the optimization on each subgraph. Given the number of subgraphs s, we run *METIS*[1] to get almost equal-sized subgraphs with minimum number of inter-subgraph edges. Each subgraph has n_s potential edges added before running the quadratic program. This phase is outlined in Algorithm 1.

5.3 Quadratic Programming

By assuming the independence of edges, the total edge variance of $\mathcal{G} = (V, E, p)$ for edit distance (Theorem 1) is:

$$Var(E) = \sum_{i=1}^{|E|} p_i(1 - p_i) = |E_{G_0}| - \sum_{i=1}^{|E|} p_i^2 \qquad (6)$$

---

[1] http://glaros.dtc.umn.edu/gkhome/views/metis.

Algorithm 1. Partition-and-Add-Edges

Input: true graph $G_0 = (V, E_{G_0})$, number of subgraphs s, number of potential edges
   per subgraph n_s
Output: list of augmented subgraphs gl
1: $gl \leftarrow \text{METIS}(G_0, s)$.
2: **for** sG in gl **do**
3:     $i \leftarrow 0$
4:     **while** $i < n_s$ **do**
5:         randomly pick $u, v \in V_{sG}$ and $(u, v) \notin E_{sG}$ with $d(u, v) = 2$
6:         $E_{sG} \leftarrow E_{sG} \cup (u, v)$
7:         $i \leftarrow i + 1$
    return gl

The last equality in (6) is due to the constraint that the expected node degrees are unchanged (i.e. $\sum_{i=1}^{d_u(\mathcal{G})} p_i = d_u(G_0)$), so $\sum_{i=1}^{|E|} p_i$ is equal to $|E_{G_0}|$. By targeting the maximum edge variance, we come up with the following quadratic program.

$$\text{Minimize} \qquad \sum_{i=1}^{|E|} p_i^2$$

$$\text{Subject to} \qquad 0 \le p_i \le 1$$

$$\sum_{v \in \mathcal{N}(u)} p_{uv} = d_u(G_0) \quad \forall u$$

The objective function reflects the privacy goal (i.e. the sampled graphs do not highly concentrate around the true graph) while the expected degree constraints aims to preserve the utility.

By dividing the large input graphs into subgraphs, we solve independent quadratic optimization problems. Because each edge belongs to at most one subgraph and the expected node degrees in each subgraph are unchanged, it is straightforward to show that the expected node degrees in G_0 are also fixed.

6 Quantifying Framework

This section introduces a unified framework for privacy and utility quantification of anonymization methods in which the concept of incorrectness is central to privacy assessment.

6.1 Privacy Measurement

We focus on structural re-identification attacks under various models of attacker's knowledge as shown in [10]. We quantify the privacy of an anonymized graph as the *sum* of re-identification probabilities of all nodes in the graph. We differentiate *closed-world* from *open-world* adversaries. For example, when a closed-world adversary knows that Bob has three neighbors, this fact is exact. An open-world adversary, in this case, would learn only that Bob has at least three neighbors. We consider the result of structural query Q on a node u as the node signature $sig_Q(u)$. Given a query Q, nodes having the same signature form an *equivalence class*. So given the true graph G_0 and an output anonymized graph G^*, the privacy score is measured as in the following example.

Example 1. Assuming that we have signatures of G_0 and signatures of G^* as in Table 3, the re-identification probabilities in G^* of nodes 1,2 are $\frac{1}{3}$, of nodes 4,8 are $\frac{1}{2}$, of nodes 3,5,6,7 are 0s. And the privacy score of G^* is $\frac{1}{3}+\frac{1}{3}+\frac{1}{2}+\frac{1}{2}+0+0+0+0 = 1.66$. Note that the privacy score of G_0 is $\frac{1}{3}+\frac{1}{3}+\frac{1}{3}+\frac{1}{2}+\frac{1}{2}+\frac{1}{3}+\frac{1}{3}+\frac{1}{3} = 3$, equal to the number of equivalence classes.

Table 3. Example 1

Graph	Equivalence classes
G_0	$s_1\{1,2,3\}, s_2\{4,5\}, s_3\{6,7,8\}$
G^*	$s_1\{1,2,6\}, s_2\{4,7\}, s_3\{3,8\}, s_4\{5\}$

We consider two privacy scores in this paper.

- **H1** score uses node degree as the node signature, i.e. we assume that the attacker knows *apriori* degrees of all nodes.
- **H2$_{open}$** uses the *set* (not multiset) of degrees of node's friends as the node signature. For example, if a node has 6 neighbors and the degrees of those neighbors are $\{1,2,2,3,3,5\}$, then its signature for $H2_{open}$ attack is $\{1,2,3,5\}$.

Higher-order scores like $H2$ (exact multiset of neighbors' degrees) or $H3$ (exact multiset of neighbor-of-neighbors' degrees) induce much higher privacy scores of the true graph G_0 (in the order of $|V|$) and represent less meaningful metrics for privacy. The following proposition claims the *automorphism-invariant* property of structural privacy scores.

Proposition 1. *All privacy scores based on structural queries [10] are automorphism-invariant, i.e. if we find a non-trivial automorphism G_1 graph of G_0, the signatures of all nodes in G_1 are unchanged.*

Proof. G_1 is an automorphism of G_0 if there exists a permutation $\pi: V \to V$ such that $(u,v) \in E_{G_0} \leftrightarrow (\pi(u), \pi(v)) \in E_{G_1}$. For $H1$ score, it is straightforward to verify that $H1_{G_1}(u) = H1_{G_0}(\pi(u))$ according to the definition of π.

For $H2_{open}$ score, we prove that $\forall d_v \in H2_{G_0}(u)$ we also have $d_v \in H2_{G_1}(\pi(u))$ and vice versa. Because $d_v \in H2_{G_0}(u) \to (u,v) \in E_{G_0} \to (\pi(u),\pi(v)) \in E_{G_1}$. Note that $d_{\pi(v)} = d_v$ ($H1$ unchanged), so $d_v \in H2_{G_1}(\pi(u))$.

The reverse is proved similarly. This argument can also apply to any structural queries (signatures) in [10]. □

6.2   Utility Measurement

Following [2] and [23], we consider three groups of statistics for utility measurement: degree-based statistics, shortest-path based statistics and clustering statistics.

Degree-Based Statistics

- Number of edges: $S_{NE} = \frac{1}{2}\sum_{v \in V} d_v$
- Average degree: $S_{AD} = \frac{1}{n}\sum_{v \in V} d_v$
- Maximal degree: $S_{MD} = \max_{v \in V} d_v$
- Degree variance: $S_{DV} = \frac{1}{n}\sum_{v \in V}(d_v - S_{AD})^2$
- Power-law exponent of degree sequence: S_{PL} is the estimate of γ assuming the degree sequence follows a power-law $\Delta(d) \sim d^{-\gamma}$

Shortest Path-Based Statistics

- Average distance: S_{APD} is the average distance among all pairs of vertices that are path-connected.
- Effective diameter: S_{ED} is the 90-th percentile distance among all path-connected pairs of vertices.
- Connectivity length: S_{CL} is defined as the harmonic mean of all pairwise distances in the graph.
- Diameter: S_{Diam} is the maximum distance among all path-connected pairs of vertices.

Clustering Statistics

- Clustering coefficient: $S_{CC} = \frac{3N_\Delta}{N_3}$ where N_Δ is the number of triangles and N_3 is the number of connected triples.

All of the above statistics are computed on sample graphs generated from the uncertain output $\mathcal{G}$. In particular, to estimate shortest-path based measures, we use Approximate Neighbourhood Function (ANF) [14]. The diameter is lower bounded by the longest distance among all-destination bread-first-searches from 1,000 randomly chosen nodes.

7 Evaluation

In this section, our evaluation aims to show the effectiveness and efficiency of the MV approach and verify its outperformance over (k, ϵ)-obfuscation. The effectiveness is measured by privacy scores (lower are better) and the relative error of utility (lower are better). The efficiency is measured by the running time. All algorithms are implemented in Python and run on a desktop PC with $Intel^{®}$ Core i7-4770@ 3.4 Ghz, 16 GB memory. We use $MOSEK^2$ as the quadratic solver.

Three large real-world datasets are used in our experiments[3]. dblp is a co-authorship network where two authors are connected if they publish at least one paper together. amazon is a product co-purchasing network. If a product i is frequently co-purchased with product j, the graph contains an undirected edge from i to j. youtube is a video-sharing web site that includes a social

---

[2] http://mosek.com/.
[3] http://snap.stanford.edu/data/index.html.

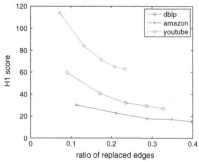

Fig. 3. $H1$ score

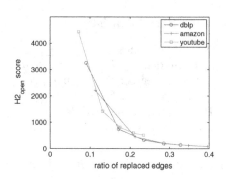

Fig. 4. $H2_{open}$ score

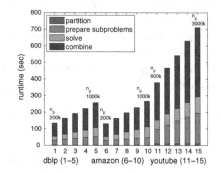

Fig. 5. Relative error

Fig. 6. Runtime of MV

network. The graph sizes $(|V|, |E|)$ of dblp, amazon and youtube are (317080, 1049866), (334863, 925872) and (1134890, 2987624) respectively. We partition dblp, amazon into 20 subgraphs and youtube into 60 subgraphs. The sample size of each test case is 20.

7.1 Effectiveness and Efficiency

We assess privacy and utility of MV by varying n_p (the number of potential edges). The results are shown in Table 4. As for privacy scores, if we increase n_p, we gain better privacy (lower sums of re-identification probabilities) as we allow more edge switches. Due to the expected degree constraints in the quadratic program, all degree-based metrics vary only a little. By contrast, (k, ϵ)-obfuscation (cf. Table 5) does not have such advantages. The heuristics used in [2] only reaches low relative errors at small values of σ. Unfortunately, these choices give rise to privacy risks (much higher $H1, H2_{open}$ scores).

We observe the near *linear* relationships between $H1$, *rel.err* and the number of replaced edges $|E_{G_0} \setminus E_G|$ in Figs. 3, 5 and near *quadratic* relationship of $H2_{open}$ against $|E_{G_0} \setminus E_G|$ in Fig. 4. The ratio of replaced edges in Figs. 3, 4 and 5 is defined as $\frac{|E_{G_0} \setminus E_G|}{|E_{G_0}|}$.

Table 4. Effectiveness of MV (k denotes one thousand)

n_p	$H1$	$H2_{open}$	S_{NE}	S_{AD}	S_{MD}	S_{DV}	S_{CC}	S_{PL}	S_{APD}	S_{ED}	S_{CL}	S_{Diam}	rel.err
dblp	199	125302	1049866	6.62	343	100.15	0.306	2.245	7.69	9	7.46	20	
200k	59.7	3257.2	1049774	6.62	342.3	100.73	0.279	2.213	7.66	9.3	7.43	19.5	0.017
400k	40.7	744.0	1049813	6.62	343.5	101.26	0.255	2.189	7.56	9.1	7.33	18.9	0.030
600k	32.1	325.7	1050066	6.62	343.4	101.73	0.235	2.173	7.46	9.0	7.25	17.7	0.045
800k	29.5	199.2	1049869	6.62	345.9	102.07	0.219	2.163	7.45	9.0	7.24	17.0	0.056
1000k	27.0	140.7	1049849	6.62	345.4	102.29	0.205	2.155	7.34	9.0	7.15	17.0	0.064
amazon	153	113338	925872	5.53	549	33.20	0.205	2.336	12.75	16	12.10	44	
200k	30.2	2209.1	925831	5.53	551.5	33.83	0.197	2.321	12.38	16.1	11.72	40.5	0.022
400k	22.8	452.4	925928	5.53	550.2	34.40	0.182	2.306	11.88	15.3	11.28	37.1	0.050
600k	17.8	188.4	925802	5.53	543.9	34.79	0.167	2.296	11.60	15.0	11.04	36.9	0.066
800k	17.2	118.8	925660	5.53	550.0	35.11	0.154	2.289	11.33	14.4	10.81	34.5	0.087
1000k	15.2	82.4	925950	5.53	551.8	35.43	0.142	2.282	11.13	14.1	10.62	31.8	0.105
youtube	978	321724	2987624	5.27	28754	2576.0	0.0062	2.429	6.07	8	6.79	20	
600k	114.4	4428.8	2987898	5.27	28759	2576	0.0065	2.373	6.19	7.8	5.97	18.6	0.030
1200k	84.2	1419.2	2987342	5.26	28754	2576	0.0064	2.319	6.02	7.2	5.82	17.9	0.042
1800k	71.4	814.4	2987706	5.27	28745	2577	0.0062	2.287	5.97	7.1	5.78	17.2	0.049
2400k	65.3	595.5	2987468	5.26	28749	2577	0.0060	2.265	5.96	7.1	5.77	16.6	0.056
3000k	62.8	513.7	2987771	5.27	28761	2578	0.0058	2.251	5.89	7.1	5.71	16.4	0.062

Table 5. (k, ϵ)-obfuscation

σ	$H1$	$H2_{open}$	S_{NE}	S_{AD}	S_{MD}	S_{DV}	S_{CC}	S_{PL}	S_{APD}	S_{ED}	S_{CL}	S_{Diam}	rel.err
dblp	199	125302	1049866	6.62	343	100.15	0.306	2.245	7.69	9	7.46	20	
0.001	72.9	40712.1	1048153	6.61	316.0	97.46	0.303	2.244	7.74	9.4	7.50	20.0	0.018
0.01	41.1	24618.2	1035994	6.53	186.0	86.47	0.294	2.248	7.82	9.5	7.59	19.8	0.077
0.1	19.7	7771.4	991498	6.25	164.9	64.20	0.284	2.265	8.08	10.0	7.85	20.0	0.128
amazon	153	113338	925872	5.530	549	33.20	0.205	2.336	12.75	16	12.10	44	
0.001	55.7	55655.9	924321	5.52	479.1	31.73	0.206	2.340	12.14	15.2	11.65	33.2	0.057
0.01	34.5	39689.8	915711	5.47	299.7	27.18	0.220	2.348	12.40	15.6	11.91	32.4	0.101
0.1	19.2	16375.4	892140	5.33	253.9	21.87	0.232	2.374	12.52	15.5	12.06	31.4	0.144
youtube	978	321724	2987624	5.27	28754	2576.0	0.0062	2.429	6.07	8	6.79	20	
0.001	157.2	36744.6	2982974	5.26	28438	2522.6	0.0062	2.416	6.24	8.0	6.01	19.5	0.022
0.01	80.0	22361.7	2940310	5.18	26900	2282.6	0.0061	2.419	6.27	8.0	6.04	19.0	0.043
0.1	23.4	5806.9	2624066	4.62	16353	970.8	0.0070	2.438	6.59	8.1	6.36	20.4	0.160

The runtime of MV consists of time for (1) partitioning G_0, (2) adding friend-of-friend edges to subgraphs, (3) solving quadratic subproblems and (4) combining uncertain subgraphs to get $\mathcal{G}$. We report the runtime in Fig. 6. As we can see, the total runtime is in several minutes and the partitioning step is nearly negligible. Increasing n_p gives rise to runtime in steps 2,3 and 4 and the trends are nearly linear. The runtime on youtube is three times longer than on the other two datasets, almost linear to their sizes.

7.2 Comparative Evaluation

Table 6 compares MV and (k, ϵ)-obfuscation. Beside the default strategy *NearBy* (nb), we include *Random* (rand) strategy for potential edges (i.e. selecting pairs of nodes uniformly on V). The column *tradeoff* is $\sqrt{H2_{open}} \times rel.err$ as we

Table 6. MV vs. (k, ϵ)-obfuscation (lower tradeoff is better)

graph	Privacy $H1$	$H2_{open}$	$|E_{G_0} \setminus E_G|$	$|E_G \setminus E_{G_0}|$	$\epsilon(k=30)$	$\epsilon(k=50)$	$\epsilon(k=100)$	Utility rel.err	tradeoff
dblp	199	125302			0.00238	0.00393	0.00694		
$\sigma = 0.001$	72.9	40712.1	6993.0	5280.2	0.00039	0.00122	0.00435	0.018	**3.61**
$\sigma = 0.01$	41.1	24618.2	19317.3	5444.9	0.00051	0.00062	0.00082	0.077	**12.03**
$\sigma = 0.1$	19.7	7771.4	65285.1	6916.8	0.00179	0.00199	0.00245	0.128	**11.33**
(nb)200k	59.7	3257.2	94508.0	94416.5	0.00033	0.00077	0.00152	0.017	**0.99**
(nb)600k	32.1	325.7	246155.6	246355.3	0.00017	0.00029	0.00085	0.045	**0.82**
(rand)200k	118.4	7390.4	69838.0	69917.2	0.00092	0.00206	0.00347	0.036	**3.09**
(rand)600k	56.4	369.4	202425.5	202530.8	0.00045	0.00077	0.00171	0.078	**1.50**
amazon	153	113338			0.00151	0.00218	0.00456		
$\sigma = 0.001$	55.7	55655.9	6158.9	4607.4	0.00048	0.00119	0.00293	0.065	**13.40**
$\sigma = 0.01$	34.5	39689.8	14962.0	4801.3	0.00038	0.00052	0.00066	0.114	**21.33**
$\sigma = 0.1$	19.2	16375.4	39382.6	5650.3	0.00068	0.00102	0.00190	0.145	**18.46**
(nb)200k	30.2	2209.1	104800.9	104759.9	0.00023	0.00032	0.00065	0.022	**1.03**
(nb)600k	17.8	188.4	266603.7	266533.7	0.00015	0.00023	0.00047	0.066	**0.91**
(rand)200k	87.8	7728.6	76417.8	76400.4	0.00071	0.00111	0.00190	0.112	**9.88**
(rand)600k	43.2	353.0	222055.3	222276.3	0.00042	0.00065	0.00106	0.175	**3.30**
youtube	978	321724			0.00291	0.00402	0.00583		
$\sigma = 0.001$	157.2	36744.6	19678.5	15028.5	0.00143	0.00232	0.00421	0.022	**4.28**
$\sigma = 0.01$	80.0	22361.7	62228.55	14914.3	0.00060	0.00105	0.00232	0.043	**6.38**
$\sigma = 0.1$	23.4	5806.9	378566.0	15007.5	0.00038	0.00052	0.00074	0.160	**12.20**
(nb)600k	114.4	4428.8	213097.3	213371.4	0.00047	0.00063	0.00108	0.030	**2.00**
(nb)1800k	71.4	814.4	521709.9	521791.6	0.00040	0.00052	0.00090	0.049	**1.38**
(rand)600k	733.5	108899.3	32325.3	32273.0	0.00092	0.00096	0.00105	0.018	**5.76**
(rand)1800k	345.0	9888.8	216297.2	216160.3	0.00107	0.00134	0.00204	0.050	**5.01**

conjecture the quadratic and linear curves of $H2_{open}$ and *rel.err* respectively (Figs. 4 and 5). Clearly, MV provides better privacy-utility tradeoffs.

In addition to the re-identification scores $H1$ and $H2_{open}$, we also compute ϵ for $k \in \{30, 50, 100\}$ to have a fair comparison with (k, ϵ)-obfuscation. Table 6 justifies the better performance of MV. Our approach results in lower relative errors (better utility), lower privacy scores as well as smaller tolerance ratio ϵ (better privacy). Moreover, the worse results of *Random* strategy confirm our second observation in Sect. 4.3.

The number of potential edges used in MV could be 20 % of $|E_{G_0}|$, much less than that of (k, ϵ)-obfuscation (100 % for $c = 2$ [2]). Columns $|E_{G_0} \setminus E_G|, |E_G \setminus E_{G_0}|$ show the difference of edge sets between G_0 and samples generated from $\mathcal{G}$. Because the expected degrees are preserved, $|E_{G_0} \setminus E_G| \simeq |E_G \setminus E_{G_0}|$ in MV and are higher than those of (k, ϵ)-obfuscation where the number of edges is preserved only at small σ, i.e. we allow more edge changes while not sacrificing the utility.

8 Conclusion

In this work, we propose a novel anonymization scheme for social graphs based on edge uncertainty semantics. To remedy the drawbacks in previous work, our

MV approach exploits two key observations: maximizing degree variance while keeping the expected values unchanged and using nearby potential edges. Furthermore, we promote the usage of incorrectness measure for privacy assessment in a unified quantifying framework rather than Shannon entropy or min-entropy (k-anonymity). The experiments demonstrate the outperformance of our method over (k, ϵ)-obfuscation. Our work may incite several directions for future research including (1) deeper analysis on the privacy-utility relationship (e.g. explaining the near-linear or near-quadratic curves) in MV (2) generalized uncertainty models for graph anonymization with constraint of unchanged expected node degrees.

A   Proof of Theorems

A.1   Proof of Theorem 1

Proof. We prove the result by induction.

When $k = 1$, we have two cases of G_1: $E_{G_1} = \{e_1\}$ and $E_{G_1} = \emptyset$. For both cases, $Var[D(\mathcal{G}_1, G_1)] = p_1(1 - p_1)$, i.e. independent of G_1.

Assume that the result is correct up to $k-1$ edges, i.e. $Var[D(\mathcal{G}_{k-1}, G_{k-1})] = \sum_{i=1}^{k-1} p_i(1 - p_i)$ for all $G_{k-1} \sqsubseteq \mathcal{G}_{k-1}$, we need to prove that it is also correct for k edges. We use the subscript notations $\mathcal{G}_k, G_k$ for the case of k edges. We consider two cases of G_k: $e_k \in G_k$ and $e_k \notin G_k$.

Case 1. The formula for $Var[D(\mathcal{G}_k, G_k)]$ is

$$Var[D(\mathcal{G}_k, G_k)] = \sum_{G'_k \sqsubseteq \mathcal{G}_k} Pr(G'_k)[D(G'_k, G_k) - E[D(\mathcal{G}_k, G_k)]]^2$$

$$= \sum_{e_k \in G'_k} Pr(G'_k)[D(G'_k, G_k) - E[D_k]]^2 + \sum_{e_k \notin G'_k} Pr(G'_k)[D(G'_k, G_k) - E[D_k]]^2$$

The first sum is $\sum_{G'_{k-1} \sqsubseteq \mathcal{G}_{k-1}} p_k Pr(G'_{k-1})[D_{k-1} - E[D_{k-1}] - (1 - p_k)]^2$.

The second sum is $\sum_{G'_{k-1} \sqsubseteq \mathcal{G}_{k-1}} (1 - p_k) Pr(G'_{k-1})[D_{k-1} - E[D_{k-1}] + p_k)]^2$.

Here we use shortened notations D_k for $D(G'_k, G_k)$ and $E[D_k]$ for $E[D(\mathcal{G}_k, G_k)]$. By simple algebra, we have $Var[D(\mathcal{G}_k, G_k)] = Var[D(\mathcal{G}_{k-1}, G_{k-1})] + q_k(1 - q_k) = \sum_{i=1}^{k} p_i(1 - p_i)$.

Case 2. similar to the Case 1.   □

References

1. Backstrom, L., Dwork, C., Kleinberg, J., Wherefore art thou r3579x?: anonymized social networks, hidden patterns, and structural steganography. In: WWW, pp. 181–190. ACM (2007)
2. Boldi, P., Bonchi, F., Gionis, A., Tassa, T.: Injecting uncertainty in graphs for identity obfuscation. Proc. VLDB Endow. **5**(11), 1376–1387 (2012)
3. Bonchi, F., Gionis, A., Tassa, T.: Identity obfuscation in graphs through the information theoretic lens. In: ICDE, pp. 924–935. IEEE (2011)

4. Cheng, J., Fu, A. W.-C., Liu, J.: K-isomorphism: privacy preserving network publication against structural attacks. In: SIGMOD, pp. 459–470. ACM (2010)
5. Chester, S., Kapron, B.M., Ramesh, G., Srivastava, G., Thomo, A., Venkatesh, S.: Why waldo befriended the dummy? k-anonymization of social networks with pseudo-nodes. Soc. Netw. Anal. Min. **3**(3), 381–399 (2013)
6. Chester, S., Kapron, B.M., Srivastava, G., Venkatesh, S.: Complexity of social network anonymization. Soc. Netw. Anal. Min. **3**(2), 151–166 (2013)
7. Dalvi, N., Suciu, D.: Management of probabilistic data: foundations and challenges. In: PODS, pp. 1–12. ACM (2007)
8. Fard, A.M., Wang, K., Yu, P.S.: Limiting link disclosure in social network analysis through subgraph-wise perturbation. In: EDBT, pp. 109–119. ACM (2012)
9. Gao, H., Hu, J., Huang, T., Wang, J., Chen, Y.: Security issues in online social networks. IEEE Internet Comput. **15**(4), 56–63 (2011)
10. Hay, M., Miklau, G., Jensen, D., Towsley, D., Weis, P.: Resisting structural re-identification in anonymized social networks. Proc. VLDB Endow. **1**(1), 102–114 (2008)
11. Leskovec, J., Kleinberg, J., Faloutsos, C.: Graph evolution: densification and shrinking diameters. ACM Trans. Knowl. Discov. Data (TKDD) **1**(1), 2 (2007)
12. Liu, K., Terzi, E.: Towards identity anonymization on graphs. In: SIGMOD, pp. 93–106. ACM (2008)
13. Mittal, P., Papamanthou, C., Song, D.: Preserving link privacy in social network based systems. In: NDSS (2013)
14. Palmer, C. R., Gibbons, P. B., Faloutsos, C.: ANF: a fast and scalable tool for data mining in massive graphs. In: KDD, pp. 81–90. ACM (2002)
15. Potamias, M., Bonchi, F., Gionis, A., Kollios, G.: K-nearest neighbors in uncertain graphs. Proc. VLDB Endow. **3**(1–2), 997–1008 (2010)
16. Sala, A., Cao, L., Wilson, C., Zablit, R., Zheng, H., Zhao, B.Y.: Measurement-calibrated graph models for social network experiments. In: WWW, pp. 861–870. ACM (2010)
17. Shokri, R., Theodorakopoulos, G., Le Boudec, J.-Y., Hubaux, J.-P.: Quantifying location privacy, In: SP, pp. 247–262. IEEE (2011)
18. Smith, G.: On the foundations of quantitative information flow. In: de Alfaro, L. (ed.) FOSSACS 2009. LNCS, vol. 5504, pp. 288–302. Springer, Heidelberg (2009)
19. Sweeney, L.: k-anonymity: a model for protecting privacy. Int. J. Uncertainty Fuzziness Knowl. Based Syst. **10**(05), 557–570 (2002)
20. Tai, C.-H., Yu, P.S., Yang, D.-N., Chen. M.-S.: Privacy-preserving social network publication against friendship attacks. In: KDD, pp. 1262–1270. ACM (2011)
21. Vázquez, A.: Growing network with local rules: preferential attachment, clustering hierarchy, and degree correlations. Phys. Rev. E **67**(5), 056104 (2003)
22. Wu, W., Xiao, Y., Wang, W., He, Z., Wang, Z.: k-symmetry model for identity anonymization in social networks. In: EDBT, pp. 111–122. ACM (2010)
23. Ying, X., Wu, X.: Randomizing social networks: a spectrum preserving approach. In: SDM, vol.8, pp. 739–750. SIAM (2008)
24. Yuan, Y., Wang, G., Wang, H., Chen, L.: Efficient subgraph search over large uncertain graphs. Proc. VLDB Endow. **4**(11), 876–886 (2011)
25. Zhou, B., Pei, J.: Preserving privacy in social networks against neighborhood attacks. In: ICDE, pp. 506–515. IEEE (2008)
26. Zou, L., Chen, L., Özsu, M.T.: K-automorphism: a general framework for privacy preserving network publication. Proc. VLDB Endow. **2**(1), 946–957 (2009)
27. Zou, Z., Li, J., Gao, H., Zhang, S.: Mining frequent subgraph patterns from uncertain graph data. IEEE Trans. Knowl. Data Eng. **22**(9), 1203–1218 (2010)

Privacy by Design: On the Conformance Between Protocols and Architectures

Vinh-Thong Ta$^{(\boxtimes)}$ and Thibaud Antignac

INRIA, University of Lyon, Lyon, France
{vinh-thong.ta,thibaud.antignac}@inria.fr

Abstract. In systems design, we generally distinguish the architecture and the protocol levels. In the context of privacy by design, in the first case, we talk about privacy architectures, which define the privacy goals and the main features of the system at high level. In the latter case, we consider the underlying concrete protocols and privacy enhancing technologies that implement the architectures. In this paper, we address the question that whether a given protocol conforms to a privacy architecture and provide the answer based on formal methods. We propose a process algebra variant to define protocols and reason about privacy properties, as well as a mapping procedure from protocols to architectures that are defined in a high-level architecture language.

1 Introduction

According to the definition provided in [6], "the architecture of a system is the set of [elements and their relations] needed to reason about the system". In the context of privacy, the elements are typically the privacy enhancing technologies (PETs) themselves and the purpose of the architecture is to combine them to achieve the privacy requirements. Generally speaking, an architecture can be seen as the abstraction of a system since an architecture abstracts away the details provided by PETs (such as message ordering, timing, complex cryptographic algorithms, etc.). Architectures only capture the main functionalities that a system should provide, for instance, which computations and communications are to be performed by the components.

Works in privacy by design mainly focus on PETs rather than architectures. In the position paper [3], the authors addressed the problem of privacy by design at the architecture level and proposed the application of formal methods that facilitate a systematic architecture design. In particular, they provided the idea of *the architecture language and logic*, a dedicated variant of epistemic logics [12], to deal with different aspects of privacy. Basically, an architecture is defined as a set of *architecture relations*, which capture the computations and communications abilities of each component. For instance, a relation $compute_i(x = t)$ specifies that a component i can compute a value t for x. Nevertheless, since [3] is a position paper, the language envisioned in the paper is mainly based on an introductory description. An extended version of this language is detailed in [2].

In this paper, we address the major question that whether the integration or combination of several different PETs conforms to a particular architecture.

© Springer International Publishing Switzerland 2015
F. Cuppens et al. (Eds.): FPS 2014, LNCS 8930, pp. 65–81, 2015.
DOI: 10.1007/978-3-319-17040-4_5

One challenge we have to face is that due to the diversity of technologies and protocols, their combination can raise a huge number of scenarios. Moreover, architectures are defined in an abstract way, while concrete implementations are more detailed, and it is challenging to define a proper abstraction from a lower to a higher level. The goal of this paper is to provide answers to this question.

Specifically, our main contributions are two-fold: first, we propose a modified variant of the applied π-calculus [13] for specifying the protocols related to PETs, and reasoning about the knowledge of components during the protocol run. Second, we propose a mapping procedure which defines the connection between the protocol specified in the calculus and the architecture defined in the architecture language. This mapping allows us to show whether a protocol (or a combination of protocols) conforms to a given architecture. To the best of our knowledge, this work is the first attempt that examines the connection between the two levels based on formal methods in the context of privacy protection.

The paper is organized as follows: in Sect. 2, we review the privacy architectures language (PAL) proposed in [2], which is a high-level language for specifying architectures and reasoning about privacy requirements in them. Sections 3 and 4 contain our contributions. The modified applied π-calculus is given in Sect. 3. Section 4 discusses the connection between each calculus process and relation in PAL, as well as the definitions and properties of the conformance between the two levels. In Sect. 5 we review the most relevant related works. Finally, we conclude the paper and discuss about the future works in Sect. 6.

2   Architecture Level

The language we review here is a simplified version of the one in [2]. The functionality of a service is defined by $\Omega = \left\{\tilde{X} = T\right\}$, where T is a term and $\tilde{X} \in Var$ represents a variable that can be either indexed (X_K) or unindexed (X). Each $\tilde{X}$ can be a single variable or an array of variables. $F \in Fun$ denotes a function, and $\odot F(X)$ defines the iterative application of F to the variables in the array X (e.g.: $\odot + (X)$ defines the summation of the variables in a given array).

$$T ::= \tilde{X} \mid F(T_1, \ldots, T_n) \mid \odot F(X); \qquad \tilde{X} ::= X \mid X_K$$

$$\mathcal{A} ::= \{\mathcal{R}\}$$
$$\mathcal{R} ::= Has_i^{arch}\left(\tilde{X}\right) \mid Receive_{i,j}\left(\{Att\}, \tilde{X}\right) \mid Compute_i\left(\tilde{X} = T\right)$$
$$\mid Check_i\left(T_1 = T_2\right) \mid Verif_j^{Attest}\left(Att\right) \mid Trust_{i,j}$$
$$Att ::= Attest_i\left(\{\tilde{X} = T\}\right)$$

An architecture $\mathcal{A}$ is defined by a set of components C_i, $i \in [1, \ldots, n]$, associated with the set of *relations* $\{\mathcal{R}\}$. Each *relation* $\mathcal{R}$ specifies a capability of the components. Subscripts i and j denote component IDs. $Has_i^{arch}(\tilde{X})$ expresses the fact that $\tilde{X}$ is a variable that component C_i initially has (i.e., an input variable of C_i). $Receive_{i,j}(\{Att\}, \tilde{X})$ expresses the possibility for C_i to receive the variable $\tilde{X}$ directly from C_j, and optionally an attestation Att related to this variable. An attestation, defined by $Attest_i(\{\tilde{X} = T\})$, captures a statement made by C_i on the set of equations. Each $\tilde{X} = T$ in the set $\{\tilde{X}{=}T\}$ expresses the integrity of $\tilde{X}$, stating that it equals to T. $Compute_i(\tilde{X} = T)$ says that C_i can compute a variable defined by an equation $\tilde{X} = T$. $Check_i(T_1 = T_2)$ states that C_i can check the satisfaction of property $T_1 = T_2$. The property $\tilde{X} = T$ in $Attest_i$ is related to the same property in $Compute_i$, namely when C_i computes $\tilde{X} = T$ it can send an attestation on this. $Verif_j^{Attest}(Att)$ says that C_j is able to successfully verify the origin of an attestation. Finally, $Trust_{i,j}$ is used to express the fact that component C_i trusts C_j, and this trust relation does not change during operations. Trust relations are pre-defined, and an attestation sent by C_i will be accepted by C_j after a successful verification only if C_j trusts C_i.

The semantics of an architecture is defined as its sets of compatible traces. A trace is a sequence of possible high-level events occurring in the system. Events can be seen as *instantiated relations* of the architecture.

$$
\begin{aligned}
\theta \;\; &::= \;\; Seq(\epsilon) \\
\epsilon \;\; &::= \;\; has_i\left(\tilde{X} : V\right) \mid receive_{i,j}\left(\{Att\}, \tilde{X} : V\right) \mid compute_i\left(\tilde{X} = T\right) \\
& \quad \mid check_i(T_1 = T_2) \mid verif_j^{Attest}(Att)
\end{aligned}
$$

To distinguish events from relations, we let events start with lowercase. For instance, event $has_i\left(\tilde{X} : V\right)$ captures the fact that C_i has the value V for $\tilde{X}$, and $compute_i\left(\tilde{X} = T\right)$ expresses the fact that C_i performes the computation $\tilde{X} = T$. The other events are interpreted based on their corresponding relations (see [2] for details). An event trace θ is *compatible* with an architecture $\mathcal{A}$, if in this trace, only events which are instantiations of components of the architecture can appear in θ – except for the *compute* events. For the case of *compute* events, besides the computation specified explicitly in the architecture, we also take into account the "background" computations (deduction) that can be performed by each component, based on the data it has. This deduction ability of each C_i is captured by its deduction system $\rhd_i$ [2]. The semantics of events is based on the *component states* and the *global state* of the architecture, given as follows:

$$
\begin{aligned}
State &= State_V \times State_P; \\
State_V &= (Var \rightarrow Val_\perp); \qquad State_P = \left\{\{\tilde{X} = T\} \cup \{T_1 = T_2\} \cup \{Trust_{i,j}\}\right\}
\end{aligned}
$$

The state of a component $(State)$ is composed of a variable state $(State_V)$ and a property state $(State_P)$. $State_V$ assigns a value (which can be undefined, $\perp$) to each variable. $State_P$ defines the set of properties $\tilde{X} = T$ and $T_1 = T_2$ known by a component.

In the sequel, σ is used to denote the global state of the architecture $\mathcal{A}$ (state of the components $\langle C_1, \ldots, C_n \rangle$) defined on $State^n$. σ_i ($\sigma_i = (\sigma_i^v, \sigma_i^{pk})$) denotes the state of the component C_i, where σ_i^v and σ_i^{pk} represent the variable state and property state of C_i, respectively. The initial state of $\mathcal{A}$, denoted by $Init^{\mathcal{A}}$, contains only the trust properties specified by the architecture. The semantics of an event trace is defined by the function $\mathcal{S}_T$, which specifies the impact of a trace of events on the states of the components, through the impact of each event on the states (defined by the function S_E).

$$S_T : \textit{Trace} \times \textit{State}^n \to \textit{State}^n; \qquad S_E : \textit{Event} \times \textit{State}^n \to \textit{State}^n;$$
$$S_T\ (\epsilon.\theta, \sigma) = S_T(\theta, S_E(\epsilon, \sigma)); \qquad S_T\ (\langle\rangle, \sigma) = \sigma;$$
$$S_E\ (\textit{compute}_i\left(\tilde{X} = T\right), \sigma) = \sigma[(\sigma_i^v[\textit{eval}(T, \sigma_i^v)/\tilde{X}], \sigma_i^{pk} \cup \{\tilde{X} = T\}) \ / \ \sigma_i\ ].$$

Due to lack of space we only present S_E for the compute event here, the full list can be found in [2]. The notation $\epsilon.\theta$ is used to denote a trace whose first element is ϵ and the rest of the trace is θ, while $\langle\rangle$ denotes the empty trace. Each event modifies only the state σ_i of the component C_i. A modification is expressed by $\sigma[(v, pk)/\sigma_i]$ that replaces σ_i^v and σ_i^{pk} of σ_i by v and pk, respectively. The effect of $\textit{compute}_i(\tilde{X} = T)$ is to set $\tilde{X}$ to the evaluation of T based on the current variable state σ_i^v, which is denoted by $\textit{eval}(T, \sigma_i^v)$. Event $\textit{compute}_i$ also results in adding the knowledge about $\tilde{X} = T$ to the property state σ_i^{pk}.

The semantics of an architecture $\mathcal{A}$ is defined as $\mathcal{S}(\mathcal{A}) = \{\sigma \in \textit{State}^n \mid \exists \theta \in T(\mathcal{A})$ such that $S_T(\theta, \textit{Init}^{\mathcal{A}}) = \sigma\}$, where $T(\mathcal{A})$ is the set of compatible traces of $\mathcal{A}$. To reason about the privacy requirements of architectures, the *architecture logic* is proposed in [2], which is based on the architecture language PAL.

$$\phi ::= \textit{Has}_i^{all}\left(\tilde{X}\right) \mid \textit{Has}_i^{none}\left(\tilde{X}\right) \mid K_i\left(T_1 = T_2\right) \mid \phi_1 \wedge \phi_2$$

This logic involves modality K_i that represents the epistemic knowledge [12] of C_i about $T_1 = T_2$. In the rest of the paper, we refer to ϕ as an architecture property. The semantics $S(\phi)$ of a property ϕ is defined as follows:

1. $\mathcal{A} \in S(\textit{Has}_i^{all}\left(\tilde{X}\right)) \Leftrightarrow \exists\ \sigma \in \mathcal{S}(\mathcal{A}),\ \sigma_i^v(\tilde{X}) \neq \bot$
2. $\mathcal{A} \in S(\textit{Has}_i^{none}\left(\tilde{X}\right)) \Leftrightarrow \forall\ \sigma \in \mathcal{S}(\mathcal{A}), \sigma_i^v(\tilde{X}) = \bot$
3. $\mathcal{A} \in S(K_i\left(Eq\right)) \Leftrightarrow \forall\ \sigma' \in \mathcal{S}_i(\mathcal{A}),\ \exists\ \sigma \in \mathcal{S}_i(\mathcal{A}),\ \exists\ Eq' : (\sigma \geq_i \sigma') \wedge (\sigma_i^{pk} \rhd_i Eq')$
$$\wedge\ (Eq' \Rightarrow Eq),$$

where Eq (Eq') represents an equation $T_1 = T_2$ $(T_1' = T_2')$. An architecture satisfies the $\textit{Has}_i^{all}(\tilde{X})$ property if and only if C_i may obtain the value of all X_k in $\textit{Range}(X)$ in at least one compatible execution trace. $\textit{Has}_i^{none}(\tilde{X})$ holds if and only if no execution trace can lead to a state in which C_i gets any value of any X_k. We note that $\textit{Has}_i$ properties only inform on the fact that C_i can get or derive some values for the variables but they do not bring any guarantee about the correctness of these values. Integrity requirements can be expressed using the property $K_i(T_1 = T_2)$, which states that the component C_i knows the truth of the integrity property $T_1 = T_2$. In $\sigma \geq \sigma'$, compared to σ', σ represents the state at the end of a longer trace. Finally, $\sigma_i^{pk} \rhd_i Eq'$ and $Eq' \Rightarrow Eq$ capture that Eq' can be deduced from σ_i^{pk} and Eq', respectively.

Example Architecture: Let us consider a very simple smart metering architecture which consists in the communication between two components: the meter (M) and the operator (O). The goal of this architecture is to ensure that the operator will get the consumption fee for a given period and to be convinced that the fee is correct. The privacy requirement says that O must not obtain the consumption data. One possible design solution is that the meter passes directly the consumption data to the operator who will compute the fee:

$$\mathcal{A}_1 = \{\text{for } i \in [1, \ldots, r]:\ Has_M^{arch}(X_c);\ Compute_M(X_{m_i} = X_{c_i});$$
$$Receive_{O,M}(Attest_M(X_{m_i} = X_{c_i}), X_{m_i});\ Verif_O^{Attest}(Attest_M(X_{m_i} = X_{c_i}));$$
$$Compute_O(X_{tf_i} = F(X_{m_i});\ Compute_O(X_{fee} = \odot + (X_{tf})),\ Trust_{O,M}\}.$$

In the architecture $\mathcal{A}_1$, the meter initially has the (input) variable X_c that represents the array of r consumption data X_{c_i}, $i \in [1, \ldots, r]$. The meter is capable to compute each metered data (X_{m_i}) based on each consumption data (X_{c_i}). Intuitively, in $X_{m_i} = X_{c_i}$, X_{m_i} will get the value of X_{c_i} . Then, the operator will receive the metered data (X_{m_i}), along with the attestation made by M on the integrity property $X_{m_i} = X_{c_i}$. After verifying the received attestation with success, due to $Trust_{O,M}$ the operator knows that $X_{m_i} = X_{c_i}$. Then for each X_{m_i}, O computes the tariff based on the function F. Finally, O computes the summation of the r tariffs (i.e., array X_{tf}) to get the fee for the period. The requirements of the architecture are modeled with the properties of the architecture logic. Namely, $Has_O^{all}(X_{fee})$ specifies that O has (all) the fee, while $Has_O^{none}(X_c)$ says that O must not have any consumption data. $\mathcal{A}_1$ fulfills the first requirement, but it does not satisfy the privacy requirement because based on $Receive_{O,M}(Attest_M(X_{m_i} = X_{c_i}), X_{m_i})$ O can obtain X_{c_i} from X_{m_i}.

3   Protocol Level

To reason about the concrete implementations of an architecture, we propose a modified variant of the applied π-calculus. We decided to modify the basic applied π-calculus [13] because thanks to its expressive syntax and semantics, it is broadly used for security verification of systems and protocols (e.g., [4,9–11,14, 17,18]). Our main goal is to modify some syntax and semantics elements of the applied π-calculus, making it more convenient to find the connection between the calculus semantics and the interpretation of architecture relations. One of such modifications is the notion of component, which is characterized by three elements: (i) the internal behavior of the component; (ii) the unique ID assigned to the component; and (iii) the set of IDs of the components who are trusted by this component. Another reason why we cannot use the basic applied π-calculus is that it focuses on reasoning about the information a Dolev-Yao attacker (who can eavesdrop on all communications) obtains. However, in our case we reason about the information that components can have, which are only aware of the communications they can take part in.

3.1   Syntax of the Modified Applied π-Calculus

We assume an infinite set of *names* $\mathcal{N}$ and *variables* $\mathcal{V}$, and a finite set of *component identifiers* $\mathcal{L}$, where $\mathcal{V} \cap \mathcal{N} \cap \mathcal{L} = \emptyset$. Terms are defined as follows:

$$t ::= c \mid l_i \mid n, m, k \mid x, y, z \mid f(t_1, \ldots, t_p).$$

The meaning of each term is given as follows: c models a communication channel. l_i represents a component ID ($l_i \neq l_j$ if $i \neq j$) that uniquely identifies a component. n, m and k denote names, which model some kind of data (e.g., a random nonce, a secret key, etc.). Terms x, y, z denote variables that represent any term, namely, any term can be bounded to variables. $f(t_1, \ldots, t_p)$ is a function, which models cryptographic primitives, e.g., digital signature can be modeled by $sign(x_m, x_{sk})$, where x_m and x_{sk} specify the message and the private key, respectively. Moreover, f can also be used to specify verification functions (e.g., the signature check is modeled by function $checksign(sign(x_m, x_{sk}), x_{pk})$, where x_{pk} represents the public key corresponding to the private key x_{sk}).

We rely on the same type system for terms as in the applied π-calculus [13]. Due to lack of space, we omit the unimportant details of this type system, and leave it implicit in the rest of the paper. We assume that terms are well-typed and that substitutions preserve types (see [22] for details).

The internal operation of components is modeled by *processes*. Processes are specified with the following syntax:

$$P, Q, R ::= \overline{c}\langle t \rangle.P \quad \| \quad \overline{c}\langle t_m, t_{sig} \rangle\rangle.P \quad \| \quad c(x).Q \quad \| \quad c(x_m, x_{sig}).Q \quad \| \quad P|Q$$
$$\| \quad \nu n.P \quad \| \quad let\ x = t\ in\ P \quad \| \quad if\ (t_1 = t_2)\ then\ P \quad \| \quad \mathbf{0}.$$

Note that for simplicity we left out the infinite replication of processes, $!P$. As a result a protocol/system run consists of a finite number of traces.

Process $\overline{c}\langle t \rangle.P$ sends the term t (where $t \neq (t_m, t_{sig})$) on channel c, and continues with the execution of P. Process $\overline{c}\langle t_m, t_{sig} \rangle.P$ models the attestation sending, where t_m and the signature t_{sig} are sent on c.

Process $c(x).Q$ waits for a term on channel c and then binds the received term to x in Q. Process $c(x_m, x_{sig}).Q$ waits for a term x_m and its signature x_{sig} on channel c, which models the attestation reception.

$P|Q$ behaves as processes P and Q running (independently) in parallel. A restriction $\nu n.P$ is a process that creates a new, bound name n, and then behaves as P. The name n is called bound because it is available only to P. Process $let\ x = t\ in\ P$ proceeds to P and binds every (free occurrence of) x in P to t.

Process $if\ (t_1 = t_2)\ then\ P$ says that if $t_1 = t_2$ (with respect to the equational theory E, discussed later) then process P is executed, else it stops. Its special case is $if\ x_m = checksign(x_{sig}, x_{l_i}^{pk})\ then\ P$, which captures the verification of an attestation (i.e., signature x_{sig} with key $x_{l_i}^{pk}$). For message authentication and integrity protection purposes digital signature and message authentication code (MAC) are used. In this paper we only consider signature.

Finally, the *nil* process $\mathbf{0}$ does nothing and specifies process termination.

Components: To make the connection between calculus processes and architecture relations more straightforward, we introduce the notion of components. $\lfloor P \rfloor_l^\rho$ defines a component with the unique identifier l, who trusts the components whose IDs are in the set ρ, and whose behavior is defined by process P. The trust relation can be either one-way or symmetric, for instance, $\lfloor P \rfloor_{l_1}^{\{l_2\}}$ and $\lfloor Q \rfloor_{l_2}^{\{l_1\}}$ represent components l_1 and l_2 who trust each other. The rationale behind this way of component specification is that the component IDs and the trust relation between them are pre-defined, and do not change during the protocol run (this is what we assumed at the architecture level). In addition, we assume that a trusted component will not become untrusted.

Systems: A *system*, denoted by S, can be an empty system with no component: $\mathbf{0}_S$; a singleton system with one component: $\lfloor P \rfloor_l^\emptyset$; the parallel composition of components: $\lfloor P \rfloor_{l_1}^{\rho_1} \mid \lfloor Q \rfloor_{l_2}^{\rho_2}$, where ρ_1 and ρ_2 may include l_2 and l_1, respectively; or a system with name restriction. To capture more complex systems, we also allow systems to be the parallel composition of sub-systems, $S_1 \mid S_2$.

$$S ::= \mathbf{0}_S \mid \lfloor P \rfloor_l^\rho \mid \nu n.S \mid (S_1 \mid S_2).$$

The name restriction $\nu n.S$ represents the creation of new name n, such as secret keys, or a random nonce which are only available to the components in S.

3.2   Semantics of the Modified Applied π-Calculus

In order to check the conformance between protocols and architectures, it suffices to consider the internal reduction rules of the calculus, which model the behavior of the protocol (without contact with its environment). Reduction rules capture the internal operations (e.g., *let* or *if* processes) and communications performed by components. We define and distinguish the following reduction rules:

(Reduction rules)

(Rcv) $\lfloor \bar{c}\langle t \rangle.P \rfloor_{l_i}^{\rho_i} \mid \lfloor c(x).Q \rfloor_{l_j}^{\rho_j} \xrightarrow{rcv(l_j, l_i, x:t)} \lfloor P \rfloor_{l_i}^{\rho_i} \mid \lfloor Q\{t/x\} \rfloor_{l_j}^{\rho_j}, \; t \neq (t_m, t_{sig})$;

(Rcv$_{att}$) $\lfloor \bar{c}\langle t_m, t_{sig} \rangle.P \rfloor_{l_i}^{\rho_i} \mid \lfloor c(x_m, x_{sig}).Q \rfloor_{l_j}^{\rho_j} \xrightarrow{rcv_{att}(l_j, l_i, x_m:t_m)}$
$\qquad\qquad\qquad\qquad\qquad\qquad\qquad\qquad \lfloor P \rfloor_{l_i}^{\rho_i} \mid \lfloor Q\{t_m/x_m, t_{sig}/x_{sig}\} \rfloor_{l_j}^{\rho_j}$;

(Verif$_{att}$) $\lfloor if \; x_m = checksign(x_{sig}, t_{l_i}^{pk}) \; then \; Q' \rfloor_{l_j}^{\rho_j} \xrightarrow{ver_{att}(l_j, \; x_m:t_m)} \lfloor Q' \rfloor_{l_j}^{\rho_j}$,
$\qquad\qquad$ where $\{t_m/x_m, t_{sig}/x_{sig}\}$. Note: l_j accepts the attestation if $l_i \in \rho_j$.

(Check) $\lfloor if \; (t_1 = t_2) \; then \; P \rfloor_{l_j}^{\rho_j} \xrightarrow{check(l_j, t_1:t_2)} \lfloor P \rfloor_{l_j}^{\rho_j} \; (t_1 = t_2 \in E, \; t_2 \neq checksign)$;

(Comp) $\lfloor let \; x = t \; in \; P \rfloor_{l_j}^{\rho_j} \xrightarrow{\omega_{comp}} \lfloor P\{t/x\} \rfloor_{l_j}^{\rho_j}, \; (t = x'$ or f, such that
$\qquad\qquad \omega_{comp} = comp(l_j, x : t)$ when $f \notin \{sign, checksign\}$, else $\omega_{comp} = \tau$);

(Has) $(\nu k.) \lfloor let \; x = k \; in \; P \rfloor_{l_j}^{\rho_j} \xrightarrow{has(l_j, x:k)} (\nu k.) \lfloor P\{k/x\} \rfloor_{l_j}^{\rho_j}$,

(Error) $\lfloor if \; (t_1 = t_2) \; then \; P \rfloor_{l_j}^{\rho_j} \xrightarrow{error} \lfloor \mathbf{0} \rfloor_{l_j}^{\rho_j} \; (if \; t_1 = t_2 \notin E)$;

(Par-C) $\lfloor P \rfloor_{l_j}^{\rho_j} \xrightarrow{\omega_c} \lfloor P' \rfloor_{l_j}^{\rho_j}$ then $\lfloor Q \mid P \rfloor_{l_j}^{\rho_j} \xrightarrow{\omega_c} \lfloor Q \mid P' \rfloor_{l_j}^{\rho_j}$;

(Res-C) $\lfloor P \rfloor_{l_j}^{\rho_j} \xrightarrow{\omega_c} \lfloor P' \rfloor_{l_j}^{\rho_j}$ then $\lfloor \nu n.P \rfloor_{l_j}^{\rho_j} \xrightarrow{\omega_c} \lfloor \nu n.P' \rfloor_{l_j}^{\rho_j}$, where
$\qquad\qquad \omega_c \in \{comp(l_j, x : t), has(l_j, x : k), check(l_j, t_1 : t_2), error, ver_{att}(l_j, x_m:t_m)\}$;

(Par-S) $S_1 \xrightarrow{\omega_s} S_1'$ then $S_2 \mid S_1 \xrightarrow{\omega_s} S_2 \mid S_1'$;

(Res-S) $S \xrightarrow{\omega_s} S'$ then $\nu n.S \xrightarrow{\omega_s} \nu n.S'$, where
             ω_s can be ω_c, and $rcv(l_j, l_i, x : t)$, $rcv_{att}(l_j, l_i, x_m : t_m)$.

Before defining the system states, we label each reduction relation (arrow) based on the name of the rule and the terms used in them. We adopt the notion of equational theory E from [13,22], which contains rules of form $t_1 = t_2 \in E$, that define when two terms are equal. For instance, the equational theory E may include rules for signature verification, decryption, MAC verification, etc. The meaning of each reduction rule is as follows:

- Rule (Rcv) captures the communication between components l_i and l_j. Namely, l_i sends value t for x on channel c, which is received by l_j. As a result, we get $Q\{t/x\}$ that binds t to every free occurrence of x in Q. It is assumed that $t \neq (t_m, t_{sig})$, which is treated as a special case.
- Rule (Rcv$_{att}$) deals with exchanging the message t_m and the signature t_{sig} on channel c, which models the reception of the attestation $Attest_{l_i}(\{x_m = t_m\})$. As a result, we get Q in which t_m and the signature are bound to x_m and x_{sig}, respectively. The reason that we distiguish (Rcv$_{att}$) from (Rcv) is because we want to make a clear distinction between the cases of receiving a message with and without an attestation.
- Rule (Verif$_{att}$) captures the case when after binding t_m and t_{sig} to x_m and the signature x_{sig}, respectively, component l_j successfully verified the signature using the corresponding public key of l_i, $t_{l_i}^{pk}$. We implicitly assume that t_m and t_{sig} contain enough information for the receiver to identify the "type" of the received message (e.g., the consumption fee in smart metering systems). Rules (Rcv$_{att}$) and (Verif$_{att}$) together specify the scenario when l_i sends to l_j the value t_m for x_m, with the signature that proves the integrity and the authenticity of this message. Then, in case l_j trusts l_i, it knows the truth about the integrity property $x_m = t_m$.
- Rule (Check) considers the case when two terms are equal in the check (with respect to the equational theory E), which leads to P as result. We assume that t_2 is not the *checksign* function, which is used for the attest verification.
- Rule (Comp) models the computation $x = t$ performed by l_j. As a result, every free occurrence of x in P is given the value t. In this rule we assume that t can be either a variable or a function (except for *sign* and *checksign*, because they are considered as parts of the attestation), but not a name.
- Rule (Has) deals with the case when t is a name. The name k, either bound (with νk) or free (without νk), represents the value of x. Here x is used to model the variable that l_j initially has to capture the input data coming from the environment (e.g., the consumption data in the smart metering).
- Rule (Error) specifies the case when two terms are not equal with respect to E. As a result, the process will continue with the *nil* process.
- Rules (Par-C) and (Res-C) say that the *if* and *let* reductions are closed under parallel composition and restriction within a component, respectively.

Rules (Par-S) and (Res-S) capture that all the reductions are closed under parallel composition and restriction on systems, respectively.

Instead of referring to the trace of reductions $\xrightarrow{\omega_s^1} \ldots \xrightarrow{\omega_s^m}$ we will refer to the trace of the corresponding labels $\omega_s^1, \ldots, \omega_s^m$ for the sake of clarity.

States of components and systems: Let us consider a system S with n components. Let $Label_S$ be the set of all labels ($\omega_s \in Label_S$) of the reduction relations defined above, and let $LTrace_S$ be the set of all possible label traces of S. We define the functions $\mathcal{V}_{ST}$, $\mathcal{V}_T$ and $\mathcal{V}_L$ that update the states of the components and the entire system. $\mathcal{V}_T$ and $\mathcal{V}_L$ are similar to $\mathcal{S}_T$ and $\mathcal{S}_E$ in PAL, but they are based on label traces and labels instead of traces of events and events. $\mathcal{V}_{ST}$ takes as input the set of all the possible label traces of S and handle each trace with $\mathcal{V}_T$. Let $State_S^n$ denote the set of global state of S and $\emptyset_{tr}$ an empty set of traces. Finally, in $\omega_s.tr$ the label ω_s is the prefix of the trace tr.

$\mathcal{V}_{ST} : \{LTrace_S\} \times State_S^n \to State_S^n;$

$\mathcal{V}_T : LTrace_S \times State_S^n \to State_S^n; \qquad\qquad \mathcal{V}_L : Label_S \times State_S^n \to State_S^n;$

$\mathcal{V}_{ST}(LTrace_S, \lambda) = \mathcal{V}_{ST}(LTrace_S \backslash \{tr\}, \mathcal{V}_T(tr, \lambda)); \quad \mathcal{V}_{ST}(\emptyset_{tr}, \lambda) = \lambda;$

$\mathcal{V}_T(\omega_s.tr, \lambda) = \mathcal{V}_T(tr, \mathcal{V}_L(\omega_s, \lambda)); \qquad\qquad \mathcal{V}_T(\langle\rangle, \lambda) = \lambda;$

$\mathcal{V}_L(has(l_i, x : k), \lambda) = \lambda[(\lambda_{l_i}^v \{k/x\}, \lambda_{l_i}^{pk}) / \lambda_i];$

$\mathcal{V}_L(rcv(l_i, l_j, x : t), \lambda) = \lambda[(\lambda_{l_i}^v \{t/x\}, \lambda_{l_i}^{pk}) / \lambda_i]$

$\mathcal{V}_L(rcv_{att}(l_i, l_j, x_m : t_m), \lambda) = \lambda[(\lambda_{l_i}^v \{t_m/x_m\}, \lambda_i^{pk}) / \lambda_{l_i}]$

$\mathcal{V}_L(comp(l_i, x : t), \lambda) = \lambda[(\lambda_{l_i}^v \{\lambda_{l_i}^v t/x\}, \lambda_{l_i}^{pk} \cup \{x = t\}) / \lambda_{l_i}]$

$\mathcal{V}_L(check(l_i, t_1 : t_2), \lambda) = \lambda[(\lambda_{l_i}^v, \lambda_{l_i}^{pk} \cup \{t_1 = t_2\}) / \lambda_{l_i}]$ if $\lambda_{l_i}^v t_1 = \lambda_{l_i}^v t_2 \in E$

$\mathcal{V}_L(ver_{att}(l_i, x_m : t_m), \lambda) = \lambda[(\lambda_{l_i}^v, \lambda_{l_i}^{pk} \cup \{\{x_m = t_m\} \text{ if } Trust_{l_i, l_j} \in \lambda_{l_i}^{pk}\}) / \lambda_i].$

We let λ_{l_i} and λ denote the state of component l_i and the global state that consists in the state of all components in the system, respectively. Each λ_{l_i} is defined by the pair $(\lambda_i^v, \lambda_{l_i}^{pk})$, which is the variable state and the property state for component l_i, respectively. In our calculus the variable state λ_i^v is defined by the set of substitutions $\{t_1/x_1, \ldots, t_m/x_m\}$, which captures the terms available to l_i, as well as the values of each variable from the perspective of l_i. $\lambda_{l_i}^v \{t/x\}$ is a shorthand for $(\lambda_{l_i}^v \cup \{t/x\}) \backslash \{t'/x\}$, if $\{t'/x\} \in \lambda_{l_i}^v$ for some t'. λ_i^{pk} is the set of integrity properties (e.g., $t_1 = t_2$) that captures the knowledge gained by l_j about these properties. $\lambda_i^v t$ represents the evaluation of t based on λ_i^v, and $\lambda_{l_i}^v t_1 = \lambda_{l_i}^v t_2 \in E$ says that the evaluation of t_1 and t_2 in λ_i^v are equal up to the equational theory E. We also consider the state update that results after a failed check (namely, $\lambda[\lambda_{Err}/\lambda_i]$, where λ_{Err} denotes the error state), though we omit the formal details here to save space.

4   From Protocols to Architectures

In the sequel, we discuss how the corresponding architecture can be extracted based on a given protocol or system. Namely, given a protocol specified in our process calculus we define an extraction procedure that extracts the corresponding architecture relations. The extraction procedure is based on the application of a set of extraction rules that we define below. Each extraction rule specifies the connection between the traces of labels of a system and the corresponding architecture relation. We assume a (initial) system S which consists in the parallel composition of r components (for a finite r), namely, $S \stackrel{def}{=} \lfloor P_1 \rfloor_{l_1}^{\rho_1} \mid \ldots \mid \lfloor P_r \rfloor_{l_r}^{\rho_r}$. The corresponding architecture relations will be extracted based on the possible traces (i.e., the trace semantics) of S. We emphasize that during the extraction of architectural properties we only consider the reduction traces to capture the communication between components, without considering the activity of the environment (i.e., the Dolev-Yao attacker). Formally, we do not take into account the labelled transitions known in the applied π-calculus [13]. The reason is that the architecture relations focus only on the abilities of the components and the communication between them.

An architecture does not not contain the *Compute* relations for background computations. The situation is similar at the protocol level, where the protocol description specifies the basic computations and communications of the components, without involving the background computations. Hence, when extracting the architecture relations, it is sufficient to consider only the protocol description and its corresponding reduction traces. The background computations will be taken into account when we discuss the mapping to the Has_j architecture logic property for reasoning about the data that can be deduced by a component.

Given a system S and the set $LTrace_S$ of (all) its possible label traces, we define the extraction function $\mathcal{X}_T$ that extracts the corresponding architecture based on $LTrace_S$. $\mathcal{X}_{ST}$ is interpreted similarly as $\mathcal{V}_{ST}$. Rel_S denotes the set of architectural relations of S. Function $\mathcal{X}_L$ extracts a relation based on a label ω_s and put it into α_S. We use α_S to denote the set of the extracted relations so far. We have the following extraction rules:

$$\mathcal{X}_{ST} : \{LTrace_S\} \times Rel_S \rightarrow Rel_S;$$

$$\mathcal{X}_T : LTrace_S \times Rel_S \rightarrow Rel_S; \qquad \mathcal{X}_L : Label_S \times Rel_S \rightarrow Rel_S;$$

$$\mathcal{X}_{ST}(LTrace_S, \alpha_S) = \mathcal{X}_{ST}(LTrace_S \backslash \{tr\}, \mathcal{X}_T(tr, \alpha_S)); \qquad \mathcal{X}_{ST}(\emptyset_{tr}, \alpha_S) = \alpha_S;$$

$$\mathcal{X}_T(\omega_s.tr, \alpha_S) = \mathcal{X}_T(tr, \mathcal{X}_L(\omega_s, \alpha_S)); \qquad \mathcal{X}_T(\langle\rangle, \alpha_S) = \alpha_S;$$

$R^{has}: \quad \mathcal{X}_L(has(l_j, x : k), \alpha_S) = \alpha_S \cup \{Has_{l_j}^{arch}(x)\};$

$R^{recv}: \quad \mathcal{X}_L(rcv(l_j, l_i, x : t), \alpha_S) = \alpha_S \cup \{Receive_{l_j, l_i}(x)\};$

$R_{att}^{recv}: \quad \mathcal{X}_L(rcv_{att}(l_j, l_i, x_m : t_m), Compute_{l_i}(x_m = t_m) \in \alpha_S) = $
$\qquad \alpha_S \cup \{Receive_{l_j, l_i}(\{Att\}, x_m)\}, \text{ where } Att = Attest_{l_i}(\{x_m = t_m\});$

$R^{comp}: \quad \mathcal{X}_L(comp(l_j, x : t), \alpha_S) = \alpha_S \cup \{Compute_{l_j}(x = t)\}, \text{ where } t \notin \{sign, checksign\};$

$R^{check}: \quad \mathcal{X}_L(check(l_j, t_1 : t_2), \alpha_S) = \alpha_S \cup \{Check_{l_j}(t_1 = t_2)\} \text{ if } t_1 = t_2 \in E;$

$R^{attver}: \quad \mathcal{X}_L(ver_{att}(l_j, x_m : t_m), \{Trust_{l_j, l_i}, Receive_{l_j, l_i}(\{Att\}, x_m)\} \subseteq \alpha_S) = $
$\qquad \alpha_S \cup \{Verif_{l_j}^{Attest}(Att)\}, \text{ where } Att = Attest_{l_i}(\{x_m = t_m\});$

All the rules above capture the communication and computation abilities of each component during the protocol run and are defined based on the trace semantics. In contrast, the $Trust_{l_i, l_j}$ relations are extracted based on the syntax. The initial set of relations is $\alpha_S^{init} = \{Trust_{l_i, l_j} \text{ if } l_j \in \rho_i \mid \forall \ l_i, l_j \in \{l_1, \ldots, l_r\}\}$. The meaning of each rule is defined as follows:

- Rule R^{has} corresponds to the relation $Has_{l_j}^{arch}(x)$, which says that l_j initially has a value for x. The name k represents an input data for x of l_j.
- R^{recv} extracts the relation $Receive_{l_j,l_i}(x)$, and describes the case when l_j receives a value t for x during the protocol run. S' and S'' represent the systems before and after the communication between l_i and l_j. S' involves the possibility for l_j to receive the variable x.
- R_{att}^{recv} extracts the relation $Receive_{l_j,l_i}(Attest_{l_i}(\{x_m = t_m\}), x_m)$, where $\{x_m = t_m\}$ contains $x_m = t_m$, along with all the equations $x_g = x_h$ computed by l_i in order to constitute t_m. Intuitively, besides attesting $x_m = t_m$, l_i attests the integrity of all the computations it performed in order to get x_m. S' includes the possibility for l_j to receive x_m, and its signature x_{sig}. Assumption $Compute_{l_i}(x_m = t_m) \in \alpha_S$ captures the fact that l_i is able to compute $x_m = t_m$, hence, it can make an attestation on this equation.
- Rule R^{comp} corresponds to the relation $Compute$, for the equations $x = f$ or $x = x'$. We do not extract the computations for signature and its verification since these computations are integrated within the $Attest$ relation.
- Rule R^{check} extracts the relation $Check$. To be able to check an equation, a component must have the ability to perform the function required in the check and it should possess the required data during the protocol run. This is determined by the equational theory E, which defines the checking abilities of a component. We do not extract $Check$ for signature check because it is considered as an attestation verification.
- Rule R^{attver} deals with the case when component l_j successfully verified the attestation sent by component l_i. However, we get the corresponding relation $Verif_{l_j}^{Attest}(Att)$ only in case $l_i \in \rho_j$ (i.e., l_j trusts l_i). The assumption $Receive_{l_j,l_i}(Att, x_m) \in \alpha_S$ captures the fact that l_j has received (Att, x_m).

The extraction procedure starts with the initial system S, then we follow the possible reduction traces from S and apply the extraction rules where possible. Although during the extraction every possible label trace of the system is examined, due to the simplifications we made on the processes (e.g., infinite process replication is leftout), the number of traces is finite, hence, the extraction procedure will terminate. In the sequel, we let $\mathcal{A}_S$ denote the extracted architecture of S (i.e., the set of relations α_S when we have examined all the possible traces).

Definition 1 *(State based semantics)*: *The state based semantics of a given system is defined as* $\mathcal{V}(S) = \{\lambda \in State_S^n \mid \exists\ tr \in T(S), \mathcal{V}_T(tr, Init^S) = \lambda\}$.

$Init^S$ is the initial state of the system S which contains only the $Trust$ relations in λ^{pk}. We adopt the Has properties used in PAL (Sect. 2), and define their semantics based on the semantics of the calculus.

$$\psi ::= Has_{l_i}^{all}(x) \mid Has_{l_i}^{none}(x) \mid K_{l_i}(t_1 = t_2) \mid \psi_1 \wedge \psi_2$$

Definition 2 *(Semantics of property ψ for systems):*

$$1.\ S \in \mathcal{V}(Has_{l_i}^{all}(x)) \Leftrightarrow \exists\ \lambda \in \mathcal{V}(S) \colon \exists\ t'\ and\ t\ such\ that$$
$$(\lambda_{l_i}^v t' = t) \in E,\ where\ BoundTo(t) = x$$

2. $S \in \mathcal{V}(Has_{l_i}^{none}(x)) \Leftrightarrow \forall \lambda \in \mathcal{V}(S)$ and $\forall t \in terms(\lambda_{l_i}^v)$:
$\not\exists t'$ such that $(\lambda_{l_i}^v t' = t) \in E$, where $BoundTo(t) = x$
3. $S \in \mathcal{V}(K_{l_i}(Eq)) \Leftrightarrow \forall \lambda' \in \mathcal{V}_{l_i}(S) \exists \lambda \in \mathcal{V}_{l_i}(S), \exists Eq'$:
$(\lambda \geq_{l_i} \lambda') \wedge (\lambda_{l_i}^{pk} \rhd_E Eq') \wedge (Eq' \Rightarrow_E Eq).$

S satisfies the property $Has_{l_i}^{all}(x)$ when during the system run, l_i can deduce or obtain a value t for x. $(\lambda_{l_i}^v t' = t) \in E$ means that l_i can deduce t based on $\lambda_{l_i}^v t'$ and the equational theory E. $BoundTo(t) = x$ captures the fact that this t has been bounded to x during the reduction trace (i.e., t is the value of x). S satisfies $Has_{l_i}^{all}(x)$ when l_i cannot deduce or obtain any value t for x. Finally, the deduction $\lambda_{l_i}^{pk} \rhd_E Eq'$ and $Eq' \Rightarrow_E Eq$ are defined on the deduction system based on the equational theory E.

To compare $\mathcal{A}_S$ and $\mathcal{A}$, we define $\mathcal{E}$, the set of *type-preserved* mappings from terms in the calculus to the terms in PAL: $\mathcal{E} = \{l_i \mapsto i; x \mapsto \tilde{X}; f(t_1, \ldots, t_m) \mapsto F(T_1, \ldots, T_m); f(x_1, \ldots, x_m) \mapsto \odot F(X), X = [X_1, \ldots, X_m]\}$. It is important to emphasize that in each mapping, the result and its preimage must have the same type. Defining an explicit type system for terms is not in the scope of this paper. Here, we only provide general type matching requirements for the mapping rules, giving the reader an intuition about the mapping to understand the definitions given below. In $\mathcal{E}$, each ID l_i can be mapped to an ID i; each x can be mapped to a $\tilde{X}$ of the same type. $f(t_1, \ldots, t_m)$ can be mapped to $F(T_1, \ldots, T_m)$ if each (t_j, T_j) pair has the same type, and the two functions return the same type, too. Similarly, $f(x_1, \ldots, x_m)$ can be mapped to $\odot F(X)$ if they return the same type, and the array X contains m variables, such that each corresponding variable pair has the same type. In the sequel, we let $\mathcal{E}\mathcal{A}_S$ denote the application of the mapping $\mathcal{E}$ to the architecture $\mathcal{A}_S$.

The property 1 discusses the connection between a system S and its extracted architecture $\mathcal{E}\mathcal{A}_S$ with respect to the *Has* and K logical properties (ϕ and ψ).

Property 1 *(Correctness of the mapping)*: *Given a system S and its extracted architecture $\mathcal{E}\mathcal{A}_S$, for some $\mathcal{E}$, we have that $\forall x, l_i, t_1, t_2$ in S and $\forall \tilde{X}, i, T_1, T_2$ in $\mathcal{E}\mathcal{A}_S$, where $\{x \mapsto \tilde{X}, l_i \mapsto i, t_1 \mapsto T_1, t_2 \mapsto T_2\} \in \mathcal{E}$: 1. $S \in \mathcal{V}(Has_{l_i}^{all}(x))$ iff $\mathcal{E}\mathcal{A}_S \in \mathcal{S}(Has_i^{all}(\tilde{X}))$; 2. $S \in \mathcal{V}(Has_{l_i}^{none}(x))$ iff $\mathcal{E}\mathcal{A}_S \in \mathcal{S}(Has_i^{none}(\tilde{X}))$; and 3. $S \in \mathcal{V}(K_{l_i}(t_1 = t_2))$ iff $\mathcal{E}\mathcal{A}_S \in \mathcal{S}(K_i(T_1 = T_2))$.*

The first point of Property 1 says that if the system S satisfies $Has_{l_i}^{all}(x)$, then the extracted architecture $\mathcal{E}\mathcal{A}_S$ of S satisfies $Has_i^{all}(\tilde{X})$, and vice versa. The second point is related to the privacy requirement capturing that when $\mathcal{E}\mathcal{A}_S$ satisfies $Has_i^{none}(\tilde{X})$, the system S satisfies $Has_{l_i}^{none}(x)$, and vice versa. The third point is related to the integrity property stating that if in the system S component l_i knows $t_1 = t_2$, then in the extracted architecture this component knows the corresponding $T_1 = T_2$, and vice versa. The proof is based on the semantics of the architecture and the state based semantics of the systems, as well as the correspondence between the deduction rules of the privacy logic and the equational theory E of the calculus.

We give two conformance definitions between protocol and architecture, a *strong* one and a *weak* one.

Definition 3 *(Strong Conformance)*: *Let us consider a system S and an architecture $\mathcal{A}$. We say that S strongly conforms to $\mathcal{A}$ up to $\mathcal{E}$ ($S \models_{\mathcal{E}}^{s} \mathcal{A}$) if $\exists \mathcal{E}$ such that $\mathcal{E}\mathcal{A}_S = \mathcal{A}$.*

In the strong case, we require that there exists a mapping $\mathcal{E}$ such that $\mathcal{E}\mathcal{A}_S$ contains exactly the same relations as $\mathcal{A}$.

Definition 4 *(Weak Conformance)*: *Let us consider a system S and an architecture $\mathcal{A}$. We say that S weakly conforms to $\mathcal{A}$ up to $\mathcal{E}$ (denoted $S \models_{\mathcal{E}}^{w} \mathcal{A}$) if (i.) $\exists \mathcal{E}$ such that $\mathcal{A} \subset \mathcal{E}\mathcal{A}_S$, and (ii.) $\forall x, \tilde{X}$ such that $\{x \mapsto \tilde{X}\} \in \mathcal{E}$: If $\mathcal{A} \in S$ $(Has_i^{none}(\tilde{X}))$ then $S \in \mathcal{V}(Has_{l_i}^{none}(x))$.*

Point (i.) of the weak case requires the more relaxed $\mathcal{A} \subset \mathcal{E}\mathcal{A}_S$. Point (ii.) says that for every $\tilde{X}$ in the privacy requirement $Has_j^{none}(\tilde{X})$ of the architecture, l_j cannot have any value t for x in the system S (where $\{x \mapsto \tilde{X}\} \in \mathcal{E}$).

Next, we provide the state simulation and bisimulation definitions in order to formulate Properties 2 and 3 about the relationship between the states of a system and states of an architecture in case of weak and strong conformance.

Definition 5 *(State simulation)*: *Let us consider a system S and an architecture $\mathcal{A}$. We say that $\lambda \in \mathcal{V}(S)$ simulates $\sigma \in \mathcal{S}(\mathcal{A})$ up to $\mathcal{E}$ (denoted by $\lambda \sqsubseteq_{\mathcal{E}} \sigma$), if $\forall l_i, x, t_1, t_2$ in S, and $\forall i, \tilde{X}, T_1, T_2$ in $\mathcal{A}$, such that $\{l_i \mapsto i, x \mapsto \tilde{X}, t \mapsto T, t_1 \mapsto T_1, t_2 \mapsto T_2\} \in \mathcal{E}$:*

- *if $\exists \sigma[(\sigma_i^v[V/\tilde{X}], \sigma_i^{pk}) / \sigma_i] \in \mathcal{S}(\mathcal{A})$, then $\exists \lambda[(\lambda_{l_i}^v \cup \{t/x\}, \lambda_{l_i}^{pk}) / \lambda_{l_i}] \in \mathcal{V}(S)$*
- *if $\exists \sigma[(\sigma_i^v[eval(T, \sigma_i^v)/\tilde{X}], \sigma_i^{pk} \cup \{\tilde{X} = T\}) / \sigma_i] \in \mathcal{S}(\mathcal{A})$, then $\exists \lambda[(\lambda_{l_i}^v \cup \{\lambda_{l_i}^v t/x\}, \lambda_{l_i}^{pk} \cup \{x = t\}) / \lambda_{l_i}] \in \mathcal{V}(S)$, and*
- *if $\exists \sigma[(\sigma_i^v, \sigma_i^{pk} \cup \{T_1 = T_2\}) / \sigma_i] \in \mathcal{S}(\mathcal{A})$, then $\exists \lambda[(\lambda_{l_i}^v, \lambda_{l_i}^{pk} \cup \{t_1 = t_2\}) / \lambda_{l_i}] \in \mathcal{V}(S)$.*

Also, we write $\lambda \sqsubseteq_{\mathcal{E}}^{(\tilde{X}, x)} \sigma$ if λ simulates σ up to $\mathcal{E}$, but with respect to only the pair $(\tilde{X}, x)$, where $\{x \mapsto \tilde{X}\} \in \mathcal{E}$.

Each point of Definition 5 captures the state simulation that results from the corresponding architecture relations. For example, the second point says that if $\exists \ Compute_i(\tilde{X} = T) \in \mathcal{A}$ then $\exists \ Compute_{l_i}(\tilde{X} = T) \in \mathcal{E}\mathcal{A}_S$.

Definition 6 *(State bisimulation)*: *Given a system S and an architecture $\mathcal{A}$:*

1. *We say that $\lambda \in \mathcal{V}(S)$ and $\sigma \in \mathcal{S}(\mathcal{A})$ simulate each other up to $\mathcal{E}$ ($\lambda \simeq_{\mathcal{E}} \sigma$), if $\lambda \sqsubseteq_{\mathcal{E}} \sigma$ and $\sigma \sqsubseteq_{\mathcal{E}} \lambda$.*
2. *We say that $\lambda \in \mathcal{V}(S)$ and $\sigma \in \mathcal{S}(\mathcal{A})$ simulate each other up to $\mathcal{E}$ and the variable pair $(\tilde{X}, x)$, $\lambda \simeq_{\mathcal{E}}^{(\tilde{X}, x)} \sigma$, if $\lambda \sqsubseteq_{\mathcal{E}}^{(\tilde{X}, x)} \sigma$ and $\sigma \sqsubseteq_{\mathcal{E}}^{(\tilde{X}, x)} \lambda$.*

Property 2. *Given a system S and an architecture $\mathcal{A}$, where $\lambda \in \mathcal{V}(S)$ and $\sigma \in \mathcal{S}(\mathcal{A})$. We have that $S \models_{\mathcal{E}}^{s} \mathcal{A}$ iff $\lambda \simeq_{\mathcal{E}} \sigma$.*

Property 2 says that when S strongly conforms to $\mathcal{A}$, then the states of l_j in S simulates the states of the corresponding component j in $\mathcal{A}$, and vice versa.

Property 3. *Given a system S and an architecture $\mathcal{A}$, where $\lambda \in \mathcal{V}(S)$ and $\sigma \in \mathcal{S}(\mathcal{A})$. We have that $S \models_{\mathcal{E}}^{w} \mathcal{A}$ iff (i.) $\lambda \sqsubseteq_{\mathcal{E}} \sigma$ and (ii.) $\lambda \simeq_{\mathcal{E}}^{(\tilde{X}, x)} \sigma$, for all $\tilde{X}$ in $Has_{j}^{none}(\tilde{X})$.*

Property 3 says that in case S weakly conforms to $\mathcal{A}$, then the states of l_j simulates the states of the corresponding component j, and these states are bisimilar for all the variable pair $(x, \tilde{X})$, such that $Has_{j}^{none}(\tilde{X})$ holds. A consequence of Properties 2 and 3 is that it is sufficient to show the state simulation and bisimulation to prove the weak and strong conformance properties. These two properties also capture the correctness of the mapping with respect to the weak and strong conformance definitions. The proof of Properties 2 and 3 is based on the defined extraction rules and the correspondence between functions $\mathcal{S}_E$ of the architecture and $\mathcal{V}_L$ of the system.

Example Conformance Check: We check the conformance between an example protocol and the architecture $\mathcal{A}_1$ at the end of Sect. 2, with $r = 1$. Let us consider the protocol description in which there are components l_M and l_O that refer to the meter and operator, respectively. The behavior of the meter is specified by the process R_M. The operator is defined by the process R_O.

$$R_M \overset{def}{=} \text{let } x_{c_1} = k_1 \text{ in } P_1; \qquad P_1 \overset{def}{=} \text{let } x_{m_1} = x_{c_1} \text{ in } P_2;$$
$$P_2 \overset{def}{=} \text{let } x_{sig} = sign(x_{m_1}, sk_m) \text{ in } P_3; \qquad P_3 \overset{def}{=} \overline{c_{mo}}\langle x_{m_1}, x_{sig}\rangle. \ \mathbf{0}.$$
$$R_O \overset{def}{=} c_{mo}(x_{m_1}, x_{sig}). \ \mathbf{0}. \qquad S \overset{def}{=} \lfloor R_M \rfloor_{l_M} \mid \lfloor R_O \rfloor_{l_O}^{l_M}.$$

Due to lack of space, we use this very simple example to demonstrate the mapping procedure and the conformance check between S and $\mathcal{A}_1$. The initial relations set α_S^{init} is $\{ Trust_{l_O, l_M} \}$. The architecture relations corresponding to S can be extracted in the following steps: From the two reductions

$$S \xrightarrow{has(l_M, \ x_{c_1}:k_1)} \lfloor P_1 \rfloor_{l_M} \mid \lfloor R_O \rfloor_{l_O}^{l_M} \xrightarrow{comp(l_M, \ x_{m_1}:x_{c_1})} \lfloor P_2 \rfloor_{l_M} \mid \lfloor R_O \rfloor_{l_O}^{l_M} \text{ and rules}$$

R^{has}, R^{comp} we have $\alpha_S = \alpha_S^{init} \cup \{Has_{l_M}^{arch}(x_{c_1})\} \cup \{Compute_{l_M}(x_{m_1} = x_{c_1})\}$. The *let*-process in P_2 has no effect on the extraction, while the channel synchronization will result in adding $Receive_{l_O, l_M}(\{x_{m_1} = x_{c_1}\}, x_{m_1})$ to α_S. Since R_O terminates right after receiving the attestation, the two $Compute_{l_O}$ relations and $Verif_{l_O}^{Attest}(Attest_{l_M}(\{x_{m_1} = x_{c_1}\}))$ cannot be extracted. This means that the system S does not conform to the architecture $\mathcal{A}_1$.

5   Related Works

Dedicated languages have been proposed to specify privacy properties (e.g., [5,7,16]) but they are complex and not intended to be used at the architectural level. In [2,3] the authors addressed the idea of applying formal methods to architecture design and proposed a simple privacy architecture language (PAL).

On the other hand, there are also many works focusing mainly on the protocol level, providing formal methods for specifying and verifying protocols, as well as reasoning about the security and privacy properties (e.g., [8, 19, 21]). For this purpose, process algebra languages are the most favoured means in the literature, because they are general frameworks to model concurrent systems.

In addition, among the process algebras, the applied π-calculus ([13, 22]) is one of the most promising language in the sense that its syntax and semantics are more expressive than the others (e.g., [1, 15, 20]). It also have been used to analyse security and privacy protocols (e.g., in [4, 9–11, 14, 17, 18]). However, we cannot use it directly for our purpose because for instance, it lacks syntax and semantics for modelling component IDs and trust relations. Some modifications and extensions of the applied π-calculus are required, which we proposed in Sect. 3.

Finally, the definition of the architecture comes before the definition of the protocol in software development cycles. Therefore, we chose to make it possible to verify the conformance of a protocol described in our language to an architecture. We used the architecture language in [2] for this purpose. Its main advantage is that (i) compared to informal pictorial methods, or semi-formal representations such as UML diagrams, it is more formal and precise, while (ii) compared to process calculi, it is more abstracted. The architecture language PAL enables designers to reason at the level of architectures, providing ways to express properties without entering into the details of specific protocols.

6 Conclusions and Future Works

In this paper, we proposed the application of formal methods to privacy by design. We provided the mapping from the protocol level to the architecture level for checking if a given implementation conforms to an architecture and showed its correctness. For this purpose, we modified the applied π-calculus and defined the connection between the semantics of the calculus and PAL. To the best of our knowledge, this is the first attempt at examining the connection between the protocol and the architecture levels in the privacy protection context.

The calculus version and the mapping procedure we proposed in this paper are based on a simplified version of the architecture language. Indeed, we only consider the attestation on equation $\tilde{X} = T$. Moreover, our proposed calculus (and mapping) does not support the modelling of zero-knowledge proofs, as well as the posibility of spot-checks used in toll pricing systems. Hence, our method can only handle simple architectures and protocols at this stage. One future direction of our work is to extend the calculus to support these such extensions.

Acknowledgements. The authors would like to thank Daniel Le Métayer for his initial idea and valuable comments during this work. This work is partially funded by the European project PARIS/FP7-SEC-2012-1, the ANR project BIOPRIV, and the Inria Project Lab CAPPRIS.

References

1. Abadi, M., Gordon, A.: A calculus for cryptographic protocols: the Spi calculus. Technical Report SRC RR 149, Digital Equipment Corporation, Systems Research Center (1998)
2. Antignac, T., Le Métayer, D.: Privacy architectures: Reasoning about data minimisation and integrity. In: Mauw, S., Jensen, C.D. (eds.) STM 2014. LNCS, vol. 8743, pp. 17–32. Springer, Heidelberg (2014)
3. Antignac, T., Le Métayer, D.: Privacy by design: From technologies to architectures. In: Preneel, B., Ikonomou, D. (eds.) APF 2014. LNCS, vol. 8450, pp. 1–17. Springer, Heidelberg (2014)
4. Backes, M., Maffei, M., Unruh, D.: Zero-knowledge in the applied pi-calculus and automated verification of the direct anonymous attestation protocol. In: Proceedings of SSP 2008. IEEE Symposium on Security and Privacy, pp. 202–215, May 2008
5. Barth, A., Datta, A., Mitchell, J., Nissenbaum, H.: Privacy and contextual integrity: framework and applications. In: IEEE Symposium on Security and Privacy, pp. 15–198, May 2006
6. Bass, L., Clements, P., Kazman, R.: Software Architecture in Practice. SEI Series in Software Engineering, 3rd edn. Addison-Wesley, Reading (2012)
7. Becker, M.Y., Malkis, A., Bussard, L.: A practical generic privacy language. Inf. Syst. Secur. **6503**, 125–139 (2011)
8. Burrows, M., Abadi, M., Needham, R.: A logic of authentication. ACM Trans. Comput. Syst. **8**, 18–36 (1990)
9. Delaune, S., Kremer, S., Ryan, M.: Verifying privacy-type properties of electronic voting protocols. J. Comput. Secur. **17**(4), 435–487 (2009)
10. Delaune, S., Ryan, M.D., Smyth, B.: Automatic verification of privacy properties in the applied pi calculus. Trust Management II. IFIP AICT, vol. 263, pp. 263–278. Springer, Boston (2008)
11. Dong, N., Jonker, H., Pang, J.: Analysis of a receipt-free auction protocol in the applied pi calculus. In: Degano, P., Etalle, S., Guttman, J. (eds.) FAST 2010. LNCS, vol. 6561, pp. 223–238. Springer, Heidelberg (2011)
12. Fagin, R., Halpern, J.Y., Moses, Y., Vardi, M.: Reasoning About Knowledge, paperback edn. MIT Press, New York (2004)
13. Fournet, C., Abadi, M.: Mobile values, new names, and secure communication. In: Proceedings of the 28th ACM Symposium on Principles of Programming, POPL 2001, pp. 104–115 (2001)
14. Fournet, C., Abadi, M.: Hiding names: Private authentication in the applied pi calculus. In: Okada, M., Babu, C.S., Scedrov, A., Tokuda, H. (eds.) ISSS 2002. LNCS, vol. 2609, pp. 317–338. Springer, Heidelberg (2003)
15. Hoare, C.A.R.: Communicating sequential processes. Commun. ACM **21**(8), 666–677 (1978)
16. Jafari, M., Fong, P.W., Safavi-Naini, R., Barker, K., Sheppard, N.P.: Towards defining semantic foundations for purpose-based privacy policies. In: Proceedings of the First ACM Conference on Data and Application Security and Privacy, CODASPY 2011, New York, USA, pp. 213–224 (2011)
17. Kremer, S., Ryan, M.D.: Analysis of an electronic voting protocol in the applied pi calculus. In: Sagiv, M. (ed.) ESOP 2005. LNCS, vol. 3444, pp. 186–200. Springer, Heidelberg (2005)

18. Li, X., Zhang, Y., Deng, Y.: Verifying anonymous credential systems in applied pi calculus. In: Garay, J.A., Miyaji, A., Otsuka, A. (eds.) CANS 2009. LNCS, vol. 5888, pp. 209–225. Springer, Heidelberg (2009)
19. Meadows, C.: Formal methods for cryptographic protocol analysis: Emerging issues and trends. IEEE Sel. Areas Commun. **21**(1), 44–54 (2003)
20. Milner, R., Parrow, J., Walker, D.: A calculus of mobile processes, parts i and ii. Inf. Comput. **100**(1), 1–77 (1992)
21. Paulson, L.C.: The inductive approach to verifying cryptographic protocols. J. Comput. Secur. **6**(1–2), 85–128 (1998)
22. Ryan, M.D., Smyth, B.: Applied pi calculus. In: Cryptology and Information Security Series, vol. 5, pp. 112–142 (2011)

Software Security and Malware Analysis

Moving Target Defense Against Cross-Site Scripting Attacks (Position Paper)

Joe Portner, Joel Kerr, and Bill Chu[⊠]

Department of Software and Information Systems, University of North Carolina,
Charlotte, NC 28223, USA
{jpportner,cjokerr}@gmail.com, billchu@uncc.edu

Abstract. We present a new method to defend against cross-site scripting (XSS) attacks. Our approach is based on mutating symbols in the JavaScript language and leveraging commonly used load-balancing mechanisms to deliver multiple copies of a website using different versions of the JavaScript language. A XSS attack that injects unauthorized JavaScript code can thus be easily detected. Our solution achieves similar benefits in XSS protection as Content Security Policy (CSP), a leading web standard to prevent cross site scripting, but can be much more easily adopted because refactoring of websites is not required.

Keywords: Cross site scripting · Moving target defense · Web security · Application security

1 Introduction

Cross-site scripting (XSS) has been a leading web attack vector for many years. XSS attacks stem from a web design feature: there is no clear demarcation separating JavaScript programs from other web data such as Hypertext Markup Language (HTML) and Cascading Style Sheets (CSS) data streams. JavaScript programs can be intermixed with other web data in very complicated ways, affording malicious Java-Script programs to be injected into a legitimate web data stream and cause malicious logic to be executed on a client device. Unfortunately there is no easy way to prevent all XSS attacks. The best practice is to encourage developers to sanitize untrusted data before placing them into the web stream [1, 5–7]. However, there is no one-size-fit-all solution to perform whitelist-based data sanitization for web data streams that can prevent XSS attacks while preserving legitimate web functions [1].

The most comprehensive industry proposal to combat XSS is part of the Content Security Policy (CSP) introduced by Mozilla Foundation in Firefox 4 and adopted as a W3C candidate in 2012 [2]. All major browsers are supporting it today. XSS protection is one of the major goals of CSP. It can be summarized by the following four components. (1) New versions of CSP-compliant browsers must be used. (2) CSP assumes legitimate JavaScript programs can be enumerated before run time. (3) Dynamic evaluation of JavaScript programs using the "eval" function is not permitted. (4) No inline JavaScript programs are permitted. All legitimate JavaScript programs must be contained in dedicated files. The website will instruct a CSP-compliant browser to load

© Springer International Publishing Switzerland 2015
F. Cuppens et al. (Eds.): FPS 2014, LNCS 8930, pp. 85–91, 2015.
DOI: 10.1007/978-3-319-17040-4_6

approved JavaScript files from approved web locations. By banning inline JavaScript programs, CSP achieves a clear separation of JavaScript programs from other web data stream. To execute a JavaScript program, a CSP-compliant site will use:

```
script-src www.acmecorp.com;
<script src="https://www.acmecorp.com/main.js"/>
```

The first line is a CSP directive indicating that JavaScript programs can be served from www.acmecorp.com. The second line invokes a particular JavaScript program from the whitelisted source. CSP has a built in XSS detection mechanism. If an inline JavaScript program is detected, a CSP-compliant browser will report this event back to the server as an indication of malicious attack behavior.

No major objections have been raised against the first three components of CSP. Legitimate JavaScript programs in most web sites reside in either static files (e.g. .html, .css, .php, .jsp, .aspx) or content management systems databases that do not change after deployment. Dynamic contents often come from either business databases (e.g. orders, accounts) or user input. They typically do not contain JavaScript programs. XSS attacks target vulnerabilities in server side scripts written in languages such as PHP, ASP, Java, and JSP.

The fourth component of CSP presents the most challenge for its wide adoption. Many small JavaScript programs are often tightly integrated into web pages as illustrated by the following example.

```
<type="text" name="email" onkeyup="doX(arg1, arg2)">
```

In this case a JavaScript function doX() is called whenever a key is released in the text box. If one were to disable inline JavaScript programs, one must refactor the webpage and move this JavaScript program out of the html file. It is a formidable task for any large website to pull out many small snippets of JavaScript code into different files. It is equally difficult to maintain such a website as these scripts will not be directly visible to a developer in the files that they are used in. The developer is forced to open separate files to view/modify a few lines of code. It is not surprising that despite efforts by browser vendors to support CSP, a 2014 study by Veracode indicated only 355 of the top 1 million Alexa web sites have adopted CSP [3]. Even for those adopting CSP, they often continue to enable inline JavaScript programs for reasons described here. Therefore in practice even the limited adoption of CSP is for reasons other than XSS protection.

2 Moving Target Defense Against XSS

In this paper we outline a new approach, based the principle of moving target defense [11], to mitigate XSS attacks with CSP-like benefits without the requirement of refactoring JavaScript programs in existing websites. Our approach, referred to as the Moving Target defense against XSS (MDX), shares the same first three assumptions as CSP but allows inline JavaScript programs. We create randomly mutated versions of JavaScript language. A server implementing MDX will maintain multiple copies of a website, each with a different version of JavaScript. For a given web page request, a random version will be served. The server will inform a compliant browser the version of mutated JavaScript language it should use. Injected JavaScript programs will fail because it cannot predict the version of JavaScript at run time. A MDX-compliant browser will report back any instances of JavaScript programs not using the agreed upon mutation. These instances suggest website vulnerabilities that should be fixed.

2.1 JavaScript Language Mutation

XSS attacks consist of injected code that modifies either state or behavior on a page. If we can defend a script from both unwanted state change and behavior, we can defeat XSS attacks. To modify behavior of a page, an attacker must use JavaScript functions, or APIs. For example, an attack script can inject page elements as shown below:

```
node.appendChild(newNode);
```

This particular attack would add the "newNode" object as a child to the "node" object. In order to make API calls, a script must use the parentheses (). We can mutate one of these tokens – for instance, the left parenthesis – in whitelisted JavaScript programs. The above example JavaScript program can be mutated to:

```
node.appendChild(123newNode);
```

Here the string "(123" will be interpreted by JavaScript interpreter as a single token representing the left parenthesis. By taking away an attacker's ability to use the left parenthesis, they are not able to attack page behavior. Only left parentheses that are syntactically correct (i.e., appropriately mutated) will be executed successfully.

To manipulate page state (without using API functions), the attackers must use the assignment operator. The browser and DOM objects provide access to key state objects that attackers could manipulate. An example of a XSS attack that manipulates page state is shown below:

```
location = "evil.com";
```

We can mutate the "=" token in whitelisted JavaScript programs. Again, the above example becomes:

```
location =123 "evil.com";
```

Similarly here the string "=123" is interpreted by the JavaScript interpreter as the token for assignment operator.

Limiting mutation to these two tokens simplifies the mutation process and keeps computation resource requirements low. We acknowledge that there is potential for an attacker to use a different JavaScript language feature to launch a successful XSS attack; however, if it was discovered that another token could be used to manipulate behavior or state, our method could easily be extended to include another token. Additionally, because the tokens themselves are being changed, filter evasion techniques, like encoding, redirection, etc., will not be successful either.

2.2 Deploying MDX

Multiple versions of the web site will be served, each using a different version of the JavaScript language. For a given web request, one of the versions will be picked randomly. This scheme fits nicely into most practical settings as websites are often replicated for load balancing, as illustrated in Fig. 1.

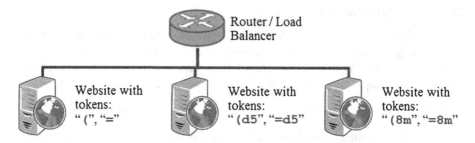

Fig. 1. Example load-balanced MDX implementation

Whitelisted JavaScript programs in a web site are mutated offline by a process that scans web content (e.g. files with extensions such as .html, .php, .jsp, .aspx, and .css, as well as databases used by a content management system), to identify JavaScript programs, and mutate the tokens for left parenthesis and assignment operator. When a web page is served, part of the header informs an MDX-compliant browser of the particular version of JavaScript being used. This is accomplished by passing a string that represents the mutated left parenthesis and assignment operator. The browser passes the mutated tokens to its JavaScript engine to interpret JavaScript programs. Our example for this scenario is seen in Fig. 2.

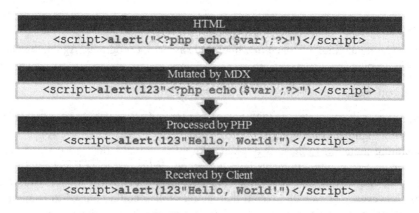

Fig. 2. MDX mutation process

Backwards compatibility can easily be maintained. If a request is made from a browser not supporting MDX, then the request will be redirected to an unmodified version of the site. Similar to CSP, an MDX-compliant browser will report JavaScript violations back to the server so XSS vulnerabilities can be identified. These reports include: the page on which the violation occurred, the page's referrer, the resource that violated the page's policy, and the specific directive it violated [2]. Our assumption is that reported vulnerabilities will be fixed in a timely manner.

With MDX, the odds are greatly in favor of the defenders. Suppose N copies of the web site are deployed at any given time. An attacker might be able to discover all versions of JavaScript available at any given moment. He can craft an attack with a probability of 1/N being successful. The probability of the attack failing, thus leading to vulnerability discovery, is 1–1/N. For example if 10 website copies are deployed the probability of a successful attack is 10 %. For any attack, its probability of being discovered is 90 %.

Each cross site scripting attacks are likely to be carried out multiple times. For example, XSS attack may involve sending a mass email with a malicious JavaScript program embedded in a link. If k attacks occur, the probability of all k attacks being successful is $(1/N)k$. The probability of at least one attack failing—leading to the detection of the vulnerability—is $1–(1/N)k$. Continuing with the email attack example, if 10 attack links were clicked, the probability of XSS vulnerability detection would be $1–(1/10)10$, or 0.999999999.

2.3 Browser Implementation

We carried out a proof of concept implementation to start exploring how to modify an open source browser to support MDX. We implemented a modified JavaScript engine inside WebKit by statically changing JavaScript tokens for the left parenthesis and assignment operators. We tested the modified WebKit JavaScript engine with a modified version of Safari browser and found it worked as planned. All known filter evasion XSS attacks [4] were defeated by our modified browser. The next steps in a future browser implementation include (1) have the browser dynamically change the symbol table used by the lexical analyzer of the JavaScript interpreter and (2) make each tab of the browser work with different versions of the lexical analyzer table within the JavaScript interpreter. Based on our experience in modifying WebKit, assistance from browser developers may be required.

3 Discussions

Much research into preventing XSS attacks has focused on offline taint analysis based on server side source code (e.g. [5–7]). However it is difficult to fix all XSS vulnerabilities using program analysis in practice because of high false positives generated. Space limitation does not permit us to reference other research proposals to protect XSS attacks at run time. Most of them are heuristics based. Our work is related to one line of such research, Instruction-Set Randomization (ISR) [8, 10], which was designed to protect languages from injection attacks without relying on any heuristics. However, as pointed out by [9] parsing all web streams on a web server to randomize JavaScript programs upon every page load introduces a prohibitive run time overhead.

To minimize performance overhead, xJS [9] was proposed to counter XSS in such way that one does not need to run JavaScript parsing on the web server. All JavaScript programs are encoded by XORing them with a random key which will be decoded by a browser plugin by XORing again with the same key. This key can be exchanged as part of response to a web request. This approach has the advantage of not requiring browser modifications. The main drawback of this approach, however, is that it does not accommodate server side scripts. It is common for JavaScript programs to contain host variables, which will be dynamically replaced with content by a server side script (e.g. PHP). By XORing all JavaScript programs blindly, xJS breaks such behavior as illustrated in Fig. 3.

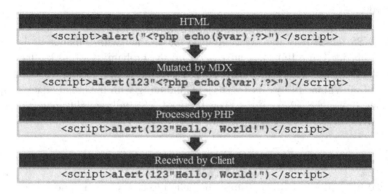

Fig. 3. xJS transformation process

In contrast, MDX preserves all server side script functions as illustrated in Fig. 2. Unlike ISR MDX mutates JavaScript programs offline. This has the advantage of avoiding run time performance penalty. Although an attacker can still craft JavaScript code to attack a specific version of the JavaScript language, such an attempt will likely to fail because the version of JavaScript language served is chosen randomly from a (potentially large) number of options, which is accomplished by leveraging commonly used load-balancing features. Furthermore XSS vulnerabilities can be discovered quickly with very high probability.

In summary, MDX is a promising new approach to defend against XSS attacks without requiring people to change their existing websites. It can be deployed efficiently by leveraging existing web delivery infrastructure without performance penalties. MDX is highly scalable, enabling those with more computing resources to offer better protection against XSS attacks by deploying more website copies. A critical success factor for wide adoption of MDX is to gain the necessary support from major browsers. Such support is possible, as in the case of support for Content Security Policy we discussed above.

Acknowledgment. This work is funded in part by NSF Grant 1129190.

References

1. OWASP: XSS (Cross Site Scripting) Prevention Cheat Sheet, 12 April 2014. https://www.owasp.org/index.php/XSS_(Cross_Site_Scripting)_Prevention_Cheat_Sheet
2. Web Application Security Working Group: Content Security Policy 1.1, 11 February 2014. http://www.w3.org/TR/2014/WD-CSP11-20140211/
3. Dawson, I.: Security Headers on the Top 1,000,000 Websites: March 2014 Report, 19 March 2014. http://blog.veracode.com/2014/03/security-headers-on-the-top-1000000-websites-march-2014-report/
4. OWASP: XSS Filter Evasion Cheat Sheet, 26 April 2014. https://www.owasp.org/index.php/XSS_Filter_Evasion_Cheat_sheet
5. Xie, J., Chu, B., Lipford, H.R., Melton, J.T.: ASIDE, p. 267. ACM Press, New York (2011)
6. Vogt, P., Nentwich, F., Jovanovic, N., Kirda, E., Kruegel, C., Vigna, G.: Cross-site scripting prevention with dynamic data tainting and static analysis. In: 14th Annual Network & Distributed System Security Symposium, 28 February 2007
7. Wassermann, G., Su, Z.: Static detection of cross-site scripting vulnerabilities, p. 171. ACM Press, New York (2008)
8. Kc, G.S., Keromytis, A.D., Prevelakis, V.: Countering code-injection attacks with instruction-set randomization, p. 272. ACM Press, New York (2003)
9. Krithinakis, A., Athanasopoulos, E., Markatos, E.P.: Isolating javascript in dynamic code environments, pp. 45–49. ACM Press, New York (2010)
10. Athanasopoulos, E., Krithinakis, A., Markatos, E.P.: An architecture for enforcing javascript randomization in web 2.0 applications. In: 13th Information Security Conference, USA, 25–28 October 2010
11. MIT Lincoln Lab: Survey of Cyber Moving Targets. Technical Report 1166, September 2013

Combining High-Level and Low-Level Approaches to Evaluate Software Implementations Robustness Against Multiple Fault Injection Attacks

Lionel Rivière[1,2]([⊠]), Marie-Laure Potet[3], Thanh-Ha Le[1],
Julien Bringer[1], Hervé Chabanne[1,2], and Maxime Puys[1]

[1] Safran Morpho, Paris, France
{lionel.riviere,thanh-ha.Le,julien.bringer,herve.chabanne,
maxime.Puys}@morpho.com
[2] Télécom Paristech, Paris, France
{lionel.riviere,herve.chabanne}@telecom-paristech.fr
[3] Verimag, Gières, France
marie-laure.potet@imag.fr

Abstract. Physical fault injections break security functionalities of algorithms by targeting their implementations. Software techniques strengthen such implementations to enhance their robustness against fault attacks. Exhaustively testing physical fault injections is time consuming and requires complex platforms. Simulation solutions are developed for this specific purpose. We chose two independent tools presented in 2014, the *Laser Attack Robustness* (Lazart) and the *Embedded Fault Simulator* (EFS) in order to evaluate software implementations against multiple fault injection attacks. Lazart and the EFS share the common goal that consists in detecting vulnerabilities in the code. However, they operate with different techniques, fault models and abstraction levels. This paper aims at exhibiting specific advantages of both approaches and proposes a combining scheme that emphasizes their complementary nature.

Keywords: Fault injection · Fault simulation · Instruction skipping · Control flow graph · Multiple fault · Smartcard · Embedded systems · Security

1 Introduction

Active physical attacks, in particular fault injections, are performed against smartcard implementations in order to reveal sensitive information or break

This work was partially funded by the French ANR project E-MATA HARI.
Identity and Security Alliance (The Morpho and Télécom ParisTech Research Center).
Maxime Puys—Work done while the author was in internship at Morpho.

© Springer International Publishing Switzerland 2015
F. Cuppens et al. (Eds.): FPS 2014, LNCS 8930, pp. 92–111, 2015.
DOI: 10.1007/978-3-319-17040-4_7

secured codes. Introduced in 1997 [1], they consist in inducing volatile faults in an operating circuit in order to generate computational errors. Several means exist to perform physical fault injections such as clock of voltage glitch [2]. Electromagnetic waves [3] and laser beams [4] improved the injection accuracy. Physical injections effects can be exploited towards Differential Fault Analysis attacks (DFA) [1,5], which aim at retrieving crucial information such as cryptographic keys by com paring faulty outputs with the correct ones. Such attacks also apply to non-cryptographic security features such as integrity checks or authentications.

In the following subsections, we describe how fault attacks threaten smartcard implementations and we propose a coarse-grained process for secure development accordingly. We emphasize actual challenges in this area and we present our contributions.

1.1 Fault Injection Attacks Threats

In the context of smartcard-based products, manufacturers have the challenge to ensure fault robustness for every embedded functionality. Sensitive data such as private keys are critical and must be securely managed. In order to provide confidentiality, integrity and authenticity to sensitive data, smartcard manufacturers design secure implementations, embedding software countermeasures, that are tested and evaluated against physical attacks.

However, performing an exhaustive physical fault injection evaluation would be time consuming, thus costly and therefore would come far too late in the development process. Moreover, if a vulnerability is found in the final sample code, it then remains mainly two options to smartcard developers. If a software countermeasure can handle the vulnerability, the product may be patched on already existing smartcards. However, if the vulnerability is not addressable with a software countermeasure, it could condemn the project. Furthermore, different products are built on different components. For each new product specifications, new dedicated evaluations are developed from scratch or adapted from existing ones. Hence, smartcard manufacturer need a generic method to cope with this multiplicity constraint and stem experiments complexity. This justifies the use of a global development process taking into account the robustness of the developed applications against fault injections.

1.2 A Coarse-Grained Process

Defining a secure development process against fault injection attacks is based on the following steps:

1. identify objects that must be protected
2. develop the functional application embedding appropriate countermeasures
3. physical testing of the robustness against fault injections

This coarse-grained process must be refined in order to detect weaknesses as soon as possible. Although physical attacks are conducted on the binary code under execution, countermeasure accuracy evaluation must take place both on the source code (for instance C code) and on the assembly code (proper to each architecture). Source code robustness evaluation offers several advantages. First, a same application can be deployed on several types of architectures and C codes can then be reused, even with some adaptations depending on the component countermeasures. Then the evaluation effort is factorized between several deployments of a same application. As illustrated below, testing a low-level code against fault injection can produced a huge amount of attacks that must be examined in detail. Attacks established at the source level abstract several low-level attacks and can be more easily classified in terms of their impacts. Nevertheless, source code robustness evaluation does not give sufficient guarantees: physical attacks take place at the binary code, which can be very different than the source code (due to the compiling process). As a consequence, a low-level code analysis is also necessary. In this paper we present such a development process, based on two tools.

1.3   Actual Challenges

There exist several tools and approaches dedicated to test implementations against fault injections [6–8]. All these works differ from the fault model that is taken into account [9] and the level of code that is targeted (C or Java bytecode for the referenced works). Nevertheless all approaches face to the same problems:

- how to evaluate the dangerousness of traces obtained by fault injection
- how to compare a set of attacks
- how to establish a final verdict both in term of vulnerability or robustness

Starting from the set of assets to be protected, the first challenge consists in stating a verifiable oracle (in white or black box approach) allowing to classify attacks that jeopardize security and are not detected by countermeasures. White box oracles can be made more precise because they imply the internal state execution. Fault injection robustness is an intrinsically brute-force process, implying all possible deviant behaviors provoked by fault injections. Generally we obtain a large amount of attacks that must be reduced, to be reasonably treated. Actually there exist no criteria for that. Finally we can distinguish two classes of tools: dynamic tools start from a given execution trace which is progressively mutated [7,10] and static tools [6,8] that do not execute code and produce programs embedding some fault injections. For the first category of tools, attacks can be effectively founded but it is not possible to state robustness verdict. On the contrary, static approaches are complete but can generate false positives (for instance unfeasible paths).

We use here two complementary tools. The first one, Lazart [11], is a static tool acting on the source code and based on symbolic execution [12] that ensures both the feasibility of founded attacks and completeness verdict. The second one [10] is a low-level embedded simulator, based on a dynamic approach, which guarantee a fine-grained attack classification due to the fact that hardware mechanisms and countermeasures are not abstracted.

1.4   Our Contributions

- We propose a global process combining high-level and low-level robustness evaluation against multiple fault injections
- We formalize the relationship between source and assembly attacks
- Based on the complementarity between source code and assembly code attacks, we propose a systematic way to reduce the set of low-level attacks in order to facilitate the verdict statement.

After the identification of sensitive code that must be protected, we propose to conduct several evaluations:

1. Use the concolic tool Lazart in order to evaluate the code robustness to produce (or prove the absence of) high-level attacks
2. Use the low-level Embedded Fault Simulator (EFS) to produce low-level attacks
3. Evaluate the coverage of the high-level attacks by the low-level attacks
4. Evaluate the divergence between high and low-level evaluation
5. State a verdict

In Sect. 2, we describe the Lazart [11] approach used to perform high-level fault injection simulation and its concolic analysis capabilities. Section 3 keeps the same structure to provide a description of the low-level Embedded Fault Simulator that simulates fault effects on the assembly code on actual smartcards. We exhibit the main advantage of each approach and show how results can be compared. In complement of [10], we propose a way to classify found attacks, through the notion of *representative* attack. Section 4 illustrates the proposed process on more significant examples. In Sect. 4, we expose our fault simulation results on a PIN verification implementation, with the Lazart and EFS tools. Finally, in Sect. 5, we explore the potential of combining the two tools to enhance the vulnerability detection rate and accuracy. Section 6 concludes the paper and gives some perspectives.

A Small Example. In the two following sections, tools are illustrated with the help of the small example given below.

```
1  // Byte array comparison
2  static bool byteArrayCompare(byte* a1, byte* a2){
3      int i       = 0;
4      int status  = BOOL_FALSE;
5      int diff    = BOOL_FALSE;
6      int size    = sizeof(a1)/sizeof(byte);
7      for (i=0; i<size; i++)
8          if (a1[i] != a2[i])
9              diff = BOOL_TRUE;
10     if ((i==size) && (diff == BOOL_FALSE))
11         status = BOOL_TRUE;
12     return status;
13 }
```

Listing 1.1. byteArrayCompare

Listing 1.1 describes a `byteArrayCompare` function, that compares two arrays of byte and return true if they match, false otherwise. The code of this function contains some countermeasures: for instance the test `i==size` allows to verify that we loop `size` times. '$a1$' and '$a2$' have the same size, which is checked prior to the function call. `BOOL_TRUE` and `BOOL_FALSE` are constant bytes define to `0xAA` and `0x55` respectively.

2   High-level Robustness Evaluation

The Lazart approach aims at evaluating the code robustness against multiple and volatile fault injections [11] and acts at the source code level (here the LLVM.3.3 intermediate representation issued from C code). The considered fault model combines an attack objective and fault injections impacting the control flow by test inversion. A test inversion consists in changing the result of a conditional jump. The originality of Lazart is to be based on a static code analysis technique, here symbolic execution. Attack paths are determined with respect to an attack objective, mastering in that the combinatorial of multiple injections. A path that fulfills the attack objective reveals a vulnerability in the code and constitutes an attack.

The main particularity of Lazart, contrary to other tools starting from a concrete trace [6–8], is to be able to positively or negatively qualify the result of the robustness evaluation. Thanks to the symbolic approach, Lazart explores all possible paths (and fault injection possibility) with respect to a set of symbolic inputs. Then it is possible to state if a targeted application resists to an attack of multiplicity n or not.

2.1   The Lazart Approach

The Lazart approach is based on the following steps, as illustrated on Fig. 1.

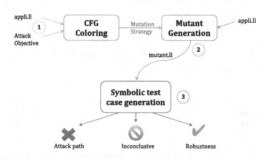

Fig. 1. The Lazart approach

1. Starting from the Control Flow Graph (CFG) and an attack objective, Lazart uses a reachability propagation algorithm that colors the CFG. An attack objective is a parameter that must be set, corresponding to a basic block to reach or not to reach.

2. Based on coloration, Lazart determines which program locations are candidate for successful fault injections. It produces a mutant that embeds these fault injection possibilities.
3. Using Klee, a symbolic test case generator aiming a path-coverage criterion, Lazart evaluates the robustness of the targeted application. It produces either some attacks, or establishes the absence of attacks or even an inconclusive response.

A more complete description of Lazart, and underlying algorithms, can be found in [11]. Here, we illustrate this approach on the byteArrayCompare example given Listing 1.1. Figure 2(a) gives the CFG associated to the byteArray Compare function. The mapping between the C code and the CFG is direct, except for the test on line 10, which is split into two conditions: the basic block for.end testing the condition (i==size) followed by the basic block land.lhs.true testing the condition (diff == BOOL_FALSE). Figure 2(b) gives the colored CFG, with the objective to reach the block if.then9 (corresponding to the assignment status=BOOL_TRUE on the line 11).

A node n is green whenever the attack objective is fatally reachable from n and red when the objective is never reachable. The yellow color corresponds to a node from which the goal could (or not) be reachable. A yellow node owning at least one red son becomes orange. Faults are possibly injected in yellow and orange nodes, forcing to reach a green block (and consequently not fall into a red one).

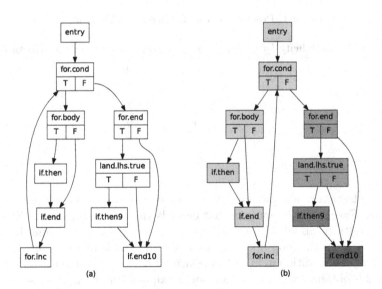

(a)   (b)

Fig. 2. Initial CFG of byteArrayCompare and after coloration

Fault injections are encoded by adding code simulating test inversions (a mutant of the initial code). A global fault number counter is added and incremented as soon as a fault is injected and each mutation is guarded by a boolean variable that indicates if the fault is injected or not. In our example, two mutations are introduced to avoid the red node if.then10 and two double mutations hijacking the flow of the block if.then in the for loop body and another one forcing (or avoiding) the exit of the for loop.

Klee [13,14] is the concolic test case generation engine used by Lazart to explore all paths and thus all combinations of fault injections. It requires to declare which variables are made symbolic. Klee makes it possible to define assertions to constrain the chosen symbolic variables. The byteArrayCompare function takes two arrays of byte a1 and a2 as input arguments. Here, the size a1 and a2 is set to 4, a1 is instantiated by an initial value and a2 is declared as symbolic with the following constraint: each byte must be different from a1. Variables guarding fault injections are implicitly declared as symbolic, as described below.

2.2   Results Analysis

Table 1 gives the results supplied by Lazart when at most 4-faults injections are performed. An n-attack is found when the corresponding path led to reach the green block introducing n faults. Attacks can be partially compared with respect to the program locations where faults are injected. An attack strictly including all locations associated to another one is considered as redundant.

Table 1. Possible attacks for byteArrayCompare

Attack multiplicity (# of fault)	# of attacks	Non-redundant attacks
0	0	0
1	1	1
2	5	1
3	10	0
4	11	1
Total	27	3

For the byteArrayCompare function, Lazart generates 17 possibilities of fault injections. Executing the mutant that embeds these fault injections, Klee produces 56 tests in about 3 s. Among them, the single attack of multiplicity 1 is obtained when the loop operates normally and the fault injection forces the inversion of the condition diff==BOOL_FALSE. The non-redundant attack of multiplicity 2 is obtained when first, the loop is skipped (inverting the test i<size) and secondly, we force the condition i==size to be true. Others 2-faults injection attacks are redundant with the attack of multiplicity 1 (we invert one of the internal test of the body and the final condition diff==BOOL_FALSE). 3-faults injections do not introduce new attacks. The attack of order 4 corresponds to the case where the internal test of comparison is inverted for each byte.

The fault model considered by Lazart encompasses several data or control flow low-level attacks, depending on the compilation process: replacing an assembly instruction by no operation (NOP) to delete a jump or a carry flag assignment, modifying values impacting the condition, etc. Nevertheless a complete and exhaustive approach does really make sense only at the binary level where all impacts of code modification can be taken into account (such as code operation mutation). On the contrary, a coarse-grain analysis, guided by some objectives in term of sensible parts of code, takes sense during the development process where threats must be early determined and proved to be taken into account. Here we focus on control flow modification impact that is generally hard to follow in a manual audit process. Some other fault models, such as data modification, can be also simulated by code mutation as described in [15] and could be integrated into Lazart, without difficulty. Furthermore, multiple fault injection must now be taken into account according to the next state-of-the art in term of laser attacks.

Finally, the main originality of Lazart is the possibility of stating a complete verdict either in term of found attacks or absence of attacks (in our example when 0 injection is targeted). A static analysis is also used in [8,15], based on a theorem proving approach, targeting single data fault injection. The use of a concolic engine allows us either to establish the robustness or to produce attacks.

3 Low-Level Robustness Evaluation

The EFS approach [10] differs from Lazart [11] as it operates in runtime mode (dynamically) in the actual smartcard. No bias is introduced by external peripherals and no code mutation is performed. It uses the whole function execution time frame to exhaustively inject cycle-wise faults. For instance, without any knowledge of the code, the EFS skips every single byte of instruction, one-by-one up to n-by-n in order to perform instruction skip even with unaligned instruction sets. The fault width n is chosen and can be wider than the size of a single instruction. It is then possible to evaluate security consequences of skipping several instructions.

3.1 The EFS Approach

Figure 3 describes the EFS workflow. The EFS operates on the smartcard Central Processing Unit (CPU) as it is embedded in the software project with other applications. On the computer side, the EFS Handler, which consists of a software program, provides functionalities to manage fault injection experiments. The host computer is in charge of the smartcard communication.

The whole process takes place in four main steps. First, the developer provides some attack parameters such as the fault characteristics, in term of fault model and fault width. He also specifies the targeted functionality such as PIN verification or an Rivest, Shamir, Adleman (RSA) signature. According to these parameters, in a second step, the EFS Handler calls its test case generation

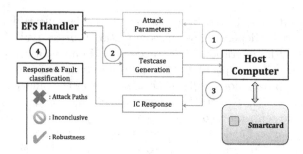

Fig. 3. The embedded fault simulator workflow

algorithm and produces a task list. A task consists in setting up the EFS and launching the targeted function.

At the third step, the host computer performs all tasks and sends back the functional smartcard responses to the EFS Handler. Finally, at the fourth step, the EFS handler sorts every functional responses into groups according to their functional behaviors. A functional response can be of four kinds: normal, faulty, countermeasure or CPU signal. A Functional response is said faulty under two conditions: it differs from the expected reference response and the program terminates.

In the faulty group, an attack is found when the corresponding attack path breaks the functional specification of the targeted program. For instance, a PIN verification program ensures that a PIN candidate matches the expected PIN value. Its output is binary (true of false), thus any output that invert the expected response is considered as an attack. A more complete description of the Embedded Fault Simulator can be found in [10].

3.2   Results Analysis

We illustrate this approach on the `byteArrayCompare` example given in Listing 1.1. As the EFS is a low-level approach, we perform our code analysis on the assembly generated from the code compilation. Chosen parameters allow to generate all paths and thus all possibilities of fault injection with respect to the instruction skip fault model.

Table 2 gives the results of the EFS according to the number of skipped contiguous instructions. In this experiment we skipped up to 16 instructions. However, 4 to 16-contiguous instructions skips, denoted as {4+} in the table, didn't reveal any new representative attacks. A detected attack is representative if it produces an unobserved functional effect leading to a successful attack.

A functional effect of an attack breaks the functional property of an instruction such as a value assignment to a register or the equality of two registers. The attack is successful if the broken assembly instruction disrupts the property of the high-level function that contains it (a comparison or a PIN Verification for instance). Several faults at the assembly level can produce the same functional effect on the high-level. We discuss this point in Sect. 4.4.

Table 2. EFS attacks on `byteArrayCompare`

# of skipped instructions	# of attacks	Representative attacks
1	4	4
2	3	1
3	2	1
4+	407	0
Total	416	6

Three of the four attacks that skipped only one instruction are obtained when some assignment instructions are skipped (`MOV`). First, two attacks occurred at the initialization phase where `status` and `diff` should have been initialized to BOOL_FALSE.

```
uint8_t status  = BOOL_FALSE; ->x97A055
   MOV       R10,#0x55
uint8_t diff    = BOOL_FALSE; ->x977055
   MOV       R7,#0x55
```

Listing 1.2. Single instruction skip 1 & 2

As these two assignments are contiguous, a double instructions skip attack also succeeds but is redundant as shown in Listing 1.2. Those attacks work when R7 or R10 contains the precise value.

The attack effect found accounts to the same 1-fault with Lazart, which consists in inverting the condition `diff==BOOL_FALSE`.

```
if (a1[i] != a2[i]) diff = BOOL_TRUE;
   xAD4B       CMP       R4,R11
   xD903       JE        0x38A1
   ->x9770AA   MOV       R7,#0xAA
```

Listing 1.3. Single instruction skip 3

The third single instruction skip attack avoids the update of the `diff` value when a difference is found during the comparison. This effect is showed in Listing 1.3. Consequently, the difference is not reported.

Replayed 4 times in a row, this attacks corresponds to the 4-fault attacks found by Lazart that consists in inverting the internal test of comparison for each byte.

Finally, the last single instruction skip attack is found in the sensitive part corresponding to the equality status assignment to true. Listing 1.4 gives the corresponding assembly code. At line 3, after the `CMP` (Compare), the Z flag (Zero) is set. In normal condition, the `JNE` (Jump Not Equal) instruction will read and reset the Z flag then continue without branching.

```
1  if ((i==array_size) && (diff==BOOL_FALSE)) status = BOOL_TRUE;
2    xAD56     CMP   R5,R6              ;(i==array_size)
3  ->xD907     JNE   0x38B2             ;return status
4    xD91F5503 CJNE  R7,#0x55,0x38B2    ;diff==BOOL_FALSE
5    x97A0AA   MOV   R10,#0xAA          ;status=BOOL_TRUE
```

Listing 1.4. byteArrayCompare Attack

However, if we skip the line 4, the Z flag is not restored and will be read by the following conditional branch CJNE (Conditional Jump Not Equal). Consequently, even if a mismatch occurs during the array comparison, the status is set to BOOL_TRUE.

The attack effect is equivalent to the 2-fault attacks found by Lazart that consists in inverting the line 10 of Listing 1.1.

A non-redundant two instructions skip attack was found. It breaks the comparison loop by avoiding the loop counter initialization (first instruction skipped) and the loop branching routine (second instruction skipped). Consequently, the diff value will never be updates and will keep its BOOL_FALSE initial value. A non-redundant three instructions skip attack was also found but is similar to the one showed in Listing 1.4. It breaks the double condition test on the line 1 by directly branching to the status=BOOL_TRUE assignment after the comparison loop (line 6). This is a second manner to produce the same effect obtained by Lazart, inverting the line 10 of Listing 1.1.

Skipping 4 up to 16 instructions does not introduce new attacks. The whole process has reported 416 attacks over 3199 tests. The subset of 9 attacks consisting of $\{1, 2, 3\}$-instructions skips provided 6 representative low-level attacks. These recover the 4 non-redundant high-level attacks found by Lazart. The equivalence between the two fault attack classes is not trivial due to the abstraction level difference. The EFS performs exhaustive testing according to a fault model and with respect to the function code, size and duration. Therefore, the output fault classification allows determining the robustness of a targeted embedded application code against a chosen fault model. Moreover, output states that differ from the reference state can be evaluated to claim if the detected attack path reveals a critical vulnerability or not.

4   Case Study

A PIN verification algorithm constitutes a valuable target of evaluation for Lazart and the EFS tools. As it provides a secret PIN to protect, and uses a try counter to avoid brute force attacks, PIN verification is sensitive to fault attacks impacting both data and control flow. With fault injections, the aim is to break the PIN verification and/or the PIN Try Counter (PTC). In this paper, we focus on the PIN comparison. Subsect. 4.1 first describes the attack scenario selected to evaluate Lazart and the EFS. Subsect. 4.2 focuses on the results obtained with Lazart while Subsect. 4.3 exhibits attacks found by the EFS. A short synthesis is proposed in Subsect. 4.4 to summarize both approach capabilities.

4.1   Secured `VerifyPIN` implementation

We analyze, in the next subsections, with both Lazart and the EFS, a secured implementation of the `VerifyPIN` functionality. First, we added the *always-decrement-first* rule [16–18], which recommends to decrement the PTC before any other operation occurs. When every conditional tests on the PIN passes, the PTC is incremented back. This prevents from tearing attacks, which consist in tearing the smartcard from the reader, or disabling the power just after the PIN comparison. Thereby, an attacker could not lead brute force attacks on the PIN value.

Our implementations are also prone to fault injection on data flow and control flow. The main methods to prevent fault attacks are redundancy and integrity checks. We provide the PTC integrity via backups for checking. We also managed operations involving the PTC, hence, increment and decrement are protected by checking the expected value after each operation. We also use double checks for sensitive conditional tests such as the PIN comparison itself to avoid single fault injection leading to instruction skip or test inverting [19]. The core of the `VerifyPIN` implementation is shown in Listing 1.5.

```
1  equal = BOOL_TRUE;
2  for(i=0 ; i<SIZE_OF_PIN; i++) {           // Main Comparison
3      equal = equal & ((buffer[i] != pin[i]) ? BOOL_FALSE : BOOL_TRUE);
4      stepCounter++;
5  }
6
7  if(equal == BOOL_TRUE) {
8      if(equal != BOOL_TRUE)                // Double test
9          goto counter_measure;             // Resets the remaining tries to max
10     triesLeft = MAX_TRIES;                // First backup
11     triesLeftBackup = -MAX_TRIES;         // Second backup
12     if(triesLeft != -triesLeftBackup)     // Verifies the new value
13         goto counter_measure;
14     authenticated = 1;                    // Authentication status update
15     if(stepCounter == INITIAL_VALUE + 4)
16         return EXIT_SUCCESS;
17 }
18 else {
19     authenticated = 0;
20     if (stepCounter == INITIAL_VALUE + 4)
21         goto failure;
22 }
```

Listing 1.5. `VerifyPIN` C code

Table 3. `VerifyPIN` implementation properties

# of lines in C code	83
# o lines in ASM code	67
ASM Code size (in Byte)	179
Constant time comparison	√
Double comparison	√
Branch balancing	×

Table 3 summarizes implementation properties. As described in Sect. 3, we perform an exhaustive testing campaign, with respect to the targeted function size and duration. Using the EFS, the test consists in skipping every single instruction and every possible block of instructions of the very same implementation on a 16-bit smartcard. The results are described in the three following subsections.

4.2 Vulnerabilities Detected by Lazart

Here, we present the results produced with Lazart for the `VerifyPIN` code, where we target the block containing the statement `authenticated=1` (Listing 1.5 line 14).

```
BYTE triesLeft = maxTries;
int i;
klee_make_symbolic(buffer,
    sizeof(char)*SIZE_OF_PIN, "buffer");
for (i = 0; i < SIZE_OF_PIN; ++i)
    klee_assume(buffer[i] != pin[i]);
```

Listing 1.6. Klee Symbolic Input

The experiment aims at establishing the robustness of PIN implementations with a permissive number of trials and when the attacker does not known any part of the PIN. Then inputs are characterized for Klee as described in Listing 1.6.

`VerifyPIN` **Robustness Evaluation.** Lazart generates 6 possibilities of fault injection. Klee takes about three second to terminate normally producing 49 tests, distributed as described in Table 4, with up to 4 fault injections.

Table 4. Lazart results for `VerifyPIN`

Fault Multiplicity	# of test	# of attack	# non- redundant
0	4	0	0
1	7	0	0
2	9	2	2
3	13	5	0
4	16	11	1
Total	49	18	3

One non-redundant attack of multiplicity 2 consists in inverting the double tests `equal==BOOL_TRUE` and `equal!=BOOL_TRUE`. The other one corresponds to a fault injection that circumvents the loop execution followed by another one that hijacks the step counter value countermeasure. The attack of multiplicity 4 corresponds to the case where the internal test of the comparison is inverted for each byte.

4.3   Vulnerabilities Detected by the EFS

With EFS attacks on `VerifyPIN` we encountered five types of functional outputs that are described in Table 5.

Table 5. Functional output behaviors distribution with the EFS tool

Functional Output	VerifyPIN
Wrong PIN / Signal or Countermeasure	79,87 %
Random output / APDU Errors	18,5 %
Right PIN → Authentication	**1,59 %**
Number of tests	4528

Wrong PIN / Signal or Countermeasure is the most recurrent case over all experiments. *Signal* stands for illegal opcode or illegal operand and is triggered by the CPU. Software *Countermeasures* are triggered by the targeted code itself, when a fault is detected. When no CPU signal nor software countermeasures are triggered, the fault injection has no effect and leads to the *Wrong PIN* status.

Internal countermeasures are triggered when function calls or register operation are targeted (`ECALL`, `MOV`). Tampering with the `DEC/CMP` or `INC/CMP` pair also leads to trigger countermeasures. When the fault width is too large, there is a possibility to jump outside of the PIN verification execution window leading to countermeasure triggering, unresponsive smartcard, random outputs and Application Protocol Data Unit (APDU) error cases.

Table 6. Detected attacks by the EFS on `VerifyPIN`

# skipped instructions	VerifyPIN
1	1 (1)
2	2 (1)
3	1 (0)
4	4 (0)
5+	64 (1)
Total	72 (3)

`VerifyPIN` **Robustness Evaluation.** Table 6 describes the fault obtained attacking `VerifyPIN`, according the number of skipped instructions. From the 72 successful attacks over 4528 tests (1.59 %), there are only 2 representative vulnerabilities found in the code under 4-instructions skips. The varying fault width explains this rate. The fault width corresponds to the number of skipped bytes of opcode. Most successes are explained by skips of conditional tests implying the `triesLeft` counter or the `BOOL_TRUE` value.

If we consider only addresses where successful attacks started from, we obtain the following Table 7. It describes the fault width according to the faulted assembly code address that led to successful authentications. The digit between parentheses corresponds to representative attacks. Several non-representative $\{1, 2\}$-instructions skip faults were found. Those results are exposed with more details on the following subsections.

Table 7. Faulted code address in `VerifyPIN`

Address (ASM code)	Fault width	#instr	Corresponding C code
0x4909	0x16	9	If (triesLeft ≤ 0)
0x490D	0x12	7	
0x490F	0x10	4	If (t1 != triesLeftBackup)
0x4914	0x0B	6	
0x4970	0x08	4	If (equal == BOOL_TRUE)
0x4974	0x04	1	

In the #instr. column we show the corresponding number of skipped instruction. Successful attacks imply to skip up to 9 contiguous instructions, which is hard to achieve with a physical injection.

Moreover, Table 7 exhibits one attack path that only requires a single instruction skip. The corresponding C code is the conditional test on the boolean value `equal` that states the equality of the two compared PINs (lines 1-5 in Listing 1.1, recalled in Listing 1.7 below).

```
equal  =  BOOL_TRUE;
for (i=0; i<SIZE_OF_PIN; i++) {              // Main Comparison
    equal = equal & (buffer[i] != pin[i]) ? BOOL_FALSE : BOOL_TRUE);
    stepCounter++;
}
```

Listing 1.7. `VerifyPIN` C code

The `equal` value is used as a part of the comparison at each step, for each byte comparison.

A single difference between the PIN value and the input PIN is sufficient to switch the `equal` value to `false`. A single instruction skip leading to an authentication with a wrong input PIN at `equal == BOOL_TRUE` is not easy to detect at the C level. The analysis has to be pushed further, at the assembly level. While reading the assembly code, we notice that neither the byte-to-byte comparison nor the PIN values is altered during the `for` loop. However, the `equal` value is initialized to the constant value `BOOL_TRUE` before the loop starts as stated in Listing 1.7 in the C code.

```
equal   =    BOOL_TRUE;
  x9710         MOV      R11,#DWR(0x10)
  x9741000A     MOV      EQUAL(0x000A),R11
```

Listing 1.8. VerifyPIN ASM `equal` Assignment

In Listing 1.8 we show how the `equal` assignment takes place at assembly level. First, the `BOOL_TRUE` constant is copied from its address `#DWR(0x10)` to the register `R11`.

Then, `R11` is immediately copied into `EQUAL(0x000A)`, which stands for the `equal` variable in the C code. During the loop, `EQUAL(0x000A)` takes part in a multi-conditional assignment formula. The `R11` register is still unused during the loop. At the end of the loop, `EQUAL(0x000A)` is written back to `R11` and compared to the `BOOL_TRUE` constant as shown in Listing 1.9.

```
1 ->x97D1000A    MOV      R11,#EQUAL(0x000A)
2    xD9101B     CJNE     R11,#DWR(0x10),AUTH(0x4996)
3    xD91024     CJNE     R11,#DWR(0x10),CTM(0x49A2)
```

Listing 1.9. VerifyPIN ASM code

Consequently, if the `MOV` responsible of that copy is skipped (line 1), the `R11` register will not be updated and will keep its latest value, namely `BOOL_TRUE`.

Therefore, this single skip leads to a successful authentication without disrupting the control flow.

4.4 Synthesis

We encountered different behaviors during our experiments. Less than 2 % of the EFS attack paths against `VerifyPIN` implementations leads to a successful authentication. Most of reported attacks are redundant. They include all attacks detected by Lazart but except 4-faults injections due to the fact that, in the current implementation of the EFS, only contiguous instructions are skipped. However, high-multiplicity faults performed by Lazart can target different lines of the C code, at different locations. This is why those two faults are not reported by the EFS. However, for each other non-redundant attack found by Lazart, there is at least one attack found by the EFS that reflect the same code vulnerability. In particular, for a given vulnerable code line detected by Lazart, there can be different explanations in the underlying assembly code, which are reported by the EFS.

As shown on Fig. 4, the first observation is that, to a statement at high-level C code corresponds several low-level assembly code lines (1). Secondly, some low-level operations are totally abstracted at the C-level and thus, they cannot be targeted. Some instructions induce implicit operations, such as flag register read/writes. To have a good insight of flag states updates (2), the developer must consider the dynamic assembly code behavior.

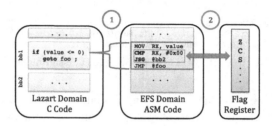

Fig. 4. Fault level differences insights

Therefore, vulnerable instructions such as CMP RX,#0x00 can be avoided. Regarding instruction skips, a careful attention must be paid to manage branching codes in order to avoid unexpected branching attacks, as illustrated in the example given in Listing 1.4.

5   Combining Lazart and the EFS to Improve the Vulnerability Detection

In this section, we expose some interesting results obtained by combining Lazart and the EFS tool in evaluating both the VerifyPIN and the byteArrayCompare implementations. The two approaches reveal some complementary despite their different operating mode. On the one hand, Lazart can locate a sensitive portion of code at the C level according to an attack goal but it does not consider the underlying mechanism. On the other hand, the EFS can perform exhaustive instruction skipping in a whole function time frame but without any predetermined security purpose. Performances, in terms of timing and accuracy differ according to the security property that the developer is trying to evaluate or reach.

Here, the main idea is to combine both approaches in order to perform a low-level exhaustive testing on assembly codes that correspond to some sensitive code blocks determined by Lazart. We proceed as described below:

(1) Determine the attack goal with Lazart. In our case study, we must ensure that the PIN authentication fulfills its security functionality.
(2) Locate sensitive portions of code according to the CFG coloring algorithm, the green basic block. If it is reached under fault injection, the goal no longer holds.
(3) Setup the EFS code range target according to the assembly code address range that corresponds to the green basic block in the source code.
(4) Perform the EFS within the restricted code area

As we first try Lazart and the EFS independently on byteArrayCompare and VerifyPIN, we propose to run the combined tests on those two implementations. To do so, we define two benchmark criteria. First, the *Detection rate* denotes the capacity of an approach to reveal distinct vulnerabilities in the code via the non-redundant attacks. It is the ratio between the number of attacks found and the number of non-redundant attacks. Secondly, the *Timing performance* criterion denotes the time spent to perform the whole process and is largely related to the total number of test.

In the rest of this section, all results are obtained under the following attack parameters. Lazart performed multiple fault injections up to four faults. The EFS performed up to four contiguous instructions skips for all implementations. Non-redundant and representative attacks are reported in parentheses.

Table 8. Lazart & EFS complementarity results on `byteArrayCompare`

Approach	# of tests	# of attacks	Detection rate	Timing performance
Lazart	56	27 (3)	11.7 %	~3 s
EFS	2652	204 (6)	2.9 %	~9 mn
Lazart + EFS	56 + 572	20 (4)	20 %	~2 mn

Table 8 describes the results obtained by the combination of Lazart and the EFS on the `byteArrayCompare` function. Chaining Lazart and the EFS greatly improves the detection rate and is 4,5 times faster than the EFS alone. There is a difference of magnitude between the Lazart and the EFS timing performance. This arises because of the operating platform. Lazart runs on powerful x86 processors clocked at several GHz whereas the EFS runs at best on 33 MHz smartcards.

Lazart performs its fault injection simulation based on code mutation. Each mutation consists in forcing a conditional test to branch or not to branch, regardless values considered in the targeted test. Thereby, whatever the conditional test, the fault will occur. However, as described in Listing 1.2, two attacks are found in the initialization phase of the `byteArrayCompare` function. Those two are not reported because Lazart does not take data mutations into account. Consequently, at the low level, the EFS alone found two non-redundant faults that are not reported with the combined approach. This highlights the importance of tracking the evolution of values that are used in conditional tests. We simply extended the portion of code spotted by Lazart with the portion of code where sensitive values are manipulated for the combined approach. Therefore, the combined approach is able to retrieve all six attacks.

Table 9 describes the results obtained on `VerifyPIN` code. The combination reduces the experiment duration by a factor of 10 thanks to the range reduction operated by Lazart. Moreover, the detection rate increases, it reflects a more accurate fault detection. Lazart and the EFS found two different sets of attacks in the same code area. This explains the better non-redundant attack detection rate.

Lazart and the EFS are two fault injection simulation tools that operate at different abstraction levels with different fault models. However, we proposed a new method to make them work together. Our experiments highlight the interest of combining them despite of their differences and show significant performance improvements. The high-level static approach helps to refine the code range of the low-level dynamic one, and altogether they improve the vulnerability detection rate of our fault simulation.

Table 9. Lazart & EFS complementarity results on `VerifyPIN`

Approach	# of tests	# of attacks	Detection rate	Timing performance
Lazart	49	18 (3)	16.6 %	<3 s
EFS	4528	72 (2)	2.7 %	~17 mn
Lazart + EFS	49 + 720	14 (3)	21.4 %	~1 mn 30 s

6   Conclusion

In this paper, we study the application of two simulation techniques to evaluate smartcards robustness against multiple fault attacks and show their complementary. Lazart performs concolic analysis on the control flow graph of a C code under the test inverting fault model. The EFS performs exhaustive instruction skip at the assembly level with respect to a targeted function. We exposed our attack results on a common PIN verification implementation. We show that software countermeasure implementations must be tested to avoid coding errors or some compiler optimizations that could lead to the countermeasure deprecation. We also took advantage of Lazart and the EFS differences by combining them. It results in a new multi-level fault injection simulation tool that improved the fault vulnerability detection rate and accuracy.

There exist several tools and approaches dedicated to test implementations against fault injections [6–8]. All these works differ from the fault model that is taken into account and the level of code that is targeted (C or Java bytecode for the referenced works). Actually, there exists no criteria allowing us to evaluate and compare such approaches. The work presented here constitutes a first step in this sense: we propose some criteria based on the number of generated tests and non-redundant attacks (number of generated attacks is not significant). Then we proposed to evaluate the efficiency of a test campaign against fault injection by a detection rate. Proposed criteria must be refined and extended for instance in taking into account coverage criteria. Another contribution of this work is the proposition of a method to combine high and low level evaluations. In [7], the authors exploit high-level attacks generation in order to evaluate a low level simulation. But it is an *a posteriori approach*. Here we propose to combine *a priori* fault injection simulations. A finer analysis must be conducted in order to estimate the gain of this combination.

References

1. Boneh, D., DeMillo, R.A., Lipton, R.J.: On the importance of checking cryptographic protocols for faults. In: Fumy, W. (ed.) EUROCRYPT 1997. LNCS, vol. 1233, pp. 37–51. Springer, Heidelberg (1997)
2. Balasch, J., Gierlichs, B., Verbauwhede, I.: An in-depth and black-box characterization of the effects of clock glitches on 8-bit MCUs. In: Breveglieri, L., Guilley, S., Koren, I., Naccache, D., Takahashi, J. (eds.) FDTC, pp. 105–114. IEEE (2011)

3. Dehbaoui, A., Dutertre, J.-M., Robisson, B., Tria, A.: Electromagnetic transient faults injection on a hardware and a software implementations of AES. In: Bertoni, G., Gierlichs, B. (eds.) FDTC, pp. 7–15. IEEE (2012)
4. Skorobogatov, S.P., Anderson, R.J.: Optical fault induction attacks. In: Kaliski Jr., B.S., Koç, Ç.K., Paar, C. (eds.) Cryptographic Hardware and Embedded Systems - CHES 2002. LNCS, vol. 2523, pp. 2–12. Springer, Heidelberg (2003)
5. Biham, E., Shamir, A.: Differential fault analysis of secret key cryptosystems. In: Kalisk Jr., B.S. (ed.) CRYPTO 1997. LNCS, vol. 1294, pp. 513–525. Springer, Heidelberg (1997)
6. Machemie, J.-B., Mazin, C., Lanet, J.-L., Cartigny, J.: SmartCM a smart card fault injection simulator. In: WIFS, pp. 1–6. IEEE (2011)
7. Berthomé, P., Heydemann, K., Kauffmann-Tourkestansky, X., Lalande, J.-F.: High level model of control flow attacks for smart card functional security. In: ARES, pp. 224–229. IEEE Computer Society (2012)
8. Christofi, M., Chetali, B., Goubin, L., Vigilant, D.: Formal verification of a CRT-RSA implementation against fault attacks. J. Cryptographic Eng. 3(3), 157–167 (2013)
9. Bar-El, H., Choukri, H., Naccache, D., Tunstall, M., Whelan, C.: The sorcerer's apprentice guide to fault attacks. Proc. IEEE 94(2), 370–382 (2006)
10. Berthier, M., Bringer, J., Chabanne, H., Le, T.-H., Rivière, L., Servant, V.: Idea: embedded fault injection simulator on smartcard. In: Jürjens, J., Piessens, F., Bielova, N. (eds.) ESSoS. LNCS, vol. 8364, pp. 222–229. Springer, Heidelberg (2014)
11. Potet, M.-L., Mounier, L., Puys, M., Dureuil, L.: Lazart: a symbolic approach for evaluation the robustness of secured codes against control flow fault injection. In: ICST (2014)
12. King, J.C.: Symbolic execution and program testing. Commun. ACM 19(7), 385–394 (1976)
13. The KLEE symbolic virtual machine. http://klee.llvm.org/
14. Cadar, C., Dunbar, D., Engler, D.R.: KLEE: unassisted and automatic generation of high-coverage tests for complex systems programs. In: OSDI, pp. 209–224 (2008)
15. Christofi, M.: Preuves de sécurité outillées d'implémentation cryptographiques. Ph.D. thesis, Laboratoire PRiSM, Université de Versailles Saint Quentin-en-Yvelines, France (2013)
16. Uguchi-Cartigny, J., Sere, A.A.-K., Lanet, J.-L.: Carte à puce Java Card : Protection du code contre les attaques en faute (2009)
17. Folkman, L.: The use of a power analysis for influencing PIN verification on cryptographic smart card. Bakalásk práce, Masarykova univerzita, Fakulta informatiky (2007)
18. Sauveron, D.: Etude et réalisation d'un environnement d'exprimentation et de modélisation pour la technologie Java Card : application à la sécurité. Ph.D. thesis, Université Bordeaux 1- Informatique et Mathématiques (2004). Thèse de doctorat dirigée par Chaumette, S
19. van Woudenberg, J.G.J., Witteman, M.F., Menarini, F.: Practical optical fault injection on secure microcontrollers. In: Breveglieri, L., Guilley, S., Koren, I., Naccache, D., Takahashi, J. (eds.) FDTC, pp. 91–99. IEEE (2011)

Malware Message Classification
by Dynamic Analysis

Guillaume Bonfante[(✉)], Jean-Yves Marion, and Thanh Dinh Ta

Lorraine University - CNRS - LORIA, Nancy, France
bonfante@loria.fr

Abstract. The fact that new malware appear every day demands a strong response from anti-malware forces. For that sake, an analysis of new samples must be performed. Usually, one tries to replay the behavior of malware in a safe environment. However, some samples activate a malicious function only if they receive some particular inputs from its command and control server. The problem is then to get some grasp on the interactions between the malware and its environment. For that sake, we propose to work in four steps. First, we enumerate all possible execution path following the reception of a message. Second, we describe for all execution path the set of corresponding messages. Third, we build an automaton that discriminate types of runs given an arbitrary word. Finally, we unify some equivalent run, and simplify the underlying automaton.

1 Introduction

The essential problem of an anti-virus software is to discriminate malware from safe programs. There are broadly two ways to perform such a task: by a syntactic analysis of the code or by a behavioral one. The first one is the key of standard anti-virus software. Indeed, the principle takes benefit from optimized pattern matching algorithms and may be tuned to avoid false positives. On the other hand, they are very sensitive to malware mutations, and thus may be easily fooled.

Behavioral analyses try to discriminate good usages from bad ones. Usually, this is done by recording interactions of the program with its operating system: file modifications, access to some drive, memory rights alteration and so on. Good/Bad behaviors are modeled by state automata or by temporal logical formulae [4,21]. Though attracting in theory, such systems suffer from an heavy slow down of the monitored machines. Furthermore, it is not that easy to distinguish good from bad behaviors leading to high false negative/positive rates. And finally, it is not that complicate to make behaviors mutate.

In this contribution, we propose an alternative form of behavioral analysis which focuses on the interactions between a program with its environment via messages. It results more technically in an analysis of the structure of input messages as read by programs. This is called *message format extraction.*

© Springer International Publishing Switzerland 2015
F. Cuppens et al. (Eds.): FPS 2014, LNCS 8930, pp. 112–128, 2015.
DOI: 10.1007/978-3-319-17040-4_8

Message format extraction can be considered also in the context of retro-engineering as a first and inevitable step to understand the communication protocols used in the malicious code. In the pioneer work [7], the authors described a method to extract formats of received messages by a pattern analysis. Using similar techniques, this work was pursued later on for respectively sent messages [6], encrypted ones [23] or hierarchically-structured ones [16], and finally for communication protocols [9].

In this line of work, messages are modeled as fields sequences. The main issue is then to detect the fields boundaries in a message. The problem is even more complicate due to fields (qualified as *directed*) which may contain informations about other fields (via length measure for instance). The authors developed algorithms that detect direction fields and *separators*. However, to do that, they make a strong assumption on the parsing algorithm of the target program itself. If one replaces the naive string matching algorithm with a more sophisticated one (e.g. Knuth-Morris-Pratt), the assumptions (described in these interpretations) are no more valid and thus the results.

Our approach relies on a different paradigm. We state that the structure of input messages can be described (or at least approximated) by finite state automata. Suppose we are given a program P which reads some input m at run time, then we provide a finite state automaton which will categorize input messages according to their corresponding execution. Actually, we will show experimentally that one retrieves the shape of messages from the automaton. Second difference, we do not make any hypothesis on the parsing algorithm of the program P.

However, from the idea to its concrete realization, there are some preliminary steps that must be crossed. Suppose we want to study the communications of a malware P. First, one must identify which instructions open a communication. This is not computable in general. But, for self-modifying program—that is almost all malware—standard heuristics will fail. This is a first reason to work dynamically. Second reason, suppose P opens a communication with its Command and Control (C&C). In that case, the C&C behaves like an oracle from our perspective and there is no way to get a simple sample of a message. Letting the communication open (and the program run) gives us access to a (hopefully informative) message from the other side.

But, in the scenario above, there are two issues. First, the C&C server may be closed. Malware managers move very quickly servers to escape traffic surveillance. Second, launching P may be observed by the C&C, thus breaking the stealth of the analysis. In the experiment we report here, we opened the communication *only once*. This can be seen as a kind of trade-off between stealth and information. However, the method we develop cope with the all scenarios, fully open or fully closed communications and all in-between ones.

So, let us suppose we run a program P which at some point receives some data. As said above, we will build an automaton which is fed by some byte sequence w (in other words, a message) will output a state witnessing the execution path in P of w. Actually, states of the automaton describe the analysis of the message by the program P, and consequently reveal the structure of messages.

To build the automaton, we proceed in four steps. First, we enumerate all execution paths from the reception instant that are reachable by message modification. This is known as a coverage issue in the context of software testing or in the context of malware retro-engineering. In recent times [15,18], the binary code is translated to some intermediate representation, and then some *concolic testing* [12] is performed with help of SMT solvers. Our approach is known as tainting driven fuzzing analysis which gave reasonably good coverage level for the experiments we made. But we already think for the near future to use techniques mentioned above, or some coming from disassembly such as the ones presented by Reps et al. [19] who developed CodeSurfer, or by Kinder and Veith [14], the authors of Jakstab, or the more recent Bardin et al. [3] which combines advantages of both latter methods.

For the second step, we proceed for each execution branch to a tainting analysis. For each conditional instructions (that are junctions in the execution tree), we describe a condition for each successor. Again, symbolic execution techniques could be used here, such as [2]. From these constraints, we build in a third step a dual automaton which serves as a basis for the fourth one. In the last step, we simplify the automaton by state sharing. Those are meant to fold execution loops.

We have implemented the constructions described all along, and tested it on several programs, but notably on the well-known malware called **Zeus**. In Sect. 5, we present the result of the approach that we obtained on the malware.

Limitations. In this contribution, we do not consider protocols. We work only on one message, not on the dialog between the program and its C&C. Thus, a malware could easily escape our analysis, simply by splitting messages. However, we think that a careful analysis of one message is a first step toward protocol analysis. Second limitation, we consider that the message analysis is done by some non-self-modifying code, globally, the code may be self-modifying, but not the parsing procedure itself. This limitation is not too harsh: during packer's decryption (that is when a malware is essentially self-modifying), there are few interactions with the environment. In his thesis, Calvet [8] showed that less than 2 % of malware interact with the system during decryption. But, a code may interpret some commands sent by a C&C, and for those ones, our method is not operant. We let that issue for further researches.

Related Work. Beside the previously cited works [6,7,9,16,23], the automata approximation can be though of as a *learning procedure*. This approach has natural relations with researches in *machine learning* [1,22] and may take benefit from results is this domain for the further development. Actually, we faced a problem very similar to the one of M. Dalla Preda et al. [10] but in a different setting. They describe execution paths of a program as automata, and at one point they compute approximations to get finite descriptions. Here, we focus on messages rather than execution paths, but actually this fact induces an underlying path approximation.

2 Background

In this contribution, we model the memory as a flat sequence of 8-bit bytes. The set of bytes is noted BYTES. The set of addresses (the address space) is noted DWORDS. Typically, the address space is the range $0..2^{32} - 1$, that is 4 BYTES. The memory is represented as a finite mapping $\mu : \text{DWORDS} \to \text{BYTES}$. Aside from the memory, there is a finite set of *registers*, next denoted REGISTERS, which contains eip, the *instruction pointer*. The state of registers is represented by a finite function $\nu : \text{REGISTERS} \to \text{DWORDS}$.

An *execution environment* (μ, ν) represents the state of the system. At each step of the computation, an *opcode* c pointed by eip is fetched from memory, and depending on it, the execution environment is updated. The couple $(\nu(\text{eip}), c)$ is the *underlying instruction* of (μ, ν) next denoted $\mathcal{I}(\mu, \nu)$.

Accordingly, the execution from an initial state (μ_1, ν_1) is the sequence $(\mu_1, \nu_1) \to (\mu_2, \nu_2) \to \cdots$. From this execution, we extract the *sequence of underlying instructions* called the *trace* $T(\mu, \nu) = \mathtt{i}_1, \mathtt{i}_2, \ldots$ where $\mathtt{i}_j = \mathcal{I}(\mu_j, \nu_j)$ for all $j \geq 1$ (see Example 1).

A running program P may ask for some inputs. To do that, it gives the control back to the operating system which will itself (a) push in memory a sequence of bytes m and (b) resume P. We call the execution environment at instant (b) an *input environment*. Input environments are characterized to be the "return" state of reading interruptions, or to follow input functions calls (e.g. WSARecv or recv on the Windows® OS). The instruction corresponding to an input environment is said to be an *input instruction*.

Let $N = (\mu, \nu)$ be an input environment. The *input message* m is stored in memory in an interval of addresses $A = [\mathtt{b}, \mathtt{b}+1, \ldots, \mathtt{b}+\ell-1]$ with ℓ the length of the message m and b some (more or less arbitrary) address. Given some message $m' = b_0 \cdots b_{\ell'-1} \in \text{BYTES}^*$, let $N[m'] = (\mu', \nu')$ be the same environment as N but the one which received m' instead of m. More technically, suppose ℓ is stored in eax then $\mu'(\mathtt{b}+i) = b_i$ for all $i < \ell'$, otherwise $\mu'(\mathtt{a}) = \mu(\mathtt{a})$ and $\nu'(r) = \nu(r)$ for all registers except eax for which $\nu'(\text{eax}) = \ell'$. For the remaining, we define $m[i] = b_i$ for all $i < \ell'$.

Given some input environment N, consider an instruction $\mathtt{i}_j$ in a trace $T(N) = \mathtt{i}_1, \ldots, \mathtt{i}_j, \mathtt{i}_{j+1}, \ldots$, we say that $\mathtt{i}_j$ is *deterministic* if for any message m such that $T(N[m]) = \mathtt{i}_1, \ldots, \mathtt{i}_j, \mathtt{i}', \ldots$, then $\mathtt{i}' = \mathtt{i}_{j+1}$. In other words, the successor of a deterministic instruction does not depend on messages. Typically, sequential instructions (e.g. mov ebp, esp), calls and unconditional jumps to some fixed address (e.g. call 0xf1b542 or jmp 0xf1ae33) enter this category.

Non deterministic instructions are called *message-triggered*. In this category, one finds calls or jumps to some register (e.g. call edx or jmp eax), but the most representative are the conditional jumps (e.g. jnz 0xf1a9ce).

2.1 Execution Tree

Let us consider a program P asking for some input m, its behavior will then depend on m. In a first step, we compute all possible run depending on m seen as a parameter. In a second step, for each execution branch, we describe the language of messages corresponding to that branch. But, for the moment, let us define the execution tree of an input environment N.

Consider an input environment N, define i_0^N to be the index of the first message triggered instruction in the trace $T(N) = \mathtt{i}_1, \ldots, \mathtt{i}_{i_0^N}, \ldots$. Actually, the prefix $\mathtt{i}_1, \ldots, \mathtt{i}_{i_0^N}$ is shared by all traces $T(N[m])$ with m a message. Indeed, by definition, $\mathtt{i}_1, \ldots, \mathtt{i}_{i_0^N}$ are deterministic but the last one, thus the sequence is uniquely determined by N. In the sequel, we shall drop the superscript N when the context is clear.

The trace $T_N(m) = \mathtt{i}_1, \ldots, \mathtt{i}_n$ is the sub-sequence of $T(N[m])$ cut after a second *input* instruction $\mathtt{i}_n$ (if such an $\mathtt{i}_n$ exists, otherwise $T_N(m) = T(N[m])$). In other words, we forget anything which would follow the analysis of a second message coming from the environment. The *trigger-trace* of m is the sequence $B_N(m) = [(\mathtt{a}_1, \mathtt{i}_{i_1}), \ldots, (\mathtt{a}_k, \mathtt{i}_{i_k})]$ where:

- $\mathtt{i}_{i_0}, \mathtt{i}_{i_1}, \ldots, \mathtt{i}_{i_k}$ is the subsequence of $T_N(m)$ containing only the *message-triggered instructions* and (if relevant) the input instruction at the end of $T_N(m)$,
- $\mathtt{a}_{\ell+1}$ is the address pointed by $\mathtt{eip}$ at step $\mathtt{i}_{i_\ell+1}$ for all $\ell \geq 0$, that is the address of the instruction following $\mathtt{i}_{i_\ell}$.

$$T_N(m) = \mathcal{I}(N) \to \cdots \to \mathtt{i}_{i_0} \to \mathtt{i}_{\mathtt{a}_1} \to \cdots \to \mathtt{i}_{i_1} \to \mathtt{i}_{\mathtt{a}_2} \to \cdots$$

One may observe that the trace $T_N(m)$ is uniquely determined by $B_N(m)$. Indeed, with the notation above, for all $\ell \geq 0$, instructions $\mathtt{i}_{i_\ell+1}, \ldots, \mathtt{i}_{i_{\ell+1}-1}$ are deterministic, thus uniquely determined by $\mathtt{a}_{\ell+1}$.

Example 1. Let us run `wget` on some `URL`, the program receives a first message from the server via the operating system. It then verifies that the first four bytes of this message are "HTTP". Figure 1 displays the corresponding piece of trace:

The notion of message-triggered instruction is relative to traces. Indeed, the instruction `cmpsb [esi],[edi]` at address `0x404f89` is message triggered the first three times, not the fourth one (that is because of `cmpsb` stops either when `[esi]` $\neq$ `[edi]` or if `ecx = 0`, and `ecx`'s value is 0 after the third time).

address	trace	trigger-trace
0x404f89	cmpsb [esi],[edi]	(0x403a20,cmpsb [esi],[edi])
0x404f89	cmpsb [esi],[edi]	(0x404f89,cmpsb [esi],[edi])
0x404f89	cmpsb [esi],[edi]	(0x404f89,cmpsb [esi],[edi])
0x404f89	cmpsb [esi],[edi]	
0x404f8b	pop edi	
0x404f8c	pop esi	
0x404f8d	jz 0x404f94	(0x404f89,jz 0x404f94)
0x404f94	test edx, edx	...

Fig. 1. Trace and its corresponding triggered-trace

Definition 1 (Trigger Execution Tree (TET)). *Given an input environment N, its trigger execution tree $\mathcal{E}_N$ is a tree with labeled vertices and labeled edges, that is defined inductively as follows:*

- *the root is labeled $\mathtt{i}_{i_0^N}$, it is associated with the empty sequence $[]$.*
- *suppose $B_N(m) = [(a_1, \mathtt{i}_{i_1}), \ldots, (a_k, \mathtt{i}_{i_k})]$ is a trigger-trace, suppose that the vertex n is associated with $[(a_1, \mathtt{i}_{i_1}), \ldots, (a_j, \mathtt{i}_{i_j})]$ for some $j < k$, then $\mathcal{E}_N$ contains a transition $n \xrightarrow{a_{j+1}} n'$ with n' a (fresh) vertex labeled $\mathtt{i}_{i_{j+1}}$ and associated to $[(a_1, \mathtt{i}_{i_1}), \ldots, (a_{j+1}, \mathtt{i}_{i_{j+1}})]$.*

The trigger execution tree is the standard execution tree once removed intermediate deterministic instructions. Each path from the root to some leaf of $\mathcal{E}_N$ corresponds to a trigger trace, thus to a trace in the original program.

Since traces are infinite in general, so may be the execution tree. Given $c > 0$, let $T_c(N)$ be the prefix of length c of the trace $T(N)$, then we define $\mathcal{E}_{N,c}$ to be the sub-tree of $\mathcal{E}_N$ cut to traces of length at most c.

Example 2. Figure 3a shows the TET of $\mathtt{wget}$ with traces limited to 50 instructions. The vertices $\perp_i$'s mark the ends of traces due to length limit.

Remark 1. From now on, the trigger execution trees are understood as to be cut at some length limit c. We then omit c in $\mathcal{E}_{N,c}$ when it is clear from the context.

3   Input Messages Analysis

3.1   Dynamic Tainting Analysis

Dynamic tainting is a well known technique which tracks the dependency of data within programs. The below is a very brief introduction, we refer the reader to [20] for details.

The semantics of an instruction $\mathtt{i} = \mathcal{I}(N)$ of some execution environment N depends on a set of registers[1] R and memory content at a set of addresses A, and modify a set register[2] R' and memory content at a set of addresses A'. For such an $\mathtt{i}$, one derives a *hyper-edge* $(R \cup A, \mathtt{i}, R' \cup A')$ where source nodes are "read" memory addresses or registers, targets are "written" ones. Source and target nodes are considered separate. We say that $\mathtt{i}$ depends on source nodes.

Let us consider a prefix $\mathtt{i}_1, \ldots, \mathtt{i}_j$ of some trace $T(N) = \mathtt{i}_1, \mathtt{i}_2, \ldots$. The *hyper-graph* $\mathcal{H}(\mathtt{i}_1, \ldots \mathtt{i}_j)$ is the chain of edges obtained by *glueing* corresponding target and sources (cf. Example 3). The sources of $\mathcal{H}(\mathtt{i}_1, \ldots, \mathtt{i}_j)$, denoted by $\mathcal{S}(\mathtt{i}_1, \ldots, \mathtt{i}_j)$, consists of source nodes that are not targets of any hyper-edge (that is source nodes which are not glued). The set $\mathcal{S}(\mathtt{i}_1, \ldots, \mathtt{i}_j)$ describes the dependency of $\mathtt{i}_1, \ldots, \mathtt{i}_j$ on N. The local sources $\mathcal{S}_\ell(\mathtt{i}_1, \ldots, \mathtt{i}_j)$ are source nodes in $\mathcal{S}(\mathtt{i}_1, \ldots, \mathtt{i}_j)$ related by a path to the targets of $\mathtt{i}_j$. They describe the dependency of $\mathtt{i}_j$ on N (supposedly it is executed).

---

[1] But $\mathtt{eip}$ which is treated apart.
[2] Idem.

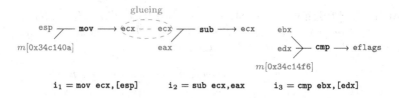

Fig. 2. Hyper-edge glueing

Example 3. Given that esp and edx have respectively the value 0x34c140a and 0x34c14f6 at the beginning. The hyper-graph $\mathcal{H}(\mathtt{i}_1, \mathtt{i}_2, \mathtt{i}_2)$ in Fig. 2 has sources $\mathcal{S}(\mathtt{i}_1, \mathtt{i}_2, \mathtt{i}_3) = \{\mathtt{esp}, m[\mathtt{0x34c140a}], \mathtt{eax}, \mathtt{ebx}, \mathtt{edx}, m[\mathtt{0x34c14f6}]\}$ and local sources $\mathcal{S}_\ell(\mathtt{i}_1, \mathtt{i}_2, \mathtt{i}_3) = \{\mathtt{ebx}, \mathtt{edx}, m[\mathtt{0x34c14f6}]\}$.

Proposition 1. *The tainting analysis leads to two main facts.*

1. *Any instruction in a finite trace depends only on finitely many input bytes from memory. It is a direct consequence from the fact that assembly instructions read and modify only locally the memory.*
2. *Given some execution environment N and some instruction $\mathtt{i}_j$ occurring in its trace $T(N) = \mathtt{i}_1, \ldots, \mathtt{i}_j, \ldots$, let N' be an environment coinciding with N on the sources of $\mathcal{H}(\mathtt{i}_1, \ldots, \mathtt{i}_j)$, then, $T(N') = \mathtt{i}_1, \ldots, \mathtt{i}_j, \ldots$ coincide with the trace of N at least up to the j-th instruction.*

3.2   Trace Formula Construction

In this section, and the following ones, N denotes an input environment and $A = [\mathtt{b}, \ldots, \mathtt{b} + \ell - 1]$ is the relative interval of addresses. A *local condition* is a subset $\gamma \subseteq \mathrm{BYTES}^S$ for some (finite) set S, called the support of γ.

Definition 2 (Trace Language). *Given a program P and some input environment N, its execution tree (possibly cut at some length c) is $\mathcal{E}_N$. Let p be a finite path in $\mathcal{E}_N$ from the root to some leaf, its language is the set of messages*

$$M_N(p) = \{m \in \mathcal{M} \mid B_N(m) = p\}.$$

A path (from the root to some leaf) p in $\mathcal{E}_N$ corresponds to a trigger-trace $B_N(m)$ of some $m \in M_N(p)$, and thus to a sub-trace $T_N(m) = \mathtt{i}_1, \ldots, \mathtt{i}_j$. Let $\mathcal{S}_p$ be the addresses of A that are sources of $\mathcal{H}(\mathtt{i}_1, \ldots, \mathtt{i}_j)$, namely $\mathcal{S}_p = A \cap \mathcal{S}(\mathtt{i}_1, \ldots, \mathtt{i}_j)$. In other words, $\mathcal{S}_p$ is the set of addresses within the message which are read by the processor along p.

Proposition 2. *For any message $m \in M_N(p)$, for any message m', if $m' =_{|\mathcal{S}_p} m$ then $m' \in M_N(p)$.*

Proposition 2 can be restated as follows: the set $M_N(p)$ is isomorphic to $\gamma_p \times \mathrm{BYTES}^{A \backslash \mathcal{S}_p}$ for some set $\gamma_p \subseteq \mathrm{BYTES}^{\mathcal{S}_p}$. In terms of languages, it means that $M_N(p)$ is a regular one.

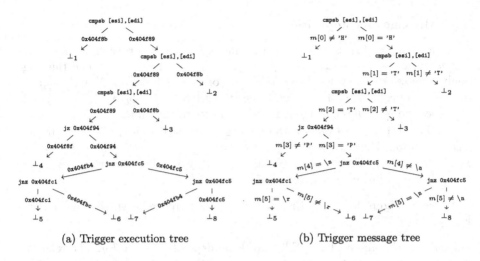

(a) Trigger execution tree   (b) Trigger message tree

Fig. 3. Trigger trees of `wget`

Example 4. In Fig. 3a, writing $[\hat{}\,\mathtt{X}]$ for $(\textsc{Bytes} \setminus \{\mathtt{X}\})$, we have $M_N\,(\bot_1) = [\hat{}\,\mathtt{H}] \cdot \textsc{Bytes}^*$, $M_N\,(\bot_2) = \mathtt{H} \cdot [\hat{}\,\mathtt{T}] \cdot \textsc{Bytes}^*$, $M_N\,(\bot_3) = \mathtt{H} \cdot \mathtt{T} \cdot [\hat{}\,\mathtt{T}] \cdot \textsc{Bytes}^*$, etc.

3.3 Message Execution Tree

A trigger execution tree can be seen as a decision tree, which gives a set of messages given a trace. Here, we consider the dual view that gives a trace given a message.

Definition 3. *A Message Execution Tree (MET) is a tree whose transitions are labeled by finite sets of bytes and leaves are labeled by a trigger path; for each vertex n and letter $b \in \textsc{Bytes}$, there is a unique vertex n' such that $n \xrightarrow{S \ni b} n'$.*

Given a MET G and a message m, let us follow m within G until we reach a leaf (if any). $G(m)$ denote the trigger path labeling that leaf. The MET G is said to be compatible with a TET $\mathcal{E}_N$ if $m \in M_N(G(m))$ for all $m \in \textsc{Bytes}^*$.

We can always build a compatible MET for any finite[3] TET $\mathcal{E}_N$. Indeed, let $L = \max\left(\cup_{p\in\mathcal{E}_N}(\mathcal{S}_p)\right) - \mathtt{b}$ as the largest offset appearing in the sources of a path $p \in \mathcal{E}_N$, and let G be the full 256-ary tree of depth L. Each leaf of G corresponds to some word in $m \in \textsc{Bytes}^L$, we associate to that leaf the path p such that $m \in M_N(p)$, then G is compatible with $\mathcal{E}_N$.

However, one may notice that the full tree G described above is very large in general, its size is of the order 256^L, thus hardly computable. We developed some heuristics to get a much more compact representation.

---

[3] Possibly due to a length limit.

3.4   Message Decomposition

Given a path $p = [(a_1, i_{i_1}), \ldots, (a_k, i_{i_k})]$ in a TET $\mathcal{E}_N$, it corresponds to a trace $T_N(m) = i_1 \rightarrow \cdots \rightarrow i_{i_0} \rightarrow i_{a_1} \rightarrow \cdots \rightarrow i_{i_1} \rightarrow i_{a_2} \rightarrow \ldots$. The tainting analysis shows that any $i \in T_N(m)$ depends on the environment N with respect to a local sources $\mathcal{S}_l(i_1, i_2, \ldots, i)$. Hence the set $\mathcal{S}^A(i) = \mathcal{S}_\ell(i_1, i_2, \ldots, i) \cup A$ describes the *local dependency* of i with respects to the input.

In the TET $\mathcal{E}_N$, we replace the label a_{j+1} of each edge $i_{i_j} \xrightarrow{a_{j+1}} i_{i_{j+1}}$ by its *local condition*, that is the set $\gamma_{a_{j+1}} = \{m_{|\mathcal{S}^A(i)} \mid m \in \text{BYTES}^* \wedge T_N(m) = i_1, \ldots, i_{a_{j+1}}, \ldots\}$. The tree thus obtained from $\mathcal{E}_N$ is called the *trigger message tree* relative to $\mathcal{E}_N$, next denoted by $\mathcal{F}_N$.

Example 5. Figure 3b shows the trigger message tree relative to the TET in Fig. 3a.

Let $\mathcal{S}_{\mathcal{F}_N}$ be the union $\bigcup_{i \in \mathcal{F}_N} \mathcal{S}^A(i)$ of local dependencies in $\mathcal{F}_N$. The relation $R_{\mathcal{F}_N} \subseteq \mathcal{S}_{\mathcal{F}_N} \times \mathcal{S}_{\mathcal{F}_N}$ is defined by $(a, a') \in R_{\mathcal{F}_N}$ if $a, a' \in \mathcal{S}^A(i)$ for some $i \in \mathcal{F}_N$.

Definition 4 (Address Closure). *The reflexive-transitive closure of $R_{\mathcal{F}_N}$ is called the address closure of $\mathcal{F}_N$, denoted by $\alpha_{\mathcal{F}_N}$.*

The address closure $\alpha_{\mathcal{F}_N}$ induces a partition $\mathcal{S}_{\mathcal{F}_N} = A_1 \cup \cdots \cup A_r \subseteq A$ of equivalence classes. Let p be some path in $\mathcal{F}_N$, from the root to some leaf, each $A_i \subseteq A$ gives a *local decomposition* of $M_N(p)$ defined by $\gamma_{p,A_i} = \{m_{|A_i} \mid m \in M_N(p)\}$. Then the path language $M_N(p)$ can be decomposed into:

Proposition 3. $M_N(p) = \gamma_{p,A_1} \times \gamma_{p,A_2} \times \cdots \times \gamma_{p,A_r} \times \text{BYTES}^{A \setminus \mathcal{S}_{\mathcal{F}_N}}$

Example 6. The path p in Fig. 4 is extracted from the execution tree of `wget` cut at length 60, it is of the form

$$i_1 \xrightarrow{m[0]=\text{'H'}} i_2 \xrightarrow{m[1]=\text{'T'}} \cdots \xrightarrow{m[4]=\backslash n} i_6 \xrightarrow{m[5] \neq \backslash n} i_7 \xrightarrow{m[5]=\backslash r} \perp$$

Both instructions i_6 and i_7 depend on the 5-th byte of the input, the local decomposition groups their local conditions into a single set $M_N(p)_{|\{5\}} = \{m[5] \neq \backslash n\} \cap \{m[5] = \backslash r\} = \{m[5] = \backslash r\}$, thus $M_N(p)$ decomposes:

$$M_N(p) = \{\text{H}\} \times \{\text{T}\} \times \{\text{T}\} \times \{\text{P}\} \times \{\backslash n\} \times \{\backslash r\} \times \text{BYTES}^{A \setminus \{0,1,2,3,4,5\}}$$

local condition	path	
$m[0] = \text{'H'}$	`cmpsb [esi],[edi]`	i1
$m[1] = \text{'T'}$	`cmpsb [esi],[edi]`	i2
$m[2] = \text{'T'}$	`cmpsb [esi],[edi]`	i3
$m[3] = \text{'P'}$	`jz 0x404f94`	i4
$m[4] = \backslash n$	`jnz 0x404fc5`	i5
$m[5] \neq \backslash n$	`jnz 0x404fc1`	i6
$m[5] = \backslash r$	`jnz 0x404fc5`	i7

Fig. 4. Path of `wget` and message decomposition

From the partition $\mathcal{S}_{\mathcal{F}_N} = A_1 \cup \cdots \cup A_r$ induced from the closure $\alpha_{\mathcal{F}_N}$ of $\mathcal{F}_N$, we derive a tree $\overline{\mathcal{F}_N}$ whose branches have the form where γ_i is a local condition on A_i. Moreover, each path in $\mathcal{E}_N$ corresponds uniquely to a leaf in $\overline{\mathcal{F}_N}$. Algorithm 1 constructs the tree $\overline{\mathcal{F}_N}$ when the following hypothesis holds.

Hypothesis 1. *For any path* $i_{i_0} \xrightarrow{\gamma_1} i_{i_1} \xrightarrow{\gamma_2} \cdots$ *in* $\mathcal{F}_N$, *let* $A_{d(k)}$ *denote the equivalence class containing the support of* γ_k. *Then, for all* $k \leq l$, $d(k) \leq d(l)$.

Proposition 4. *Let* s_0 *be the root of the trigger message tree* $\overline{\mathcal{F}_N}$. *For any path* p *in* $\mathcal{E}_N$, *there is a unique path* $\overline{p} = s_0 \xrightarrow{\gamma_1} \cdots \xrightarrow{\gamma_r} s_r$ *in* $\overline{\mathcal{F}_N}$ *such that* $M_N(p) = \gamma_1 \times \cdots \times \gamma_r \times \text{BYTES}^{\complement A_1 \cup \cdots \cup A_r}$.

Input: $\mathcal{P} = \{M_N(p) = \gamma_{p,A_1} \times \cdots \times \gamma_{p,A_r} \times \gamma_{p,\complement} \mid p \text{ is a path on } \mathcal{F}_N\}$.
Output: the tree $\overline{\mathcal{F}_N}$.
begin
 $\overline{\mathcal{F}_N} \leftarrow \{\text{initial state } s\}$;
 foreach $M_N(p) \in \mathcal{P}$ **do**
  $i \leftarrow 1, s_1 \leftarrow s$; **while** *edge* $e = s_i \xrightarrow{\gamma_{p,A_i}} s_i'$ *for some* s_i' *exists on* $\overline{\mathcal{F}_N}$ **do**
   $i \leftarrow i + 1$; $s_1 \leftarrow$ source of e; $s_2 \leftarrow$ target of e;
  end
  while $i \neq j$ **do**
   $s_1 \leftarrow s_2$;
   if $i + 1 \leq n$ **then**
    $s_2 \leftarrow$ new state;
   else
    $s_2 \leftarrow$ new state labeled $\bot$;
   end
   add new edge $s_1 \xrightarrow{\gamma_{p,A_i}} s_2$ into $\overline{\mathcal{F}_N}$; $i \leftarrow i + 1$;
  end
 end
end

Algorithm 1: Tree construction

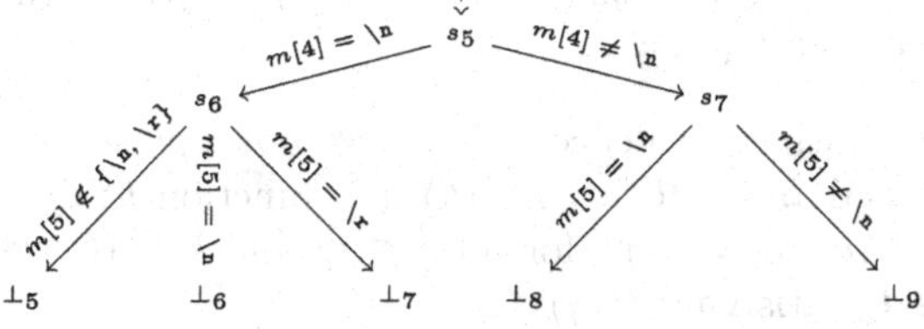

Fig. 5. Decomposition tree

Finally, local conditions in the tree $\overline{\mathcal{F}_N}$ can be reordered to follow the progression of a MET. We end with a message execution tree, next denoted $\mathcal{A}_N$.

Example 7. Figure 5 shows the tree $\overline{\mathcal{F}_N}$ corresponding to the $\mathcal{E}_N$ discussed in Example 6. To save space, we grouped transitions of the first four characters, that is from s_1 to s_4. One can observe that $\overline{\mathcal{F}_N}$ in this case is indeed $\mathcal{A}_N$.

4   Message Classification

In Sect. 3, we showed how to relate messages to traces of execution using path languages and their dual representation by message execution trees. With this analysis, some messages m and m' that are not treated in the same manner are not in the same path language, even if they are clearly related. For example, consider a program which looks for the first newline character by examining each byte, then the execution traces of the parsing of `"aaa\n"` and the one of `"aaaa\n"` fall into different categories. In this section, we propose a method to avoid such irrelevant details. The principle is to gather equivalent path languages with respect to the remaining execution of the program.

4.1   Message Automaton

Definition 5 (Message Automaton (MA)). *A message automaton $\mathcal{A}$ is a quadruple $\langle Q, \iota, E, P \rangle$ where*

- *Q is a set of states, $\iota \in Q$ being the one qualified to be initial,*
- *$E \subseteq Q \times \text{BYTES} \to Q$ is a transition function which is totally determined at some states, and totally undetermined at other states.*
- *$P : Q \to 2^{\mathcal{B}}$ maps each state to a set of trigger paths (in general, the trigger paths of $\mathcal{B}$ are distinguished from the paths within $\mathcal{A}$).*

In other words, it is a pair made of a (deterministic) automaton and the path function P. Given some word m, $E(\iota, m)$ and $Q(\iota, m)$ denote respectively the state and the path (within the automaton) following the word m along the transition function E from the initial state ι.

Proposition 5. *The message execution tree $\mathcal{A}_N$ has form of a message automaton $\langle Q, \iota, E, P \rangle$ where Q consists of all vertices, ι is the root vertex, E consists of $s \times \gamma \to s'$ whenever $s \xrightarrow{\gamma} s'$ is an edge of $\mathcal{A}_N$, and $P(q) = \{$the path from root to q$\}$ for any leaf q, otherwise $P(q) = \emptyset$.*

Given some trigger path equivalence $\approx \subseteq \mathcal{B} \times \mathcal{B}$, a *morphism* $h \colon \mathcal{A} \to \mathcal{A}'$ where $\mathcal{A} = \langle Q, \iota, E, P \rangle$ and $\mathcal{A}' = \langle Q', \iota', E', P' \rangle$ is a function $h \colon Q \to Q'$ satisfying: $1.h(\iota) = \iota'$, $2.E'(h(q), b) = h(q')$ for all $q \in Q$ and $b \in \text{BYTES}$, $3.P'(h(q)) \approx P(q)$[4] for any $q \in Q$ satisfying $P(q) \neq \emptyset$.

---

[4] This is the set equality up to the equivalence $\approx$.

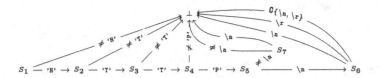

Fig. 6. Message automaton constructed from a morphism

Definition 6 (Observational Approximation). *Given a MA $\mathscr{A} = \langle Q, \iota, E, P \rangle$, a MA $\mathscr{A}' = \langle Q', \iota', E', P' \rangle$ is said to approximate observationally $\mathscr{A}$ if $E(\iota, m)$ exists[5] then $E'(\iota', m)$ exists, moreover if $P(E(\iota, m)) \neq \emptyset$ then $P'(E'(\iota', m)) \approx P(E(\iota, m))$ and if $Q(\iota, m_1) \neq Q(\iota, m_2)$ then $Q'(\iota', m_1) \neq Q'(\iota', m_2)$, for all $m, m_1, m_2 \in \text{BYTES}^*$.*

Intuitively, the message automaton $\mathscr{A}'$ recognizes and distinguishes at least the paths of $\mathscr{A}$. Morphisms justify the observational approximation:

Proposition 6. *If there is a morphism $h\colon \mathscr{A} \to \mathscr{A}'$, then $\mathscr{A}'$ approximates observationally $\mathscr{A}$.*

Example 8. The automaton $\mathscr{A}$ in Fig. 6 is constructed from $\mathcal{A}_N$ in Example 7 using the morphism that maps $s_i \mapsto S_i$ and $\perp_i \mapsto \perp$ for all $1 \leq i \leq 7$. On $\mathscr{A}$, set the path function to be $\perp \mapsto \cup_{i \leq 7} \perp_i$ (with the identification of $\perp_i$ with its corresponding path in $\mathcal{A}_N$) and $S_i \mapsto \emptyset$ otherwise. One can observe that $\mathscr{A}$ approximates observationally $\mathcal{A}_N$.

Definition 7 (State Equivalence). *Given a MA $\mathscr{A} = \langle Q, \iota, E, P \rangle$, a state equivalence relative to $\approx$ is an equivalence $\sim \subseteq Q \times Q$ satisfying: if $q_1 \sim q_2$ then*

- *if there is a transition $q_1 \xrightarrow{t} q_1'$*
  - *then either q_2 has no outgoing transitions,*
  - *or there is a state q_2' with transition $q_2 \xrightarrow{t} q_2'$ and $q_1' \sim q_2'$.*
- *if $P(q_1), P(q_2) \neq \emptyset$ then $P(q_1) \approx P(q_2)$.*

The co-recursive definition of the state equivalence is constructive. Indeed, to look for a state equivalence we can start the verification from any pair (q_1, q_2): first, add it as the first element of the relation whenever q_1 or q_2 has no transition, or both of them have similar transitions, then continue verifying pairs of corresponding states (q_1', q_2') or some pair obtained from the transitive closure of the current constructed relation. At any verification step, if states of the verified pair invalidate the definition, then the relation cannot be a state equivalence. In this case, we will restart verifying with another pair until an equivalence is completely constructed. This construction is given in the technical report.

---

[5] Because E is a partial function, $E(\iota, m)$ does not always exist for any $m \in \text{BYTES}^*$.

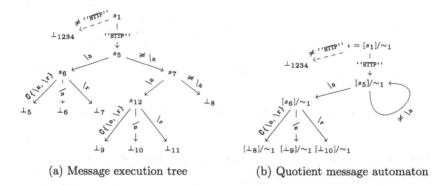

(a) Message execution tree   (b) Quotient message automaton

Fig. 7. Message automaton and its quotient

Example 9. Figure 7a shows the MET of `wget` with traces cut to length 70. Given the path equivalence $\perp_5 \approx \perp_9$, $\perp_6 \approx \perp_{10}$, $\perp_7 \approx \perp_{11}$, we have a state equivalence $s_5 \sim_1 s_7 \sim_1 \perp_8$, $s_6 \sim_1 s_{12}$, $\perp_5 \sim_1 \perp_9$, $\perp_6 \sim_1 \perp_{10}$ and $\perp_7 \sim_1 \perp_{11}$.

Given a MA $\mathscr{A} = \langle Q, \iota, E, P \rangle$, let $\sim$ be a state equivalence relative to some path equivalence $\approx$, then the MA $\mathscr{A}/\sim = \langle Q', \iota', E', P' \rangle$ constructed as follows

- $Q' = \{[q]/\sim \mid q \in Q\}$, $\iota' = [\iota]/\sim$,
- $E' = \{[q_1]/\sim \xrightarrow{t} [q_2]/\sim \mid q_1 \xrightarrow{t} q_2 \in E\}$
- $P' : [q]/\sim \mapsto \bigcup_{q' \in frac[q]\sim} P(q')$.

is called the *quotient of $\mathscr{A}$ by $\sim$*. This construction leads to:

Proposition 7. *The function $[]/\sim : Q \to Q'$ defines a morphism $\mathscr{A} \to \mathscr{A}/\sim$, then $\mathscr{A}/\sim$ approximates observationally $\mathscr{A}$.*

Example 10. The MA in Fig. 7b is constructed from the state equivalence $\sim_1$ in Example 9, it approximates observationally the MET in Fig. 7a.

4.2   Minimal Message Automaton

Let $\mathscr{A}$ be a message automaton, let $\sim$ be a nontrivial[6] equivalence on $\mathscr{A}$ then the quotient $\mathscr{A}/\sim$ has fewer state than $\mathscr{A}$. A message automaton $\mathscr{A}$ is said to be irreducible if there is no nontrivial equivalence on $\mathscr{A}$.

Proposition 8. *The composition $f \circ g$ of two morphisms is a morphism.*

Consider a sequence of morphisms $\mathcal{A}_N \xrightarrow{\text{id}} \mathscr{A}_1 \xrightarrow{h_1} \mathscr{A}_2 \xrightarrow{h_2} \dots$ where the h_i's are induced from some nontrivial state equivalence on $\mathscr{A}_i$, then this sequence is always finite (the number of states is strictly decreasing). It ends on an irreducible machine automaton $\mathscr{A}_{n+1}$. By Proposition 7 and Proposition 8, $h = h_n \circ h_{n-1} \circ \dots \circ h_1$ is a morphism. By Proposition 6, $\mathscr{A}_{n+1}$ approximates observationally $\mathcal{A}_N$. Moreover, since $\mathscr{A}_{n+1}$ is not reducible, it is minimal:

---
[6] Namely $\sim$ is not the equality.

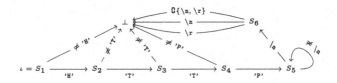

Fig. 8. Minimal message automaton

Proposition 9. *There is no message automaton that approximates observationally $\mathcal{A}_N$ but has less states than $\mathcal{A}_{n+1}$.*

Example 11. The MA in Fig. 8 is reduced from the MA in Fig. 7b using the morphism constructed from the state equivalence $\perp_1 \sim_2 \perp_2 \sim_2 \perp_3 \sim_2 \perp_4 \sim_2 [s_8]/\!\sim_1 \sim_2 [s_9]/\!\sim_1 \sim_2 [s_{10}]/\!\sim_1$, it approximates observationally the MET in Fig. 7a. We let the reader verify that it is minimal.

5 Implementation and Experiments

To verify the relevance of the approach, we have implemented a *binary code coverage module* that builds the execution tree by a fuzzing techniques optimized by means of a tainting analysis; then the results are fed to an *automaton construction module* that constructs a minimal message automaton that represents the language of input messages for each examined program. We repeatedly apply non trivial state equivalence transformations up to a non reducible automaton.

The implementation of both consists in about 16500 lines of C++ code and is freely available online at [5]. The binary code coverage module is implemented with the help of the Pin DBI framework [17].

5.1 Experiments

The results given here obtained by our modules when examining Zeus, a well-known family of malwares disclosed in 2009. Some previous analyses [11,13] have shown that this malware steals private informations on infected hosts. Below, we provide some details on Zeus that, as far as we know, are not published.

With an initial dynamic analysis, we could observe that Zeus hooks the API send and WSASend. Then it parses the data at the hooked socket to collect the informations. Figure 9 shows the message automaton obtained from a message execution tree where traces are limited to the length 450 (for the path equivalence $\approx$, again, we identify all pending vertices $\perp_i$). Actually, the automaton classifies data that Zeus is interested in. First, one reads keywords directly within the automaton. Let us consider now the languages corresponding to path between the state mentioned as "initial" and the one as "terminal":

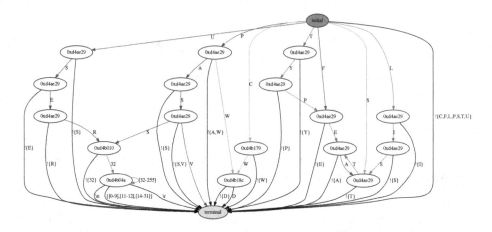

Fig. 9. Message automaton of Zeus

$$M_1 = \text{`U'.`S'.`E'.`R'}.\{32\}.\{32, 33, \ldots, 255\}^*$$
$$M_2 = \text{`P'.`A'.`S'.`S'}.\{32\}.\{32, 33, \ldots, 255\}^*$$
$$M_3 = \text{`P'.`A'.`S'.`V'}.\text{Bytes}^*$$
$$M_4 = \text{`P'.`W'.`D'}.\text{Bytes}^*$$
$$M_5 = \text{`C'.`W'.`D'}.\text{Bytes}^*$$
$$M_6 = \text{`T'.`Y'.`P'.`E'}.\{!`A'\}.\text{Bytes}^*$$
$$M_7 = \text{`F'.`E'.`A'.`T'}.\{!`A'\}.\text{Bytes}^*$$
$$M_8 = \text{`S'.`T'.`A'.`T'}.\{!`A'\}.\text{Bytes}^*$$
$$M_9 = \text{`L'.`I'.`S'.`T'}.\{!`A'\}.\text{Bytes}^*$$

The observed words USER, PASS, PASV, PWD, CWD, TYPE, FEAT, STAT, LIST are commands defined in the ftp protocol. That may be interpreted as an insight that Zeus steals information concerned with ftp communications. Moreover, besides these words there is no more commands of ftp occurring in the automaton, so we may think that Zeus is interested only in this subset of ftp commands. In the following languages that occur also within the automaton:

$$M_{10} = \text{`U'.`S'.`E'.`R'}.\{!32\}.\text{Bytes}^*$$
$$M_{11} = \text{`U'.`S'.`E'.`R'}.\{32\}.\{32, 33, \ldots, 255\}^k.\backslash\text{r}.\text{Bytes}^*$$
$$M_{11} = \text{`U'.`S'.`E'.`R'}.\{32\}.\{32, 33, \ldots, 255\}^k.\backslash\text{n}.\text{Bytes}^*$$
$$M_{12} = \text{`U'.`S'.`E'.`R'}.\{32\}.\{32, 33, \ldots, 255\}^k.(\{1, 2 \ldots, 31\} \setminus \{\backslash\text{r}, \backslash\text{n}\}).\text{Bytes}^*$$
$$M_{13} = \text{`P'.`A'.`S'.`S'}.\{!32\}.\text{Bytes}^*$$
$$M_{14} = \text{`P'.`A'.`S'.`S'}.\{32\}.\{32, 33, \ldots, 255\}^k.\backslash\text{r}.\text{Bytes}^*$$
$$M_{15} = \text{`P'.`A'.`S'.`S'}.\{32\}.\{32, 33, \ldots, 255\}^k.\backslash\text{n}.\text{Bytes}^*$$
$$M_{16} = \text{`P'.`A'.`S'.`S'}.\{32\}.\{32, 33, \ldots, 255\}^k.(\{1, 2, \ldots, 31\} \setminus \{\backslash\text{r}, \backslash\text{n}\}).\text{Bytes}^*$$

we notice that 32 is the ASCII code of the space character, and the set $\{1, 2, \ldots, 31\}$ contain all control characters. So these languages show clearly how Zeus parses a USER or PASS command: it checks whether the next character is space or not, if yes then it collects the bytes until a control character is detected. In other words, we retrieved the delimiter-oriented analysis of Caballero et al. [7].

6 Conclusion

The experiments we made so far showed that the hypothesis we made are generally speaking fulfilled. The parsing methods look more or less transparent. However, the shape of the automaton depends largely on the choice on the length of traces. At the same time, the computation time is more or less exponential in the size of the execution tree, thus, usually exponential in the length of traces. There a good reasons to optimize the computation of the execution tree and all derived ones, we think of symbolic execution, SMT-solvers and advanced tainting techniques. Finally, there is a parameter that we did not really used, namely the path equivalence $\approx$. Again, some first tries showed that this must be deepened.

References

1. Angluin, D.: Inductive inference of formal languages from positive data. Inf. Control **45**(2), 117–135 (1980)
2. Bardin, S., Philippe, H.: OSMOSE: automatic structural testing of executables. Softw. Test. Verification Reliab. **21**(1), 29–54 (2011)
3. Bardin, S., Herrmann, P., Védrine, F.: Refinement-based CFG reconstruction from unstructured programs. In: Jhala, R., Schmidt, D. (eds.) VMCAI 2011. LNCS, vol. 6538, pp. 54–69. Springer, Heidelberg (2011)
4. Beaucamps, P., Gnaedig, I., Marion, J.-Y.: Abstraction-based malware analysis using rewriting and model checking. In: Foresti, S., Yung, M., Martinelli, F. (eds.) ESORICS 2012. LNCS, vol. 7459, pp. 806–823. Springer, Heidelberg (2012)
5. Bonfante, G., Marion, J.-Y., Ta, T.D.: PathExplorer
6. Caballero, J., Poosankam, P., Kreibich, C., Xiaodong Song, D.: Dispatcher: enabling active botnet infiltration using automatic protocol reverse-engineering. In: CCS (2009)
7. Caballero, J., Yin, H., Liang, Z., Song, D.: Polyglot: automatic extraction of protocol message format using dynamic binary analysis. In: CCS (2007)
8. Calvet, J.: Analyse Dynamique de Logiciels Malveillants (2013)
9. Comparetti, P.M., Wondracek, G., Krügel, C., Kirda, E.: Prospex: protocol specification extraction. In: SSP (2009)
10. Preda, M.D., Giacobazzi, R., Debray, S., Coogan, K., Townsend, G.M.: Modelling metamorphism by abstract interpretation. In: Cousot, R., Martel, M. (eds.) Static Analysis. LNCS, vol. 6337, pp. 218–235. Springer, Heidelberg (2010)
11. Falliere, N., Chien, E.: Zeus: King of the Bots. Technical report (2009)
12. Godefroid, P., Klarlund, N., Sen, K.: DART: directed automated random testing. In: PLDI (2005)
13. IOActive. Reversal and Analysis of Zeus and SpyEye Banking Trojans. Technical report (2012)

14. Kinder, J., Zuleger, F., Veith, H.: An abstract interpretation-based framework for control flow reconstruction from binaries. In: Jones, N.D., Müller-Olm, M. (eds.) VMCAI 2009. LNCS, vol. 5403, pp. 214–228. Springer, Heidelberg (2009)
15. Lecomte, S.: Élaboration d'une représentation intermédiaire pour l'exécution concolique et le marquage de données sous Windows (2014)
16. Lin, Z., Jiang, X., Xu, D., Zhang, X.: Automatic protocol format reverse engineering through context-aware monitored execution. In: NDSS (2008)
17. Luk, C.-K., Cohn, R.S., Muth, R., Patil, H., Klauser, A., Lowney, P.G., Wallace, S., Reddi, V.J., Hazelwood, K.M.: Pin: building customized program analysis tools with dynamic instrumentation. In: PLDI (2005)
18. Moser, A., Krügel, C., Kirda, E.: Exploring multiple execution paths for malware analysis. In: SSP (2007)
19. Reps, T., Balakrishnan, G.: Improved memory-access analysis for X86 executables. In: Hendren, L. (ed.) Compiler Construction. LNCS, vol. 4959, pp. 16–35. Springer, Heidelberg (2008)
20. Schwartz, E.J., Avgerinos, T., Brumley, D.: All you ever wanted to know about dynamic taint analysis and forward symbolic execution. In: SSP (2010)
21. Song, F., Touili, T.: Pushdown model checking for malware detection. STTT **16**(2), 147–173 (2014)
22. Valiant, L.G.: A theory of the learnable. CACM **27**, 1134–1142 (1984)
23. Wang, Z., Jiang, X., Cui, W., Wang, X., Grace, M.: ReFormat: automatic reverse engineering of encrypted messages. In: Backes, M., Ning, P. (eds.) ESORICS 2009. LNCS, vol. 5789, pp. 200–215. Springer, Heidelberg (2009)

Network Security and Protocols

A Game Approach for an Efficient Intrusion Detection System in Mobile Ad Hoc Networks

Myria Bouhaddi[1]([✉]), Mohammed Saïd Radjef[1], and Kamel Adi[2]

[1] Research Unit of LaMOS, Department of Operational Research,
Faculty of Exact Sciences, University of Bejaia, Bejaia, Algeria
[2] Department of Computer Science and Engineering, University of Quebec
in Outaouais, Quebec, Canada
myria.bouhaddi@gmail.com, radjefms@yahoo.fr,
Kamel.Adi@uqo.ca

Abstract. Intrusion Detection Systems (IDS) have become a necessary complement to any security infrastructure and are widely deployed as an additional line of defense to conventional security techniques. Intrusion detection techniques have been widely studied in the literature for the conventional networks. However, due to the specific characteristics of the mobile ad hoc networks (MANET), such as the lack of a fixed infrastructure and a centralized management, the implementation of an IDS presents several new challenges that must be addressed. In this paper, we present a game-based approach to implement an intrusion detection system in MANETs. We consider the selfish node behavior and discuss mechanisms that stimulate cooperation between nodes while reducing the consumption of energy due to deployment of the IDS. We also address the problem of increasing the effectiveness of security mechanism by developing a network packet sampling strategy, to effectively detect network intrusions with respect to a given total sampling budget, and find the right moment for notifying specific nodes to launch countermeasures. Finally, we evaluate the proposed approach via simulations where the results show the effectiveness of the proposed intrusion detection model.

Keywords: MANETs · IDS · Clustering · Selfish nodes · Game theory · Nash equilibrium

1 Introduction

Mobile Ad-hoc NETworks (MANET) are, nowadays, a vital complement to traditional networks. They are generally built around a set of wireless mobile nodes forming a temporary network and that can be deployed spontaneously without requiring any pre-existing network infrastructure or centralized administration. Hence, network operations are fully distributed among mobile nodes that act as relays to support multi-hop communications. The unique characteristics of MANET such as infrastructure-less nature make them very interesting for a growing number of situations and applications, in particular, when the deployment of a network infrastructure is unfeasible or prohibitively expensive.

© Springer International Publishing Switzerland 2015
F. Cuppens et al. (Eds.): FPS 2014, LNCS 8930, pp. 131–146, 2015.
DOI: 10.1007/978-3-319-17040-4_9

Unlike traditional networks, MANETs have no specific station where an Intrusion Detection System (IDS) can be deployed. Hence, a node may need to run its own IDS [3,4] and cooperate with others to ensure security. This is very inefficient in terms of resource consumption since the nodes, typically, have limited autonomy in term of energy. To overcome this difficulty, a common approach is to divide a MANET into a set of 1-hop clusters where each node belongs to at least one cluster. Nodes in each cluster have a leader node (cluster-head) to serve as an IDS for the entire cluster.

All these election procedures do not take into account the residual energy that ensure the longevity of the network, and in the case where they do it, it remains very difficult to collect this data because the information regarding the node's energy is private to the node, and thus, not verifiable. Since cluster-head is more energy consuming, some selfish nodes will be tempted to keep the information hidden to avoid being cluster-head while they still taking advantage from network services.

Game theory has been developed and extensively used in the context of economy and biology. It is very powerful mathematical tool for analyzing and predicting the behavior of rational and selfish entities [1]. Due to its interesting and sometimes unexpected results, its popularity reached the field of communications and networking technology. In this paper, we use game theory as a central tool for modeling two problems: (i) encourage nodes to declare themselves as leaders in the clustering procedure and assume the IDS functions (leader-IDS) (ii) increase the detection efficiency of malicious packets in the network by finding an optimal sampling rate in accordance with a given total sampling budget and members' reputation, and determine the optimal probability for an attacker to launch an attack, i.e.: when it would be more profitable for it to attack a target node, the IDS informs the victim node to launch countermeasures (for instance, activate its own Host Intrusion Detection System HIDS) once the probability of attack exceeds this threshold.

The remainder of this paper is organized as follows. Section 2 presents the related work. Section 3 describes the problem statement and proposed model which is consists of the leader election procedure and the intrusion detection mechanism. In Sect. 4, we present the results of the simulation and we evaluate our model based on these results. Finally, Sect. 5 draws a conclusion with a future work.

2   Related Work

This section reviews the related work on the application of the game theory for the intrusion detection in ad hoc network and the clustering procedure, then summarizes the work on selfishness in wireless networks.

Several proposals address the use of game theory in order to model and solve intrusion detection problems. In [5], the authors considered the problem of intruding packets in a network by means of network packets sampling. The intrusion detection game is played between two players: the service provider and the intruder. They take into consideration the scenario where the adversary has significant information about the network. The attack is accomplished when the adversary sends a malicious packet via a path to the victim node and the packet is not sampled. The intruder objective is to minimize chances of detection and the provider maximizes it. This is a min-max approach, where the solution is a max flow problem from which the stable points will be obtained. This work have been extended in [9], where the authors considered the problem of intrusion over multiple packets in a network. Note that, a single packet belonging to an attack may look as normal if sampled alone, while a series of these packets could be marked as an intrusion. In the modeling process, the authors considered the case where the IDS needs all the malicious fragments to detect the intrusion.

In [6], the authors used game theory to analyze the clustering problem and propose a clustering mechanism called CROSS. In this model, each node is modeled as player, who can hear all other players' messages and know how many players there are. According to this number of players, every player calculates an equilibrium probability, which is used to decide whether a player declares itself to be a cluster-head. So, the idea is to have a self-election process where a node has a great benefit when it transmits data, while it wants to avoid being a cluster-head. The setup of the game and its rules create a natural cooperation between nodes. A node is then "forced" to cooperate and declare itself, because it has more benefit from transmitting its data than declaring itself as CH. Moreover, if all its neighbors have already declared themselves, then the only way to transmit own data is to declare itself, and no other node will declare itself until this node has done so.

Selfishness in wireless networks has been given a particular attention in the research community. The activation of an IDS imply a cost in terms of energy consumption and the use other resources to the nodes. So, a selfish node will need an inducement or reward for being cluster-head and keep its IDS active. To encourage selfish nodes in ad hoc network to cooperate, one way to address the problem is to use the incentive mechanisms. Various approaches have been used in the literature such as credit-exchange schemes and reputation-based systems. In credit-exchange schemes [8], nodes receive a credit payment to compensate the energy consumption during their participation in services of the network and this credit can later be used by these nodes to encourage other nodes to cooperate. In the reputation-based schemes [7], a node's behavior is measured by its neighbors, and selfishness is deterred by the threat of partial or total disconnection from the network.

3   Problem Statement and Proposed Model

The approach set-up is outlined in two steps. First, we elaborate a game theoretic model to form and analyze the problem of clustering in ad hoc networks where we consider the conflicting interests of nodes in their appointment to the role of leader-IDS. Furthermore, we introduce another game theoretic framework to represent the interaction between a leader-IDS and an attacker with incomplete information as a non-zero sum non-cooperative game.

3.1 Game Theoretic Model for Leader Selection

Amongst other things, the responsibility of a cluster-head is to offer the IDS services to its cluster members. Since a cluster-head consumes much more energy to maintain the security of the whole cluster, a selfish node may refuse to declare itself as CH. To solve this problem, we consider the CH declaration as a game and adopt a game theoretic model to promote cooperation of selfish nodes.

The idea to use the game theory to designate cluster-heads in considering the misbehavior of selfish nodes takes inspiration from the work presented in [6] where the cluster-head is responsible for the packets transmission of its members to the sink in wireless sensors network. Unlike to the transmission function of the cluster-head considered in [6], the task of the leader here is to run its IDS to sample the incoming packets to its whole cluster for detecting the malicious ones. In the case where there is no node declare itself cluster-head, then the security will be compromised and the losses with the damage caused will be considered and appear in the game structure. The authors in [6] also assume that the game is played with all nodes of the network, this hypothesis is unrealistic, because all nodes of a network cannot be neighbors. In addition, they didn't take into account the nodes energy level during the leader selection process which is a decisive factor in the lifespan of the network.

We consider an ad hoc network as a graph $G = (N, X)$, where N is the set of nodes and X is the set of bidirectional links in the network. Each node $i \in N$ is characterized by a level energy E_i and it is assumed that it has an IDS. Each link is characterized by a value of a reputation R_x, $x \in X$ ($0 \le R_x \le 1$) initialized to 1. We consider the presence of selfish nodes that are not willing to participate in detecting network intrusions in order not to consume resources such as battery, memory and CPU time. The reputation value is calculated by the leader-IDS for each incoming link to its members according to the number of tested packets and it allows to reflect the behavior of nodes. This value depends on the number of malicious messages detected w.r.t. the total number of messages tested. We denote by $V(i)$ the set of i's neighbors, with $|V(i)|$ the number of these neighbors. The energy, reputation and the list of neighbors are updated at each time interval T_{elec}. The reputation of node i will be the average reputation at each interval. We assume nodes are rational in the sense that they want to maximize their own benefice.

We define the problem of the self-organization of nodes into groups in an ad hoc network with presence of selfish behavior as a game which is formally defined by:

$$CG^{(i)} =< \zeta^{(i)}, \{S_k^{(i)}\}_{k \in \zeta^{(i)}}, \{U_k^{(i)}\}_{k \in \zeta^{(i)}} >, \quad \text{where:}$$

- $\zeta^{(i)}$ is the set of players containing the node i and its neighbors ($|V(i)|$) i.e.:

$$\zeta^{(i)} = \{i\} \cup V(i)$$

- a node (player) has a choice between two decisions: a node decides to either declare itself as CH (D) or not (ND)

$$S_k^{(i)} = \{D, ND\}, \forall i, \forall k$$

- regarding payoffs, if a player chooses to not become CH, then if no other node becomes a CH either, security will be compromised and hence the losses incurred will be estimated at value l. If at least one neighbor declares itself as CH, nodes will get a reward r for having their data secured. Finally, if the player declares itself as CH, its reward for securing its data will be reduced by an amount equal to the cost c corresponding to the IDS activation (ex. energy consumption). In this case, the final payoff for this node will be $r - c$. We suppose that $r > c$ and $l > c$, otherwise the node is not motivated to declare itself as a leader.

The game is played by $|V(i)|+1$ players. Let $s^{(i)} = \{s_1^{(i)}, \cdots, s_{|V(i)|}^{(i)}, s_{|V(i)|+1}^{(i)}\}$ be the vector profile of the strategies followed by the players. The utility function $U_k^{(i)}(s)$ of an arbitrary node k playing to the $CG^{(i)}$ has the following form:

$$U_k^{(i)}(s) = \begin{cases} -l, & \text{if } s_k^{(i)} = ND, \forall\, k \in \zeta^{(i)} \\ r & \text{if } s_k^{(i)} = ND \text{ and } \exists\, j \in \zeta^{(i)}, \ s_j^{(i)} = D \\ r - c & \text{if } s_k^{(i)} = D \end{cases} \tag{1}$$

When the game is played between two players, it will admit two Nash equilibria (D, ND) and (ND, D). Although, these two Nash equilibria are not symmetrical. Since these players are nodes, this implies that they have the same reasoning. So, we calculate the Nash equilibria in a mixed strategies to find a symmetrical equilibrium. If we assume that each player is allowed a probability distribution on its strategies set, a mixed strategy Nash equilibrium can be found. In other words, every player has now a probability of declaring itself as CH and a probability to not doing so. We denote the probability of playing D as p and the probability of playing ND as $1 - p$. According to Theorem 1 in [6], there exists an equilibrium probability p^* based on a symmetric mixed strategies Nash equilibrium. Using the procedure found in [10], the symmetric mixed strategy Nash equilibrium is given by the following formula:

$$p_i^* = 1 - \left(\frac{c}{l+r}\right)^{\frac{1}{|V(i)|}} \tag{2}$$

with: $\frac{c}{r+l} < 1$.

Note that p_i^* decreases as the number of players increases. This can be interpreted by the fact that players become less cooperative when the number of their neighbors increases.

Once the Nash equilibrium is found, an interesting point is to look at the variation of this equilibrium depending on the losses l.

In order to study the variation of the cooperation w.r.t. the loss l of the node i in its participation in the clustering game, we made an implementation under MATLAB to compute the optimal probability a node i should have to declare itself as a leader. For this implementation, we set the following game parameters $r = 30$ $c = 15$ and l varying in $[1, 30]$. We also varied the number of neighbors $|V(i)|$ by considering the values 5, 15, 25 and 35 (Fig. 1).

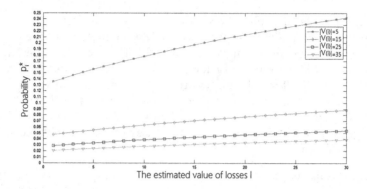

Fig. 1. Variation of the p_i^* according to losses l and the number of neighbors $|V(i)|$.

Based on this figure, we remark that:

- The optimal probability p_i^* decreases when the number of neighbors increases. This means that when the number of neighbors increases, the nodes become less cooperative to declare themselves as cluster-head.
- p_i^* increases when the value of l increases, which means that when the insecurity increase, the node are more cooperating by playing "De", independently of values of $|V(i)|$.

The probability of at least one player declares itself as CH is:

$$
\begin{aligned}
p_A &= Pr\{at\ least\ one\ node\ plays\ De\} \\
&= 1 - Pr\{no\ one\ plays\ De\} \\
&= 1 - (1 - p)^{|V(i)|+1} \\
&= 1 - (\frac{c}{r+l})^{\frac{|V(i)|+1}{|V(i)|}}
\end{aligned}
\tag{3}
$$

Let $\omega = \frac{c}{r+l}$. By representing the variation of the two probabilities (p_i^*, p_A) for the different values of ω with respect to the number of neighbors of an arbitrary node i, we get the following figure.

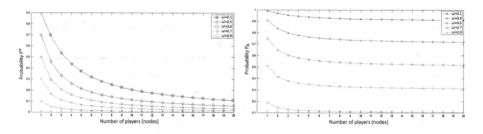

Fig. 2. Evaluation of p_i^* and p_A for different values of ω.

Figure 2 gives a graphic illustration of Eqs. 2 and 3. When the number of players $|V(i)|$ increases, the probabilities p_i^* and p_A decrease. Moreover, what is interesting to note also is that p_A is closely related to the parameter ω. The probability that there is at least one node that declares itself cluster-head is large when the value of omega is small. This means in a practical sense that a node is encouraged to declare itself as a leader when the gain in security and losses are much bigger than the cost ($c << r + l$).

These characteristics of the computed probabilities can be very useful in the designation of a clustering mechanism based on the rationality of the selfish nodes to encourage cooperation without integrating a mandatory mechanism.

The expected average payoff of an arbitrary node i is:

$$\overline{U^{(i)}} = -l(1-p)^{|V(i)|+1} + (r-c)p + r(1-p) - r(1-p)^{|V(i)|+1} \qquad (4)$$

By substituting in Eq. (4) the equilibrium probability p_i^*, the average payoff for the equilibrium strategy $\overline{U_{NE}^{(i)}}$ is:

$$\overline{U_{NE}^{(i)}} = -(l+r)(\frac{c}{r+l})^{\frac{|V(i)|+1}{|V(i)|}} + c(\frac{c}{r+l})^{\frac{1}{|V(i)|}} + r - c = r - c \qquad (5)$$

However, this average payoff is not the optimum value. For indeed, as in [6], the optimal case would correspond to the situation that only one player plays D and all others play ND. Since, we do not differentiate the players, the optimum solution during a period of $|V(i)| + 1$ rounds corresponds to the case where each player plays D in only one round, and no other player does so. The probability corresponding to this situation is:

$$(p(1-p)^{|V(i)|})^{(|V(i)|+1)} \qquad (6)$$

In this optimum case, the average payoff is:

$$\overline{U_{opt}^{(i)}} = \frac{r - c + r|V(i)|}{|V(i)| + 1} \qquad (7)$$

What is interesting to note here is that $\overline{U_{NE}^{(i)}}$ is less than $\overline{U_{opt}^{(i)}}$, which means that the probability that maximizes the average gain of a player is suboptimal. Using these results, we develop a clustering algorithm that evolve in this direction, where the role of cluster-head is cyclic, i.e.: a node declares itself cluster-head once every $|V(i)| + 1$ round. During the $|V(i)|$ other rounds, its neighbors will assume the function of leader-IDS by turns.

Now, we calculate the Price of Anarchy (PoA), which measures the inefficiency of the equilibrium p^* and corresponds to the payoff loss due to this suboptimum choice:

$$PoA = \overline{U_{opt}^{(i)}} - \overline{U_{NE}^{(i)}} = \frac{r - c + r|V(i)|}{|V(i)| + 1} - r + c = \frac{|V(i)|c}{|V(i)| + 1} \qquad (8)$$

From this result, the PoA depends only on the cost c of playing D and not to the gain r or the loss l. In order to adjust the average gain given by the Nash equilibrium towards the optimum average gain, the cost c must be small.

Clustering Algorithm. Based on these mathematical results, the proposed clustering algorithm is summarized as follows:

1. In the first round, each node $i \in N$ broadcasts a "Hello" message to discover its neighborhood $V(i)$ in which he attaches its different characteristics, namely its energy level E_i.
2. Thereafter, each node i which is in the same location as its neighbors, plays in the clustering game, i.e.: the $CG^{(i)}$ non-cooperative game defined above. Each node i calculates the equilibrium probability p_i^*, given by the equation. 2, for becoming CH according to the parameters of the game but also the number of its neighbor $|V(i)|$ participating in the game.
3. If the probability p_i^* for a node is nonzero, then the node joins the list of potential cluster-heads N_{CHP}.
4. From the list (N_{CHP}) of the CH-potential, the node for which the residual energy is greater than or equal to the threshold E_r:

$$E_r = \frac{\sum_{j \in N_{CHP}} E_j}{|N_{CHP}|}$$

and having the lowest physical media address will immediately announce itself to be a CH and joins the set of cluster-heads (N_{CH}).
5. To form the clusters, the node with the lowest ID belonging to N_{CH} announces its new status as a leader and the closest nodes will join it to form a cluster. This operation will be iterated until all nodes are affiliated to clusters, be it as leader or member.
6. After a predetermined time T_{elec} (1 round), the current cycle ends and the next cycle begins with the formation of new clusters.
7. The nodes that have already served as CH (N_{CH}), will be awarded a probability to declare themselves as CH equal to zero until there are no more neighbors which choose to designate itself cluster-head.
8. The game for the next round will take place between a node i which does not have served as CH yet and its neighbors which are in the same case, i.e.: $V(i) = V(i) - NCH$.

When there are several potential cluster-heads, a first test is used to select nodes whose residual energy exceeds a certain threshold. Among these nodes, a second test is applied for selecting the node with the lowest ID as a cluster head.

Thus, as the rounds pass, the number of nodes that have not been cluster-heads decreases, so this probability increases.

3.2   Intruder-Defender Game Theoretical Model

To have a best management of energy resources of the network when deploying of the IDSs, we consider them installed only on the cluster-heads. So, we suppose that the whole network is partitioned into clusters following the previously presented algorithm. After finding the appropriate sample rate for each link, the leader-IDS calculates the optimal probability of attack to warn the target node for taking appropriate action when its beliefs exceed this threshold.

Each cluster-head is responsible for the cluster members' security by sampling some packets circulating the incoming links to a cluster members in accordance to the sampling budget (B_{CH}) available to the leader-IDS and the reputation of each incoming link. Reputations are needed to locate whom to inspect among the nodes in the network. This budget can be defined as the number of packets that a cluster-head can sample during a certain time. The reputation value is calculated by the leader-IDS for each incoming link to its each member node $T \in MCH$[1]. Initially, the reputation value for each link is set to 1, i.e.: we assume at the beginning that all links are well reputed. If the leader-IDS detects a malicious message on an incoming link to its cluster, then the reputation corresponding to this link decreases, otherwise it may increase or remain unchanged. So, the reputation value $R_x(t)$ represents the evaluation of good behavior of the link x during the interval $[0, t]$, with $0 \leq R_x(t) \leq 1$.

$$R_x(t) = \begin{cases} 1 & \text{, if } t = 0 \\ 1 - \frac{\text{Number of messages tested malicious } (t)}{\text{Number of all tested messages } (t)} & \text{if } t > 0 \end{cases} \quad (9)$$

Each leader-IDS maintains a reputation list about the incoming links of each target node for which it is liable. The leader-IDS divides the time interval T_{elec} in which it has the security responsibility of the cluster. Each time interval, it updates its data about the reputation of its neighbors links. We define the sampling rate s_x on the link x as the number of packets to be examined during a particular interval. The sampling rate is based on the reputation of the link x and the total sampling budget of the leader-IDS. Our goal is to give more attention to the less reputable links. So, the sampling rate allowed to the incoming link x by CH during the period $[0, t]$ is:

$$s_x^*(t) = \frac{(1 - R_x(t)) \times B_{CH}}{\sum_{x \in \eta}(1 - R_x(t))}, \qquad \eta = \bigcup_{T \in MCH} X_T \quad (10)$$

with η the set of the all incoming links to the members nodes MCH.

The interpretation of the Eq. 10 is that more the reputation is small, more the link should be monitored. So, since the goal of the attacker is to attack without being detected, it is pushed to improve its reputation.

3.2.1 The Game Definition

At this stage, we suppose that our network is fully clustered with a leader-IDS designated in each cluster. We consider the interaction between the coalition (leader-IDS and target node T) and the sender node as a two-player static Bayesian game. The coalition leader-IDS and target node maintain the security of communications by attempting to detect any intrusion from an attacker. The sender node having the private type Malicious (M) or Normal (N), tries

---

[1] MCH: represents the set of the cluster members with CH as cluster-head.

to attack a target node when its type is malicious. The goal of the game is to find the optimal probability for which the sender (Intruder) would be tempted to attack the target node. This probability will be very useful in the intrusion detection because if this probability is high, the victim node should launch its own countermeasures to thwart the intrusion.

We formalize the efficiency of the intrusion detection as a game where the leader-IDS evaluates the risk of attack to notify or not the target node to take the necessary measures. In contrast to the method given in [11], the leader-IDS, here, considers all sender nodes, even those who are part of its cluster as potential attackers. This leads to detect internal and external intrusion in the network. For more efficiency, we consider the believes of a leader-IDS about all the sender nodes directly related to their reputation.

A malicious sender has two pure strategies: *Attack* and *Not Attack*. A normal sender has one pure strategy: *Not Attack*. On the other hand, the coalition leader-IDS/Target node has two pure strategies: *Notify* and *Not Notify* which means either the leader-IDS notifies the target node to launch its countermeasures (HIDS) or not.

We suppose that the leader-IDS/Target player (player 2) assigns a probability μ to a sender player being malicious. At each beginning of a game, the defender considers that the probability that a sender is malicious or not is equivalent to the calculated reputation corresponding to the incoming link x, we set $\mu = 1 - R_x(t)$.

Figure 3 illustrates the game payoff of the attacker and leader-IDS/target node interactions for the activation or not of the target's IDS in the extensive form. In this figure, we have the following game parameters:

- a (resp. a') denotes the detection rate of the leader-IDS (resp. the detection rate of the target-IDS),
- b (resp. b') denotes the false alarm rate of the leader- IDS (resp. target-IDS), with $a, a', b, b' \in [0, 1]$.
- The gain for the secured data when the target node is protected is r.
- The cost of an attacker, leader-IDS and target-HIDS for attacking and monitoring (e.g., energy cost) are denoted by C_a, C_{CH} and C_T respectively, where $C_a > 0$, $C_{CH} > 0$ and $C_T > 0$. It is reasonable to assume that $r > C_a$, $r > C_{CH}$ and $r > C_T$, since otherwise attacker does not have incentive to attack and leader-IDS/target node do not have incentive to monitor,
- $C_{f_{CH}}$ and C_{f_T} denote the loss for a false alarm of the leader-IDS and the target-HIDS respectively, where $C_{f_{CH}}, C_{f_T} > 0$.

From the Fig. 3, we note that for the strategy combination (*Attack, Notify*), the payoff of the coalition leader IDS/ target node is the expected gain of detecting the attack minus the monitoring cost ($C_{CH} + C_T$). The expected gain for detecting the attack depends on the values a and a', which is $ar - (1 - a)r = (2a - 1)r$ and $a'r - (1 - a')r = (2a' - 1)r$. Note that $1 - a$ and $1 - a'$ are the false negative rate for the leader-IDS and Target node respectively. In contrast, the gain of a malicious sender is the loss of the leader-IDS and the target node $(1 - 2a)r + (1 - 2a')r$. Thus, the payoff of the player 1 is his gain minus the attacking cost. For the other two strategy combinations, when the malicious

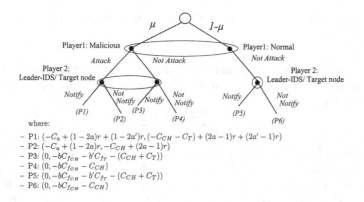

Fig. 3. Extensive form of attacker/coalition leader-IDS/target node game.

where:

- P1: $(-C_a + (1-2a)r + (1-2a')r, (-C_{CH} - C_T) + (2a-1)r + (2a'-1)r)$
- P2: $(-C_a + (1-2a)r, -C_{CH} + (2a-1)r)$
- P3: $(0, -bC_{f_{CH}} - b'C_{f_T} - (C_{CH} + C_T))$
- P4: $(0, -bC_{f_{CH}} - C_{CH})$
- P5: $(0, -bC_{f_{CH}} - b'C_{f_T} - (C_{CH} + C_T))$
- P6: $(0, -bC_{f_{CH}} - C_{CH})$

node plays *Not Attack*, his payoff is always 0. In both cases, the payoff of the coalition leader-IDS/target node if the leader-IDS decides to *Notify* the target node is the cost of monitoring of the coalition and an expected loss $-bC_{f_{CH}}$ and $-b'C_{f_T}$ due to false alarms, and a payoff of $-bC_{f_{CH}} - C_{CH}$ if he decides to *Not Notify*. For the strategy combination (*Attack*, *Not Notify*), the payoff of the leader-IDS is only the gain of his detection minus cost of his monitoring, and the payoff of the malicious player is his gain of success minus the attacking cost.

3.2.2 The Game Solution

The objective of both players is to maximize their own payoffs. It can be shown that the game has a pure strategy Bayesian Nash Equilibrium only when $\mu < \frac{b'C_{f_T} + C_T}{(2a'-1)r + b'C_{f_T}}$, which is ((Attack if malicious, Not Attack if Normal), Not Notify, μ).

When $\mu > \frac{b'C_{f_T} + C_T}{(2a'-1)r + b'C_{f_T}}$, a mixed strategy Nash Equilibrium can be derived as follows.

We set β as the probability to notify the target node to launch its own HIDS and α the probability for an attack by the Intruder.

To solve the game and find the overall payoffs of the attacker, we compute the corresponding utility functions followed by the first derivative of these functions. From Fig. 3, we define the leader-IDS utility function $U_{CH/T}$ as follows:

$$U_{CH/T} = \mu[\alpha\beta((-C_{CH} - C_T) + (2a-1)r + (2a'-1)r) +$$
$$\alpha(1-\beta)(-C_{CH} + (2a-1)) + (1-\alpha)\beta(-bC_{f_{CH}} -$$
$$b'C_{f_T} - C_{CH} - C_T) - (1-\alpha)(1-\beta)(C_{CH} + bC_{f_{CH}})] +$$
$$(1-\mu)[\beta(-bC_{f_{CH}} - b'C_{f_T} - C_{CH} - C_T) -$$
$$(1-\beta)(C_{CH} + bC_{f_{CH}})]$$

(11)

The main objective of the leader-IDS is to maximize this utility function by choosing for a fixed β^*, a α^* strategy that maximizes the probability of protecting the target node. This leads to an equilibrium where the following holds:

$$U_{CH/T}(\alpha^*, \beta^*) \geq U_{CH/T}(\alpha^*, \beta)$$

To attain this aim, the leader-IDS calculates the optimal value of α^* by finding the first derivative with respect to β^* and setting it to zero. This results to the following:

$$\alpha^* = \frac{b'C_{f_T} + C_T}{\mu((2a' - 1)r + b'C_{f_T})}. \tag{12}$$

The value of β^* is used by the leader-IDS to decide whether to inform the victim node to active its own HIDS or not. The leader-IDS is monitoring and analyzing the traffic via sampling, it calculates its believes about all the incoming links to a target node T, if $\sum_{x \in X_T}(1 - R_x) > \sum_{x \in X_T} \alpha_x^*$ so it notifies the target node to run its HIDS for more security.

The utility function U_a of the attacker is defined as follows:

$$U_a = \alpha\beta(-C_a + (1 - 2a)r + (1 - 2a')r) + \\ \alpha(1 - \beta)(-C_a + (1 - 2a)r) \tag{13}$$

The main objective of the attacker is to maximize this utility function by choosing for a fixed β^*, an α^* that maximizes the probability for compromising the victim node. By following the same procedure as for the leader-IDS, we have:

$$\beta^* = \frac{C_a + (2a - 1)r}{(1 - 2a')r} \tag{14}$$

From the solution of the game, the attacker best strategy is to attack when the probability of activating the HIDS by the victim node is less than β^*. To achieve this goal, the attacker observes the behavior of the leader-IDS to determine whether it attacks or not by comparing its observations with the determined threshold.

4   Simulation

In this section, we evaluate the performances of our detection intrusions approach by simulating it under Matlab. The idea is to compare the effectiveness of our intrusion detection model where only the cluster-heads are concerned with the safety of their clusters with a standard model. We remind that in our model a target node is invited to activate its HIDS when the risk of intrusion goes beyond a certain threshold. For the validation of our model we use the detection rate and the lifetime of the secure network.

In our simulation, initially, we assign a residual energy chosen randomly in [40, 100] Joules. The node's energy decreases by 10 J [2] per 10 s, respectively 5 J/10 s in the case of the activation the NIDS, respectively the HIDS. The data traffic flow is randomly fixed in [10, 50] packets per node per session. The expended energy during the transmission of one packet is fixed to 0.0368 J [12] and we consider as negligible the energy expended for the reception of a packet.

The simulation parameters are summarized in Table 1.

Table 1. Simulation parameters.

Parameter	Value
Simulation area	$500\,m \times 500\,m$
Number of nodes	15
Transmission range	$150\,m$
Residual energy	Random value in $[40\,..\,100]$ Joules
Energy to forward one packet	$0.0368\,J$
Energy to activate an NIDS/10 s	$10\,J$
Energy to activate an HIDS/10 s	$5\,J$
Sampling budget	$20\,packets/10\,s$
T_{elec}	$100\,s$
Simulation run time	$100\,s$
Time step	$10\,s$

4.1 Simulation Results

We apply our clustering algorithm presented in the first part of this work, with the following parameters set: $r = 30$, $l = 20$ and $c = 10$. The result of this simulation within T_{elec} time is summarized in the following figure (Fig. 4).

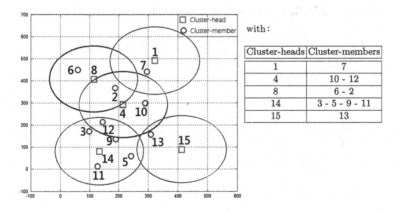

Fig. 4. The clustered network.

4.2 Approach Evaluation

In the sequel, we evaluate our model of a collaborative approach between NIDSs running in the network cluster-heads and HIDSs running in the target nodes. This simulation evaluates the detection rate the lifetime of the secured network. We fix the game parameters as described in the following table (Table 2).

Table 2. Game parameters.

Game parameter	value	Game parameter	value
a	0.9	C_{CH}	15
a'	0.83	C_T	10
b	0.05	C_a	5
b'	0.05	C_{fCH}	3
r	20	C_{fCH}	3

We compare our collaborative NIDS-HIDS game based approach with a standard approach in which the IDS is activated only in the cluster-heads and we use the same parameters in the two models.

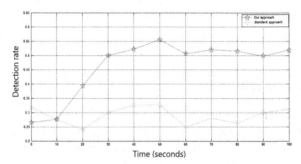

Fig. 5. Comparison in terms of detection rate.

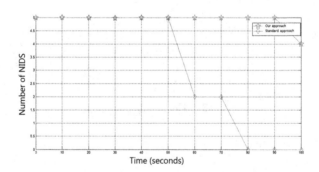

Fig. 6. Comparison in terms of the secured network lifetime.

The Fig. 5 shows that our approach gives better results for the detection rate since our model is more efficient and allows to sample more packets and hence to detect more malicious attacks.

The Fig. 6 shows that in our model the network stays secured much more than in the standard model. This is explained by the fact that when an HIDS is activated, there is a reduction of the energy consumption of the corresponding cluster-head, allowing it, then, to remain active much longer.

5 Conclusion

The tradeoff between security and resource consumption of IDSs has motivated us to propose a game theoretical solution for preserving the longevity of nodes while increasing their security.

In the first step, we have proposed a clustering algorithm based on game theory. Nodes play a clustering game with the purpose of selecting a cluster-head which will be responsible of the security of the whole cluster. The game has been developed so that its setup and its rules lead to a natural cooperation of the nodes in the self-election process. A node is "forced" to cooperate and declare itself, because it has greater benefit for being cluster-head, i.e.: it is aware that if all its neighbors have already declared themselves, then the only way to secure its data is to declare itself.

The second step of the model consists in managing sparingly the resources of cluster-head by finding the optimal sampling rate based on the contribution of each node in the cluster. Hence, a nonzero-sum non cooperative game was formulated to analyze the interaction between the leader-IDS and the intruder in order to find the threshold from which the leader-IDS notifies the target node to launch countermeasures (activate an HIDS), once the probability of attack is greater than the game derived threshold.

The simulation carried out showed that our model is able to increase the intrusion detection rate while keeping the secure of the network for longer.

References

1. Altman, E., Boulogne, T., Azouzi, R.-E., Jimenez, T., Wynter, L.: A survey on networking games in telecommunications. Comput. Oper. Res. **33**, 286–311 (2006)
2. Bhattacharya, P., Debbabi, M., Mohammed, N., Otrok, H., Wang, L.: Mechanism design-based secure leader election model for intrusion detection in MANET. IEEE Trans. Dependable Secure Comput. **8**, 89–103 (2011)
3. Da Silva, A-P-R., Martins, M-H-T., Rocha, B.P.S., Loureiro, A.A.F., Ruiz, L.B., Wong, H.C.: Decentralized intrusion detection in wireless sensor networks. In: Proceedings of the 1st ACM International Workshop on Quality of Service and Security in Wireless and Mobile Networks, pp. 16–23(2005)
4. Kamhoua, C.-A., Makki, K., Pissinou, N.: Game theoretic modeling and evolution of trust in autonomous multi-hop networks application to network security and privacy, pp. 1–6. IEEE Communications Society (2011)
5. Kodialam, M., Lakshman, T.: Detecting network intrusions via sampling: a game theoretical approach. Bell Laboratories Lucent Technologies (2003)
6. Koltsidas, G., Pavlidou, F.-N.: A game theoretical approach to clustering of ad hoc and sensor networks. Telecommun. Syst. **47**, 81–93 (2011)
7. Komathy, K., Narayanasamy, P.: Study of cooperation among selfish neighbors in MANET under evolutionary game theoretic model. In: IEEE- ICSNC, pp. 133–138 (2007)
8. Li, F., Wu, J.: Hit and run: a Bayesian game between malicious and regular nodes in MANETs. In: IEEE SECON, pp. 432–440 (2008)

146 M. Bouhaddi et al.

9. Mahrandish, M., Assi, C., Debbabi, M.: A game theoritic model to handle network intrusions over multiple packets. In: Proceedings of IEEE International Conference on Communications (ICC), Turkey (2006)
10. Osborne, M.-J.: An Introduction to Game Theory. Oxford University Press, New York (2000)
11. Otrok, H., Mohammed, N., Wang, L., Debbabi, M., Bhattacharya, P.: A moderate to robust game theoretical model for intrusion detection in MANETs. In: Wireless Communications and Networking Conference (WCNC), pp. 608–612 (2008)
12. Robert, J.-M., Otrok, H., Chriqi, A.: RBC-OLSR: reputation-based clustering OLSR protocol for wireless ad hoc networks. Comput. Commun. 35, 487–499 (2012)

Optimizing TLS for Low Bandwidth Environments

Diego A. Ortiz-Yepes[1,2]([✉])

[1] IBM Research – Zurich Laboratory, Säumerstrasse 4, 8803 Rüschlikon, Switzerland
[2] Digital Security Group, Institute for Computing and Information Sciences,
Radboud University Nijmegen, Nijmegen, The Netherlands
ort@zurich.ibm.com

Abstract. This paper explores alternatives to minimize the overhead of Transport Layer Security (TLS) towards making it usable in bandwidth-constrained environments. Several areas are identified where overhead can be reduced while remaining fully compatible with standard Transport Layer Security. The most relevant one consists of moving to Elliptic Curve Cryptography (ECC) from RSA in the certificates, which reduces the overhead of the TLS handshake between 22 % and 60 % depending on the chosen security level.

We also propose two TLS extensions that further reduce the size of the handshake: *using a more compact certificate format* and *certificate caching*. Using compact certificates instead of ECC based X.509 certificates reduces the overhead of the handshake between 11 % and 20 % depending on the security level. Using *certificate caching* avoids exchanging certificates more than once irrespective of the number of times that the handshake is performed.

Keywords: Transport Layer Security · Embedded systems security · Optimization of secuity protocols

1 Introduction

The research described in this paper is motivated by research into the Mobile ZTIC (MZTIC) [23], a companion security device intended to be used with mobile devices via the 3.5 mm Tip-Ring-Ring-Sleeve (TRRS) audio interface. We found that the theoretical bidirectional bandwidth that can be reliably achieved using this analogue interface across different types of mobile devices was rather low, in the order of a few hundred bytes per second. Therefore, we decided to use an ad-hoc light weight message-based security protocol ensuring integrity, authenticity and confidentiality of the data exchanges between the MZTIC and the server instead of Transport Layer Security (TLS), as we did in the original ZTIC [32]. However, it remains an interesting question whether TLS could be used on top of such a low bandwidth channel as it would allow an identical back-end to be used for both the ZTIC and the MZTIC, and for the code of the ZTIC to be reused for the MTZIC.

© Springer International Publishing Switzerland 2015
F. Cuppens et al. (Eds.): FPS 2014, LNCS 8930, pp. 147–167, 2015.
DOI: 10.1007/978-3-319-17040-4_10

We note that the applicability of this research goes far beyond MZTIC: low bandwidth environments are increasingly encountered, e.g. in sensors and smart electricity meters. Moreover, such environments are expected to be more prevalent in the Internet-of-Things, where security should not be neglected [30]. Even mobile phones and tablets with fast Internet connections can benefit from a bandwidth optimized TLS setting because it would help them preserve power and possibly allow for security-sensitive network-enabled applications to be executed more efficiently.

The rest of this paper is structured as follows: Sect. 2 examines the TLS handshake overhead, suggesting optimizations to avoid it without deviating from the protocol. Section 3 outlines two complementary extensions aimed to reduce the certificate related overhead. Section 4 presents approaches related to our research. Section 5 concludes and outlines future work. The main concepts of TLS are summarized in Appendix A. Readers unfamiliar with TLS are encouraged to familiarize themselves with the concepts presented in this appendix as they are used throughout the rest of this paper.

2 Optimizing the TLS Handshake

This section identifies overhead areas in the TLS handshake, suggesting optimizations for minimizing such overhead.

2.1 Resumed vs. Full Handshake

The goal of the resumed handshake is to reduce the performance cost of the full handshake in terms of CPU processing and the number of required round trips [26], therefore using resumed sessions is encouraged. However, there is a clear trade off between the efficiency gained by using the resumed handshake and the security provided by performing a full handshake, which is required when starting a new session. Consequently, a maximum session length of 24 h is suggested in [9]. In practice, most web servers use sessions of a few minutes [1]. For embedded applications, something in between should be considered. The rationale is that the prospects of successfully performing an attack increases with the transmitted data volume. A hint towards a "reasonable" amount of data to be exchanged during a single session of five megabytes is provided in [5]. For embedded applications the amount of data exchanged may be relatively low, and therefore the session length can be allowed to span for a longer amount of time. In fact, instead of having a relatively short maximum session length, it would be best to allow the server to perform a full handshake whenever a certain amount of data has been exchanged using the session.

2.2 Client Hello

Each listed cipher suite uses a couple of bytes. Therefore, the client should include the minimum possible number of cipher suites in the ClientHello message.

Support for compression [8] is only worthwhile when large volumes of data are to be exchanged. Furthermore, it only makes sense to include the compression method in the `ClientHello` if message sizes are expected to be large and contain low-entropy information. If the size of the exchanged messages is small, then using compression may actually increase the processing time. Furthermore, using compression is prone to implementation errors [17] and is a precondition for the CRIME attack [27]. Therefore, unless there is a clear benefit in terms of bandwidth savings by enabling compression, it should be disabled.

It is recommended to avoid listing non-essential extensions. For example, the mechanism that enables the TLS server to resume sessions and avoid keeping per-client session state [28] should be avoided because it adds a few hundred bytes to the handshake. Similarly, when the Elliptic Curve Cryptography (ECC) Cipher Suites for TLS extension is used [3], then it is recommended to list as few curves and as few point formats as possible in the `elliptic_curves` and `point_formats` messages, respectively.

2.3   Certificates

Encoding Overhead. Most of the TLS handshake overhead is in the certificates exchanged during the handshake protocol. Standard TLS servers use X.509 certificates [7]. These certificates are constructed and stored using ASN.1 and exchanged using Distinguished Encoding Rules (DER). Consequently, each certificate contains metadata describing its structure as well as the types of each primitive data element constituting it. The amount of overhead that the certificate encoding brings is non-negligible, for example the server certificate sent by the server when connecting to https://www.google.com is 1151 bytes long, of which 310 bytes (27 %) are encoding overhead. Section 3.2 (p. 8) provides an alternative which suggests using Card Verifiable Certificates (CVCs) instead of X.509 certificates to avoid this issue.

Server Certificates. Sending a server certificate *chain* should be avoided. If possible, clients should be provisioned with all required certificates to validate a single certificate sent by the server during the handshake.

Certificate Keys and Signature Schemes. RSA keys and signatures have been traditionally used in X.509 certificates [7]. However, using ECC keys and signatures (fully compatible with X.509) is more appropriate on computational and transport efficiency grounds. The reason is that for equivalent security the required key lengths for ECC are smaller than their RSA counterparts yielding shorter signatures, which result in smaller certificates taking less time to transport. ECC keys and certificates are supported by many browsers [33] and smart card applications, particularly by ePassports [18] and (chipped) driver licenses [21]. The study of ECC based cryptosystems is certainly younger than the study of RSA, but mature enough to be used with confidence in real-world applications.

A rough comparison between ECC key sizes and RSA moduli sizes for comparable security is shown in the first two columns of Table 1. The resulting certificate sizes without changing certificate fields other than `signatureAlgorithm`, `signatureValue`, and `subjectPublicKeyInfo` (cf. [7]) are also shown after the slash. The last column shows the substantial savings in certificate size when ECC is used instead of RSA.

Table 1. Comparison between RSA and ECC keys and the resulting certificates.

RSA key length (bits)/certificate size (bytes)	ECC key size (bits)/certificate size (bytes)	Savings
1024/589	160/291	51 %
2048/845	224/315	63 %
3072/1101	256/331	70 %

Issuer and Subject. The *Issuer* and *Subject* fields identify the entities *issuing* and being *issued* the certificate, respectively. It is useful for these fields to have a well-defined structure that can be used to automatically index them in a directory service and to be readable and understandable by a human in case that they need to be "manually" checked. In most situations involving Machine-to-Machine (M2M) communication and embedded devices, such as considered in this paper, certificates are not intended for human validation. Hence, these fields can still be constructed following the conventions in [20], yet making them as short as possible, e.g. each consisting of a single attribute pair, `NAME = PKId`, where `NAME` correspond to the *common name* attribute, and `PKId` is the *public key identifier* of the corresponding entity, e.g. a digest of the public key object encoded, for example, as a `UniversalString`. We note that using `UniversalStrings` is discouraged in [15]. However, they allow the most succinct encoding of a public key identifier (binary data) and *must* be supported [7]. Alternatively a `UTF8` or `Teletext` string could be used, but then a printable (and expanded!) representation of the public key identifier would be stored.

Certificate Revocation. When an entity receives a certificate during the handshake, it must check that the certificate's signature is valid, that it has been issued by a trusted Certification Authority (CA), that it is within its validity period, and that it has not been revoked. In order to check the revocation status of the certificate, the entity can either retrieve the Certificate Revocation List (CRL) and check that the certificate in not included in it [7], or submit a query to the Online Certificate Status Protocol (OCSP) server, which will indicate whether the certificate is revoked [29]. Given that less information is exchanged and most of the processing is done by the (OCSP) server, if revocation is checked it is suggested to use OCSP instead of CRLs.

2.4   Certificate Request

Distinguished Names. The number of trusted CA root certificate names should be kept to a minimum. The names themselves should be kept as short as possible, e.g. following the optimization presented in Sect. 2.3. Furthermore, if a single trusted CA root is supported by the server, then this field should be omitted altogether. Even when there is more than one supported trusted CA root this field can be omitted by configuring clients to *implicitly* signal the server which client CA they are planning to use, for example, by selecting a certain port or using a specific url suffix.

Key Exchange Algorithm. It is suggested to use Elliptic Curve Diffie-Hellman (ECDH) instead of RSA or Diffie-Hellman (DH). The rationale is that ECDH is based in ECC, while RSA and DH are based in Finite Field Cryptography (FFC) [22]. As discussed in Sect. 2.3 (p. 3), the size of ECC keys are smaller and the associated public key operations take less time to compute than using comparable RSA or DH keys [16]. Thus, by using ECDH not only the sizes of the `ClientKey Exchange` and `ServerKeyExchange` can be reduced (with respect to DH), but also the computation of the pre-master secret can be performed using less resources, and eventually more efficiently.

2.5   Combining the Handshake Optimizations

A *base* handshake size can be estimated by adding the sizes of the messages exchanged during the handshake, excluding those pertaining certificate exchanges and cryptographic related extensions, e.g. ECC extensions [3]. This base handshake size (about 630 bytes) can be used to estimate the size of several handshake scenarios using different cryptosystems in the X.509 certificates. Table 2 shows these estimations.

The last four columns of Table 2a and b consider the following handshake scenarios:

- **Handshake (only server authentication, no chain):** The client authenticates the server. The server sends its certificate. The server does *not* authenticate the client.
- **Handshake (only server authentication, chain):** The client authenticates the server. The server sends its certificate and the certificate of its issuer. The server does *not* authenticate the client.
- **Handshake (mutual authentication, no chain):** The client authenticates the server. The server sends its certificate. The server authenticates the client. The client sends its certificate.
- **Handshake (mutual authentication, chain):** The client authenticates the server. The server sends its certificate and the certificate of its issuer. The server does authenticates the client. The client sends its certificate.

Table 2. Using X.509 certificates: RSA vs. ECC.

RSA Key Size (bits)	X.509 Certificate Size (bytes)	Handshake (only server authentication, no chain)	Handshake (only server authentication, chain)	Handshake (mutual authentication, no chain)	Handshake (mutual authentication, chain)
1024	589	1225	2073	1817	2665
2048	845	1481	2585	2329	3433
3072	1101	1737	3097	2841	4201
4096	1357	1993		3353	

(a) *Handshake sizes (in bytes) using X.509 certificates with RSA.*

ECC Key Size (bits)	X.509 Certificate Size (bytes)	Handshake (only server authentication, no chain)	Handshake (only server authentication, chain)	Handshake (mutual authentication, no chain)	Handshake (mutual authentication, chain)
160	291	959	1277	1253	1571
224	315	983	1317	1301	1635
256	331	999	1349	1333	1683
288	347	1015		1365	

(b) *Handshake sizes (in bytes) using X.509 certificates with ECC.*

Key Sizes (bits) RSA → ECC	Handshake (only server authentication, no chain)	Handshake (only server authentication, chain)	Handshake (mutual authentication, no chain)	Handshake (mutual authentication, chain)
1024 → 160	22%	38%	31%	41%
2048 → 224	34%	49%	44%	52%
3072 → 256	42%	56%	53%	60%

(c) *Handshake savings from replacing RSA with security-comparable ECC.*

For calculating the certificate sizes, each of the two entities (i.e. client and server) are assumed to have a key of the size indicated in the first column. The signature of the certificate uses a key of the size indicated in the first column of the next row. In practice, CAs tend to have larger keys than the entities that they certify, so it makes sense to incorporate this consideration in the size estimation model.

Table 2c compares the values in Table 2a and b showing the bytes saved with ECC as a percentage relative to the base RSA. Note that the savings in Table 2c increase with the security level in a similar way than the savings in Table 1. This is not surprising because the savings are directly related to the certificate, and ultimately to the differences of the key and signature sizes.

3   Reducing TLS Handshake Certificate Exchange Overhead

We have already pointed out that most of the TLS handshake overhead can be attributed to the exchanged certificates. We propose in this section two complementary extensions towards reducing such overhead while preserving the ability and flexibility of the end points to mutually authenticate using Public Key Infrastructures (PKIs). The first extension consists of *End-point certificate caching* (Sect. 3.1); and the second of *Replacing X.509 with CVCs* (Sect. 3.2).

3.1 End Point Certificate Caching

The goal of this extension is to minimize the number of times that a certificate is exchanged between the end points. Ideally, a certificate should be sent only once over the network, and then cached by the receiving end point. Initially, each of the end points would start with an empty cache and a list of trusted certificates. When a given end point receives and validates an entity certificate, it caches it. The next time that a full handshake occurs, using the extension would proceed as follows:

`ClientHello` The client indicates support for the *End point certificate caching* extension by including at least one of the following two elements:
  `CachedServerCertificates` Lists the hashes of the server certificates that the client has received and validated in previous handshakes. Note that this list only contains entity certificates.
  `ClientCertificates` Lists the hashes of the client certificates. If the client does not support client authentication, it does not include this element.
`ServerHello` The server indicates support for the *End point certificate caching* extension by including at least one of the following two elements:
  `UsingServerCertificate` Offset in `CachedServerCertificates` of the certificate that shall be used by the server to authenticate itself to the client. If this is not a valid offset, the client shall terminate the connection sending a `HANDSHAKE_FAILURE` alert (or a custom alert defined by the extension). If this message is included, then the Server shall not send any `Certificate` handshake message to the client.
  `UsingClientCertificate` Offset in `ClientCertificates` of the certificate that the server expects the client to use for client authentication. If this is not a valid offset, the client shall terminate the connection sending an appropriate alert. If this message is included, then client authentication shall take place during the handshake and the client shall use the certificate signaled by the server. Note that the semantics of this element is that the server already has the certificate. Consequently, if it is the first time that the client intends to use the certificate, the server shall not send this element, i.e. to allow the client to send the certificate (chain) to the server for the first time. In this case, the server shall send a `CertificateRequestMessage`.

When an extension such as outlined above is used, there may be an initial lengthy handshake, but all subsequent handshakes would not include any certificate, thus making them short. When the server rolls its certificate over, it would simply not send a `UsingServerCertificate` element. Instead, it would send its new certificate as traditionally done. Conversely, if a client is rolling its certificate, it would refrain from including the old certificate hash in the `ClientCertificates` list.

`CachedServerCertificates` and `ClientCertificates` can be seen as *dynamic white-lists* leveraging the dynamism and flexibility of PKIs, while at the same time avoiding wasteful certificate exchanges and checks. Managing the caches is left to each of the end points. At the client side, there is little need to have more than a single client certificate and associated private key, resulting in a succinct `ClientCertificates` containing a single element. Caching server certificates may prove difficult for embedded devices (clients) with limited memory. We note that end points do not need to store the full certificate: just the certificate hash, expiration date and associated public key. For embedded devices that communicate repeatedly with the same set of known servers, this solution would bring large overhead savings. At the server side, implementing the cache should be easier to accommodate due to larger amounts of resources being available.

Note that certificate caching does not reduce the level of security already attained with the TLS handshake. This follows from the fact that ultimately each of the end points has to prove possession of the corresponding private keys. The extension merely avoids having to exchange certificates that have already been exchanged in the past between the end points.

3.2   Using Card Verifiable Certificate (CVC) with TLS

A large part of the TLS handshake overhead is a consequence of X.509 certificates being represented in ASN.1 and encoded using DER. Besides the actual certificate information, there is a non-negligible amount of structuring data (e.g. tags and lengths), as well as data type descriptors for each of the primitive certificate fields as already alluded to in Sect. 2.3 (p. 3). To address this issue, we now describe a TLS extension replacing X.509 certificates with CVCs in order to not just make certificate exchanges less frequent (the goal of the extension presented in the previous section), but also smaller.

CVCs are widely used in smart card based applications. They have been designed to have a small footprint to enable them to be sent to the smart card in as few—if possible, just one—Application Protocol Data Units (APDUs). A single APDU can carry at most 255 bytes of application data, and even less when a secure channel [14] is established. There are mechanisms to allow longer payloads, e.g. extended length APDUs and APDUs chaining, but these mechanisms are not necessarily supported by all smart cards. Consequently, these certificates are very good candidates to replace X.509 certificates in the context of TLS entity authentication. The main components of a CVC are defined in [19]. However, this standard falls short of providing an actual certificate format *per se*. Consequently, there are several, not necessarily interoperable CVC formats. The most widely used formats are Extended Access Control (EAC) and Extended Access Protection (EAP) certificates, described below.

Extended Access Control (EAC) Certificates. EAC certificates are defined in [18]. They are used by Machine Readable Travel Document (MRTD)—commonly known as electronic passports—to check the entitlements of a terminal, e.g. at border control, to read sensitive biometric information. The main mechanism for checking such entitlements is *Terminal Authentication*, a protocol in which the terminal must sign a challenge sent by the passport using the private key associated to the certificate that it sends to the passport.

According to [18], EAC certificates may use RSA for keys and signatures, but in practice ECC is always used because when using relatively small curves (e.g. less than 256 bits) it is possible to fit the certificates in a single APDU.

It would be possible to use EAC certificates *out-of-the-box* with TLS. The main advantage of such an approach is that existing PKI management tools such as [10,12,25] could be used to create and manage them. However, the following peculiarities—and to some extent, limitations— would need to be considered:

References. The structure and semantics of both the *Certification Authority Reference* and the *Certificate Holder Reference* are prescribed in [18]: a 2 letter country code, a variable length (at most 9 characters) *holder mnemonic*, and a 5 digit sequence number. Sticking to such a convention does not make sense in the context of TLS authentication and would break compatibility with existing PKI management tools.

Hierarchy. [18] defines a 3-layer hierarchy: Country Verifying Certification Authority (CVCA) → Document Verifier (DV) → Inspection System (IS), which is not related to the purposes of TLS authentication. Such a hierarchy could be kept, providing the TLS entities (servers and clients) with IS certificates. For server authentication, depending on the setting, clients could be provided beforehand with the CVCA certificate, the DV certificate (or both), which would act as the roots of trust for authenticating the server. For client authentication, the Server could send the Certification Authority Reference(s) of any of the certificates that it trusts in the `CertificateRequest` message. As discussed in Sect. 2.4, it would be recommended to provide a single reference, or at most two, in case of rollover periods.

Certificate Holder Authorization Template. This field would need to be ignored. It uses up only a few bytes, which does not make it problematic.

Extended Access Protection (EAP) Certificates. EAP certificates are defined in [21], which standardizes, among others, mechanisms to control access to the information stored in electronic driver licenses. Particularly, these certificates are used for the driver license (chip) to check the entitlements of a terminal to read its sensitive information, in a similar manner than described in Sect. 3.2. The structure of an EAP certificate is rather similar to that of an EAC certificate. Further, again ECC is used for keys and signatures for the same reason as with EAC certificates.

Unlike EAC certificates, however, EAP certificates do not use ASCII References as their EAC counterparts do. This neatly avoids the *References* issue discussed for EAC certificates. In order to identify the holder and the issuer of a given EAP certificate, public key identifiers (in the guise suggested in Sect. 2.3, p. 4) are used. Further, EAP certificates do not restrict the hierarchy to three tiers, which makes them more flexible than EAC certificates, thus overcoming the *Hierarchy* issue alluded to when discussing EAC certificates.

On the downside, the *Certificate Holder Authorization* field also has information that would need to be ignored. Besides, to the best of our knowledge, other than sample and test implementations around ISO 18013, there are no tools geared to generate and/or manage EAP certificate hierarchies.

A TLS Extension Using CVCs. There does not seem to be a clean, nice way to either use EAC or EAP certificates "out-of-the-box" for the purposes of TLS entity authentication. The former are widely supported by existing tools that could be leveraged to create and manage them. However, they are inflexible regarding the entity naming conventions. On the other hand, EAP certificates do not have such naming limitations, but tools supporting them are close to non-existent. In both cases, there are semantics in the holder authorization field that would need to be ignored. Also, using them for TLS authentication feels like an *abuse* as it is a scenario that they were not originally designed for. Consequently, in the context of TLS entity authentication there is room for creating a TLS extension such that:

- The client indicates support for the extension in the `ClientHello` message
- The server acknowledges support for the extension in the `ServerHello` message
- Any `Certificate` message contains a certificate following the TLS CVC format. Such a format would be essentially the same as the EAP certificate format, except for the fact that the *Certificate Holder Authorization* is replaced for a Object Identifier (OID) indicating that it is a certificate to be used for generic public key remote authentication.

By simulating usage of an extension with the properties described above, we have created Table 3a, which illustrates handshake sizes using CVCs with different ECC key/signature sizes[1]. Table 3b compares the values of Tables 2a and 3a, corresponding to the savings resulting from moving from X.509 to CVCs (both using ECC). Table 4 compares the values of Tables 2a and 3b, corresponding to the savings resulting from moving from X.509 (RSA) to Card Verifiable (CV) (ECC) certificates.

The following observations can be made regarding Tables 2, 3 and 4:

- There is more improvement in Table 2c than in Table 3b because the former changes RSA keys and signatures to ECC, while the latter just changes the certificate format (but not the underlying cryptosystem).

---

[1] Note that in the case of Table 2a and b, the signature of the certificate uses a key of the size indicated in the first column of the next row. In Table 3a that is not the case. Particularly, the key of the certificate and the one used to sign the certificate have the same size because the whole CVC chain is expected to use the same curve.

Table 3. ECC: X.509 vs. CVC.

ECC Key Size (bits)	CV Certificate Size (bytes)	Handshake (only server authentication, no chain)	Handshake (only server authentication, chain)	Handshake (mutual authentication, no chain)	Handshake (mutual authentication, chain)
160	179	844	1026	1026	1208
224	211	876	1090	1090	1304
256	227	892	1122	1122	1352
288	243	908	1154	1154	1400

(a) Handshake sizes (in bytes) using CVC certificates with different (ECC) key lengths.

ECC Key Sizes (bits) X.509 → CVC	Handshake (only server authentication, no chain)	Handshake (only server authentication, chain)	Handshake (mutual authentication, no chain)	Handshake (mutual authentication, chain)
160	12%	20%	18%	23%
224	11%	17%	16%	20%
256	11%	17%	16%	20%

(b) Handshake reductions from replacing X.509 (ECC) certificates with CVCs.

Table 4. X.509 (RSA) vs. CVC.

Key Sizes (bits) X.509 RSA → CVC (ECC)	Handshake (only server authentication, no chain)	Handshake (only server authentication, chain)	Handshake (mutual authentication, no chain)	Handshake (mutual authentication, chain)
1024 → 256	31%	51%	44%	55%
2048 → 320	41%	58%	53%	62%
3072 → 384	49%	64%	61%	68%

- The improvements in Table 3b are flat irrespective of increasing the security size, while they grow with the security level in Table 2c. This follows from the fact that the gains of changing the cryptosystem grow with the security level, whereas the gain from changing the certificate format are constant and do not depend on the security level.
- The combined improvement shown in Table 4 is quite substantial, especially when mutual authentication takes place and with increasing security level.
- Moving from X.509 ECC to CVC (Table 3b) brings modest improvement, but it is not comparable to the gain when moving from X.509 RSA to CVC (Table 4), which is much larger. This is visible in Fig. 1 by noting that the distance between dark gray and black lines is smaller than the distance between the gray ones. Consequently, if X.509 ECC certificates are already in use, there is little gain, and possibly a lot of necessary work to use CVCs instead.

4 Related Work

The closest related work to this paper is the TLS Pre-Shared Keys (PSK) extension [13], which allows TLS entities to authenticate each other using symmetric

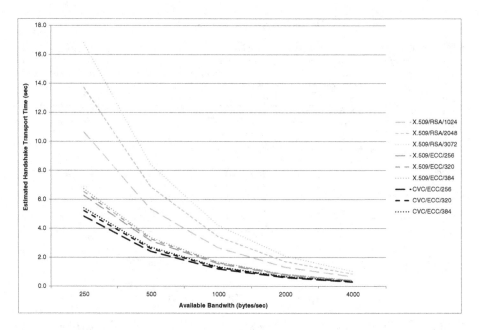

Fig. 1. Mutually authenticated handshake transport time as a function of a given bandwidth (based on the third columns of Tables 2a, b and 3a): the light gray lines illustrate using RSA X.509 certificates ; the dark gray lines using ECC X.509 certificates, and the black lines using CVC certificates. The vertical difference between two lines of the same dashing pattern, associated to the security level, represent the amount of time saved during the handshake between the corresponding certificate/cryptosystem combination. Absolute time savings are higher as bandwidth is decreased and the security level is increased. In these scenarios, applying the optimizations presented in this paper is highly advisable.

keys shared in advance instead of the traditional combination of private keys and X.509 certificates. The PSK extension aims to avoid computationally expensive public key operations and certificate exchanges, which result in faster handshakes. If no certificates are exchanged, the total handshake size is in the order of the *base handshake size* described in Sect. 2.5, p. 5, which is—not surprisingly— lower than any entry in the last 4 columns of Tables 2a, b and 3a. As noted in [13], PSKs are better suited for *"closed environments where the connections are mostly configured manually in advance"*, and geared towards a *"rather limited set of applications, usually involving only a very small number of clients and servers"*.

There are situations where the level of authentication provided by a shared key may be insufficient, and stronger, public key based alternatives are needed. When clients need to be authenticated, PSK does not provide cipher suites allowing public keys to be used for that purpose. Therefore, "traditional" certificate-based TLS still has to be used. In these cases, the handshake and certificate optimizations discussed in Sects. 2 and 3.2 remain fully applicable.

Table 5. Optimizations for reducing TLS overhead. The shading of the first column indicates the amount of overhead saved: the darker the color, the more overhead is saved by implementing the optimization.

Optimization	Category
Listing as few cipher suites as possible in the `ClientHello` message	Client side
Using ECDH as the Key Exchange algorithm (instead of DH or RSA)	Both sides
Not including certificate extensions	Certification Authority
Not listing support for additional extensions, e.g., TLS Session resumption without server-side state [28]	Client side
Sending as few distinguished names as possible in the `CertificateRequest` message	Server side
Only using compression when large messages of low-entropy data are exchanged	Both sides
Listing as few curves and point formats as possible when the ECC cipher suites for TLS extension is used	ECC support
Making the Distinguished Names or the Holder/Issuer references as short as possible	Certification Authority
Replacing X.509 certificates with CVCs	Extensions
Performing full handshakes as sporadically as possible	Server side
Sending at most one certificate in each direction	Both sides
Using ECC cryptography with X.509 certificates	ECC support
Using the End-point certificate caching extension	Extensions

Secure Messaging [14] is widely used to establish secure channels between a remote entity and a smart card. In order to establish the secure channel (encrypted, authenticated, or both), the remote entity and the smart card must share a set of symmetric, usually 3-DES, keys. The overhead of Secure Messaging consists of a 8-byte MAC appended to each APDU, plus a few bytes used to agree on the security parameters of the channel. Using secure messaging may be an option, but server support for it is rare outside of the smart card world. Further, being based on symmetric cryptography, has the same shortcomings as discussed for PSKs.

5   Conclusions and Future Work

We have shown that there are areas where the TLS protocol overhead can be reduced by following certain optimizations, summarized in Table 5. The "Client side", "Server side" and "Both sides" optimizations listed in this table are easy to implement and bring small to moderate reductions in the TLS handshake size. If supporting ECC is an option, the "ECC support" optimizations can be implemented. These optimizations bring moderate to large benefits. As the largest amount of handshake overhead is in the certificates themselves, we found that just by using ECC X.509 certificates the total handshake sizes can be shrunk between 22 % and 60 % depending on the chosen security level, e.g. reduced from 1225 bytes to 959 bytes at the lowest security level (1024 bit RSA keys/160 bit ECC keys) and from 4201 bytes to 1683 bytes at the highest security level (4096 bit RSA keys/288 bit ECC keys). Such a gain comes at relatively little "cost" and is therefore strongly encouraged.

X.509 certificates have been shown to bring considerable overhead due to their representation and encoding. Because of that, we have suggested to replace them with compact, Card Verifiable (CV) certificates, which by design use a more succinct representation. We have explored the feasibility of using EAC and EAP certificates for TLS authentication, concluding that these certificates are not interoperable with each other and carry semantics that would be undesirable to reuse. For that reason we have proposed a complementary CVC format to be used for generic entity authentication. *Replacing X.509 ECC certificates with CVCs* would yield a further decrease between 11 % and 20 % on the handshake size depending on the chosen security level, e.g. from 983 to 876 bytes, and from 1571 to 1208 bytes. Such a gain is modest compared with the gain obtained by moving from RSA to ECC X.509 certificates and may not justify implementing the extension. On the other hand, we have found the *End point certificate caching* extension to be extremely useful and promising because it enables exchanging the end point certificates a single time between the client and the server. This may be a relatively "heavy" handshake, but subsequent handshakes will be negligible and will take place much faster, even with limited available bandwidth. In fact, these handshakes would combine the authentication strength of using PKIs with the transport efficiency of using a purely symmetric PSK cipher suite.

In summary, we conclude that following most of the optimizations summarized above, particularly using ECC X.509 certificates and implementing the *End point certificate caching* extension, would render feasible using TLS in the MZTIC (the initial motivating purpose of our work) without negatively impacting usability. However, replacing X.509 certificates with CVCs may not be worth the effort. Similarly, using compression is also not warranted because the messages that are sent back and forth are rather small.

We consider *properly* defining the *End point certificate caching* extension and implementing it accordingly as the next steps derived from our research as presented in this paper.

Acknowlegements. The author wishes to thank *Michael Kuyper* for the pointer to EAP certificates; *Tamas Visegrady, Erik Poll, Peter Schwabe* and *Reto Hermann* for providing feedback and suggestions based on draft versions of this paper.

A   Transport Layer Security (TLS)

The TLS protocol suite, specified in RFC 5426 [9], aims at providing confidentiality and integrity between a client and a server—the *end points*—communicating over an untrusted network.

This appendix summarizes the most important elements of TLS for the purposes of this paper. Focus will be given to the latest version (i.e. TLS v. 1.2). We refer to [9, 26] for more authoritative and detailed descriptions of TLS.

A.1   TLS Goals

End Point Authentication. The client can authenticate the server to make sure that it is not communicating with a third party trying to impersonate the server. This authentication takes place using an X.509 [7] public key certificate provided by the server, which the client must validate. Once the client has validated the server certificate, it authenticates the server by requesting it to prove possession of the associated private key. The server may request the client to authenticate using an analogous mechanism.

The roots of trust for end point authentication are the trusted Certification Authorities (CAs), whose certificates must be provisioned to each end point. These trusted certificates need to be distributed or configured by some offline means. Additional intermediate certificates in the certificate chain can be either provisioned using the same means, or sent during the handshake (cf. Appendix A.4).

End point authentication is not mandatory in TLS. It is possible—albeit rare—to find anonymous TLS connections providing only confidentiality and integrity (but not entity authentication). Usually in TLS the client authenticates the server. The connection is said to be *mutually authenticated* when both client and the server have authenticated to one another.

Data Confidentiality and Integrity. Once established, TLS protects the integrity and confidentiality of the application data exchanged between the end points. This is achieved by encrypting the application data exchanged using the record protocol (cf. Appendix A.5) and adding a Hash-based Message Authentication Code (HMAC), using key material derived during the handshake (cf. Appendix A.4).

The secure tunnel that TLS provides not only guarantees integrity of the *individual messages* exchanged, but also of the *session*, i.e. the sequence of messages. This is an important benefit, as weaknesses in security protocols due to so-called Man-in-the-Middle attacks where an attacker replays, reorders, or manipulates some individual messages are not uncommon, even in security-critical protocols used for financial transactions, e.g. see [2, 4, 11, 31].

A.2   TLS Requirements

To use TLS a bidirectional, reliable link is required. If the link is not reliable, then TLS can be used only on top of a protocol ensuring reliability. Additionally, the end points must be able to perform cryptographic operations, including public key cryptography. If they do not have resources to perform such operations, then "traditional" TLS is not suitable[2].

---

[2] Unless the Pre-Shared Keys (PSK) extension is used, cf. Sect. 4.

A.3   Benefits of Using TLS

Using TLS is advantageous because there are existing and well maintained implementations. In addition, these implementations and the protocol itself receive wide scrutiny from the security community. TLS is very flexible regarding the security levels that can be achieved. There are known attacks, e.g. [6,24], but most of them can be avoided by fine tuning the implementations and enabling only essential extensions. In the case of Machine-to-Machine (M2M) communication, the focus of this paper, Man In The Middle (MITM) and impersonation attacks can be prevented by having certificate checks strictly and automatically enforced.

A.4   TLS Handshake

Execution of the TLS handshake achieves the following three goals: the end points (1) agree on a cipher suite, (2) calculate a *master secret*, and (3) may have authenticated to each other.

A cipher suite is a combination of the following four algorithms:

Key exchange used by the end points to agree on the *pre-master secret*, a shared bit string only known by the end points. There are fundamentally three key exchange mechanisms: RSA, Diffie-Hellman (DH) and Elliptic Curve Diffie-Hellman (ECDH)[3]. The pre-master secret is used in conjunction with random values generated by the end points to generate the *master secret*, which is then used to derive the keys that will subsequently be used to encrypt the application layer data and generate the HMAC to protect its integrity.

Server authentication used by the server to authenticate to the client. The most frequent are RSA and DSS.

Bulk encryption used to encrypt the application layer data, e.g. RC4, 3DES-EDE, Advanced Encryption Standard (AES).

Digest used to hash the application layer data, e.g. MD5, SHA1.

A full handshake is illustrated in Fig. 2a. It is initiated by the client, who sends the `ClientHello` message to the server. This message lists the cipher suites and extensions supported by the client. It also includes a client-generated random value.

Upon receiving the `ClientHello`, the server responds with a `ServerHello` message. This message selects the cipher suite and a subset of the extensions that shall be used during the rest of the session, along with a server-generated random value and a server-assigned session identifier (*Session ID*). If the server is to authenticate to the client (which is usually the case), it sends its X.509 public key certificate in a `Certificate` message. It may send more than one certificate in the chain to allow the client to properly validate its certificate. The server sends a `ServerKeyExchange` message to provide the client with its public

---

[3] The last two used in conjunction with Digital Signature Standard (DSS) [22].

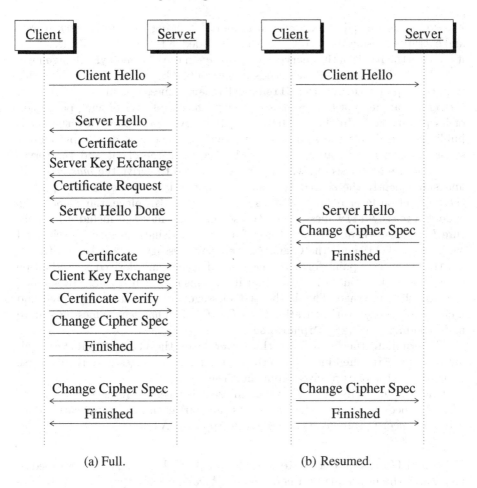

(a) Full.   (b) Resumed.

Fig. 2. TLS handshake.

key to be used for deriving the pre-master secret. This message is only sent when (EC)DH is used for key exchange. The key included in the ServerKeyExchange message is signed by the server using the private key associated to the public key included in the server certificate that was sent to the client. If the server requires the client to also authenticate (to the server), then it sends the CertificateRequest message. The server signals the end of its messages by sending a ServerHelloDone message.

The client checks the messages received from the server. It makes sure that the cipher suite and extensions are actually supported and that the server certificate is valid. If the server sent a ServerKeyExchange message, it checks that the signature of the server's public key is valid. If the server requested the client to authenticate, then the client sends its X.509 certificate in a Certificate message. The client then sends the ClientKeyExchange message. If RSA is used for key exchange, this client generates a random bit string (the *pre-master secret*) and encrypts it using the server public key included in the server certificate. Then it includes the result of the encryption operation in the `ClientKeyExchange` message. If (EC)DH is used, it just sends its DH public key to the server using this message. Upon receiving the `ClientKeyExchange` message, in the RSA case, the server can decrypt the pre-master secret (thus implicitly proving possession of its private key). In the (EC)DH case, the server can simply use the client public key to derive the shared secret, which is then used as the pre-master secret. In either case, after receiving this message, the client and the server share the pre-master secret, which can then be used to derive the *master secret*, and subsequently the shared key material that is later to be used to protect the application layer data. If client authentication takes place, the client sends a `CertificateVerify` message to the server. This message includes a signature (using the client's private key) of all the handshake messages exchanged so far. The client sends the `ChangeCipherSpec` message[4] to the server, to signal that from this point forth the negotiated cipher and derived keys shall be used. The client notifies the server that it has finished the handshake by sending the `Finished` message. This is the first message to be actually encrypted and includes a Message Authentication Code (MAC) of all handshake messages up to and including the `ChangeCipherSpec`.

To terminate the handshake, the server sends the `ChangeCipherSpec` followed by the `Finished` message to the client. These messages have the converse semantics as the ones received from the client.

Once the server initiated `Finished` message is received by the client (and its MAC has been validated), the end points can start exchanging application data using the record protocol, as described in Appendix A.5.

Resumed Handshake and Rehandshake. A *full* handshake (as described so far) marks the beginning of a new *session*. A *session* may span several *connections* between the client and the server. For example, when accessing a web site using HTTP on top of TLS (HTTPS), each object is fetched using a different connection, but most of these connections belong to the same session.

When a new connection is established, the client may indicate to the server its willingness to *reuse* an existing session by including the *Session ID* field in the `ClientHello` message. If the server accepts, it echoes the same *Session ID* in the `ServerHello` message. In this case a *resumed handshake* as illustrated in Fig. 2b takes place.

The resumed handshake reuses the master secret that has been previously calculated, but uses the new random values exchanged in the `*Hello` messages to calculate new session keys. Clearly, the resumed handshake is much more efficient than the full handshake because neither certificates are exchanged nor public key operations are performed.

---

[4] Strictly speaking, the `ChangeCipherSpec` is not a message but a protocol. However, for the purposes of this description, it can be seen a message sent during the handshake.

When the client wants to negotiate a new cipher suite or refresh the session keys, it can request a *rehandshake* by simply sending a `ClientHello` to the server. Conversely, if the server decides to initiate the rehandshake, it may do so by sending a `HelloRequest` message to the client. Whether the subsequent handshake is *full* or *resumed* depends on the *Session ID* being present in the *Hello messages.

A.5 TLS Record Protocol

Application layer data is split into *fragments* by the TLS record protocol. Each of these fragments is appended with an HMAC, which is used to protect the integrity of the fragment and the stream. The fragment payload and the HMAC are then encrypted in order to ensure confidentiality (cf. Appendix A.1). A record is then built by prepending a header (record type = application data, protocol version, length) to the encrypted fragment. Once assembled, the record is handled to the lower (transport) layer for delivery to the receiving end point.

A.6 TLS Alert Protocol

Whenever an anomaly is detected by one of the end points, the alert protocol is used to signal it to the other one. The alert protocol builds on the record layer and includes a level (warning or fatal) and an alert code. If the level is fatal, the connection must be terminated.

References

1. Apache: Apache Module mod_ssl, January 2014. http://httpd.apache.org/docs/2.2/mod/mod_ssl.html
2. Barisani, A., Bianco, D., Laurie, A., Franken, Z.: Chip & PIN is definitely broken. In: Presentation at CanSecWest Applied Security Conference, Vancouver 2011 (2011). Slides available at http://dev.inversepath.com/download/emv/emv_2011.pdf
3. Blake-Wilson, S., Bolyard, N., Gupta, V., Hawk, C., Moeller, B.: Elliptic Curve Cryptography (ECC) Cipher Suites for Transport Layer Security (TLS). RFC 4492 (Informational), May 2006. http://www.ietf.org/RFC/RFC4492.txt, updated by RFCs 5246, 7027
4. Blom, A., de Koning Gans, G., Poll, E., de Ruiter, J., Verdult, R.: Designed to fail: a USB-connected reader for online banking. In: Jøsang, A., Carlsson, B. (eds.) NordSec 2012. LNCS, vol. 7617, pp. 1–16. Springer, Heidelberg (2012)
5. Bundesamt für Sicherheit in der Informationstechnik : Schutzprofil für die Kommunikationseinheit eines intelligenten Messsystems für Stoff- und Energiemengen, March 2013
6. Codenomicon: The Heartbleed Bug, April 2014. http://heartbleed.com/
7. Cooper, D., Santesson, S., Farrell, S., Boeyen, S., Housley, R., Polk, W.: Internet X.509 Public Key Infrastructure Certificate and Certificate Revocation List (CRL) Profile. RFC 5280 (Proposed Standard), May 2008. http://www.ietf.org/RFC/RFC5280.txt, updated by RFC 6818

8. Deutsch, P.: DEFLATE Compressed Data Format Specification version 1.3. RFC 1951 (Informational), May 1996. http://www.ietf.org/RFC/RFC1951.txt
9. Dierks, T., Rescorla, E.: The Transport Layer Security (TLS) Protocol Version 1.2. RFC 5246 (Proposed Standard), August 2008. http://www.ietf.org/RFC/RFC5246.txt, updated by RFCs 5746, 5878, 6176
10. Digital Security group Radboud University Nijmegen, et al.: JMRTD: An Open Source Java Implementation of Machine Readable Travel Documents, January 2014. http://jmrtd.org/index.shtml
11. Drimer, S., Murdoch, S.J., Anderson, R.: Optimised to fail: card readers for online banking. In: Dingledine, R., Golle, P. (eds.) FC 2009. LNCS, vol. 5628, pp. 184–200. Springer, Heidelberg (2009)
12. Entrust: Consolidated Certificate Issuance and Management, January 2014. http://www.entrust.com/solutions/certificate-management/
13. Eronen, P., Tschofenig, H.: Pre-Shared Key Ciphersuites for Transport Layer Security (TLS). RFC 4279 (Proposed Standard), December 2005. http://www.ietf.org/RFC/RFC4279.txt
14. GlobalPlatform: Card Specification, January 2001
15. Gutmann, P.: X.509 Style Guide (2000). https://www.cs.auckland.ac.nz/~pgut001/pubs/x509guide.txt
16. Hankerson, D., Menezes, A.J., Vanstone, S.: Guide to Elliptic Curve Cryptography. Springer, Heidelberg (2004)
17. Hollenbeck, S.: Transport Layer Security Protocol Compression Methods. RFC 3749 (Proposed Standard), May 2004. http://www.ietf.org/RFC/RFC3749.txt
18. Advanced Security Mechanisms for Machine Readable Travel Documents-Part 3, Technical report, Bundesamt für Sicherheit in der Informationstechnik: Advanced Security Mechanisms for Machine Readable Travel Documents - Part 3 July 2013
19. ISO/IEC: ISO 7816-8. Identification cards Integrated circuit cards Part 8: Commands for security operations (2004)
20. ISO/IEC: ISO/IEC 9594-1:2005, Information technology - Open Systems Interconnection - The Directory: overview of concepts, models and services (2005)
21. ISO/IEC: ISO 18013-3. Information technology Personal identification ISO-compliant driving licence. Part 3: Access Control, authentication and integrity validation (2009)
22. National Institute of Standards and Technology: FIPS PUB 186-4 – Digital Signature Standard (DSS), July 2013
23. Ortiz-Yepes, D., Hermann, R., Steinauer, H., Buhler, P.: Bringing strong authentication and transaction security to the realm of mobile devices. IBM J. Res. Dev. Cybersecurity Smarter Planet **58**(1), 4:1–4:11 (2014)
24. Polk, T., McKay, T., Chokhani, S.: NIST Special Publication 800-52 - Guidelines for the Selection, Configuration, and Use of Transport Layer Security (TLS) Implementations, April 2014
25. PrimeKey: EJBCA - Open Source PKI Certificate Authority, January 2014. http://www.ejbca.org/
26. Rescorla, E.: SSL and TLS: Designing and Building Secure Systems. Addison-Wesley, Reading (2000)
27. Rizzo, J., Duong, T.: The CRIME attack. In: Ekoparty (2012)
28. Salowey, J., Zhou, H., Eronen, P., Tschofenig, H.: Transport Layer Security (TLS) Session Resumption without Server-Side State. RFC 5077 (Proposed Standard), January 2008. http://www.ietf.org/RFC/RFC5077.txt

29. Santesson, S., Myers, M., Ankney, R., Malpani, A., Galperin, S., Adams, C.: X.509 Internet Public Key Infrastructure Online Certificate Status Protocol - OCSP. RFC 6960 (Proposed Standard), June 2013. http://www.ietf.org/RFC/RFC6960.txt
30. Scheier, B.: The Internet of Things Is Wildly Insecure And Often Unpatchable. Wired (2014). http://www.wired.com/opinion/2014/01/theres-no-good-way-to-patch-the-internet-of-things-and-thats-a-huge-problem/
31. Szikora, J.P., Teuwen, P.: Banques en ligne: à la découverte d'EMV-CAP. MISC (Multi-System & Internet Security Cookbook) 56, 50–62 (2011)
32. Weigold, T., Kramp, T., Hermann, R., Höring, F., Buhler, P., Baentsch, M.: The Zurich Trusted information channel – an efficient defence against man-in-the-middle and malicious software attacks. In: Lipp, P., Sadeghi, A.-R., Koch, K.-M. (eds.) Trust 2008. LNCS, vol. 4968, pp. 75–91. Springer, Heidelberg (2008)
33. Zoller, T.: TLS/SSL hardening and compatibility report 2011 (2011)

Automating MAC Spoofer Evidence Gathering and Encoding for Investigations

Serguei A. Mokhov[1,3,4]($\boxtimes$), Michael J. Assels[4], Joey Paquet[1,4],
and Mourad Debbabi[2,3,4]

[1] Computer Science and Software Engineering, Concordia University,
Montreal, QC, Canada
[2] Concordia Institute for Information Systems Engineering, Montreal, QC, Canada
[3] NCFTA Canada, Montreal, QC, Canada
[4] Faculty of Engineering and Computer Science Concordia University,
Montreal, QC, Canada
{mokhov,mjassels,paquet,debbabi}@encs.concordia.ca

Abstract. Following up on the previous work, we elaborate on the
details of the design and implementation of the live and dead digital
evidence gathering and its encoding into FORENSIC LUCID by the corresponding *MAC Spoofer Analyzer*'s (MSA's) components in an actual
operational environment. We monitor over a 1000 analyst-managed computers on the Faculty's network to help network system administrators in
daily network security monitoring. The common FORENSIC LUCID evidence encoding format represents a consistent evidence representation
and allows specification of reasoning functions over the evidence in a
context-oriented manner.

Keywords: MAC spoofing · FORENSIC LUCID · Digital evidence

1 Introduction

We have laid out the introductory and background setting of this work in a recent
short paper [11]. Here we add extra detail to that discussion reducing some of
the background repetition, while keeping it reasonably stand-alone. The readers
wishing to get more details on the related work, please refer to that short piece.

It is simple to spoof a MAC address by changing the network card settings
in most operating systems, via a bridged virtual machine, or most house-grade
routers that allow setting an arbitrary MAC address for a variety of legitimate
needs [10,11]. On the analyst-managed subnets on campus, however, a MAC
spoofer presents a significant security concern if a MAC address of a MAC-based port security setting of a security-hardened desktop in a managed lab
or office gets spoofed by a visiting laptop (where the user is in full control).
Among other things, it may potentially gain unauthorized access to restricted
services/resources and/or increase the Faculty's liability if, for example, the laptop is infested with malware [10,11].

© Springer International Publishing Switzerland 2015
F. Cuppens et al. (Eds.): FPS 2014, LNCS 8930, pp. 168–183, 2015.
DOI: 10.1007/978-3-319-17040-4_11

Our existing *MAC Spoofer Watcher* tool (msw) detects many of such possibilities and alerts the network group's security *Request Tracker* (RT) [19] queue together with cellphone notifications after a series of probes and checks [10,11]. It spends good effort in filtering out the common false positives identified commonly through several iterations of the deployed tool in daily network operations [11]. However, more often than not, a false positive report is generated. Analysts had to manually and sequentially double-check for true or a false positive right after the alert is generated (to the RT ticket as well as cellphones at any time of the day or night). A large volume of such events is overwhelming to the limited human resources dealing with such events while attending to many other duties [10,11].

The msw's processing is triggered by switch port events registered in the switchlog that msw observes, such as when LINK-UP events occur at Layer 2 of the OSI model [8]. If all of its preliminary false-positiveness tests incrementally fail, msw generates the RT email alert at the time [10,11]. This alert triggers a follow-up investigation by the MSA tool presented in this paper to automate the process and establish the likelihood of a genuine spoofer or a false positive with high confidence to assist the network security crew in their daily operations by supplying the evidential results back to the same RT ticket [10,11].

This follow-up includes two types of digital forensics: live and "dead" (passive) [5,9,14], simultaneously [10]. The process re-examines the evidence used by msw as well as performing additional live probes as explained further [10,11]. The live forensics includes re-examining the switch port status, ARP [15] cache, ping, and finger replies, etc. In parallel, we also examine the past logs on the switch port link activity, user activity syslog, DHCP logs, netflows surrounding the time of the incident. These tools, daemons, and their logs act as *witnesses* and their witness accounts of the relevant events are a part of the *evidential statement* in our case [10,11]. All evidence is gathered in the common format of FORENSIC LUCID, and is fed to the eduction-based analysis engine (in our case based on GIPSY presented in [10]).

There is a possibility that more than one alert is generated for the same host in a short period of time—currently that means all such offences will be processed concurrently with the gradually growing body of evidence with each subsequent incident. That means the current and the recent past evidence will have a disadvantage of multiple processing of logically the same case. The later runs, however, gather all the previous and the new evidence, thereby increasing the confidence in the subsequent analyses [10,11] that we can live with. Likewise, there is no synchronization between the multiple concurrently running investigations working independently on the same logical case; however, the "phase 2" design calls to leverage GIPSY's implementation of the eductive computation model [10], where the already-computed event reconstruction results at the same forensic contexts [10] are cached in the Demand Store Tier DST [10] speeding up later runs and avoiding duplicate work. This implies, a GIPSY instance should be running on a standby waiting to process such things, whereas currently we spawn a GIPSY instance each run [10,11].

2   Methodology

2.1   MAC Spoofer RT Alert

At the arrival of the MAC spoofer report we construct a primary claim "there is a MAC spoofer" with some initial facts and evidence from the ticket [10,11]. In the long run, we want to automatically verify its true- or false-positiveness to some degree of certainty by gathering all the supporting evidence from various sources (e.g., `switchlog`, activity log, argus/netflow data, etc.) in one common format of FORENSIC LUCID and reason about it. Subsequently, we send a follow-up report results to the ticket [10,11]. In case of a likely true positive, other things are to be possibly automatically verified/established, such as who is the likely perpetrator and their malignity, whether privileged resources access was attempted, etc [10,11].

2.2   Report Analysis by Human Experts

An investigator, usually a network administrator, manually examining the evidence and doing an investigation usually goes sequentially through some of the steps occasionally taking shortcuts by omitting some of the steps if something is obvious or performing them to increase confidence in the analysis results [10,11]:

1. Check the switch port is still up [10,11]
2. Check the host responds to `telnet` with `memory` and `hardware` commands (the custom commands are designed to return expected values) [10,11]
3. Check `switchlog` for LINK-UP events regarding the switch port in question [10,11]
4. Delete ARP entry for the host from the ARP cache with `arp` (for further checks) [10,11]
5. Check the host responds to `ping`, `finger` (both should respond as expected, else the firewall configuration is non-standard) [10,11]
   (a) If `ping` answers, check the TTL values for likely Linux (64) or Windows (128) hosts, or someone plugged in a router (63 or 127, i.e., decremented by 1 at each hop) [3,10,11,18]
   (b) No answer to `ping` nor ARP cache entry re-appears, likely machine no longer up due to a quick reboot or ghosting; often leading to a false-positive [11]
   (c) No answer to `ping`, but ARP query returns successfully. A good indicator of a likelihood of a real MAC spoofer (the machine acquired an IP, is up, but does not reply as it should) [10,11]
6. Check the host responds to `nbtscan` for Windows hosts (should return one of the known strings) [10,11]
7. Attempt to `ssh` to the host (should accept certain logins and respond appropriately) [10,11]
8. Check activity log for boot and login events for the host [10,11]
9. Optionally check for swpvios for this port in the recent past [10,11]
10. Check argus/netflow logs for connections made from the host after the spoofer report for potential illicit network activity [10,11]

2.3   Automated Algorithm

We automated and enhanced the manual process presented in the preceding section with a parallel algorithm for MSA that does extra verification, evidence gathering, and subsequent reporting, all in near-realtime [10,11].

The algorithm for the automated solution is in Algorithm 1 [10,11]. In the general case, it consists of both live- (probing and checking the active MAC-spoofer-accused on the network) and dead-forensics (examining some of the logs after the fact) techniques simultaneously [10,11]. It should be noted while the algorithm is depicted in the traditional sequential manner, many of steps related to both live and dead forensics data gathering are designed to be done concurrently, which will commonly yield a performance improvement compared to the human expert doing the same [10,11].

Additional evidence is gathered with an nmap scan to fingerprint the OS and ports [11]. Then, gather the DHCP requests made to see if the offending laptop by default (suddenly) queries DHCP for the IP while not too long ago the legitimate host did its own DHCP requests (with known intervals or, if rebooted frequently, with the additional log entries "booted successfully in OS") [10,11]. This will not work if the laptop has been intentionally configured with static IP, but could provide additional confidence, if the DHCP was used (which is the default in many cases) [10,11]. An additional query to nbtscan for additional evidence, à la msw is also made [10,11].

2.4   Use and Misuse Cases

The UML Use Case diagram in Fig. 1 depicts most common use and misuse cases of the ENCS network in the context of MAC spoofer investigations. Misuse cases are in gray. Following Alexander's notion of Misuse Cases for requirements specification ([1]) to visualize the threat and mitigation scenarios as well as the primary and supporting actors involved. A lot of investigative work is shared between the network administrator and the *MAC Spoofer Analyzer* (MSA), where the latter automatically gathers all the evidence in one place, encodes, invokes the analysis computation via GIPSY and then generates two reports: the summarized evidence and designed upcoming automated reasoning report. The MAC spoofer misuse cases illustrate the typical actions a person with a UM laptop would do to spoof a MAC address. While presently MSA is not downing the switch port, the design includes this use case to be complete; this action depends on the result of the analysis and confidence in it. In Sect. 2.6 is the description of the corresponding sequence diagram (Fig. 3).

2.5   False Positives

The typical false positive (we have about 2–3 per week excluding semester-bound re-imaging season) spoofer detections include [11]:

1. Unusually slow booting (and often patching right afterward and rebooting of) Windows hosts.

```
begin
    Trigger start by an RT alert of a possible MAC spoofer via the procmail handler;
    // In the below live and dead evidence gathering in the begin-end blocks is done in
       parallel processes.
    // Each check/evidence collector as a product, encodes its output in FORENSIC
       LUCID as an observation sequence. All such sequences are combined into an
       evidential statement for further analysis.
    // Live network MAC spoofer evidence gathering
    begin
        Check the switch port status;
        // SL6 and Windows 7 only should be there
        Check host OS and ports open with nmap;
        Check how the host responds to telnet with memory and hardware commands;
        // Should respond as expected, else the firewall configuration is non-standard
        Delete ARP entry for the host from the ARP cache with arp;
        Check how the host responds to ping, finger;
        begin
            if ping answers then
                Check the TTL values for likely Linux (64) or Windows (128) hosts, or
                someone plugged in a router (63 or 127);
            end
            else
                No answer to ping nor ARP cache entry re-appears, likely machine no
                longer up due to a quick reboot or ghosting; often leading to a
                false-positive;
            end
            // May increase confidence in false-positiveness
            begin
                Reaffirm possible boot and patching in the activity log;
            end
            No answer to ping, but ARP query returns successfully. A good indicator of a
            likelihood of a real MAC spoofer (the machine acquired an IP, is up, but does
            not reply as it should);
        end
        Check how the host responds to nbtscan;
        // Should be allowed internally
        Attempt to ssh to the host;
    end
    // "Dead" network MAC spoofer evidence gathering
    begin
        Check switchlog for
        LINK-UP events regarding the switch port in question;
        Check activity log for boot and login events for the host;
        Optionally check for swpvios [2] for this port in the recent past;
        Check argus/netflow logs for connections made from the host after the spoofer
        report for potential illicit network activity;
        Check the DHCP requests for the host;
    end
    // Analysis
    begin
        Gather evidence from all the checks and encode it in FORENSIC LUCID;
        Invoke analysis engine;
    end
    Generate a report;
end
```

Algorithm 1. MAC spoofer checking algorithm [11].

2. Older outdated images of OS's that were rarely booted to and unpatched/not re-imaged for a long time [11].
3. Accidental user-managed (UM) host (with the UM image) on a trusted virtual LAN (VLAN) [2,7] (either mistaken OS image/IP address or switch port configuration settings) [11].

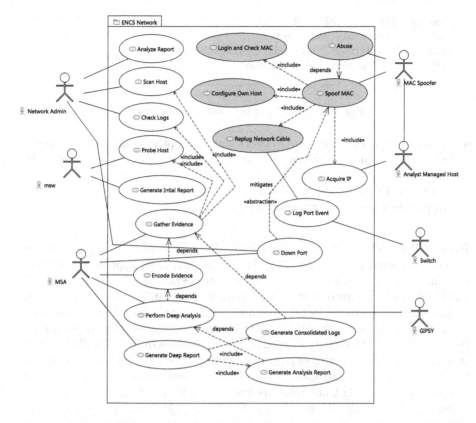

Fig. 1. Use and Misuse Cases in MAC spoofer investigations

4. Host in the middle of ghosting or in the ghosting console without a recognized NetBIOS string on a trusted VLAN [11].
5. Exceptional printers on the trusted VLAN [11].
6. Malfunctioning host (hard drive or memory going bad) [11].

While not all can be handled in an automated manner easily, the proposed MSA tool is designed to be able to identify cases 1, 2, and 6 in its follow-up investigation [11].

2.6   Components

The MSA system's design consists of the following components/modules acting together in unison (sequentially or in parallel) [11]:

1. Procmail [4] handler
2. RT ticket email to FORENSIC LUCID encoder
3. Live and log data collector/FORENSIC LUCID encoder (activity, switchlog, argus [16], DHCP, and others)

```
:0c:mac-spoofer-analyzer.lock
* ^Subject: .*Possible MAC spoofer
* ^From: .*(nobody|root(\+[a-z\d-]+)?|nag(db)?)@
| $HOME/bin/mac-spoofer-alert-handler | ...
```

Fig. 2. Procmail handler trigger recipe (rule)

4. (under design consideration) Network database query component for previously known information on the hosts, locations, switch ports, and MAC addresses
5. FORENSIC LUCID processor (GIPSY) invocator
6. Output/conclusion report generator

Procmail Handler. This component consists of two parts: the .procmailrc recipe for procmail [4] (see Fig. 2) looking for Possible MAC spoofer and From: matching a regular expression .*(nobody|root(+[a-z-]+)?|nag(db)?)@ [17] and handing over a copy of that RT ticket email to the handler (the variable $HOME is appropriately set to the installation directory); and the handler is a script that (1) parses the Subject: header for RT ticket number, host, switch and port number, (2) checks in its internal storage if this ticket has already been handled to avoid duplicate or useless handling of replies or comments to the ticket by people in case the From: didn't filter enough in (1), (3) if this is a new spoofer report claim, save the RT email into a .rt file, which is a text file with the name of the RT ticket number containing the RT email, e.g., 123456.rt, (4) ssh to primary compute and control host and start the Collector/Encoder component there.

Collector/Encoder. The collector/encoder script consists of multiple modules and subcomponents that collect information from various data sources (mostly logs or probes on different hosts) and convert them into an evidential statement *es* context format encoded in FORENSIC LUCID [11]. The script, mac-spoofer-evidence-collector is a multiprocess PERL application that calls upon various modules (listed below) to gather the corresponding evidence available [11].

There are three primary API methods that the main collector/encoder dynamically discovers and calls for each of the following modules are collect(), encode(), and getType() [11]. The collect() method implements a specific data gathering mechanism (from a log file on some host or a direct live probe around the *initial contextual point* of interest in meta-LUCID terms as initial filtering criteria), and stores the gathered data (RT-number.collector-type) [11]. The encode() methods selectively encode the collected data into FORENSIC LUCID with some preprocessing and filtering following the Occam's razor principles and normalization (for easier co-relation of timestamps and other data items of the same type, such as MAC addresses). Something that is not encoded or not recognized by the encoder for a particular data log, is still preserved either as a simple observation in an observation sequence or in a comment section of the corresponding FORENSIC LUCID fragment, such that a human investigator can review and fine-tune it later [11]. The getType() is simply a way for the main collector/encoder to tell apart which module was called to use as an extension [11]. All encoded files have an additional extension of .ctx, that is context files (that have observation sequences of interest). The main script then check-sums all the collected and encoded data with sha1sum [11].

1. RTForensicLucidEncoder is the module that is the very first to be invoked to parse and encode the initial RT ticket into a claim [11]. In particular, it extracts the date, hostname, IP, switch, and port context point data that are used for subsequent lookups in the related logs, live data, and database entries that follow to gather all relevant contextual evidence surrounding the initial RT report [11]. The other concrete collector/encoder modules search for data temporally near this context point [11].

2. SwitchLogForensicLucidEncoder uses the date, switch, and port information to look for related events in the switchlog and encode the events of interest such as link state changes, *swpvios*, etc. [11]

3. ActivityLogForensicLucidEncoder uses the date and host information to look for host bootups, shutdowns, patching, and user logins/logouts [11].

4. MSWForensicLucidEncoder encodes log entries produced by msw. The older msw did not produce non-STDERR log file entries, only errors and email notifications. To be able to replay some of the data (that are normally real-time) from the past, we need an event trace/decision log. This is especially relevant for development and testing on past cases while no actual spoofing is going on [11]. Thus as a part of this work, msw was itself augmented to add extra logging functionality, and, while at it, making it in a more FORENSIC LUCID-friendly manner to simplify extraction by logging sub-expressions directly in the FORENSIC LUCID context format [11]. This approach compensates somewhat for the fact that real-time data for nbtscan and other probes and the like are not available in the offline playback. Furthermore, those data serve as additional evidential observations to improve the confidence in the subsequent analysis [11].

5. DHCPLogForensicLucidEncoder uses the date and host information to look for the host's DHCP requests and the corresponding DHCP protocol exchange messages [11].

6. ARPPingForensicLucidEncoder uses arp and ping to gather the live host presence evidence, which is especially useful in the presence of a firewall on the spoofing host [11].

7. NmapForensicLucidEncoder uses nmap to gather the live OS and open ports evidence [11].

8. FingerForensicLucidEncoder uses finger to gather the live OS and login evidence [11].

9. SSHForensicLucidEncoder uses ssh to gather the live "genuineness" test evidence [11].

10. ArgusForensicLucidEncoder uses Argus commands to gather netflow summaries, etc., as evidence of network activity prior the report arrival time t_{ar},

such as at least $t_{ar} - t_{linkup}$ primarily because a number of probes are done between the LINK-UP event [6,7,12,13] and the ticket arrival time to weed out the majority of false positives [11].

11. `NbtscanForensicLucidEncoder` uses `nbtscan` to gather the live NetBIOS evidence (for Windows hosts) for work groups and the MAC address [11].

12. `SWMForensicLucidEncoder` uses the switch management `swm` [2] to check the live current port status at the time of the check if it is up [11].

13. `EncodingUtils` module was developed as a helper module for many of the above to uniformly encode data such as timestamps, MAC addresses, and hostnames, which sometimes vary in their lexical representation in different logs or probes. It, therefore, has `timestampformat()`, `macformat()`, and `hostnameformat()` methods [11]. For example, timestams formatted similar to `"Jul 7 15:10:18"`, `"2013-07-07 13:10:55497751"`, `"2013-07-07 16:24 EDT"`, or `"201307020450"`, become `"Tue Jul 9 08:56:56 2013"` in the human-readable form for reporting and as a long epoch integer internally [11]. Likewise, MAC addresses have different legal lexical representations used by different vendors, like `00bb335588ff` in raw, `0:bb:33:55:88:ff` in Argus (stripping leading zeroes), `00-BB-33--55-88-FF` by Microsoft, or `00bb.3355.88ff` by Cisco are folded into the DCHP ethers format, such as `00:bb:33:55:88:ff`. Hosts are simply formatted into fully-qualified domain names (FQDNs) [11].

Encoding the RT Ticket Claim. The RT ticket claim's evidence is primarily the following:

- Ticket arrival timestamp `t_ar`, e.g., `Wed, 1 Aug 2012 07:07:07 -0400`, is a contextual point in time from which to move forward and backward to extract relevant events in other evidential sources [11].
- `ipaddr` – possible spoofer's IP address; filter for logs that use IP addresses only. This works well if the spoofer uses the same IP address as the legitimate host, via DHCP or statically [11]. This partially breaks if the spoofer changes an IP address to be of another host on the same subnet after checking, which IPs are unused. (Such behavior is a sign of extreme deliberation and possibly malice of someone who knows what they are doing as opposed to "scriptkiddie" tools for "mere Internet access" with a laptop.) This case can still be caught via the other evidential sources and logs that do not use IPs, and primarily host/switch/port based checks [11]. The extra `arp` checks for the investigation if the MAC address in DHCP matches the expected IP address talking on the port or not, will confidently tell if the spoofer is genuine [11].
- `hostname`–possible spoofer's DNS name; filter for logs that use hostnames [11].
- `switch`–uplink switch DNS name where the host is/was connected to [11].
- `port`–uplink port on the switch where the host is/was connected to [11].
- `mac`–the MAC address being spoofed; for lookups in DHCP, switch, database, and other sources that have it [11].

The so-called secondary context, encoded hierarchically (primarily for reporting to humans and possibly other uses) includes a room number, jack number on the wall, and (possibly in the future) hardware/memory/OS information extracted [11]. The primary context point is used to construct the two-claim solution [11] and gather the evidence from the log files surrounding that context filtered by t_ar ± 24 hrs, ipaddr, hostname, switch, port, and mac further. The RT two-claim is made indirectly by msw, as a "prosecution witness" [11].

Encoding Log and Probe Evidence. Collection of other pertinent evidence depends on the context of the initial report described in the preceding section. The modules described earlier collect both live and dead evidence from probes and logs. Not everything possible is collected to avoid unnecessary complexity in encoding and evaluation, so only information is kept that is likely to be helpful in the decision making. The data selection is made by the typical criteria a human expert selects the data for the same task. Following the examples presented in [10], we illustrate some of the examples of the encoded evidence in FORENSIC LUCID for the modules mentioned. Context calculus operators [10] help with additional filtering of deemed unnecessary data during computation.

In Listing 1.1 is the msw evidence encoding example. In Listing 1.2 is the empty (no-observation) activity log example. In the regular cases, activity log features operating system booted and users logged on. perp_o in the presence of users can be set to the most likely perpetrator in a follow-up investigation. finger and ssh live evidence supplements the activity log evidence with similar information on expected banners and possible users, if available. No-observations are recorded similarly.

```
// ...
// msw evidence, encoded: Jul 22 09:17:31 2013
observation sequence msw_os =
{
  msw_encsldpd_o_1,
  msw_ghost_o_2,
  msw_arp_o_3
};

observation msw_encsldpd_o_1 = ([switch:"switch1",port:"FastEthernet0/1",
    ipaddr:"123.45.44.252",hostname:"flucid-44.private.local",encsldpd:
    false], 1, 0, 1.0, "Jul 13 14:33:37 2013");
observation msw_ghost_o_2 = ([switch:"switch1",port:"FastEthernet0/1",
    ipaddr:"123.45.44.252",hostname:"flucid-44.private.local",ghost:false],
    1, 0, 1.0, "Jul 13 14:33:38 2013");
observation msw_arp_o_3 = ([switch:"switch1",port:"FastEthernet0/1",ipaddr:
    "123.45.44.252",hostname:"flucid-44.private.local",arp:true], 1, 0,
    1.0, "Jul 13 14:33:39 2013");
// end of msw evidence
// ...
```

Listing 1.1. msw encoded evidence example

Live probes by nmap (and similarly complementary by nbtscan) give a list of open ports and other aspects that are compared to the minimum expected ports and other values. In Listing 1.4 is an example of captured and encoded nmap evidence. The samples of ignored lines are in the comment section; they play no role in evaluation but recorded anyway in case the investigator wants to include some of that data later on.

```
// ...
// activity log evidence, encoded: Jul 22 09:17:25 2013
observation perp_o = $;
observation sequence activity_os =
{
  activity_o_1
};

observation activity_o_1 = $;
// end of activity log evidence
// ...
```

Listing 1.2. `activity` encoded no-observation evidence example

In Listing 1.3 is an example of the evidence encoded from the DHCP logs to supplement the investigation and provide visibility into the situation.

Collection/Encoding Summary. All the encoded evidence, e.g., for the ticket RT12345 is saved into the appropriate files: `12345.rt.ctx`,`12345.switchlog.ctx`, `12345.activity.ctx`, `12345.nmap.ctx`, and others plus the incident modeling transition functions ψ (forward tracing) and Ψ^{-1} (optimized backtracing, see [10] for their description and definition) in the file `mac-spoofer-transition.ipl` for the case into the case file `12345.spoofer.ipl` for the primary claim "there is a spoofer" and `12345.notspoofer.ipl` as "defence" claim that "this is a false positive" for parallel evaluation.

In case of reasonable true-positiveness, the design calls for subclaims to be created and evaluated as well: `12345.perp.ipl`, `12345.nfs.ipl` to determine who (*attribution*) and how malicious they are based on the previously extracted evidence (e.g., via activity and Argus logs).

At the end of its operation, Collector/Encoder (after checksumming everything) passes all the collected and encoded data to the FORENSIC LUCID processor (see the following section) to do the actual reasoning and event reconstruction computations. A GIPSY instance is spawned per claim to be evaluated.

FORENSIC LUCID **Processor.** The FORENSIC LUCID Processor presently includes the `mac-spoofer-flucid-processor` script feeding the encoded evidence to GIPSY [10] that has a FORENSIC LUCID parser and a distributed run-time system, implemented in JAVA. This component is designed to do the heavy weight computation, model-checking, and event reconstruction. The Collector/Encoder then gathers its report for analysis and notifies the analysts. The MSA design includes a provision to act on the results of analysis if the confidence is high by, e.g., shutting down the switch port or quarantining the IP address. Presently this aspect is under development.

Output/Conclusion Generator. In MSA, this corresponds to the `mac-spoofer-reporter` to report the findings to system administrators. Presently, 1 is already in production; 2 reports in the development environment.

– Decision tree, findings, conclusions; mail with the proper RT subject (under active development).

```
// ...
// DHCP evidence, encoded: Jul 14 21:08:13 2013
observation sequence dhcpd_os =
{
  dhcp_log_o_1,
  dhcp_log_o_2,
  dhcp_log_o_3,
  dhcp_log_o_4,
  dhcp_log_o_5
};

observation dhcp_log_o_1 = ([dhcpmsg:"DHCPOFFER", direction1:"on", ipaddr:"
    xxx.xxx.xx.xx", direction2:"to", mac:"xx:xx:xx:xx:xx:xx", via:"xxx.xxx.
    xx.x"], 1, 0, 1.0, "Jul 14 11:58:03 2013");
observation dhcp_log_o_2 = ([dhcpmsg:"DHCPREQUEST", direction1:"for",
    ipaddr:"xxx.xxx.xx.xx", dhcpd:"xxx.xxx.xx.xxx", direction2:"from", mac:
    "xx:xx:xx:xx:xx:xx", via:"xxx.xxx.xx.x"], 1, 0, 1.0, "Jul 14 11:58:03
    2013'');
observation dhcp_log_o_3 = ([dhcpmsg:"DHCPACK", direction1:"on", ipaddr:"
    xxx.xxx.xx.xx", direction2:"to", mac:"xx:xx:xx:xx:xx:xx", via:"xxx.xxx.
    xx.x"], 1, 0, 1.0, "Jul 14 11:58:03 2013");
observation dhcp_log_o_4 = ([dhcpmsg:"DHCPINFORM", direction1:"from",
    ipaddr:"xxx.xxx.xx.xx", via:"xxx.xxx.xx.x"], 1, 0, 1.0, "Jul 14
    11:58:07 2013");
observation dhcp_log_o_5 = ([dhcpmsg:"DHCPACK", direction1:"to", ipaddr:"
    xxx.xxx.xx.xx", mac:"xx:xx:xx:xx:xx:xx", via:"bond0"], 1, 0, 1.0, "Jul
    14 11:58:07 2013");
// end of DHCP evidence
// ...
```

Listing 1.3. dhcp log encoded evidence example

- Multi-stage reporting mailings as data become available:
  1. Gathered evidence first; grouped together in one place. (This is already in operation and is of help earlier on to any active network security people watching in.)
  2. Analysis, that may computationally take a longer time, will be delivered in a follow-up analysis update (in progress).

The UML sequence diagram shown in Fig. 3 depicts the design of a series of synchronous and asynchronous calls by the modules involved. It is based on the components mentioned earlier in Sect. 2.6 and further, their API, and on Algorithm 1. All the encoders work asynchronously as child processes (fork()) started by mac-spoofer-evidence-collector. This is because there is no particular ordering for their execution required (except for the RT ticket encoding as there is a data dependency on the context point from it used by the other modules as well as preferential start up of live forensics modules first to do their probes sooner). All modules produce intermediate raw files and encoded timestamped files; the latter are subsequently collected into one FORENSIC LUCID script when all the modules return, which is then fed to GIPSY to compile and evaluate for reasoning purposes. When GIPSY returns, the final analysis report is generated.

```
// ...
// 'nmap' evidence, encoded: Jul 14 21:09:23 2013
observation sequence nmap_os = os_nmap_entries;

observation sequence os_nmap_entries =
{
  ([protocol_port:135, protocol:"tcp"], 1, 0),
  ([protocol_port:139, protocol:"tcp"], 1, 0),
  ([protocol_port:445, protocol:"tcp"], 1, 0),
  ([protocol_port:49152, protocol:"tcp"], 1, 0),
  ([protocol_port:49157, protocol:"tcp"], 1, 0),
  ([protocol_port:6002, protocol:"tcp"], 1, 0),
  ([protocol_port:49153, protocol:"tcp"], 1, 0),
  ([protocol_port:49154, protocol:"tcp"], 1, 0),
  ([protocol_port:49156, protocol:"tcp"], 1, 0),
  ([protocol_port:7001, protocol:"tcp"], 1, 0),
  ([protocol_port:7002, protocol:"tcp"], 1, 0),
  ([protocol_port:49155, protocol:"tcp"], 1, 0),
  ([protocol_port:135, protocol:"tcp"] => "open   msrpc      Microsoft
      Windows RPC", 1, 0),
  ([protocol_port:139, protocol:"tcp"] => "open   netbios-ssn", 1, 0),
  ([protocol_port:445, protocol:"tcp"] => "open   netbios-ssn", 1, 0),
  ([protocol_port:6002, protocol:"tcp"] => "open   http       SafeNet
      Sentinel License Monitor httpd 7.3", 1, 0),
  ([protocol_port:7001, protocol:"tcp"] => "open   tcpwrapped", 1, 0),
  ([protocol_port:7002, protocol:"tcp"] => "open   hbase-region Apache
      Hadoop Hbase 1.3.0 (Java Console)", 1, 0),
  ([protocol_port:49152, protocol:"tcp"] => "open   msrpc      Microsoft
      Windows RPC", 1, 0),
  ([protocol_port:49153, protocol:"tcp"] => "open   msrpc      Microsoft
      Windows RPC" 1, 0),
  ([protocol_port:49154, protocol:"tcp"] => "open   msrpc      Microsoft
      Windows RPC", 1, 0),
  ([protocol_port:49155, protocol:"tcp"] => "open   msrpc      Microsoft
      Windows RPC", 1, 0),
  ([protocol_port:49156, protocol:"tcp"] => "open   msrpc      Microsoft
      Windows RPC", 1, 0),
  ([protocol_port:49157, protocol:"tcp"] => "open   msrpc      Microsoft
      Windows RPC", 1, 0),
  ([mac:"00:13:72:xx:xx:xx"] => "(Dell)", 1, 0),
  ([os:"Microsoft Windows 7|2008"], 1, 0),
  ([hops:1], 1, 0)
};

// Unencoded data
/*
  Starting Nmap 6.25 ( http://nmap.org ) at 2013-07-14 21:08 EDT
  NSE: Loaded 106 scripts for scanning.
  NSE: Script Pre-scanning.
  Initiating ARP Ping Scan at 21:08
  Scanning xxx.xxx.xx.xx [1 port]
  Completed ARP Ping Scan at 21:08, 0.00s elapsed (1 total hosts)
  Initiating SYN Stealth Scan at 21:08
  Scanning xxx.xxx.xx.xx [1000 ports]
*/
// end of 'nmap' evidence
// ...
```

Listing 1.4. nmap encoded evidence example

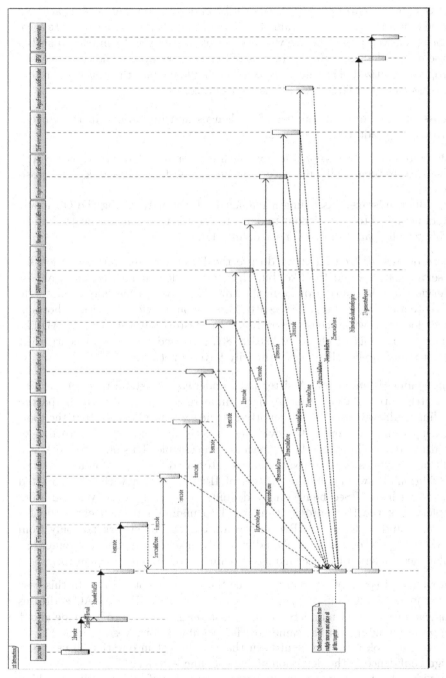

Fig. 3. MAC spoofer analyzer UML sequence diagram

3   Conclusion

MSA is already a part of the `nagtools` set [2] in production that is being actively designed, developed, and maintained in iterative builds [11]. The `nagtools` have not been released publicly since we have not estimated yet the impact of such a release on the details of the operations of our network even if the code released is properly sanitized. The interested readers should contact the first two authors to discuss this. The GIPSY's code is open-source.

Discussion. There are a number of challenges and limitations in the current approach to be addressed:

- Short-lived spoofer sessions, so not much live forensic data are available [11].
- Need to systematically measure true negatives, false negatives, false positives [11].
- Sysadmin mistakes (assigning a managed VLAN or replacing the OS image from managed to UM without updates to the VLAN), which is nearly impossible to tell apart from genuine spoofing [11].

A note on RADIUS/802.1X: we do use the latter for user authentication for the server consoles and the like, but that service does not uniformly scale for all services and hosts we provide in the labs and servers, especially we are only moving to an AD-based service recently. Some of our services are tied to hosts in specific locations with license restrictions, and historically without any AD-like domains and a mix of clients RADIUS/802.1X-based machine authentication was not really applicable on our primarily Layer-2 network.

Ongoing and Future Work. A sister work underway to extend this approach to the switch port violations that are more numerous in volume with the partial encoding is already done (being reported in the same way) except that the tools are being taught to report the evidence directly in FORENSIC LUCID due to its natural readability while being machine-processable. This ongoing work as a result also includes the FORENSIC LUCID automated formal reasoning aspects.

Additionally, we are in the process of IPv6 migration with all associated benefits, such as IPSec being on by default. We are, however, very far from completion of the IPv6 project, and need to maintain the current setup for some time and evaluate the IPv6 impact on our entire network not only from the MAC spoofer perspective. We additionally, need to implement a somewhat similar mechanism in the user-managed realm. Furthermore, we plan to:

- provide a direct hook for `msw` to invoke the reasoner not via RT. In this case one can group relevant `.ctx`, etc. files by the hostname, IP, or MAC addresses instead of RT ticket numbers. Some adjustments will need to be made about duplicate handling for the same host for possible prior investigations [11]
- provide a hook to `swm` to shutdown the switch port in question in case of a high confidence in the detection of the spoofing activity [11]
- provide a hook to the account management in case of high severity and high confidence, autoblock the account of the offender (long term future goal) [11]

References

1. Alexander, I.: Misuse Cases: Use Cases with hostile intent, November 2002. http://www-dse.doc.ic.ac.uk/Events/BCS-RESG/Aleksander.pdf
2. Assels, M.J., Echtner, D., Spanner, M., Mokhov, S.A., Carrière, F., Taveroff, M.: Multifaceted faculty network design and management: practice and experience. In: Desai, B.C., Abran, A., Mudur, S. (eds.) Proceedings of C^3S^2E 2011, pp. 151–155. ACM, New York, May 2010–2011. short paper; full version online at http://www.arxiv.org/abs/1103.5433
3. Bejtlich, R.: The Tao of Network Security: Beyond Intrusion Detection. Addison-Wesley, New York (2005). ISBN: 0-321-24677-2
4. van den Berg, S.R., Guenther, P.A.: procmail v3.22, September 2001. http://www.procmail.org/
5. Carrier, B.D.: Risks of live digital forensic analysis. Commun. ACM **49**(2), 57–61 (2006). http://www.d.umn.edu/~schw0748/DigitalForensics/p56-carrier.pdf
6. Cisco Systems Inc: Catalyst 2950 Switch Hardware Installation Guide, October 2003
7. Clark, K., Hamilton, K.: Cisco LAN Switching. Cisco Press (1999). ISBN: 1-57870-094-9
8. Day, J.D.: The (un)revised OSI reference model. SIGCOMM Comput. Commun. Rev. **25**(5), 39–55 (1995)
9. McDougal, M.: Live forensics on a Windows system: using Windows Forensic Toolchest (WFT) (2003–2006). http://www.foolmoon.net/downloads/Live_Forensics_Using_WFT.pdf
10. Mokhov, S.A.: Intensional Cyberforensics. Ph.D. thesis, Department of Computer Science and Software Engineering, Concordia University, Montreal, Canada, September 2013. http://arxiv.org/abs/1312.0466
11. Mokhov, S.A., Assels, M.J., Paquet, J., Debbabi, M.: Toward automated MAC spoofer investigations. In: Proceedings of C3S2E 2014, pp. 179–184. ACM, August 2014 (short paper)
12. Odom, W.: CCENT/CCNA ICND1: 640–822 Official Cert Guide, 3rd edn. Cisco Press (2012). ISBN: 978-1-58720-425-8
13. Odom, W.: CCNA ICND2: 640–816 Official Cert Guide, 3rd edn. Cisco Press (2012). ISBN: 978-1-58720-435-7
14. Pearce, C.: Computing forensics: a live analysis, April 2005. http://www.linux.org.au/conf/2005/security_miniconf/presentations/crpearce-lca2005.pdf
15. Plummer, D.C.: RFC 826: An Ethernet Address Resolution Protocol, November 1982. http://tools.ietf.org/html/rfc826, viewed in December 2012
16. QoSient, LLC.: Argus: Auditing network activity (2000–2013). http://www.qosient.com/argus/
17. RJK: Regexp syntax summary, June 2002. http://www.greenend.org.uk/rjk/2002/06/regexp.html, last viewed May 2008
18. Tanenbaum, A.S., Wetherall, D.J.: Computer Networks, 5th edn. Prentice Hall (2011). ISBN: 978-0-13-212695-3
19. Vincent, J., Rolsky, D., Chamberlain, D., Foley, R., Spier, R.: RT Essentials. O'Reilly Media, Inc., August 2005

Access Control Models
and Policy Analysis

HGABAC: Towards a Formal Model of Hierarchical Attribute-Based Access Control

Daniel Servos[✉] and Sylvia L. Osborn

Department of Computer Science, Western University, London, ON, Canada
dservos5@uwo.ca, sylvia@csd.uwo.ca

Abstract. Attribute-based access control (ABAC) is a promising alternative to traditional models of access control (i.e. discretionary access control (DAC), mandatory access control (MAC) and role-based access control (RBAC)) that is drawing attention in both recent academic literature and industry application. However, formalization of a foundational model of ABAC and large scale adoption are still lacking. This paper seeks to aid in the transition by providing a formal model of hierarchical ABAC, called Hierarchical Group and Attribute-Based Access Control (or HGABAC), which includes attribute inheritance through user and object groups as well as environment, connection and administrative attributes. A formal specification and an attribute-based policy language are provided. Finally, several example configurations (which demonstrate the versatility of the model) are presented and evaluated.

1 Introduction

Until recently, access control research and real world access control implementations have largely fallen under one of the three traditional models of access control: discretionary access control (DAC) [11], mandatory access control (MAC) [1,5] or role-based access control (RBAC) [6,14]. In these models, access control decisions are largely based on the identity of the user. In DAC this often takes the form of an access control list (ACL) mapping users to permissions on an object, while MAC is based around a security lattice controlling the direction of information flow. In dynamic environments where information sharing between systems and users from different security domains is common, these identity-based access control models are inadequate. While RBAC provides a more generalized model than MAC or DAC [13], it also falls short in cases where users and their respective roles in the system are poorly defined beforehand. A secondary issue, common among these models, is the simplicity of the access control policies. In the case of RBAC, all access control policies must fit the form of "if a user is assigned a role X they are granted the set of permissions Y". However, this is insufficiently flexible for many real world scenarios. For example, a bank may only permit an employee with the role "teller" to access clients' accounts during set times of the day and week or limit their access to accounts based on a systemwide threat level. In both cases, the policy would be too complex to express in a traditional RBAC model.

© Springer International Publishing Switzerland 2015
F. Cuppens et al. (Eds.): FPS 2014, LNCS 8930, pp. 187–204, 2015.
DOI: 10.1007/978-3-319-17040-4_12

To date, researchers have largely approached this problem by extending foundational RBAC models to compensate for inadequate flexibility required for their particular use case (e.g. [3,4,10,15]). However, there has been a growing demand from both government and industry for a more general and dynamic model of access control, namely attribute-based access control (ABAC). Rather than basing access control decisions on a user's identity like the traditional methods, ABAC bases access control around the attributes of a user, the objects being accessed, the environment and a number of other attribute sources. Ideally, these are all properties of the elements already existing in the system and do not need to be manually entered by administration (e.g. many of the attributes about a document come from its existing metadata; author, title, etc.). Access policies can be created, limiting access to certain resources or objects, based on the result of a boolean statement comparing attributes, for example "user.age >= 18 OR object.owner == user.id". This allows for flexible enforcement of real world policies, while only requiring knowledge of some subset of attributes about a given user.

Despite the demand for and potential advantages of ABAC, little has been accomplished in the way of formalizing foundational models and large scale adoption is still in its early stages. The work detailed in this paper seeks to provide a formalized hierarchical model of ABAC, entitled Hierarchical Group and Attribute-Based Access Control (or HGABAC), which introduces a group based hierarchical representation of object and user attributes that is lacking in current models. HGABAC is intended to be a starting point that is detailed enough for real world use but generic enough to emulate traditional models of access control.

The rest of this paper is organized as follows. Section 2 reviews the existing work related to attribute-based access control models and current efforts towards standardization. Section 3 outlines our proposed model of ABAC, HGABAC, and provides a formal specification, as well as details of the policy language used and the group hierarchy. Section 4 gives an example use case and evaluates the solution HGABAC provides. Section 5 demonstrates how HGABAC can be configured to emulate DAC, MAC and RBAC access control policies. Finally, Sect. 6 details our conclusions and plans for future work.

2   Related Work

One of the most frequently referenced works in the ABAC literature is the eXtensible Access Control Markup Language (XACML) standard [7]. XACML is an XML-based access control policy language that is notable for its support of attribute-based policies and use in multiple access control products. While XACML supports attribute-base access control concepts and hierarchical resources, it intently lacks any kind of formal model (simply being a policy language) and instead relies on the implementing system to apply an underlying model of access control. Another related but distinct research area from ABAC is attribute-based encryption (ABE), where objects are encrypted based on attribute related access policies. In ciphertext-policy (CP-ABE) style ABE

Table 1. Comparison of notable models of attribute-based access control.

	Logic-based framework for ABAC [18]	ABAC$_\alpha$ [8]	ABAC for web services [19]	WS-ABAC [17]	ABMAC [12]	HGABAC
Hierarchical	Hierarchical attributes, no user groups					√
Object attributes		√	√	√	√	√
User attributes	√	√	√	√	√	√
Environment attributes			√	√	√	√
Connection attributes					Shown in example but not model	√
Administrative attributes						√
General model	√	√	For web services	For web services	For grid computing	√
Formal model	Only models policies and evaluation	√	Simplistic	Simplistic	√	√
Can model DAC, MAC, and RBAC	Not demonstrated	√	Not demonstrated	Not demonstrated	Not demonstrated	√

an attribute-based policy is used to encrypt an object and user's keys consist of a set of attributes relating to that user [2, 16]. While ABE, much like XACML, lacks any kind of formal ABAC model and has rather simplified access policies, it does provide an interesting means of enforcing ABAC policies outside of the security domain in which they originate.

Various works have attempted to informally describe ABAC or have taken the first steps towards formalization. The most notable of these are summarized and compared to our model in Table 1. Yuan and Tong [19] describe the ABAC model in terms of authorization architecture and policy engineering and give an informal comparison between ABAC and traditional role-based models. Shen and Hong [17] present WS-ABAC, an ABAC model designed for web services based around XACML. However, the model presented in this work is limited and mostly describes an architecture to use XACML and attribute-based policies to provide authentication for web services. Lang et al.'s ABMAC model [12] aims to bring ABAC like access control to grid computing. While this model is based on attribute-based policy decisions, it has several key differences in the policy description and policy evaluation methods. This work is of note as it mentions ABAC's ability to represent the traditional models using a single policy language.

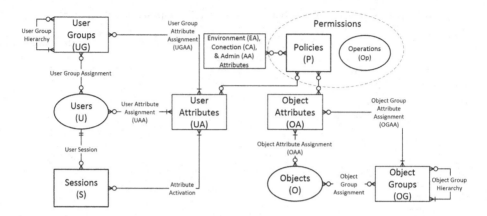

Fig. 1. HGABAC components and relations using Crow's Foot Notation to denote cardinality of relationships. Primitive components are shown in ovals.

Wang et al. [18] propose a logic-based framework for ABAC based on logic programming where policies are specified as "stratified constraint flounder-free logic programs that admit primitive recursion". While their framework introduces hierarchical attributes (something lacking from other models), it is largely focussed on the representation, consistency and performance of attribute-based policies and their evaluation over providing a workable model of ABAC. Several critical components required for a usable model are absent, including object attributes (the only attributes considered are user attributes) and they omit any kind of formalization of ABAC aspects outside of policies and their evaluation (e.g. there is no mention of objects and only access control on services/operations is considered).

Lastly, and most promising is the work by Jin et al. [8] towards a generalized and formalized model of ABAC with constraints for the traditional models, which they call $ABAC_\alpha$. Their model provides a first step "to develop a formal ABAC model that is just sufficiently expressive to capture DAC, MAC and RBAC" which allows configuration of constraints on attributes at creation and modification time as well as policies. While this work provides a sufficient basis for new models of ABAC, it (intentionally) lacks components that would be necessary for a real world implementation, such as attribute and object hierarchies, a simplistic policy language and environment attributes.

Our model, HGABAC, is distinct from other models in several regards. Most notably, the graph based user group hierarchy provides several new interesting means of representing the traditional models in an ABAC framework (allowing the hierarchy to model MAC and RBAC in an intuitive way, rather than a partially ordered set as is done in $ABAC_\alpha$ [8]). These hierarchical representations of MAC and RBAC are demonstrated in Sect. 5. The object group hierarchy allows for objects to be categorized into collections of similar types of objects (e.g. a collection of only health care record objects) and have common attributes applied to all members of the group. This reduces the amount of manual intervention required to tag similar objects with a common attribute and value pairs and reduces the number of object attribute assignments required (as evaluated in Sect. 4.2). Additionally, several efforts are made to create a model more suited to real world application without losing descriptive power or flexibility in terms of policies that may be enforced; a fully specified and intuitive policy language is presented (in Sect. 3.2) loosely based on C style boolean statements and a more rich selection of attribute sources is allowed. Attributes based on the user's current connection to the system and administrative attributes are supported which are lacking in other models. Finally, HGABAC uses a strongly typed system to represent attribute values (i.e. an attribute must have a predefined data type, e.g. integer, floating point, set, etc.). This helps enforce consistency in policies and attribute value assignments as well as helping to prevent any possible ambiguity in policies (e.g. preventing any type mismatches).

3 HGABAC Model

3.1 Formal Model

Basic Elements and Definitions. We define the base elements of the HGABAC model, as shown in Fig. 1, as follows:

- **Users (U):** set of current human and non-human entities that may request access on system resources through sessions.
- **Objects (O):** finite set of system resources (files, database records, devices, etc.) for which access should be limited.
- **Operations (Op):** finite set of all operations provided by the system that may be applied to an object (e.g. read, write, create, delete, update etc.).
- **Policies (P):** set of all current policy strings following the format of our policy language defined in Sect. 3.2.
- **Sessions (S):** set of all user sessions, such that each element, s is a tuple of the form $s = (u \in U, a \subseteq effective(u \in U), con\_atts)$ where u is the user who activated the session, con_atts is the set of connection attributes for the session such that $\forall c \in con\_atts : c = (name, values)$ and a is the subset of the user's effective attributes they wish to activate for the given session ($effective(u)$ is the set of all attributes a user is assigned either directly through the UAA relation or indirectly through group membership). Policies are evaluated on the basis of the activated attributes in a user's session rather than the total set of the user's assigned and inherited attributes.
- **Permissions:** pairing of a policy string and an operation, such that $perm = (p \in P, op \in Op)$. Access to perform an operation, op, on a given object is only allowed if there exists a permission that contains a policy, p, that is satisfied by a given set of attributes corresponding to the requesting user's session, object being accessed and the current state of the connection, environment and administrative attributes in the system. For example, a policy paired with a read operation, "$user.id = object.author$", would allow read access to all objects for which the user is also the author.

Attributes. HGABAC defines attributes to be (name, value, type) triples where the name is a unique identifier and value is an unordered set of atomic values of a given type or the *null* set. Type restricts the data type of the atomic values (e.g. string, integer, boolean, etc.) to a system defined data type. Attributes represent some descriptive characteristic of the entity to which they are assigned. For example, a user might have attributes describing their name, age, employee id, etc., while an object might have attributes describing its author, owner, file type, etc. The set of all attributes (TA) is divided into five subsets based on their origin and to which entity or object they may be applied:

- **User Attributes (UA):** the set of attribute name, type pairs that may be applied to users such that $\forall a \in UA : a = (name, type)$ and each element of UA has a globally unique name (i.e. there cannot be two elements with the same name but different types). Note that value is left out of the definition of UA as user attributes are given a set of values when assigned to users directly or to groups (in the UAA and UGAA relations).
- **Object Attributes (OA):** the set of attribute name, type pairs that may be applied to objects such that $\forall a \in OA : a = (name, type)$ and each element of OA has a globally unique name (i.e. there cannot be two elements with the same name but different types). As with UA, value is left out of the definition of OA as object attributes are given a set of values when assigned to objects directly or to groups (in the OAA and OGAA relations).
- **Environment Attributes (EA):** the set of attribute (name, value, type) triples that represent the current state of the system's environment (e.g. the current time, number of active users, etc.) such that $\forall a \in EA : a = (name, value, type)$ and each element of EA has a globally unique name (i.e. there cannot be two elements with the same name but different types or values). What properties of a system's environment are available as environment attributes is left to the implementation.
- **Connection Attributes (CA):** the set of attribute name, type pairs that correspond to attributes derived from and available for each connection to the system such that $\forall a \in CA : a = (name, type)$ and each element of CA has a globally unique name (i.e. there cannot be two elements with the same name but different types). What properties of the connection are available as connection attributes is left as a implementation decision; however, at a minimum some kind of unique session id should be included.
- **Administrative Attributes (AA):** the set of attribute (name, value, type) triples that are defined by administrators (including automated administrative tasks and programs) that rarely change and apply to all policies which reference them such that $\forall a \in AA : a = (name, value, type)$ and each element of AA has a globally unique name. What administrative attributes are available will change at runtime based on both the implementation and actions of administrators.
- **Total Attributes (TA):** set of all attributes that exist in a given system such that $TA = UA \cup OA \cup CA \cup EA \cup AA$.

Groups. Groups and their hierarchies both simplify administration tasks, allowing attributes to be assigned to groups of users or objects at once rather than directly, and allow for more intuitive and expressive configuration possibilities than allowed in current ABAC models (including in the task of emulating the traditional models as shown in Sect. 5). Section 3.1 details the group hierarchy, while user and object group definitions and membership are defined below:

- **User Groups (UG):** set of all current user groups, where each element is comprised of a tuple, g, such that $g = (name, u \subseteq U, p \subseteq UG)$ where $name$ is a globally unique identifier, u is the set of members of the group, and p is the set of the group's parents in the user group graph.
- **Object Groups (OG):** set of all current object groups, where each element is comprised of a tuple, g, such that $g = (name, o \subseteq O, p \subseteq OG)$ where $name$ is a globally unique identifier, o is the set of members of the group, and p is the set of the group's parents in the object group graph.

Relations. We define the following relations between the base elements, groups and attributes:

- **Direct User Attribute Assignment (UAA):** user attribute assignment relation containing user, attribute name, value triples such that:

$$\forall uaa \in UAA : uaa = (u \in U, att\_name, values)$$

where $att\_name \in \{name \mid (name, type) \in UA\}$ and $values$ is some set of elements such that each element of $values$ is of the same data type $(type)$ and $(att\_name, type) \in UA$. There may exist only one tuple in UAA for every user, att_name pair.
- **Direct Object Attribute Assignment (OAA):** object attribute assignment relation containing object, attribute name, value triples such that:

$$\forall oaa \in OAA : oaa = (o \in O, att\_name, values)$$

where $att\_name \in \{name \mid (name, type) \in OA\}$ and $values$ is some set of elements such that each element of $values$ is of the same data type $(type)$ and $(att\_name, type) \in OA$. There may exist only one tuple in OAA for every object, att_name pair.
- **User Group Attribute Assignment (UGAA):** user group attribute assignment relation containing user group name, attribute name, value triples such that:

$$\forall ugaa \in UGAA : ugaa = (group\_name, att\_name, values)$$

where $group\_name \in \{name \mid (name, u, p) \in UG\}$ and $att\_name \in \{name \mid (name, type) \in UA\}$. $values$ is some set of elements such that each element of $values$ is of the same data type $(type)$ and $(att\_name, type) \in UA$. There may exist only one tuple in UGAA for every group_name, att_name pair.

- **Object Group Attribute Assignment (OGAA):** object group attribute assignment relation containing object group name, attribute name, value triples such that:

$$\forall ogaa \in OGAA : ogaa = (group\_name, att\_name, values)$$

where $group\_name \in \{name \mid (name, u, p) \in OG\}$ and $att\_name \in \{name \mid (name, type) \in OA\}$. $values$ is some set of elements such that each element of $values$ is of the same data type $(type)$ and $(att\_name, type) \in OA$. There may exist only one tuple in OGAA for every group_name, att_name pair.

Mappings. The following are the most important formal functions in the HGABAC model.

- **direct:** Mapping of a user, object, or group to the attribute name, value pairs directly assigned to it in the UAA, OAA, UGAA or OGAA relation (i.e. not including inherited attributes or attributes from group membership). *direct* is defined as:

$$direct(x) = \begin{cases} \{(n, v) \mid (x, n, v) \in UAA\}, & \text{if } x \in U \\ \{(n, v) \mid (x, n, v) \in OAA\}, & \text{if } x \in O \\ \{(n, v) \mid (name(x), n, v) \in UGAA\}, & \text{if } x \in UG \\ \{(n, v) \mid (name(x), n, v) \in OGAA\}, & \text{if } x \in OG \end{cases}$$

where $name(x)$ is the name of the given group, n is an attribute name, v is a set of valid values for that attribute and $x \in U \cup O \cup UG \cup OG$.
- **consolidate:** Mapping of a set of attribute name, value pairs which may contain multiple instances of the same name to a set of attribute name, value pairs where each name occurs only once. Value sets are unioned together for pairs with the same attribute name. *consolidate* is defined as:

$$consolidate(x) = \{(n, v_1 \cup v_2) \mid (n, v_1) \in x \wedge (n, v_2) \in x\}$$

where x is sets of attribute name, value pairs, n is an attribute name, v_1 and v_2 are sets of values.
- **member:** Mapping of a User or Object to the set of groups for which they are a member. *member* is defined as:

$$member(x) = \begin{cases} \{(n, u, p) \mid (n, u, p) \in UG \wedge x \in u\}, & \text{if } x \in U \\ \{(n, o, p) \mid (n, o, p) \in OG \wedge x \in o\}, & \text{if } x \in O \end{cases}$$

where n is the name of a group, u is a subset of U, o is a subset of O, p is a subset of UG or OG and $x \in U \cup O$.
- **inherited:** Mapping of a user, object or group to its set of inherited attributes (i.e. the set of attributes assigned indirectly through the group hierarchy or group membership). *inherited* is defined as:

$$inherited(x) = consolidate($$
$$\begin{cases} \{(n, v) \mid g \in member(x) \wedge (n, v) \in consolidate(direct(g) \cup inherited(g))\}, & \text{if } x \in U \cup O \\ \{(n, v) \mid g \in parents(x) \wedge (n, v) \in consolidate(direct(g) \cup inherited(g))\}, & \text{if } x \in UG \cup OG \\ \emptyset, & \text{if } name(x) = min\_group \end{cases}$$
$$)$$

where $parents(x)$ is the set of parents for the given group, n is an attribute name, v is a set of valid values for n and $x \in O \cup U \cup UG \cup OG$.

- **effective:** Mapping of a user, object, or group to their effective attributes (i.e. all attributes inherited or directly assigned). *effective* is defined as:

$$effective(x) = consolidate(direct(x) \cup inherited(x))$$

where x is a user, object or group (i.e. $x \in U \cup O \cup OG \cup UG$).

- **name:** Mapping of a group or attribute to its assigned name. *name* is defined as:

$$name(x) = x_{(1)}$$

that is, the name is the first element of the tuple in both the case of groups and attributes, and $x \in OG \cup UG \cup TA$.

- **parents:** Mapping of a group to its set of parents. *parents* is defined as:

$$parents(x) = x_{(3)}$$

that is, the set of a groups where parents is the third element of the tuple in both the case of user and object groups, and $x \in OG \cup UG$.

- **authorized:** $P, S, O \rightarrow \{true, false, undef\}$
  Function which determines if a user session passes the given policy given the current value of the environment and administrative attributes for a given object, where P is the set of all policies, S is the set of all sessions and O is the set of all objects. *true* and *false* are returned as expected based on the evaluation of the boolean policy rule; *undef* is returned if the policy cannot be evaluated (e.g. an object or user attribute referred to in the policy is not present in the attribute sets or incompatible types are compared).

Group Graph. HGABAC represents the group hierarchy as a directed acyclic graph with each group a vertex and each edge a parent/child relation between the groups such that the edge is directed to the parent. Additionally, all paths in the graph must eventually end at a special *min_group* that has no parents and no assigned attributes. A group, g, can only have *min_group* as a parent if it has one and only one parent such that $effective(g) = direct(g)$ and $inherited(g) = \emptyset$. The parent/child relation between any two related groups is defined such that group c is a child of group p iff:

$$\forall (n, v_1) \in \text{effective(p)}:$$
$$\exists! a \in \text{effective(c)}: a = (n, v_2) \text{ and } v_1 \subseteq v_2$$

A child group must have one attribute for each effective attribute assigned to the parent group, such that the attribute has the same name and the parent's attribute's value is a subset of the child's attribute's value. Thus, the effective attributes for a group, g, are calculated as:

$$effective(g) = consolidate(direct(g) \cup inherited(g))$$

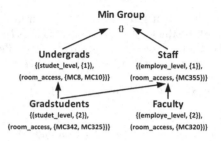

Fig. 2. Example user group hierarchy represented as a graph. The large bold text denotes the group's name, beneath which the set of directly assigned attributes is shown.

Users' and objects' effective attributes are calculated in a similar way, consolidating the values of directly assigned and inherited attributes.

An example user group hierarchy is shown in Fig. 2. In this example the set of effective attributes of groups *Undergrad* and *Staff* are the same as their set of direct attributes as they both inherit from *min_group*. The group *Faculty* inherits the attributes (*employe_level*, {1}) and (*room_access*, {MC355}) from the group *Staff* such that the effective attributes of *Faculty* will be (*employe_level*, {2, 1}) and (*room_access*, {MC320, MC355}). Similarly, the group *Gradstudents* inherits attributes from both the groups *Undergrads* and *Staff* such that the set of effective attributes for *Gradstudents* is {(*employe_level*, {1}), (*student_level*, {1, 2}), (*room_access*, {MC325, MC342, MC8, MC10, MC355})}.

The object group hierarchy has the same properties as the user group hierarchy (being a directed acyclic graph, etc.), and is set up in a similar way with a *min_group* place holder being the ancestor of all object groups. In implementations, of HGABAC it is likely that both the user and object group graphs could be consolidated into a single graph with the same *min_group* and treated similarly (e.g. with the same functions/operations) so long as constraints are enforced so no object group may inherit from a user group and no object group may have a user attribute assigned (and vice versa).

3.2   Policy Language

In HGABAC access control decisions are based on a boolean rule based policy language comparing attributes and constants. The result of logical operations (AND, OR, NOT) on ternary values (TRUE, FALSE, UNDEF) are determined based on the AND, OR and NOT truth tables from Kleene K3 logic [9]. A policy evaluated to UNDEF is equivalent to FALSE in terms of access control decisions (i.e. access is denied). Comparison operations ($<$, $>$, etc.) result in TRUE or FALSE as expected when value types are comparable (e.g. $1 < 2$ results in TRUE) and UNDEF when incomparable (e.g. *"Pizza"* > 3.1415). The following definition of the policy language is given using ABNF syntax:

```
policy   = exp [ bool_op policy ]
         / ( policy )
```

```
exp        =  var op var
           /  [ "NOT" ] bool_var
           /  [ "NOT" ] "(" policy ")"
var        =  const / att_name
bool_var   =  boolean / att_name
op         =  ">" / "<" / "=" / ">=" / "<=" / "! =" / "IN" / "SUBSET"
bool_op    =  "AND" / "OR"
att_name   =  user_att_name / object_att_name / env_att_name / admin_att_name
           /  connect_att_name
user_att_name    =  "user." id
object_att_name  =  "object." id
env_att_name     =  "env." id
admin_att_name   =  "admin." id
connect_att_name =  "connect." id
atomic     =  int / float / string / "NULL"
const      =  atomic / set
boolean    =  "TRUE" / "FALSE" / "UNDEF"
set        =  "{" "}" / "{" setval "}"
setval     =  atomic / atomic "," setval
id         =  +(ALPHA / DIGIT / "_")
int        =  ["-"] ( 1-9 ) *( DIGIT ) / "0"
float      =  int "." +( DIGIT )
string     =  DQUOTE *( %x20-21 / %x23-7E ) DQUOTE
```

user_att_name and *object_att_name* correspond to attribute names in *UA* and *OA* respectively, while *env_att_name*, *admin_att_name* and *connect_att_name* correspond to attribute names in EA, AA and CA respectively. *string* are c-style strings limited to printable characters. Otherwise, our policy language functions like c-style boolean statements where the only variables are attributes.

The following are example policy strings using the HGABAC policy language:

(a) *user.id* IN {5, 72, 4, 6, 4} OR *user.id = object.owner*

(b) *object.required_perms* SUBSET *user.perms* AND *user.age* $>=$ 18

(c) *user.admin* OR (*user.role* = "doctor" AND *user.id* ! $=$ *object.patient*)

Policy string *a* would only return true when processed by the *authorized* function, if the user attribute *id* is present and has at least one value matching an element in the given set {5, 72, 4, 6, 4} or has a value that is equal to a value in *object.owner*. Note that the value of the attribute *user.id* may be a set of multiple values, which would still pass the policy so long as $\exists e \in user.id$: $e \in \{5, 72, 4, 6, 4\}$ or $e = object.owner$. Policy string *b* would limit access to a user who is at least 18 and has the set of permissions such that the object's *required_perms* is a subset. Finally, policy string *c* demonstrates a possible use case, where you desire to give doctors access to any medical record but their own (as well as allow a user with the admin attribute to access any record).

4 Examples and Evaluation

4.1 Example: The Library

This section outlines how HGABAC may be used to provide access control for a hypothetical university library. In the following use cases it is assumed that access control is desired on four different kinds of resources provided by the library; books, course material (textbooks, lecture notes, etc.), periodicals, and archived records.

Case 1: Undergraduate students may check out any unrestricted book and any course materials for a course in which they are enrolled.

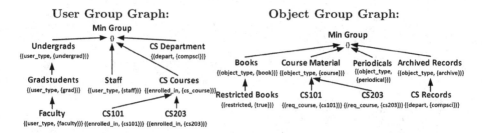

Fig. 3. User and object group hierarchies to support the cases given in Sect. 4.1.

Case 2: Graduate students may check out any unrestricted book or periodical but may only check out course materials for courses in which they are a teaching assistant or enrolled.

Case 3: Faculty may check out any book, periodical or course material as well as any archived record from their department.

Case 4: Staff may access any resource between the hours of 8:00 and 17:00 on weekdays.

Case 5: Students enrolled in a computer science course may access periodicals from the university network.

Group Graphs. Figure 3 shows the the user and object group hierarchies that would be created by an administrator for the above example and cases.

Group Membership. Users are assigned to one of the four user_type groups (Undergrads, Gradstudents, Faculty or Staff) as expected (i.e. undergraduate students are members of the "Undergrads" group, graduate students to the "Gradstudents" group, etc.). Students are also assigned membership in a user group for each course they are enrolled in (e.g. if a student is enrolled in CS203 they would be a member of the user group "CS203"). Graduate students and faculty also belong to a department group (for the purposes of these cases, only a computer science department group, "CS Department", is considered). For example a computer science graduate student taking the course CS203 would be a member of the "Gradstudents","CS203" and "CS Department" groups and would have the effective attributes {{ *user_type*, { *undergrad, grad*}}, { *enrolled_in*, { *cs_course, cs203*}}, { *depart*, { *compsci*}}.

Resources are assigned membership in one of the four object_type groups or one of their children as expected (i.e. books are assigned to the "Books" group or the "Restricted Books" group, course material to one of the course object groups (e.g. "CS101"), etc.). For example a textbook for the course CS101 would be assigned to the "CS101" object group and would have the following effective attributes {{ *object_type*, { *course*}}, { *req_course*, { *cs101*}}}.

Case 1. One permission pair would be sufficient for meeting the requirements of the case: $PERMS=\{\{$ ""*undergrad*" IN *user.user_type* AND (($object.object\_type$ = "*book*" AND NOT $object.restricted$) OR ($object.object\_type$ = "*course*" AND *user.enrolled_in IN object.req_course))"*, *check_out_book*}} where "check_out_book" is the operation that allows a resource to be read/viewed.

Case 2. In this case each graduate student would be assigned an attribute "teaching" containing the set of courses the graduate student is assigned to as a TA. The following permission pair combined with the pair from Case 1 would be sufficient for meeting the requirements of the case: *PERMS = {{ ""grad" IN user.user_type AND (object.object_type = "periodical" OR (object.object_type = "course" AND object.req_course IN user.teaching))"*, *check_out_book*}}. As the "Gradstudents" group is a child of the "Undergrads" group, graduate students are granted access to unrestricted books and course materials for courses they are enrolled in through the policy permission pair in Case 1 (as they have both the values "grad" and "undergrad" for their user_type attribute).

Case 3. As this case is less restrictive than the previous it can be met by a straightforward permission pair: *PERMS = {{ ""faculty" IN user.user_type AND (object.object_type IN { "book", "periodical", "course"} OR (object.object_type = "archive" AND object.depart IN user.depart))"*, *check_out_book*}}.

Case 4. For this case at least two environment attributes are required. "time_of_day_hour", that represents the current hour (1 to 24) and, "day_of_week", that represents the current day of the week (1 to 7). Then the following permission pair would be sufficient for meeting the requirements for the case: *PERMS = {{ ""staff" IN user.user_type AND env.time_of_day_hour >= 8 AND env.time_of_day_hour <= 16 AND env.day_of_week IN {2, 3, 4, 5, 6}"*, *check_out_book*}}.

Case 5. It is assumed that four connection attributes exist which represent the user's IP address; "ip_octet_1" represents the first digit of the user's IP address, "ip_octet_2", the second and so on up to "ip_octet_4". It is also assumed that all IP addresses matching the pattern "192.168.*.*" are internal addresses on the university's network. The following permission pair would then be sufficient for meeting the requirements of the case: *PERMS = {{ ""cs_course" IN user.enrolled_in AND connect.ip_octet_1 = 192 AND connect.ip_octet_2 = 168 AND object.object_type = "periodical" "*, *check_out_book*}}.

4.2 Evaluation

To evaluate whether the hierarchical user and object groups of the HGABAC model provides an advantage over more traditional non hierarchical models of ABAC in terms of simplifying administration and reducing complexity, we evaluate HGABAC based on the number of attribute and group assignments needed to fulfill the requirements of each use case given in Sect. 4.1. These results are compared to the number of attribute assignments that would be required in a non hierarchical model of ABAC such as $ABAC_\alpha$ [8] (if $ABAC_\alpha$ supported environment and connection attributes required to model cases 4 and 5).

Table 2 outlines the results of this comparison. The worst case (each user is enrolled in each course and each object is of an object_type such that it will

Table 2. Number of attribute and group assignments required for each case in Sect. 4.1. U is the number of users and O is the number of objects.

	Case 1		Case 2		Case 3	
	HGABAC	ABAC	HGABAC	ABAC	HGABAC	ABAC
User attribute assignments	4	$4U$	$U + 5$	$5U$	4	$2U$
Object attribute assignments	5	$2O$	6	$2O$	8	$2O$
User group assignments	$3U$	0	$3U$	0	$2U$	0
Object group assignments	O	0	O	0	O	0
Total assignments	$3U + O + 9$	$4U + 2O$	$4U + O + 11$	$5U + 2O$	$2U + O + 12$	$2U + 2O$
	Case 4		Case 5			
	HGABAC	ABAC	HGABAC	ABAC		
User attribute assignments	1	U	1	U		
Object attribute assignments	0	0	1	O		
User group assignments	U	0	U	0		
Object group assignments	0	0	O	0		
Total assignments	$U + 1$	U	$U + O + 2$	$U + O$		

have the most attributes) is assumed as well as a constant number of courses and departments (the same number shown in the group graphs in Fig. 3). In cases 1, 2 and 3 where it is required that multiple attributes be assigned to each object and user, HGABAC has a noticeable advantage as hierarchical groups allow multiple attributes to be assigned with a single group membership assignment. This also has significant advantages for administration of ABAC systems, for example if an administrative tasks required adding an attribute to every student in a given course, only a single additional attribute assignment to the course's user group would be required in HGABAC, while a new attribute assignment for every user in the course would be required in traditional ABAC. Cases 4, and 5 take less advantage of HGABAC's group hierarchy, instead making use of connection and environment attributes, and as such results in HGABAC having a comparable performance to traditional ABAC but with a slight overhead due to the object and user groups.

5   Emulating Traditional Models

5.1   DAC Style Configuration

HGABAC can be configured to emulate DAC by assigning each user an "id" attribute with a single value equal to a unique identifier for that user and assigning each object an attribute for each access mode (e.g. "read" and "write") that contains the set of user ids corresponding to users who have access to that object for the given access mode. The set of permissions are then simply: $PERMS = \{($ "user.id IN object.read", read$), ($ "user.id IN object.write", write$)\}$. To model DAC style administration, an "owner" attribute maybe added to objects that contains a single user id corresponding to the owner of the object. The permission to grant access on administrative operations is then simply: ("user.id = object.owner", admin_operation).

5.2 MAC Style Configuration

HGABAC's user groups allow configurations that emulate MAC style lattice based access control. For example given the following MAC lattice:

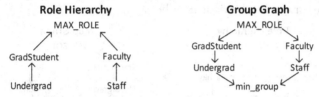

The user group graph may be configured as follows to enable MAC with a liberal *-property where each user is assigned only to a single read group and a single write group. This is similar to how RBAC is configured to emulate MAC in [13]. Each read group is assigned a single attribute named "read" and each write group is assigned a single attribute named "write" both with a single value equal to its clearance level (e.g. group UR is assigned the value { "UR"} for its "read" attribute). Each object is assigned a security level attribute named "level". The set of permissions are then simply: $PERMS = \{($ "object.level IN user.read", read$), ($ "object.level IN user.write", write$)\}$. Users are limited to only activating attributes inherited from groups of a single security level in any given session. The following table shows direct(g) and effective(g) for each group:

g	direct(g)	effective(g)
min_group	∅	∅
UR	"UR"	"UR"
C_1R	"C1R"	"UR", "C1R"
C_2R	"C2R"	"UR", "C2R"
S_1R	"S1R"	"UR", "C1R", "S1R"
S_2R	"S2R"	"UR", "C1R", "C2R", "S2R"
S_3R	"S3R"	"UR", "C2R", "S3R"
TSR	"TSR"	"UR", "C1R", "C2R", "S1R", "S2R", "S3R", "TSR"
TSW	"TSW"	"TSW"

(Continued)

g	direct(g)	effective(g)
S_1W	"S1W"	"TSW", "S1W"
S_2W	"S2W"	"TSW", "S2W"
S_3W	"S2W"	"TSW", "S3W"
C_1W	"C1W"	"TSW", "S1W", "S2W", "C1W"
C_2W	"C2W"	"TSW", "S2W", "S3W", "C2W"
UW	"UW"	"TSW", "S1W", "S2W", "S3W", "C1W", "C2W", "UW"

5.3 RBAC Style Configuration

HGABAC's user groups can also effectively enforce hierarchical RBAC style access control by having each user group represent a role and its assigned attributes, represent permissions. For example given the following role hierarchy, the user group graph on the right may be used:

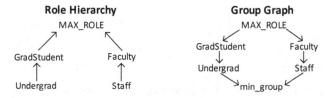

Each group is assigned a single attribute named "perms" that contains the set of permissions that group grants. Objects are tagged with an attribute for each access mode whose value contains the set of permissions that grant permission to perform that access mode on the object. For example, an object may have a "read" attribute with values p_1 and p_4 and a "write" attribute with values p_2 and p_3. The set of permissions are then simply: $PERMS = \{($"user.perms IN object.read", read$), ($"user.perms IN object.write", write$)\}$ assuming the only access modes are read and write.

If the roles in the above example role hierarchy have the following directly assigned permissions, then the groups in the user group graph will have the following direct and effective values for the attribute "perms":

Role	Direct Permissions
Undergrad	P_1
Staff	P_2
GradStudent	P_3, P_4
Faculty	P_5, P_6
MAX_ROLE	$\emptyset$

g	direct(g)	effective(g)
min_group	$\emptyset$	$\emptyset$
$Undergrad$	P_1	P_1
$Staff$	P_2	P_2
$GradStudent$	P_3, P_4	P_1, P_3, P_4
$Faculty$	P_5, P_6	P_2, P_5, P_6
MAX_ROLE	$\emptyset$	$P_1, P_2, P_3, P_4, P_5, P_6$

While this enables HGABAC to emulate core and hierarchical RBAC (as defined in the NIST RBAC standard [6]), work towards emulating the separation of duty style constraints possible in NIST RBAC is left to future work.

6 Conclusions and Future Work

We have introduced a new model of ABAC, entitled HGABAC, that supports boolean rule based ABAC, hierarchical user and object groups, as well as environment, connection and administrative attributes. We show that adding user and object groups enables greater flexibility when modelling real world situations in addition to simplifying administration.

Future work in terms of formalizing a model of ABAC should largely consist of extending HGABAC to support features required for real world use of ABAC systems. Some potential additions include support for separation of duty, delegation, and access control for administrative functions. Expanding the policy language defined in Sect. 3.2 or alternatively exploring using XACML in it's place could lead to greater flexibility in supported policies. To achieve the full potential of ABAC, further automation is needed in terms of attribute assignment and group membership. The addition of conditional user and object group membership could also have interesting applications and implications that are worthy of future research.

References

1. Bell, D., Padula, L.: Secure Computer Systems: Mathematical Foundations and Model. Mitre, Bedford (1974)
2. Bethencourt, J., Sahai, A., Waters, B.: Ciphertext-policy attribute-based encryption. In: IEEE Symposium on Security and Privacy, SP 2007, pp. 321–334. IEEE (2007)
3. Chandran, S.M., Joshi, J.B.D.: *LoT-RBAC*: a location and time-based RBAC model. In: Ngu, A.H.H., Kitsuregawa, M., Neuhold, E.J., Chung, J.-Y., Sheng, Q.Z. (eds.) WISE 2005. LNCS, vol. 3806, pp. 361–375. Springer, Heidelberg (2005)
4. Chen, L., Crampton, J.: Risk-aware role-based access control. In: Meadows, C., Fernandez-Gago, C. (eds.) STM 2011. LNCS, vol. 7170, pp. 140–156. Springer, Heidelberg (2012)
5. Denning, D.E.: A lattice model of secure information flow. Commun. ACM **19**(5), 236–243 (1976)
6. Ferraiolo, D.F., Sandhu, R., Gavrila, S., Kuhn, D.R., Chandramouli, R.: Proposed NIST standard for role-based access control. ACM Trans. Inf. Syst. Secur. (TISSEC) **4**(3), 224–274 (2001)
7. Godik, S., Anderson, A., Parducci, B., Humenn, P., Vajjhala, S.: OASIS extensible access control 2 markup language (XACML) 3. Technical report, OASIS (2002)
8. Jin, X., Krishnan, R., Sandhu, R.: A unified attribute-based access control model covering DAC, MAC and RBAC. In: Cuppens-Boulahia, N., Cuppens, F., Garcia-Alfaro, J. (eds.) DBSec 2012. LNCS, vol. 7371, pp. 41–55. Springer, Heidelberg (2012)
9. Kleene, S.C.: On notation for ordinal numbers. J. Symb. Log. **3**(4), 150–155 (1938)
10. Kuhn, D.R., Coyne, E.J., Weil, T.R.: Adding attributes to role-based access control. IEEE Comput. **43**(6), 79–81 (2010)
11. Lampson, B.W.: Protection. ACM SIGOPS Oper. Syst. Rev. **8**(1), 18–24 (1974)
12. Lang, B., Foster, I., Siebenlist, F., Ananthakrishnan, R., Freeman, T.: A flexible attribute based access control method for grid computing. J. Grid Comput. **7**(2), 169–180 (2009)
13. Osborn, S., Sandhu, R., Munawer, Q.: Configuring role-based access control to enforce mandatory and discretionary access control policies. ACM Trans. Inf. Syst. Secur. (TISSEC) **3**(2), 85–106 (2000)

14. Sandhu, R.S., Coyne, E.J., Feinstein, H.L., Youman, C.E.: Role-based access control models. Computer **29**(2), 38–47 (1996)
15. Servos, D.: A role and attribute based encryption approach to privacy and security in cloud based health services. Master's thesis, Lakehead University (2012)
16. Servos, D., Mohammed, S., Fiaidhi, J., Kim, T.-H.: Extensions to ciphertext-policy attribute-based encryption to support distributed environments. Int. J. Comput. Appl. Technol. **47**(2), 215–226 (2013)
17. Shen, H.-B., Hong,F.: An attribute-based access control model for web services. In: Seventh International Conference on Parallel and Distributed Computing, Applications and Technologies, PDCAT 2006, pp. 74–79. IEEE (2006)
18. Wang, L., Wijesekera, D., Jajodia,S.: A logic-based framework for attribute based access control. In Proceedings of the 2004 ACM Workshop on Formal Methods in Security Engineering, pp. 45–55. ACM (2004)
19. Yuan, E., Tong, J.: Attributed based access control (ABAC) for web services. In: Proceedings of the 2005 IEEE International Conference on Web Services, ICWS 2005. IEEE (2005)

Logical Method for Reasoning About Access Control and Data Flow Control Models

Luigi Logrippo[⊠]

Département d'informatique et d'ingénierie,
Université du Québec en Outaouais, Gatineau, QC J8X 3X7, Canada
luigi@uqo.ca

Abstract. Some logic definitions applicable to a variety of access control and data flow control models are proposed. A formalization of concepts of confidentiality and integrity is provided, on the basis of predicates CanKnow and CanStore. The application of these concepts is demonstrated for simplified versions of the following models: Coalitions, Multi-Level Systems, Role-Based Access Control, High Water Mark, Chinese Wall. Formal definitions and proofs of invariant properties of these models in terms of our concepts are given. It will then appear that these models have many possible variations and combinations of which only few have been studied. These concepts can be useful for developing proofs on access control models, automatically or manually, for developing new models, and for teaching access control and data flow control concepts.

Keywords: Access control · Flow control · Formal methods · Logic · Invariants

1 Introduction

In order to perform operations on data *objects* (typically, *reading* from them or *writing* on them, according to the well-known UNIX data protection primitives) *subjects* must secure the authorization of access control systems. Some of these systems are concerned not only about single accesses, but also about propagation of data (*flow control*).

The theory of access control systems has generated extensive literature. Given the importance of the access control function, it is generally agreed that such systems have to be built according to solid *formal methods*. Many such methods have been proposed. The logic of the *models* underlying such systems has often been specified in formal terms, and proofs have been provided of their soundness.

However, there is no agreement on what kind of logic methods can be used in order to prove properties of these models. Different authors use different concepts and methods, tailored to the specific model they are discussing. In standard textbooks [5], the various models are presented with different formalisms. The result is conceptual fragmentation in the area, which makes it difficult to isolate basic concepts and to combine solutions.

In this paper, we identify some basic access control and data flow control concepts that can be used for characterizing the properties of abstract models and for providing their proofs. The concepts are intuitive and are shown to be general enough to deal with

© Springer International Publishing Switzerland 2015
F. Cuppens et al. (Eds.): FPS 2014, LNCS 8930, pp. 205–220, 2015.
DOI: 10.1007/978-3-319-17040-4_13

several of the classical models of access control. In order to keep proofs simple and the paper within page limits, these models have been reduced to their minimal characteristics and adapted to our method. Also, proofs are sketchier or omitted for the more complex models.

We concentrate on proving properties of confidentiality and integrity, for which we propose our own formal definitions. According to an often cited source [17], *confidentiality* is related to disclosure of information, while *integrity* is related to modification of information. In our formal method, confidentiality defines what subjects can know, and integrity defines what objects can contain. We are aware of the fact that these two terms are often used with more complex meanings. Our definitions arise from our concepts and do not attempt to fully capture these meanings.

These properties can be also seen as *requirements* that can be proven to be *invariant* for the models because of the access control rules.

After a brief literature review in Sect. 2, the main ideas of this paper are presented in Sect. 3. The following sections present case studies to show the range of applicability of the method and can be read independently, with the exception mentioned in Sect. 11. An easy application is coalitions, Sect. 4. Upward multilayer models, with their counterpart, downward multilayer models, are presented in Sects. 5 and 6. Section 7 presents a model for categories or domain powersets as we call them. If incompatibilities between domains are defined, then we obtain a sort of static Chinese Wall model, presented in Sect. 8. A very simplified RBAC model is presented in Sect. 9. In Sects. 10 and 11, we deal with the dynamic models of High Water Mark and Chinese Wall. Section 12 presents prospectives of research.

2 Literature Review

Over the years, there have been many contributions on logic formalisms and formal methods for access control models. Most of these contributions addressed specific models and applications. Others were more general but went in directions that are orthogonal to ours. Abadi has written many papers on this general subject, but addressing subjects such as authentication, cryptography, security protocols and languages for programming security policies. A survey paper published in 2003 can be used as introduction to his work [1]. Bertino et al. [4] developed a logical framework "to evaluate and compare the expressive power of access control models", which is not the purpose of our paper. Similar goals inspired the work of Habib, Jaume and Morisset [9, 12]. Barker [2, 3] has developed a general logic framework for the modeling of access control, but his main focus were policy systems, rather than reasoning about access control and flow control properties of models as in our paper. Crampton et al. [6] presented a logic for automated tools "to assist in reasoning about the effects of an access control mechanism on the computations performed by an operating system". Cuppens and Demolombe [7] developed a modal logic framework to specify confidentiality policies. They addressed indirect channels such as deductive and abductive ones.

Combining these approaches with ours will be the subject of future research.

The access control models we discuss are well-known textbook models [5, 8]. We refer to these sources for citations and background information. As mentioned, the usual definitions are adapted to our method.

3   Basic Concepts for Our Logical Method

Our method uses seven basic concepts:

- Three kinds of entities: Subjects, Objects, Data Variables. The objects model files or databases, and data variables stand for data values contained in the objects.
- Two relationships between subjects or objects and data variables, respectively CanKnow and CanStore
- Two relationships that express access control constraints or rules between subjects and objects: CanRead, CanWrite.

We will see that this is enough to define several basic access control models and prove some of their main properties. Other more complex models may require additional concepts. We will see that the High Water Mark and Chinese Wall models will require the notions of state and state transitions caused by read and write operations.

We use the letters S, O and x with various primes or numerals to denote variables over respectively subjects, objects and data items (indexes will be used later to express states). We also use the following abbreviations:

CK for CanKnow, CS for CanStore, CR for CanRead, CW for CanWrite

A simple example will introduce the idea of our method. Consider a system with two subjects S1, S2 and two objects, O1 and O2. Suppose that we have the following access control relationships:

CR(S1,O1), CW(S1,O2), CR(S2,O2).

Suppose also that CS(O1,x) is given unconditionally, so we know that x is in O1. Then S1 can read x from O1 and store it in O2. S2 can then read x from O2. We can conclude that CS(O2,x) and CK(S2,x).

In other words, subjects can know values by reading them from the data objects they are authorized to read, and objects can store values that are written on them by subjects authorized to do so. In order for something to be known or stored at all in a system we must also assume that some subjects can know something or some objects can store something at some point and this will be expressed by *unconditional relationships*.

Security research knows methods for passing information between subjects without using intermediate objects, as first discussed in [13]. A reference that uses a logical point of view is [7]. Our method does not consider explicitly these methods, and so does not attempt to cover information flow in its generic meaning but is open to the addition of other entities and rules.

Table 1 defines the deduction rules for our method. The rule for CK expresses the fact that if there exists an object that can store a value and a subject can read that object, then the subject can know the value. The rule for CS deals with storing and is similar. The rules of Table 1 will be used throughout this paper, although for readability we will use their intuitive meaning in place of their logic formulation. A translation into symbolic notation should always be possible.

We also use the auxiliary functions CSS and CKS, as follows:

For any S, *CanKnowSet(S)* or *CKS(S)* is the set of data variables x for which CK (S,x) is true: $CKS(S) =_{def} \{x \mid CK(S,x) = true\}$

For any O, *CanStoreSet(O)* or *CSS(O)* is the set of data variables x for which CS (O,x) is true: $CSS(S) =_{def} \{x \mid CS(S,x) = true\}$.

We will use both the notation based on CS and CK binary predicates and the notation based on CKS and CSS sets. These two notations are equivalent, e.g. the deductive rules of Table 1 could be expressed in terms of sets, but in intuitive terms one notation is sometimes more clear than the other. E.g. it may be easier to say: S can know x rather than saying: x is in the set that can be known by S. On the other hand it is easier to say that S can know everything that S' can rather than saying that for all x, etc. The set notation will be used in order to define the confidentiality and integrity properties.

Concerning logical notation, in order to simplify the expressions, we omit universal quantifiers. Variables that are not existentially quantified should be assumed to be universally quantified outside the expression. This implies that several free occurrences of the same variable in an expression refer to the same entity. This is a common convention in algebra and logic.

A key element of our logic method is the use of *variable labelling*, e.g. in the next section we use the notation *O:D* to denote object O belonging to domain D. These labels can be thought of as types, since they regulate the use of read and write operations for the variables that are associated with them, by means of CR and CW predicates. However we will not make use of type theory concepts. Our use of labels is inspired by [14] but we are not attempting in this paper to establish a relationship between our method and the method of [14].

We should clarify the role of these labels in implementations of the models described by our method. If a label is used in the access control rules of a model, then it should be available in the implementation, e.g. for the model of the next section the implementation should have available the labels indicating the domains of subjects S or objects O. Otherwise, the label is there only for our proofs, to show the provenance of entities, e.g. in the next section x:D means that data variable x belongs to domain D but an implementation of the model does not need to know this, since the access control rules do not use it. There are security models in which the labels of data variables should be available to the implementation, such is the one of [14].

To lighten the notation we also write variables without labels. This means: any possible label, according to the context. For example in Table 1, x, S and O have no labels which means that the rules apply for any labels, still subject to the rule that if there are several free occurrences of the same variable in an expression, they refer to the same entity and so all such occurrences are understood to have the same label.

Table 1. Deductive system

• *Unconditional relationships* are expressed in the form: CK(S,x) or CS(O,x)
• The *inference rule for CK* is:
$\qquad \exists O\ (CS(O,x) \wedge CR(S,O)) \Rightarrow CK(S,x)$
$\qquad$ (if O can store x and S can read from O, then S can know x)
• The *inference rule for CS* is:
$\qquad \exists S\ (CK(S,x) \wedge CW(S,O)) \Rightarrow CS(O,x)$
$\qquad$ (if S can know x and S can write on O, then O can store x)
• All CS or CK relationships must be true either unconditionally or by one of the two inference rules above.

4   Coalitions

The study of coalitions is a first application of our method. It is very simple, but introduces a concept that is useful in practice and provides a good introduction to our method. The main properties of coalitions will hold, with appropriate changes, for other models that will be discussed later.

Coalitions model collaborating organizations that share data. A *coalition* is a set of *domains* that are mutually compatible. Data, subjects and objects belong to specific domains but subjects can read or write from or to other objects of their coalition. So an object will store values only from its own coalition. For example, in a coalition of banks, each bank has its own customers, but all banks can read from each other's databases and so can know and store all the data of all the members of the coalition.

Coalitions in their elementary form presented here are not mentioned in the literature. Some papers have considered information sharing schemes with relation to Role-Based Access Control. Other papers study organizational and collaborative issues related to coalitions, spontaneous coalitions, coalitions in social networks, etc., issues which are beyond the scope of this paper. We give coalitions their place in our catalogue of basic models of access control.

To formalize the notion of coalitions, we use the following notation and conventions:

- S:D, O:D, x:D are variables for subjects, objects and values belonging to domain D
- For each D, we assume that there is at least one S:D, one O:D and one x:D
- $D \approx D =_{def} D$ and D' belong to the *same coalition*: this an equivalence relation that is supposed to be known for a given system.

We assume that for each data variable x:D we have at least one of the following two:

- an unconditional relationship of the form CK(S:D, x:D) stating that subject S:D can know x:D
- an unconditional relationship of the form CS(O:D, x:D) stating that object O:D can store x:D

The access control rules and the confidentiality and integrity properties for coalitions are given in Table 2:

Table 2. Access control rules and properties for coalitions

- (Read rule) CR(S:D, O:D') ↔ D≈D'   (a subject can read from an object iff they are in the same coalition)
- (Write rule) CW(S:D, O:D') ↔ D≈D'   (a subject can write on an object iff they are in the same coalition)
- (Confidentiality property): x:D∈CKS(S:D') ↔ D≈D' (a value belonging to one domain can be known in another domain iff the two domains are members of the same coalition).
- (Integrity property): x:D∈CSS(O:D') ↔ D≈D' (a value belonging to one domain can be stored in another domain iff the two domains are members of the same coalition).

The contents of Table 2 can be taken in one of two ways: one could start from the access control rules and prove that the confidentiality and integrity properties are invariant by the rules. Or one could start from the desired properties and derive the rules. Here we take the first avenue and we leave the second for future research. We have the following results, note that several of them are independent of the label of x.

Property 1: (Pervasiveness of data values in a domain): CK(S:D, x) ↔ CS(O:D, x)

Proof: Any S:D can write on any O:D and any S:D can read from any O:D.   □

The following properties extend the pervasiveness to all domains in a coalition

Property 2: D ≈ D' → (CK(S:D, x) ↔ CK(S:D', x))

Property 3: D ≈ D' → (CS(O:D, x) ↔ CS(O:D', x))

Property 4: D ≈ D' → (CK(S:D, x) ↔ CS(O:D', x))

Proofs: They are similar for all three. If a subject in a coalition can know any value, then it can write the value in an object in the same coalition, from which it can be read by another subject in the coalition, etc.   □

Property 5: (Main coalition property): (CK(S:D, x:D') ∨ CS(O:D, x:D')) ↔ D ≈ D'

Proof for → : This property can be true unconditionally and then D = D'. Other CK or CS relationships can be inferred from the unconditional ones only by using CK or CS inference rules. The access control rules ensure that D ≈ D' at each inference, and ≈ is transitive.

Proof for ← : Both consequences are simultaneously true, and the proofs are similar. Let us prove only D ≈ D' → CK(S:D, x:D'). By the unconditional relationships, there must exist a subject S:D' that knows x:D' or an object O:D' that stores it. In the first case, x:D' can be written on a O:D'. Since D ≈ D', S:D can read from it. In the second case, no write is necessary and S:D can read directly from O:D'.   □

The following corollary is another way to write the confidentiality and integrity properties of Table 2.

Corollary: CK(S:D, x:D') ↔ D ≈ D' and CS(O:D, x:D') ↔ D ≈ D'

In view of the previous results, we can strengthen the three pervasiveness properties to 'if and only if'. Let us take the first one, and the other two follow in similar ways:

Property 2': (CK(S:D, x) ↔ CK(S:D', x)) ↔ D ≈ D'

Proof: the ← part was Property 2, now for (CK(S:D, x) ↔ CK(S:D', x)) → D ≈ D'. This means proving: (CK(S:D, x:D") ↔ CK(S:D', x:D")) → D≈D'. By the Corollary, D ≈ D" and D' ≈ D" so D ≈ D'. □

This model can be varied in various ways, which we propose for further study. For example, subjects can read only from their own domain, but can write anywhere in the coalition, or: subjects can read from anywhere in the coalition, but write only in their own domain, or yet: subjects in different domains can have different read and write properties, e.g. we can have 'master' and 'slave' domains. This last variation brings us to the models considered in the next section.

5   Upward Multi-level Models (UML)

The *upward multi-level models* (UML) are characterized by partially ordered sets of security levels. On the low (high) end of the ordering we find the low (high) security classifications. These models are characterized by the requirement: *information can only move upward*, i.e. from lower to higher security classifications [17]. The well-known Bell-La Padula model (BLP henceforth) belongs to this category. The main simplification we make here is that a single set of levels is used for both security clearance and security classification. So if TopSecret > Secret, subject Alice:TopSecret can read from but not write on object MedFile:Secret.

Furthermore:

- S:L, O:L, x:L are variables for subjects, objects and data belonging to level L
- For each level L, we assume that there is at least one S:L, one O:L and one x:L

This assumption allows us to avoid having to consider some limit cases, such as levels among which no information could flow, levels holding no information of their own, etc. Without it the essential results would remain valid, but with more complicated formulation and proofs. However we don't assume that the number of levels is finite and we don't require them to form a lattice.

We assume that for each x:L we have at least one of the following two:

- an unconditional relationship of the form CK(S:L, x:L) stating that a subject S:L can know x:L
- an unconditional relationship of the form CS(O:L, x:L) stating that an object O:L can store x:L

The access control rules and the confidentiality and integrity properties for UML are given in Table 3. The latter state that a value of a certain security level cannot be known or stored at a lower security level, which is another way of saying that information can only move up.

Table 3. Access control rules and properties for Upward Multi-level models

• CR(S:L, O:L') ↔ L≥L'   (Subjects can read only at the same level or lower)
• CW(S:L, O:L') ↔ L'≥L   (Subjects can write only at the same level or higher)
• (Confidentiality) : x:L∈CKS(S:L') ↔ L≤L'
• (Integrity) :   x:L∈CSS(O:L') ↔ L≤L'

We have the following results, which should be obvious. They state the pervasiveness of data values in a level and the upward monotonicity of knowledge. They are independent of the label of x.

Property 1: CK(S:L, x) ↔ CS(O:L, x)

Property 2: L ≥ L' → (CK(S:L', x) → CK(S:L, x))

Property 3: L ≥ L' → (CS(O:L', x) → CS(O:L, x))

Property 4: L ≥ L' → (CK(S:L', x) → CS(O:L, x))

Proof of Property 2: By Property 1, an O:L' can store x. By the CR rule, S:L can read it and know it.   □

Property 5: (Main UML property): (CK(S:L, x:L') ∨ CS(O:L, x:L')) ↔ L ≥ L'

Proof for → : This property can be true unconditionally and then L = L'. Otherwise, it can be true only by CK and CR inference rules. But then L ≥ L' must be true at each inference by the access control rules and then the result follows by transitivity.

Proof for ← : By the unconditional relationships, CK(S:L', x:L') ∨ CS(O:L', x:L') for some S:L' or O:L'. Since L ≥ L', (CK(S:L, x:L') ∨ CS(O:L, x:L')) can be derived by repeated use of CK or CS inference rules. We have assumed that there are subjects and objects at every level, so data can move up.□

Property 6: (Strong monotonicity): (CK(S:L',x) → CK(S:L,x)) ↔ L ≥ L'

Proof. The ← is Property 2 and the → can be proven by contradiction. (CK(S:L', x) → CK(S:L,x)) ∧ L < L' is impossible since we have assumed that at each level, such as L', there is a variable x:L' that cannot be read from level L.   □

Property 7 and **Property 8** are corresponding 'iff' strengthening of Properties 3 and 4 and can be proven in similar ways.

We can express the same properties in terms of sets, with the *proper inclusion* operator ⊂ :

Property 6': (CKS(S:L) ⊂ CKS(S:L')) ↔ L < L'

Property 7': (CSS(O:L) ⊂ CSS(O:L')) ↔ L < L'

Property 8': (CKS(S:L) ⊂ CSS(O:L')) ↔ L < L'

The confidentiality and integrity properties of Table 3 follow as corollaries.

6 Downward Multi-level Models (DML)

We have just seen that UML models allow values to migrate to higher levels. Therefore, higher levels are not protected against information coming from lower levels. This
is usually expressed by saying that UML leads to high confidentiality but low integrity.
To protect the integrity of the upper layers, the Biba model was invented, where
information can only move downward [17]. The duality of *downward multi-level
models* (DML) with respect to UML is well-known, and we leave the proof of the
corresponding properties as an easy exercise.

We propose as interesting cases study a 'maximum integrity model' that we have
found in a company. Some important documents of this company are placed in a security
level that can be read by all, but cannot be written on. Furthermore, information
belonging to this level cannot be stored anywhere else. In this way, these documents do
not risk becoming corrupted. Note that in this model we don't have the symmetry
between confidentiality and integrity that characterizes the previous models: all levels
can know but only one can store this information. Unlike the previous models, the labels
of the data variables seem to be important in implementations of this model.

7 Domain Powerset Models (DP)

Domain powerset models (DP) are often called *category* or *compartment* models and
are combined with the UML model in the usual presentation of the BLP model.
However they deserve a place of their own because they can be combined with other
models than UML.

Let us assume that in an organization there are three domains (or categories or
compartments) of data, for example: NUC, EUR, US. Some subjects can be allowed to
access only data classified NUC, others only data classified EUR, other yet only data
classified US. We label them {NUC},{EUR},{US}. But then there may be subjects
allowed to access data classified NUC or EUR, they will be labeled {NUC, EUR} and
so upward in the powerset lattice until we find the label {NUC, EUR, US}. There may
also be subjects not allowed to access anything, labeled { }. See for this [5]. We extend
this labeling method to objects, to specify what are the domains of the values that can
be stored in them.

We will continue using D with primes for variables for domain names. Labels
Δ, Δ'... will denote sets of domains. A subject S:Δ has clearance to know only data
variables in the domains in Δ. An object O:Δ can store data belonging to any of the
domains in Δ. We also assume that there is at least one object, subject and data variable
in each of the domains.

For each variable x:D we have at least one of the following two:

- An unconditional relationship of the form CK(S:{D}, x:D)
- An unconditional relationship of the form CS(O:{D}, x:D)

The access control rules and the properties for this model are given in Table 4 and
their proofs follow by methods similar to those we have seen.

Table 4. Access control rules and properties for Domain Powerset Models

• CR(S:Δ, O:Δ') ↔ Δ'⊆Δ (a subject can read from an object iff the object can contain only data variables that the subject can know)
• CW(S:Δ, O:Δ') ↔ Δ⊆Δ' (a subject can write on an object iff the subject can know only data variables that the object can contain).
• (Confidentiality): x:D∈CKS(S:Δ) ↔ D∈Δ
• (Integrity) x:D∈CSS(O:Δ) ↔ D∈Δ

8 Domain Powersets with Conflicts (DPC)

The existence of conflicts between domains motivates this model, which is a 'static' version of the Chinese Wall model (see Sect. 11). Starting from the domain powerset model (DP), we define conflicts between domains, and then we stipulate that *subjects (objects) may not know (store) values belonging to mutually conflicting domains*: this phrase expresses the confidentiality (integrity) properties of this model. This means that labels containing conflicting domains are not allowed in DPC, neither for subjects, nor for objects. Note that after this removal, the powerset lattice of labels of the DP model is no longer a lattice. References [16, 17] present a lattice construction for Chinese Wall. This is possible for our model as well, if we agree that there could be unassignable labels.

Rather than using a conflict relationship we prefer to use its complement, the compatibility relationship, which is reflexive and symmetric. For domains D and D' we write D ~ D' if the two domains are compatible. We suppose that this relationship is known in a given organizational context. We still use labels Δ as for the DP model, but with the condition that for D, D' ∈ Δ, D ~ D'.

Because of this fact, the CR and CW relationships for the DPC model can be the same as those of the DP model in Table 4, and the confidentiality and integrity properties follow.

As an example, consider a system with two subjects, Alice and Bob, and three domains, Bank1, Bank2 and Oil. The domains are all pairwise compatible, with the exception of Bank1 and Bank2. So allowed labels are: {}, {Bank1}, {Bank2}, {Oil}, {Bank1, Oil}, {Bank2, Oil} and forbidden labels are: {Bank1, Bank2}, {Bank1, Bank2, Oil}. A possible label assignment is: Alice: {Bank1, Oil}; Bob: {Oil}; Bank1: {Bank1,Oil}; Bank2: {Bank2, Oil};Oil: {Oil}. We'll leave it as an exercise for the reader to determine the resulting CR and CW relationships.

An issue in this model is that a conservative label assignment could assign to all subjects only empty labels. This of course would come into conflict with "need to know" and availability requirements, and is a reason for the model of Sect. 11.

9 Role-Based Access Control (RBAC)

In order to present the essential idea in one page, we will consider here a drastically simplified RBAC with only subjects, objects and data variables. We will take the concept of RBAC's *role* to correspond to our concept of *subject* and subjects-roles will be called R1, R2 etc.

Subjects-roles will be labeled with their sets of permissions P, each of which will be of the form (CR,O) or (CW,O). Normally objects are not labeled in RBAC. The access control rules for RBAC are given in Table 5.

Table 5. Access control rules for RBAC

•   CR(R:P, O) ↔ CR(R,O)∈P
•   CW(R:P,O) ↔ CW(R,O)∈P

Example:

- R1:{(CR,O1),(CW,O2)}
- R2: {(CR,O1),(CR,O2)}
- R3: {(CR,O1), (CR,O2), (CW,O2), (CW,O3)}
- R4: {(CR,O3)}

We assume unconditional relationships of the form CK(Oi, xi:Oi) for each Oi. By application of the inference rules of Table 1 and the access control rules of Table 5 in the example above the following can be derived:

- CKS(R1) = {x1:O1};
- CKS(R2) = CKS (R3) = {x1:O1, x2:O2};
- CKS(R4) = {x1:O1, x2:O2, x3:O3}
- CSS(O1) = {x1:O1};
- CSS(O2) = {x1:O1, x2:O2};
- CSS(O3) = {x1:O1, x2:O2, x3:O3}

Constraints can be defined in RBAC according to the application. Here are two constraints that are violated in the previous example:

- (Confidentiality) No subject-role should be allowed to know both x1:O1 and x2:O2
- (Integrity) No object should be able to store both x1:O1 and x2:O2

A practical case for this integrity constraint could be: no cheque can bear two accountant signatures. This constraint is violated if O2 is a cheque and x1:O1, x2:O2 are accountant signatures.

Other possibilities exist for the application of this method in RBAC, but this should be the subject of another paper.

A more complete presentation requires considering mappings between users, subjects and roles, as well as mappings between roles and sets of permissions. See [15] for a thorough discussion of data flow in RBAC.

10 High Water Mark (HWM)

HWM is our first example of a dynamic model. In dynamic models, some read or write operations that are not allowed by the access control rules are still possible and lead to state changes, i.e. label changes for subjects and objects.

The HWM model is a variation of the UML model. We define it as follows (note that the usual definition is somewhat different). Writing down is possible but when this happens, the level of the object which has received the information from higher up is moved up to the level of the subject that has just written on it. Reading up is possible but as soon as a subject does this, its level is moved up correspondingly.

This model can be formalized by a state machine whose transitions are determined by read and write operations. As a consequence of the operations, subjects or objects can change levels so that the confidentiality and integrity properties of UML models can remain true. Data variables don't change labels.

We have an unbounded set of states M_0, M_1 ... $L_i(S)$ or $L_i(O)$ are the labels of S or O at state M_i. The labels denote levels as in UML and the set of levels is the same for all states. The notation CKS_i, CSS_i has similar meaning. Each one of these sets is determined by what can be read or stored at state M_i according to the access control rules of the UML model.

Note that although now the notation $S:L_i(S)$ or $O:L_i(O)$ would be formally more appropriate, we will continue to use the notation $S:L_i$ or $O:L_i$ for simplicity. A consequence is the fact that L_i is not the same in $S:L_i$ and $O:L_i$.

For the initial state M_0 and each x:L we have one of the unconditional relationships: $x:L \in CKS_0(S:L_0)$ or $x:L \in CSS_0(O:L_0)$ where $L_0 = L$.

R(S,O) and W(S,O) are respectively read and write operations of a subject on an object which cause state transitions. They are not constrained by the access control rules and have no pre-conditions, but have post-conditions.

The post-condition of a $R(S:L_i, O:L'_i)$ operation is:

- For $S:L_{i+1}$, L_{i+1} is the greatest of L_i and L'_i
- However for $O:L'_{i+1}$, $L'_{i+1} = L'_i$ (Upgrade security level of subject, but the object does not change level)
- $CKS_{i+1}(S:L_{i+1}) = CKS_i(S:L_i) \cup CSS_i(O:L'_i)$ and $CSS_{i+1}(O:L'_{i+1}) = CSSi(O:L'_i)$ (Add to what subject can know, but the object's knowledge is unchanged)

Correspondingly, the post-condition of a $W(S:L_i, O:L'_i)$ operation is:

- For $O:L'_{i+1}$, L'_{i+1} is the greatest of L_i and L'_i
- However for $S:L_{i+1}$, $L_{i+1} = L_i$
- $CKS_{i+1}(O:L'_{i+1}) = CKS_i(S:L_i) \cup CSS_i(O:L'_i)$ and $CSS_{i+1}(S:L_{i+1}) = CSS_i(S:L_i)$

Given these definitions, the confidentiality and integrity properties of Table 6 seem to be intuitively true for the HWM model, although a detailed proof will have to consider all the cases. The properties hold for the unconditional relationships at the initial state and the post-conditions for each state transition ensure their invariance.

Note that R(S,O) (or W(S,O)) operations could be executed when the access control conditions CR(S,O) (or CW(S,O)) are true. However then the initial and final states of the transition are identical.

The theory knows also a "low water mark" model in connection with DML models and the same concepts apply, with the appropriate modifications.

Table 6. Properties for HWM

• x:L∈CKS$_i$(S:L$_i$) ↔L≤L$_i$ (Confidentiality) (a variable can be known by a subject at some state iff the classification of the variable does not exceed the classification of the subject at that state) • x:L∈CSSi(O:L$_i$) ↔ L≤L$_i$ (Integrity) (a variable can be stored in an object at some state iff the classification of the variable does not exceed the classification of the object at that state)

11 Chinese Wall (ChW)

The usual definitions of ChW characterize this model in terms of constraints on reading and writing expressed by 'simple' and '*' properties [5, 16]. We start instead from the requirements, which are the same as for our DPC model, with its confidentiality and integrity properties. Unlike the DPC model, in our version of ChW subjects initially know nothing, and objects know only one domain. Subjects (objects) are allowed to acquire new information by read (write) operations and then their labels change, but these operations are allowed only if they lead to allowed labels.

There would be much to say about this model, but we limit ourselves to the minimum necessary to illustrate the application of our method. So we consider only the case where the sets of domains, subjects and objects are fixed.

The understanding of our version of ChW depends on the understanding of the DPC model (Sect. 8) and the HWM model (Sect. 10). We have a set of domains {D1, … Dn}, with a compatibility relation ~ between domains as in the DPC model. The state model is similar to the one of HWM and similar notation will be used, however here there are both pre-conditions and post-conditions for reading and writing.

Labels Δ_i are subsets of the set of domains. For S:Δ_0, Δ_0 = {} and CKS$_0$(S:Δ_0) = {}. For O:Δ_0, Δ_0 = {Dk} for some k and CSS(O:Δ_0) is the set of all x:Dk. So at the beginning subjects know nothing, and each object stores information about one domain. At each state, the access control rules are the same as for the DPC (or DP) model and determine the CKS$_i$, CSS$_i$ sets but reading and writing operations R and W are not constrained by them, they are only constrained by their pre-conditions. In S:Δ_i, Δ_i is the set of labels of data variables in CKS$_i$(S:Δ_i) and similarly for O:Δ_i.

We write Δ ~ Δ' if for D∈Δ, D'∈Δ', D ~ D'. Δ ~ Δ' is the pre-condition for both R (S:Δ, O:Δ') and W(S:Δ, O:Δ'). In the case of operation R this means that all the information that S already can know must be compatible with the all the information that O already can store, and similarly in the case of operation W.

The post-condition for R(S:Δ_i, O:Δ'_i) describes the fact that S can now know anything in O:

- For S:Δ_i, Δ_{i+1} = $\Delta_i \cup \Delta'_i$
- For O:Δ_i, Δ_{i+1} = Δ_i
- CKS$_{i+1}$(S:Δ_{i+1}) = CKS$_i$(S:Δ_i) ∪ CSS$_i$(O:Δ'_i)
- CSS$_{i+1}$(O:Δ'_{i+1}) = CSS$_i$(O:Δ_i)

The post-condition for W(S:Δ_i, O:Δ'_i) describes the fact that O can now store anything that S knows:

- For $O:\Delta_i$, $\Delta_{i+1} = \Delta_i \cup \Delta'_i$
- For $S:\Delta_i$, $\Delta_{i+1} = \Delta_i$
- $CSS_{i+1}(O:\Delta_{i+1}) = CSS_i(O:\Delta_i) \cup CSS_i(O:\Delta'_i)$
- $CKS_{i+1}(S:\Delta'_{i+1}) = CSS_i(S:\Delta_i)$

Note that the CR and CW access control rules for the DPC model imply the preconditions for the R and W operations. If these are executed when the access control rules are true, the initial and final states of the transition will be identical.

Following is an example of execution of such a system, similar to the example of Sect. 8.

We have four objects and four domains. At the beginning each object contains one domain, which has the same name as the object:

Bank1:{Bank1}, Bank2:{Bank2}; Oil:{Oil}; Auto:{Auto}

We suppose that we have only one conflict, between domains Bank1 and Bank2. We have two subjects, Alice and Bob, who know nothing at the beginning, their labels are { }. A possible sequence of state transitions is:

Alice reads from Bank1, now Alice:{Bank1}.

Bob reads from Bank2, now Bob:{Bank2}.

Alice reads from Oil, now Alice:{Bank1,Oil}.

Bob writes on Oil, now Oil:{Oil,Bank2}.

(Henceforth, Alice cannot read from Oil, since it may contain Bank2 data).

Alice writes on Auto, now Auto:{Auto,Bank1,Oil}

(Henceforth, Bob cannot read from Auto, since it may contain Bank1 data)

Each one of the above is a R or W operation that changes the state. After a number of such operations we will reach a state after which no new labels can be generated. But in a real execution after this and between state transitions other read and write operations are possible, which agree with the DPC (or DP) access control rules and therefore do not change the state.

The confidentiality and integrity properties for ChW are the same as those for the DPC model, extended to the set of all possible states. It is clear in this example that it is not possible to reach a state where Alice or Bob can know both x:Bank1 and y:Bank2, and similarly for what objects can store.

Note that according to the original definition of ChW Alice would be prevented to write on Auto. This example shows that the two shortcomings of this definition identified in [16] are not present in our version of ChW. Similar results were shown in [16, 18] by using different models.

12 Future Research: Variations and Combinations of the Models

Once a basic common reasoning method has been developed, and once some basic models have been identified, it is possible to start playing with variations and combinations of the models. We have mentioned that by combining the UML model with the DP model we obtain the most commonly referenced variety of the BLP model. It is also known that we can further combine this with the DML models to obtain a model where UML is used for certain types of information (e.g. sales statistics), and DML for others (e.g. directives). Since these models have been invented, many variations for them have been proposed in the literature and it will be interesting to see which ones fit in our framework, and if not what extensions will be necessary.

Aspects of *Discretionary Access Control* (DAC) models can be described by using labels to describe capabilities of subjects or access control lists for objects, where label changes result in state changes.

New models can also be invented. For example, one can think of combinations of the RBAC model with layered models, if subject and object variables are given levels in additions to permissions. Such models can be made dynamic if labels can change by effect of operations, as a consequence of user action or administrative intervention.

References [10, 19] propose Attribute Based Access Control (ABAC) as a very general access control model where each one of these new combined models could find its place. Applications of these models can perhaps be found in the Web and in the Cloud, where there is a need for multi-functional access control models [11].

Of course, many concepts can be added to our model: operations different from reading and writing, creation and deletion of subjects and objects, etc.

13 Conclusions

We have presented a new formalized reasoning method for expressing and proving properties of access control and data flow control models. This method is based on simple and intuitive concepts, but has been shown to be usable for a number of classical access control models. The properties proven were already known in their essence, but with reference to different conceptual frameworks.

Some classical proof methods in this area deal with subject and objects and only implicitly with data. Our method deals explicitly with data, making it possible to prove that data values originating from certain levels or domains cannot cross certain boundaries.

In all the examples we have used essentially the same reasoning method. Each model has access control rules that are defined to ensure the invariance of the model's confidentiality and integrity properties, but this invariance must be proven. Unconditional relationships are specified to populate the model and they are such that the desired properties are true in a base case. Then the fact that the properties are invariant is proven by an induction step showing that, because of the access control rules, each use of an inference rule produces results that preserve the properties. The proofs in this paper were straightforward but they will not necessarily be so for the combined models proposed in Sect. 12.

The use of our method has allowed us to determine that some of the classical models can be decomposed into more elementary models. Our common logic framework allows these basic models to be varied and combined in many ways, leading to other models that have not been studied in the literature but can be practically useful. Their properties can be proven with our framework.

One interesting question towards which progress can now be made is the following: given certain desired flow control properties, find a labeling principle and a combination of reading and writing authorizations that can be used to achieve it.

Our method can be at the basis of automatic proof methods for more complex models and can be an asset for teaching systematically access control and flow control theory.

Acknowledgment. This research was supported in part by the Natural Sciences and Engineering Research Council of Canada. I would like to thank Frédéric Cuppens and Nora Cuppens-Boulahia for having hosted me during a phase of this project. I would also like to thank my PhD students Sofiene Boulares, Omar Abahmane and Jamal Abd-Ali for many inspiring discussions.

References

1. Abadi, M.: Logic in access control. In: Proceedings of the 18th IEEE Symposium on Logic in Computer Science (LCS 2003), pp. 228–233 (2003)
2. Barker, S.: Access control for deductive databases by logic programming. In: Stuckey, P.J. (ed.) ICLP 2002. LNCS, vol. 2401, pp. 54–69. Springer, Heidelberg (2002)
3. Barker, S.: The next 700 access control models or a unifying meta-model? In: Proceedings of the 14th ACM Symposium on Access Control Models and Technologies (SACMAT 2009), pp. 187–196 (2009)
4. Bertino, E., Catania, B., Ferrari, E., Perlasca, P.: A logical framework for reasoning about access control models. ACM Trans. Inform. Syst. Secur. (TISSEC) **6**(1), 71–127 (2003)
5. Bishop, M.: Computer Security – Art and Science. Addison-Wesley, USA (2003)
6. Crampton, J., Loizou, G., O'Shea, G.: A logic of access control. Comput. J. **44**(2), 137–149 (2001)
7. Cuppens, F., Demolombe, R.: A modal logical framework for security policies. In: Proceedings of the 10th International Symposium on Foundations of Intelligent Systems (ISMIS 1997), pp. 579–589 (1997)
8. Jaeger, T.: Operating System Security. Morgan and Claypool, San Rafael (2008)
9. Jaume, M., Morisset, C.: Un cadre sémantique pour le contrôle d'accès. Technique et Science Informatique **27**(8), 951–976 (2008)
10. Jin, X., Krishnan, R., Sandhu, R.: A Unified Attribute-Based Access Control Model Covering DAC, MAC and RBAC. In: Cuppens-Boulahia, N., Cuppens, F., Garcia-Alfaro, J. (eds.) DBSec 2012. LNCS, vol. 7371, pp. 41–55. Springer, Heidelberg (2012)
11. Khamadja, S., Adi, K., Logrippo, L.: Designing flexible access control models for the Cloud. In: Proceedings of the 6th International Conference on Security of Information and Networks (SIN 2013), pp. 225–232 (2013)
12. Habib, L., Jaume, M., Morisset, C.: Formal definition and comparison of access control models. J. Inform. Assur. Secur. **4**, 372–381 (2009)
13. Lampson, B.W.: A note on the confinement problem. Comm. ACM **16**(10), 613–615 (1973)
14. Myers, A.C., Liskov, B.: Protecting privacy using the decentralized label model. ACM Trans. Softw. Eng. Methodol. (TOSEM) **9**(4), 410–442 (2000)
15. Osborn, S.: Information flow analysis of an RBAC system. In: Proceedings of the 7th ACM Symposium on Access Control Models and Technologies (SACMAT 2002), pp. 163–168 (2002)
16. Sandhu, R.S.: Lattice-based enforcement of Chinese Wall. Comput. Secur. **11**(8), 753–763 (1992)
17. Sandhu, R.S.: Lattice-based access control models. Computer **26**(11), 9–19 (1993)
18. Sharifi, A., Tripunitara, M.V.: Least-restrictive enforcement of the Chinese Wall security policy. In: Proceedings of the 18th ACM Symposium on Access Control Models and Technologies (SACMAT 2013), pp. 61–72 (2013)
19. Wang, L., Wijsekera, D., Jajodia, S.: A logic-based framework for Attribute-Based Access Control. In: Proceedings of the ACM Workshop on Formal Methods in Security Engineering (FMSE 2004), pp. 45–55 (2004)

A Formal Approach to Verify Completeness and Detect Anomalies in Firewall Security Policies

Ahmed Khoumsi[1]([✉]), Wadie Krombi[2], and Mohammed Erradi[2]

[1] Department of Electrical and Computer Engineering,
University of Sherbrooke, Sherbrooke, Canada
ahmed.khoumsi@usherbrooke.ca
[2] ENSIAS, Mohammed V University, Rabat, Morocco
krombi@yahoo.com, erradi@ensias.ma

Abstract. Security policies are a relevant solution to protect information systems from undue accesses. In this paper, we develop a formal and rigorous automata-based approach to design and analyze security policies. The interest of our approach is that it can be used as a common basis for analyzing several aspects of security policies, instead of using a distinct approach and formalism for studying each aspect. We first develop a procedure that synthesizes automatically an automaton which implements a given security policy. Then, we apply this synthesis procedure to verify completeness of security policies and detect several types of anomalies in security policies. We also study space and time complexities of the developed procedures.

1 Introduction

In this paper, we develop a formal automata-based approach to study firewall security policies described by filtering rules. Our fundamental contribution is the development of a procedure that synthesizes an automaton which implements a security policy given as a table of filtering rules. Then, we apply our automata-based approach for verifying completeness of security policies and detecting several types of anomalies in security policies. We also detect and correct an error in the commonly used definition of redundancy anomaly. Finally, we give a precise and accurate evaluation of space and time complexities of our developed procedures.

Our results are presented as 14 propositions which have all been formally proved. Due to space limitation, we do not present the proofs.

The rest of this paper is organized as follows. Section 2 presents related work on modeling and analyzing firewall security policies. In Sect. 3, we present preliminaries on firewall security policies. Section 4 contains a procedure that synthesizes an automaton which implements a security policy given as a table of filtering rules. In Sects. 5, 6, 7, and 8, we apply the synthesis procedure to verify completeness and detect various types of anomalies in a security policy. Section 9 evaluates space and time complexities of the procedures we have developed throughout Sects. 4, 5, 6, 7, and 8. We conclude in Sect. 10.

© Springer International Publishing Switzerland 2015
F. Cuppens et al. (Eds.): FPS 2014, LNCS 8930, pp. 221–236, 2015.
DOI: 10.1007/978-3-319-17040-4_14

2   Related Work

Many studies on security policies focus on firewalls. In [1,2], the authors present techniques and algorithms to detect anomalies in the filtering policy of a firewall. Firewall policy anomaly is defined in [3] as the existence of two or more filtering rules that match the same packet. The security policy is described by a tree called *Policy tree* in [1] and *Decision tree* in [2], where each node represents a field of a filtering rule and each link corresponds to a possible value of a field. A path from the root to a leaf describes a filtering rule of the policy. A leaf specifies the action (Accept, Deny) to be taken when the corresponding filtering rule is satisfied. The authors of [4] also study anomaly detections, but we find their categorization of anomalies less rigorous than in [1]. While in [1,2] the study of anomaly detection is limited to stateless firewalls, in [5,6] the authors provide solutions to analyze and handle stateful firewall anomalies.

In [7], the authors propose a method to detect functional discrepancies between various implementations of a security policy of a firewall. The data structure used to model the security policy is a tree called *Firewall Decision Diagram* (FDD) [8] which maps each packet to the decision to be taken by the firewall for such a packet. Each non-terminal node in a FDD specifies a test performed on a field of the packet, and each branch descending from this node corresponds to possible values of this field.

In [9], the authors introduce *Fireman*, which is a toolkit for modeling and analyzing firewalls. Fireman detects errors such as violation of a policy and inconsistency in a policy of a firewall. Fireman is implemented using *Binary Decision Diagrams* (BDD) [10] to represent predicates and perform all the set of the available operations.

In [11], the authors propose a framework to generate automatically test sequences to validate the conformance of a security policy. In such a framework, the behavior of the system is specified by an extended finite state machine [12] and the security policy is specified with the model OrBAC [13].

In [14], the authors present a visualization tool to analyze firewall configurations. To use this visualization, the firewall policy is modeled using a specific hierarchical way. The first level after the root in that model consists of the names of the different rules. The second level contains the action to execute, the third one the protocol, followed by the source and destination address. The hierarchical representation of the firewall is formed from rules data by grouping identical rule elements in a recursive manner.

In [15], the authors develop a method to verify equivalence between two security policies by extracting and comparing equivalent policies whose filtering rules are disjoint.

In each of the above works, the security policy is modeled by a data structure designed to solve a specific problem. To study a given security policy, we need to model it: by a policy tree to study anomalies, by a FDD to study discrepancies, by a BDD to study policy violation and inconsistency in a policy of a firewall, etc. This observation motivated the recent work of [16] which develops an automata-based approach to design and analyze several aspects of firewall security policies, instead of using a distinct approach and formalism for studying each aspect. The present article adds the following contributions:

- We improve our synthesis procedure, in particular by defining formally the product of automata and labeling the transitions by intervals instead of values, which implies an enormous reduction of the number of transitions.
- We develop detection procedures, not only for shadowing anomaly, but also for generalization, correlation, and redundancy anomalies.
- We detect and correct an error in the definition commonly used for redundancy anomaly.
- We compute space and time complexities of our developed procedures.

3   Preliminaries on Firewall Security Policies

As defined in [17], firewalls are devices or programs that control the flow of network traffic between networks or hosts that employ differing security postures. The main objective of a firewall is to separate logically networks that have distinct security requirements. This is done by using rules on which communications are permitted between networks. The behavior of a firewall is controlled by its security policy which is specified by an ordered list of filtering rules defining the decisions and actions to be taken each time a packet arrives at the firewall. The packets arriving at the firewall are specified by an n-tuple of headers that are taken into account by the security policy. Examples of headers: source IP address, destination IP address, port number, protocol.

A firewall security rule (also called filtering rule) is expressed in the form: *if some conditions are satisfied, then a given action must be taken to authorize or refuse the access.* A rule can be represented as a couple (*Condition, Action*):

- *Condition* is a set of filtering fields $F^0, \cdots, F^{m-1}$ corresponding to respective headers $H^0, \cdots, H^{m-1}$ of a packet arriving at the firewall. Each F^j defines the set of values that are authorized to H^j. *Condition* is satisfied for a given packet P, if for every $j = 0, \cdots m-1$ the value of the header H^j of P belongs to the field F^j. We say that P matches a rule R (we may also say: R matches P) when the condition of R is satisfied for P. Otherwise, we say that P does not match R (or R does not match P).
- The field *Action* is *Accept* or *Deny*, to authorize or forbid a packet to go through the firewall, respectively.

Table 1 shows a structure of table that describes a security policy by a list of filtering rules $R_1, \cdots, R_n$. Each line of the table corresponds to a rule R_i ($1 \leq i \leq n$) which is defined by: (1) its condition consisting of m filtering fields $F_i^0, \cdots, F_i^{m-1}$; and (2) its action a_i. The rules are given in decreasing priority order, that is, when a packet P arrives at the firewall, matching of P and R_1 is verified: if P matches R_1, then action a_1 is executed; if P does not match R_1, then matching of P and R_2 is verified. And so on, the process is repeated until a rule R_i matching P is found or all the rules are examined. If none of the rules

R_1 to R_n matches P, then usually a default rule is used for P. Such a default rule has its condition equal to True, that is, it matches any packet.

A security policy of a firewall is said *complete* if for any packet P arriving at the firewall, there exists at least one of its filtering rules which matches P. Note that a security policy is complete if we integrate at the end of its list of rules a default rule with condition True.

Table 1. Structure of a table of filtering rules

Rule	F^0	...	F^j	...	F^{m-1}	Action
R_1	F_1^0	...	F_1^j	...	F_1^{m-1}	a_1
...	...	...	...	...	...	...
R_n	F_n^0	...	F_n^j	...	F_n^{m-1}	a_n

Table 2 contains an example of security policy with four rules R_1 to R_4, where each line of the table corresponds to a rule. The condition of each rule R_i is defined by four fields named IPsrc, IPdst, Port and Protocol, and its action is the last field. The term *Any* in the column of a field F^j means any value in the domain of F^j. The term a.b.c.0/x is a usual notation that denotes an interval of IP addresses obtained from the 32-bit address a.b.c.0 by keeping constant the first x bits and varying the other bits. A packet P arriving at the firewall matches a rule R_i if the following four points are satisfied:

- P comes from an address belonging to IPsrc,
- P is destined to an address belonging to IPdst,
- P is transmitted through a port belonging to Port,
- P is transmitted by a protocol belonging to Protocol.

This security policy is complete because R_4 has the condition True (i.e., it matches every packet). Consider for example a packet P specified by the headers $(88.120.10.15), (65.22.23.11), (25), (\text{TCP})$, that is, P comes from 88.120.10.15, is destined to 65.22.23.11, and is transmitted through the port 25 by the protocol TCP. Only R_4 matches P which is accepted because the action of R_4 is *Accept*.

The example of Table 2 has been constructed specifically to illustrate the detections of all the anomalies studied in Sects. 7 and 8.

Table 2. Example of security rules

Rule	IPsrc	IPdst	Port	Protocol	Action
R_1	*Any*	81.10.10.0/24	*Any*	*Any*	*Accept*
R_2	192.168.10.0/24	81.10.10.0/24	21, 80	TCP	*Deny*
R_3	192.168.10.0/24	81.10.10.0/24	21, 85	*Any*	*Accept*
R_4	*Any*	*Any*	*Any*	*Any*	*Accept*

4   Synthesis Procedure

In this section, we develop a procedure that synthesizes an automaton which implements a security policy. The input of the procedure is a firewall security policy $\mathcal{F}$ specified by an array of n filtering rules $R_1, \cdots, R_n$ ordered in decreasing priority, where each R_i is defined by a condition consisting of m fields and by an action a_i. The result is an automaton $\Gamma_\mathcal{F}$ implementing $\mathcal{F}$ which is generated in three steps which are presented below and illustrated by the example of Table 2.

Due to space limitation, we omit theoretical details on automata. An automaton $\mathcal{A}$ consists of states related by labeled transitions, and will be represented by a graph whose nodes and arcs are the states and the transitions of $\mathcal{A}$, respectively. An arc from node q to node r labeled by the event σ represents the transition $q \xrightarrow{\sigma} r$. There is one initial state (with a small incoming arrow) and one or more final states (in bold).

We will use the following notation of intervals of integers: $[a, b] = \{x \,|\, a \leq x \leq b\}$, $[a, b[= \{x \,|\, a \leq x < b\}$, $]a, b] = \{x \,|\, a < x \leq b\}$ and $]a, b[= \{x \,|\, a < x < b\}$. For the sake of clarity, in Figs. 1 and 2 we will use the shorthands of Table 3.

Table 3. Shorthands in Figs. 1 and 2

Figure 1	$\alpha_1 = 192.168.10.0$	$\beta_1 = 81.10.10.0$
	$\alpha_2 = 192.168.10.255$	$\beta_2 = 81.10.10.255$

Figure 2	$I_1 = [0, \alpha_1[$	$I_2 = [\alpha_1, \alpha_2]$	$I_3 =]\alpha_2, 2^{32}[$	
	$J_1 = [0, \beta_1[$	$J_2 = [\beta_1, \beta_2]$	$J_3 =]\beta_2, 2^{32}[$	
	$K_1 = [0, 21[$	$K_2 =]21, 80[$	$K_3 =]80, 85[$	$K_4 =]85, 2^{16}[$

4.1   Step 1: Automaton for Each Filtering Rule

In Step 1, for each rule R_i, we synthesize an automaton $\mathcal{A}_i$ that has $m + 1$ consecutive states $q_i^0, q_i^1, \cdots, q_i^m$, where q_i^0 is the initial state and q_i^m is the final state. Every pair of consecutive states q_i^j and q_i^{j+1} ($0 \leq j < m$) are linked by as many as transitions as the number of intervals defining the values of the field F_i^j. The transitions are labeled by the respective interval names. Then, each automaton $\mathcal{A}_i$ is completed as follows:

- A new final state E_i is added.
- In every non final state q_i^j of $\mathcal{A}_i$, we add the transitions labeled by the intervals which are complementary to the intervals labeling the transitions leading from q_i^j to q_i^{j+1}. All the added transitions lead to state E_i.

As we will explain it in Proposition 1, the intuition of E_i is that it is reached when a packet does not match rule R_i.

Step 1 is illustrated in Fig. 1 which represents the automata $(\mathcal{A}_i)_{i=1\cdots 4}$ obtained from the rules of Table 2. We assume that IP addresses are in 32 bits, port numbers are in 16 bits, and only two protocols are possible: TCP and UDP. Note that some intervals consist of a single value, e.g. 21, 80, 85, TCP and UDP.

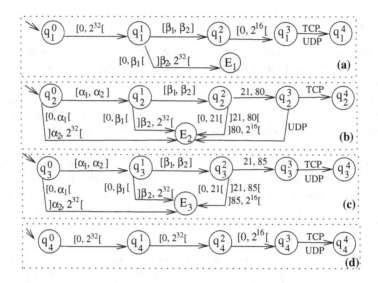

Fig. 1. Automata $(\mathcal{A}_i)_{1\cdots 4}$ obtained from Table 2.

4.2 Step 2: Uniform Intervals

We say that a state is of level i if it is reached after i transitions from the initial state. Hence, each automaton $\mathcal{A}_i$ has $m+1$ states, from level 0 to level m. The automata $(\mathcal{A}_i)_{i=1\cdots n}$ constructed in Step 1 do not use the same intervals in the same level. For example, at level 0 (i.e. from q_i^0) of Fig. 1, we have the following intervals: $[0, 2^{32}[$ in $\mathcal{A}_1$ and $\mathcal{A}_4$; and $[\alpha_1, \alpha_2]$, $[0, \alpha_1[$ and $]\alpha_2, 2^{32}[$ in $\mathcal{A}_2$ and $\mathcal{A}_3$.

To be able to combine the n automata in Step 3, the objective of Step 2 is to rewrite the n automata so that at each level, they all use the same intervals. For that purpose, for each level j, the domain of the field F^j is partitioned into a set of disjoint intervals, so that every interval that labels a transition of level j of $\mathcal{A}_i$ is an union of intervals of the partition. We proceed as follows:

- For every automaton $\mathcal{A}_i$ and level j, we consider the set of the intervals labeling the transitions from state q_i^j. We construct the list L_i^j consisting of the values of the extremities of the considered intervals. The values in L_i^j are sorted in increasing order.
  Consider for example the level 0 of Fig. 1: in $\mathcal{A}_1$ and $\mathcal{A}_4$ we obtain the list $L_1^0 = L_4^0 = \langle 0, 2^{32} \rangle$ from the interval $[0, 2^{32}[$; in $\mathcal{A}_2$ and $\mathcal{A}_3$ we obtain the list $L_2^0 = L_3^0 = \langle 0, \alpha_1, \alpha_2, 2^{32} \rangle$ from the intervals $[0, \alpha_1[$, $[\alpha_1, \alpha_2]$, $]\alpha_2, 2^{32}[$.
- For every level j, the lists $(L_i^j)_{i=1\cdots n}$ are merged into a single increasing sorted list L^j. Then, we construct a set of disjoint intervals whose extremities are consecutive elements of L^j (we may have to define some single-value intervals). The obtained set of intervals is a partition of the domain of the field F^j, because the set of outgoing transitions in each state q_i^j of an automaton $\mathcal{A}_i$ constitute the whole domain of the field F^j.

For example, if we merge the above $(L_i^0)_{i=1\cdots4}$, we obtain the sorted list: $L^0 = \langle 0, \alpha_1, \alpha_2, 2^{32} \rangle$, from which we construct the three disjoint intervals I_1, I_2 and I_3, which constitute a partition of the domain $[0, 2^{32}[$ of IPsrc.

- For every automaton $\mathcal{A}_i$ and level j, each transition labeled by an interval I is replaced by several transitions labeled by the intervals of the partition that constitute I.

Consider for example the level 0 of $\mathcal{A}_1$ in Fig. 1. The transition labeled $[0, 2^{32}[$ is replaced by 3 transitions labeled I_1, I_2 and I_3, respectively.

Step 2 is illustrated in Fig. 2 which represents the automata $(\mathcal{A}_i^*)_{i=1\cdots4}$ obtained from the automata $(\mathcal{A}_i)_{i=1\cdots4}$ of Fig. 1. The constructed intervals are: I_1, I_2, I_3 at level 0; J_1, J_2, J_3 at level 1; $K_1, K_2, K_3, K_4, 21, 80, 85$ at level 2; and TCP, UDP at level 3.

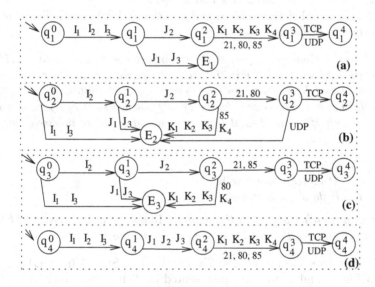

Fig. 2. Automata $(\mathcal{A}_i^*)_{1\cdots4}$ obtained from automata $(\mathcal{A}_i)_{1\cdots4}$ of Fig. 1.

4.3   Step 3: Product and Association of Actions

Consider two automata $\mathcal{A}_1^*$ and $\mathcal{A}_2^*$ constructed in Step 2. The product $\mathcal{A}_1^* \otimes \mathcal{A}_2^*$ is defined inductively as follows:

- Its initial state $\langle q_1^0, q_2^0 \rangle$ is a combination of the initial states q_1^0 and q_2^0 of $\mathcal{A}_1^*$ and $\mathcal{A}_2^*$.
- For every state $\langle r_1, r_2 \rangle$ of $\mathcal{A}_1^* \otimes \mathcal{A}_2^*$ and label σ:
  1. If $\mathcal{A}_1^*$ and $\mathcal{A}_2^*$ have $r_1 \xrightarrow{\sigma} s_1$ and $r_2 \xrightarrow{\sigma} s_2$ respectively, then $\mathcal{A}_1^* \otimes \mathcal{A}_2^*$ has the state $\langle s_1, s_2 \rangle$ and the transition $\langle r_1, r_2 \rangle \xrightarrow{\sigma} \langle s_1, s_2 \rangle$.
  2. If $\mathcal{A}_1^*$ has $r_1 \xrightarrow{\sigma} s_1$ and $r_2 = E_2$, then $\mathcal{A}_1^* \otimes \mathcal{A}_2^*$ has the state $\langle s_1, E_2 \rangle$ and the transition $\langle r_1, E_2 \rangle \xrightarrow{\sigma} \langle s_1, E_2 \rangle$.

3. If $\mathcal{A}_2^*$ has $r_2 \xrightarrow{\sigma} s_2$ and $r_1 = E_1$, then $\mathcal{A}_1^* \otimes \mathcal{A}_2^*$ has the state $\langle E_1, s_2 \rangle$ and the transition $\langle E_1, r_2 \rangle \xrightarrow{\sigma} \langle E_1, s_2 \rangle$.
 - $\mathcal{A}_1^* \otimes \mathcal{A}_2^*$ has no other state and transition.

The product of all automata $\mathcal{A}_1^*, \cdots, \mathcal{A}_n^*$ is an iteration of products of two automata. Let $\Gamma_\mathcal{F}$ denote the product of the n automata. Each state of $\Gamma_\mathcal{F}$ is defined in the form $(r_1, \cdots, r_n)$, where each r_i may be q_i^j or E_i, for $i = 1 \cdots n$ and $j = 0 \cdots m$. We define two types of final states:

 - A *match* state $(r_1, \cdots, r_n)$ is such that $r_i = q_i^m$ for at least one i;
 - The (unique) *no-match* state is $(E_1, \cdots, E_n)$.

To each match state $u = (r_1, \cdots, r_n)$ of $\Gamma_\mathcal{F}$, we associate the action a_i of the rule R_i that has the smallest index i such that $r_i \neq E_i$.

The fundamental characteristics of $\Gamma_\mathcal{F}$ is that it implements $\mathcal{F}$ as stated by the following proposition:

Proposition 1. *Consider a packet P arriving at the firewall, and let $H^0, \cdots, H^{m-1}$ be its headers. From the initial state of $\Gamma_\mathcal{F}$, we execute the m consecutive transitions labeled by the intervals $\sigma_0, \cdots, \sigma_{m-1}$ that contain $H^0, \cdots, H^{m-1}$, respectively. Let $r = \langle r_1, \cdots, r_n \rangle$ be the (final) reached state of $\Gamma_\mathcal{F}$. r is a match state if and only if P matches at least one rule of $\mathcal{F}$. More precisely, for every $i = 1, \cdots, n$:*

 - $r_i = q_i^m$ *or* $r_i = E_i$,
 - *if* $r_i = q_i^m$, *P matches the rule* R_i,
 - *if* $r_i = E_i$, *P does not match* R_i.

And if r is a match state, then the action (Accept or Deny) associated to r is the action dictated by the most priority rule matching P.

Figure 3 represents the automaton $\Gamma_\mathcal{F}$ obtained in Step 3 from $(\mathcal{A}_i^*)_{i=1\cdots 4}$ of Fig. 2. In Figs. 1 and 2, we have represented explicitly each interval labeling a transition, because that was useful to understand the operations of Step 2. In Fig. 3, we use a simpler and more symbolic notation based on the expressions *Any* and *not(X)* where X is one or more intervals. A transition labeled *Any* from a state q_i^j is a symbolic representation of the transitions labeled by all the intervals defined at level j in Step 2. For example, the transition *Any* from $\langle q_1^2, E_2, E_3, q_4^2 \rangle$ represents the 7 transitions labeled $K_1, K_2, K_3, K_4, 21, 80, 85$. *not(X)* corresponds to *Any* without the transitions labeled by the intervals in X. For example, the transition labeled *not(192.168.10.0/24)* (i.e. *not(I_2)*) represents the 2 transitions labeled I_1 and I_3, and the transition labeled *not(21, 80, 85)* represents the 4 transitions labeled K_1, K_2, K_3 and K_4. The 5 match states of $\Gamma_\mathcal{F}$ are in bold, there is no no-match state. Let us illustrate the fact that $\Gamma_\mathcal{F}$ of Fig. 3 implements $\mathcal{F}$ of Table 2. Consider a packet P which arrives at the firewall and assume that its four headers H^0 to H^3 are $(192.168.10.12), (81.10.10.20), (25), (TCP)$, respectively. We start in the initial state $\langle q_1^0, q_2^0, q_3^0, q_4^0 \rangle$. The transition labeled 192.168.10.0/24 (comprising H^0) is executed and leads to state $\langle q_1^1, q_2^1, q_3^1, q_4^1 \rangle$. Then, the transition labeled 81.10.10.0/24 (comprising H^1) is executed and leads to state $\langle q_1^2, q_2^2, q_3^2, q_4^2 \rangle$. Then, the transition labeled $]21, 80[$ (comprising H^2) is executed and leads to state $\langle q_1^3, E_2, E_3, q_4^3 \rangle$. Finally, the transition labeled TCP (comprising H^3) is executed and leads to the match state $\langle q_1^4, E_2, E_3, q_4^4 \rangle$. Since the reached match state is associated to *Accept*, the packet is accepted.

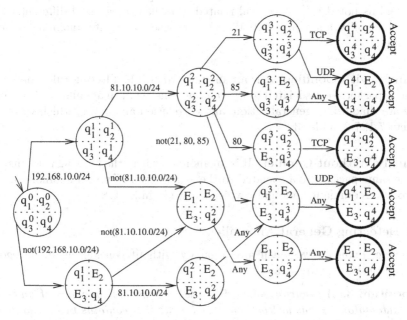

Fig. 3. Automaton $\Gamma_{\mathcal{F}}$ synthesized from automata $(\mathcal{A}_i^*)_{1\cdots4}$ of Fig. 2.

In the following four Sects. 5, 6, 7, and 8, we show how our 3-step synthesis procedure can be applied for verifying completeness of security policies and detecting several types of anomalies in security policies.

5   Verifying Completeness

We consider a security policy $\mathcal{F}$ defined by a table of n filtering rules R_1 to R_n and its corresponding automaton $\Gamma_{\mathcal{F}}$. A firewall security policy is said *complete* if every packet reaching the firewall matches at least one of the rules R_1 to R_n. From Proposition 1, we obtain:

Proposition 2. *A security policy $\mathcal{F}$ is complete if and only if its automaton $\Gamma_{\mathcal{F}}$ has no no-match state.*

For example, the security policy of Table 2 is complete because all final states of $\Gamma_{\mathcal{F}}$ in Fig. 3 are match states. If we remove rule R_4, we obtain an incomplete security policy because the corresponding automaton contains the no-match state, which is reached for any packet whose header IPdst does not belong to 81.10.10.0/24.

6   Anomaly Categorization, General Anomaly Detection

6.1   Categories of Anomalies

Recall that an anomaly in a firewall security policy is defined as the existence of two or more filtering rules matching the same packet. From this basic definition, and as noted in [18], several related work has categorized different types of firewall policy anomalies [1,9,19]. We propose to classify anomalies in two categories:

Anomaly with Conflict: It is an anomaly where the filtering rules matching the same packet are associated to *different* actions. Typical anomalies of this category are shadowing, generalization, and correlation anomalies, which we study in Sects. 7.1, 7.2, and 7.3.

Anomaly Without Conflict: It is an anomaly where the filtering rules matching the same packet are associated to the *same* action. Typical anomaly of this category is redundancy anomaly, which we study in Sect. 8.

6.2   Detecting General Anomalies

By *general anomaly* we mean any anomaly without considering its category. From Proposition 1, we obtain:

Proposition 3. *A security policy $\mathcal{F}$ contains a general anomaly if and only if the automaton $\Gamma_{\mathcal{F}}$ has at least one match state that contains two or more q_i^m.*

Intuitively, the presence of several q_i^m in a match state means the existence of packets that are accepted by several filtering rules. For example, the security policy of Table 2 contains several general anomalies, because the automaton of Fig. 3 has four match states with two or more q_i^m.

The nonexistence of general anomaly implies obviously the nonexistence of any category of anomalies. On the other hand, the existence of general anomaly is a symptom (but not a guarantee) of the existence of specific anomalies. In the following two Sects. 7 and 8, we show how to detect anomalies with conflict and without conflict, respectively.

7   Detecting Anomalies with Conflict

7.1   Detecting Shadowing Anomaly

A rule R_j is shadowed by a preceding rule R_i (i.e. $i < j$) if, on the one hand R_i matches all the packets that match R_j, and on the other hand actions of R_i and R_j are distinct [19]. In this case, all the packets that R_j intends to deny (resp. accept) are accepted (resp. denied) by R_i; thus, R_j never takes effect. It is important to discover shadowed rules and alert the administrator to correct this error by reordering or removing these rules [1]. Based on this definition and Proposition 1, we obtain:

Proposition 4. *In a security policy $\mathcal{F}$, rule R_j is shadowed by rule R_i if and only if the following three conditions hold: (1) $i < j$; (2) $a_i \neq a_j$; and (3) for every match state $\langle r_1, \cdots, r_n \rangle$ of $\Gamma_{\mathcal{F}}$, if $r_j = q_j^m$ then $r_i = q_i^m$.*

For example, in Table 2, R_2 is shadowed by R_1 because: $1 < 2$, $a_1 = Accept \neq a_2 = Deny$, and $\Gamma_{\mathcal{F}}$ of Fig. 3 has no match state with q_2^4 and without q_1^4. Consequently, R_2 never takes effect and hence its action $Deny$ is never taken. Assume that the administrator decides to remove this anomaly by switching the orders of rules R_1 and R_2. After this switch, it is not necessary to construct a new automaton $\Gamma_{\mathcal{F}}$ from the beginning. Since R_1 becomes R_2 and vice versa, we have just to switch between r_1 and r_2 in all states to give priority to R_2 over R_1, and then to re-assign actions to match states. As a result, in Fig. 3 we will have the action $Deny$ associated to the first and third match states from the top, and the action $Accept$ associated to the three other match states.

7.2 Detecting Generalization Anomaly

A rule R_j generalizes a preceding rule R_i (i.e. $i < j$) if, on the one hand R_j matches more packets than R_i, and on the other hand actions of R_i and R_j are distinct [19]. Based on this definition and Proposition 1, we obtain:

Proposition 5. *In a security policy $\mathcal{F}$, rule R_j generalizes rule R_i if and only if the following four conditions hold: (1) $i < j$; (2) $a_i \neq a_j$; (3) for every match state $\langle r_1, \cdots, r_n \rangle$ of $\Gamma_{\mathcal{F}}$, if $r_i = q_i^m$ then $r_j = q_j^m$; and (4) there exists a match state $\langle r_1, \cdots, r_n \rangle$ of $\Gamma_{\mathcal{F}}$ such that $r_i = E_i$ and $r_j = q_j^m$.*

For example, in Table 2, R_4 generalizes R_2 because: $2 < 4$, $a_2 = Deny \neq a_4 = Accept$, and $\Gamma_{\mathcal{F}}$ of Fig. 3 has no match state with q_2^4 and without q_4^4 and has 3 match states with E_2 and q_4^4.

We have seen in Sect. 7.1 that R_2 is shadowed by R_1 and that the shadowing anomaly can be removed by switching the orders of R_1 and R_2. It can be easily checked that after this reordering, the shadowing anomaly is transformed into a generalization anomaly: R_1 (which becomes R_2) generalizes R_2 (which becomes R_1).

7.3 Detecting Correlation Anomaly

Rules R_i and R_j correlate if their actions are distinct and:

– there exist packets that match R_i and not R_j,
– there exist packets that match R_j and not R_i,
– there exist packets that match both R_i and R_j [19].

Based on this definition and Proposition 1, we obtain:

Proposition 6. *In a security policy $\mathcal{F}$, rules R_i and R_j correlate if and only if the following five conditions hold: (1) $i \neq j$; (2) $a_i \neq a_j$; (3) there exists a match state $\langle r_1, \cdots, r_n \rangle$ of $\Gamma_{\mathcal{F}}$ such that $r_i = E_i$ and $r_j = q_j^m$; (4) there exists a match state $\langle r_1, \cdots, r_n \rangle$ of $\Gamma_{\mathcal{F}}$ such that $r_i = q_i^m$ and $r_j = E_j$; and (5) there exists a match state $\langle r_1, \cdots, r_n \rangle$ of $\Gamma_{\mathcal{F}}$ such that $r_i = q_i^m$ and $r_j = q_j^m$.*

For example, in Table 2, rules R_2 and R_3 correlate because: $2 \neq 3$, $a_2 = Deny \neq a_3 = Accept$, and the automaton $\Gamma_{\mathcal{F}}$ of Fig. 3 has the three match states $\langle q_1^4, q_2^4, q_3^4, q_4^4 \rangle$, $\langle q_1^4, E_2, q_3^4, q_4^4 \rangle$, $\langle q_1^4, q_2^4, E_3, q_4^4 \rangle$.

8   Redefining and Detecting Redundancy Anomaly

In the present section, we study redundancy anomaly which has been defined in [1] as follows: A rule R_i is redundant to a rule R_j if: (1) R_j is associated to the same action as R_i and matches the same or more packets than R_i, and (2) the security policy will not be affected if R_i is removed.

We have detected that the formal definition of redundancy anomaly given by [1] is incompatible with this informal definition. Indeed, there are situations where a rule is diagnosed by [1] as redundant to another rule, while its removal affects the security policy.

We will distinguish two cases of redundancy, LP-redundancy and MP-redundancy, which are compatible with the informal definition. We will show how to detect each of them. Then, we will show why the formal definition of [1] is problematic.

8.1   Definition and Detection of LP-Redundancy Anomaly

Redundancy of the Least Priority (LP) of the Two Rules: R_j is LP-redundant to R_i if the following three conditions hold: (1) $i < j$; (2) $a_i = a_j$; and (3) R_i matches all the packets matching R_j.

The intuition of LP-redundancy is that if R_j has less priority than R_i and matches less packets than R_i, then R_j is obviously useless and can be removed.

Detecting LP-Redundancy Anomaly: Based on the definition of LP-redundancy and Proposition 1, we obtain:

Proposition 7. *In a security policy $\mathcal{F}$, rule R_j is LP-redundant to R_i if the following three conditions hold: (1) $i < j$; (2) $a_i = a_j$; and (3) for every match state $\langle r_1, \cdots, r_n \rangle$ of $\Gamma_{\mathcal{F}}$, if $r_j = q_j^m$ then $r_i = q_i^m$;*

For example, in Table 2, R_3 is LP-redundant with R_1 because: $1 < 3$, $a_1 = a_3 = Accept$, and in the automaton $\Gamma_{\mathcal{F}}$ of Fig. 3, the two match states that contain q_3^4 contain also q_1^4.

8.2   Definition and Detection of MP-Redundancy Anomaly

Redundancy of the Most Priority (MP) of the Two Rules: R_i is MP-redundant to R_j if the following four conditions hold: (1) $i < j$; (2) $a_i = a_j$; (3) R_j matches more packets than R_i; (4) there exists no rule R_k satisfying the following three sub-conditions: (4.a) $i < k < j$, (4.b) $a_k \neq a_i$, and (4.c) there exist packets matching both R_i and R_k.

The intuition of MP-redundancy is that if R_i has more priority than R_j but matches less packets than R_j, then R_i is useless if its removal does not give the chance to another rule R_k to take an effect different from the effect of R_i.

The following proposition expresses MP-redundancy by using the three anomalies with conflict.

Proposition 8. R_i *is MP-redundant to* R_j *if:* $i < j$; $a_i = a_j$; R_j *matches more packets than* R_i; *and there exists no rule* R_k *between* R_i *and* R_j *satisfying one of the following three conditions:* R_k *is shadowed by* R_i, R_k *generalizes* R_i, *or* R_k *and* R_i *correlate.*

Detecting MP-Redundancy Anomaly: Based on the definition of MP-redundancy and Proposition 1, we obtain:

Proposition 9. *In a security policy* $\mathcal{F}$, *rule* R_i *is MP-redundant to* R_j *if the following five conditions hold: (1)* $i < j$; *(2)* $a_i = a_j$; *(3) for every match state* $\langle r_1, \cdots, r_n \rangle$ *of* $\Gamma_{\mathcal{F}}$: *if* $r_i = q_i^m$, *then* $r_j = q_j^m$; *(4) there exists a match state* $\langle r_1, \cdots, r_n \rangle$ *of* $\Gamma_{\mathcal{F}}$ *such that:* $r_i = E_i$ *and* $r_j = q_j^m$; *and (5) for every* k *such that* $i < k < j$ *and* $a_k \neq a_i$, *there exists no match state* $\langle r_1, \cdots, r_n \rangle$ *of* $\Gamma_{\mathcal{F}}$ *such that:* $r_i = q_i^m$ *and* $r_k = q_k^m$.

For example, in Table 2, R_3 is MP-redundant with R_4 because: $3 < 4$, $a_3 = a_4 = Accept$, and in the automaton $\Gamma_{\mathcal{F}}$ of Fig. 3: the two match states that contain q_3^4 contain also q_4^4, there exist three match states containing E_3 and q_4^4, and there exists no k between 3 and 4.

8.3 Difference with [1]

The difference between our definition of MP-redundancy and the definition of [1] is in the condition related to R_k. In our definition, the condition is that for every rule R_k between R_i and R_j that has a different action than R_i, the set of packets matching R_i must be *disjoint* with the set of packets matching R_k. In the definition of [1], the condition is weaker because its permits that the set of packets matching R_k be included in or equal to the set of packets matching R_i. In other words, we obtain the definition of [1] by removing the line "R_k is shadowed by R_i" in Proposition 8. Consequently, there are situations where a rule is diagnosed by [1] as redundant to another rule while in reality its removal affects the security policy.

To illustrate the problematic definition of MP-redundancy of [1], let us consider R_1 and R_4 of Table 2. With our definition, R_1 is not MP-redundant to R_4, because R_1 accepts all the packets accepted by R_2, while R_2 is between R_1 and R_4 and has a different action than R_1. But with the definition of [1], R_1 is MP-redundant to R_4, because the definition of [1] accepts that between R_1 and R_4 there exists a rule (R_2) which is shadowed by R_1. This is problematic because in reality removing R_1 affects the security policy.

9   Space and Time Complexities

Recall that n and m are the number of rules and fields, respectively. We call *great field* a field whose domain contains more than n values, and *small field* a field whose domain contains at most n values. Consider for example the four fields IPsrc, IPdst, Port and Protocol and assume $n = 1000$. IPsrc, IPdst and Port are great fields, because their domains contain 2^{32}, 2^{32} and 2^{16} values, respectively, hence more than 1000 values. Protocol is a small field, because its domain contains much less than 1000 values (the number of considered protocols is negligible to 1000). In addition to n and m, we will use the following parameters:

d_i = number of bits necessary to code the values of field F^i, for $i = 0, \cdots, m-1$,
    hence 2^{d_i} is the number of possible values of F^i;
D = sum of the number of bits to code all the fields, i.e. $D = d_0 + \cdots + d_{m-1}$;
μ = number of great fields, hence $\mu \leq m$;
δ = sum of the number of bits to code the small fields, hence $\delta \leq D$.

In our computation of complexities, we assume that $d_i \geq 1$ (i.e. several possible values for each field), $n > D$ (hence $n > m$) and $2^n > n^m$ which is realistic when we have hundreds or thousands of filtering rules.

For example, for the $m = 4$ fields IPsrc, IPdst, Port and Protocol, we have used $d_0 = d_1 = 32$ (each IPsrc and IPdst is coded in 32 bits), $d_2 = 16$ (Port is coded in 16 bits), $d_3 = 1$ (Protocol is coded in 1 bit since we consider only TCP and UDP), and $D = 32 + 32 + 16 + 1 = 81$. For $81 < n < 2^{16}$, the above assumptions (all $d_i \geq 1$, $n > 81$ and $2^n > n^4$) are obviously satisfied. IPsrc, IPdst and Port are great fields (theirs domains have more than n values), and Protocol is a small field (its domain has less than n values). We obtain $\mu = 3$ (number of great fields) and $\delta = d_3 = 1$ (1 bit is used to code the unique small field Protocol).

Proposition 10. *The space and time complexities of the synthesis procedure are in* $O(n^{\mu+1} \times 2^{\delta})$, *which is bounded by both* $O(n^{m+1})$ *and* $O(n \times 2^D)$.

Proposition 11. *The space and time complexities for verifying completeness of a security policy are in* $O(n^{\mu+1} \times 2^{\delta})$, *which is bounded by both* $O(n^{m+1})$ *and* $O(n \times 2^D)$.

Proposition 12. *The space and time complexities for detecting general anomalies in a security policy are in* $O(n^{\mu+1} \times 2^{\delta})$, *which is bounded by both* $O(n^{m+1})$ *and* $O(n \times 2^D)$.

Proposition 13. *The space and time complexities for detecting anomalies with conflict (shadowing, generalization, correlation) and LP-redundancy anomalies are in* $O(n^{\mu+2} \times 2^{\delta})$, *which is bounded by both* $O(n^{m+2})$ *and* $O(n^2 \times 2^D)$.

Proposition 14. *The space complexity for detecting MP-redundancy anomalies is in* $O(n^{\mu+2} \times 2^{\delta})$, *which is bounded by both* $O(n^{m+2})$ *and* $O(n^2 \times 2^D)$. *The time complexity for detecting MP-redundancy anomalies is in* $O(n^{\mu+3} \times 2^{\delta})$, *which is bounded by both* $O(n^{m+3})$ *and* $O(n^3 \times 2^D)$.

By using results in [20], the authors of [21] prove that several fundamental problems encountered in analysis and design of firewalls are NP-hard. In our context, their result is that the time complexity is at least in $O(n \times 2^D)$. Our contribution here is that the expression $O(n \times 2^D)$ is an upper bound of our more precise expression $O(n^{\mu+1} \times 2^\delta)$ which shows explicitly the influence of the size of fields (through μ and δ) on the complexity.

10   Conclusion and Future Work

We have first proposed a procedure that synthesizes an automaton which implements a security policy. This synthesis procedure can be a common basis to design and analyze several aspects of firewall security policies, instead of using a distinct approach and formalism for studying each aspect. We have demonstrated this statement by applying our synthesis procedure for verifying completeness of security policies and detecting several types of anomalies in security policies. Another contribution is that we have identified and corrected an error in the commonly used definition of redundancy anomaly. Last but not least, we have evaluated precisely space and time complexities of our developed procedures.

As near future work, we intend to use our automata-based approach to design security policies that can adapt dynamically to the filtered traffic. The approach we will adopt is that from a given security policy, we extract a new equivalent policy whose filtering rules can be put in any order without influencing the semantics of the policy. When the filtered traffic varies, the filtering rules will be reordered dynamically in order to keep a low average delay of determining the rule that is applied for an arriving packet.

References

1. Al-Shaer, E., Hamed, H.: Modeling and management of firewall policies. IEEE Trans. Netw. Serv. Manage. **1**(1), 2–10 (2004)
2. Karoui, K., Ben Ftima, F., Ben Ghezala, H.: Formal specification, verification and correction of security policies based on the decision tree approach. Int. J. Data Netw. Secur. **3**(3), 92–111 (2013)
3. Madhuri, M., Rajesh, K.: Systematic detection and resolution of firewall policy anomalies. Int. J. Res. Comput. Commun. Technol. (IJRCCT) **2**(12), 1387–1392 (2013)
4. Chen, Z., Guo, S., Duan, R.: Research on the anomaly discovering algorithm of the packet filtering rule sets. In 1st International Conference on Pervasive Computing, Signal Processing and Applications (PCSPA), Harbin, China, pp. 362–366, September 2010
5. Garcia-Alfaro, J., Cuppens, F., Cuppens-Boulahia, N., Martinez Perez, S., Cabot, J.: Management of stateful firewall misconfiguration. Comput. Secur. **39**, 64–85 (2013)
6. Cuppens, F., Cuppens-Boulahia, N., Garcia-Alfaro, J., Moataz, T., Rimasson, X.: Handling stateful firewall anomalies. In: Gritzalis, D., Furnell, S., Theoharidou, M. (eds.) SEC 2012. IFIP AICT, vol. 376, pp. 174–186. Springer, Heidelberg (2012)

7. Liu, A.X., Gouda, M.G.: Diverse firewall design. IEEE Trans. Parallel Distrib. Syst. **19**(9), 1237–1251 (2008)
8. Liu, A.X., Gouda, M.G.: Structured firewall design. Comput. Netw. Int. J. Comput. Telecommun. Netw. **51**(4), 1106–1120 (2007)
9. Yuan, L., Mai, J., Su, Z., Chen, H., Chuah, C.-N., Mohapatra, P.: FIREMAN: a toolkit for firewall modeling and analysis. In: IEEE Symposium on Security and Privacy (S&P), Berkeley/Oakland, May 2006
10. Bryant, R.E.: Graph-based algorithms for boolean function manipulation. IEEE Trans. Comput. **35**(8), 677–691 (1986)
11. Mallouli, W., Orset, J., Cavalli, A., Cuppens, N., Cuppens, F.: A formal approach for testing security rules. In: 12th ACM Symposium on Access Control Models and Technologies (SACMAT), Sophia Antipolis, France, June 2007
12. Lee, D., Yannakakis, M.: Principles and methods of testing finite state machines - a survey. Proc. IEEE **84**, 1090–1126 (1996)
13. El Kalam, A.A., El Baida, R., Balbiani, P., Benferhat, S., Cuppens, F., Deswarte, Y., Miège, A., Saurel, C., Trouessin, G.: Organization based access control. In: IEEE 4th International Workshop on Policies for Distributed Systems and Networks (POLICY), Lake Come, Italy, June 2003
14. Mansmann, F., Göbel, T., Cheswick, W.: Visual analysis of complex firewall configurations. In: 9th International Symposium on Visualization for Cyber Security (VizSec), Seattle, pp. 1–8, October 2012
15. Lu, L., Safavi-Naini, R., Horton, J., Susilo, W.: Comparing and debugging firewall rule tables. IET Inf. Secur. **1**(4), 143–151 (2007)
16. Krombi, W., Erradi, M., Khoumsi, A.: Automata-based approach to design and analyze security policies. In: International Conference on Privacy, Security and Trust (PST), Toronto, Canada (2014)
17. Scarfone, K., Hauffman, P.: Guidelines on Firewalls and Firewall Policy, Recommendations of the National Institute of Standards and Technology (NIST). Special Publication 800–41, Revision 1, 2–1, September 2009
18. Madhavi, S., Raghu, G.: Segment generation approach for firewall policy anomaly resolution. Int. J. Comput. Sci. Inf. Technol. (IJCSIT) **5**(1), 6–11 (2014)
19. Hu, H., Ahn, G., Kulkarni, K.: Detecting and resolving firewall policy anomalies. IEEE Trans. Dependable Secure Comput. **9**(3), 318–331 (2012)
20. Garey, M.R., Johnson, D.S.: Computers and Intractability: A Guide to the Theory of NP-Completeness. A.W.H. Freeman, San Francisco (1979)
21. Elmallah, E., Gouda, M.G.: Hardness of firewall analysis. In: International Conference on NETworked sYStems (NETYS), Marrakesh, Morocco, May 2014

Protocol Verification

Debating Cybersecurity or Securing a Debate?
(Position Paper)

Fabio Martinelli and Francesco Santini[(✉)]

Istituto di Informatica e Telematica, IIT-CNR, Pisa, Italy
{fabio.martinelli,francesco.santini}@iit.cnr.it

Abstract. Although inheriting from a well-established literature, Argumentation is currently emerging more and more as a prosperous field of Artificial Intelligence. This paves the way to applications different from traditional ones, as legal reasoning. This paper sets the scene of a large-scale work whose purpose is to develop an Argumentation-based reasoning tool dedicated to the assessment of Cybersecurity and its (re)configuration. Concurrently, and for the first time, we plan to extend the same framework in order to check the vulnerabilities of a debate itself, preventing those attacks aimed at manipulating the result of a decision-making process (e.g., an attack/countermeasure analysis).

1 Introduction

Decisions about network/system security are increasingly complex, involving tradeoffs between keeping systems secure, maintaining system operation, escalating costs, and compromising functionality. We suggest the use of Argumentation to provide automated support for Cybersecurity decisions. Argumentation is a formal approach to decision-making that has proved to be effective in a number of domains, for instance, reasoning in Law, Medicine (diagnosis and treatment of patients), and e-Democracy.

The main benefit of using Argumentation is that it specifically supports reasoning when direct resolution is not possible due to inherent, unresolved logical conflicts. This well adapts to problems where multiple causes for a specific anomalous behaviour are possible, and multiple countermeasures can be taken to solve/mitigate it (as, in general symptom diagnosis, and treatment/mitigation of a problem). In case of a Cybersecurity attack, or policy violation, these problems along with their solution involve *(i)* the integration of information from multiple sources (e.g., sensors), *(ii)* the need to handle information that is noisy and may be inconsistent (or somehow manipulated), and, finally, *(iii)* the requirement to explain the outcome of such integration to humans, in order to support a decision in a way clear to the end-user (see Sect. 3).

But a second issue naturally arises with this approach. How much is the cost of manipulating a final decision by acting on the decision process itself (Sect. 3.1)? In fact, it is possible to study the key arguments of a debate and try

The author 'F. Santini' is supported by MIUR PRIN "Security Horizons".

© Springer International Publishing Switzerland 2015
F. Cuppens et al. (Eds.): FPS 2014, LNCS 8930, pp. 239–246, 2015.
DOI: 10.1007/978-3-319-17040-4_15

to make them weaker or stronger with the purpose to bring the result in favour of the desired side (i.e., persuasion). Knowing this, an attacker can try to forge sensor-data, and consequently to pop up the expected argument in a system. Such cost can be measured in terms of the number of arguments to add to or remove from a discussion, or, in case of weighted frameworks [5], the number of fake votes on arguments/attacks, an uncertainty score associated with them, or, in general, a related strength-level to be manipulated.

2   Preliminaries

In this section we briefly summarise the background information related to classical Abstract Argumentation Frameworks (AAFs) [8]. First we give the definition of AAF (see Definition 1), the definition of defence (Definition 2), of extension-based semantics (Definition 3), and, finally, of the acceptance state for an argument (Definition 4).

Definition 1 (AAF). *An Abstract Argumentation Framework (AAF) is a pair $F = \langle A, R \rangle$ of a set A of arguments and a binary relation $R \subseteq A \times A$, called the attack relation. $\forall a, b \in A$, aRb (or, $a \rightarrowtail b$) means that a attacks b. An AAF may be represented by a directed graph (an interaction graph) whose nodes are arguments and edges represent the attack relation. A set of arguments $S \subseteq A$ attacks an argument a, i.e., $S \rightarrowtail a$, if a is attacked by an argument of S, i.e., $\exists b \in S . b \rightarrowtail a$.*

Definition 2 (Defence). *Given $F = \langle A, R \rangle$, an argument $a \in A$ is defended (in F) by a set $S \subseteq A$ if for each $b \in A$, such that $b \rightarrowtail a$, also $S \rightarrowtail b$ holds.*

The "acceptability" of an argument can be defined under different semantics, depending on the frequency of its membership to some sets, called *extensions*: such semantics characterise a collective "acceptability" for arguments. In Definition 3 we only report the original semantics given by Dung [8] (successive proposals can be found in the literature [9, Chap. 2.5]). Respectively, *adm*, *com*, *prf*, *stb*, and *gde* stand for admissible, complete, preferred, stable, and grounded semantics.

Definition 3 (Semantics [8]). *Let $F = \langle A, R \rangle$ be an AAF. A set $S \subseteq A$ is conflict-free (in F), denoted $S \in cf(F)$, iff there are no $a, b \in S$, such that $a \rightarrowtail b$ or $b \rightarrowtail a \in R$. For $S \in cf(F)$, it holds that*

- *$S \in adm(F)$, if each $a \in S$ is defended by S;*
- *$S \in com(F)$, if $S \in adm(F)$ and for each $a \in A$ defended by S, $a \in S$ holds;*
- *$S \in prf(F)$, if $S \in adm(F)$ and there is no $T \in adm(F)$ with $S \subset T$;*
- *$S \in stb(F)$, if for each $a \in A \backslash S$, $S \rightarrowtail a$;*
- *$S = gde(F)$ if $S \in com(F)$ and there is no $T \in com(F)$ with $T \subset S$.*

We also recall that the requirements in Definition 3 define an inclusion hierarchy on the corresponding extensions, from the most to the least stringent: $stb(F) \subseteq prf(F) \subseteq com(F) \subseteq adm(F)$. Moreover, $\sigma(F) \neq \emptyset$ always holds for each considered semantics σ (except stable). Finally, $gde(F)$ is always unique.

Definition 4 (Arguments acceptance-state). *Given one of the semantics σ in Definition 3 and a framework F, an argument a is (i) sceptically accepted in iff $\forall S \in \sigma(F), a \in S$, (ii) a is credulously accepted if $\exists S \in \sigma(F), a \in S$ and a is not sceptically accepted, and (iii) a is rejected if $\nexists S \in \sigma(F), a \in S$.*

Consider $F = \langle A, R \rangle$ in Fig. 1, with $A = \{a, b, c, d, e\}$ and $R = \{a \rightarrowtail b, c \rightarrowtail b, c \rightarrowtail d, d \rightarrowtail c, d \rightarrowtail e, e \rightarrowtail e\}$. In F we have $adm(F) = \{\emptyset, \{a\}, \{c\}, \{d\}, \{a, c\}, \{a, d\}\}$, $com(F) = \{\{a\}, \{a, c\}, \{a, d\}\}$, $prf(F) = \{\{a, d\}, \{a, c\}\}$, $stb(F) = \{\{a, d\}\}$, and $gde(F) = \{a\}$. Hence, argument a is sceptically accepted in $com(F)$, $prf(F)$ and $stb(F)$, while it is only credulously accepted in $adm(F)$.

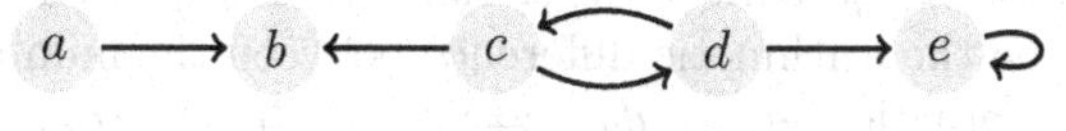

Fig. 1. An example of AAF.

2.1 Decision-Making with Arguments

In this section we simplify part of the content in [9, Chap. 15]. Solving a decision problem amounts to defining a pre-ordering, usually a complete one, on a set $D = \{d_1, \ldots, d_n\}$ of n candidate options. Argumentation can be a means for ordering this set D, that is to define a preference relation $\succcurlyeq$ on D.

Two categories of arguments are distinguished: *(i)* epistemic arguments (A_e) justify beliefs and are themselves based only on beliefs, while *(ii)* practical arguments (A_p) justify options and are built from both beliefs and preferences or goals; moreover, we have that $A_e \cup A_p = A$, and $A_e \cap A_p = \emptyset$. We also define the subsets of practical arguments that are respectively in favour $(\mathcal{F}_f)$, or against $(\mathcal{F}_c)$ a given option $d \in D$:

- $\mathcal{F}_f : D \rightarrow 2^{A_p}$ is a function that returns the arguments in favour of a candidate decision. Such arguments are said pros the option.
- $\mathcal{F}_c : D \rightarrow 2^{A_p}$ is a function that returns the arguments against a candidate decision. Such arguments are said cons the option.

These functions need to satisfy some side-conditions, usually *(i)* $\forall d \in D, \nexists \delta \in A_p$ s.t. $\delta \in \mathcal{F}_f(d)$ and $\delta \in \mathcal{F}_c(d)$, *(ii)* if $\delta \in \mathcal{F}_f(d)$ and $\delta \in \mathcal{F}_p(d')$ (resp. if $\delta \in \mathcal{F}_c(d)$ and $\delta \in \mathcal{F}_c(d')$), then $d = d'$, and *(iii)* $D = \{d_1, \ldots, d_n\}$, $A_p = (\bigcup \mathcal{F}_f(d_i)) \cup (\bigcup \mathcal{F}_c(d_i))$, with $i = 1, \ldots, n$.

In Definition 5 we present one of the possible ways to prefer $(\succcurlyeq)$ one decision instead of another. This *unipolar* principle only refers to either the arguments pros or cons.

Definition 5 (Counting arguments pros/cons). *Let $DS = (D, F)$ be a decision system, where F is an AAF, and $Acc_{stb}(F)$ collects the sceptically accepted arguments of a framework F under the stable semantics. Let $d_1, d_2 \in D$, then:*

$$d_1 \succcurlyeq d_2 \iff |\mathcal{F}_f(d_1) \cap Acc_{stb}(F)| \geq |\mathcal{F}_f(d_2) \cap Acc_{stb}(F)|$$

242   F. Martinelli and F. Santini

In some applications, the arguments in favour of and against a decision are aggregated into a unique meta-argument having a unique strength value. In Definition 6 we present a *non-polar* principle, where h is a generic aggregation function.

Definition 6. *Let* $DS = (D, F)$, $Acc_{stb}(F)$, *and* $d_1, d_2 \in D$. *Let* $(\delta_1, \ldots, \delta_n)$ *and* $(\delta'_1, \ldots, \delta'_m)$ *(resp.* $(\gamma_1, \ldots, \gamma_l)$ *and* $(\gamma'_1, \ldots, \gamma'_k))$ *the vectors of the arguments in* A_p *pros and cons the decision* d_1 *(resp.* d_2*). Then:*

$$d_1 \succcurlyeq d_2 \iff h(\delta_1, \ldots, \delta_n, \delta'_1, \ldots, \delta'_m) \geq_p h(\gamma_1, \ldots, \gamma_l, \gamma'_1, \ldots, \gamma'_k)$$

Relation $\geq_p \subseteq A_p \times A_p$ defines a preference (partial) order on A_p. A simple example can just be the arithmetic difference between the number of arguments pros and cons: in practice, $d_1 \succcurlyeq d_2 \iff |\mathcal{F}_f(d_1) \cap Acc_{stb}(F)| - |\mathcal{F}_c(d_1) \cap Acc_{stb}(F)| \geq |\mathcal{F}_p(d_2) \cap Acc_{stb}(F)| - |\mathcal{F}_c(d_2) \cap Acc_{stb}(F)|$.

3 An Example for Adopting Cybersecurity Countermeasures

Consider an AAF, $F_{worm} = \langle \{a, b, c, d, e, f, g\}, \{b \rightarrowtail a, c \rightarrowtail b, d \rightarrowtail b, e \rightarrowtail d, f \rightarrowtail a, g \rightarrowtail f\} \rangle$, where the arguments correspond to the following statements:

a. A worm is attacking our web server.
b. Disabling Web traffic mitigates worms.
c. Web traffic can be blocked only if loss >70 %.
d. Traffic should not be blocked if the alarm is faulty.
e. Evidence shows that the alarm is reliable.
f. The antivirus has been recently updated.
g. Virus definitions are no longer maintained.

Such AAF is visually represented in Fig. 2a. We consider a related decision-making problem with two options, $D = \{disable\_port80, \neg disable\_port80\}$, which respectively represent the action of disabling or not disabling traffic through port 80. A_p is $\{b, c, d\}$, since these arguments are directly associated with actions in D. Then we have that $\mathcal{F}_f(disable\_port80) = \{b\}$, while $\mathcal{F}_f(\neg disable\_port80) = \{c, d\}$.[1] The set of stable extensions is $stb(F_{worm}) = \{\{a, c, e, g\}\}$ (only one extension), and consequently $Acc(F_{worm}) = \{a, c, e, g\}$ (in grey in Fig. 2b). These arguments are therefore sceptically (i.e., always) accepted in stable extensions, and, for this reason, they represent the strongest arguments possible in such formalisation. Since, the final goal is to reason in presence of conflict, this set of arguments represents our truth: even if attacked (e.g., argument a), they can be considered as "enough" defended (e.g., by d).

---

[1] For the sake of simplicity, in our example we allow attacks among practical arguments (e.g., $d \rightarrowtail b$), and attacks between a practical and an epistemic argument (e.g., $b \rightarrowtail a$). In general, this should be avoided to prevent wishful thinking [9, Chap. 15.2.3].

Following the unipolar principle in Definition 5, we have that $|\mathcal{F}_f(disable\_port$ $80) \cap Acc_{stb}(F_{worm})| = 0$ and $|\mathcal{F}_f(\neg disable\_port80) \cap Acc_{stb}(F_{worm})| = 1$. Therefore, the final result is $\neg disable\_port80 \succcurlyeq disable\_port80$, and the system-security administrator is recommended not to disable traffic on port 80.

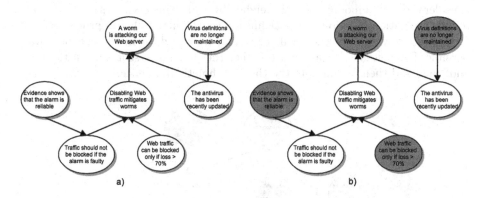

Fig. 2. (a) F_{worm}, and (b), in grey, the arguments in the unique stable extension

3.1 Forgery of a Discussion

The goal of this section is to briefly introduce how the same framework can also be used by an attacker to reach an intended goal, e.g., to block traffic on port 80. Such attacker can study the vulnerabilities of the decision-making process (knowing the security policy of a company, or altering sensor output) and exploit them for his own sake. Considering the same example in Fig. 2a, by attacking argument c with a new argument h, we obtain a completely different result, as sketched in Fig. 3: A_p is still $\{b, c, d\}$, but the set of stable extensions changes to $stb(F_{worm}) = \{\{b, e, g, h\}\}$, and $Acc_{stb}(F_{worm}) = \{b, e, g, h\}$. Following Definition 5, we now have that $|\mathcal{F}_f(disable\_port80) \cap Acc_{stb}(F_{worm})| = 1$ and $|\mathcal{F}_f(\neg disable\_port80) \cap Acc_{stb}(F_{worm})| = 0$. The result is the opposite: $disable\_port80 \succcurlyeq \neg disable\_port80$, and the system-security administrator is thus recommended to disable traffic on port 80. To achieve this behaviour, an attacker could try to keep the loss percentage of Web traffic below 70 %, for instance by reducing the activity of the worm. In this way, the worm is maintained alive and spreading to other computers through a different port/service; nevertheless, Web traffic is blocked, consequently causing a double damaging-effect.

Clearly, the manipulation of this reasoning process comes with a cost in terms of the chosen metrics. First, an attacker is interested in what arguments to attack in order to bring the decision to the desired result, that is only c in this case (but they can be more than one). Then, among such arguments, the goal is to choose the least expensive one to attack, in terms of e.g., money or possibility. This cost also depends on the available actions that can be executed on an AAF. For example, removing argument e in Fig. 2a enforces the decision of keeping port 80 open, since $Acc_{stb}(F_{worm}) = \{a, c, d, g\}$ $(A_p = \{b, c, d\})$ and $|\mathcal{F}_f(disable\_port80) \cap Acc_{stb}(F_{worm})| = 0$, $|\mathcal{F}_f(\neg disable\_port80) \cap Acc_{stb}(F_{worm})| = 2$. With respect to Fig. 2b, the preference of decision $disable\_port80$ is increased from 1 to 2.

In addition, further actions can be the insertion or deletion of attacks, or if either arguments or attacks are associated with a preference score, we can consider the cost of modifying such weights: by evaluating decisions in accordance to an aggregation function h (see Definition 6), the manipulation process is now focused on how to alter the result of h, and how to do it in the cheapest way possible. For instance, h can sum together the preference scores of all the pros and cons, and then to compute the their arithmetic difference.

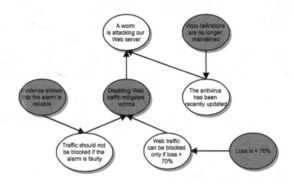

Fig. 3. A forged F_{worm} with a new augment h: "Loss is $<70\,\%$".

4   From Raw Data to Decision

In Fig. 4 we show the architecture of the tool we want to develop to deal with the process presented in Sect. 3: circles represent outputs or inputs that are outside the direct scope of such implementation. One of these inputs is the Cybersecurity case-studies we want to manage, while a second one is represented by other reasoning-engines to plug-in besides our own tool, named $ConArg^2$ [6], which is already capable to find Acc_{stb} [4]. Round rectangles represent software that does not need any interactive input from a user (e.g., translators between different formats), while octagons represent the core modules where we implement the intelligence of the tool, as ConArg, the Decision-Making module (which implements the process designed in Sect. 2.1), and the *Reasoner*. In the Reasoner we realise the intelligence to solve higher-level problems, as evaluating and optimising the cost of manipulation. All the other components in Fig. 4 represent human-interaction through GUIs. For instance, a Security Expert can directly add the information for a particular Cybersecurity case-study she/he has in mind, without having an automated translation from offline cases. On the other side, the System Security Administrator can visually examine Cybersecurity decisions to be taken on the considered problem, and graphically manipulate

---

them with the purpose to see what happens in case new arguments are added. Since arguments/attacks can be weighted, a module is dedicated to the analysis/ extraction of costs and their representation in *WAML*, which is a weighted extension of *Argument Markup Language* (based on XML). WAML will be the lingua-franca format to represent (weighted) AAFs.

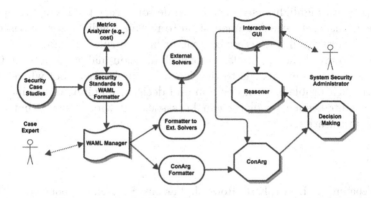

Fig. 4. An architecture to manage Cybersecurity case-studies and their manipulation.

5   Related Work

Since the application of Argumentation to Cybersecurity-related issues is relatively a new field (or, at least, not deeply investigated), there is a few related work to be mentioned. A bunch of works applying Argumentation-based conflict-resolution to the specific case of firewall rules are [1–3]. In our approach, however, we would like to provide a general reasoning-tool.

In [7] the authors formalise the reasoning about access control using a planning theory formalised in Dung's abstract argumentation framework [8]; such planning is based on an adaptation of Dung's notion of defence. Their formal argumentation framework allows arguments about the backward derivation of plans from objectives and policy rules (abduction), as well as arguments about the forward derivation of goals from general objectives. Parties negotiate to find an agreement about which policy to apply, even though there may be more than one way to achieve a security objective.

A first general and introductory work on Argumentation and Cybersecurity is proposed in [10]. There the authors suggest the use of Argumentation to provide automated support for Cybersecurity decisions. Three different tasks where Argumentation can contribute are surveyed in the paper: first, the establishment of a security policy, drawing from a range of information on best practice and taking into account likely attacks and the vulnerability of the system to those attacks. Secondly, the process diagnosis to determine if an attack is underway after some apparent anomaly in system operation is detected; the final goal is to decide what action, if any, should be taken to ensure system integrity. At last,

Argumentation can be used to reconfigure a security policy in the aftermath of a successful attack: this reconfiguration needs to ensure protection against future similar-attacks, without creating new vulnerabilities.

6   Conclusion

As related work highlights (see Sect. 5), while some very preliminary steps have been accomplished to use Argumentation to resolve conflicts in rule-based policies (e.g., security policies, access control, or firewall rule-set), no real effort has been spent to avoid the manipulation of such decision-making process in Cybersecurity scenarios. Our goal is to develop a comprehensive tool where to deal with both such problems, i.e., decision and decision manipulation. Since AAFs can be weighted, such problems can be associated with a score that enables solution-optimisation.

References

1. Applebaum, A., Levitt, K.N., Rowe, J., Parsons, S.: Arguing about firewall policy. In: Verheij, B., Szeider, S., Woltran, S. (eds.) COMMA. Frontiers in Artificial Intelligence and Applications. IOS Press, Amsterdam (2012)
2. Bandara, A.K., Kakas, A.C., Lupu, E.C., Russo, A.: Using argumentation logic for firewall policy specification and analysis. In: State, R., van der Meer, S., O'Sullivan, D., Pfeifer, T. (eds.) DSOM 2006. LNCS, vol. 4269, pp. 185–196. Springer, Heidelberg (2006)
3. Bandara, A.K., Kakas, A.C., Lupu, E.C., Russo, A.: Using argumentation logic for firewall configuration management. In: Integrated Network Management, pp. 180–187. IEEE (2009)
4. Bistarelli, S., Rossi, F., Santini, F.: Benchmarking hard problems in random abstract AFs: The stable semantics. In: Proceedings of the Fifth International Conference on Computational Models of Argument, FAIA, IOS Press (2014, to appear)
5. Bistarelli, S., Santini, F.: A common computational framework for semiring-based argumentation systems. In: 19th European Conference on Artificial Intelligence, ECAI 2010, FAIA, vol. 215, pp. 131–136. IOS Press (2010)
6. Bistarelli, S., Santini, F.: Conarg: a constraint-based computational framework for argumentation systems. In: Proceedings of the 2011 IEEE 23rd International Conference on Tools with Artificial Intelligence, ICTAI 2011, pp. 605–612. IEEE Computer Society (2011)
7. Boella, G., Hulstijn, J., van der Torre, L.W.N.: Argumentation for access control. In: AI*IA, pp. 86–97 (2005)
8. Dung, P.M.: On the acceptability of arguments and its fundamental role in non-monotonic reasoning, logic programming and n-person games. Artif. Intell. **77**(2), 321–357 (1995)
9. Rahwan, I., Simari, G.R.: Argumentation in Artificial Intelligence, 1st edn. Springer Publishing Company, Incorporated, New York (2009)
10. Rowe, J., Levitt, K., Parsons, S., Sklar, E., Applebaum, A., Jalal, S.: Argumentation logic to assist in security administration. In: Proceedings of the 2012 Workshop on New Security Paradigms, NSPW 2012, pp. 43–52. ACM (2012)

Formal Verification of e-Reputation Protocols

Ali Kassem[2]([✉]), Pascal Lafourcade[1], and Yassine Lakhnech[2]

[1] LIMOS, Université d'Auvergne, Clermont-ferrand, France
[2] CNRS, VERIMAG, Université Grenoble Alpes, Saint-Martin-d'Hères, France
ali.kassem@imag.fr

Abstract. Reputation systems are often useful in large online communities in which most of the users are unknown to each other. They are good tools to force the users to act in truthfulness way. However, for a reputation system to work effectively users have to be willing to provide rates. In order to incentivize the users to provide honest rates, a reputation system have to ensure their privacy and anonymity. Users are also concerned about verifying the correctness of the reputation score. In the applied pi-calculus, we define a formal framework and several fundamental privacy, authentication, and verifiability properties suitable for the security analysis of e-reputation protocols. As proof of concept, using ProVerif, we analyze a simple additive decentralized reputation protocol proposed to ensure rate privacy if all users are honest.

Keywords: Reputation protocols · Formal verification · Privacy · Authentication · Verifiability · Applied pi-calculus · ProVerif

1 Introduction

Electronic reputation (in short, *e-reputation*) systems are tools for the users to quantify the trust between each other. Electronic commerce, social news, peer-to-peer routing, and collaborative environments are examples of applications highly benefit from using e-reputation systems. Indeed, similar to the word-of-mouth reputation, an e-reputation system allows users to form an opinion on the behavior of an unknown user service provider through a reputation score. A reputation score is a mathematical value[1] (*e.g.,* the number of all users that provided a positive feedback, or the percentage of those provided a positive one from all the users that provided feedback) computed from the opinions of users that have been interacted with the service provider. For example, users may rate a service provider on eBay or a restaurant on Yelp as useful, and those ratings allow other to identify more easily the best service provider (or product). In the following, whatever the type

---

This research was conducted with the support of the "Digital trust" chair from the Foundation of the University of Auvergne.

[1] Note that, the reputation score could be a vector computed from detailed opinions of the users, where each value reflects the quality of a specific task such as item describing accuracy, shipping speed, etc.

© Springer International Publishing Switzerland 2015
F. Cuppens et al. (Eds.): FPS 2014, LNCS 8930, pp. 247–261, 2015.
DOI: 10.1007/978-3-319-17040-4_16

of parties (clients, service providers, nodes, website, etc.) involved in a reputation system we call them *users*, and the opinions or feedbacks they provide about each other are called *rates*. We explicitly distinguish the user that is currently receiving a rate by calling him *target user*.

E-reputation protocols are becoming an important tool in online communities. However, many adversarial behaviors can affect such systems [8]. Users may collude to collectively subvert the system either by giving a negative (unfair) rates on the victim in order to destroy its reputation–what is called *bad-mouthing* attack [10], or by advertising the quality of service of a certain user more than its real value to increase his reputation–what is called *ballot-stuffing* attack [10]. Moreover, reputation systems may have to face *Sybil attack*, that is users that pollute the system by creating numerous fake identities [13]. In the worst case, some parties (*e.g.*, authority, or users) may act dishonestly and modify the rates to obtain a wrong reputation score. To limit such behavior, users have to be able to check for irregularities, or to prove their absence. Target user may wish to ensure verifiability too. He may want to be transparent to inspire trustworthiness in his reputation score.

For reputation systems to be effective, in addition to their correctness, users have to be willing to provide rates. In order to incentivize the users to provide honest rates, e-reputation protocols have to ensure their privacy and anonymity. Usually, users wish to remain anonymous as they would like to be sure that the rate they provide cannot be used in a way that can affect them in the future. Actually, it has been shown that preserving the privacy of users encourage them to feed the reputation systems with honest ratings without fearing retaliation [22].

Contributions: In this paper, we provide the means to analyze the privacy of e-reputation protocols and verify their correctness. Precisely, we model e-reputation protocols in the applied pi-calculus [1], we define four privacy properties: *Rate Privacy*, rates provided by the users are kept secret; *Rate Anonymity*, an attacker cannot relate a certain rate to the user provided it; *Receipt-Freeness*, a user cannot prove to an attacker that he provided a certain rate about the target user; *Coercion-Resistance*, even when interacting with a coercer, the user can still provide a rate of his choice. We also give two authentication properties: *Rate Integrity*, the rate is recorded as sent (casted) by the user unmodified; *User Eligibility*, only eligible users (those who accomplish a successful interaction) can cast rates, and two verifiability properties: *Reputation Score Verification*, any one can verify the validity of a certain user score; *User Eligibility Verification*, any one can verify that every counted rate is casted by an eligible users (those who accomplish a successful interaction). Finally, we validate the effectiveness of the proposed approach by analyzing the security of an e-reputation protocol [21] using ProVerif [7].

The proposed properties still cannot detect attacks such as bad-mothing and ballot-stuffing attacks, but properties such as: *User Eligibility Verification*, *Receipt-Freeness*, and *Coercion-Resistance* can minimize them. As *User Eligibility Verification* imposes some constraints on the users in order to provide a rate (*e.g.*, accomplish a successful interaction); *Receipt-Freeness* can limit the bribing and positive rate exchange between users as they cannot provide a proof that they provided a certain rate; similarly does *Coercion-Resistance* even when interacting with a coercer.

Related Work: As an example of simple reputation system is the one used by eBay. After the exchange is accomplished between users (a client and a service provider), they can rate each other with a rating, -1, 0, or $+1$ in accordance with their satisfaction. A more sophisticated reputation systems have been recently proposed. Androulaki *et al.* propose an reputation protocol relies on trusted central authority to demonstrate the validity of rates in [4]. Pavlov *et al.* [21] were the first ones to propose a decentralized reputation protocol to preserve users privacy. Other try to have privacy preserving protocols [2,24,25] by dealing with *unlinkability* that is to ensure that an attacker cannot distinguish whether the same user is involved in two interactions or not. Bethencourt *et al.* [6] formally define the anonymity of both the users and the target user, and propose a protocol argued informally to satisfy those definitions. Anceaume *et al.* extend their work in [3] to handle non-monotonic ratings and mention additional security properties concerned in reputation scores correctness.

However, to best of our knowledge no general formal framework that allows the verification of the security properties in e-reputation protocols have been given. In some related domains, there are numerous papers presenting the formalization and verification of the security properties, for instance in e-voting [5,9, 16,17], in e-auction systems [12,15,18], and in e-exams [14]. Some of the security properties therein studied seem to relate with those we present for e-reputation protocols. For instance, user eligibility is analogous to voter, bidder, and student eligibility. Rate privacy reminds vote, bid, and mark privacy.

However, still there are fundamental differences. In voting, the candidates and the voters (and thus the maximum possible number of votes) are already known, and after voting process the total number of votes and that taken by each candidate will be publicly available. Thus, there is a certain leakage of information. For example, if a candidate does not receive any vote, the attacker can exclude this previously possible option. While in reputation all users can rate each other playing two rules at the same time (rate provider and target user). Also, the number of provided rates is not (necessarily) publicly known. Thus, having a reputation score does not give us any information about the number of the rates provided for the other users. Also, in protocols that support both negative and positive rates, a score zero does not means zero rates. Even in case of only positive rates, a score zero could due to the fact that this user did not make any interaction with the others yet, not necessarily means that users provides their rates to other target users like in voting. Actually, in reputation a user do not have to choose between different target users as he can provides rates for all users he interacted with. Note that, providing a rate for a certain user is not always good like when you vote for a certain candidate in voting, as the rate could be a bad one. Hence, reputation systems have many differences from voting systems.

Furthermore, the threat models for reputation, voting, auctions and exams are different: in voting collusion between the voters and the candidates (bribing) aims to see a candidate win; in reputation collusion between the users by bribing, by exchanging good rates or even making fake interaction aims to increase their reputation scores; similarly in exams collusion between the student and the examiner aims to get the highest possible mark; it is different in auction since bidders want to win with the lowest possible price, but seller want to sell with the highest possible one.

Outline: In Sect. 2, we model e-reputation protocols in the applied pi-calculus. We formally express the security properties in Sect. 3. In Sect. 4, we validate our framework by analyzing the security of an e-reputation protocol [21]. Finally, we conclude and outline the future work in Sect. 5.

2   Modelling

We model e-reputation protocols in the applied pi-calculus [1], a process calculus designed for the verification of cryptographic protocols. To perform the automatic protocol verification, we use ProVerif [7]. This tool uses a process description based on the applied pi-calculus, but has syntactical extensions and is enriched by events to check reachability and correspondence properties. Besides, it can check equivalence properties. We use the *labeled bisimilarity* ($\approx_l$) to express the equivalence between two processes [1]. Informally, two processes are equivalent if an observer has no way to distinguish between them.

Precisely, honest parties are modeled as processes in the applied pi-calculus. These processes can exchange messages on public or private channels, create keys or fresh random values and perform tests and cryptographic operations, which are modeled as functions on terms with respect to an equational theory describing their properties.

The Dolev-Yao attacker [11] has complete control of the network, except the private channels: he can eavesdrop, remove, substitute, duplicate and delay messages that the parties are sending one another, and insert messages of his choice on the public channels. To capture threats due to collusions and coercions, we assume dishonest parties. They cooperate with the attacker, revealing their secret data (*e.g.*, secret keys) to him, or taking orders from him (*e.g.*, what rate to provide). We model such dishonest parties as in Definition 10 and 15 from [9]: if the process P is an honest party, then the process P^{c_1} or P^{c_1,c_2} is its dishonest version. The process P^{c_1} is a variant of P which shares with the attacker channels c_1. Through c_1, P^{c_1} sends all its inputs and freshly generated names (but not other channel names). The second process P^{c_1,c_2} does not only reveal the secret data on channel c_1, but also takes orders from the attacker on the channel c_2 before sending a message or branching. This models a completely corrupted party. To hide the outputs of an extended process (a process which may contain an active substitutions $\{^m/_x\}$) on a certain channel, we use the Definition 11 from [9]: if A is an extended process, then the process $A^{\setminus out(ch,\cdot)}$

is a variant of A that hides all the outputs on channel ch, it is defined by $\nu ch.(A|!in(ch, x))$. For more details about the applied pi-calculus, its standard results and all the definitions used in this paper, we refer to the papers [1,9].

Reputation protocols have some important differences. However, a large class of them can be represented as follows.

Definition 1 (Reputation Protocol). *A reputation protocol is defined by a tuple $(U, T, A_1, \ldots, A_l, \tilde{n}_p)$, where U is the process executed by the users, T is the process executed by the target user; the one we looking for his reputation score, A_i's are the processes executed by the authorities, and $\tilde{n}_p$ is the set of private channel names.*

A reputation protocol involves users who provide the rates about the target user, and the protocol authorities who often handle the rates, calculate the reputation score, distribute the scores, etc. Note that all users execute the same process, but with different variable values, *e.g.*, keys, identities, and rates. In some protocols, especially decentralized ones such as [21], reputation scores are computed upon request by a certain user; the one looking to know the reputation score of the target user (due to a potential interaction with him), this user is represented as on of the authorities as usually his task involve some organizational work.

To reason about privacy, we talk about *reputation processes*; instances of a reputation protocol.

Definition 2 (Reputation Process). *Given a reputation protocol a reputation process is a closed process $\nu\tilde{n}.(U\sigma_{id_1}\sigma_{r_1}, \ldots, U\sigma_{id_n}\sigma_{r_n}, T, A_1, \ldots, A_m)$ where $\tilde{n}$ is the set of all restricted names, which includes the set of the protocol's private channels; $U\sigma_{id_i}\sigma_{r_i}$'s are the processes run by the users, the substitution σ_{id_i} specifies the user's identity and σ_{r_i} specifies the rate given by the user id_i; T is the process runs by the target user; and $A_1, \ldots, A_m$ are the processes run by the authorities.*

As a notation, we use what in applied pi-calculus is called "context". The context $RP_I[\_]$ is the process RP without the processes whose identities are in the set I; they are replaced by "holes". We use this notation when we need to specify exactly, for instance, the processes of the users id_1 and id_2 without repeating the entire reputation process. This is done by rewriting RP as $RP_{\{id_1,id_2\}}[U\sigma_{id_1}\sigma_{r_1}|U\sigma_{id_2}\sigma_{r_2}]$.

3   Security Properties

In the following, we formally define our security properties.

3.1   Privacy Properties

We model our four privacy properties; *Rate Privacy, Rate Privacy, Receipt-Freeness,* and *Coercion-Resistance* as observational equivalence, a standard choice for such kind of properties [23]. We use the labeled bisimilarity to express the equivalence between two processes.

The first property, *Rate Privacy*, says that user rates have to be secret. Keeping the rates secret gives the users more incentive to provide honest rates.

Definition 3 (Rate Privacy). *A reputation protocol ensures* Rate Privacy *if for any reputation process RP, any user id, and any two rates r, r', we have that:* $RP_{\{id\}}[U\sigma_{id}\sigma_r] \approx_l RP_{\{id\}}[U\sigma_{id}\sigma_{r'}]$.

Rate Privacy states that two processes with different rates have to be observationally equivalent. Note that, such a property can be defined as a reachability property: an attacker can not reach a state where the rate r is in his knowledge. However, modeling it as an equivalence property is stronger, as this prevents the attacker from obtaining any information about the rate.

Here, we can consider dishonest target user, as he might be interested in knowing the rates provided by the others users about him. We can do this by replacing honest T with dishonest one. If we assume that T has an identity id_t, we obtain $RP_{\{id,id_t\}}[U\sigma_{id}\sigma_r|T^{c_1,c_2}] \approx_l RP_{\{id,id_t\}}[U\sigma_{id}\sigma_{r'}|T^{c_1,c_2}]$. We can also add another dishonest users using the same technique, however the user who provides the two different rates has to be honest. Otherwise the property can be trivially violated by him revealing his rate to the attacker. This technique can be used in all the following properties if we want to add some dishonest parties.

The previous definition of *Rate Privacy* ensures that the attacker cannot know the rates of the users. However, in practice the rates could be publicly available, *e.g.*, in some sites we could find that n users provide a certain rate without mentioned the identities of these users. Another variant of *Rate Privacy* is *Rate Anonymity*, *i.e.*, the attacker might know the list of all rates, but is unable to associate a certain rate to its corresponding user.

Definition 4 (Rate Anonymity). *A reputation protocol ensures* Rate Anonymity, *if for any reputation process RP, any users id_1, id_2, and any rates r_1, r_2, we have that:* $RP_{\{id_1,id_2\}}[U\sigma_{id_1}\sigma_{r_1}|U\sigma_{id_2}\sigma_{r_2}] \approx_l RP_{\{id_1,id_2\}}[U\sigma_{id_1}\sigma_{r_2} |U\sigma_{id_2}\sigma_{r_1}]$.

This definition states that the process where user id_1 provides a rate r_1 and user id_2 provides a rate r_2 is equivalent to the process where id_1 provides a rate r_2 and id_2 provides a rate r_1. This prevents the attacker from obtaining the identity of the user who provides a certain rate.

A protocol that ensures *Rate Privacy* also ensures *Rate Anonymity*. We have $RP_{\{id_1,id_2\}}[U\sigma_{id_1}\sigma_{r_1}|U\sigma_{id_2}\sigma_{r_2}] \approx_l RP_{\{id_1,id_2\}}[U\sigma_{id_1}\sigma_{r_2}|U\sigma_{id_2}\sigma_{r_2}]$ using *Rate Privacy* since only the rate provided by the user id_1 is changed from r_1 in the left side to r_2 in the right one. Similarly, by changing the rate of id_2, we have: $RP_{\{id_1,id_2\}}[U\sigma_{id_1}\sigma_{r_2}|U\sigma_{id_2}\sigma_{r_2}] \approx_l RP_{\{id_1,id_2\}}[U\sigma_{id_1}\sigma_{r_2}|U\sigma_{id_2}\sigma_{r_1}]$.

For *Receipt-Freeness* and *Coercion-Resistance* we follow the definitions introduced in [9].

A protocol is receipt-free, if an attacker cannot distinguish between a situation where a user id_1 provides a rate r_c according to the attacker's wishes and reveals his data on a channel ch, and a situation where id_1 actually provides a rate r_1 of his choice and pretends to reveal his secret data (this is modeled by process U'). The process U' is a process in which user id_1 provides a rate r_1, but communicates with the attacker (coercer) to trick him by saying that his desired rate r_c is provided. This can be done by providing the attacker a fake receipt, *e.g.*, using a trapdoor to generate a different opening key. Note that, user id_2 swaps the rates with id_1 to avoid the case where the attacker can distinguish the situations by counting the rates, if possible.

Definition 5 (Receipt-Freeness). *A reputation protocol ensures* Receipt-Freeness *if for any reputation process RP, any users id_1, id_2, and any rates r_1, r_c, there exists a closed plain process U' such that:*

- $U'^{\backslash out(ch,.)} \approx_l U\sigma_{id_1}\sigma_{r_1}$, *and*
- $RP_{\{id_1,id_2\}}[(U\sigma_{id_1}\sigma_{r_c})^{ch}|U\sigma_{id_2}\sigma_{r_1}] \approx_l RP_{\{id_1,id_2\}}[U'|U\sigma_{id_2}\sigma_{r_c}].$

Coercion-Resistance is a stronger property than *Receipt-Freeness*, as the attacker can not only ask for a receipt, but is also allowed to interact with the user during the rating process and to provide the messages the user should send.

Definition 6 (Coercion-Resistance). *A reputation protocol ensures* Coercion-Resistance *if for any reputation process RP, there exists a closed plain process U' such that for any $\sigma_?$, and context $C = \nu c_1.\nu c_2.(\_|P)$ satisfying $\tilde{n} \cap fn(C) = \emptyset$ and $RP_I[C[(U\sigma_{id_1}\sigma_?)^{c_1,c_2}]|U\sigma_{id_2}\sigma_{r_1}] \approx_l RP_I[(U\sigma_{id_1}\sigma_{r_c})^{ch}|U\sigma_{id_2}\sigma_{r_1}]$, where $I = \{id_1, id_2\}$, we have that:*

- $C[U']^{\backslash out(ch,.)} \approx_l U\sigma_{id_1}\sigma_{r_1}$, *and*
- $RP_I[C[(U\sigma_{id_1}\sigma_?)^{c_1,c_2}]|U\sigma_{id_2}\sigma_{r_1}] \approx_l RP_I[C[U']|U\sigma_{id_2}\sigma_{r_c}].$

Here, the context C models the attacker's behaviors which tries to force the user to provide the rate r_c. Note that, no matter what rate the user id_1 intends to provide ($\sigma_?$), the attacker will force him to provide the rate r_c.

3.2 Authentication Properties

We model the authentication properties as correspondence properties, a well-known approach [23]. Correspondence properties capture relationships between events, which may have the same structure *"if a event e is executed the event e''s has been previously executed"*. Events are annotations that do not change a process behavior, but are inserted at precise locations to allow reasoning about the authentication properties.

To define our two authentication properties, we use the following events:

- Event $sent(id_u, id_t, r)$ emitted when the user id_u send a rate r (or sum of rates) for the authority (or responsible party) to evaluate the target user id_t. This event is emitted just before sending the message containing the rate.

- Event $record(id_u, id_t, r)$ emitted when the rate r (or sum of rates) from the user id_u provided about the target user id_t is received by the authority (or the intended party). This event is placed after receiving the rate and perform the required checks before accepting it, if any.
- Event $eligible(id_u, id_t)$ emitted when the user id_u is certified as an eligible user to provide a rate about the target user id_t. It is placed just before providing the credential by the responsible party.

After placing these events inside the reputation process, the authentication properties can then defined as follows:

First, *Rate Integrity*, which ensures that the rate is not altered and received by the responsible party as it provided by the user.

Definition 7 (Rate Integrity). *A reputation protocol ensures* Rate Integrity, *if for every reputation process RP each occurrence of the event* $record(id_u, id_t, r)$ *is preceded by a distinct occurrence of the corresponding event* $sent(id_u, id_t, r)$ *on every possible execution trace.*

The second property is *User Eligibility*, which ensures that only the users have a certain credential can provide a rate. The credential can be a certificate from an authority, a proof that he has been interacted with the target user, or marked in some database as interacted with the target user. It is defined using the following two events:

Definition 8 (User Eligibility). *A reputation protocol ensures* User Eligibility, *if for any reputation process RP each occurrence of the event* $record(id_u, id_t, r)$ *(for any r) is preceded by a distinct occurrence of the corresponding event* $eligible$ (id_u, id_t) *on every possible execution trace.*

3.3   Verifiability Properties

Similar to [15], we define a verification test as an efficient terminating algorithm that takes as input the data visible to a participate of the reputation protocol and returns a boolean value (*true* or *false*). To reason about verifiability properties, we extend the reputation process with the following functions and variables:

- rs is a variable referring to the reputation score assigned to the target user;
- L: $List(ERate)$ is a list of (encrypted or anonymized) rates provided by the users about the target user;
- $getRate$: $ERate \mapsto Rate$ is a function that maps the (encrypted or anonymized) rates to a regular rates (*e.g.*, an integer). This function does not need to be computable for any party, as it is only used to define the verification test;
- $compRep$ is a function that computes the reputation score given a list of rates. This might be simply the summation of all the rates, but there may be more complex operations to determine this value;
- $isEligible$: $ID \times ID \mapsto \{true, false\}$ is a function which takes a rate and returns *true* if the rate was provided by a certified user (user which interacted with the target user).

We write $getRate(L)$ for $getRate(L[1]), \ldots, getRate(L[n])$, where $L[i]$ is the ith entry of the list L.

Users would like to verify the validity of the reputation score of the target, this is ensured by *Reputation Score Verification*.

Definition 9 (Reputation Score Verification). *A reputation protocol ensures* Reputation Score Verification, *if we have a test RSV respecting the following:*

- *Soundness: $RSV = true \Rightarrow rs = compRep(getrate(L))$;*
- *Completeness: if all participants follow the protocol correctly, then $rs = comp$* $Rep(getrate(L)) \Rightarrow RSV = true$.

Another interesting verifiability property is *User Eligibility Verification* which allows anyone to check if every counted rate is provided by an eligible user.

Definition 10 (User Eligibility Verification). *A reputation protocol ensures* User Eligibility Verification, *if we have a test UEV respecting the following conditions:*

- *Soundness: $UEV = true \Rightarrow \forall r \in L, isEligible(r) = true$;*
- *Completeness: if all participants follow the protocol correctly, then $\forall r \in L, is$* $Eligible(r) = true \Rightarrow UEV = true$.

Note that, this property is different from the *User Eligibility* presented before. A protocol satisfying *User Eligibility* means that it authenticates the users and only allows eligible ones to provide rates, but this does not necessarily means that anyone (*e.g.,* another user) can himself verify that the rates were provide by an eligible users as the protocol might not provide a proof for that. In the protocols that satisfy *User Eligibility* but not *User Eligibility Verification*, users usually have to trust a certain authority about the eligibility of the users, however in those satisfying *Use Eligibility Verification* a user can himself verify the eligibility of the users and thus detecting any error or cheating, and does not have to trust any authority concerning this point as the authority itself might act dishonestly.

4   Case Study

Using ProVerif [7], we applied the previously explained definitions on the first protocol proposed by Pavlov *et al.* in [21]. This protocol was designed to provide privacy of the rates in decentralized additive reputation systems, if all users flow the protocol correctly *i.e.,* all users are honest. It also assumes that all users provide honest rating about the target user (*i.e.,* rating that correctly reflects their satisfaction), as the protocol cannot prevent the users from providing an unfair rating to increase (or decrease) the reputation score of the target user more (or less) than its real value. The authors argue that the protocol preserves the secrecy of all the rates if the users do not collude with each others.

Informal Description. The basic idea behind this protocol is to consider the rate provided by each user to be his secret information. The rates are cumulatively added to each other, without revealing them, to obtain a sum represents the reputation score of the target. The protocol is initiated by a querying agent A_q looking to know the reputation score of the target user, and proceeded as follows:

1. Initialization Step: the querying agent A_q orders the users in a ring: $A_q \rightarrow U_1 \rightarrow, \ldots, \rightarrow U_n \rightarrow A_q$, and sends to each user U_i the identity of his successor in the ring, *i.e.*, for $i \in \{1, \ldots, n-1\}$ it sends the identity of U_{i+1} to U_i, and for U_n it sends its identity.
2. A_q chooses a random number $r_q \neq 0$ and sends it to U_1.
3. Upon reception of r_p from his predecessor in the ring, each user U_i for $i \in \{1, \ldots, n\}$ calculates $r_p + r_i$ and sends the obtained value to his successor in the ring, where r_i is the reputation rate of the user U_i about the target user.
4. Upon reception of the feedback from U_n, A_q subtracts r_q from it in order to obtain the reputation score of the target user represented by the sum of all rates.

To ensure secrecy and authentication, the designers of the protocol assume an authenticated secure channel between every two users.

Formal Model. Generally, it is difficult to model arithmetic operations in formal protocol provers such as ProVerif. However, we build a simple equational theory which handles the required arithmetics to verify the protocol for the case where we have two users U_1 and U_2 in addition to the querying agent.

We modeled the protocol in ProVerif using a standard equational theory for symmetric encryption (functions `senc` and `sdec`), `senc(m, k)` represents the symmetric encryption of the message m with the key k and `sdec` represents the decryption function; and an equational theory for arithmetic addition and subtraction (functions `sum` and `sub`). The function `sum` takes two values and return their sum. Having `x` or `y` we can obtain the other one from `sum(x, y)` using the function `sub`. Similarly, we can obtain `sum(y,z)` and `sum(x,z)` from `sum(sum(x, y), z)` having `x` and `y` respectively. Note that with this equational theory, having `x` or `y`, one cannot obtain `sum(z, y)` or `sum(z,x)` from `sum(z, sum(x, y))`. Solving this requires two additional equations similar to the last two equations presented below. One could also says why not modeling `sum` as a commutative function, *i.e.*, `sum(x, y) = sum(y, x)`, which solves this problem and moreover allows us to represent the subtraction using only two equations instead of four. This is due to a ProVerif problem as both solutions cause non termination. Actually, it is well known that ProVerif has difficulties with commutative operations. However, we overcome this weakness by giving the value r_p received by the user process U_i as the first argument to the function `sum`, and his rate r_i as the second argument. Thus, such a term `sum(z, sum(x, y))` does not appear between the messages involved in the protocol.

$$\texttt{sdec(senc(m,k),k)} = \texttt{m}$$
$$\texttt{sub(sum(x, y), x)} = \texttt{y}$$
$$\texttt{sub(sum(x, y), y)} = \texttt{x}$$
$$\texttt{sub(sum(sum(x, y), z), x)} = \texttt{sum(y,z)}$$
$$\texttt{sub(sum(sum(x, y), z), y)} = \texttt{sum(x,z)}$$

An alternative equational theory could be modeling the sum of two numbers x and y as their exclusive-or (XOR), *i.e.*, xor(x, y) instead of sum(x, y). In this case the subtraction will represented by another XOR application, *i.e.*, xor(xor(x, y), y) = x. ProVerif, originally does not handel the XOR operator, however Küsters *et al.* show how to reduce the derivation problem for horn theories with XOR to the XOR-free case in [20]. Their reduction allows one to carry out the analysis of the protocols that involve XOR operator using tools, such as ProVerif. We belive that their result allows us to carry out the analysis (possiblly for more than two users) with ProVerif, using the XOR operator to model the summation and subtraction. However, we kept this for future work.

All the parties (querying agent and users) are modeled as honest parties. To model the authenticated secure channel, all the messages are exchanged encrypted with a symmetric key shared between all the users, for a secure communication. For authentication, the unique identities of the sender and the receiver are included in the message to authenticate the sender, and ensure that only the intended receiver will receive the message. Note that, the attacker can still block, or re-play the messages.

Analysis. The results of our analysis are detailed below.

Rate Privacy: In case of only one user, it is clear that we do not have *Rate Privacy* as the reputation score will be equal to the rate of this user, and thus the querying agent can knows this rate. We show, using ProVerif, that the protocol ensures *Rate Privacy* in the case of two users (other than the querying agent). As we mentioned, to model the authenticated channel we add the identities to the messages. Note that, if the identity of the receiver is removed from the messages, the attacker can re-direct the message sent by the first user, which contains $sum(r_q, r_1)$, to the querying agent instead of the second user, and thus the rate of the first user will be enclosed to the querying agent even if he acts honestly. A similar attack will enclose the rate of the last user (herein user two) if the attacker re-direct the first message by querying agent, which contains r_q to the last user. To make the attack on the intermediate users (in case of more than two users) the attacker needs two sessions to be initiated by the same querying agent. Note that, in all these attacks the rate will only enclosed to the querying agent and not to the attacker unless that the obtained reputation score is published by the querying agent.

Rate Anonymity: ProVerif was able to show that the protocol ensures *Rate Anonymity* in the case of two users (other than the querying agent).

Receipt-Freeness: The protocol does not ensure Receipt-Freeness since the shared key k can be used as a receipt which allows the attacker to enclose the value of the message received by the victim user and that sent by him, then subtract them from each other to check whether the difference is equal to the rate r_c he wants, or not. Note that, the user cannot lie about the key by giving the attacker an different key k' since, for any keys $k' \neq k$ and rates $r_c \neq r_i$, we cannot have that $r_c = sub(sdec(senc(sum(r_p, r_i), k), k'), sdec(senc(r_p, k), k'))$.

Coercion-Resistance: As *Receipt-Freeness* does not hold, then *Coercion-Resistance* also does not hold since by Proposition 18 of [9], if a protocol ensures *Coercion-Resistance* then it also ensures *Receipt-Freeness.*

Rate Integrity: We check the integrity of the messages exchanged between the parties (querying agent and users). Thus events are placed in both querying agent and user processes. ProVerif shows that the integrity of the messages is preserved if the correspondance is modeled without injectivity, and terms types (sorts) are respected. Note that, the injectivity does not hold since the attacker can re-play the message several times, and thus we will have several emission of the event *record* preceded by only one emission of event *sent.* Note also that a flaw attack exists if we ignore the types of the terms: for example, the first message sent by the querying agent to the first user to inform him about the identity of his successor, which has a type ID, might be received by this user as a rate r_q, which has another type Rate. Thus, the event *record* will emitted but not the event *sent.*

User Eligibility: We show with ProVerif that *User Eligibility* is ensured by the protocol. We assume that the users included in the ring are eligible as they are registered in a certain database. Thus, the event *eligible* is emitted when the querying agent chooses the user as a node in the ring. The event *record* emitted when the rate is received by his successor in the ring (actually the summation of all privious rates is received).

Reputation Score Verification: The users can only get the reputation score, however they have no means to check if this score is calculated correctly from the users rates. However, if the rates and the score are published encrypted with the shared key in a Bulletin Board, then we can design a test that allows the users to verify the reputation score. The test takes users rates and the reputation score of the target user, and simply checks if the summation of all rates is equal to the score. Note that, verifability could destroys the privacy of the rates. We show using ProVerif that the test is sound and complete.

User Eligibility Verification: Users that provides rates are not publicly known. Also, users do not provide any proof (*e.g.,* certificate from authority) which could allow us to verify their eligibility. Note that, as user eligibility is ensured, according to the definition of *User Eligibility Verification* the test that always gives true is sound and complete. However, this test is dummy as it does not provide any information for the users to remove their doubts, trusting the authority is all what they have to do instead.

5 Conclusion and Future Work

We set the first research step on the formal understanding of e-reputation systems, and establishes a framework for the automatic analysis of their security requirements. In particular, we show how to model reputation protocols in the applied pi-calculus, and how security properties such as privacy, authentication, and verifiability properties can be expressed.

We validate our model and definitions by analyzing, using ProVerif, the security of an e-reputation protocol, the protocol by Pavlov *et al.* [21]. It has been informally argued to preserve rate privacy. Our analysis shows that it ensured *Rate Privacy*, *Rate Anonymity*, and *User Eligibility*. It fails to satisfy *Receipt-Freeness*, *Coercion-Resistance*, and *User Eligibility Verification*, and presents some weakness concerning *Rate Integrity*, and *Reputation Score Verification* but satisfies them with some assumptions.

As a future work we intend to analyze more e-reputation protocols. Several e-reputation protocols are highly depends on algebraic properties such as arithmetic operations and homomorphic encryptions, *e.g.* [3,6,19,21]. Developing automatic tools that can deal with these properties is still a real challenge for the community. However, researches goes some way in the direction of finding solutions for such a problem, for instance the result obtained by Küsters *et al.* [20] allows us to analyze protocols with XOR operator using ProVerif. Note that, this result could help us in analyzing protocols with arithmetic operations, which is the case of many e-reputation protocols, if used to model summation and subtraction.

Other interesting research works include the study of the relation between our security properties as well as the definition of novel properties such as correctness of the reputation score, prevent double rating, accountability, reliability (*e.g.,* to prevent Sybil attacks), and addressing false unfair rates.

References

1. Abadi, M., Fournet, C.: Mobile values, new names, and secure communication. In: Hankin, C., Schmidt, D. (eds.) POPL, pp. 104–115. ACM (2001)
2. Anceaume, E., Guette, G., Lajoie-Mazenc, P., Prigent, N., Tong, V.V.T.: A privacy preserving distributed reputation mechanism. In: ICC, pp. 1951–1956. IEEE (2013)
3. Anceaume, E., Guette, G., Lajoie-Mazenc, P., Sirvent, T., Viet Triem Tong, V.: Extending signatures of reputation. In: Hansen, M., Hoepman, J.-H., Leenes, R., Whitehouse, D. (eds.) Privacy and Identity 2013. IFIP AICT, vol. 421, pp. 165–176. Springer, Heidelberg (2014)
4. Androulaki, E., Choi, S.G., Bellovin, S.M., Malkin, T.: Reputation systems for anonymous networks. In: Borisov, N., Goldberg, I. (eds.) PETS 2008. LNCS, vol. 5134, pp. 202–218. Springer, Heidelberg (2008)

5. Backes, M., Hritcu, C., Maffei, M.: Automated verification of remote electronic voting protocols in the applied pi-calculus. In: CSF, pp. 195–209 (2008)
6. Bethencourt, J., Shi, E., Song, D.: Signatures of reputation. In: Sion, R. (ed.) FC 2010. LNCS, vol. 6052, pp. 400–407. Springer, Heidelberg (2010)
7. Blanchet, B.: An efficient cryptographic protocol verifier based on prolog rules. In: 14th IEEE Computer Security Foundations Workshop (CSFW-14 2001), Cape Breton, Nova Scotia, Canada, 11–13 June 2001, pp. 82–96. IEEE Computer Society (2001)
8. Carrara, E., Hogben, G.: Reputation-based systems: a security analysis (2007)
9. Delaune, S., Kremer, S., Ryan, M.: Verifying privacy-type properties of electronic voting protocols. J. Comput. Secur. 17(4), 435–487 (2009)
10. Dellarocas, C.: Immunizing online reputation reporting systems against unfair ratings and discriminatory behavior. In: EC, pp. 150–157 (2000)
11. Dolev, D., Yao, A.C.: On the security of public key protocols. IEEE Trans. Inf. Theory 29(2), 198–208 (1983)
12. Dong, N., Jonker, H., Pang, J.: Analysis of a receipt-free auction protocol in the applied pi calculus. In: Degano, P., Etalle, S., Guttman, J. (eds.) FAST 2010. LNCS, vol. 6561, pp. 223–238. Springer, Heidelberg (2011)
13. Douceur, J.R.: The sybil attack. In: Druschel, P., Kaashoek, M.F., Rowstron, A. (eds.) IPTPS 2002. LNCS, vol. 2429, pp. 251–260. Springer, Heidelberg (2002)
14. Dreier, J., Giustolisi, R., Kassem, A., Lafourcade, P., Lenzini, G., Ryan, P.Y.A.: Formal analysis of electronic exams. In: Samarati, P. (ed.) SECRYPT 2014 - Proceedings of the 11th International Conference on Security and Cryptography, Vienna, Austria, 28–30 August, 2014. SciTePress (2014)
15. Dreier, J., Jonker, H., Lafourcade, P.: Defining verifiability in e-auction protocols. In: Chen, K., Xie, Q., Qiu, W., Li, N., Tzeng, W.-G. (eds.) ASIACCS, pp. 547–552. ACM (2013)
16. Dreier, J., Lafourcade, P., Lakhnech, Y.: Vote-independence: a powerful privacy notion for voting protocols. In: Garcia-Alfaro, J., Lafourcade, P. (eds.) FPS 2011. LNCS, vol. 6888, pp. 164–180. Springer, Heidelberg (2012)
17. Dreier, J., Lafourcade, P., Lakhnech, Y.: A formal taxonomy of privacy in voting protocols. In: ICC, pp. 6710–6715 (2012)
18. Dreier, J., Lafourcade, P., Lakhnech, Y.: Formal verification of e-Auction protocols. In: Basin, D., Mitchell, J.C. (eds.) POST 2013 (ETAPS 2013). LNCS, vol. 7796, pp. 247–266. Springer, Heidelberg (2013)
19. Hasan, O., Brunie, L., Bertino, E., Shang, N.: A decentralized privacy preserving reputation protocol for the malicious adversarial model. IEEE Trans. Inf. Forensics Secur. 8(6), 949–962 (2013)
20. Küsters, R., Truderung, T.: Reducing protocol analysis with xor to the xor-free case in the horn theory based approach. J. Autom. Reasoning 46(3–4), 325–352 (2011)
21. Pavlov, E., Rosenschein, J.S., Topol, Z.: Supporting privacy in decentralized additive reputation systems. In: Jensen, C., Poslad, S., Dimitrakos, T. (eds.) iTrust 2004. LNCS, vol. 2995, pp. 108–119. Springer, Heidelberg (2004)
22. Resnick, P., Zeckhauser, R.: Trust among strangers in internet transactions: Empirical analysis of ebay's reputation system. In: Baye, M.R. (ed.) The Economics of the Internet and E-commerce (Advances in Applied Microeconomics), vol. 11, pp. 127–157. Emerald Group Publishing Limited (2002)
23. Ryan, M., Smyth, B.: Applied pi calculus. In: Formal Models and Techniques for Analyzing Security Protocols, chapt. 6. IOS Press (2011)

24. Steinbrecher, S.: Design options for privacy-respecting reputation systems within centralised internet communities. In: Fischer-Hübner, S., Rannenberg, K., Yngström, L., Lindskog, S. (eds.) Security and Privacy in Dynamic Environments. IFIP AICT, vol. 201, pp. 123–134. Springer, Boston (2006)
25. Steinbrecher, S.: Enhancing multilateral security in and by reputation systems. In: Matyáš, V., Fischer-Hübner, S., Cvrček, D., Švenda, P. (eds.) The Future of Identity. IFIP AICT, vol. 298, pp. 135–150. Springer, Heidelberg (2009)

(In)Corruptibility of Routing Protocols

Raphaël Jamet[1]([✉]) and Pascal Lafourcade[2]

[1] Univ. Grenoble Alpes, CNRS, VERIMAG, 38000 Grenoble, France
raphael.jamet@imag.fr
[2] LIMOS, Université d'Auvergne, Clermont-Ferrand, France
pascal.lafourcade@udamail.fr

Abstract. Analyses of routing protocols security are nearly always supported by simulations, which often evaluate the ability to deliver messages to a given destination. Several competing definitions for secure routing exist, but to our knowledge, they only address source routing protocols. In this paper, we propose the notion of *corruptibility*, a quantitative computational definition for routing security based on the attacker's ability to alter the routes used by messages. We first define *incorruptibility*, and we follow with the definition of *bounded corruptibility*, which uses two routing protocols as bounds for the evaluated protocol. These definitions are then illustrated with several routing algorithms.

1 Introduction

Internet is made out of several independent entities controlling their own networks. To be routed, packets need to get through several networks until they reach their destination, and so the Internet can be seen as a large ad hoc network. In this context, routing relies on several protocols, including the Border Gateway Protocol (BGP, [10]). This protocol ensures the dissemination of routing information between autonomous systems (AS), and is notoriously insecure [9,12,13].

For instance, the AS 7007 incident [3] caused an internet-wide outage in 1997 because this AS declared itself able to route to the whole Internet. This declaration was made in a way that ensured most networks would choose the AS, as the preferred gateway to the rest of the Internet. This misconfiguration then propagated through the Internet, overloading the faulty AS, and causing huge packet losses.

Another example, still related to BGP, has been seen more recently in the wild [7]. In this incident, China Telecom's subnetwork declared itself preferential for the routing to more than 50,000 IPs, including some strategic subnetworks for the USA. Unlike the previous example, the infrastructure of the problematic subnetwork still managed to route packets to their destination.

In the context of wireless ad hoc networks (WANET), attacks and misconfigurations are not as well studied as in traditional networks. For instance, in [15],

This research was conducted with the support of the "Digital trust" Chair from the Foundation of the University of Auvergne.

© Springer International Publishing Switzerland 2015
F. Cuppens et al. (Eds.): FPS 2014, LNCS 8930, pp. 262–276, 2015.
DOI: 10.1007/978-3-319-17040-4_17

the authors present some usual routing protocol vulnerabilities. In [8], the analysis is more specific to the security of routing protocols on wireless sensor networks, which are a subset of the WANET family with more limited resources and specific protocols.

Our intuition is that a secure routing protocol should guarantee that malicious parties cannot influence the routes a message will take, or at least that this influence is limited in a clearly stated way. We call such protocols *incorruptible*, and using an incorruptible routing protocol would have prevented both previously mentioned incidents. We do not consider confidentiality or integrity of the data, as they are properties which are not necessarily tied to the routing layer. Furthermore, this study is centered on wireless networks, but we believe the notion can easily be transposed to the context of wired networks.

Contribution: We propose the first steps towards a computational notion for the security of routing protocols, based on the ability for an attacker to influence how messages are routed. We provide three measures. The first one quantifies the difference between routing protocols in a safe context. The second one, denoted *routing protocol corruption*, quantifies how much an attacker is able to change how messages are routed. The last definition allows one to prove that an attacker can only corrupt a protocol within some limits. We only consider protocols where the nodes memories do not evolve once the attack begins. Finally, we illustrate these definitions with the analysis of a simple protocol.

Related Work: In [14], the authors proposed the Source Routing Protocol (SRP), which is an on-demand route discovery protocol. In on-demand routing protocols, route discovery is the process of building a valid path for a given data message. Using BAN logic [4], they claimed that routes generated by this protocol are correct and their integrity is respected. An attack has been found later on that protocol by [11], who argued that the results of the analysis are flawed because such an analysis is "*a misuse of BAN*", as this logic has been designed to study trust relationships, and not security notions.

The authors of [1] provide a definition of provably secure on-demand route discovery. They assume the adversary has compromised a few nodes in the network which gives him full control of their actions and memories. To prove security of protocols, they use the *simulation paradigm*, which uses two models: the *real-world model*, and an *ideal-world model* where the protocol is idealized. This way, they can detect specific problems in the protocol, while avoiding the inherent problems of such routing protocols. In their model, a protocol is considered secure if the executions set in the real-world model are indistinguishable from those set in the ideal-world version. This model was expanded in [5], where the authors provided an automated way to check protocols in this model.

The main differences between our model and theirs lie in the limitations on the evaluated protocols, and the property being evaluated. Regarding protocols, their model is able to track of the evolution of the internal states on nodes and to model broadcasts, while we do not consider these situations. Regarding the properties, the one we verify is universal to routing protocols, and could be applied to any, while their property of secure route discovery only makes sense on source routing protocols.

Outline: In Sect. 2, we model networks and protocols in our formalism, and in Sect. 3 we provide some routing protocols. We present our definitions of an incorruptible routing protocol in Sect. 4, along with the analysis of one of the protocols given in Sect. 3. Finally, we conclude and present the perspectives of this work in Sect. 5.

2 Definitions

To represent the network *topology*, we use a vertex-labeled directed graph named the *topology*, and denoted by $T = \{V, E, f\}$, where vertices V represent network nodes, and edges E represent their connectivity. We consider only static networks, and we suppose that nodes cannot send messages to themselves. The function f associates labels to nodes, which are used to model pre-existing distinctions between nodes, such as sinks and sensors in the case of a wireless sensor network. We denote by $\mathcal{N}eig_v$ the set of neighbors of a node v (that is, the nodes at one hop of v). We notice that $v \notin \mathcal{N}eig_v$.

2.1 Routing Protocols

To forward messages, all the nodes follow a routing protocol $\mathcal{P}$. This protocol must verify that all messages are routed independently at the time of the analysis. The path that a message will take should not be influenced by what other messages have been routed before. Note that acknowledgments can be modeled by considering they are the continuation of the route of the initial message.

We define K as the array of individual node memories, denoted by $K[v]$ for any node $v \in V$. Once initialized, a node's memory is never modified again. This is a strong restriction, and it reduces the range of protocols that can be modeled. On the other hand, for a given message, these protocols generate routes that do not depend on the past messages, which is an important property for the following security proofs, and we embrace that assumption in the rest of this paper. We discuss ways to lift this restriction in the conclusion.

We denote by η_d the data size, and by η the security parameter for cryptographic functions. $a \overset{\$}{\leftarrow} X$ denotes that a is a random value obtained according the distribution represented by X. If X is a set, a is randomly drawn using the uniform law on X. Similarly, if X is a probabilistic algorithm, a is drawn at random using the algorithm.

We define a routing protocol $\mathcal{P}$ as the set of four oracles $\{\mathcal{P}^I, \mathcal{P}^G, \mathcal{P}^R, \mathcal{P}^D\}$ which respectively model the initialization, message generation, routing and the depacketing phases. They are defined in Definitions 1 through 4.

Definition 1 (Initialization oracle). *Let $T = \{V, E, f\}$ be a topology, which contains nodes $v_1 \ldots v_n \in V$. The initialization oracle $\mathcal{P}^I(T, \eta)$ models the setup* *phase of* $\mathcal{P}$ *on the topology represented by* T, *with security parameter* η, *which initializes the memories of the nodes. This oracle call returns* K, *an array associating to each node its memories.*

Definition 2 (Message generation oracle). *Let* $T = \{V, E, f\}$ *be a topology with* $o, d \in V$. *Once memories* K *have been initialized, the* message generation oracle $\mathcal{P}_K^G(o, d, \eta_d)$ *models the generation of a new random data of length* η_d *to route by* o, *for* d. *This oracle call returns a message* m, *and does not modify* K.

Definition 3 (Routing oracle). *Let* $T = \{V, E, f\}$ *be a topology with* $v \in V$. *Once memories* K *have been initialized, the routing oracle* $\mathcal{P}_K^R(v, m)$ *models how* v *would route* m *given the initialization* K. *This oracle call returns either* $\perp$ *if no message is forwarded, or* (w, m') *if a message* m' *is forwarded to* w *(with* $w \in \mathcal{N}eig_v$). *That call does not modify* K.

Definition 4 (Depacketing oracle). *Let* $T = \{V, E, f\}$ *be a topology with* $d \in V$. *Once memories* K *have been initialized, the depacketing oracle* $\mathcal{P}_K^D(d, m)$ *models how* d *would unpack the message* m *given the initialization* K. *This oracle call returns either the Data contained in the message if extractable, or* $\perp$ *if that operation is not possible. That call does not modify* K.

2.2 Message Lifecycle and Routes

We now present how to model the natural lifecycle of a message. First, the network needs to be initialized by calling $K \xleftarrow{\$} \mathcal{P}^I(T, \eta)$. Then, a new message containing a random data is generated by a node o with destination d using the generation oracle $m_0 = \mathcal{P}_K^G(o, d, \eta_d)$. That message is first routed by the node o with the routing oracle $\mathcal{P}_K^R(o, m_0) = (h_1, m_1)$, assuming that message is not dropped. We then continue with its first hop, h_1, who reacts accordingly: $\mathcal{P}_K^R(h_1, m_1) = (h_2, m_2)$. This process continues until the message finally reaches a node h_n such that $\mathcal{P}_K^R(h_n, m_n) = \perp$: at this point, the message is stopped. We refer to such a sequence $[h_0, \ldots, h_n] = \mathbf{R}$ as a *route*, which can be empty, in which case it is denoted by $[\,]$.

Definition 5 (GENROUTE($m_0, h_0, \mathcal{P}_K^R$)). *Given a message* m_0, *a node identifier* h_0, *and a routing oracle* $\mathcal{P}_K^R$ *initialized with node memories* K, *we define* GENROUTE($m_0, h_0, \mathcal{P}_K^R$) *the function that generates a route for* m_0 *starting at* h_0. *This function calls* $\mathcal{P}_K^R$, *first with arguments* (h_0, m_0), *and then with the pair* (h_i, m_i) *returned by the previous call, until the oracle returns* $\perp$. *The function returns the route* $[h_1, \ldots, h_n]$.

As $\mathcal{P}$ can be probabilistic, making several calls to GENROUTE with the same arguments can result in different routes. However, since we require message routing independence, the probabilistic distribution of routes should stay the same, no matter what messages have been routed before. Finally, we define a predicate on routes which we denote by Φ.

Definition 6 ($\Phi(\mathbf{R}, a, b)$). *Given a route* $\mathbf{R}$ *and two nodes* a *and* b, $\Phi(\mathbf{R}, a, b)$ *is a function that returns true if and only if a route R contains a and that a appears before any occurrence of b.*

3 Examples of Routing Protocols

We now provide some routing protocols in our formalism. Given a message m and the initialized memories array K, the $\mathcal{P}^D$ oracles return the *Data* that is contained in m.

Let S be a signature scheme with three functions: GENASYMKEYPAIR(η) generates asymmetric key pairs given the security parameter η, SIGN(x, sk) generates a signature of x using the key sk, VERIFY(x, pk, S) verifies a signature S against the input x with key pk. The function SHORTROUTE(o, d, T) takes as input an origin, a destination, and a topology, and returns uniformly at random one of the shortest routes between the origin and destination. Finally, FINDNEXT($\mathbf{R}, v$) is the function that returns the node identifier coming right after v in the route $\mathbf{R}$, or $\perp$ otherwise.

The null protocol $\mathcal{P}\emptyset$ is defined in Fig. 1. It drops all messages, and adds no information in the packets it generates. The uniform random walk $\mathcal{RW}$ is defined in Fig. 2. The following protocol is called $\mathcal{SI}$ (for Shortest-Insecure) and it is described in Fig. 3. That protocol stores routes in messages without protecting them.

We define two other protocols, which stem from $\mathcal{SI}$, and use the signature scheme S. First, $\mathcal{S}\emptyset$ (Fig. 4) is a secured version of $\mathcal{SI}$, which prevents any alteration to the route stored in a message by using signatures. The route is signed by the message sender, and if that signature does not verify, then the message is discarded. The next protocol, $\mathcal{SR}$ (Fig. 5), works in a similar way, but instead of discarding the message, it routes it randomly until the message reaches the destination.

4 Incorruptibility

We now present how our notion of incorruptibility is formalized, and how it can be used to show the security of routing protocols. We begin by defining what is an attacker in our context, and follow with the measures of distance, incorruptibility, and bounded corruptibility.

4.1 Attacker

Our model deals with an attacker external to the network, who did not compromise any honest node. This entity controls the network links, and is able to intercept, create and manipulate messages. Its goal is to alter how a challenge message is routed. Notice that manipulating communications implies the possibility of forging messages to observe how nodes would react, and to observe which messages are generated in the network. However, since we suppose the attacker is external to the network, it does not have any direct access to the node's memories.

This adversary is modeled as a probabilistic polynomial-time Turing machine. It can query the oracles $\mathcal{P}_K^G$, $\mathcal{P}_K^R$ and $\mathcal{P}_K^D$ a polynomial number of times, but does not have direct access to the array of node memories K. None of its actions can modify K by hypothesis, but the adversary has its own memory. Note that we provide access to $\mathcal{P}_K^D$ to the adversary, as we are not concerned by confidentiality.

We denote the trivial attacker that returns its given input message by $\mathcal{A}_{safe}$. We name it *"safe"* as it is a placeholder attacker that effectively does nothing.

4.2   Measuring How Routing Protocols Operate

We define an experiment named $\mathbf{Expt}_{\mathcal{P}}^{Rt}$, which allows us to reason on an adversary's ability to influence how a message is routed.

Definition 7 ($\mathbf{Expt}_{\mathcal{P}}^{Rt}(\mathcal{A}, T, o, d, s, a, b, \eta, \eta_d)$). *Let $\mathcal{P}$ be a routing protocol. Let $\mathcal{A}$ be an adversary and $T = \{V, E, f\}$ a topology with $o, d, s, a, b \in V$. We define:*

$$\mathbf{Expt}_{\mathcal{P}}^{Rt}(\mathcal{A}, T, o, d, s, a, b, \eta, \eta_d) :$$

$$K \xleftarrow{\$} \mathcal{P}^I(T, \eta)$$

$$m \xleftarrow{\$} \mathcal{P}_K^G(o, d, \eta_d)$$

$$m' \xleftarrow{\$} \mathcal{A}^{\mathcal{P}_K^R, \mathcal{P}_K^G, \mathcal{P}^I, \mathcal{P}_K^D}(m, o, d, s, a, b, T)$$

$$\mathbf{If}\ \mathcal{P}_K^D(d, m') \neq \mathcal{P}_K^D(d, m)$$

$$m' \leftarrow m$$

$$\mathbf{R} \xleftarrow{\$} \textsc{GenRoute}(m', s, \mathcal{P}_K^R)$$

$$\mathbf{Return}\ \varPhi(\mathbf{R}, a, b)$$

First, the initialization is done by calling $\mathcal{P}^I(T, \eta)$, which returns the array of node memories K that is used through the experiment. A challenge message m is generated using K, and given to the adversary. The adversary should then change m in a new message m', containing the same data as m. The experiment returns a value $\varPhi(\mathbf{R}, a, b)$ with $\mathbf{R}$ a route generated for m' from the node s. The predicate $\varPhi(\mathbf{R}, a, b)$ is true when the route passes through a before b. We use the equality of depacketed messages as a way to prevent replay attacks: an attacker has no incentive in returning new messages containing random data, as their answer would get replaced by the challenge message, which they could have output in the first place. Note that we do not take into account the messages formats or contents because we focus only on their route.

For instance, the return value of $\mathbf{Expt}_{\mathcal{P}}^{RT}(\mathcal{A}_{safe}, T, o, d, s, a, b, \eta, \eta_d)$ models whether a random message m generated by o in destination of d gets routed by a before b when sent first from s, when all those nodes follow the routing protocol $\mathcal{P}$. When we use an arbitrary adversary $\mathcal{A}$, then the experiment $\mathbf{Expt}_{\mathcal{P}}^{RT}(\mathcal{A}, T, o, d, s, a, b, \eta, \eta_d)$ represents the same observation, except that m has been tampered with by $\mathcal{A}$ before being routed by s. We remark that $\mathcal{P}\emptyset$ has an interesting property here: for any $\mathcal{A}, T$ and o, d, s, a, b, the probability $Pr[\mathbf{Expt}_{\mathcal{P}\emptyset}^{Rt}(\mathcal{A}, T, o, d, s, a, b, \eta, \eta_d)] = 0$.

We then compare two such measures in order to define the *distance* between a tuple protocol, attacker and another.

Initialization $\mathcal{P}\emptyset^I(T, \eta)$:
1: **Return** $\emptyset$

Message generation $\mathcal{P}\emptyset^G_K(o, d, \eta_d)$:

1: $Data \xleftarrow{\$} \{0, 1\}^{\eta_d}$
2: **Return** $Data$

Message routing $\mathcal{P}\emptyset^R_K(m, v)$:
1: **Return** $\perp$

Fig. 1. Protocol $\mathcal{P}\emptyset$

Initialization $\mathcal{RW}^I(T, \eta)$:
1: **Return** $\emptyset$

Message generation $\mathcal{RW}^G_K(o, d, \eta_d)$:

1: $Data \xleftarrow{\$} \{0, 1\}^{\eta_d}$
2: **Return** $next, (Data, d)$

Message routing $\mathcal{RW}^R_K(m, v)$:

1: $(Data, d) \leftarrow m$
2: **if** $v \neq d$ **then**
3:     $next \xleftarrow{\$} \mathcal{N}eig_v$
4:     **Return** $next, (Data, d)$
5: **else**
6:     **Return** $\perp$
7: **end if**

Fig. 2. Protocol $\mathcal{RW}$

Initialization $\mathcal{SI}^I(T, \eta)$:
1: **for all** nodes v in T **do**
2:     $K[v] \leftarrow T$
3: **end for**
4: **Return** K

Message generation $\mathcal{SI}^G_K(o, d, \eta_d)$:

1: $Data \xleftarrow{\$} \{0, 1\}^{\eta_d}$
2: $\mathbf{R} \leftarrow \textsc{ShortRoute}(o, d, K[o])$
3: **Return** $(Data, \mathbf{R}, d)$

Message routing $\mathcal{SI}^R_K(m, v)$:

1: **if** $v \neq d$ **then**
2:     $next \leftarrow \textsc{FindNext}(\mathbf{R}, v)$
3:     **Return** $(next, (Data, \mathbf{R}, d))$
4: **end if**
5: **Return** $\perp$

Fig. 3. Protocol $\mathcal{SI}$

Initialization $\mathcal{S}\emptyset^I(T, \eta)$:
1: **for all** nodes v in T **do**
2:     $(pk[v], sk[v]) \leftarrow \textsc{GenAsymKeyPair}(\eta)$
3:     $K[v] \leftarrow (T, pk, sk[v])$
4: **end for**
5: **Return** K

Message generation $\mathcal{S}\emptyset^G_K(o, d, \eta_d)$:

1: $Data \xleftarrow{\$} \{0, 1\}^{\eta_d}$
2: $\mathbf{R} \leftarrow \textsc{ShortRoute}(o, d, K[o])$
3: $S \leftarrow \textsc{Sign}((Data, \mathbf{R}, o, d), sk[o])$
4: **Return** $(Data, \mathbf{R}, o, d, S)$

Message routing $\mathcal{S}\emptyset^R_K(m, v)$:

1: $(Data, \mathbf{R}, o, d, S) \leftarrow m$
2: **if** $v \neq d$ **then**
3:     **if** $\textsc{Verify}((Data, \mathbf{R}, o, d), pk[o], S)$ **then**
4:        $next \leftarrow \textsc{FindNext}(\mathbf{R}, v)$
5:        **Return** $(next, (Data, \mathbf{R}, o, d, S))$
6:     **end if**
7: **end if**
8: **Return** $\perp$

Fig. 4. Protocol $\mathcal{S}\emptyset$

Initialization $\mathcal{SR}^I(T, \eta)$:
1: **for all** nodes v in T **do**
2:     $(pk[v], sk[v]) \leftarrow \textsc{GenAsymKeyPair}(\eta)$
3:     $K[v] \leftarrow (T, pk, sk[v])$
4: **end for**
5: **Return** K

Message generation $\mathcal{SR}^G_K(o, d, \eta_d)$:

1: $Data \xleftarrow{\$} \{0, 1\}^{\eta_d}$
2: $\mathbf{R} \leftarrow \textsc{ShortRoute}(o, d, K[o])$
3: $S \leftarrow \textsc{Sign}((Data, \mathbf{R}, o, d), sk[o])$
4: **Return** $(Data, \mathbf{R}, o, d, S)$

Message routing $\mathcal{SR}^R_K(m, v)$:

1: $(Data, \mathbf{R}, o, d, S) \leftarrow m$
2: **if** $v \neq d$ **then**
3:     **if** $\textsc{Verify}((Data, \mathbf{R}, o, d), pk[o], S)$ **then**
4:        $next \leftarrow \textsc{FindNext}(\mathbf{R}, v)$
5:     **else**
6:        $next \xleftarrow{\$} \mathcal{N}eig_v$
7:     **end if**
8:     **Return** $(next, (Data, \mathbf{R}, o, d, S))$
9: **end if**
10: **Return** $\perp$

Fig. 5. Protocol $\mathcal{SR}$

Definition 8 (Distance). *For a topology $T = \{V, E, f\}$ with nodes $o, d, s, a, b \in V$, two adversaries $\mathcal{A}_1$ and $\mathcal{A}_2$, two protocols $\mathcal{P}_1$ and $\mathcal{P}_2$, we define the distance $Dist((\mathcal{P}_1, \mathcal{A}_1), (\mathcal{P}_2, \mathcal{A}_2), T, o, d, s, a, b, \eta, \eta_d)$ as*

$$\left| Pr[\mathbf{Expt}^{Rt}_{\mathcal{P}_1}(\mathcal{A}_1, T, o, d, s, a, b, \eta, \eta_d)] - Pr[\mathbf{Expt}^{Rt}_{\mathcal{P}_2}(\mathcal{A}_2, T, o, d, s, a, b, \eta, \eta_d)] \right|.$$

The notion of distance is a way to compare the routes being generated by $(\mathcal{P}_1, \mathcal{A}_1)$ and $(\mathcal{P}_2, \mathcal{A}_2)$, given T and o, d, s, a, b. We now present how to measure observable differences between routing protocols using this experiment.

4.3   Routing Similarity

We begin by expressing the similarity of routing protocols using $Dist$. We recall that stating that a function $\mu(x) : \mathbb{N} \to \mathbb{R}$ is negligible in x means that for every positive polynomial P there exists an integer I such that for all $x > I$, $\mu(x) < |\frac{1}{P(x)}|$, as given in [2].

Definition 9 (Routing protocols similarity). *For a topology $T = \{V, E, f\}$, we say that two protocols $\mathcal{P}_1$ and $\mathcal{P}_2$ route messages similarly on the topology T if $\forall o, d, s, a, b \in V$, $Dist((\mathcal{P}_1, \mathcal{A}_{safe}), (\mathcal{P}_2, \mathcal{A}_{safe}), T, o, d, s, a, b, \eta, \eta_d)$ is negligible in η and in η_d.*

Intuitively, two protocols route messages similarly on a topology if the routes generated for random messages are computationally indistinguishable for all origins o, destinations d, and senders s. For instance, $\mathcal{RW}$ and $\mathcal{SI}$ are not similar for all topologies, as the latter generates distinguishably shorter routes. However, on a topology T_2 consisting of two connected nodes, they are similar, as messages are either routed to the neighbor if $o \neq d$ and not routed at all otherwise.

Fig. 6. Topology T_s

Consider for instance $\mathcal{S\emptyset}$ and $\mathcal{P\emptyset}$ on a topology T_s as described in Fig. 6. We observe that on this topology, the probability $Pr[\mathbf{Expt}^{Rt}_{\mathcal{S\emptyset}}(\mathcal{A}_{safe}, T_s, o, d, s, a, b, \eta, \eta_d)] = 0.5$, as there are two shortest routes from o to d and only one reaches a before b. We know that $Pr[\mathbf{Expt}^{Rt}_{\mathcal{P\emptyset}}(\mathcal{A}_{safe}, T_s, o, d, s, a, b, \eta, \eta_d)] = 0$, since null routes will never reach any of the two nodes. So, we can deduce that $Dist((\mathcal{S\emptyset}, \mathcal{A}_{safe}), (\mathcal{P\emptyset}, \mathcal{A}_{safe}), T_s, o, d, s, a, b, \eta, \eta_d) = 0.5$, which means that those two protocols are not similar on T_s, and we can conclude that $\mathcal{P\emptyset}$ and $\mathcal{S\emptyset}$ are not *similar on every topology*, as they differ on at least T_s.

Notice that this definition does not include attackers: two protocols routing messages similarly may not behave in the same way in presence of an *active* adversary. This allows us to show that a secure version of a protocol is similar to its original counterpart. For instance, $\mathcal{SR}$, $\mathcal{S\emptyset}$ and $\mathcal{SI}$ are all similar.

4.4   Incorruptibility of a Protocol

We propose a measure which evaluates whether an attacker can alter a message m into another message m' in order to make its routing distinguishably different. We call this measure the *incorruptibility* of a routing protocol, the related advantage is denoted by $\mathbf{Adv}_{\mathcal{P}}^{INC}$, and we define it using *Dist*.

Definition 10 ($\mathbf{Adv}_{\mathcal{P}}^{INC}(\mathcal{A}, T, o, d, s, a, b, \eta, \eta_d)$). *For an adversary $\mathcal{A}$, a topology $T = \{V, E, f\}$ with five nodes $o, d, s, a, b \in V$, we define $\mathbf{Adv}_{\mathcal{P}}^{INC}(\mathcal{A}, T, o, d, s, a, b, \eta, \eta_d) = Dist((\mathcal{P}, \mathcal{A}), (\mathcal{P}, \mathcal{A}_{safe}), T, o, d, s, a, b, \eta, \eta_d)$.*

Definition 11 (Incorruptible protocol). *If for any adversary $\mathcal{A}$, any topology $T = \{V, E, f\}$, and any five nodes $o, d, s, a, b \in V$, the value of the advantage $\mathbf{Adv}_{\mathcal{P}}^{INC}(\mathcal{A}, T, o, d, s, a, b, \eta, \eta_d)$ is negligible in η and in η_d, we say that $\mathcal{P}$ is incorruptible.*

Informally, a protocol is corruptible if an adversary's alterations of a message can result in distinguishably different routes. For instance, the $\mathcal{P}\emptyset$ protocol is incorruptible, as it always generates null routes. Similarly, $\mathcal{RW}$ is incorruptible: it is not influenced by any information contained in the messages, and so intuitively an attacker which can only alter the content of a message is not able to influence in any way how a message is routed.

However, this definition is too restrictive for some protocols that intuitively cannot be attacked, such as $\mathcal{S}\emptyset$. Most protocols whose behavior depends on the message contents can be influenced, as an attacker can use that dependency in order to differ from the safe behavior of the protocol. We now provide an attacker for $\mathcal{S}\emptyset$ to illustrate this reasoning, and in the next subsection, we provide a generalization of the incorruptibility advantage to answer those concerns.

In order to show the corruptibility of $\mathcal{S}\emptyset$ (which is described in Fig. 4), we use the adversary $\mathcal{A}_{zero}$ that takes as input the message $m = (Data, \mathbf{R}, o, d, S)$, and returns the altered $m' = (Data, \mathbf{R}, o, d, 0)$. Intuitively, this attacker destroys the signature S of the message m, which ensures the protocol drops it at the next hop. This behavior differs significantly from how the original m would have been routed.

We recall the definition of $\mathbf{Adv}_{\mathcal{S}\emptyset}^{INC}(\mathcal{A}_{zero}, T, o, d, s, a, b, \eta, \eta_d) = \Big| Pr[\mathbf{Expt}_{\mathcal{S}\emptyset}^{Rt}$

$(\mathcal{A}_{zero}, o, d, s, a, b, \eta, \eta_d)] - Pr[\mathbf{Expt}_{\mathcal{S}\emptyset}^{Rt}(\mathcal{A}_{safe}, o, d, s, a, b, \eta, \eta_d)] \Big|$.

We omit T, o, d, s, a, b, and η, η_d from the parameters list when it is clear from the context. We are first interested in the left part of this subtraction. $\mathcal{A}_{zero}$ changes the signatures of messages it is given. Let us consider what happens with an altered message m'_{zero} (containing S_{zero}) and its corresponding $\mathbf{R}_{zero}$, generated in the $\mathbf{Expt}_{\mathcal{S}\emptyset}^{Rt}(\mathcal{A}_{zero}, o, d, s, a, b, \eta, \eta_d)$ experiment. We separate the case where S is valid and where it is not. We have:

$$Pr[\mathbf{Expt}_{\mathcal{S}\emptyset}^{Rt}(\mathcal{A}_{zero}, o, d, s, a, b, \eta, \eta_d)] =$$
$$Pr[\Phi(\mathbf{R}_{zero}, a, b) | \text{VERIFY}((Data, \mathbf{R}_{zero}, o, d), pk[o], S_{zero})] \times$$
$$Pr[\text{VERIFY}((Data, \mathbf{R}_{zero}, o, d), pk[o], S_{zero})] +$$
$$Pr[\Phi(\mathbf{R}_{zero}, a, b) | \neg\text{VERIFY}((Data, \mathbf{R}_{zero}, o, d), pk[o], S_{zero})] \times$$
$$Pr[\neg\text{VERIFY}((Data, \mathbf{R}_{zero}, o, d), pk[o], S_{zero})]$$

If we assume that $\mathcal{S}\emptyset$ uses a secure (UF-CMA in the sense of [6]) signature scheme $\mathcal{S}$ of security parameter η, then we know that the probability ϵ of the signature being forged by an intruder (*i.e.* VERIFY$((Data, \mathbf{R}, o, d), pk[o], S)$ returns true) becomes *negligible* in η. Therefore:

$$Pr[\mathbf{Expt}_{\mathcal{S}\emptyset}^{Rt}(\mathcal{A}_{zero}, o, d, s, a, b, \eta, \eta_d)] =$$
$$Pr[\varPhi(\mathbf{R}_{zero}, a, b)|\text{VERIFY}((Data, \mathbf{R}_{zero}, o, d), pk[o], S_{zero})] \times \epsilon +$$
$$Pr[\varPhi(\mathbf{R}_{zero}, a, b)|\neg\text{VERIFY}((Data, \mathbf{R}_{zero}, o, d), pk[o], S_{zero})] \times (1 - \epsilon)$$

We first consider the case where the signature is invalid. Consider the oracle $\mathcal{S}\emptyset_K^R$ described in Fig. 4. If the signature of the message is not valid, then the message is dropped. Therefore, all the routes generated for m' in this context are equal to the empty route [ ]. We know that $\varPhi([\ ], a, b)$ is always false for any a and b. We can therefore conclude that the experiment returns 0 with a probability $(1 - \epsilon)$, and remove it from the equation.

$$Pr[\mathbf{Expt}_{\mathcal{S}\emptyset}^{Rt}(\mathcal{A}_{zero}, o, d, s, a, b, \eta, \eta_d)] =$$
$$Pr[\varPhi(\mathbf{R}_{zero}, a, b)|\text{VERIFY}((Data, \mathbf{R}_{zero}, o, d), pk[o], S_{zero})] \times \epsilon$$

We denote by p the probability of the experiment returning 1 when the signature is valid. Going back to the advantage, we have:

$$\mathbf{Adv}_{\mathcal{S}\emptyset}^{INC}(\mathcal{A}_{zero}) = \left|(0 + \epsilon \times p) - Pr[\mathbf{Expt}_{\mathcal{S}\emptyset}^{Rt}(\mathcal{A}_{safe})]\right|$$

The first part of the subtraction is negligible in η, as p is a probability and ϵ is negligible in η. However, $Pr[\mathbf{Expt}_{\mathcal{S}\emptyset}^{Rt}(\mathcal{A}_{safe}, T, o, d, s, a, b)]$ may not be negligible, depending on T and o, d, s, a, b (as we have shown using the topology in Fig. 6). Intuitively, without attacker interference, $\mathcal{S}\emptyset$ actually routes messages to their destination, which ensures the existence of such nodes. Therefore, there exist some topologies T (T_s being one of them) where the advantage $\mathbf{Adv}_{\mathcal{S}\emptyset}^{INC}(\mathcal{A}_{zero}, T, o, d, s, a, b, \eta, \eta_d)$ is not negligible in η and in η_d, and so $\mathcal{S}\emptyset$ is not *incorruptible on all topologies*.

4.5 Bounded Corruptibility

We generalize the notion of corruptibility to a definition using two reference protocols. We define another advantage, called $\mathbf{Adv}_{\mathcal{P},\mathcal{B}_1,\mathcal{B}_2}^{BINC}$. It follows the same principle as $\mathbf{Adv}_{\mathcal{P}}^{INC}$, but instead of considering how an attacker can force $\mathcal{P}$ to behave differently, we consider how it can be corrupted to the outside of a reference routing *interval*, defined by the safe execution of two protocols $\mathcal{B}_1$ and $\mathcal{B}_2$ on T, measured for the parameters o, d, s, a, b.

Definition 12 ($\mathbf{Adv}_{\mathcal{P},\mathcal{B}_1,\mathcal{B}_2}^{BINC}(\mathcal{A}, T, o, d, s, a, b, \eta, \eta_d)$). *Let $\mathcal{A}$ be an attacker, and let $T = \{V, E, f\}$ be a topology with nodes $o, d, s, a, b \in V$. We consider a protocol $\mathcal{P}$, which is compared with two protocols $\mathcal{B}_1$ and $\mathcal{B}_2$. We define $\mathbf{Adv}_{\mathcal{P},\mathcal{B}_1,\mathcal{B}_2}^{BINC}$ $(\mathcal{A}, T, o, d, s, a, b, \eta, \eta_d)$ as:*

$$max(\ Dist((\mathcal{B}_1, \mathcal{A}_{safe}), (\mathcal{B}_2, \mathcal{A}_{safe}), T, o, d, s, a, b, \eta, \eta_d),$$
$$Dist((\mathcal{P}, \mathcal{A}), (\mathcal{B}_1, \mathcal{A}_{safe}), T, o, d, s, a, b, \eta, \eta_d),$$
$$Dist((\mathcal{P}, \mathcal{A}), (\mathcal{B}_2, \mathcal{A}_{safe}), T, o, d, s, a, b, \eta, \eta_d)\ )$$
$$)\ -\ Dist((\mathcal{B}_1, \mathcal{A}_{safe}), (\mathcal{B}_2, \mathcal{A}_{safe}), T, o, d, s, a, b, \eta, \eta_d)$$

Informally, $\mathbf{Adv}_{\mathcal{P}, \mathcal{B}_1, \mathcal{B}_2}^{BINC}(\mathcal{A}, T, o, d, s, a, b, \eta, \eta_d)$ is a measure of the maximal distance the behavior of $\mathcal{P}$ attacked by $\mathcal{A}$ can get from the outside of the interval determined by the safe behavior of $\mathcal{B}_1$ and $\mathcal{B}_2$. Remark that if the attacked protocol's behavior is in the interval, then the advantage is 0.

Definition 13 (Bounded corruptibility). *If for any adversary $\mathcal{A}$, for any topology T, and for all o, d, s, a, b, $\mathbf{Adv}_{\mathcal{P}, \mathcal{B}_1, \mathcal{B}_2}^{BINC}(\mathcal{A}, T, o, d, s, a, b, \eta, \eta_d)$ is negligible in η and in η_d, we say that $\mathcal{P}$'s corruptibility is bounded between $\mathcal{B}_1$ and $\mathcal{B}_2$.*

Remark that this definition has some interesting properties:

- $\mathbf{Adv}_{\mathcal{P}, \mathcal{B}_1, \mathcal{B}_2}^{BINC}(\mathcal{A}, T, o, d, s, a, b, \eta, \eta_d) = \mathbf{Adv}_{\mathcal{P}, \mathcal{B}_1, \mathcal{B}_2}^{BINC}(\mathcal{A}, T, o, d, s, a, b, \eta, \eta_d)$:
  The bounds for bounded corruptibility are commutative.
- $\mathbf{Adv}_{\mathcal{P}, \mathcal{P}, \mathcal{P}}^{BINC}(\mathcal{A}, T, o, d, s, a, b, \eta, \eta_d) = \mathbf{Adv}_{\mathcal{P}}^{INC}(\mathcal{A}, T, o, d, s, a, b, \eta, \eta_d)$:
  Stating that a protocol is bounded between itself and itself is the same as stating its incorruptibility.
- $Dist(\mathcal{B}_1, \mathcal{B}_2, T, o, d, s, a, b, \eta, \eta_d) = 0 \Rightarrow \forall \mathcal{B}_3,\ \mathbf{Adv}_{\mathcal{P}, \mathcal{B}_1, \mathcal{B}_3}^{BINC}(\mathcal{A}, T, o, d, s, a, b, \eta, \eta_d) = \mathbf{Adv}_{\mathcal{P}, \mathcal{B}_2, \mathcal{B}_3}^{BINC}(\mathcal{A}, T, o, d, s, a, b, \eta, \eta_d)$:
  If two protocols route messages identically, then those protocols are equivalent for bounding purposes.

Example: Bounded Corruptibility of $\mathcal{S}\emptyset$: We try to bound $\mathcal{S}\emptyset$ using itself and $\mathcal{P}\emptyset$. We assume that $\mathcal{S}\emptyset$ uses a secure UF-CMA signature scheme [6] S of security parameter η. By definition, $\mathbf{Adv}_{\mathcal{S}\emptyset, \mathcal{S}\emptyset, \mathcal{P}\emptyset}^{BINC}(\mathcal{A}, T, o, d, s, a, b)$ equals:

$$max(Dist((\mathcal{S}\emptyset, \mathcal{A}_{safe}), (\mathcal{P}\emptyset, \mathcal{A}_{safe})),$$
$$Dist((\mathcal{S}\emptyset, \mathcal{A}), (\mathcal{S}\emptyset, \mathcal{A}_{safe})),$$
$$Dist((\mathcal{S}\emptyset, \mathcal{A}), (\mathcal{P}\emptyset, \mathcal{A}_{safe})),$$
$$)-Dist((\mathcal{S}\emptyset, \mathcal{A}_{safe}), (\mathcal{P}\emptyset, \mathcal{A}_{safe}))$$

By using the fact that $Pr[\mathbf{Expt}_{\mathcal{P}\emptyset}^{Rt}(\mathcal{A}_{safe})] = 0$, we get the following:

$$max(|Pr[\mathbf{Expt}_{\mathcal{S}\emptyset}^{Rt}(\mathcal{A}_{safe})]|,$$
$$|Pr[\mathbf{Expt}_{\mathcal{S}\emptyset}^{Rt}(\mathcal{A}_{safe})] - Pr[\mathbf{Expt}_{\mathcal{S}\emptyset}^{Rt}(\mathcal{A})]|,$$
$$|Pr[\mathbf{Expt}_{\mathcal{S}\emptyset}^{Rt}(\mathcal{A})]|$$
$$)-|Pr[\mathbf{Expt}_{\mathcal{S}\emptyset}^{Rt}(\mathcal{A}_{safe})]|$$

Probabilities are positive, which allows us to remove some of the absolute values. We also rewrite $|a|$ as $max(a, -a)$ in the last case, to remove all absolute values:

$$max(Pr[\textbf{Expt}_{S\emptyset}^{Rt}(\mathcal{A}_{safe})],$$
$$Pr[\textbf{Expt}_{S\emptyset}^{Rt}(\mathcal{A}_{safe})] - Pr[\textbf{Expt}_{S\emptyset}^{Rt}(\mathcal{A})],$$
$$Pr[\textbf{Expt}_{S\emptyset}^{Rt}(\mathcal{A})] - Pr[\textbf{Expt}_{S\emptyset}^{Rt}(\mathcal{A}_{safe})],$$
$$Pr[\textbf{Expt}_{S\emptyset}^{Rt}(\mathcal{A})]$$
$$)-Pr[\textbf{Expt}_{S\emptyset}^{Rt}(\mathcal{A}_{safe})]$$

We include the subtraction in the maximum and simplify further:

$$max(0,\ 0 - Pr[\textbf{Expt}_{S\emptyset}^{Rt}(\mathcal{A})],$$
$$Pr[\textbf{Expt}_{S\emptyset}^{Rt}(\mathcal{A})] - 2Pr[\textbf{Expt}_{S\emptyset}^{Rt}(\mathcal{A}_{safe})],$$
$$Pr[\textbf{Expt}_{S\emptyset}^{Rt}(\mathcal{A})] - Pr[\textbf{Expt}_{S\emptyset}^{Rt}(\mathcal{A}_{safe})])$$

We know $Pr[\textbf{Expt}_{S\emptyset}^{Rt}(\mathcal{A})] - 2Pr[\textbf{Expt}_{S\emptyset}^{Rt}(\mathcal{A}_{safe})] \leq Pr[\textbf{Expt}_{S\emptyset}^{Rt}(\mathcal{A})] - Pr[\textbf{Expt}_{S\emptyset}^{Rt}(\mathcal{A}_{safe})]$, and therefore we can remove the right part of the inequation from the maximum. Similarly, $0 - Pr[\textbf{Expt}_{S\emptyset}^{Rt}(\mathcal{A})] \leq 0$. We therefore simplify the maximum to:

$$max(0, Pr[\textbf{Expt}_{S\emptyset}^{Rt}(\mathcal{A})] - Pr[\textbf{Expt}_{S\emptyset}^{Rt}(\mathcal{A}_{safe})])$$

We want to prove that this is negligible in η and in η_d for all $T = \{V, E, f\}$ and $o, d, s, a, b \in V$. We reformulate this as $Pr[\textbf{Expt}_{S\emptyset}^{Rt}(\mathcal{A})] - Pr[\textbf{Expt}_{S\emptyset}^{Rt}(\mathcal{A}_{safe})] \leq \epsilon$, with ϵ negligible in η and in η_d. Looking at the experiment, this means that

$$Pr[\Phi(\textsc{GenRoute}(m', s, S\emptyset_K^R), a, b))] - Pr[\Phi(\textsc{GenRoute}(m, s, S\emptyset_K^R), a, b))] \leq \epsilon$$

The difference between these probabilities is null unless the routes generated from attacked messages m' and the routes generated from m are different. Looking at the route generation process, the only factors influencing the oracle $S\emptyset_K^R$ (defined in Fig. 4) are the validity of the signature, the contents of $\textbf{R}$, and the identity of the receiver (which cannot be modified by the attacker). Furthermore, all those solutions require $S\emptyset_K^D(m') = S\emptyset_K^D(m)$, as otherwise the experiment would have run as if the attacker output m.

We therefore know that the advantage is null unless the attacker either made the signature invalid, or it altered the route stored in the message and the signature is still valid. In that first case, the invalid signature forces the message to be dropped. Consequently, the generated route is equal to the empty route [ ]. Since $\Phi([\ ], a, b) = 0$, then the probability of the experiment returning true is null, and so this strategy does not provide an higher advantage. In the other case, the attacker managed to alter the route stored in the message, while keeping the same data, and keeping the signature valid. To have a valid signature for an altered message, the attacker has either forged it, or recovered it from

$\mathcal{S}\emptyset_K^G(o, d)$. Note that it cannot create a valid signature for a key it created, as that key would not be present in any node's K.

We first consider the case of the attacker trying to forge the signature. We proceed by assuming it manages to forge or guess the signature with a probability p_F when running on T', o', d', s', a', b'. This adversary $\mathcal{A}$ could also be used to build an adversary $\mathcal{A}_S$ who breaks the UF-CMA experiment with probability p_F. $\mathcal{A}_S$ needs to emulate $\mathcal{S}\emptyset$ on T', creating its own initialization on the network except for the node o', who uses the challenge's key. As $\mathcal{A}_S$ does not know the keys of o', it should use the chosen-plaintext oracle and verification oracle provided in the UF-CMA experiment to simulate its knowledge. $\mathcal{A}$ will therefore be in the right simulated context for $\mathbf{Expt}_{\mathcal{S}\emptyset}^{Rt}(\mathcal{A}, T', o', d', s', a', b')$, and will be provided a message m originating from o' (which costs $\mathcal{A}_S$ one call to its chosen-plaintext oracle). By assumption, this adversary will therefore return a message m' containing a valid forged signature with probability p_F. In the end, given an adversary $\mathcal{A}$ for $\mathbf{Expt}_{\mathcal{S}\emptyset}^{Rt}$ who makes q_G queries to $\mathcal{S}\emptyset_K^G$ and q_R queries to $\mathcal{S}\emptyset_K^R$ to forge signatures with probability p_F, we built an adversary $\mathcal{A}_S$ making $q_G + 1$ queries ($\mathcal{A}$'s queries, plus one to create the setting) to the chosen-plaintext oracle, and q_R queries to the verification oracle such that $\mathbf{Adv}_S^{UFCMA}(\mathcal{A}_S, \eta) = p_F$. As we supposed the signature scheme $\mathcal{S}$ secure, we know that p_F is negligible in η.

The attacker can also try to obtain the signature without forging it. The only source of valid signatures for $\mathcal{A}$ is $\mathcal{S}\emptyset_K^G(o, d)$, but this oracle provides packets containing random data. Therefore, given the attacker does q_G queries, the probability of obtaining a valid packet m' verifying $\mathcal{S}\emptyset_K^D(m') = \mathcal{S}\emptyset_K^D(m)$ is $\left(\frac{2^{\eta_d}-1}{2^{\eta_d}}\right)^{q_G}$, which is negligible in η_d. Summing all the possibilities before:

$$Pr[\Phi(\textsc{GenRoute}(m', s, \mathcal{S}\emptyset_K^R), a, b))] - Pr[\Phi(\textsc{GenRoute}(m, s, \mathcal{S}\emptyset_K^R), a, b))]$$

$$\leq \mathbf{Adv}_S^{UFCMA}(\mathcal{A}_S, \eta) + \left(\frac{2^{\eta_d}-1}{2^{\eta_d}}\right)^{q_G}$$

Therefore, we can say that for all adversaries $\mathcal{A}$ making a polynomial number of queries to $\mathcal{S}\emptyset_K^G(o, d)$ and $\mathcal{S}\emptyset_K^R(m, v)$, $\mathbf{Adv}_{\mathcal{S}\emptyset, \mathcal{S}\emptyset, \mathcal{P}\emptyset}^{BINC}(\mathcal{A}, T, o, d, s, a, b)$ is negligible in η and in η_d.

5   Conclusion

In this paper, we have presented a notion of routing security, named *incorruptibility*. Incorruptibility is a quantitative measure, based on the ability of an attacker to influence how messages are routed. We provide a few example protocols in our modelization, and proved that some of them are indeed incorruptible. However, some protocols require a broader notion: after showing why one of them is corruptible, we propose the notion of *bounded corruptibility*, a generalization of the previous measure. This more accommodating notion allows us to prove that some routing protocols can only be influenced between given limits, which are exprimed using routing protocols. We finally provide a proof of the bounded corruptibility of one of our example routing protocols.

Perspectives: There are several ways this work could be expanded. Modeling node state changes is possible, but this would require more complex proof techniques to obtain results given messages influence how the next ones are routed. This would be an important step towards more complex protocols.

Insider attacks on routing protocols suppose one or more nodes in the network are controlled by the attacker. To model this, our first intuition was to allow the attacker some degree of access to K, for instance $K[s]$ (as s represents the last hop before attacker alteration of m). However, this simple modification of the game does not work because of the $\mathcal{P}_K^D(d, m') \neq \mathcal{P}_K^D(d, m)$ check: if the attacker has enough access to K, most protocols get trivially broken in this model as the attacker can create a completely new message containing the data of its choice. However, this attack, based on building from scratch another packet, is not meaningful as all protocols relying on cryptography are vulnerable to it. Our goal is to ensure the attacker's m' is based on m, without blocking any legitimate alteration of the message that would change its route.

Finally, it may be interesting to consider dynamic topologies, which correspond better to what may be actually found in a network, either because of varying wireless transmission quality, or because of an intruder actively disrupting the connections. To do this, the attacker could be able to actively choose the topology used by the network during initialization and evaluation of the challenge message.

References

1. Ács, G., Buttyán, L., Vajda, I.: Provably secure on-demand source routing in mobile ad hoc networks. Trans. Mob. Comput. **5**(11), 1533–1546 (2006)
2. Bellare, M.: A note on negligible functions. J. Cryptol. **15**(4), 271–284 (2002)
3. Bono, V.J.: 7007 explanation and apology. Appears in NANOG mailing list (1997)
4. Burrows, M., Abadi, M., Needham, R.M.: A logic of authentication. Proc. Roy. Soc. Lond. A. Math. Phys. Sci. **426**(1871), 233–271 (1989)
5. Buttyán, L., Thong, T.V.: Formal verification of secure ad-hoc network routing protocols using deductive model-checking. In: Wireless and Mobile Networking Conference (WMNC 2010), pp. 1–6. IEEE (2010)
6. Goldwasser, S., Micali, S., Rivest, R.L.: A digital signature scheme secure against adaptive chosen-message attacks. SIAM J. Comput. **17**(2), 281–308 (1988)
7. Hiran, R., Carlsson, N., Gill, P.: Characterizing large-scale routing anomalies: a case study of the China Telecom incident. In: Roughan, M., Chang, R. (eds.) PAM 2013. LNCS, vol. 7799, pp. 229–238. Springer, Heidelberg (2013)
8. Karlof, C., Wagner, D.: Secure routing in wireless sensor networks: attacks and countermeasures. Ad Hoc Netw. **1**(2–3), 293–315 (2003)
9. Kent, S.T.: Securing the border gateway protocol: a status update. In: Lioy, A., Mazzocchi, D. (eds.) CMS 2003. LNCS, vol. 2828, pp. 40–53. Springer, Heidelberg (2003)
10. Lougheed, K., Rekhter, Y.: Border Gateway Protocol (BGP). RFC 1105 (Experimental), June 1989. Obsoleted by RFC 1163
11. Marshall, J.: An analysis of SRP for mobile ad hoc networks. In: International Multiconference in Computer Science (IMECS 2002), pp. 18–21 (2002)

12. Murphy, S.: BGP Security Vulnerabilities Analysis. RFC 4272, January 2006
13. Nordström, O., Dovrolis, C.: Beware of BGP attacks. ACM SIGCOMM Comput. Commun. Rev. **34**(2), 1–8 (2004)
14. Papadimitratos, P., Haas, Z.J.: Secure routing for mobile ad hoc networks. In: Communication Networks and Distributed Systems Modeling and Simulation Conference (CNDS 2002), pp. 193–204 (2002)
15. Wu, B., Chen, J., Wu, J., Cardei, M.: A survey of attacks and countermeasures in mobile ad hoc networks. In: Xiao, Y., Shen, X.S., Du, D.-Z. (eds.) Wireless Network Security, pp. 103–135. Springer, New York (2007)

Cryptographic Technologies

Decentralized CRT-Based Efficient Verifiable (*n*, *t*, *n*) Multi-secret Sharing Scheme

Wen Wen$^{(\boxtimes)}$, Binod Vaidya, Dimitrios Makrakis,
and Carlisle Adams

School of Electrical Engineering and Computer Science,
University of Ottawa, Ottawa, ON, Canada
{wwen085, cadams}@uottawa.ca, bnvaidya@gmail.com,
dimitris@eecs.uottawa.ca

Abstract. Secret sharing is critical to most applications making use of security and remains one of the most challenging research areas in modern cryptography. In this paper, we propose a novel efficient multi-secret sharing scheme that is based on the (*n*, *t*, *n*) secret sharing technique. We use the Chinese remainder theorem (CRT) to generate secret shares and the reconstruction of secrets instead of using the Lagrange polynomial interpolation. In addition, we discuss the security of the scheme, and provide a new method to generate verifiable shares that make the proposed scheme a verifiable secret sharing scheme.

Keywords: Security · (*n, t, n*) secret sharing · Multi-secret sharing · Verification

1 Introduction

The Secret Sharing (SS) scheme was independently proposed by Shamir [1] and Blakley [2] in 1978 for safeguarding cryptographic keys. Since then, secret sharing has been intensively studied and has been used in various applications.

In Shamir's scheme, the dealer shares a secret with multiple shareholders; however, any entity, including the shareholders, cannot retrieve the secret unless it obtains the help from a certain number of shareholders. Secret sharing schemes with this property are called (*t, n*) threshold secret sharing schemes, where *t* represents the minimum number of shareholders that are required to retrieve the secret and *n* stands for the total number of existing shareholders. This threshold property is an important feature when applying secret sharing in practical cases.

In 1982, Mignotte [3] proposed a new secret sharing scheme that is based on the Chinese Remainder Theorem (CRT) [14]. However, with this scheme, the exposure of any individual share reveals some information of the original secret, thus it is not perfectly secure. In 1983, Asmuth and Bloom [4] proposed another secret sharing scheme that is also based on CRT. According to [10], the computational complexity of the secret reconstruction from *t* shares for Asmuth-Bloom's scheme is $O(t)$ while it is $O(t(\log^2 t))$ for Shamir's.

Both Shamir's scheme and Asmuth-Bloom's scheme can only share a secret by distributing shares once. This is not efficient when sharing multiple secrets. In 1994,

© Springer International Publishing Switzerland 2015
F. Cuppens et al. (Eds.): FPS 2014, LNCS 8930, pp. 279–293, 2015.
DOI: 10.1007/978-3-319-17040-4_18

He and Dawson [5] proposed a multi-stage secret sharing scheme which was soon proved to be one-time secret sharing scheme. Afterwards, many multi-secret sharing schemes (MSSS) have been proposed and the design of all of them is based on the Lagrange polynomial interpolation Most of the existing multi-secret sharing schemes, such as those described in [6–8], are relatively effective and efficient when sharing multiple secrets. Harn and Lin [9] proposed their strong (n, t, n) verifiable secret sharing scheme in 2010. This scheme led to the (n, t, n) multi-secret sharing scheme proposed by Liu, Harn, Yang and Zhang in 2012 [13].

To the best of our knowledge, no multi-secret sharing scheme based on CRT has been designed. In this paper, we propose an efficient and CRT based decentralized (n, t, n) multi-secret sharing scheme. We also propose a new way of generating verifiable shares to make the proposed scheme a verifiable multi-secret sharing scheme without revealing information about the final secret.

The rest of the paper is organized as follows. Section 2 gives the background of secret sharing by introducing two well-known secret sharing schemes. Section 3 describes the (n, t, n) secret sharing architecture and the previous (n, t, n) multi-secret sharing scheme based on Lagrange Polynomial Interpolation. We present our multi-secret sharing scheme in Sect. 4. The Sect. 5 presents the conclusions and directions for further works.

2   Background

This section introduces two basic and well known schemes of secret sharing. Most of the secret sharing schemes are extended or built on them.

2.1   Shamir's Secret Sharing Scheme

Shamir's secret sharing scheme uses the Lagrange Polynomial Interpolation. Denote the subject who wants to share a secret as the dealer D, sometimes called the secret-holder, and name the subjects who keep one share of the secret as participants P_i, sometimes referred to as share-holders.

Share generation/distribution stage. Dealer D randomly selects $\{S, a_1, ..., a_{t-1}\}$, where S is the secret that is to be shared later. S and a_i are used to construct a random polynomial $f(x)$ of degree $(t - 1)$:

$$f(x) = S + a_1 x + ... + a_{t-1} x^{t-1} (\bmod p) \tag{1}$$

S and all a_i belong to the finite field GF(p) with $p > S$, where p is a large prime number. D computes n shares: $\{s_1 = f(x_1), s_2 = f(x_2), ..., s_n = f(x_n)\}$. D then distributes each share s_i to the corresponding shareholder P_i through a secret channel.

Reconstruction stage. Assume there are t participants, $P_1, ..., P_t$, which wish to reconstruct the secret S. Set $x = 0$; the final secret S can be derived by simply applying the Lagrange Interpolation formula [1] as shown in Eq. (2):

$$S = f(0) = \sum_{j=1}^{t} f(x_j) \left(\prod_{r=1, r \neq j}^{t} \frac{-x_r}{x_j - x_r} \right) \pmod{p} \tag{2}$$

2.2 Asmuth-Bloom's Secret Sharing Scheme

In this scheme, two integers t and n are given, with $1 \leq t \leq n$ and $n \geq 2$. Then select a sequence of pair-wise co-prime positive integers $m_0 < m_1 < \cdots < m_n$ such that:

$$m_0 \prod_{i=n-t+2}^{n} m_i < \prod_{i=1}^{t} m_i.$$

We note that the regulations above give the secret sharing scheme (t, n)-consistency. This (t, n)-consistency is the key to achieve the threshold property and will be used to test the correctness of the collected shares of the final secret. We will discuss (t, n)-consistency in the next sub-section.

The shares used to share a secret S are generated as follows:

$$y = S + \alpha m_0$$
$$Sh_i \equiv (S + \alpha m_0) \pmod{m_i}$$

Here, α is a positive integer randomly selected subject to the condition $1 \leq y \leq M$ where $M = \prod_{i=1}^{t} m_i$.

According to CRT [14], we could reconstruct the secret by applying the following processing:

$$S + \alpha m_0 \equiv \left(\sum_{i=1}^{t} Sh_i \cdot c_i \right) \pmod{M} \tag{3}$$

$$S \equiv (S + \alpha m_0) \pmod{m_0} \tag{4}$$

where $M = \prod_{i=1}^{t} m_i$, $M_i = M/m_i$, $c_i = M_i \times (M_i^{-1} \bmod m_i)$, $1 \leq i \leq t$.

Quisquater et al. [10] analyzed the schemes based on CRT and indicated that Asmuth-Bloom's scheme is asymptotically ideal and perfect zero-knowledge if the parameters of the system satisfy a natural condition. That means, any $(t - 1)$ shares of such a (t, n) threshold secret sharing scheme will give no information about the secret; in other words, the revealing of $(t - 1)$ or fewer shares will not narrow down the search space for S.

2.3 (t, n)-Consistency Test

A set of n shares is (t, n) consistent only if all the combinations of at least t shares (each combination could be called an access structure) within the set can reconstruct the same secret.

The (t, n)-consistency test could be done by reconstructing the secret using all the possible combinations. That means the process for the reconstruction of the secret needs to be done C_t^n times, which is not efficient for large t and n.

However, in [15], Harn and Lin proposed testing the (t, n)-consistency by reconstructing the secret only once. This approach is based on Shamir's secret sharing scheme, and if the interpolation of the collected n points (x_1, s_1), (x_2, s_2), ..., (x_n, s_n) yields a polynomial with degree $(t - 1)$, then all the shares pass the (t, n)-consistency test and all the proxies are considered legitimate and honest.

This is achieved using all the n points to do the following calculation:

$$S_n = f(0) = \sum_{j=1}^{n} f(x_j) \left(\prod_{r=1, r \neq j}^{n} \frac{-x_r}{x_j - x_r} \right) (\operatorname{mod} p) \qquad (5)$$

If $S_n = S$, then all the collected shares are legitimate, and they all pass the (t, n)-consistency test.

3   Architecture and Previous Related Work

In this section, we first explain the communication architecture used by the (n, t, n) multi-secret sharing scheme. Then we introduce the Verifiable (n, t, n) Multi-Secret Sharing Scheme. Finally, we discuss the security of the Verifiable (n, t, n) Multi-Secret Sharing Scheme and explain the limitation of this multi-secret sharing approach.

3.1 (n, t, n) Secret Sharing Architecture

As shown in Fig. 1, the traditional architecture only involves two entities with a secure channel established between them. However, in our proposed scheme, there are three kinds of entities involved: dealer, proxy, and reader. Instead of the direct communication between reader and dealer, the proxies work as an intermediate layer to help both sides to exchange information.

As depicted in Fig. 1, there are two kinds of secure channels. The first one is a secure channel between the proxies and the dealer. In fact, each dealer has a secure channel with every proxy, and every pair of proxies shares a unique secure channel. This secure channel can be achieved by symmetric encryption. Later in our scheme, we choose AES-256 [14]. The shared secret key is given before deployment by a trusted third party or the manufacturer. Every pair of participants share a unique secret private key, so they can use that key to encrypt their communication. In this way, participants can communicate with each other without revealing any information to others.

The second one is a secure channel between proxies and the reader. This kind of secure channel is achieved by asymmetric cryptography, such as RSA and Elliptic Curve algorithm, since the proxies and readers do not share private keys. In our scheme, the readers and proxies are relatively more powerful than the dealer. They can afford the costs of the heavy asymmetric encryption/decryption.

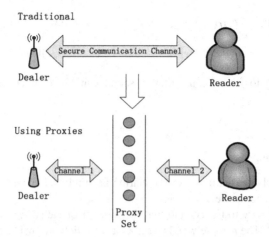

Fig. 1. Communication architecture of (n, t, n) threshold secret sharing scheme

(n, t, n) multi-secret sharing schemes based on this architecture can be used in different applications, such as key establishment in Internet of Things and key management in WSNs. The proxies are expected to help both sides of the communication to secretly exchange information without having a pre-shared key or using expensive asymmetric encryption techniques.

3.2 (n, t, n) Multi-secret Sharing Scheme [13]

Master Secret Generation Phase. Given a set of participants $\{P_1, P_2, \ldots, P_n\}$, each randomly selects a $(t-1)$ degree sub-polynomial $f_i(x)$, thus the corresponding sub-secret is $S_i = f_i(0)$.

All the participants work together to select a set of n-tuple weight vectors, denoted as $e_i = (e_{i,1}, e_{i,2}, \ldots, e_{i,n})$, for $i = 1, 2, \ldots, n - t + 1$. All e_i are linearly independent so that there would be $(n - t + 1)$ different master secrets shared among the participants; the l-th master secret will be: $M_l = \sum_{i=1}^{n} e_{l,i} S_i$.

Master Shares Generation Phase

- Each P_i computes sub-shares: $s_{i,j} = f_i(x_j) \Rightarrow \{s_{i,1}, s_{i,2}, \ldots, s_{i,n}\}$, where the x_j could be used as identifications, and $j = 1, 2, \ldots, n, i \neq j, x_i \neq x_j$.
- P_i sends each $s_{i,j}$ to a corresponding P_j secretly by encrypting the message using the shared key between these two participants.
- Each P_i computes the master shares as $ms_{i,l} = \sum_{j=1}^{n} e_{l,j} s_{j,i}$.

Master Secret Reconstruction Phase. Any t master shares can reconstruct the interpolating polynomial because:

$$ms_{i,l} = e_{l,1}f_1(x_i) + e_{l,2}f_2(x_i) + \cdots + e_{l,n}f_n(x_i) = F(x_i) \tag{6}$$

$$F_l(x) = e_{l,1}f_1(x) + e_{l,2}f_2(x) + \cdots + e_{l,n}f_n(x) \tag{7}$$

And according to Eq. (2), the master secret can be obtained as: $M_l = F_l(0) = \sum_{i=1}^{n} e_{l,i}S_i$.

3.3   Security Analysis

As was indicated above, the multi-secret sharing is simply achieved by multiplying the sub-shares by an n-tuple weight vector.

Here it is necessary to understand that the number of the secrets shared by one set of shares is limited. The n-tuple weight vectors are publicly known to every participant. Each participant only knows the sub-shares generated for itself, and participant P_i could only receive $ms_{i,l} = \sum_{j=1}^{n} e_{l,j}s_{j,i}$.

This final reconstructed secret itself will leak no information to the attackers. However, the master shares could be calculated if the attacker collected enough reconstructed secrets. The final polynomial is represented as $F_l(x) = \sum_{i=1}^{n} e_{l,i}f_i(x)$.

After reconstructing n secrets, a polynomial system could be revealed:

$$
\begin{aligned}
F_1(x) &= e_{1,1}f_1(x) + e_{1,2}f_2(x) + \cdots e_{1,n}f_n(x) \\
F_2(x) &= e_{2,1}f_1(x) + e_{2,2}f_2(x) + \cdots e_{2,n}f_n(x) \\
&\ \vdots \\
F_n(x) &= e_{n,1}f_1(x) + e_{n,2}f_2(x) + \cdots e_{n,n}f_n(x)
\end{aligned}
\tag{8}
$$

If the reconstruction is done by an outside attacker, since all the $F_i(x)$ and $e_{i,j}$, where $1 \leq i \leq l, 1 \leq j \leq n$, are known, this attacker can solve the polynomial system and get all the $f_j(x)$. Next time, it could calculate the master secret by itself using all the $f_j(x)$ and the public n-tuple weight vector.

The above is the best case for such an attacker; since this is an (n, t, n) threshold multi-secret sharing scheme, we needs to ensure that the scheme can still work when there are no more than $(t - 1)$ colluders. Here, assuming that $p_1, p_2, \ldots, p_{t-1}$ are colluders, so $f_1(x), f_2(x), \ldots, f_{t-1}(x)$ are known; deleting the known elements, it is easy to get the following polynomial system:

$$
\begin{aligned}
F_1'(x) &= e_{1,t}f_t(x) + e_{1,t+1}f_{t+1}(x) + \cdots e_{1,n}f_n(x) \\
F_2'(x) &= e_{2,t}f_t(x) + e_{2,t+1}f_{t+1}(x) + \cdots e_{2,n}f_n(x) \\
&\ \vdots \\
F_l'(x) &= e_{n,t}f_t(x) + e_{n,t+1}f_{t+1}(x) + \cdots e_{l,n}f_n(x)
\end{aligned}
\tag{9}
$$

There are only $(n - t + 1)$ unknowns, so the system can be solved if there are at least $(n - t + 1)$ equations. In other words, using this scheme, at most $(n - t + 1)$ secrets can be shared using one set of the shares.

As a result, this (n, t, n) multi-secret sharing scheme needs to update the master shares frequently, and every time a new master secret is about to be shared, the dealer needs to select and broadcast an n-tuple weight vector.

In order to further reduce the workload for the resource-constrained devices and eliminate the limitation of the number of shares that can be reused, we propose our decentralized (n, t, n) threshold multi-secret sharing scheme. The new scheme also exploits the idea of using (n, t, n) threshold secret sharing to achieve multi-secret sharing while introducing CRT and a one-way hash function.

4 Proposed Efficient Decentralized (n, t, n) Multi-secret Sharing Scheme Based on CRT

We denote the dealer as D, and each proxy as P_i, where $i = 1, 2, \ldots, n$. All the proxies form a set of P_i: $\{P_1, P_2, \ldots, P_n\}$. There is also a reader R_r outside the local network who wants to initiate the r-th communication session and get the secret S_r; here r is the session number, $r = 1, 2, \ldots, l$ and $S_1 \neq S_2 \neq \ldots \neq S_l$.

Assuming that dealer D is the extremely resource constrained device, so the workload for dealer should be as small as possible. In the best case, we can outsource most of the work to the proxies to establish a decentralized secret sharing scheme. While outsourcing the workload to the proxies, we also need to keep in mind that the

Table 1. Notifications and corresponding descriptions

Notation	Description
P_i/P_j	The i-th/j-th proxy, $i, j = 1, 2, 3, \ldots, n, i \neq j$
R_r	Reader in the r-th communication session with $r = 1, 2, 3, \ldots$
m_0	Large positive integer selected to set up the upper bound of the key space
m_i	Large randomly selected positive integers, $i = 1, 2, 3, \ldots, n$
S	Master secret, S is an integer and $0 < S < m_0$
S'	Pseudo master secret
SH_i	Secret shares of the master secret S, $SH_i \equiv S' \pmod{m_i}$
S_r	Secret generated and reconstructed in the r-th communication session
$H(x_1, x_2)$	One-way hash function with two inputs, $x_1 \neq x_2$
$h_{i,r}$	Pseudo-random number generated by P_i in the r-th session using one-way hash function
$Sh_{i,r}^j$	Sub-share generated by P_i in the r-th session which will be sent to P_j
Sh_r^j	Reconstruction share generated by P_j for secret S_r
N_y	Number of possible secrets
ShV_r^j	P_j's verification share
P_x	Cheater, or corrupted proxy, $x = 1, 2, 3, \ldots, n$

proxies have relatively more resources but are still resource-constrained devices; only the reader R which wants to initialize a communication session with D is powerful.

We list all the involved notation and their corresponding descriptions in Table 1; this notation will be used in the rest of the paper.

4.1 Detailed Scheme

Dealer Centralized Distribution Phase. As can be seen in Fig. 2, which shows the centralized distribution phase, only the dealer and all the proxies are involved in this phase.

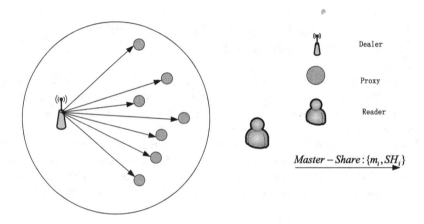

Fig. 2. Communication flow during dealer centralized distribution phase

For Dealer D:

- D randomly selects $(n + 1)$ positive pair-wise co-prime integers: $m_0, m_1, m_2, \ldots, m_n$, the boundaries are defined as follows: $m_0 \left(\prod_{i=n-t+2}^{n} m_i \right) < \prod_{i=1}^{t} m_i$.
- D then selects the master secret S. Here $0 < S < m_0$, so if m_0 is large enough, the key space will be sufficient to achieve required computational security. After S is selected, D computes $S' = S + Am_0$, where A is a randomly selected positive integer, and $0 < S' < M$, $M = \prod_{i=1}^{n} m_i$.
- D computes shares for all the proxies: $SH_i \equiv S' \bmod m_i$.
  (m_i, SH_i) is the actual share which will be sent to the corresponding proxy P_i, and all the $m_0, m_1, m_2, \ldots, m_n$ will be public to all members.

Proxy Sub-shares Distribution Phase. In this phase, proxies become senders and receivers at the same time, and when a proxy is in the Sender mode, its behavior will be similar to the dealer. The real dealer and the reader will not participate in the process. As shown in Fig. 3, the dealer and the reader are both waiting, and all the proxies start to distribute the generated sub-shares. We use one proxy as an example of sender state proxy and show this proxy as a square in order to distinguish it from others in Fig. 3. In later discussion, in order to distinguish two proxy states, we use P_i to represent the proxies in sender mode, and use P_j to represent the proxies in receiver mode.

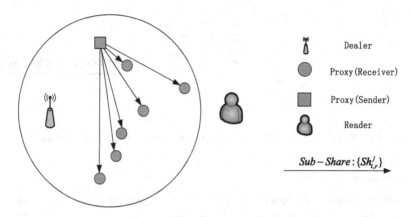

Fig. 3. Proxy P_i distribute sub-shares to other proxies

For Proxy P_i:

- When R_r wants to reconstruct S_r, P_i uses a two-variable one-way hash function $H(x_1, x_2)$ to generate a random number: $H(r, SH_i) = h_{i,r}$. By using one-way hash function, we can easily compute $h_{i,r}$ but the reverse computation is extremely difficult.

- P_i computes sub-shares $Sh_{i,r}^j \equiv SH_i \cdot h_{i,r} \pmod{m_j}$, then distributes each sub-share to corresponding proxy P_j $(j = 1, 2, \ldots, n, j \neq i)$.

For Proxy P_j:

- P_j will obtain n sub-shares from both other proxies and itself: $\left\{ Sh_{1,r}^j, Sh_{2,r}^j, \ldots, Sh_{1,r}^j \right\}$.

- P_j then adds all sub-shares together: $Sh_r^j \equiv \left(\sum_{i=1}^{n} Sh_{i,r}^j \right) \pmod{m_j}$; we call this Sh_r^j the reconstruction share for secret S_r.

Final Reconstruction Phase. After receiving all the sub-shares and generating the final construction share, the reader will first request reconstruction shares from t or more proxies. The dealer will locally perform the same one-way hash function operations as the proxies did, and compute the final secret without the help from the proxies. This method requires more memory space while reducing the communication and computation costs.

Figure 4 shows the final reconstruction phase. Proxies can provide reconstruction shares to both the dealer and the reader. However, the dealer may choose not to get the final secret by using reconstruction shares.

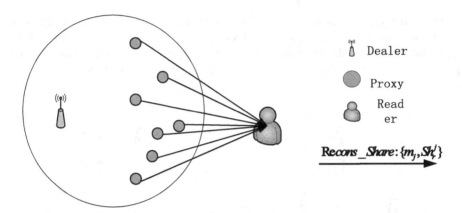

Fig. 4. Dealer and reader collecting reconstruction shares from proxies

For Receiver or Reader R_r:

- R_r selects a group of proxies: $\{P_1, P_2, \ldots, P_t\}$. Each proxy will send its own reconstruction share to R_r through the secret channel, so that R_r gets $\{Sh_r^1, Sh_r^2, \ldots, Sh_r^t\}$ and $\{m_1, m_2, \ldots, m_t\}$.

- Let $M_r = \sum_{i=1}^{t} m_i$, $M_{i,r} = M_r/m_i$, $y_{i,r} = M_{i,r}^{-1}(\bmod\, m_i)$. Then, based on CRT, R_r can compute the unique solution:

$$S_r' \equiv (\sum_{i=1}^{t} Sh_i^r \cdot M_{i,r} \cdot y_{i,r})(\bmod\, M_r) \tag{10}$$

$$S_r \equiv S_r'(\bmod\, m_0) \tag{11}$$

Note: $S_r' \equiv (\sum_{i=1}^{n} SH_i \cdot h_{i,r})(\bmod\, M)$, since $h_{i,r}$ will change every time, S_r will be different accordingly.

Performance Analysis. There are several resource consuming processes: primality test; secret reconstruction; communication; and encryption/decryption. As we see from the details of the proposed scheme, the heavy computation does not frequently happen on the dealer side.

The primality test is one of the operations that takes a long time, especially when the device is not powerful. However, we only need one set of well tested prime numbers, so over a long period of time, this type of computation would only happen once on the dealer.

The exponential operation is another resource-consuming process. It will be introduced when calculating the multiplicative inverse during the secret reconstruction phase. Since the dealer possesses all the required information, so the new secret can be reconstructed locally, this means that the exponential operation will only executed by the resourceful reader.

Since the master shares are reusable, once the master shares are distributed; the dealer has no need to communicate with proxies which omits the frequent communication as well as the heavy encryption operations.

That means that for each communication session, the dealer only needs to perform lightweight hash function computation and multiplication while in the previous scheme the dealer still has to communicate with proxies and periodically update the polynomials possessed by all the proxies.

Our scheme therefore adjusts the workload distribution to make the workloads further outsourced from the dealer to the proxies and the reader. This is an important feature for the resource-constrained devices such as small sensor nodes. However, in order to reduce the workload of the dealer, we introduced more operations on the proxies and the reader, which will potentially increase the overall cost of the system. Due to the page limitation, we do not give the details here.

4.2 Security and Verification

Security Analysis. The security analysis on Asmuth-Bloom's scheme has been done by [10], which indicates that as long as no more than $(t - 1)$ shares (s_i, m_i) are revealed, the secret S is secure. Here, we reused part of the shares, so it is necessary to discuss the possible influence of revealing of all the m_i, for $i = 1, 2, 3, \ldots n$.

In the worst case, assume $(t - 1)$ shares, which correspond to prime numbers $m_{n-t+2}, m_{n-t+3}, \ldots, m_n$, are known to the attacker, and all the co-prime numbers $m_0, m_1, m_2, \ldots, m_n$ are publicly exposed. S is the selected secret within the range $(0, m_0)$, and S' is in the range of $\left(0, \prod_{i=1}^{t} m_i\right)$ with $S' \equiv S + a m_0 (\text{mod } M)$, $M = \prod_{i=1}^{t} m_i$. The generated shares are $s_i \equiv S' (\text{mod } m_i)$.

Since the adversary has only $(t - 1)$ shares, together with the corresponding m_i, the adversary could perform CRT reconstruction operation on $(t - 1)$ shares to get all the information that $(t - 1)$ shares could reveal.

The multiplicative inverse of m_i is $M_i^{-1} = [(\prod_{i=n-t+2}^{n} m_i)/m_i]^{-1}$. Denote the reconstructed result as X; the computation of X is shown in Eq. (12).

$$X \equiv \left(\sum_{i=n-t+2}^{n} M_i \times (M_i^{-1} \bmod m_i) \times s_i \right) (\bmod \prod_{i=n-t+2}^{n} m_i) \qquad (12)$$

We could know that $X < \prod_{i=n-t+2}^{n} m_i$, which means there is only one possible value of S', and S' cannot be smaller than X. We assume there is an integer Y such that $S' = X + Y$, and in order to meet the requirement that $s_i \equiv S' (\text{mod } m_i)$ for m_{n-t+2}, $m_{n-t+3}, \ldots, m_n$, Y is divisible by $m_{n-t+2}, m_{n-t+3}, \ldots, m_n$, since they are co-prime to each other, so $Y = b \prod\limits_{i=n-t+2}^{n} m_i$, where b is a non-negative integer; thus $S' = X +$ $b \prod\limits_{i=n-t+2}^{n} m_i$.

Next, if we could get the value of b, we can obtain S'. Within the search space for S', the number of possible values for b is $N = (\prod\limits_{i=1}^{t} m_i - X)/ \prod\limits_{i=n-t+2}^{n} m_i$.

Because $m_0 \left(\prod\limits_{i=n-t+2}^{n} m_i \right) < \prod\limits_{i=1}^{t} m_i$, $N > (m_0 \prod\limits_{i=n-t+2}^{n} m_i - X)/ \prod\limits_{i=n-t+2}^{n} m_i$. Since $X < \prod\limits_{i=n-t+2}^{n} m_i$, we conclude that at least $N > (m_0 \prod\limits_{i=n-t+2}^{n} m_i - \prod\limits_{i=n-t+2}^{n} m_i)/ \prod\limits_{i=n-t+2}^{n} m$ $i = (m_0 - 1)$.

That means that despite the adversary knowing all the prime numbers and $(t-1)$ shares, it still needs to try at least $(m_0 - 1)$ times to learn the real secret. Considering that the conclusions above are based on the fact that all the m_i, for $i = 1, 2, 3, \ldots n$, are known, then as long as m_0 is big enough, the key space will not be narrowed down to an unacceptable level.

Also because both SH_i and $h_{i,r}$ are unknown, it is hard for an adversary to compute SH_i from the received $Sh_{i,r}^{j} \equiv SH_i \cdot h_{i,r} (\bmod m_j)$.

Two Methods of Generating Verifiable Shares. Although the algorithm itself appears to be secure, as demonstrated above, it is still important to consider the possibility that not all the received shares are correct. Some errors may occur during the transmission, or the proxies may intentionally send false shares to hamper the operation of the system.

We assume that the majority of the proxies are trustworthy, and the shares could be verified through the test of (t, n)-consistency. In order to do the test, we need to collect shares and perform the reconstruction operation to see if the reconstruction result of every set of t shares is the same. But this also means the reconstruction shares and the final secret are both exposed.

Here in this sub-section, we present two methods to generate verifiable shares without revealing any information about the final secret.

Using Uniform Vectors for Verifiable Shares Generation. The first method of generating verifiable shares is using uniform vectors. This method was proposed by Liu, Harn, Yang and Zhang in 2012 [13].

They proposed to ask the dealer to broadcast two n-tuple weight vectors at the same time. One of them is used to generate the reconstruction shares, the other is used to form the verifiable shares. However, since the publicly exposed n-tuple weight vectors will reveal some information about the secret as we illustrated in Sect. 3, the dealer needs to more frequently updates the privately kept polynomials.

Here, we simply ask the proxies to locally generate two sets of random numbers by performing the hash function, then following the similar steps in the reconstruction share generation. Reader receives two sets of shares, one is used for secret reconstruction purpose, the other one is for verification.

Exploits Special Property of CRT for Verifiable Shares Generation. The second method exploits a special property of CRT, and helps the verifier to get reconstruction shares and verifiable shares at the same time without asking the dealer to broadcast an *n*-tuple weight vector as done in the first method.

As we mentioned before, in the proxy sub-distribution phase, proxy P_j receives the following information: $\{Sh_{1,r}^j, Sh_{2,r}^j, \ldots, Sh_{n,r}^j\}$. The verifiable shares are simply generated by using the following operation: $ShV_r^j \equiv (\prod Sh_{i,r}^j)(\bmod m_j)$.

If all the verification shares have the (t, n)-consistency property, then the reconstruction shares reveal the correct secret.

In our scheme, we choose the second method because it is more efficient and simple to be exploited.

Here, we could also use the verification shares as the reconstruction shares while using the reconstruction ones to do the verification. How to decide which one to be used as reconstruction shares? That is according to the actual application requirements. Since the multiplication operation requires more computational resources and more time, and the verification does not need to happen frequently, we shall use $ShV_r^j \equiv$

$(\prod_{i=1}^{n} Sh_{i,r}^j)(\bmod m_j)$ as the verification share.

Cheater Detection. Cheater could be a compromised legitimate node or an attacker disguised itself as a legitimate node. The main purpose of a cheater is launching attacks from the inside and those attacks have different kinds.

The passive attacks are intended to eavesdrop and steel the shared secret. In our distributed approach, every proxy only possess part of the secret. A successful attack requires at least t cheaters to collude with each other, which is difficult to achieve. As long as the number of cheaters is up to $t - 1$, the risk of leaking the secret can be ignored since $t - 1$ shares cannot construct the secret as we discussed in this section.

The active attacks are trying to degrade the quality of service by modifying the messages or simply denying the request of information. If the attackers are so powerful that they can make the honest proxies to obliviously collude with the fellow cheaters, in the worst case, there is no way to detect nor identify the cheaters when $n = 2t - 1$ and up to $t - 1$ proxies are compromised [16].

We highlight our assumption again, which is that the majority of the proxies are honest and trustworthy. Because of the similarities shared by the Lagrange Polynomial Interpolation and the Chinese Remainder Theorem, in our scheme, we can use the similar technique as we mentioned earlier in Sect. 2 to test the (t, n)-consistency of all the collected reconstruction shares.

This test can be done as follows. We use all the received reconstruction shares to reconstruct the final secret:

$$Sn_r' \equiv (\sum_{i=1}^{n} Sh_i^r \cdot M_{i,r} \cdot y_{i,r})(\bmod M_r) \tag{13}$$

Here $M_r = \sum_{i=1}^{n} m_i$, $M_{i,r} = M_r/m_i$, $y_{i,r} = M_{i,r}^{-1} (\text{mod } m_i)$. If $S_r' = Sn_r'$, all the reconstruction shares are legitimate.

However, since the CRT operation involves exponential computations, we propose to reconstruct the secret by randomly selecting t shares from all the collected shares pool first. Then, instead of using all the shares to do the reconstruction again, we use the reconstructed secret to re-generate a copy for the unselected reconstruction shares:

$$Sh_r^{t+1'} \equiv S_r'(\text{mod } m_{t+1}), \ldots, Sh_r^{n'} \equiv S_r'(\text{mod } m_n)$$

If all the calculated reconstruction shares equal the collected corresponding ones, then all the shares are legitimate; otherwise, there are one or more cheaters among the majority-honest proxies.

5 Conclusion and Future Work

In this paper, we reviewed the existing multi-secret sharing schemes, and proposed our own CRT-based efficient (n, t, n) multi-secret sharing scheme with two verifiable scheme approaches. The use of CRT reduces the computational expense compared to Lagrange Polynomial Interpolation, and by allowing the proxies and the dealer to compute the one-way hash function locally, our scheme further omits the requirement of obtaining the n-tuple weight vector from the dealer and the periodically updating of the secret distributed polynomials.

Further analysis of the performance of this scheme is underway. The communication and computation costs of our scheme will be carefully simulated and tested. This scheme can be used in multiple applications such as Internet of Things and WSNs. However, in order to adapt this scheme to various applications, further security enhancements and performances improvements should be done as well.

References

1. Shamir, A.: How to share a secret. Commun. ACM **22**(11), 612–613 (1979)
2. Blakley, G.R.: Safeguarding cryptographic keys. In: National Computer Conference, 1979, ser. American Federation of Information Processing Societies Proceedings, vol. 48, pp. 313–317 (1979)
3. Mignotte, M.: How to share a secret? In: Beth, T. (ed.) EUROCRYPT 1982. LNCS, vol. 149, pp. 371–375. Springer, Heidelberg (1983)
4. Asmuth, C.A., Bloom, J.: A modular approach to key safeguarding. IEEE Trans. Inf. Theor. **IT-29**(2), 208–210 (1983)
5. He, J., Dawson, E.: Multistage secret sharing based on one-way function. Electron. Lett. **30**(19), 1591–1592 (1994)
6. He, J., Dawson, E.: Multisecret-sharing scheme based on one-way function. Electron. Lett. **31**(2), 93–95 (1995)
7. Lin, H.Y., Yeh, Y.S.: Dynamic multi-secret sharing scheme. Int. J. Contemp. Math. Sci. **3**(1), 37–42 (2008)

8. Chang, T., Hwang, M., Yang, W.: A new multi-stage secret sharing scheme using one-way function. ACM SIGOPS Oper. Syst. Rev. **39**(1), 48–55 (2005)
9. Harn, L., Lin, C.: Strong (n, t, n) verifiable secret sharing scheme. Inf. Sci. **180**(16), 3059–3064 (2010)
10. Quisquater, M., Preneel, B., Vandewalle, J.: On the security of the threshold scheme based on the chinese remainder theorem. In: Naccache, D., Paillier, P. (eds.) PKC 2002. LNCS, vol. 2274, pp. 199–210. Springer, Heidelberg (2002)
11. Herranz, J., Ruiz, A., Sáez, G.: New results and applications for multi-secret sharing schemes. Des. Codes Crypt. **73**, 841–864 (2013)
12. Waseda, A., Soshi, M.: Consideration for multi-threshold multi-secret sharing schemes. In: 2012 International Symposium on Information Theory and Its Applications (ISITA). IEEE (2012)
13. Liu, Y., Harn, L., Yang, C., Zhang, Y.: Efficient (n, t, n) secret sharing schemes. J. Syst. Softw. **85**, 1325–1332 (2012)
14. Stallings, W.: Cryptography and Network Security, 4th edn. Pearson Education India, New Delhi (2006)
15. Harn, L., Lin, C.: Detection and Identification of cheaters in (t, n) secret sharing scheme. Des. Codes Cryptogr. **52**(1), 15–24 (2009)
16. Ghodosi, H.: Comments on Harn–Lin's cheating detection scheme. Des. Codes Crypt. **60**(1), 63–66 (2011)

Composable Oblivious Extended Permutations

Peeter Laud[(✉)] and Jan Willemson

Cybernetica AS, Tallinn, Estonia
{peeter.laud,jan.willemson}@cyber.ee

Abstract. An extended permutation is a function $f : \{1, \ldots, m\} \to \{1, \ldots, n\}$, used to map an n-element vector $\boldsymbol{a}$ to an m-element vector $\boldsymbol{b}$ by $b_i = a_{f(i)}$. An *oblivious* extended permutation allows this mapping to be done while preserving the privacy of $\boldsymbol{a}$, $\boldsymbol{b}$ and f in a secure multiparty computation protocol. Oblivious extended permutations have several uses, with private function evaluation (PFE) being the theoretically most prominent one.

In this paper, we propose a new technique for oblivious evaluation of extended permutations. Our construction is at least as efficient as the existing techniques, conceptually simpler, and has wider applicability. Our technique allows the party providing the description of f to be absent during the computation phase of the protocol. Moreover, that party does not even have to exist — we show how to compute the private representation of f from private data that may itself be computed from the inputs of parties. In other words, our oblivious extended permutations can be freely composed with other privacy-preserving operations in a multiparty computation.

Keywords: Secure multiparty computation · Private function evaluation · Extended permutations

1 Introduction

In Secure Multiparty Computation (SMC), k parties compute $(y_1, \ldots, y_k) = f(x_1, \ldots, x_k)$, with the party P_i providing the input x_i and learning no more than the output y_i. Private Function Evaluation (PFE) is a special case of SMC, where the function f is also private, and its description, typically in the form of a circuit, is provided as input by one of the parties. One will thus obtain a solution for PFE, if one designs an SMC system for a universal function f. In SMC systems, f is usually represented as a Boolean or arithmetic circuit. Universal circuits are large (compared to circuits they can execute), hence this approach has not been practical so far.

Supported by the European Union Seventh Framework Programme (FP7/2007–2013) under grant agreement no. 284731 "Usable and Efficient Secure Multiparty Computation (UaESMC)", by Estonian Research Council through grant no. IUT27-1, and by European Regional Development Fund through the Estonian Center of Excellence in Computer Science (EXCS).

© Springer International Publishing Switzerland 2015
F. Cuppens et al. (Eds.): FPS 2014, LNCS 8930, pp. 294–310, 2015.
DOI: 10.1007/978-3-319-17040-4_19

Recently, Mohassel and Sadeghian [39] have split the task of oblivious circuit evaluation into two parts — obliviously evaluating the gates, and hiding the topology of the circuit in a manner that allows the outputs of the gates to be passed to the inputs of next gates. They introduce *oblivious extended permutations (OEP)* for the second subtask. Their approach increases the performance of PFE over the state of the art by a couple of orders of magnitude, making the private execution of small circuits a realistic proposition.

SMC techniques have seen significant maturation in last years, with the appearance of several frameworks [1,2,5,8,14,23,37] that allow the private computation of certain tasks with practically relevant sizes. There have been a number of successful applications of these frameworks [3,6,7,28,33]. A common tenet of all existing and in-progress applications is their client-server nature, where the participating entities are partitioned into *input parties* providing the private inputs to a SMC system, *computing parties* that execute the SMC protocols for computing the function f, and *output parties* that receive the results of the computation [4] (these sets of parties may overlap). This flexibility is certainly required in practice, as the active participation of all input parties in all stages of computation is unwanted both for efficiency (if the number of input parties is large), as well as organizational (if the input parties do not have the ability to execute complex protocols) reasons.

Mohassel's and Sadeghian's OEP construction does not fit into the model with input, computing and output parties. In their construction, the party providing the description of the private function must participate in the computation, i.e. it must be both an input and a computing party.

In this paper, we propose a multiparty OEP construction that allows the extended permutation to be input to the private computation by a non-computing input party or constructed *during* the computation from other private values, thereby removing the need to treat them in any special manner. In fact, all our constructions will be presented in the Arithmetic Black Box (ABB) model [13], making their use in larger applications straightforward, and also greatly simplifying the security proofs. Our construction is conceptually simpler than [39], and, if the number of computing parties is small, also potentially more efficient (even though a fair comparison is difficult due to different operational profiles). It increases the variety of deployment scenarios for PFE applications, among which credit evaluation and background checks have been proposed [29]. With our construction, the private computation can be outsourced, and the evaluated function itself may be obtained through secure computation. We have implemented our proposed construction and provide benchmarking results.

This paper has the following structure. We review the related work in Sect. 2 and give the necessary preliminaries, including the ABB model, in Sect. 3. In Sect. 4 we present the desired ideal functionality for OEPs, as well as the actual protocol set (together with security proofs), with the most complicated protocol appearing in Sect. 5. In Sect. 6 we present the benchmarking results of our implementation of the OEP protocol; according to our knowledge, this is the first such implementation. In Sect. 7, we discuss some further research directions opened up by our OEP construction.

2   Related Work

A number of existing OEP constructions are based on switching networks employing 2×2 switches that may either pass their inputs unmodified, swap the inputs, or copy one input to both outputs. The network is commonly obtained from Waksman's construction [42]; it is evaluated with SMC techniques. Such constructions appear in [24,29,39]. In [38], the construction of [39] is amended to give it security against malicious adversaries. All such constructions require one of the computing parties to know the extended permutation.

An OEP can also be constructed with homomorphic encryption [24, Sect. 5.3.2]. This construction has better asymptotic complexity than the ones based on switching networks, but it requires many expensive public-key operations. Again, one computing party has to know the extended permutation.

Oblivious RAM (ORAM) [17,19,41] is a functionality that allows a server's memory to be read and written according to a client's private address. It is a more flexible construction than OEP, which fixes the indices ahead of time and performs many reads in parallel. The implementation of ORAM algorithms on top of SMC (which would be necessary to emulate OEP) is non-trivial and brings high overheads [12,36].

A very simple construction for *shuffling* (permuting) the elements of a vector is given by Laur et al. [34]. Hamada et al. [21,22] have used this construction to give fast sorting algorithms. Our constructions are also based on this form of shuffling protocols.

3   Preliminaries

Universal composability (UC) [9] is a standard theoretical framework for stating and proving security of cryptographic constructions. In this framework, a protocol π is defined secure if it is *as secure as* some ideal functionality $\mathcal{F}$ embodying the desired functional and non-functional properties of π in an abstract manner. A functionality $\mathcal{F}_1$ is at least as secure as $\mathcal{F}_2$, if for every user of these functionalities, and every adversary of $\mathcal{F}_1$, there is an adversary of $\mathcal{F}_2$, such that the user cannot see the difference in interacting with $\mathcal{F}_1$ or $\mathcal{F}_2$. UC framework derives its usefulness from the composability of the *"at least as secure as"* relation: If protocol π_1 is at least as secure as the (ideal) functionality $\mathcal{F}_1$, and protocol π_2 incorporating $\mathcal{F}_1$ (i.e. π_2 has been realized in the $\mathcal{F}_1$-*hybrid model*) is at least as secure as $\mathcal{F}_2$, then π_2, where the calls to $\mathcal{F}_1$ have been replaced with the invocations of π_1, is also at least as secure as $\mathcal{F}_2$.

Arithmetic black box. For SMC, the standard ideal functionality is the Arithmetic Black Box (ABB) $\mathcal{F}_{ABB}$ [13]. It provides an interface for users $P_1, \ldots, P_k$, up to t of which may be corrupted (for simplicity, we only consider static corruptions), to perform computations without revealing intermediate values. Here t depends on the protocol set π_{ABB} implementing $\mathcal{F}_{ABB}$. The functionality $\mathcal{F}_{ABB}$ is given in Fig. 1. Depending on the implementation π_{ABB}, the adversary and/or

Internal state: a finite map **S** from variable names to values (initially empty)
Exposed commands:

Input data. On input (input, v, x) from some P_i and (input, v) from all other parties,
    add $\{v \mapsto x\}$ to **S**.
Classify. On input $(\mathsf{classify}, v, x)$ from all parties, add $\{v \mapsto x\}$ to **S**.
Compute. On input $(\mathsf{compute}, \otimes, v_1, v_2, v_3)$ from all parties, look up $x_1 = \mathbf{S}(v_1)$ and
    $x_2 = \mathbf{S}(v_2)$, and add $\{v_3 \mapsto x_1 \otimes x_2\}$ to **S**.
Declassify. On input $(\mathsf{declassify}, v)$ from all parties, answer with $\mathbf{S}(v)$ to all parties.

When receiving any command except input, the whole command, as well as its answer
is also sent to the adversary. For input-commands, (input, v) is sent to the adversary. I.e.
one does not attempt to hide from the adversary, which protocols are executed (who
could determine it through traffic analysis). Only the processed values are hidden.
Some of the parties may be *corrupted*. For any command $(c, \ldots)$ listed above, $\mathcal{F}_{\mathsf{ABB}}$
accepts the command $(\mathsf{masq}^i, c, \ldots)$ from the adversary, for a corrupted party P_i. Such
commands are processed as commands $(c, \ldots)$ from P_i.
The execution of $\mathcal{F}_{\mathsf{ABB}}$ takes place in *rounds*, with each party submitting its command
for the current round, and the adversary submitting commands for corrupt parties. In
implementations π_{ABB}, many rounds may take place in parallel.

Fig. 1. The ideal functionality $\mathcal{F}_{\mathsf{ABB}}$

certain coalitions of users may also be able to stop the execution of $\mathcal{F}_{\mathsf{ABB}}$. We
will not define the behaviour of $\mathcal{F}_{\mathsf{ABB}}$ in exceptional situations (e.g. undefined
variables), because their occurrence can be detected from public information.

The interface of $\mathcal{F}_{\mathsf{ABB}}$ does not correspond well to the partitioning of parties
into input, computing, and output parties. Still, it can be modeled by precisely
defining, which parties are needed to execute different commands, and which
parties receive the results.

The values $\mathcal{F}_{\mathsf{ABB}}$ operates on are elements of some algebraic structure depending on π_{ABB}, typically some finite field or ring. The operations $\otimes$ supported by
$\mathcal{F}_{\mathsf{ABB}}$ also depend on the actual protocols that are available. Many protocol sets
π_{ABB} for SMC have been proposed [11,15,16,18,26,40,43], several of them also
providing security against malicious adversaries. All sets support at least the addition and multiplication of values stored in **S**. Based on them, one can implement
a rich set of arithmetic and relational operations [10], enjoying the same security
properties. The protocols we present in this paper need to compare the values in
S, and we assume that "equals" and "less than" operations are available in $\mathcal{F}_{\mathsf{ABB}}$.

For a variable name v, it is customary to denote its value, as stored in **S**, by
$[\![v]\!]$. Also, in the description of algorithms executed together with $\mathcal{F}_{\mathsf{ABB}}$, notation
$[\![w]\!] = \otimes([\![u]\!], [\![v]\!])$ denotes the calling of $(\mathsf{compute}, \otimes, u, v, w)$ on $\mathcal{F}_{\mathsf{ABB}}$.

Shuffling. An oblivious shuffle, introduced by Laur et al. [34] allows to permute
the elements of a private array of length m according to a private permutation $\sigma \in S_m$. The functionality and security of oblivious shuffle can be likewise
presented through the notion of ABB. Let the variable names be partitioned

Input a shuffle. On input (input, s, σ) from some P_i and (input, s, m) from all other
   parties, if $\sigma \in S_m$ then add $\{s \mapsto \sigma\}$ to **S**.
Classify a shuffle. On input (classify, s, σ) from all parties, add $\{s \mapsto \sigma\}$ to **S**.
Make a random shuffle. On input (rand_shuffle, s, m) from all parties, pick $\sigma \in_R S_m$
   and add $\{s \mapsto \sigma\}$ to **S**.
Compose private and public shuffle. On input (compose_left, s_1, s_2, τ) from all
   parties, look up $\sigma = \mathbf{S}(s_2)$ and add $\{s_1 \mapsto \tau \circ \sigma\}$ to **S**. On input
   (compose_right, s_1, s_2, τ) do the same, but add $\{s_1 \mapsto \sigma \circ \tau\}$ to **S**.
Apply a shuffle. On input (apply, $u_1, \ldots, u_m; v_1, \ldots, v_m; s$) from all parties, look up
   $\sigma = \mathbf{S}(s)$ and $x_i = \mathbf{S}(v_i)$ for all $i \in \{1, \ldots, m\}$. Add $\{u_i \mapsto x_{\sigma(i)}\}$ to **S** for all i.
Invert a shuffle. On input (invert, s_1, s_2) from all parties, look up $\sigma = \mathbf{S}(s_1)$ and add
   $\{s_2 \mapsto \sigma^{-1}\}$ to **S**.

Similarly to Fig. 1, all commands are also sent to the adversary, except for input, where
only (input, s, m) is sent. Also, (masq^i, ...) commands are accepted from the adversary.

Fig. 2. Shuffle-related operations in $\mathcal{F}_{\mathsf{ABB}}$

into two — names for scalars, and shuffles. In Fig. 1, each variable name refers
to a scalar. In Fig. 2 we list the shuffling-related commands of the ABB. Here
u, v denote scalar variables, and s denotes shuffle variables.

For ABB implementations based on secret sharing, Laur et al. [34] introduce
a construction, where a shuffle $\sigma \in S_m$ is represented as $[\![\sigma]\!] = ([\![\sigma]\!]_1, \ldots, [\![\sigma]\!]_l)$,
where $[\![\sigma]\!]_i \in S_m$ are random permutations subject to $[\![\sigma]\!]_1 \circ \cdots \circ [\![\sigma]\!]_l = \sigma$. Each
$[\![\sigma]\!]_i$ is known by all parties in some set A_i. In the shuffling protocol, the values
$x_1, \ldots, x_m$ are shuffled using $[\![\sigma]\!]_1, \ldots, [\![\sigma]\!]_l$ (sequentially). Before shuffling with
$[\![\sigma]\!]_i$, the current values are shared among the parties in A_i only. The sets A_i
have to be carefully selected for the scheme to be secure. For $k = 3$ and $t = 1$,
we may take $l = 3$ and $A_i = \{1, 2, 3\} \backslash \{i\}$.

It is straightforward to securely implement other operations in Fig. 2, based
on the protocol of Laur et al. [34]. Note that inverting a shuffle also inverts
the sequence of the party sets A_i applying the consecutive permutations in $[\![\sigma]\!]$.
Laur et al. also show how to make the protocols secure against malicious adversaries. Alternatively, recent proposals for making passively secure protocols verifiable [25,31] are readily applicable to described shuffling protocols.

Oblivious shuffles are instrumental for fast sorting algorithms on private val-
ues [22]. To sort a vector $[\![u]\!] = ([\![u_1]\!], \ldots, [\![u_m]\!])$, where all values are known to
be different, one may generate a random shuffle $[\![\sigma]\!]$ and apply it on $[\![u]\!]$. Afterwards, the elements of $[\![u]\!]$ are randomly ordered and their comparison results
may be declassified. In this way expensive, data-oblivious sorting methods [27]
do not have to be employed. Sorting, in turn, can be used to transform a vector
of values $([\![v_1]\!], \ldots, [\![v_m]\!])$ to a shuffle $[\![\sigma]\!]$, such that $\sigma(i) = v_i$, provided that the
private values are a permutation of $(1, \ldots, m)$. See Algorithm 1. The algorithm
is secure because the only values output by $\mathcal{F}_{\mathsf{ABB}}$ during its execution are the

---

Algorithm 1. Vector2Shuffle, From a vector of private values to private shuffle

---

Data: Vector of values $(\llbracket v_1 \rrbracket, \ldots, \llbracket v_m \rrbracket)$, with $\{v_1, \ldots, v_m\} = \{1, \ldots, m\}$
Result: A shuffle $\llbracket \sigma \rrbracket$, such that $\sigma(i) = v_i$
$\llbracket s \rrbracket \leftarrow$ rand_shuffle(m)
$(\llbracket u_1 \rrbracket, \ldots, \llbracket u_m \rrbracket) \leftarrow$ apply$(\llbracket v_1 \rrbracket, \ldots, \llbracket v_m \rrbracket; \llbracket s \rrbracket)$
Sort $(\llbracket u_1 \rrbracket, \ldots, \llbracket u_m \rrbracket)$, using declassify$(\llbracket \cdot \rrbracket \le \llbracket \cdot \rrbracket)$ as the comparison function
Let $\tau \in S_m$ be the sorting permutation, i.e. $u_{\tau(i)} = i$.
return invert$(\llbracket s \rrbracket \circ \tau)$

---

results of comparisons; these may be made public by the security arguments for sorting algorithms. It is easy to verify that Algorithm 1 is also correct.

As sorting turns out to be a useful operation in our protocols, we opt to make it a part of $\mathcal{F}_{ABB}$. See Fig. 3 for the exact specification of lexicographically, stably sorting the rows of a $m \times l$ table. For ease of use, we let our sorting functionality to not actually sort its input, but to output a private shuffle that would sort the input if applied to it. The protocol for computing such a shuffle in π_{ABB} is identical to Algorithm 1, except for the omission of the last inversion.

Sort. On input $(\text{sort}, u_1^1, \ldots, u_1^l; \ldots; u_m^1, \ldots, u_m^l; s)$, look up the values $x_i^j = \mathbf{S}(u_i^j)$ for all $i \in \{1, \ldots, m\}$ and $j \in \{1, \ldots, l\}$. Find $\sigma \in S_m$, such that
- for all $1 \le i \le j \le n$: $(x_{\sigma(i)}^1, \ldots, x_{\sigma(i)}^l) \le (x_{\sigma(j)}^1, \ldots, x_{\sigma(j)}^l)$, where the ordering of tuples is defined lexicographically;
- for all $1 \le i < j \le n$: if $(x_i^1, \ldots, x_i^l) = (x_j^1, \ldots, x_j^l)$, then $\sigma(i) < \sigma(j)$.

Add $\{s \mapsto \sigma\}$ to $\mathbf{S}$ and forward the sort-command to the adversary.

Fig. 3. Sorting in $\mathcal{F}_{ABB}$

4   Our OEP Functionality

The notion of *extended permutation (EP)* was introduced in [39] for encoding the topology of arithmetic or Boolean circuits. Mathematically, an EP ϕ from a length-n to a length-m sequence is just a function from $\{1, \ldots, m\}$ to $\{1, \ldots, n\}$. Applying ϕ to a sequence $(x_1, \ldots, x_n)$ produces a sequence $(y_1, \ldots, y_m)$, such that $y_i = x_{\phi(i)}$ for each i. Similarly to shuffles, we want to apply EPs in an oblivious manner, such that the values to which ϕ is applied, as well as ϕ itself remain private.

Let $F_{n,m}$ denote the set of all mappings from $\{1, \ldots, m\}$ to $\{1, \ldots, n\}$. Our intended ideal functionality for an ABB with EPs is given in Fig. 4. The functionality maps variables to either private values, private shuffles or private EPs, and allows operations on them. Let the variable names be partitioned into three — names for scalars, shuffles, and EPs. In Fig. 4, u, v denote scalar variables, while f denotes EP variables.

Include the state **S** and commands of $\mathcal{F}_{\mathsf{ABB}}$ in Fig. 1 and Fig. 2.
Additional commands are given below.

Input an EP. On input (input, f, ϕ) from some P_i and (input, f, n, m) from all other
  parties, if $\phi \in F_{n,m}$ then add $\{f \mapsto \phi\}$ to **S**.
Classify an EP. On input (classify, f, ϕ) from all parties, add $\{f \mapsto \phi\}$ to **S**.
Apply an EP. On input (apply, $u_1, \ldots, u_m; v_1, \ldots, v_n; f$) from all parties, look up $\phi = $
  S(f) and $x_i = $ **S**(v_i). Add $\{u_j \mapsto x_{f(j)}\}$ to **S** for all $j \in \{1, \ldots, m\}$. The mapping
  ϕ must be an element of $F_{n,m}$.
Convert a vector to an EP. On input (convert, $u_1, \ldots, u_m, n, f$) from all parties,
  look up $x_i = $ **S**(u_i) for all $i \in \{1, \ldots, m\}$. If $1 \le x_i \le n$ holds for all i, let $\phi \in F_{n,m}$
  be defined by $\phi(i) = x_i$ and add $\{f \mapsto \phi\}$ to **S**. Otherwise, the behaviour of $\mathcal{F}_{\mathsf{OEP}}$
  is undefined.

The commands are sent to the adversary, and accepted from the adversary similarly
to Fig. 1 and Fig. 2.

Fig. 4. The ideal functionality $\mathcal{F}_{\mathsf{OEP}}$

The representation of oblivious extended permutations used by our imple-
mentation π_{OEP} of $\mathcal{F}_{\mathsf{OEP}}$ is based on the following simple result.

Theorem 1. *For any $m, n \in \mathbb{N}$ there exist $\ell_{n,m} = (1 + o(1))m \ln m$ and $g_{n,m} :$
$\{1, \ldots, \ell_{n,m}\} \to \{1, \ldots, n\}$, such that for any function $\phi \in F_{n,m}$, there exist
$\sigma \in S_n$ and $\tau \in S_{\ell_{n,m}}$, such that $\phi(x) = (\sigma \circ g_{n,m} \circ \tau)(x)$ for all $x \in \{1, \ldots, m\}$.*

Proof. Define $\ell_{n,m}$ by

$$\ell_{0,m} = 0$$
$$\ell_{n,m} = \ell_{n-1,m} + \lfloor m/n \rfloor.$$

Then $\ell_{n,m} = (1 + o(1))m \ln m$ [35]. Define $g_{n,m}$ by

$$g_{n,m}(x) = k \Leftrightarrow \ell_{k-1,m} < x \le \ell_{k,m}.$$

Let $\phi \in F_{n,m}$ be given. For each $y \in \{1, \ldots, n\}$, let $\phi^{-1}(y) = \{x \mid \phi(x) = y\}$.
Let the permutation $\sigma \in S_n$ be such, that $|\phi^{-1}(\sigma(i))| \ge |\phi^{-1}(\sigma(i+1))|$ for all i.
Note that $|\phi^{-1}(\sigma(i))| \le \lfloor m/i \rfloor$.

Let $D_i = \{\ell_{i-1,m} + 1, \ldots, \ell_{i,m}\}$. Note that $|D_i| = \lfloor m/i \rfloor$ and $g_{n,m}(z) = $
i for all $z \in D_i$. Let the permutation $\tau \in S_{\ell_{n,m}}$ be defined so, that for all
$i \in \{1, \ldots, n\}$, we have $\tau(\phi^{-1}(\sigma(i))) \subseteq D_i$. Such permutation τ exists, because
$|\phi^{-1}(\sigma(i))| \le |D_i|$ and different sets D_i are disjoint.

For each $x \in \{1, \ldots, m\}$, we now have $\tau(x) \in D_{\sigma^{-1}(\phi(x))}$, implying $g_{n,m}(\tau(x)) = $
$\sigma^{-1}(\phi(x))$ or $\sigma(g_{n,m}(\tau(x))) = \phi(x)$.   □

We see that σ sorts the elements of $\{1, \ldots, n\}$ according to their number of
preimages with respect to ϕ. The mapping $g_{n,m}$ creates a sufficient number of
copies of each element. These copies are brought to their correct places by τ.

Theorem 1 immediately suggests the private encoding for an OEP ϕ. In our implementation π_{OEP} for $\mathcal{F}_{OEP}$, we will store them as pairs of private shuffles (σ, τ), defined as in the proof of Theorem 1. Figure 5 depicts the protocol set π_{OEP} (except for the convert-protocol, which is given in Sect. 5), defined in the $\mathcal{F}_{ABB}$-hybrid model.

There are machines $M_1, \ldots, M_k$ executing the protocols on behalf of the parties $P_1, \ldots, P_k$ participating in the protocol. These machines have access to the functionality $\mathcal{F}_{ABB}$.

There is a public function $f \mapsto (s_f, t_f)$ mapping variable names for EPs to pairs of variable names for shuffles. We assume that these variable names for shuffles are not used outside this protocol set.

A machine M_i responds to the various commands as follows.

Commands for $\mathcal{F}_{ABB}$. When receiving a command for $\mathcal{F}_{ABB}$ from the environment, M_i forwards it to $\mathcal{F}_{ABB}$ and gives back the result.

Input an EP. On input $(\mathsf{input}, f, \phi)$, the machine M_i constructs the shuffles σ and τ corresponding to ϕ according to the proof of Thm. 1. It will then send commands $(\mathsf{input}, s_f, \sigma)$ and $(\mathsf{input}, t_f, \tau)$ to $\mathcal{F}_{ABB}$.

Input an EP. On input $(\mathsf{input}, f, n, m)$, the machine M_i sends commands (input, s_f, n) and $(\mathsf{input}, t_f, \ell_{n,m})$ to $\mathcal{F}_{ABB}$.

Classify an EP. On input $(\mathsf{classify}, f, \phi)$, the machine M_i constructs the shuffles σ and τ corresponding to ϕ according to the proof of Thm. 1. Any indeterminacies in the proof are solved in the same, public manner by all parties. Machine M_i will then send the commands $(\mathsf{classify}, s_f, \sigma)$ and $(\mathsf{classify}, t_f, \tau)$ to $\mathcal{F}_{ABB}$.

Apply an EP. On input $(\mathsf{apply}, u_1, \ldots, u_m; v_1, \ldots, v_n; f)$, machine M_i will pick $\ell_{n,m}$ new variable names $w_1, \ldots, w_{\ell_{n,m}}$ (for scalars). After that, it will

  1. send $(\mathsf{apply}, w_1, \ldots, w_n; v_1, \ldots, v_n; s_f)$ to $\mathcal{F}_{ABB}$;
  2. copy $w_1, \ldots, w_n$ to $w_1, \ldots, w_{\ell_{n,m}}$ according to $g_{n,m}$, i.e. w_i after copying will be equal to $w_{g_{n,m}(i)}$ before copying (note that this is an operation of $\mathcal{F}_{ABB}$);
  3. send $(\mathsf{apply}, u_1, \ldots, u_m, w_{m+1}, \ldots, w_{\ell_{n,m}}; w_1, \ldots, w_{\ell_{n,m}}; t_f)$ to $\mathcal{F}_{ABB}$.

Fig. 5. The protocol set π_{OEP} for k parties (partially)

Theorem 2. *The protocol set π_{OEP}, as depicted in Fig. 5, is at least as secure as $\mathcal{F}_{OEP}$ without convert-commands.*

Proof. We have to show a simulator $\mathcal{S}$ that can translate between the messages at the adversarial interface of $\mathcal{F}_{OEP}$ and the messages at the adversarial interface of π_{OEP}. The simulator $\mathcal{S}$ has no long-term state and works as follows:

– On an input $(c, \ldots)$ from $\mathcal{F}_{OEP}$ that corresponds to a command for $\mathcal{F}_{ABB}$, the simulator forwards this input to the adversary.
– On input $(\mathsf{input}, f, n, m)$ from $\mathcal{F}_{OEP}$, the simulator forwards the commands (input, s_f, n) and $(\mathsf{input}, t_f, \ell_{n,m})$ to the adversary.

- On input (classify, f, ϕ) from $\mathcal{F}_{\mathsf{OEP}}$, the simulator computes the permutations σ and τ according to the proof of Theorem 1, and forwards (classify, s_f, σ) and (classify, t_f, τ) to the adversary.
- On input (apply, $u_1, \ldots, u_m; v_1, \ldots, v_n; f$) from $\mathcal{F}_{\mathsf{OEP}}$, the simulator forwards the commands for applying s_f, copying the variables and applying t_f to the adversary. The commands are the same as in Fig. 5.
- On input (masq$^i, c, \ldots$) from the adversary to $\mathcal{F}_{\mathsf{ABB}}$, the simulator $\mathcal{S}$ forwards that command to $\mathcal{F}_{\mathsf{OEP}}$, unless the command is part of an adversarial party's activity in the protocols of π_{OEP}. These are recognized through the inclusion of variable names s_f and t_f.
- On input (masq^i, input, s_f, n) from the adversary, followed by (masq^i, input, $t_f, \ell_{n,m}$): send (masq^i, input, f, n, m) to $\mathcal{F}_{\mathsf{OEP}}$.
- On input (masq$^i, c, s_f, \sigma$) from the adversary, followed by (masq$^i, c, t_f, \tau$), where c is either input or classify: the simulator constructs $\phi = \sigma \circ g_{n,m} \circ \tau$ (where n, m are found from the descriptions of σ and τ), and sends (masq$^i, c, f, \phi$) to $\mathcal{F}_{\mathsf{OEP}}$.
- On input (masq^i, apply, $w_1, \ldots, w_n; v_1, \ldots, v_n; s_f$) from the adversary, followed by the requests to copy the variables w_j according to $g_{n,m}$ and the input (masq^i, apply, $u_1, \ldots, u_m, w_{m+1}, \ldots, w_{\ell_{n,m}}; w_1, \ldots, w_{\ell_{n,m}}; t_f$): send (masq^i, apply, $u_1, \ldots, u_m; v_1, \ldots, v_n; f$) to the adversary.

Quite clearly, this simulator provides the necessary translation. Actually, the only non-trivial part of this simulator is the construction of ϕ from σ and τ provided by the adversary. Fortunately, there exists a ϕ for any σ and τ (of correct types). Hence π_{OEP} is secure even against active adversaries (if the protocol set implementing $\mathcal{F}_{\mathsf{ABB}}$ is secure against such adversaries). □

The provided simulator $\mathcal{S}$ is valid for any attacks by the adversary. It can cope with active attacks and with dishonest majority. Hence π_{OEP} provides the same security guarantees as the protocol set π_{ABB} implementing $\mathcal{F}_{\mathsf{ABB}}$.

5   Converting a Private Vector to an OEP

Suppose we are given the numbers m, n, and a vector $(\llbracket v_1 \rrbracket, \ldots, \llbracket v_m \rrbracket)$, such that $1 \leq v_i \leq n$ for all i. We want to construct $\llbracket \phi \rrbracket$, such that $\phi \in F_{n,m}$ and $\phi(i) = v_i$ for all i. For this, we have to construct private shuffles $\llbracket \sigma \rrbracket$ and $\llbracket \tau \rrbracket$ of correct size, such that $\phi = \sigma \circ g_{n,m} \circ \tau$. As we show below, the functionality provided by $\mathcal{F}_{\mathsf{ABB}}$ is sufficient for this construction. However, the construction is more complex than what we have seen before.

Partially specified shuffles. The following subtask occurs in the construction of both σ and τ. Let a vector $(\llbracket v_1 \rrbracket, \ldots, \llbracket v_n \rrbracket)$ be given, such that $v_i \in \{0, 1, \ldots, n\}$ and for each $j \in \{1, \ldots, n\}$ there exists at most one i, such that $v_i = j$. Construct $\llbracket \sigma \rrbracket$, where $\sigma \in S_n$ and $\forall i \in \{1, \ldots, n\} : v_i > 0 \Rightarrow \sigma(i) = v_i$.

Algorithm 2. FillBlanks, filling the blank squares of a shuffle

---

Data: Bounds $L, H \in \mathbb{N}$

Data: $[\![v_L]\!], [\![v_{L+1}]\!], \ldots, [\![v_H]\!]$, where $v_i \in \{0, L, \ldots, H\}$, and for each
$\quad\quad\;\; j \in \{L, \ldots, H\}$, there is at most one i, such that $v_i = j$

Result: $[\![u_L]\!], [\![u_{L+1}]\!], \ldots, [\![u_H]\!]$, where $\{u_L, \ldots, u_H\} = \{L, \ldots, H\}$ and
$\quad\quad\;\; v_i > 0 \Rightarrow u_i = v_i$

1 **if** $L = H$ **then**
2 $\quad$ **return** $[\![L]\!]$

3 $\;\; M \leftarrow \lfloor (L + H)/2 \rfloor$
4 $\;\; [\![\xi]\!] \leftarrow \mathsf{sort}([\![v_L]\!]; [\![v_{L+1}]\!]; \ldots; [\![v_H]\!])$; $\hspace{3cm}$ // Fig. 3
5 $\;\; ([\![v'_L]\!], \ldots, [\![v'_H]\!]) \leftarrow \mathsf{apply}([\![v_L]\!], \ldots, [\![v_H]\!]; [\![\xi]\!])$
6 **foreach** $i \in \{1, \ldots, H - M\}$ **do**
7 $\quad [\![b_i]\!] \leftarrow [\![v'_{M+i}]\!] \leq M$
8 $\quad ([\![v'_{L+i-1}]\!], [\![v'_{M+i}]\!]) \leftarrow [\![b_i]\!] ? ([\![v'_{M+i}]\!], [\![v'_{L+i-1}]\!]) : ([\![v'_{L+i-1}]\!], [\![v'_{M+i}]\!])$

9 $\;\; ([\![v'_L]\!], \ldots, [\![v'_M]\!]) \leftarrow \mathsf{FillBlanks}(L, M; [\![v'_L]\!], \ldots, [\![v'_M]\!])$
10 $\;\; ([\![v'_{M+1}]\!], \ldots, [\![v'_H]\!]) \leftarrow \mathsf{FillBlanks}(M + 1, H; [\![v'_{M+1}]\!], \ldots, [\![v'_H]\!])$
11 **foreach** $i \in \{1, \ldots, H - M\}$ **do**
12 $\quad ([\![v'_{L+i-1}]\!], [\![v'_{M+i}]\!]) \leftarrow [\![b_i]\!] ? ([\![v'_{M+i}]\!], [\![v'_{L+i-1}]\!]) : ([\![v'_{L+i-1}]\!], [\![v'_{M+i}]\!])$

13 $\;\; ([\![u_L]\!], \ldots, [\![u_H]\!]) \leftarrow \mathsf{apply}([\![v'_L]\!], \ldots, [\![v'_H]\!]; \mathsf{invert}([\![\xi]\!]))$
14 **return** $([\![u_L]\!], \ldots, [\![u_H]\!])$

We cannot directly apply Algorithm 1 to obtain the shuffle, because this algorithm assumes that the input vector is a permutation of $\{1, \ldots, n\}$. In particular, the correctness of Algorithm 1 hinges on the sorted vector being equal to $(1, \ldots, n)$.

We will hence first fill the zeroes in the vector $v_1, \ldots, v_n$ with the missing numbers. We use Algorithm 2 for that, making the call $\mathsf{FillBlanks}(1, n; [\![v_1]\!], \ldots, [\![v_n]\!])$. After that, we can apply Algorithm 1 and obtain a suitable $[\![\sigma]\!]$.

In Algorithm 2, we have used a few conventions that have appeared elsewhere in the specifications of privacy-preserving algorithms. In line 7, the variable $[\![b_i]\!]$ will store either 1 or 0, depending on whether the comparison returns true. The line 8 contains an instance of the *binary choice* operator $[\![b]\!] ? [\![x]\!] : [\![y]\!]$. Its result is equal to $[\![x]\!]$ if $b = 1$, and $[\![y]\!]$ if $b = 0$. It is typically computed as $[\![b]\!] \cdot ([\![x]\!] - [\![y]\!]) + [\![y]\!]$. In lines 8 and 12 we are actually using pairs of values in place of $[\![x]\!]$ and $[\![y]\!]$. Hence the effect of these lines is to swap $[\![v'_{L+i-1}]\!]$ and $[\![v'_{M+i}]\!]$ if $b_i = 1$, and otherwise leave them as is.

A number of operations in Algorithm 2 can be performed in parallelized fashion. We use the convention that **foreach**-statements indicate vectorized computations. In addition to that, the recursive calls in lines 9 and 10 are executed in parallel.

Clearly, Algorithm 2 is secure — it does not declassify any values. Also, it does not input any values from a particular party, hence there are no issues in making sure that these values are valid. Algorithm 2 invokes a number of commands of $\mathcal{F}_{\mathsf{ABB}}$ in order to transform a private vector to a different private vector. The adversary's view of Algorithm 2 consists of the sequence of the names of these commands. This sequence can be derived from L, H, and the names of the variables input to Algorithm 2.

Due to the need to preserve the privacy of $[\![v_i]\!]$, Algorithm 2 is quite non-trivial, working in the divide-and-conquer fashion. The main case starts in line 3, and the lines 3–8 are used to rearrange the elements of $v_L, \ldots, v_H$ so, that $v_L, \ldots, v_M$ only contain elements in $\{0, L, \ldots, M\}$, and $v_{M+1}, \ldots, v_H$ only contain elements in $\{0, M+1, \ldots, H\}$. We record ξ and $b_1, \ldots, b_{H-M}$ that are sufficient to undo this rearrangement later. Through recursive calls in lines 9 and 10, we fill in the zeroes among $v'_L, \ldots, v'_H$ with missing numbers. Finally, in lines 11–13 we undo the rearrangement we introduced at the beginning.

Assuming that the complexity of sorting is $O(n \log n)$, the overall complexity of FillBlanks is $O(n \log^2 n)$. We could actually simplify the algorithm somewhat — in line 10, the vector that is the argument to the recursive call is already sorted, hence there is no need to sort it again in line 4. This does not reduce the asymptotic complexity, though, as the FillBlanks-call in line 9 still needs to sort its argument vector. In the full version of this paper [32] we show that for certain implementations of the ABB, this vector (which is just a private rotation away from being sorted) can also be sorted more efficiently, bringing the overall complexity of FillBlanks down to $O(n \log n)$, the same as Algorithm 1.

Finding vector representations of $[\![\sigma]\!]$ and $[\![\tau]\!]$. With the help of Algorithm 2, we are now ready to present the computation of $[\![\sigma]\!]$ and $[\![\tau]\!]$, such that $\phi = \sigma \circ g_{n,m} \circ \tau$. Algorithm 3 depicts this computation. In the description of this algorithm, we will heavily use the notation $[\![v]\!]$ for vectors with private components (but note that the length of the vector is public). Algorithm 3 is secure for the same reasons as Algorithm 2.

The algorithm to convert the vector $[\![v^{(1)}]\!] = ([\![v_1^{(1)}]\!], \ldots, [\![v_m^{(1)}]\!])$ to the private shuffles $[\![\sigma]\!], [\![\tau]\!]$ performs the following steps. First, it counts how many times each value $x \in \{1, \ldots, n\}$ occurs among $v_1, \ldots, v_m$. We first sort the vector $v^{(1)}$, giving the vector $v^{(1')}$. In this vector, the different values x occur in continuous segments. Vector $v^{(2')}$ marks the start of each segment and $v^{(3')}$ additionally records the positions, where different segments start. Sorting according to $v^{(3')}$ (a stable sort according to $v^{(2')}$ would have had the same effect) brings the start positions together and their differences, recorded in $v^{(4'')}$ are the counts of the values x (the lengths of the segments).

Second, the algorithm computes the vector representing σ, to be used as the argument to Vector2Shuffle. As we sort the vectors in non-decreasing order, the counts end up in the last n elements of $v^{(4'')}$. We want to sort them in non-increasing order, hence we collect their negations in the vector $u^{(2)}$. We apply the sorting permutation to the actual values, whose counts were in $u^{(2)}$. We collect the actual values in $u^{(1)}$, but we must be careful, because not all n values are necessary there. Fortunately, in vector $v^{(2'')}$, there is exactly one "1" for each possible value. Thus we obtain zeroes instead of missing values and can use the FillBlanks-algorithm to fill them out.

Algorithm 3. From a vector of private values to an OEP

Data: $m, n \in \mathbb{N}$

Data: $[\![\boldsymbol{v}^{(1)}]\!] = ([\![v_1^{(1)}]\!], \ldots, [\![v_m^{(1)}]\!])$, where $1 \leq v_i^{(1)} \leq n$

Result: $[\![\sigma]\!], [\![\tau]\!]$, such that $(\sigma \circ g_{n,m} \circ \tau)(i) = v_i$ for all $i \in \{1, \ldots, m\}$

1 $[\![\xi_1]\!] \leftarrow \mathsf{sort}([\![\boldsymbol{v}^{(1)}]\!])$

2 $[\![\boldsymbol{v}^{(1')}]\!] \leftarrow \mathsf{apply}([\![\boldsymbol{v}^{(1)}]\!]; [\![\xi_1]\!])$

3 $[\![v_1^{(2')}]\!] \leftarrow 1$

4 **foreach** $i \in \{2, \ldots, m\}$ **do** $[\![v_i^{(2')}]\!] \leftarrow 1 - ([\![v_i^{(1')}]\!] \overset{?}{=} [\![v_{i-1}^{(1')}]\!])$;

5 **foreach** $i \in \{1, \ldots, m\}$ **do** $[\![v_i^{(3')}]\!] \leftarrow i \cdot [\![v_i^{(2')}]\!]$;

6 $[\![\xi_2]\!] \leftarrow \mathsf{sort}([\![\boldsymbol{v}^{(3')}]\!])$

7 $[\![\boldsymbol{v}^{(1'')}]\!] \leftarrow \mathsf{apply}([\![\boldsymbol{v}^{(1')}]\!]; [\![\xi_2]\!])$

8 $[\![\boldsymbol{v}^{(2'')}]\!] \leftarrow \mathsf{apply}([\![\boldsymbol{v}^{(2')}]\!]; [\![\xi_2]\!])$

9 $[\![\boldsymbol{v}^{(3'')}]\!] \leftarrow \mathsf{apply}([\![\boldsymbol{v}^{(3')}]\!]; [\![\xi_2]\!])$

10 **foreach** $i \in \{1, \ldots, m-1\}$ **do** $[\![v_i^{(4'')}]\!] \leftarrow [\![v_i^{(2'')}]\!] ? ([\![v_{i+1}^{(3'')}]\!] - [\![v_i^{(3'')}]\!]) : 0$;

11 $[\![v_m^{(4'')}]\!] \leftarrow m + 1 - [\![v_m^{(3'')}]\!]$

12 **foreach** $i \in \{1, \ldots, n\}$ **do**

13    $\quad [\![u_i^{(1)}]\!] \leftarrow m - n + i > 0 \wedge [\![v_{m-n+i}^{(2'')}]\!] ? [\![v_{m-n+i}^{(1'')}]\!] : 0$

14    $\quad [\![u_i^{(2)}]\!] \leftarrow m - n + i > 0 ? -[\![v_{m-n+i}^{(4'')}]\!] : 0$

15 $[\![\xi_3]\!] \leftarrow \mathsf{sort}([\![\boldsymbol{u}^{(2)}]\!])$

16 $[\![\boldsymbol{u}^{(1')}]\!] \leftarrow \mathsf{apply}([\![\boldsymbol{u}^{(1)}]\!]; [\![\xi_3]\!])$

17 $[\![\sigma]\!] \leftarrow \mathsf{Vector2Shuffle}(\mathsf{FillBlanks}(1, n; [\![\boldsymbol{u}^{(1')}]\!]))$

18 **foreach** $i \in \{1, \ldots, n\}$ **do** $[\![u_i^{(3')}]\!] \leftarrow \ell_{i-1,m} + 1$;

19 $[\![\boldsymbol{u}^{(3)}]\!] \leftarrow \mathsf{apply}([\![\boldsymbol{u}^{(3')}]\!]; \mathsf{invert}([\![\xi_3]\!]))$

20 **foreach** $i \in \{1, \ldots, m\}$ **do**

21    $\quad j_i \leftarrow i - m + n$

22    $\quad [\![v_i^{(5'')}]\!] \leftarrow \begin{cases} 1, & \text{if } i \leq 0 \vee \neg[\![v_i^{(2'')}]\!] \\ [\![u_{j_i}^{(3)}]\!], & \text{if } [\![v_i^{(2'')}]\!] \wedge \neg[\![v_{i-1}^{(2'')}]\!] \\ [\![u_{j_i}^{(3)}]\!] - [\![u_{j_i-1}^{(3)}]\!] + [\![u_{j_i-1}^{(2)}]\!] + 1, & \text{if } [\![v_{i-1}^{(2'')}]\!] \end{cases}$

23 $[\![\boldsymbol{v}^{(5')}]\!] \leftarrow \mathsf{apply}([\![\boldsymbol{v}^{(5'')}]\!]; \mathsf{invert}([\![\xi_2]\!]))$

24 $[\![v_1^{(6')}]\!] \leftarrow [\![v_1^{(5')}]\!]$

25 **for** $i = 2$ **to** m **do** $[\![v_i^{(6')}]\!] \leftarrow [\![v_{i-1}^{(6')}]\!] + [\![v_i^{(5')}]\!]$;

26 $[\![\boldsymbol{v}^{(6)}]\!] \leftarrow \mathsf{apply}([\![\boldsymbol{v}^{(6')}]\!]; \mathsf{invert}([\![\xi_1]\!]))$

27 **foreach** $i \in \{m+1, \ldots, \ell_{n,m}\}$ **do** $[\![v_i^{(6)}]\!] \leftarrow 0$;

28 $[\![\tau]\!] \leftarrow \mathsf{invert}(\mathsf{Vector2Shuffle}(\mathsf{FillBlanks}(1, \ell_{n,m}; [\![\boldsymbol{v}^{(6)}]\!])))$

29 **return** $[\![\sigma]\!], [\![\tau]\!]$

Third, the algorithm computes the vector representing τ^{-1}. This vector must have the values $\ell_{i-1,m}+1, \ell_{i-1,m}+2, \ldots$ in the positions where the original vector $[\![v^{(1)}]\!]$ had the i-th most often occurring values among $\{1, \ldots, n\}$. We intend to compute this vector through prefix summation; this takes place in lines 24–25. While doing this prefix summation, we assume that $v^{(1)}$ is sorted, we undo the sorting afterwards. In lines 18–23 we set up the vector $v^{(5')}$ that serves as the argument to prefix summation. We know that in the middle of continuous segments of $v^{(1')}$, the values in $v^{(5')}$ have to be "1". At the border from i-th most to i'-th most occurring value, however, there should be jumps from the segment $[\ell_{i-1,m}+1, \ldots, \ell_{i,m}]$ to $[\ell_{i'-1,m}+1, \ldots, \ell_{i',m}]$. The length of these jumps depends on i, i', and on the length of the ending segment. These lengths of jumps are computed in line 22 (clearly, the expression there can be converted into a sequence of "? :"-operations). Different cases in this line correspond to the middle of continuous segments, the start of the first segment, and to the starts of following segments, respectively. The vector $u^{(2)}$ contains the *negations* of the lengths of the continuous segments.

The running time of Algorithm 3 is dominated by the call to FillBlanks in line 28. As the size of its argument is $O(m \log m)$, the running time of the algorithm is $O(m \log^3 m)$. For ABB implementations based on additive sharing, it can be reduced to $O(m \log^2 m)$ [32].

Algorithm 3 is used in the protocol set π_{OEP} for converting a private vector to an OEP. The security of this protocol trivially follows from universal composability (π_{OEP} provides the same security guarantees as π_{ABB} with regards to the number of parties the adversary can corrupt, and the kinds of attacks they can perform). Indeed, as declassification is not used in Algorithms 2 and 3 (we assume that Vector2Shuffle is implemented with the help of the sort-command), the entire communication on the interface between the protocol and the adversary consists of the names of the commands $\mathcal{F}_{\mathsf{ABB}}$ is executing. The sequence of these commands depends only on the problem size and can be trivially generated by the simulator.

6 Benchmarks

The asymptotic complexity of our OEP protocol (both communication and computation) is $O(m \log m)$ for an extended permutation $f \in F_{n,m}$ (assuming that m is at least $O(n)$) and for a constant number of parties. The asymptotic complexity of converting a vector of indices to an OEP is $O(m \log^3 m)$.

We have implemented protocols in Fig. 5 on the SHAREMIND secure multiparty computation platform (providing security against passive attacks by one party out of three in total) and tested their performance. In performance testing, we kept in mind the scenario of private function evaluation. For a circuit with I inputs, K binary gates and O outputs, the topology of the circuit is represented by an extended permutation in $F_{I+K,2K+O}$.

Our performance tests are performed on a cluster of three computers with 48 GB of RAM and a 12-core 3 GHz CPU with Hyper Threading running Linux (kernel v.3.2.0-3-amd64), connected by an Ethernet local area network with link speed of 1 Gbps. On this cluster, we have benchmarked the execution time of the OEP application protocol for extended permutations in $F_{200+K,2K+100}$ (for various values of K), simulating the oblivious evaluation of a circuit with 200 inputs and 100 outputs. The permutations were applied to 32-bit values. The running times are presented in Table 1. The running time $t(K)$ (in seconds) is very well approximated by $4.54 \cdot 10^{-7} \cdot K \ln K$. As this has been the first implementation of OEPs (as far as we know), these numbers constitute the baseline for comparing further realizations.

Table 1. Execution times for applying an OEP from $(K + 200)$ inputs to $(2K + 100)$ outputs (times in seconds)

$K/10^6$	0.1	1	5	7	8
Running time	0.5	6	35	49	58

The benchmarking of Algorithm 3 is outside the scope of this paper.

7   Discussion

We have proposed a new, efficient construction for oblivious extended permutations, that is fully integrable with secure multiparty computation protocols for other operations. Practically usable private function evaluation is a possible application of our techniques, if combined with private evaluation of the gates in circuits. Recent advances in private function evaluation may make it a practical tool for certain subtasks in secure multiparty computation, e.g. for handling the branching on private values.

It is reasonable to assume that any application of PFE will still attempt to use as much information that can be publicly deduced about the computed function. Flexibility of PFE techniques is necessary, in order to absorb all available information. The oblivious extended permutations proposed in this paper allow a much greater multitude of potential usage scenarios than [39]. It is possible to evaluate a function without anyone knowing which function is being evaluated. This allows us to obliviously select the representation of a private function and then evaluate it, enabling branching on private values. In this case, we still need to construct private representations of both branches, but this computation can be moved to the offline phase. The actual selection of the privately executed branch can be very efficient [30].

OEPs can be used for purposes other than PFE. Guanciale et al. [20] have implicitly applied them in the minimization of finite automata obtained through the product construction.

References

1. SecureSCM. Technical report D9.1: Secure Computation Models and Frameworks, July 2008. http://www.securescm.org
2. Ben-David, A., Nisan, N., Pinkas, B.: FairplayMP: a system for secure multi-party computation. In: CCS 2008: Proceedings of the 15th ACM Conference on Computer and Communications Security, pp. 257–266. ACM, New York (2008)
3. Bogdanov, D., Kalu, A.: Pushing back the rain–how to create trustworthy services in the cloud. ISACA J. **3**, 49–51 (2013)
4. Bogdanov, D., Kamm, L., Laur, S., Pruulmann-Vengerfeldt, P.: Secure multi-party data analysis: end user validation and practical experiments. Cryptology ePrint Archive, Report 2013/826 (2013). http://eprint.iacr.org/
5. Bogdanov, D., Laur, S., Willemson, J.: Sharemind: a framework for fast privacy-preserving computations. In: Jajodia, S., Lopez, J. (eds.) ESORICS 2008. LNCS, vol. 5283, pp. 192–206. Springer, Heidelberg (2008)
6. Bogdanov, D., Talviste, R., Willemson, J.: Deploying secure multi-party computation for financial data analysis. In: Keromytis, A.D. (ed.) FC 2012. LNCS, vol. 7397, pp. 57–64. Springer, Heidelberg (2012)
7. Bogetoft, P., et al.: Secure multiparty computation goes live. In: Dingledine, R., Golle, P. (eds.) FC 2009. LNCS, vol. 5628, pp. 325–343. Springer, Heidelberg (2009)
8. Burkhart, M., Strasser, M., Many, D., Dimitropoulos, X.: SEPIA: privacy-preserving aggregation of multi-domain network events and statistics. In: USENIX Security Symposium, Washington, DC, USA, pp. 223–239 (2010)
9. Canetti, R.: Universally composable security: a new paradigm for cryptographic protocols. In: FOCS, pp. 136–145. IEEE Computer Society (2001)
10. Damgård, I.B., Fitzi, M., Kiltz, E., Nielsen, J.B., Toft, T.: Unconditionally secure constant-rounds multi-party computation for equality, comparison, bits and exponentiation. In: Halevi, S., Rabin, T. (eds.) TCC 2006. LNCS, vol. 3876, pp. 285–304. Springer, Heidelberg (2006)
11. Damgård, I., Keller, M., Larraia, E., Pastro, V., Scholl, P., Smart, N.P.: Practical covertly secure MPC for dishonest majority – or: breaking the SPDZ limits. In: Crampton, J., Jajodia, S., Mayes, K. (eds.) ESORICS 2013. LNCS, vol. 8134, pp. 1–18. Springer, Heidelberg (2013)
12. Damgård, I., Meldgaard, S., Nielsen, J.B.: Perfectly secure oblivious RAM without random oracles. In: Ishai, Y. (ed.) TCC 2011. LNCS, vol. 6597, pp. 144–163. Springer, Heidelberg (2011)
13. Damgård, I.B., Nielsen, J.B.: Universally composable efficient multiparty computation from threshold homomorphic encryption. In: Boneh, D. (ed.) CRYPTO 2003. LNCS, vol. 2729, pp. 247–264. Springer, Heidelberg (2003)
14. Geisler, M.: Cryptographic protocols: theory and implementation. Ph.D. thesis, Aarhus University, February 2010
15. Gennaro, R., Rabin, M.O., Rabin, T.: Simplified VSS and fast-track multiparty computations with applications to threshold cryptography. In: PODC, pp. 101–111 (1998)
16. Gentry, C.: Fully homomorphic encryption using ideal lattices. In: Mitzenmacher, M. (ed.) STOC, pp. 169–178. ACM (2009)
17. Gentry, C., Goldman, K.A., Halevi, S., Julta, C., Raykova, M., Wichs, D.: Optimizing ORAM and using it efficiently for secure computation. In: De Cristofaro, E., Wright, M. (eds.) PETS 2013. LNCS, vol. 7981, pp. 1–18. Springer, Heidelberg (2013)

18. Goldreich, O., Micali, S., Wigderson, A.: How to play any mental game or a completeness theorem for protocols with honest majority. In: STOC, pp. 218–229. ACM (1987)
19. Goldreich, O., Ostrovsky, R.: Software protection and simulation on oblivious RAMs. J. ACM **43**(3), 431–473 (1996)
20. Guanciale, R., Gurov, D., Laud, P.: Private intersection of regular languages. In: Proceedings of the 12th Annual Conference on Privacy, Security and Trust, pp. 112–120. IEEE (2014)
21. Hamada, K., Ikarashi, D., Chida, K., Takahashi, K.: Oblivious radix sort: an efficient sorting algorithm for practical secure multi-party computation. Cryptology ePrint Archive, Report 2014/121 (2014). http://eprint.iacr.org/
22. Hamada, K., Kikuchi, R., Ikarashi, D., Chida, K., Takahashi, K.: Practically efficient multi-party sorting protocols from comparison sort algorithms. In: Kwon, T., Lee, M.-K., Kwon, D. (eds.) ICISC 2012. LNCS, vol. 7839, pp. 202–216. Springer, Heidelberg (2013)
23. Henecka, W., Kögl, S., Sadeghi, A.R., Schneider, T., Wehrenberg, I.: TASTY: tool for automating secure two-party computations. In: CCS 2010: Proceedings of the 17th ACM Conference on Computer and Communications Security, pp. 451–462. ACM, New York (2010)
24. Huang, Y., Evans, D., Katz, J.: Private set intersection: are garbled circuits better than custom protocols? In: NDSS. The Internet Society (2012)
25. Ikarashi, D., Kikuchi, R., Hamada, K., Chida, K.: Actively private and correct MPC scheme in $t < n/2$ from passively secure schemes with small overhead. Cryptology ePrint Archive, Report 2014/304 (2014). http://eprint.iacr.org/
26. Ishai, Y., Paskin, A.: Evaluating branching programs on encrypted data. In: Vadhan, S.P. (ed.) TCC 2007. LNCS, vol. 4392, pp. 575–594. Springer, Heidelberg (2007)
27. Jónsson, K.V., Kreitz, G., Uddin, M.: Secure multi-party sorting and applications. Cryptology ePrint Archive, Report 2011/122 (2011). http://eprint.iacr.org/
28. Kamm, L., Bogdanov, D., Laur, S., Vilo, J.: A new way to protect privacy in large-scale genome-wide association studies. Bioinformatics **29**(7), 886–893 (2013)
29. Kolesnikov, V., Schneider, T.: A practical universal circuit construction and secure evaluation of private functions. In: Tsudik, G. (ed.) FC 2008. LNCS, vol. 5143, pp. 83–97. Springer, Heidelberg (2008)
30. Laud, P.: A private lookup protocol with low online complexity for secure multiparty computation. In: Shi, E., Yiu, S.M. (eds.) ICICS. LNCS. Springer, Heidelberg (2014, to appear)
31. Laud, P., Pankova, A.: Verifiable computation in multiparty protocols with honest majority. In: Chow, S.S.M., Liu, J.K., Hui, L.C.K., Yiu, S.M. (eds.) ProvSec 2014. LNCS, vol. 8782, pp. 146–161. Springer, Heidelberg (2014)
32. Laud, P., Willemson, J.: Composable oblivious extended permutations. Cryptology ePrint Archive, Report 2014/400 (2014). http://eprint.iacr.org/
33. Laur, S., Talviste, R., Willemson, J.: From oblivious AES to efficient and secure database join in the multiparty setting. In: Jacobson, M., Locasto, M., Mohassel, P., Safavi-Naini, R. (eds.) ACNS 2013. LNCS, vol. 7954, pp. 84–101. Springer, Heidelberg (2013)
34. Laur, S., Willemson, J., Zhang, B.: Round-efficient oblivious database manipulation. In: Lai, X., Zhou, J., Li, H. (eds.) ISC 2011. LNCS, vol. 7001, pp. 262–277. Springer, Heidelberg (2011)

35. Lejeune Dirichlet, J.P.G.: Über die Bestimmung der Mittleren Werthe in der Zahlentheorie. Abhandlungen der Köninglich Preussischen Akademie der Wissenschaften, pp. 69–83 (1849)
36. Lu, S., Ostrovsky, R.: Distributed oblivious RAM for secure two-party computation. In: Sahai, A. (ed.) TCC 2013. LNCS, vol. 7785, pp. 377–396. Springer, Heidelberg (2013)
37. Malka, L., Katz, J.: VMCrypt - modular software architecture for scalable secure computation. Cryptology ePrint Archive, Report 2010/584 (2010). http://eprint.iacr.org/
38. Mohassel, P., Sadeghian, S., Smart, N.P.: Actively secure private function evaluation. Cryptology ePrint Archive, Report 2014/102 (2014). http://eprint.iacr.org/
39. Mohassel, P., Sadeghian, S.: How to hide circuits in MPC an efficient framework for private function evaluation. In: Johansson, T., Nguyen, P.Q. (eds.) EUROCRYPT 2013. LNCS, vol. 7881, pp. 557–574. Springer, Heidelberg (2013)
40. Shamir, A.: How to share a secret. Commun. ACM **22**(11), 612–613 (1979)
41. Stefanov, E., van Dijk, M., Shi, E., Fletcher, C.W., Ren, L., Yu, X., Devadas, S.: Path ORAM: an extremely simple oblivious RAM protocol. In: Sadeghi, A.R., Gligor, V.D., Yung, M. (eds.) ACM Conference on Computer and Communications Security, pp. 299–310. ACM (2013)
42. Waksman, A.: A permutation network. J. ACM **15**(1), 159–163 (1968)
43. Yao, A.C.C.: Protocols for secure computations (extended abstract). In: FOCS, pp. 160–164. IEEE (1982)

Benchmarking Encrypted Data Storage in HBase and Cassandra with YCSB

Tim Waage$^{(\boxtimes)}$ and Lena Wiese

Institute of Computer Science, University of Göttingen,
Goldschmidtstrasse 7, 37077 Göttingen, Germany
{tim.waage,lena.wiese}@uni-goettingen.de

Abstract. Using cloud storage servers to manage large amounts of data has gained increased interest due to their advantages (like availability and scalability). A major disadvantage of cloud storage providers, however, is their lack of security features. In this article we analyze a cloud storage setting where confidentiality of outsourced data is maintained by letting the client encrypt all data records before sending them to the cloud storage. Our main focus is on benchmarking and quantifying the performance loss that such a cloud storage system incurs due to encrypted storage. We present results based on a modification of the Yahoo! Cloud Serving Benchmark using the AES implementation of the Bouncy Castle Java Cryptography Provider for the encryption and decryption steps. The results show that for single read and write operations the performance loss is acceptable (even for stronger encryption with 256 bit keylength) while for range scans the impact can be quite severe.

Keywords: YCSB · Encrypted data storage · Benchmarking · Cassandra · HBase

1 Introduction

Cloud computing has been devised as an alternative to intra-company data processing by outsourcing administration tasks to cloud service providers. Individual users take advantage of external processing resources, too, to store and share data. Cloud service providers might in particular offer storage space which can be booked flexibly on demand. The basic application setting we consider in this paper is using cloud storage servers for larger data records to relieve data owners from the storage burden.

One of the main obstacles of a wider adoption of cloud storage is its lack of security. Usually no functionality is provided to ensure confidentiality of the data stored in the cloud. Confidentiality can be endangered by administrators of the cloud storage provider, by malicious intruders or even by other users of the data store. Our main security target is to ensure confidentiality of the externally stored data record against any illegitimate read accesses. That is, we assume a semihonest behavior of attackers that are curious about the content of the stored

© Springer International Publishing Switzerland 2015
F. Cuppens et al. (Eds.): FPS 2014, LNCS 8930, pp. 311–325, 2015.
DOI: 10.1007/978-3-319-17040-4_20

records. To achieve protection against these attackers, we provide the data owner with a symmetric cryptographic key that is used to encrypt any outgoing data and decryption only takes place at the data owner site. This symmetric key must be secured at the data owner site.

We assume that attackers do not further interfere with the stored data. In particular, the data store should return the correct records to a client request. Malicious attacks like manipulation of the encrypted data is hence in general still possible – but provided that the employed encryption scheme is secure, manipulation will result in arbitrary distortion of data such that they no longer can be decrypted.

In this paper, we focus on benchmarking this form of encrypted data storage with one symmetric encryption key. The performance results will be obtained with the Yahoo! Cloud Serving Benchmark (YCSB; see [1]). Encryption will be executed by the Java Cryptography Provider offered by the Legion of the Bouncy Castle [2]. The benchmarking results presented in this paper are part of a larger environment where index-based keyword search will be supported as follows: Having a short synopsis of a longer data record (a summary, or simply a list of tags or keywords for the content of the document), and the large record itself, we produce a small clear text index (which can easily be stored at the owner's computer); however the actual record will be stored remotely in a data store hosted by some cloud storage provider as shown in Fig. 1.

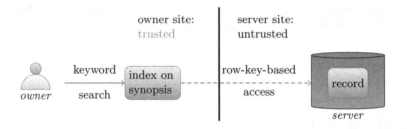

Fig. 1. Data outsourcing with keyword search

In order to comply with the confidentiality requirement, all data leaving the owner site (for being stored at the cloud server) are encrypted. The client is responsible for keeping both the encryption key and the keyword index secret at his own trusted site as shown in Fig. 2. After retrieving data from the cloud server, the client has to decrypt the data before processing them.

In this paper we make the following contributions:

– We compare the performance of two data stores (HBase and Cassandra) in both the encrypted and the non-encrypted case in a single-server environment.
– We present three tests of the data stores using a modification of the Yahoo! Cloud Serving Benchmark (YCSB) to compare the throughput and latency of the system with and without the encryption system.

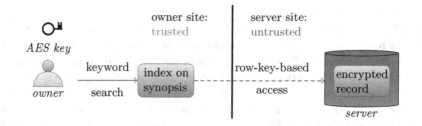

Fig. 2. Data outsourcing with encryption and confidential index

- The tests executed analyze the two systems when (1) increasing the number of parallel worker threads, (2) increasing the target throughput and (3) increasing the total number of operations.

1.1   Organization of the Article

This article is organized as follows: Sect. 2 describes the main features of the tested data stores. Section 3 introduces the Bouncy Castle Java Cryptography Provider as well as the encryption primitives used in our settings. In Sect. 4 the general architecture of the Yahoo! Cloud Serving Benchmark and its different workloads are presented. Our modifications to the original YCSB are described in Sect. 5. Section 6 describes our three test cases and discusses the outcomes. Related work is surveyed in Sect. 7. Section 8 concludes the paper with a summary of our results and briefly discusses options for future work.

2   The Data Stores

The Yahoo! Cloud Serving benchmark can be considered as a test environment for key-value stores because accesses are only done by row key (that is, the key identifying an individual record in the data store). Key-value stores have been conjectured to be good candidates when storing big data. Most of them were created as part of Web 2.0 services. From an abstract point of view, they expose a very simple interface consisting of the three operations: put, get and delete.

Because the retrieval and storage operations of a key-value store are so simple, most key-value stores do not have to bother with transactions, isolation of concurrent accesses or complex combinations (like joins) of values. However, in a multi-master setting, several clients can concurrently write to different servers and in this case the key-value store has to provide a strategy for conflict resolution (for example, using vector clocks).

Where key-value stores excel is their distribution features. Basing on the background of research done for distributed hash tables, data in key-value stores can be flexibly partitioned and automatically replicated among several independent (shared-nothing) servers. Hence, key-value stores are popular when it comes to fast and parallel processing of large amounts of non-interlinked data records.

Typically for the so-called NoSQL data stores most key-value stores also share a lack of certain security features, for example they do not offer user, role or access rights management. It is assumed that a frontend (for example, the cloud storage interface) offers the appropriate authentication and authorization features before letting users access the storage backend. Hence, there is no extra level of protection and a break-in in the frontend will leave the entire data store more vulnerable to attacks than a database product offering more sophisticated user management. A certain level of security could still be achieved by storing the data in an encrypted form, but both systems do not have any native mechanisms for providing encryption. The scope of this article is the examination of the performance impact, if such an additional encryption/decryption step is added.

In our work we focus on Cassandra [3,4] and HBase [5,6], which share a couple of commonalities. Both can be considered as key-value stores as well as column family stores (sometimes also called table stores, extensible record stores or wide column stores). They offer high availability by distributing and replicating data. Both are implemented in the Java programming language. A common feature of these systems is their storage organization in *log-structured merge trees* which implement an *append-only* storage: in-memory tables store the most recent writes to the system; once these tables are flushed to disk, no data in these tables will ever be modified again (they are *immutable*). The only modification that is taking place is merging several flushed tables into larger ones – this process is called *compaction*.

Despite the similarities of Cassandra and HBase there are fundamental differences in their design. Cassandra follows a strictly symmetric peer-to-peer concept using the Gossip protocol for coordination purposes, while HBase relies on a master-slave structure. Thus Cassandra runs in a single Java process per node and can make use of the local file system, while HBase needs the database process per node itself, a properly configured Hadoop Distributed File System (HDFS) and a Zookeeper system in order to manage different HBase processes. That means concerning the CAP Theorem [7,8] Cassandra offers availability and partition-tolerance, while HBase is designed for consistency and availability.

3   Java Cryptography API and the Bouncy Castle Provider

In the Java programming language, the Java Cryptography API (JCA) provides the basic architecture when using cryptographic algorithms; it specifies the interfaces with which cryptographic algorithms can be used in a Java program. The actual implementations are then provided by so-called cryptography providers. The Legion of the Bouncy Castle package for Java implements of most of the interfaces defined in the JCA – in particular, it implements the Java Cryptography Provider class and hence smoothly integrates with the JCA. The Bouncy Castle provider offers several encryption and decryption routines including the Advanced Encryption Standard (AES). AES is a symmetric encryption algorithm. It uses the Rijndael cipher with a block size of 128 bit. Possible key sizes are 128, 192 and 256 bit. As it turned out in various tests that we conducted the Legion of the Bouncy Castle package is the fastest choice of all cryptography providers that offer at least the same flexibility as the standard Java Cryptography Extension (SunJCE). In particular it also provides AES encryption in cipher feedback mode (CFB), which is important for our future work (e.g. when implementing searchable encryption with flexible word lengths [9]).

In our experiments we employ AES in cipher block chaining (CBC) mode using PKCS7 padding – as provided by the Bouncy Castle provider; other modes can be configured on demand. CBC mode produces a chain of ciphertext blocks by interlinking each block with its predecessor in an XOR operation. More precisely, the initial plain text block is XORed with an initialization vector; the output is encrypted with the AES key. Subsequent plain text blocks are XORed with the encrypted text from the previous block; the output is encrypted with the key. Block cipher algorithms require their input to be a multiple of the block size. Since this is not the case for the lengths of keys, field names and values in YCSB's output (see Sect. 5 for details), we use PKCS7 padding [10], which allows any block size from 2 to 255 bytes.

For decryption, the initial cipher text block is decrypted with the key, and the output is XORed with the initialization vector. Subsequent cipher text blocks are first decrypted with the key; the output is then XORed with the cipher text from the previous block to result in a plaintext block.

4   YCSB Benchmark

The Yahoo! Cloud Serving Benchmark (YCSB) is a framework for evaluating the performance of different key-value stores. It comes with the *Core Package*, consisting of six workloads. Each workload is a specific mix of read and write operations, using different data sizes and request/popularity distributions in order to simulate certain scenarios. Besides those provided workloads there are two ways of creating own custom workloads. On the one hand one can modify the existing Core Package by changing the values in the workload's parameter file. On the other hand it is possible to extend the com.yahoo.ycsb. Workload class and write new code for interacting with different databases. In this work we modify the provided parameter files and introduce some new parameters in order to deal with the aspects of encryption. Thus, in contrast to the original work we added parameters for example for turning the encryption on/off and for specifying encryption key lengths.

A workload in YCSB runs in two phases. Phase one is the *loading phase* that fills the database with records. Every record has a name, also referred to as the record's primary key, which is a string like "userxxx", where xxx is a random number. Such a record contains a set of ⟨field name, value⟩ pairs. Thereby field name is a string like "fieldxxx", where xxx again is a random number and value is a random String. For our tests we leave the defaults unchanged, which leads to 100 records, each containing ten ⟨field name, value⟩-pairs, where every value has a length of 100 bytes. While YCSB has been used for a performance evaluation of Cassandra [11], there are no workloads on real-world datasets readily available (in both Cassandra and HBase dialects) that would allow for a direct performance comparison. The second phase is the *transaction phase* in which the workload's specified insert/update/read/scan operations are actually executed.

In this work we use the six workloads of the Core Package, because they already give a good impression of the performance aspects we want to examine. Their characteristics are as follows:

- Workload A is a 50/50 mix of read and write operations.
- Workload B focuses heavily on reading and has only a small amount of writing.
- Workload C even only utilizes read operations.
- Workload D inserts a specified number of records and focuses on reading the most recently added ones preferably.
- Workload E is the only core workload not dealing with individual records, but with short ranges of records.
- Workload F combines read and write operations in the way that records are read, modified and then written back into the database.

Reference [12] gives examples for real world applications.

As it turned out, in the majority of examined cases the results for workloads A, B, C, D and F are always very similar in terms of overall throughput, as well as read and write latency, when the recommended order of workloads is obeyed. Only workload E appears to have different characteristics. Thus for the sake of simplicity and scope of this article, we narrow the analysis of the results down to workload A (as representative of the workloads A, B, C, D and F) for making statements on single read/write operations, as well as workload E for making statements on range queries.

5   Running YCSB on Encrypted Data

The necessary changes to run YCSB on encrypted data are as follows.

We added a new class that encapsulates all methods for encrypting and decrypting byte arrays and Strings. As mentioned earlier that class utilizes the Bouncy Castle Provider. One symmetric AES key is generated that is used throughout each run of the workload for encryption and decryption of all stored and retrieved records. A Cipher object is created (and initialized) that executes the block-wise encryption or decryption using CBC mode and PKCS7-padding by calling `Cipher.getInstance("AES/CBC/PKCS7Padding", "BC");`

For the load phase we proceed as follows. After the generation of random field values, we add an encryption step: each generated record key ("userxxx"), field name ("fieldxxx") and field value gets encrypted and collected in a HashMap. A record then consists of a set of such ⟨encrypted field name, encrypted value⟩ pairs. In the load phase a set of records is finally stored (batch loaded) into the database. In a similar manner, before an individual record is stored in the database (for an insertion of a new value or an update of an existing value during the transaction phase), an encryption step is added. Thus for every point in time the database contains only encrypted data, except for the corresponding timestamps. Since in CBC mode the length of the cipher-text has to be a multiple of the key length, the database gets slightly bigger compared to its size storing the same data unencrypted.

For retrieving records from the database the process is straight forward: the requested record's primary key gets encrypted and is then used in order to find the corresponding ⟨encrypted field name, encrypted value⟩ pairs for decryption.

6   Results

We performed three tests in order to examine the impact of different parameters on the performance of Cassandra and HBase. In every scenario measurements are taken with no encryption, as well as with AES encryption using key lengths of 128, 192 and 256 bits. For every test an analysis of the overall throughput, average read and write latencies is given for workload A (single read/write operations) and workload E (range queries). The latency overhead in the read case consists of the time required to encrypt the record's primary key for lookup purposes, retrieve the ciphertexts of increased length from the database and the additional decryption step of field name and value. The latency overhead in the write case consists of the encryption step as well as the additional time required to store the encrypted data of increased length (compared to non-encrypted data). All tests measure individual read/scan/insert/update calls to the database. We conducted our measurements in a single-server environment, which means the database's different replication strategies can not have any distorting effect. The database server is equipped with an Intel Core i7-4600U CPU (Haswell) @ 2.10 GHz (4 Cores), 8 GB DDR3 RAM and a Samsung PM851 256 GB SSD.

6.1   Test 1: Increasing Number of Parallel Worker Threads

Per default the YCSB client uses a single worker thread for communicating with the database. However it is possible to specify an arbitrary number of threads in order to put more load against the database and to simulate how several clients interact with the database simultaneously. Figures 3 (Cassandra) and 4 (HBase) show the performance impact, if the number of threads is increased to two, four and finally eight threads. However the total number of operations remains fixed at 30000, since all threads share the same operation counter.

As can be seen the number of worker threads has no major impact, neither on the overall throughput, nor on read and write latencies, whether encryption is enabled or not. The results are basically constant. An exception appears to be the read latency for single read/write operations, being slightly lower when performing on two or four threads. The AES encryption key length has no significant impact in all cases.

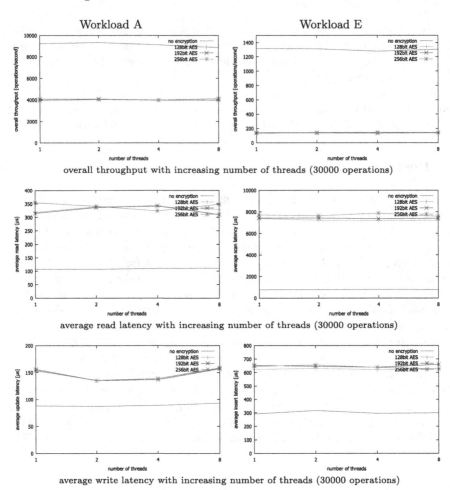

overall throughput with increasing number of threads (30000 operations)

average read latency with increasing number of threads (30000 operations)

average write latency with increasing number of threads (30000 operations)

Fig. 3. Test 1: Cassandra - Increasing the number of parallel worker threads

6.2 Test 2: Increasing the Target Number of Operations per Second

Usually the YCSB client tries to do as many operations as possible, but the number of operations per second can be throttled in order to perform latency tests. If a target parameter is specified the YCSB client executes 1-ms sleep operations to reduce the throughput accurately until the target throughput is reached. Different target throughputs may result in better or worse latency results.

Figures 5 and 6 show that enabling encryption leads much earlier to a point, where the databases are saturated and the overall throughput stops increasing. When performing range queries this point is reached very fast compared to working with single read/write operations. For both, read- and write-latencies, can be stated that increasing the targeted number of operations results in lower latencies up to a certain level, when single read/write operations are performed,

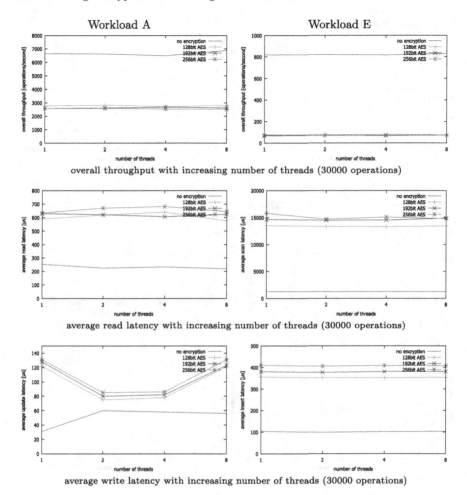

Fig. 4. Test 1: HBase - Increasing the number of parallel worker threads

but no impact can be observed on range queries. Here only HBase shows a sudden increase of write latency, when encryption is enabled and the targeted number of operations exceeds a certain level. As already observed in the first test the length of the AES key does not make any significant difference.

6.3 Test 3: Increasing the Number of Operations

The total number of operations per transaction phase can be increased in order to examine the databases performance when it comes to larger amounts of operations.

The results are presented in Figs. 7 and 8. In both databases increasing the number of operations leads to a higher overall throughput up to a certain level

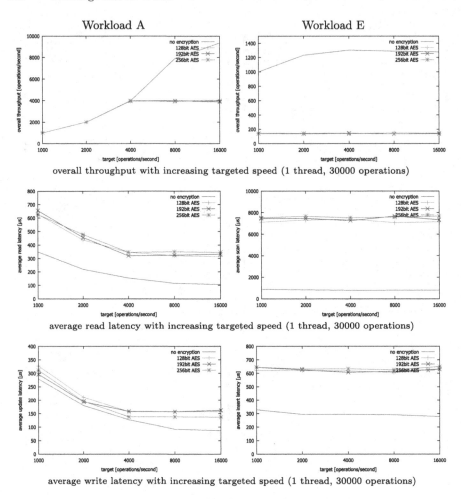

Fig. 5. Test 2: Cassandra - Throttle the target number of operations per second

for unencrypted and encrypted operation, except for range queries, when encryption is enabled. For single read/write operations a higher number of operations results in less read/write latency. This effect is even stronger, when encryption is enabled. The same is true for write latencies, when it comes to range queries, while read latencies remain on a constant level.

6.4   General Observations

It can be stated that turning on encryption reduces the overall throughput down to approximately 40 % on average for single read/write operations and only 10 % when it comes to range scans. The chosen AES key length has almost no impact, the only noticeable difference occurs in read/write latencies in range queries. With encryption enabled, read latencies are 2–3x higher on average for single

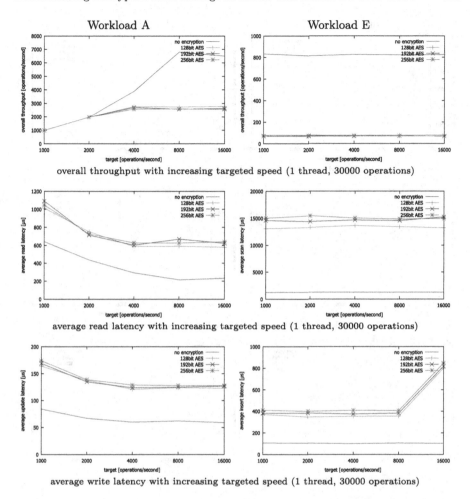

Fig. 6. Test 2: HBase - Throttle the target number of operations per second

read/write operations, even up to 10–12x higher for range queries. However this effect is not so strong for write latencies, which are only 2x higher in every scenario, except for range queries with a higher number of operations, where they can be up to 4x higher. Thus it can be stated that enabling encryption increases latency for read operations more than for write operations.

However the number of parallel worker threads seems to have no consequences for the databases performances. Targeting a higher number of operations per second slightly decreases read/write latencies to a certain point in all cases, except for write latencies in range queries with encryption enabled. Comparing the two databases Cassandra and HBase themselves, it can be stated that Casandra's overall throughput is generally higher in every scenario, in most cases by approximately 50 % on average. As mentioned earlier enabling encryption slows down both databases nearly equally. Concerning read/write latencies,

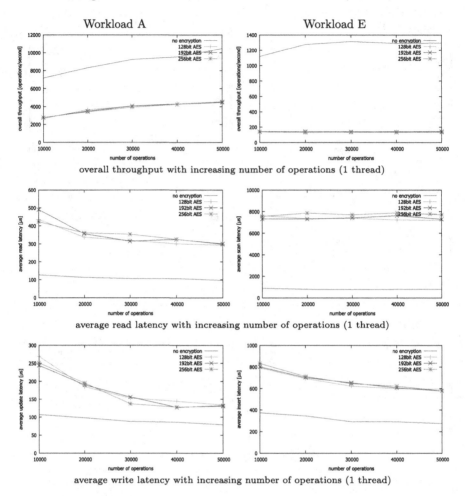

overall throughput with increasing number of operations (1 thread)

average read latency with increasing number of operations (1 thread)

average write latency with increasing number of operations (1 thread)

Fig. 7. Test 3: Cassandra - Increasing the total number of operations

it can be observed that on the one hand Cassandra's latencies are lower for read operations. On the other hand latencies of HBase are lower when it comes to write operations. This is true for every tested scenario.

The effect that latency is reduced (when increasing the target throughput or the operation count) has also been observed in [13]. Their analysis revealed that this effect is owed to increased amount of compactions (see Sect. 2) for smaller operation count.

7   Related Work

The original YCSB description can be found in [1]. There, the different workloads are described in detail. The article presents benchmark results for HBase and

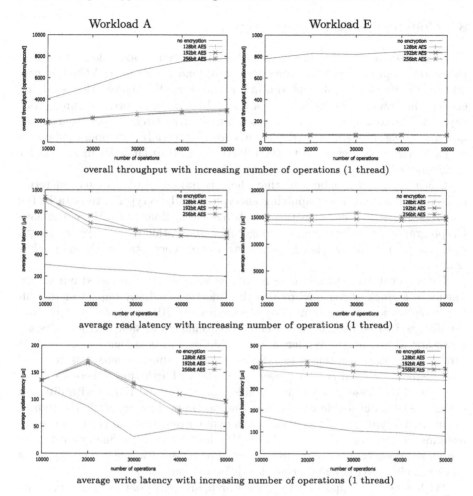

Fig. 8. Test 3: HBase - Increasing the total number of operations

Cassandra (among others) – with the overall result that Cassandra had the best throughput. Elasticity of the systems is tested by adding new servers at runtime.

The so-called YCSB++ benchmark is presented in [13] and used to analyze HBase and Accumulo. The benchmark extends the original YCSB benchmark for example to support real multi-client accesses instead of only providing the option to run multiple worker threads. Its focus lies on measuring consistency; from a security perspective, it analyzes the performance of Accumulos cell-level access control lists for read accesses. No encryption is considered there.

Reference [14] pinpoint vulnerabilities in the Cassandra gossip protocol that may reduce availability by introducing zombie or ghost nodes. Reference [15] analyze other security weaknesses in Cassandra. Hence appropriate security measures should be taken already at the client side in order to not expose sensitive data to the database server that might fall victim to attacks due to weaknesses in the database implementation.

8   Conclusion and Future Work

We examined the performance impact of adding an encryption/decryption step to the two popular key-value stores Cassandra and HBase using YCSB by presenting the impact of different runtime parameters. We showed that enabling encryption slows the entire system down to 10–40% of its original throughput capacity. The consequences for the system's read/write latency reach from almost no impact (e.g. Cassandra's write latency for single read/write operations) to a major increase of latency up to 1000–1500% (e.g. read latencies in general for range queries).

Conclusively, it can be said that there is indeed a price to pay in terms of increased latency when applying encryption and decryption to data in the YCSB workloads. However with our settings (with Bouncy Castle as the Java Cryptography Provider) using a stronger AES encryption with longer key length does not incur more overhead than using weaker encryption with shorter key length.

Future work can extend these results as follows. We conducted our experiments in a single-server environment in order to avoid any impact of the different replication strategies used by Cassandra and HBase. However since both are designed to be used in multi-server environments as well, further tests are necessary. Moreover YCSB offers a lot of additional options that can be used for further analysis. Interesting is a modification of the value field length as well as of the different read/scan/update/insert proportions. Furthermore there are many more cloud database architectures besides Cassandra and HBase with different design decisions available for testing. Another important aspect is the impact of different cryptographic systems, both symmetric (for example Blowfish) or asymmetric (for example RSA). As another field of research, fine-grained cryptographic access control can be implemented by more advanced key management (for example, using key hierarchies for different users [16]).

With regard to support for keyword search, an appropriate indexing program (for example, SOLR or ElasticSearch) shall be employed to obtain the confidential keyword index on the client site. Further benchmarking can then quantify the performance loss for this kind of advanced search-based interaction (than merely row-key-based access).

Acknowledgements. This work was partially funded by the DFG under grant number WI 4086/2-1.

References

1. Cooper, B.F., Silberstein, A., Tam, E., Ramakrishnan, R., Sears, R.: Benchmarking cloud serving systems with YCSB. In: Proceedings of the 1st ACM Symposium on Cloud Computing, pp. 143–154. ACM (2010)
2. The Legion of the Bouncy Castle. http://bouncycastle.org/
3. Lakshman, A., Malik, P.: Cassandra: a decentralized structured storage system. ACM SIGOPS Operating Syst. Rev. **44**(2), 35–40 (2010)

4. The Apache Software Foundation. http://cassandra.apache.org
5. Borthakur, D., Gray, J., Sarma, J.S., Muthukkaruppan, K., Spiegelberg, N., Kuang, H., Ranganathan, K., Molkov, D., Menon, A., Rash, S., et al.: Apache hadoop goes realtime at facebook. In: Proceedings of the 2011 ACM SIGMOD International Conference on Management of Data, pp. 1071–1080. ACM (2011)
6. The Apache Software Foundation. http://hbase.apache.org
7. Brewer, E.A.: Towards robust distributed systems. In: PODC, p. 7 (2000)
8. Brewer, E.: A certain freedom: thoughts on the cap theorem. In: Proceedings of the 29th ACM SIGACT-SIGOPS Symposium on Principles of Distributed Computing, p. 335. ACM (2010)
9. Song, D.X., Wagner, D., Perrig, A.: Practical techniques for searches on encrypted data. In: Proceedings of the 2000 IEEE Symposium on Security and Privacy, S&P 2000, pp. 44–55. IEEE (2000)
10. Kaliski, B.: Rfc 2315: Pkcs# 7: Cryptographic message syntax. Request for Comments (RFC) **2315** (1998)
11. Dede, E., Sendir, B., Kuzlu, P., Hartog, J., Govindaraju, M.: An evaluation of cassandra for hadoop. In: 2013 IEEE Sixth International Conference on Cloud Computing (CLOUD), pp. 494–501. IEEE (2013)
12. Cooper, B.F.: https://github.com/brianfrankcooper/YCSB/wiki/Core-Workloads/
13. Patil, S., Polte, M., Ren, K., Tantisiriroj, W., Xiao, L., López, J., Gibson, G., Fuchs, A., Rinaldi, B.: Ycsb++: benchmarking and performance debugging advanced features in scalable table stores. In: Proceedings of the 2nd ACM Symposium on Cloud Computing, pp. 9:1–9:14. ACM (2011)
14. Aniello, L., Bonomi, S., Breno, M., Baldoni, R.: Assessing data availability of cassandra in the presence of non-accurate membership. In: Proceedings of the 2nd International Workshop on Dependability Issues in Cloud Computing, pp. 2:1–2:6. ACM (2013)
15. Okman, L., Gal-Oz, N., Gonen, Y., Gudes, E., Abramov, J.: Security issues in nosql databases. In: 10th International Conference on Trust, Security and Privacy in Computing and Communications (TrustCom), pp. 541–547. IEEE (2011)
16. Zhu, Y., Ahn, G.J., Hu, H., Ma, D., Wang, S.: Role-based cryptosystem: a new cryptographic RBAC system based on role-key hierarchy. IEEE Trans. Inf. Forensics Secur. **8**(12), 2138–2153 (2013)

Short Papers

Data Confirmation for Botnet Traffic Analysis

Fariba Haddadi[✉] and A. Nur Zincir-Heywood

Faculty of Computer Science, Dalhousie University, Halifax, NS, Canada
{haddadi,zincir}@cs.dal.ca

Abstract. In this paper, we propose a systematic approach to generate botnet traffic. Given the lack of benchmarking botnet traffic data, we anticipate that such an endeavour will be beneficial to the research community. To this end, we employ the proposed approach to generate the communication phase of the Zeus and Citadel botnet traffic as a case study. We evaluate the characteristics of the generated data against the characteristics of a sandbox Zeus botnet, as well as the Zeus and Citadel botnet captures in the wild provided by NETRESEC and Snort. Our analysis confirms that the generated data is comparable to the data captured in the wild.

Keywords: Botnet traffic analysis · Traffic generation and evaluation

1 Introduction

In the world of fast growing Internet having a secure infrastructure is the primary need to protect users' identity and information. Botnets- among various types of malware- are recognized as one of the main threats against cyber security. A botnet is a set of compromised hosts that are under the remote control of a botmaster. To detect botnets, various detection mechanisms have been proposed by researchers where many rely on network traffic behaviour analysis. Some focus on specific types of botnets while others attempt to build general models. However, in all cases, the first challenge, is to obtain realistic data that represents botnets traffic (behaviour). Due to the malicious nature of such data, there are very few publicly available data sets in the field. Therefore, different approaches have been explored by the researchers to obtain the necessary data for their research purposes. These approaches include (but not limited to): (i) Running botnet binaries (that are publicly available or modifying such binaries) in sandbox environments and capturing the traffic [1–4]; (ii) Obtaining captured Honeynet traffic [5,6]; or (iii) Obtaining traffic from a network operator or a security company [7]. The first approach employs publicly available botnet binaries. This implies that any traffic obtained represents the old behaviours because only older versions of such binaries are publicly available. The second approach employs honeynets. Even though this method can catch newer botnet behaviours, it is also challenging to set up honeynets that can simulate real applications in normal behaviour. So there is no guarantee on the quality of the traffic attracted to the honeynet. The third

© Springer International Publishing Switzerland 2015
F. Cuppens et al. (Eds.): FPS 2014, LNCS 8930, pp. 329–336, 2015.
DOI: 10.1007/978-3-319-17040-4_21

approach is the only case where most up to date behaviours can be analyzed by obtaining data from network companies. However, this type of data has privacy issues so such data might not be made public for further benchmarking and evaluation purposes. We anticipate that if a systematic approach can be found, then potentially publicly available benchmarking data sets can be generated without such problems. Thus, in this work, we propose a systematic approach to generate botnet traffic data representing the connection phase of botnet traffic. In this phase, the infected host intends to locate the C&C server and starts a connection with the server. Once we generate such data using the proposed approach, we demonstrate that such an approach could indeed generate realistic behaviours of the botnet traffic. To this end, we evaluated our approach and confirm that the data generated represent similar behaviour to the botnet traffic that is captured in the wild and the botnet traffic that is generated in a sandbox environment based on publicly available bot binaries. To the best of our knowledge, this is the first work with such a goal. To achieve our goal, we follow two steps to evaluate the data after it is generated: (i) Analysis via flow measurements; and (ii) post-classification analysis via decision tree.

2   Related Work

Gu et al. developed BotMiner based on group behaviour analysis to detect botnets [5]. They collected the botnet data sets by employing publicly available botnet binaries as well as using Honeynet data sets. As for the normal traffic, university campus network traces were employed. Wurzinger et al. proposed an approach to detect botnets by correlating the commands and responses in the C&C channels of the monitored network traces [1]. Running a publicly available bot binary in a controlled environment, they collected the data sets used in this work. Kirubavathi et al. designed specifically an HTTP-based botnet detection system using a multilayer Feed-Forward Neural Network [2]. To evaluate the proposed system, botnet binaries were used in the lab. Strayer et al. developed an IRC botnet detection framework that makes use of classification and clustering techniques [3]. Again, they captured their data in the lab by running bot binaries. Francois et al. proposed a NetFlow monitoring framework that leverages a simple host dependency model to track communication patterns and employed linkage analysis and clustering techniques to identify similar botnet behavioral patterns [7]. They obtained traffic traces from an Internet operator company. Zhao et al. investigated a botnet detection approach based on flow intervals [6]. They also employed botnet binaries in the lab and Honeynet project data as for the normal traces, they used Lawrence Berkeley National Laboratory data sets. Haddadi et al. designed a machine learning based detection system [8]. Network traces representing malicious and normal behaviour were generated in the lab based on botnet and legitimate public data.

3   Methodology

A typical advanced botnet has five phases (i.e. lifecycle): (1) the initial infection phase where exploitation techniques are used to find the vulnerabilities and to infect the target host, (2) the secondary infection phase where the botnet shell-code is executed on the victim machine to fetch the image of the bot binary to install, (3) the connection phase where the bot binary establishes the C&C channel, (4) the malicious C&C phase in which the established C&C channel is utilized by the bot master to send the command and (5) the update and maintenance phase where the botmaster updates the bots when required. It is known that to enhance their functionality and to avoid detection systems, botnets tend to use automatic algorithms in different phases of their lifecycle. Fluxing techniques are one of such methods that botnets use to hide the C&C servers using automatic Domain Generation Algorithms (DGAs). Citadel and Zeus are just two of the recent examples of such botnets. A DGA is designed to periodically generate a large list of domain names. The infected computer (bot) may locate the C&C server by querying (sending a DNS query to retrieve the associated IP address) a list of domain names. However, only one of the domain names from the list is valid at a given time. Once a response is received for the query, the bot establishes a connection to the C&C server to receive updates and commands. The list of domain names provided to the bot is large enough so that blacklisting (blocking) at the firewall level is not straight forward. Therefore, the domain fluxing technique is highly utilized in current botnets. Since there are publically available lists of domain names generated by botnet DGAs, we implemented a systematic approach to generate network traffic using these botnet domain names to represent the botnet communication during the connection phase of the botnet lifecycle.

Once the botnet communication traffic is generated, we analyze and evaluate it against three publicly available botnet traffic data that are captured in the wild and one botnet binary based traffic data captured in the sandbox environment. In doing so, our aim is to confirm that our generated traffic is representative of the publicly available ones and the sandbox ones.

We generate the representative botnet traffic flows using the publicly available (from legitimate resources) C&C domain name lists. As for generating the representative legitimate (normal) traffic, we use a legitimate domain name list. This ensures that both the attack and the normal traffic are generated using the publically available domain name lists to enable re-engineering of the approach for benchmarking purposes. For the malicious domain name lists, the two of the most recent botnets, namely Citadel and Zeus are used. The domain name lists for these two botnets are obtained from ZeusTracker and DNS-BH project websites [9,10]. As for the legitimate name list, some of the most frequently requested domain names from Alexa lists (domain names of the high ranked web sites) are used [11]. Both the malicious and legitimate behaviour data use the HTTP protocol as their communication protocol. So, to generate the traffic, we developed a program to establish HTTP connections with the domain names from the aforementioned lists. First, this program sends out DNS queries for the domain names in the lists. If in return it receives a proper DNS response,

Table 1. Data specification

Data set	No. of Packets	No. of Exported Flows
Alexa (NIMS)	21210	7473
Citadel (NIMS)	79516	5772
Citadel (NETRESEC)	15239	226
Zeus-1 (NIMS)	108947	14884
Zeus (NETRESEC)	7453	361
Zeus (Snort)	6995	145
Zeus-2 (NIMS)	32818	874

Table 2. Softflowd feature set

Softflowd Features							
Duration	Src-AS	Dst-AS	In-If	Out-If	Total-Pkt	F-Pkt	B-Pkt
Total-Byte	F-Byte	B-Byte	Flows	ToS	Src-ToS	Dst-ToS	Src-Msk
Dst-Msk	FWD	Src-Vlan	Dst-Vlan	bps	pps	Bpp	

this indicates that the domain name is registered and is associated with a valid IP address. Then, our program attempts to establish an HTTP connection with that IP address. Hereafter, we will refer to our generated data sets using this approach as Zeus-1 (NIMS) and Citadel (NIMS) botnet data sets.

In addition, we employed the few botnet traffic data sets available at NETRESEC [12] and Snort [13] web sites for Zeus and Citadel botnets. Since many works in the literature employed running publicly botnet binaries in the lab (sandbox), we also run a Zeus botnet in a controlled environment and captured the traces [4]. This toolkit is also analyzed and employed in [14]. However, we could not do the same for the Citadel botnet given that there is no publicly available free kit, to the best of our knowledge. Hereafter, this Zeus data is referred to as Zeus-2 (NIMS).

4 Evaluation

As a case study, we focus on generating Zeus and Citadel traffic data using our proposed system. For analyzing the traffic data generated, features are extracted using IP-flow technology. Specifically, we employ Softflowd [15], which is an open source tool based on the NetFlow standard [16]. Table 1 presents the number of captured packets and the corresponding extracted flows for each of the data sets employed in this work. Table 2 presents the features that are utilized in our approach.

4.1 First Step–Analysis via Flow Measurements

As a first step, we anticipate that it will be beneficial to analyze the data sets on some of the most important features (used by other researchers [1,3,4,6]) of a flow. These features are: the flow duration (Duration), the number of bytes per flow (Total-Byte) and the number of packets per flow (Total-Pkt).

Given the wide range of the HTTP usage on the Internet, most recent botnets employ HTTP protocol to hide their malicious activities among the normal web traffic. Citadel and Zeus utilize HTTP protocol to communicate with their bots, too. Thus, to analyze and compare the aforementioned data sets, we filter out the non-HTTP flows. This way all the background information is removed from the data and therefore, the data sets can be compared on their fundamental properties.

The analysis show that the majority of flows durations (96 %, 70 %, 91 % in Zeus (NIMS), Zeus (Snort) and Zeus (NETRESEC), respectively) are less than 50 s long (placed in the first bucket). However, 20 % of Zeus (Snort) and 67 % of Zeus-2 (NIMS) flows last longer than the other two Zeus data sets. Zeus-2 (NIMS), Zeus (Snort) and Zeus (NETRESEC) have more flows with higher number of transmitted packets (30 packets or more) and more bytes, respectively. We predict that these differences are due to the connection time, because we do not keep the connection between our system and botnet C&C servers open long. Basically, we close the connection once this phase of communication is finished.

Moreover, the analysis also shows that the pattern for duration of flows for the Citadel (NIMS) botnet, is different from the pattern of the duration of the flows for Citadel (NETRESEC). On the other hand, there is almost no difference (among the two data sets) between the number of packets and the number of bytes transmitted per flow. Therefore, we can conclude that the Citadel C&C connections in NETRESEC data were kept open without any actual client-server command and response communication. Since keeping a connection open for a long time is one of the signs of malicious activities, botnets tend to close the connection when the necessary information is sent/received and open a new connection for the next round when needed. However, a high number of connections also raises flags for malicious behaviour. Therefore, there is a trade-off between these two parameters when the botnets aim to hide their malicious activity in the normal traffic. Thus, in our approach, we decided to keep the communication duration with the C&C servers as short as possible, because it gives us a good balance for the aforementioned trade-offs. In summary, the analysis of the important features of the flows of the generated traffic and the flows of the traffic captured in the wild seem to be similar except the durations of the flows as explained above. More detailed analysis and the visualizations can be found at [17].

4.2 Second Step–Post-classification Analysis via Decision Tree

To further analyze how similar the generated data (by our proposed approach) is to the data captured in the wild and the data generated in the sandbox, we employed a post-classification analysis using a decision tree. To this end, we trained a C4.5 classifier on the proposed data generation approach and tested the trained model on the botnet data from the NETRESEC and Snort web sites as well as on the sandbox data. Table 3 presents the results of this step.

Table 3. C4.5 decision tree classification results

Training data set	Testing data set	DR	Botnet		Legitimate	
			TPR	FPR	TNR	FNR
Citadel (NIMS)	Citadel (NETRESEC)	100 %	100 %	0 %	0 %	0 %
Zeus-1 (NIMS)	Zeus (Snort)	81 %	81 %	0 %	0 %	19 %
Zeus-1 (NIMS)	Zeus (NETRESEC)	79 %	79 %	0 %	0 %	21 %
Zeus-1 (NIMS)	Zeus-2 (NIMS)	88 %	88 %	0 %	0 %	12 %
Zeus-1 (NIMS)	Zeus-1 (NIMS-unseen)	84 %	84 %	0 %	0 %	16 %

In traffic classification, two metrics are typically used in order to quantify the performance of the classifier: Detection Rate (DR) and False Positive Rate (FPR). In this case, DR reflects the number of botnet flows correctly classified and is calculated using: $DR = TP/(TP+FN)$; whereas FPR reflects the number of legitimate flows incorrectly classified as botnet flows. FPR is calculated using: $FPR = FP/(FP + TN)$. Naturally, a high DR and a low FPR are the most desirable outcomes. On the other hand, False Negative Rate (FNR) indicates that botnet flows are classified as legitimate flows, whereas TNR, True Negative Rate, indicates the correctly classified legitimate flows. As shown in Table 3, the trained model on NIMS Citadel could detect all of the NETRESEC Citadel correctly (100 % TP rate).

In this case, our post-classification analysis show that the main features that the C4.5 classifier employ for the Citadel trained model are: Duration, Total-Pkt, Total-Byte, bps, pps and Bpp (from Table 2). Moreover, in the first step of our analysis, duration feature of a flow presented the most discrepancy between the NIMS botnet data set and the one captured in the wild. However, the classification results indicate that this discrepancy does not seem to have a negative effect on the identification of Citadel botnet behaviour in a given traffic trace. This might be because of the importance of the other features employed. This implies that NIMS Citadel data set is similar to the real-life NETRESEC Citadel data set. Therefore, we can confirm that the proposed approach seems to generate realistic Citadel botnet traffic.

Table 3 also presents the classification results on the Zeus botnet traffic. Again, we trained a C4.5 classifier on Zeus-1 (NIMS) data set, which is generated by the proposed approach. Then, we tested the trained model against the Zeus-2 (NIMS) and Zeus data sets from Snort and NETRESEC. As the results indicate, the DRs of the Zeus-2, Snort and NETRESEC data sets vary between 79 % to 88 %. This is lower than the DR for Citadel, but still a promising performance[1].

To further analyze the generated data by the proposed approach on Zeus botnet, we run another experiment. Since NIMS Zeus generated traffic was bigger than Alexa legitimate data (and therefore had more flows), we only used a

---

[1] Since these test data sets are one class data sets (only malicious), there is no TNR and FPR.

fraction of the Zeus HTTP traffic to build a balanced Zeus-Alexa training data set for the results presented in Table 3. Hence, we had some unseen Zeus flows that were not included in the training process. Thus, we also tested the trained Zeus model on these unseen Zeus flows. As the result shows, we obtained the DR of 84 %, Table 3. The performance is almost the same as the classification result when testing the trained model on other data sets such as NETRESEC and Snort. This seems to indicate the complicated behaviour of Zeus botnet and confirm that the results are not side effects of the generated data being different (or unrealistic), but rather the classifier performs the same on both the generated data and the data captured in the wild for Zeus botnet. This experiment also indicates that Zeus botnet behaviour is more complicated than Citadel botnet behaviour. Moreover, it seems to hide in the legitimate HTTP behaviour better than Citadel could.

In short, our 2-step analysis indicates that the traffic generated using our proposed approach is valid and comparable to the botnet traffic captured in real life (Snort and NETRESEC data) as well as the traffic captured in a sandbox environment (Zeus-2 NIMS). In other words, traffic generated based on the proposed approach can be employed in botnet behaviour analysis for representing real data. We provide our NIMS data sets for further benchmarking purposes at the following URL:

https://web.cs.dal.ca/~haddadi/data-analysis.htm

5   Conclusion

Due to the high reported botnet infection rate and its wide range of illegal activities, botnets are one of the main threats against the cyber security. One problem of this field is the availability of public data sets for meaningful benchmarks and comparisons among the botnet identification systems. In this work, we propose a systematic approach to generate botnet traffic and analyze its properties against that of available botnet traffic captures in the field. To this end, we explore a 2-step analysis. In the first step, we analyzed the data sets using the main features of the botnet traffic reported in the literature [1,3,6]. The results of this step show that the data generated by the proposed approach and the data captured in the wild by NETRESEC and Snort, are not very different in terms of their main measured features. However, the sandbox traffic data has noticeable differences (compared to the data captured in the wild) in terms of most of the measured features. In the second step, we perform a post-classification analysis on the data sets using the C4.5 classifier. In this step, we train the classifier with the data generated by the proposed approach, and test the trained model on the NETRESEC, Snort and the sandbox data sets. The results indicate that the trained model could classify the unseen data captured in the wild and the sandbox data with a high DR and a low FPR. This suggests that the botnet data generated by the proposed approach confirms to the botnet data captured in the wild or in the sandbox. We anticipate that this can further enable benchmarking and evaluation efforts in this research area. Future work will explore employing the proposed traffic generation approach for other botnets.

Acknowledgments. This research is supported by the Natural Science and Engineering Research Council of Canada (NSERC) grant, and is conducted as part of the Dalhousie NIMS Lab at https://projects.cs.dal.ca/projectx/.

References

1. Wurzinger, P., Bilge, L., Holz, T., Goebel, J., Kruegel, C., Kirda, E.: Automatically generating models for botnet detection. In: Backes, M., Ning, P. (eds.) ESORICS 2009. LNCS, vol. 5789, pp. 232–249. Springer, Heidelberg (2009)
2. Kirubavathi Venkatesh, G., Anitha Nadarajan, R.: HTTP botnet detection using adaptive learning rate multilayer feed-forward neural network. In: Askoxylakis, I., Pöhls, H.C., Posegga, J. (eds.) WISTP 2012. LNCS, vol. 7322, pp. 38–48. Springer, Heidelberg (2012)
3. Strayer, W.T., Lapsely, D., Walsh, R., Livadas, C.: Botnet detection based on network behavior. Adv. Inf. Secur. **36**, 1–24 (2008)
4. Haddadi, F., Runkel, D., Zincir-Heywood, A.N., Heywood, M.I.: On botnet behaviour analysis using GP and C4.5. In: GECCO Comp, pp. 1253–1260 (2014)
5. Gu, G., Perdisci, R., Zhang, J., Lee, W.: BotMiner: clustering analysis of network traffic for protocol- and structure- independent botnet detection. In: 17th USNIX Security Symposium, pp. 139–154 (2008)
6. Zhao, D., Traore, I., Ghorbani, A., Sayed, B., Saad, S., Lu, W.: Peer to peer botnet detection based on flow intervals. In: Gritzalis, D., Furnell, S., Theoharidou, M. (eds.) Information Security and Privacy Research. IFIP Advances in Information and Communication Technology, vol. 376, pp. 87–102. Springer, Heidelberg (2012)
7. François, J., Wang, S., State, R., Engel, T.: BotTrack: tracking botnets using netflow and pagerank. In: Domingo-Pascual, J., Manzoni, P., Palazzo, S., Pont, A., Scoglio, C. (eds.) NETWORKING 2011, Part I. LNCS, vol. 6640, pp. 1–14. Springer, Heidelberg (2011)
8. Haddadi, F., Morgan, J., Filho, E.G., Zincir-Heywood, A.N.: Botnet behaviour analysis using IP flows with HTTP filters using classifiers. In: Seventh International Workshop on Bio and Intelligent Computing, pp. 7–12 (2014)
9. Zeus Tracker. https://zeustracker.abuse.ch/
10. DNS-BH- Malware Domain Blocklist. http://www.malwaredomains.com/
11. Alexa. http://www.alexa.com/topsites
12. Publicly available PCAP files. http://www.netresec.com/?page=PcapFiles
13. Zeus Trojan Analysis. https://labs.snort.org/papers/zeus.html
14. Binsalleeh, H., Ormerod, T., Boukhtouta, A., Sinha, P., Youssef, A., Debbabi, M., Wang, L.: On the analysis of the zeus botnet crimeware toolkit. In: Eighth Annual International Conference on Privacy, Security and Trust, pp. 31–38 (2010)
15. Softflowd project. http://www.mindrot.org/projects/softflowd/
16. Cisco IOS NetFlow. http://www.cisco.com/en/US/products/ps6601/products_ios_protocol_group_home.html
17. Haddadi, F., Zincir-Heywood, A.N.: Data confirmation for botnet traffic analysis. Technical report (2014). https://www.cs.dal.ca/research/techreports/cs-2014-01

Detection of Illegal Control Flow in Android System: Protecting Private Data Used by Smartphone Apps

Mariem Graa[1,2]([⊠]), Nora Cuppens-Boulahia[1], Frédéric Cuppens[1], and Ana Cavalli[2]

[1] Telecom-Bretagne, 2 Rue de la Chataigneraie, 35576 Cesson Sévigné, France
{mariem.benabdallah,nora.cuppens,frederic.cuppens}@telecom-bretagne.eu
[2] Telecom-SudParis, 9 Rue Charles Fourier, 91000 Evry, France
{mariem.graa,ana.cavalli}@it-sudparis.eu

Abstract. Today, security is a requirement for smartphone operating systems that are used to store and handle sensitive information. However, smartphone users usually download third-party applications that can leak personal data without user authorization. For this reason, the dynamic taint analysis mechanism is used to control the manipulation of private data by third-party apps [9]. But this technique does not detect control flows. In particular, untrusted applications can circumvent Android system and get privacy sensitive information through control flows. In this paper, we propose a hybrid approach that combines static and dynamic analysis to propagate taint along control dependencies in Android system. To evaluate the effectiveness of our approach, we analyse 27 free Android applications. We found that 14 of these applications use control flows to transfer sensitive data. We successfully detect that 8 of them leaked private information. Our approach creates 19 % performance overhead that is due to the propagation of taint in the control flow. By using our approach, it becomes possible to detect leakage of personal data through control flows.

Keywords: Android system · Smartphones · Dynamic analysis · Static analysis · Control dependencies · Leakage of sensitive information

1 Introduction

Smartphone operating systems use has been increasing at an accelerated rate in recent years. Android surpassed 80 % market share in the third quarter of 2013 [17] and it is the most targeted OS by the cyber criminals with more than 98 % of malware applications [9]. This is due to the prevalence of third party app stores (48 billion apps have been installed from the Google Play store in May 2013 [19]). These applications are used to capture, store, manipulate, and access to data of a sensitive nature in mobile phone. An attacker can launch control flow attacks to compromise confidentiality of the Android system and can leak private information without user authorization. In the study presented

© Springer International Publishing Switzerland 2015
F. Cuppens et al. (Eds.): FPS 2014, LNCS 8930, pp. 337–346, 2015.
DOI: 10.1007/978-3-319-17040-4_22

```
1.boolean b = false;
2.boolean c = false;
3.if (!a)
4. c = true;
5.if (!c)
6. b = true;
```

Fig. 1. Implicit flow example.

in the Black Hat conference, Daswani [21] analyzed the live behavior of 10,000 Android applications and showed that more than 800 of them were found to be leaking personal data to an unauthorized server. Therefore, there is a need to provide adequate security mechanisms to control the manipulation of private data by third-party apps. Many mechanisms are used to protect sensitive data in the Android system, such as the dynamic taint analysis that is implemented in TaintDroid [9].

The principle of dynamic taint analysis is to "taint" some of the data in a system and then propagate the taint to data for tracking the information flow in the program. Two types of flows are defined: explicit flows such as $x = y$, where we observe an explicit transfer of a value from x to y, and implicit flows (control flows) shown in Fig. 1 were there is no direct transfer of value from a to b, but when the code is executed, b would obtain the value of a. The dynamic taint analysis mechanism does not detect control flows which can cause an under tainting problem *i.e.* that some values should be marked as tainted, but are not. The under tainting problem can cause a failure to detect a leak of sensitive information. Thus, malicious applications can bypass the Android system and get privacy sensitive information through control flows. In a previous work [12], we have proposed an approach that combines static and dynamic taint analysis to propagate taint along control dependencies and to track implicit flows in the Google Android operating system. Our approach enhances the TaintDroid approach by tracking control flows in the Android system to solve the under-tainting problem. In this paper, we present implementation details and experimental results of the proposed approach. We show effectiveness of our approach to propagate taint in the conditional structures of real Android applications and to detect leakage of sensitive information. This paper is organized as follows: Sect. 2 presents a motivating example. We discuss related work about static and dynamic taint analysis and we analyze existing solutions to solve the under tainting problem in Sect. 3. Section 4 describes the proposed approach and the corresponding implementation details. We analyse a number of Android applications to test the effectiveness of our approach and we study our approach taint tracking overhead in Sect. 5. Finally, Sect. 6 concludes with an outline of future work.

2   Motivating Example

An attacker can exploit an indirect control dependencies to leak private data. Let us consider the control dependence attack shown in Fig. 2. The variable

```
String X = contact_name;
String Y="";
char[] TabAsc;
 int k=0;
TabAsc = new char [96];

while (codeAsc < 0x80) {

   for (column = 0; column < 16; column++) {
       TabAsc[k] = codeAsc;
       codeAsc++;
       k++;
   }
   row++;
}

for (int i = 0;i< X.length(); i++)
{
    char x=X.charAt(i);

    for (int j=1;j<TabAsc.length;j++)
    {
        if (x==TabAsc[j])
           Y=Y+TabAsc[j];
    }

}

NetworkTransfer(Y);
```

Fig. 2. Control dependence attack

X contains the private data that is the user contact. The attacker tries to get the user contact name by comparing it with symboles of Ascii table in the second loop. He stored the character of private data founded in Y. At the end of the loop, the variable Y contains the correct value of the user contact and it is not tainted because taint is not propagated in the control flow statement. The attacker exploits untainted variable that should be tainted (under tainting problem) to leak private data. Thus, Y is leaked through the network without being detected. Therefore, an attacker can leak a sensitive information by exploiting control flows.

3   Related Work

Many security mechanisms are used to protect sensitive data in smartphones. TaintDroid [9], an extension of the Android mobile-phone used to control in realtime the manipulation of users personal data by third-party applications. It implements a dynamic taint tracking and analysis system to track the information flow and to detect when sensitive data leaves the system. AppFence [15] extends Taintdroid to implement enforcement policies. One limit of Taint-Droid and AppFence approaches is that they cannot propagate taint in control dependencies. The methods proposed in [5,8,11] statically analyze third party application code for detecting data leaks. But, these static analyses approaches cannot capture all runtime configuration. Some approaches combine static and dynamic analysis to solve the under-tainting problem. BitBlaze [20] presents a novel fusion of static and dynamic taint analysis techniques to track all information flow. DTA++ [16] uses Bitblaze and enhances the dynamic taint analysis to limit the under-tainting problem. However DTA++ is evaluated only on benign applications. Trishul [18] correctly identifies control flow to detect a leak of sensitive information. Furthermore, these approaches are not implemented in smartphones application. Fenton [10] defined a Data Mark Machine, an abstract model, to handle control flows. This model does not take into account the implicit flow when the branch is not executed. Denning [7] enhances the run time mechanism used by Fenton with a compile time mechanism to solve the under-tainting problem. Denning inserts updating instructions whether the branch is taken or not. We draw our inspiration from the Denning approach, but we define formally a set of taint propagation rules to solve the under-tainting problem. In [12], we propose a hybrid approach that tracks control flows in smartphones. We define a set of formal propagation rules to solve the under-tainting problem. We prove the correctness and completeness of these rules and we propose a correct and complete algorithm to solve the under tainting problem [13]. In [14], we show that our approach can resist to code obfuscation attacks based on control dependencies in the Android system using the taint propagation rules. But, we do not evaluate the overhead and effectiveness of our approach and do not test a real Android applications. We provide test exprimental results and we evaluate the overhead and the false positives of our approach. We show that it successfully detects sensitive information leakage by untrusted Android applications.

4   Approach Overview and Implementation

Our objective is to detect private information leakage by untrusted smartphone applications exploiting implicit flows. We control the manipulation of private data by third party application in realtime.

Our approach consists of two main components: the *StaticAnalysis* component and the *DynamicAnalysis* component (see Fig. 3). We implement our proposed approach in the TaintDroid operating system. We add a *StaticAnalysis* component in the Dalvik virtual machine verifier that statically analyzes instructions of third party application Dex code at load time. Also, we modify the Dalvik virtual machine interpreter to integrate the *DynamicAnalysis* component.

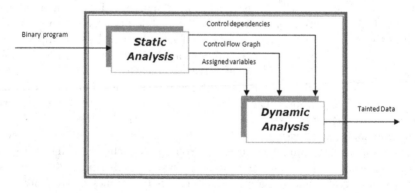

Fig. 3. Our Approach Architecture

We implement the two additional rules using native methods that define the taint propagation.

4.1   Static Analysis Component

In this component, we check the instructions of methods to create the control flow graph (CFG). A CFG is composed of basic blocks and edges. The basic blocks represent nodes of the graph. The directed edges represent jumps in the control flow. For each control instruction, we insert a *BasicBlock* at the end of the basic blocks list. Then, we specify the target of basic blocks. We perform the post dominator analysis (A node v is post-dominated by a node w in the control flow graph G if every path from v to *Exit*, not including v, contains w) on the control flow graph to determine the flow of the condition dependencies from different blocks. After this, we allocate a *BitmapBits* for tracking condition dependency. We store the control flow graph using the DOT language of graphviz tool [4] in the data directory of the smartphone.

4.2   Dynamic Analysis Component

The dynamic analysis is performed at run time by instrumenting the Dalvik virtual machine interpreter. We assign a *context_taint* to each basic block. The *context_taint* includes the taint of the condition on which the block depends. We compare arguments in the condition using the following instruction: *res_cmp= ((s4) GET_REGISTER(vsrc1) _cmp (s4) GET_REGISTER(vsrc2))*. Based on the comparison result, we verify wether the branch is taken or not. We Combine the taints of different variables of the condition as follows: *SET_REGISTER_ TAINT(vdst,(GET_REGISTER_TAINT(vsrc1)|GET_REGISTER_TAINT (vsrc2)))* to obtain the *Context_Taint*. If *res_cmp* is not null then the branch is not taken. Thus, we adjust the ordinal counter to point to the first instruction of the branch by using the function *ADJUST_PC(2)*. Otherwise, it is the second branch (else) which is not taken then we adjust the ordinal counter to point to the first instruction in this branch by using the function *ADJUST_PC(br)* where *br* represents the branch pointer. We instrument different instructions in the interpreter to handle conditional statements. For each instruction, we taint the variable to which we associate a value (destination register). In the case of *for* and *while* loops, we process by the same way but we test whether the condition is still true or not in each iteration. We make a special treatment for *Switch* instructions. We deal with all case statements and all instructions which are defined inside *Switch* instructions. Note that, we only taint variables and do not modify their values. Once we handle all not taken branches, we restore the ordinal counter to treat the taken branches and we assign taints to modified variables in this branch. We make a special exception handling to avoid leaking information. If the type of exception that occurred is listed in a catch block, the exception is passed to the catch block. So, an edge is added in the CFG from the throw statement to the catch block to indicate that the throw statement will transfer control to the appropriate catch block. If an exception occurs, the

current context taint and the exception's taint are stored. The variables assigned
in any of the catch blocks will be tainted depending on the exception's taint.

5   Evaluation

In this section, we analyse a number of Android applications to test the effectiveness of our approach. Then, we study our taint tracking approach overhead
using standard benchmarks. We evaluate the false positives that could occur
using our approach. We use a Nexus One mobile device running Android OS
version 2.3 enhanced to track implicit flows.

5.1   Effectiveness

To evaluate the effectiveness of our approach, we analyse 27 free Android applications downloaded from the Android Market [1] that manipulated private data.
As shown in Table 1, five applications require permissions for contacts and five
applications require permissions for camera at install time.

Most of these applications access to locations and phones identity. Also, our
analysis showed that these permissions are acquired by the implicit or explicit
consent of the user. For example, in the weather application, when the user
selects the option "use my location", she gives permission to the application to
use and to send this information to the weather server. We found that 14 of these
25 analyzed Android applications (marked with * in the Table 1) leak private
information:

- The IMEI numbers that identify a specific cell phone on a network is one of
  the information that is transmitted by 11 applications. Nine of them do not
  present an End User License Agreement (EULA).
- Two applications transmitted the device's phone number, the IMSI and the
  ICC-ID number to their server.

Table 1. Third party applications grouped by the requested permissions (L: location,
Ca: camera, Co: contacts, P: phone state)

Third party applications	Permissions			
	L	Ca	Co	P
The Weather Channel*; Cestos; Solitaire; Babble; Manga Browser (5)	x			
Bump; Traffic Jam; Find It*; Hearts; Blackjack; Alchemy; Horoscope*; Bubble Burst Free; Wisdom Quotes Lite*; Paper Toss*; Classic Simon Free; Astrid* (12)	x			x
Layar*; Knocking*; Coupons*; Trapster*; ProBasketBall (5)	x	x		x
Wertago*; Dastelefonbuch*; RingTones*; Yellow Pages*; Contact Analyser (5)	x		x	x

Table 2. Third party applications used control flows

Category	Application name	Leaked data
Contact and Phone Identity	Wertago	x
	Dastelefonbuch	x
	Yellow Pages	x
Camera	Knocking	x
	ProBasketBall	
Location and Phone Identity	The Weather Channel	x
	Cestos	
	Classic Simon Free	
	Bubble Burst Free	
	Bump	
	Traffic Jam	
	Horoscope	x
	Paper Toss	x
	Find It	x

- The location information is leaked by 15 third-party applications to advertisement servers. These applications do not require implicit or explicit user consent. Just two applications require an EULA.

We use dex2jar tool [2] to translate dex files of different applications to jar files. Then, we use jd-gui [3] to obtain the source code that will be analysed. As shown in Table 2, we found that 14 of tested Android applications listed by types of accessed sensitive data use control flows to transfer private information. Eight of them leaked private data. Sensitive data is used in the *if*, *for* and *while* control flow instructions. We verify that variables to which a value is assigned in these instructions and that depend on a condition containing private data are not tainted using TaintDroid. Our approach has succesfully propagated taint in these control instructions and detected leakage of tainted sensitive data that is reported in the alert messages.

5.2 Performance

In this part of the paper, we study our taint tracking approach overhead. The static analysis is performed at load and verification time. At load time, our approach adds 33 % overhead with respect to the unmodified system. At verification and optimization time, our approach adds 27 % overhead with respect to the unmodified system. This time increase is due to the verification of method instructions and the construction of the control flow graphs in the static analysis phase. We install the CaffeineMark application [6] in our Nexus One mobile device to determine the java microbenchmark. Note that the CaffeineMark scores roughly correlate with the number of Java instructions executed per second and

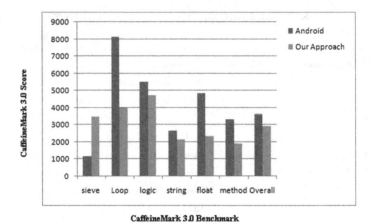

Fig. 4. Microbenchmark of java overhead

do not depend significantly on the amount of memory in the system or on the speed of a computers disk drives or internet connection [6].

Figure 4 presents the execution time results of a Java microbenchmark. We propagate taint in the conditional branches especially in the loop branches and we add instructions in the processor to solve the under tainting problem. Then, the loop benchmark in our approach presents the greatest overhead. We taint results of arithmetic operations in explicit and control flows. Thus, the arithmetic operations present the greatest overhead. The string benchmark difference between unmodified Android system and our approach is due to the additional memory required in the string objects taint propagation. We observe that the unmodified Android system had an overall score of 3625 Java instructions executed per second. Whereas, our approach had an overall score of 2937 Java instructions executed per second. Therefore, our approach has a 19 % overhead with respect to the unmodified system.

5.3   False Positives

Our analysis and tests indicated that almost of 50 % of studied Android applications use control flows and leak sensitive data. Our approach generates 25 % of false positives. We detect an IMSI leakage vulnerability when it is really used as a configuration parameter in the phone. Also, we detect that the IMEI is transmitted outside of smartphone but it is the hash of the leaked IMEI. Thus, we can not treat these applications as privacy violations.

6   Conclusion

In order to detect the leakage of sensitive information by third-party apps exploiting control flows in smartphones, we have proposed a hybrid approach that propagates taint along control dependencies to solve under-tainting problem. We have analysed 27 free Android applications to evaluate the effectiveness of our approach. We found that 14 applications use control flows to transfer sensitive data and 8 leak private information. We showed that our approach generates significant false positives that can be reduced by considering expert rules (ad hoc rules). Also, we can use an access control approach to authorize or not the transmission of the data outside the system. Our approach incurs 19 % performance overhead that is due to the propagation of taint in the control flow. To improve performance of our system, we suggest implementing the taint propagation mechanism in Just In Time Compiler (JIT) that provides better performance than the interpreter such as a minimal additional memory usage. By implementing our approach in Android systems, we successfully protect sensitive information and detect most types of software exploits caused by control flows.

References

1. Android. http://www.android.com/
2. dex2jar. http://code.google.com/p/dex2jar/
3. Java decompiler. http://jd.benow.ca/
4. AT&T Research: Graphviz. http://www.graphviz.org/
5. Chin, E., Felt, A.P., Greenwood, K., Wagner, D.: Analyzing inter-application communication in android. In: Proceedings of the 9th International Conference on Mobile Systems, Applications, and Services. pp. 239–252. ACM (2011)
6. P.S. Corporation: Caffeinemark 3.0. http://www.benchmarkhq.ru/cm30/
7. Denning, D.: Secure information flow in computer systems. Ph.D. thesis, Purdue University (1975)
8. Egele, M., Kruegel, C., Kirda, E., Vigna, G.: PiOS: detecting privacy leaks in iOS applications. In: Proceedings of the Network and Distributed System Security Symposium (2011)
9. Enck, W., Gilbert, P., Chun, B., Cox, L., Jung, J., McDaniel, P., Sheth, A.: Taintdroid: an information-flow tracking system for realtime privacy monitoring on smartphones. In: Proceedings of the 9th USENIX Conference on Operating Systems Design and Implementation. pp. 1–6. USENIX Association (2010)
10. Fenton, J.: Memoryless subsystem. Comput. J. $17(2)$, 143–147 (1974)
11. Fuchs, A.P., Chaudhuri, A., Foster, J.S.: Scandroid: automated security certification of android applications. Manuscript, University of Maryland (2009). http://www.cs.umd.edu/~avik/projects/scandroidascaa
12. Graa, M., Cuppens-Boulahia, N., Cuppens, F., Cavalli, A.: Detecting control flow in smarphones: combining static and dynamic analyses. In: Xiang, Y., Lopez, J., Jay Kuo, C.-C., Zhou, W. (eds.) CSS 2012. LNCS, vol. 7672, pp. 33–47. Springer, Heidelberg (2012)
13. Graa, M., Cuppens-Boulahia, N., Cuppens, F., Cavalli, A.: Formal characterization of illegal control flow in android system. In: 9th International Conference on Signal Image Technology & Internet Systems (2013)
14. Graa, M., Cuppens-Boulahia, N., Cuppens, F., Cavalli, A.: Protection against Code obfuscation attacks based on control dependencies in android systems. In: 8th International Workshop on Trustworthy Computing (2014)

15. Hornyack, P., Han, S., Jung, J., Schechter, S., Wetherall, D.: These aren't the droids you're looking for: retrofitting android to protect data from imperious applications. In: Proceedings of the 18th ACM Conference on Computer and Communications Security, pp. 639–652. ACM (2011)
16. Kang, M., McCamant, S., Poosankam, P., Song, D.: Dta++: dynamic taint analysis with targeted control-flow propagation. In: Proceedings of the 18th Annual Network and Distributed System Security Symposium, San Diego, CA (2011)
17. Rob van der Meulen, J.R.: Gartner says smartphone sales accounted for 55 percent of overall mobile phone sales in third quarter of 2013 (2013). http://www.gartner.com/newsroom/id/2623415
18. Nair, S., Simpson, P., Crispo, B., Tanenbaum, A.: A virtual machine based information flow control system for policy enforcement. Electron. Notes Theoret. Comput. Sci. **197**(1), 3–16 (2008)
19. News, B.: Bbc google activations and downloads update, May 2013. http://www.bbc.com/news/technology-22542725
20. Song, D., Brumley, D., Yin, H., Caballero, J., Jager, I., Kang, M., Liang, Z., Newsome, J., Poosankam, P., Saxena, P.: Bitblaze: A new approach to computer security via binary analysis. In: Information Systems Security, pp. 1–25 (2008)
21. Wilson, T.: Many android apps leaking private information, July 2011. http://www.informationweek.com/security/mobile/many-android-apps-leaking-private-inform/231002162

A Responsive Defense Mechanism Against DDoS Attacks

Negar Mosharraf[1,2]([✉]), Anura P. Jayasumana[1,2],
and Indrakshi Ray[2]([✉])

[1] Department of Electrical and Computer Engineering,
Colorado State University, Fort Collins, CO 80523, USA
negar@engr.colostate.edu,
anura.jayasumana@colostate.edu
[2] Department of Computer Science, Colorado State University,
Fort Collins, CO 80523, USA
iray@cs.colostate.edu

Abstract. Distributed Denials of Service (DDoS) attacks are among the most serious threats on the Internet. With large-scale DDoS attacks, it is necessary to stop malicious traffic closer to the attack sources with minimal disruption of legitimate traffic. A responsive defense mechanism that filters potential attack traffic and prevents it from reaching the victim network is developed. First we investigate the features of network traffic that can be used for discriminating attacks from normal traffic, and then use the identified features to develop an accurate and robust signature-based filtering model that forms the basis of a responsive defense mechanism. A Bloom filter based mechanism is proposed to efficiently implement and disseminate the signature-based model; it helps reduce the communication overhead and the computation and storage requirements at the upstream routers that check for malicious traffic. The approach is verified and evaluated using the DARPA dataset. Experimental results show the effectiveness of the proposed scheme in blocking attack traffic and allowing most of the legitimate traffic at upstream routers.

1 Introduction

Distributed Denial-of-Service (DoS) attacks on Internet based systems and infrastructure have become quite common. Multiple machines, which typically are compromised themselves, flood the victim at fast rates. Detecting these machines and isolating the attacks in a timely manner is non-trivial. From the incidents of DDoS attacks against commercial websites like Yahoo, E-bay and E*Trade, it is evident that all the computer systems connected to the Internet are vulnerable to DDoS attacks [11]. A coordinated DDoS attack within a single day on Yahoo, eBay, Amazon.com, E*trade, ZDnet, buy. com, the FBI and several other websites resulted in millions of dollars in damages and inconveniences [14]. Recent examples include a record 400 Gbit/s DDoS attack against CloudFlare, a rate about 100 Gbit/s more than the largest previously seen DDoS attack [15]. The trends indicate Terabps DDoS attacks in the near future. The impact of DDoS attacks that prevent legitimate users from using the network may vary from minor inconvenience to disastrous consequences. The frequencies and the impact of DDoS

© Springer International Publishing Switzerland 2015
F. Cuppens et al. (Eds.): FPS 2014, LNCS 8930, pp. 347–355, 2015.
DOI: 10.1007/978-3-319-17040-4_23

attacks have motivated the Internet security community to provide techniques for preventing, detecting, and surviving such attacks [2]. Yet, as the magnitude of the attacks scale, new approaches are needed to protect the victim as well as reduce the impact on the networking infrastructure. Towards this end, we demonstrate an effective method to distinguish attack traffic from legitimate traffic closer to attack sources and allow legitimate traffic access to the victim node in the event of an attack.

Researchers have worked on providing mechanisms that use traffic features to distinguish attack traffic from legitimate ones. These mechanisms are able to detect only the attacks having those specific features [1, 3]. Moreover, an attacker who knows the features that are of interest to the detection mechanism can develop strategies that bypass the detection mechanisms. For example, consider the scheme based on the abrupt change [5,7,9]. In this approach, the attacker can bypass the detection mechanism by sending out attack flow to change the statistics of the traffic. Moreover, a major drawback of these approaches is that they cannot discriminate flash crowd traffic from DDoS attack traffic. History-based IP Filtering (HIF) [11] is an efficient approach proposed to discriminate good traffic from bad traffic. This approach is based on monitoring the number of the new source IP addresses instead of the volume of the traffic. HIF keeps a history of the legitimate IP addresses that have appeared before and applies filters based on this history at the edge routers. However, an adversary can bypass this mechanism by starting to send packets with its IP address frequently and establish TCP connections. Therefore, we need a more robust and efficient defense mechanism. The goal of this paper is to introduce and evaluate a responsive defense mechanism against DDoS attacks. The first challenge is how to detect attack traffic without misclassifying legitimate traffic. We look into multiple features of DDoS attacks and normal traffic to extract characteristics that provide information about the occurrence of the DDoS attack. These features and their relationships are used to establish a high confidence IP address history. The high confidence IP history will be used to create filters. When the attack is blocked by an efficient and good filtering mechanism, the victim node can continue to receive most of the normal traffic and remain operational. This feature makes filtering technique a desirable solution; however, filtering has additional overheads. During an attack, the filters must be propagated to the upstream routers and these routers must check each packet to determine whether it is legitimate or not. Towards this end, we propose an efficient approach based on Bloom filter data structure, which facilitates a distributed response from routers closer to attack nodes and serves to prohibit attack packets from reaching the victim node while allowing the legitimate traffic to pass through.

The rest of the paper is organized as follows. Section 2 describes the proposed method to discriminate DDoS attacks from normal traffic in details. Section 3 validates our model using DARPA dataset. Section 4 concludes the paper with pointers to future directions.

2 Responsive Defense Mechanism

In this section, we explain our approach for classifying normal and attack traffic. To successfully respond to attack the approach must accurately detect the attacks and respond by minimally blocking legitimate traffic. It should also have low communication, computation, and storage overheads. An unusually high traffic volume may not be a good indicator of a DDoS attack, as it can occur due to flash crowds as well. We need to consider other features that help distinguish DDoS attacks from normal traffic. During bandwidth attacks, most source IP addresses are new to the victim, whereas most IP addresses in a flash crowd have appeared at the victim before [4]. Peng et al. [10] advocate the use of network connection history to distinguish good packets from bad ones. Many enterprises, e.g., universities, banks, etc., also have a large fraction of users that access their services regularly. Although the user base fluctuates with new additions and deletions, such a base changes at a much slower time scale compared to attacks and disruptions. These observations often form the basis of mechanisms to filter out the attack traffic. However, the attacker can bypass the history-based IP filtering if the attacker establishes a history by communicating with the victim prior to conducting the attack. We address this problem by using multiple features that help distinguish normal and attack traffic and by developing accurate normal traffic signatures and a scoring mechanism based on these features.

2.1 Feature Selection

We investigated DDoS attacks in details in order to find the features that help distinguish between attacks and normal traffic. Lee et al. [6] mention some parameters such as source/destination IP address, port number, and packet type (ICMP, TCP, UDP) that have been used to detect DDoS attacks. We will use them together with packet size to form the features in our identification model. The other feature is the frequency of an IP address. Recall that, Jung et al. [4] determined that most source IP addresses are new to the victim during bandwidth attacks, whereas with flash crowd traffic known source IP addresses are most common. Moreover, since our goal is in creating a history based only on legitimate and valid IP addresses, we only consider those IP addresses with a successful TCP handshake. Note that, a spoofed IP address will not have a complete three-way handshake [10]. Our approach uses a much more comprehensive set of features compared to existing identification approaches, and use them in an integrated manner to create filters as described later in Sect. 2.2.

2.2 History Capture

With the set of relevant parameters $p = \{p_i | i \in [0, n]\}$, our model maintains the frequency and Cumulative Distribution Function (CDF) metrics.

1. *Frequency:* The frequency f_i is the fraction of packets matching parameter p_i within a time window to create a signature.

$$f_i = \frac{F_i}{\sum\limits_{j=1}^{n} F_j} \tag{1}$$

F_i is the number of packets that matches on the basis of parameter P_i during the window. The frequency distribution is then defined as $f = \{f_1, \ldots, fn\}$.

2. *Cumulative Distribution Function (CDF):* The CDF $C_X(x)$ measures the probability that the variable X takes on a value less than or equal to x

$$CDFC_X(x) = P(X \leqslant x) \tag{2}$$

Our goal is to define a good signature to make the IP address database accurate and robust and make it hard to pass by an attacker. A key observation that can be used for defense against DDoS attack is that the DDoS attacks tend to use randomly spoofed IP addresses [12] and the other packet features, such as, port number and size of packet, which are selected randomly as well. Moreover, the interaction of these features also exhibits some anomaly when compared to that of the normal traffic. Therefore, we make use of the individual features, and also the interactions, in defining the signature. The signature is based on the CDF of each parameter's frequency during the training period. For instance, the signature of port number is CDF of each port number's frequency and measure the probability that the each port number's frequency can take value equal or less than it. This signature for each feature determines which frequent value is more reliable during normal traffic conditions. This signature assists us in selecting reliable IP addresses during the training period. The next step is assigning scores to packets in the training period and generating the source IP address history. The score value for each packet depends on the frequencies and the signatures of its selected features. Frequency threshold α_j, which indicates the level of reliability in our model, for the various levels and the corresponding scores are presented in Table 1. If the value of a selected feature is more than α_j in the related signature, it is assigned a score b_j indicating the confidence level. Four levels $b_4 > b_3 > b_2 > b_1$ (Table 1) are defined to select different levels of reliable IP addresses,). In our model, α_j defined as 70 %, 50 %, and 30 % indicate how the selected feature follows the signature of normal traffic condition and different cases are presented in Table 1. Note the value of frequency threshold α_j can be adjusted dynamically for each victim node. According to our model, when the selected feature follows the signature of normal traffic more strongly, we provide it a higher weight by assigning the score b_4.

Table 1. The score manager

Case	Frequency	Conclusion	Score
1	$\geq \alpha_1$ (=70%)	High Confidence	$b_4 = 4$
2	$\geq \alpha_2$ (=50%)	Medium	$b_3 = 3$
3	$\geq \alpha_3$ (=30%)	Low	$b_2 = 2$
4	$< \alpha_4$ (=30%)	Potential threat	$b_1 = 1$

s_i is defined as the score value for each IP address i and is determined according to the frequency distribution f_i and confidence degree b_j in Eq. 3 and the overall score S_{IP} is computed from Eq. 4. Where the n is the number parameters.

$$S_i = f_i * b_j \tag{3}$$

$$S_{IP} = \sum_{i=1}^{n} S_i \tag{4}$$

The IP addresses that have an overall score S_{IP} higher than a threshold v are selected as legitimate IP addresses.

Since the filtering mechanism is to be applied closer to the victim point, and the network bandwidth may already be saturated during an attack, transferring the entire history and looking it up in the upstream routers during the attack may be extremely high cost to pay since upstream routers must also process all the packets targeted towards the victim node. This will impose an additional overhead on the routers. To overcome this problem, we use the Bloom filter [8] mechanism to represent efficiently the filtering mechanism. This way, the victim node does not transfer the full list of IP addresses in the history to the upstream routers, but instead transfers a Bloom filter that represents the contents of the IP address history. It causes a significant reduction of message traffic and introduces an efficient filtering mechanism. This approach reduces the overhead cost significantly in the ingress routers since every packet that comes to a victim node during attack must be checked.

3 Model Validation

The objective of this experiment is to evaluate the accuracy and robustness of our filtering model to protect against DDoS attacks. To illustrate the effect of signature to distinguish attack and normal traffic we examined the DARPA 1998 Intrusion Detection dataset [15]. It contains 7 weeks of training datasets to generate signatures and establish an IP address history and 2 weeks of testing data set to evaluate our technique. The training part of the dataset consists of normal traffic as well as labeled attacks. This data set therefore provides features important for our evaluation as our goal is evaluate how signature and score mechanism is robust in discriminating malicious and normal traffic without misclassifying them.

3.1 Results

The first step is to create the IP address history from the training dataset according to the generated signatures and the overall score of selected features. The second step constructs the Bloom filter based on the results of the first step. In the first step, the signature of the port number, the size of the packet and IP address's frequency rate are created for each traffic type (ICMP, TCP, UDP) separately. In the next step, the IP address history is created based on the overall score and threshold value of v. In our experiment, v is determined to be 0.36. This value means the signature of at least two selected features should have α_j more than 50 % and one should have it more than 30 % at training time; however, this value can be set to a higher value for more protection. The value of v is a trade-off among history size, history accuracy, and protection rate. I Increasing the value of increases the size of history and protection rate, while decreasing the accuracy of history to pass legitimate traffic. Signature-based IP address history is evaluated on the basis of these parameters: (i) *Attack detection rate* (ii) *Normal traffic detection rate* (iii) *False negative rate*. Figure 1 shows the effectiveness of using signature to distinguish attack and normal traffic for different types of traffic. It is interesting to see that the false negative rate is around 1 % for TCP, UDP and ICMP when we consider all selected features in our model. We evaluate the effectiveness of each selected feature to create accurate and robustness filtering as well. As shown in Fig. 1, the false negative rate decreases as we use more features. Note that, in the figures simple history refers to creating history just based on frequency of IP addresses that were presented in [10]. It shows how the signature and score mechanism could be more effective for determining an accurate filter compared with another existing approach.

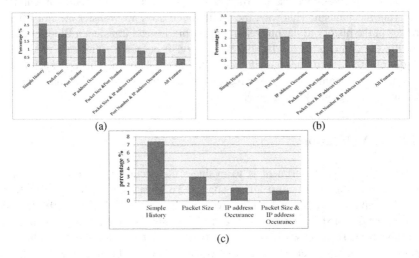

(a)   (b)

(c)

Fig. 1. False Negative Rate: (a) TCP, (b) UDP, (c) ICMP

The Bloom filter is evaluated with 2 weeks testing DARPA dataset. As shown in Fig. 2, attack detection rate is around 99.2 % for TCP traffic and 99.6 % and 99.8 % for UDP and ICMP traffic if we consider all selected features to create the history. Note that, the attack detection rate decreases if we consider fewer features and it goes down to 88 % for simple history condition.

The other important parameter to consider is how many normal packets can pass through the Bloom filter. As shown in Fig. 3, normal traffic detection rate is around 70 % for TCP and UDP traffic and it is more than 82 % for ICMP. This demonstrates that the signature based IP address performance is highly reliable for aborting malicious packets and withholding only little legitimate traffic. Normal traffic detection rate increases to around 75 % to 85 % if fewer features are used to generate IP address history, but the attack detection rate decreases at the same time. Thus, there is a tradeoff between accuracy of the attack detection rate and normal traffic detection rate. The evaluation part shows effective results in successful filtering of attack traffic and

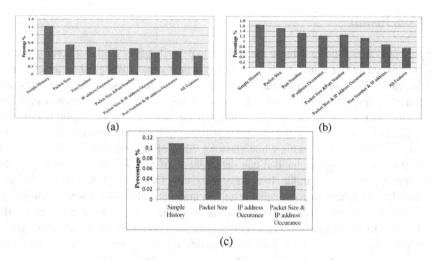

(a)   (b)

(c)

Fig. 2. Percentage of attack that can pass filtering (a) TCP, (b) UDP, (c) ICMP

permitting the normal traffic during the attack time. The experiment result verifies that our signature mechanism can be deployed in real networks as it has addressed some critical drawbacks of the previous approaches.

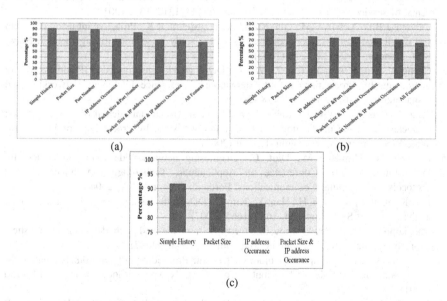

(a)   (b)

(c)

Fig. 3. Normal traffic detection rate (a) TCP, (b) UDP, (c) ICMP

4 Conclusion

We presented a responsive defense mechanism to defend against denial of service attacks. We introduced a signature-based filtering mechanism that distinguishes attacks from normal traffic. We have demonstrated how to form a history based filter that takes into account a rich set of header fields of traffic. We then presented a filtering mechanism based on Bloom filter structure that can be rapidly distributed to responsive points closer to attack sources. Our experiment indicates that our filtering model can protect the victim node from 99 % of attack traffic while allowing 70 % of legitimate traffic. In addition, it shows that the filtering mechanism can detect 99 % of attacks that want to bypass the filtering during the normal traffic. In contrast to existing DDoS attack detection techniques such as HIF, our scheme is more reliable and accurate, and also has a lower overhead. An mechanism to determine how bloom filters can distribute through the network to stop the attack close to the source of attack is our next step and will be presented in future publication. as a future work, we plan to test the efficacy of our approach on real networks. In addition, our future work includes extending our scheme for IPv6.

References

1. Beitollahi, H., Deconinck, G.: Analyzing well known countermeasures against distributed denial of service attacks. Comput. Commun. 35(11), 1312–1332 (2012)
2. Cabrera, J.B.D., Lewis, L.M., Qin, X.Z., Lee, W., Mehra, R.K.: Proactive intrusion detection and distributed denial of service attacks - a case study in security management. J. Netw. Syst. Manage. 10(2), 225–254 (2002)
3. Cheng, J., Yin, J., Liu, Y., Cai, Z., Wu, C.: DDoS attack detection using IP address feature interaction. In: Proceedings of 1st International Conference Intelligent Networking and Collaborative Systems, pp. 113–118 (2009)
4. Jung, J., Krishnamurthy, B., Rabinovich, M.: Flash crowds and denial of service attacks: characterization and implications for CDNs and web sites. In: Proceedings of 11th World Wide Web conference, Honolulu, Hawaii (2002)
5. Lakhina, A., Crovella, M., Diot, C.: Diagnosing network-wide traffic anomalies. In: Proceedings of 2004 Conference on Applications, Technologies, Architectures, and Protocols for Computer Communications, Portland, Oregon, USA (2004)
6. Lee, K., Kim, J., Kwon, K.H., Han, Y., Kim, S.: DDoS attack detection method using cluster analysis. Expert Syst. Appl. 34, 1659–1665 (2007)
7. Manikopoulos, C., Papavassiliou, S.: Network intrusion and fault detection: a statistical anomaly approach. IEEE Commun. Mag. 40(10), 76–82 (2002)
8. Mitzenmacher, M.: Compressed bloom filters. In: Proceedings of the 20th Annual ACM Symposium on Principles of Distributed Computing, Newport, Rhode Island, pp. 144–150 (2001)
9. Noh, S., Jung, G., Choi, K., Lee, C.: Compiling network traffic into rules using soft computing methods for the detection of flooding attacks. J. Appl. Soft Comput. 8(3), 1200–1210 (2008)
10. Peng, T., Leckie, C., Ramamohanarao, K.: Protection from distributed denial of service attack using history-based IP filtering. In: Proceedings of IEEE International Conference on Communications, Anchorage, Alaska, pp. 482–486 (2003)

11. Peng, T., Leckie, C., Ramamohanarao, K.: Proactively detecting distributed denial of service attacks using source ip address monitoring. In: Mitrou, N.M., Kontovasilis, K., Rouskas, G. N., Iliadis, I., Merakos, L. (eds.) NETWORKING 2004. LNCS, vol. 3042, pp. 771–782. Springer, Heidelberg (2004)
12. Peng, T., Leckie, C., Ramamohanarao, K.: Survey of network-based defense mechanisms countering the DoS and DDoS problems. ACM Comput. Surv. **39**(1), 1–42 (2007)
13. RioRey, Inc.: 2009–2012, RioRey Taxonomy of DDoSAttacks, RioRey_Taxonomy_ Rev_2.3_2012 (2012). http://www.riorey.com/x-resources/2012/RioRey_Taxonomy_DDoS_ Attacks2012.eps
14. Waikato Applied Network Dynamics Research Group. Auckland university data traces. http://wand.cs.waikato.ac.nz/wand/wits/
15. http://www.darkreading.com/attacks-and-breaches/ddos-attack-hits-400-gbit-s-breaks-record/d/d-id/1113787

Automated Extraction of Vulnerability Information for Home Computer Security

Sachini Weerawardhana, Subhojeet Mukherjee,
Indrajit Ray$^{(\boxtimes)}$, and Adele Howe

Computer Science Department, Colorado State University,
Fort Collins, CO 80523, USA
{sachini,mukherje,indrajit,howe}@cs.colostate.edu

Abstract. Online vulnerability databases provide a wealth of information pertaining to vulnerabilities that are present in computer application software, operating systems, and firmware. Extracting useful information from these databases that can subsequently be utilized by applications such as vulnerability scanners and security monitoring tools can be a challenging task. This paper presents two approaches to information extraction from online vulnerability databases: a machine learning based solution and a solution that exploits linguistic patterns elucidated by part-of-speech tagging. These two systems are evaluated to compare accuracy in recognizing security concepts in previously unseen vulnerability description texts. We discuss design considerations that should be taken into account in implementing information retrieval systems for security domain.

Keywords: Security · Vulnerability · Information extraction · Named entity recognition

1   Introduction

Hardening a home computer against malicious attacks requires identifying the different ways in which the system can be attacked, and then enacting security controls to prevent these attacks. This, in turn, requires deeper analysis to understand the contribution of different vulnerabilities towards an attack on the system, the role of a specific system configuration, the actions that an attacker must take to exploit the vulnerabilities, and, perhaps most importantly, the advertant / inadvertent contributions that home-user activities make in a successful exploit.

Researchers, including our group, have been investigating ways to capture these relationships and merge them into models of system security risk. On-line vulnerability databases, such as the National Vulnerability Database (NVD - http://nvd.nist.gov), contain a wealth of information that is needed for creating

This material is based upon work supported by the National Science Foundation under Grant No. 0905232.

F. Cuppens et al. (Eds.): FPS 2014, LNCS 8930, pp. 356–366, 2015.
DOI: 10.1007/978-3-319-17040-4_24

these system risk models. Unfortunately, these vulnerability databases (VDs) have been created by humans primarily for the use of humans. A major problem is that VDs store vulnerability descriptions as natural language plaintexts. Important information, such as attacker actions and user actions, are seldom explicitly stated but rather remain implicit. A human expert is able to infer this from the description but this is challenging for an automated tool. Automating the extraction is further complicated by the fact that these descriptions vary significantly in how they describe the different pieces of information.

Roschke et al. [12] investigate the problem of extracting vulnerability information from semi-structured plaintexts with a goal of comparing and merging vulnerability information from multiple sources. However, this scheme requires developing customized extraction rule-sets for each individual databases, and is limited in its ability to extract information buried in natural language phrases. Urbanska et al. [15] also describe a similar approach for extracting information from VDs, based on designing customized extraction filters. Although this approach is able to extract crucial information such as attacker actions, it performs very poorly in extracting user action information. Moreover, the accuracy of the approach is heavily dependent on the quality of filters developed, which is a manual process.

A Named Entity Recognition (NER) system, employing a large corpus of hand annotated data extracted from different sources (vulnerability databases, blogs and news articles) is described in [5,11]. A Conditional Random Fields (CRF) classifier [17] is trained on the corpus to identify portions of the text describing the concepts. Each portion is then processed to build associations between the concepts using an IDS Ontology specifically created for the security domain. A problem with this approach is that it is not able to extract information such as user or attacker actions. A bootstrapping algorithm called PACE is used for NER in computer security [10]. Its learning algorithm is pre-trained on a small set of known entity names (Exploit Effect, Software Name, Vulnerability Potential Effects, Vulnerability Category) and known patterns. A limitation of this approach is that the model needs to be trained on a large corpus (usually in the millions).

In this paper, we describe our efforts to design a tool to automatically extract severity information from natural language descriptions. Our work is designed to populate a model that we had proposed earlier [16], called the Personalized Attack Graph (PAG). Our approach is based on designing a NER that identifies key PAG parameters embedded in the text of a vulnerability description: software name, version, impact, attacker action, and user action. We experiment with two different NER approaches, one using machine-learning (ML) techniques, and the other exploiting lexical patterns in a parts-of-speech (POS) tagged text. The two approaches are then evaluated to compare their accuracy in recognizing security concepts embedded within newly encountered vulnerability descriptions.

Two labeled corpora are available for security vulnerability descriptions [1,5]. We use Joshi et al.'s corpus [5] to validate the performance of one of our approaches that is similar to their approach. However, the PAG representation requires identification of security concepts not supported by Joshi et al.'s corpus, most notably attacker and user actions. We, therefore, constructed our own corpus comprising of 210 randomly selected vulnerability descriptions taken from NVD as of April 2014. We used the BRAT web based annotation tool [7] to manually annotate the descriptions with the labels required for our PAG model. The annotation task was done by a computer science graduate student with substantial knowledge of computer security. We chose BRAT because it could be easily configured to allow for annotation of custom entity types. Our corpus consists of 8409 labeled tokens: 3821 default label tokens and 4588 security concept label tokens.

2   Our Approach to Extracting Computer Vulnerability Information

We implemented two independent NER solutions: a machine learning module and a part-of-speech, rule-based component. Machine learning is less brittle and may be able to accommodate examples never before seen. However, it requires training examples and a well selected set of features to support generalization. Rule systems can be efficient and well tailored to the domain; however, the accuracy drops quickly when new examples fail to match previous ones.

2.1   Machine Learning Module

The process of producing a machine-learning (ML) model for the task can be divided into two parts: feature selection and model training.

Feature Selection: We adopted the same features as in [5]: Taggy-sequences, N-grams, UsePrev, UseNext, Word-pairs, and Gazette. For the gazette, we compiled a list of software and operating systems consisting of 48709 entries using the product information repository available at www.secunia.com.

Model Training: We chose the Stanford Named Entity Recognizer (Stanford NER), that implements a CRF classifier [4]. It has the chosen features already built-in, and its CRF classifier has been widely adopted for custom NERs [13]. CRF takes into account contextual information by considering sequences of tokens, a property that can be specifically exploited by the structure of vulnerability descriptions.

2.2   Part-of-Speech Tagging

POS tagging allowed us to discover patterns in the grammatical structure of a vulnerability description and define a set of rules.

Identifying Software Names and Versions: POS tagging labels a word in text based on its role in the sentence (e.g., noun, verb, adjective, etc.) and the context in which it is used. We manually analyzed a sample of 30 vulnerability descriptions from NVD to identify persistent patterns of POS. We found that software names are typically tagged as NNP (proper nouns) and version numbers are tagged as CD (cardinal numbers). This rule was applicable to 100 % of the sample.

Software names are often followed by an IN tag (a preposition or subordinating conjunction), e.g., "Adobe Reader *before* 10.3". About half (45 %) of the descriptions followed this rule. A variation to this rule happens when a software name is preceded by an IN tag and followed by another IN tag (e.g., "index.html in Mozilla Firefox 5.4 through 6.0"), which accounted for another 30 % of the examples. For 17 %, a software name is immediately followed by a CD tag (e.g., "Adobe Reader 9.3"). The remaining 6 % were rare or erroneous structures (e.g., software name without a version number), which suggests that it would be difficult to achieve 100 % accuracy.

Our POS tag processing algorithm is based on the observed patterns. We use 3-grams because they best match the length of common software names (e.g., "Adobe Acrobat Reader"). The Stanford coreNLP POS Tagger [14] provide the POS mappings. For each sequence of 3-grams, the algorithm checks for the specific patterns. If one of the patterns is found, then a gazette (see Sect. 2.1) lookup is performed to identify the selected NNP tag as a software name. If none of the conditions are satisfied, a regular expression matching is performed. The 3-grams are then processed to identify any tokens tagged as CDs to find version numbers.

Identifying File Names, Modifiers and Vulnerability Type: File names in vulnerability descriptions typically denote a specific system artifact in which vulnerabilities are present. We try to identify modifiers, i.e., words that are used to indicate specific information about vulnerable software versions, as well as vulnerability types. File names are matched to a regular expression for

```
base_name.file_extension:
[[A-Z][a-z]{1, }]*[_-]?[[A-Z][a-z]{1,}0-9]*\\. [A-Z]?[a-z]{1,4}
```

Modifiers typically follow version numbers (e.g. "version 4.0 through 5.1") and are tagged as IN. Each description is separated into POS Tag - Value pairs (e.g. {before, IN},{2.0, CD}). To find phrases with version numbers, the description is scanned to find words that have been tagged as CD. If a word tagged as CD is found in the description, POS tag of the word preceding a version number is checked. If this POS tag is of type IN, then the associated word is identified as a modifier. Identifying vulnerability type was done by searching for keywords: "vulnerability", "vulnerabilities" and "in". Then, the adjacent adjectives (POS tag JJ) are extracted.

Identifying Attacker Actions, Impacts, User Actions: To extract attacker, user actions and impact entities, we first partition a description into separate sentences and then discard information such as "*aka Bug id ...*", "*related to ..vulnerability*" etc., which we know for sure can not be included as a part of the final result.

Identifying human actors is a two step process, which includes the use of the Stanford Parser [6], the Stanford Typed Dependency Representation [9], and

WordNet Glosses [3], via the API RiWordNet(http://rednoise.org/rita/reference/ RiWordNet.html). First, we identify actors as the nominal subject, agent or the direct object of a verb. In case of a passive nominal subject dependency, we consider the passive agent as an indirect actor. We extract the WordNet Glosses [3] for these subjects, and if the glosses contain terms like *"human"*, *"person"* or *"someone"*, we classify these as human actors.

However, at this point, we do not have enough evidence to identify the indirect actors as humans. Hence, we perform a search across the generated parsed dependency tree, pushing verbs into a stack, if they are directly related to both the passive nominal subjects and their governing verbs. As each verb is popped from the stack, it is verified whether its dependent is a non-human nominal subject or agent. If so, the concerned indirect actor is considered non-human and the iteration ends; else the verb is added to the stack and the iteration continues. If at the end of the search process, an indirect actor is found to have no direct or indirect relation with another non-human subject or agent, it is added to the list of human actors for further processing.

Each actor is attributed with a set of verbs and modifiers which are directly or indirectly related to this actor. If the actor is indirect, the set of verbs and modifiers for that actor can be enumerated as: $humanActor.VerbList \leftarrow$ $\{governing\ verb,\ open\ clausal\ complements\ of\ governing\ verb\}$ and $humanActor.ModifierList \leftarrow \{adjective\ modifiers\ for\ direct\ object\ of\ governing\ verb\}$ respectively, else, as $humanActor.VerbList \leftarrow \{governing\ verb,\ reduced\ non - finite\ verbal\ modifiers\ of\ the\ dependent,\ open\ clausal\ complements\ of\ governing\ verb\}$ and $humanActor.ModifierList \leftarrow \{adjective\ modifiers\ for\ direct\ object\ of\ governing\ verb,\ adjective\ modifiers\ of\ the\ dependent\}$ respectively.

Since, in vulnerability summaries, the actor is not always referred to as "attacker", our next step involves identifying the actor as a "malicious attacker" or a "benign user"/"victim." In these cases, we analyze the sentiment value, obtained using SentiWordNet [2], of each of the verbs and modifiers attributed to the actor. This step assumes that the actors are malicious if the set of verbs or modifiers attributed to them contains at least one verb or modifier with a negative sentiment. We assign such actors as attackers, and others as victims.

To identify attacker actions, impact, and user actions, we consider each verb that has been attributed to each actor and identify the minimal verb phrases or sub-sentences they belong to. The term "minimal phrases/sub-sentence" refers to phrases or sub-sentences that do not contain any nested phrases or sub-sentences of the same type. Each phrase/sub-sentence is then considered individually and added to the *impacts*; any nested minimal verb and/or preposition phrase is extracted from it. The nested verb phrases are tested for starting verbs like "resulting" and "using" to denote them as *impact* or *attacker-action* respectively. The preposition phrases are first extended to the end of the verb-phrase/sub-sentence, and then verified for a starting preposition like "by", "through", "with", "via", etc. to be judged as *attacker-action*.

Finally, we perform a clean-up procedure. In this phase, for all actors, and for the three categories – user actions, impacts, and attacker actions – we verify whether any of these strings is a complete sub-string of another. If so, we completely remove the smaller string from the larger string. However, we do not remove an *attacker action* from a different *attacker action* if both of them belong to the same actor. If any of these strings contain a minimal noun phrase enclosing the noun that identifies the actor, that section is also removed. Also, if the final strings start or end with stopwords and/or whitespaces/punctuations we remove them.

3 Evaluating the Extraction

A completely automatic extraction process requires a level of natural language understanding that is not currently feasible. Our evaluation focuses on what can currently be done. Thus, we ran two experiments to examine the following questions: What is the accuracy of the two approaches? How much can we reasonably automate? Are some concepts harder to automate than others? Are the two approaches complementary, favoring a hybrid approach as was done in [5]? The experiments were:

1. Validate that the performance of the re-implementation of the NER solution is similar to results reported by authors in [5].
2. Compare the performance of the two approaches with a focus on identifying trade-offs and possible complementarity.

We compute precision (Prec), recall (Rec) and F-measure (F1) [8] on a particular testing data set and for different entity labels to determine whether some labels are more difficult to automatically extract and whether the approaches differ in how accurately they extract each type.

3.1 Validate Implementation

The performance reported in [5] was computed on their own corpus (referred to as "Joshi corpus".) As the first part of validation, we computed the performance of our ML approach using the "Joshi corpus" and following their procedure (five-fold cross-validation) as closely as possible. Next, we trained our ML approach on our corpus and compared the performance to see whether the corpora differences led to significant differences in performance.

The most salient difference between the two corpora was in the labels extracted; because our labels were derived from the PAG model, our token set and "Joshi corpus"'s were not identical although had considerable overlap. Performance was calculated based only on the labels in the intersection: software, operating system, file name, NER-modifier, and consequence/impact.

Validation Experiment Setup: The Joshi corpus was partitioned into five equal sized sets: four sets for training and one set for testing. This corpus comprised four different sources – NVD, security blogs, Microsoft product specific vulnerabilities, and Adobe product specific vulnerabilities; the partitioning ensured that each source contributed uniformly to the set of descriptions in each partition. Our corpus (which we call "NVD") included labels from 210 vulnerability descriptions extracted from NVD. Both corpora were trained using the CRF Classifier with 5-fold cross validation..

Validation Experiment Results: Table 1 shows the results reported in [5] ("Orig") compared to the results of our ML approach (mean and standard deviation over the five folds) when trained/tested on different corpora. Our solution on the Joshi corpus performs similarly to the reported results on Operating System and File (difference is less than the standard deviation); our precision was lacking on NER-Modifier and Impact.

For each metric (precision, recall and F1) we ran two-tailed t-tests to test for statistically significant differences in the accuracies. At the $\alpha < 0.05$ level, we found significant differences in eight out of 15; however, a Bonferroni adjustment would reduce the threshold to 0.003 leading to significant differences on only NER-Modifier and F1 for File. While we cannot use this analysis to confirm that there is no difference, it is likely that the differences were due to the disparate sizes of the corpora and to differences in the sources. Performance on NER-Modifier and Impact were improved on our corpus, while the others were worsened.

Table 1. Accuracy metrics and t-test results for validation. Orig is as reported in [5].

Label	Metric	Orig	Joshi Corpus Mean	Joshi Corpus SD	NVD Corpus Mean	NVD Corpus SD	t-test $P <$
File	Prec	1.00	1.00	0.00	0.96	0.09	0.35
	Rec	1.00	1.00	0.00	0.35	0.22	0.36
	F1	1.00	1.00	0.00	0.58	0.14	0.002
Impact	Prec	0.71	0.45	0.08	0.58	0.08	0.20
	Rec	0.69	0.57	0.09	0.79	0.11	0.01
	F1	0.70	0.54	0.08	0.67	0.09	0.04
NER Modifier	Prec	0.79	0.48	0.15	0.94	0.02	0.002
	Rec	0.67	0.61	0.12	0.82	0.40	0.002
	F1	0.72	0.52	0.13	0.96	0.01	0.001
Operating System	Prec	0.95	0.91	0.04	0.54	0.40	0.25
	Rec	0.95	0.97	0.01	0.63	0.40	0.29
	F1	0.95	0.94	0.03	0.56	0.39	0.24
Software	Prec	0.86	0.65	0.05	0.53	0.05	0.008
	Rec	0.84	0.81	0.08	0.75	0.03	0.13
	F1	0.85	0.72	0.06	0.62	0.04	0.01

3.2   Compare Approaches

The second experiment compares the relative merits of our two approaches for the labels needed to represent our PAG model.

Comparison Experiment Setup: Essentially, the same procedure was followed for the ML approach as in the validation experiment. To assess the POS approach, we followed the same procedure except that no training was required;

Table 2. Accuracy metrics and t-test results for the two approaches on our corpus. "Diff" is the ML minus POS – difference between the two approaches on that metric; "Max" is the maximum value for the two.

Label	Metric	ML Mean	SD	POS Mean	SD	Diff	Max	t-test P <
File	Prec	0.96	0.09	0.72	0.15	0.24	0.96	0.015
	Rec	0.35	0.22	0.96	0.06	-0.60	0.96	0.001
	F1	0.58	0.14	0.81	0.12	-0.24	0.81	0.021
Impact	Prec	0.58	0.08	0.94	0.06	-0.36	0.94	0.001
	Rec	0.79	0.11	0.80	0.11	-0.01	0.80	0.880
	F1	0.67	0.09	0.86	0.08	-0.19	0.86	0.007
NER-Modifier	Prec	0.94	0.02	0.99	0.01	-0.05	0.99	0.003
	Rec	0.82	0.40	0.97	0.02	-0.14	0.97	0.132
	F1	0.96	0.01	0.98	0.01	-0.02	0.98	0.108
Operating System	Prec	0.54	0.40	0.26	0.08	0.28	0.54	0.348
	Rec	0.63	0.40	0.90	0.10	-0.26	0.90	0.377
	F1	0.56	0.39	0.40	0.10	0.16	0.56	0.551
Software	Prec	0.53	0.05	0.71	0.06	-0.17	0.71	0.001
	Rec	0.75	0.03	0.77	0.07	-0.02	0.77	0.509
	F1	0.62	0.04	0.74	0.04	-0.11	0.74	0.003
Attacker	Prec	0.12	0.12	0.94	0.04	-0.82	0.94	0.001
	Rec	0.30	0.30	0.76	0.07	-0.46	0.76	0.001
	F1	0.17	0.17	0.84	0.05	-0.67	0.84	0.001
User	Prec	0.00	0.00	0.48	0.69	-0.48	0.48	0.158
	Rec	0.00	0.00	0.60	0.55	-0.60	0.60	0.040
	F1	0.00	0.00	0.27	0.27	-0.27	0.27	0.054
Version	Prec	0.90	0.05	0.94	0.02	-0.05	0.94	0.070
	Rec	0.97	0.03	0.90	0.03	0.07	0.97	0.006
	F1	0.93	0.04	0.92	0.03	0.01	0.93	0.572
Vulnerability	Prec	0.31	0.11	0.59	0.11	-0.28	0.59	0.004
	Rec	0.62	0.14	0.73	0.06	-0.11	0.73	0.133
	F1	0.42	0.12	0.65	0.08	-0.24	0.65	0.007

the POS approach was tested on the test set for each of the five folds. The label set was expanded to encompass other labels in our corpus : attacker action (e.g., send a crafted image file), user action (e.g., opens a crafted image file), version and vulnerability (e.g., buffer overflow).

Comparison Results: Table 2 shows the results for each token type and approach. Component has been omitted because it was not implemented for POS; the reason was that there was no unique POS pattern to identify "components" in vulnerability descriptions. For ML, $Prec = .22$, $Rec = .29$ and $F1 = .25$. As shown by "Diff", POS is usually more accurate (in 22 out of 27 cases Diff is negative). ML has better precision for File and Operating System, better recall for Version and better F1 for Operating System and Version. This is somewhat surprising given that POS was constructed based on analyzing a small number of descriptions and encoding the observed patterns. On the other hand, it is using considerable knowledge about the language.

A two-tailed t-test on each of the metrics comparing the accuracy of the two approaches overall shows statistically significant differences in 15 out of 27 using $\alpha = 0.05$ and 6 out of 27 using a Bonferroni adjustment of 0.002. Although using POS is most often effective, the five cases where ML excels suggest that the combination may lead to slightly high accuracy. Overall the accuracy is good; max ranges from 0.27 for F1 for User to 0.99 for Precision for NER-Modifier.

Both approaches had difficulty in identifying user-action concepts. This is because vulnerability descriptions we analyzed do not explicitly mention user action in the description. For this reason, from the dataset we collected to train and test the learning model, we observed precision, recall and F1 measures of 0. However, false positives were generated in some of the scenarios for both machine learning and POS solutions. The reason for this, in the case of the POS tagging solution, is inaccurate sentiment values obtained from SentiNet 3.0. Since we rely on sentiments corresponding to verbs related to an actor in a sentence or its modifiers, if the sentiment of each word is either positive or neutral, even though the subject "user" in the sentence acts as the attacker, the action of that subject is classified as user action rather than attacker action.

4   Conclusion and Future Work

This work presents two approaches to automatically extracting information related to vulnerabilities that is buried in the natural language plaintexts in vulnerability databases – a machine learning approach and a POS tagging approach. Our experiments show that the POS approach is generally better (*Prec.* and *F1*) at identifying implicit entities in vulnerability descriptions such as attacker action and impact. These implicit entities exhibit limited presence in vulnerability descriptions, which affects the model training. POS solution overcomes this weakness because it relies on grammatical patterns in the sentence and not its frequency of occurrence. In addition, the POS solution outperforms the machine learning solution in identifying explicit entities such as file names (better *Rec.*

and *F1*), software names (better *Prec.*, *Rec.* and *F1*) and versions (better *Prec.*). Therefore, we can conclude that POS tagging approach provides a feasible alternative to ML in security domain without the need for creating and maintaining large corpora.

References

1. Bridges, R.A., Jones, C.L., Iannacone, M.D., Goodall, J.R.: Automatic labeling for entity extraction in cyber security. Computing Research Repository (2013). http://arxiv.org/abs/1308.4941
2. Esuli, A., Sebastiani, F.: SentiWordNet: A publicly available lexical resource for opinion mining. In: Proceedings of the 5th Conference on Language Resources and Evaluation, Genoa, Italy, May 2006
3. Fellbaum, C.: WordNet: An Electronic Lexical Database. Bradford Books, Cambridge (1998)
4. Finkel, J.R., Grenager, T., Manning, C.: Incorporating non-local information into information extraction systems by Gibbs sampling. In: Proceedings of the 43rd Annual Meeting on Association for Computational Linguistics, Ann Arbor, MI, June 2005
5. Joshi, A., Lal, R., Finin, T., Joshi, A.: Extracting cybersecurity related linked data from text. In: Proceedings of the 7th IEEE International Conference on Semantic Computing, Irvine, CA, September 2013
6. Klein, D., Manning, C.D.: Accurate unlexicalized parsing. In: Proceedings of the 41st Annual Meeting on Association for Computational Linguistics, Sapporo, Japan, July 2003
7. Lab, N.: BRAT annotation tool (2010). http://brat.nlplab.org/
8. Makhoul, J., Kubala, F., Schwartz, R., Weischedel, R.: Performance measures for information extraction. In: Proceedings of DARPA Broadcast News Workshop, Herndon, VA, March 1999
9. de Marneffe, M.C., et al.: Generating typed dependency parses from phrase structure parses. In: Proceedings of the International Conference on Language Resources and Evaluation, Genoa, Italy, May 2006
10. McNeil, N., Bridges, R.A., Iannacone, M.D., Czejdo, B.D., Perez, N.: PACE: Pattern accurate computationally efficient bootstrapping for timely discovery of cybersecurity concepts. Computing Research Repository (2013). http://arxiv.org/abs/1308.4648
11. Mulwad, V., Li, W., Joshi, A., Finin, T., Viswanathan, K.: Extracting information about security vulnerabilities from web text. In: Proceedings of the 2011 IEEE/WIC/ACM International Conferences on Web Intelligence and Intelligent Agent Technology, Lyon, France, August 2011
12. Roschke, S., Cheng, F., Schuppenies, R., Meinel, C.: Towards unifying vulnerability information for attack graph construction. In: Samarati, P., Yung, M., Martinelli, F., Ardagna, C.A. (eds.) ISC 2009. LNCS, vol. 5735, pp. 218–233. Springer, Heidelberg (2009)
13. Settles, B.: Biomedical named entity recognition using conditional random fields and rich feature sets. In: Proceedings of the International Joint Workshop on Natural Language Processing in Biomedicine and Its Applications, Geneva, Switzerland, August 2004

14. Toutanova, K., Manning, C.D.: Enriching the knowledge sources used in a maximum entropy part-of-speech tagger. In: Proceedings of the 2000 Joint SIGDAT Conference on Empirical Methods in Natural Language Processing and Very Large Corpora, Hong Kong, October 2000
15. Urbanska, M., Ray, I., Howe, A., Roberts., M.: Structuring a vulnerability description for comprehensive single system security analysis. In: Rocky Mountain Celebration of Women in Computing, Fort Collins, CO, USA, November 2012
16. Urbanska, M., Roberts, M., Ray, I., Howe, A., Byrne, Z.: Accepting the inevitable: Factoring the user into home computer security. In: Proceedings of the Third ACM Conference on Data and Application Security and Privacy, San Antonio, TX, USA, February 2013
17. Wallach, H.M.: Conditional random fields: An introduction. CIS Technical report MS-CIS-04-21, University of Pennsylvania (2004)

A Formal Approach to Automatic Testing of Security Policies Specified in XACML

Mohamed H.E. Aouadi[✉], Khalifa Toumi, and Ana Cavalli

Télécom SudParis, 91011 Evry, France
{mohamed.aouadi,khalifa.toumi,Ana.Cavalli}@it-sudparis.eu

Abstract. Nowadays, security policies are the key point of every modern infrastructure. The specification and testing of such policies are the fundamental steps in the development of a secure system. To address both challenges, we propose a framework that automatically generates test sequences to validate the conformance of a security policy. The functional behavior of the system is specified using a formal description technique based on Extended Finite-State Machines (EFSMs), while security requirements are specified using XACML. We develop specific algorithms to integrate the security rules into the functional system specification. In this way, we obtain a complete specification of the secured system. Then, automatic test generation is performed using a dedicated tool called TestGen-IF which was developed in our laboratory. This generation is based on the security properties as test objectives. Finally, a case study is presented to demonstrate the reliability of our framework.

1 Introduction

Nowadays, ensuring that detailed information can be securely exchanged between different platforms is a real and pressing need. To maintain a certain level of security, the system behavior must be restrained by a security policy. A security policy [1,2] is a set of rules that defines the desired behavior of a user within an information system. The main objective of this policy is to describe how data and other critical system resources are protected. Generally, a security policy is written by means of a natural language specification containing statements such as "this file must be accessible to regular users between 9:00 am and 5:00 pm" or "only premium users can access the DRP." The main problem is how to verify whether system implementation conforms to its policy. However, if one cannot ensure this conformance, global security can no longer be guaranteed.

In this paper, we propose an approach that makes it possible to validate security rules. Our approach manipulates three different inputs: a functional specification of the system based on a well-known mathematically based formalism, the Extended Finite State Machine; a specification of the security policy (based on XACML [3]) that we wish to apply to this system; and an implementation of the system. Our solution provides a new specification of the system that takes into account the security policy (we call it secure functional specification),

© Springer International Publishing Switzerland 2015
F. Cuppens et al. (Eds.): FPS 2014, LNCS 8930, pp. 367–374, 2015.
DOI: 10.1007/978-3-319-17040-4_25

and then it generates tests to check whether the implementation of the system conforms with the secure functional specification.

The main contributions of this paper are as follows:

- The specification and implementation of an approach to integrate XACML security rules into a functional model described by an EFSM.
- The proposition of a method to automatically derive test sequences from a set of rules. The test generation is automatically driven through a dedicated test generation tool developed by our team.
- The application of our solution in a case study to demonstrate its reliability.

The rest of this paper is organized as follows. In Sect. 2 we discuss related work. In Sect. 3, we explain the approach to integrating these security rules with an existing specification in EFSM as well as related algorithms. In Sect. 4, we present a case study, a DRP service with security features, as well as the results through the generated test cases for the validation of security rules and the experimental results. Finally, Sect. 5 presents our conclusions and some directions for future work.

2   Related Work

Most previous work has focused either on the description of the policy itself or on the verification of rules. Security rules are defined with modalities (such as permission, prohibition, and obligation) that express possible constraints on the behavior of the system.

In [4] the authors propose a testing strategy for automatically deriving test requests from an XACML policy and describe their pilot experience in test automation using this strategy. In [5] the authors give an overview of existing security testing approaches and, based on that, develop a novel classification for model-based security tests along two dimensional-risk and automated test generation. In other works [6,7], the authors propose approaches based on active testing.

Our approach distinguishes itself from these propositions by assumptions on the policy and the method used to generate test sequences. First, we make no assumption about the description language of the policy. Instead, we propose a framework to specify rules in XACML so that we can apply them to our mathematical model. XACML supports Attribute-Based Access Control (ABAC) and can implement an access control model based on RBAC or OrBAC models, making our study more general than [8] where authors use OrBAC and than [9] where authors use O2O. Then, we generate a whole set of test cases automatically using a different test generation tool developed in our laboratory. This latter is well adapted to the EFSM formalism which makes our approach different from [7] and [8].

3   Integration Methodology

3.1   Permission Integration

This process of the algorithm begins by seeking for transitions with a permission rule to integrate. Once this transition is found, the algorithm can either create a new predicate or strengthen an existing predicate depending on the existence or the absence of a predicate in that transition. The strengthening or creation of a predicate is done by adding the conditions in the XACML security rule. This algorithm is described below.

Algorithm 1. Permissions integration

Require: The transition Tr that maps the permissions.
Each $permission_i$ applies to a $condition_i$
1: if ($\exists$ associated predicate P) then
2:      $P := P \wedge (\vee_i (condition_i))$
3: else
4:      create predicate $P := \vee_i (condition_i)$
5: end if

Figure 1 gives an example. In the left transition, the system can pass from S1 to S2 when it receives input A. If the permission involves a condition C, the transition is modified by creating a predicate, as in the left transition. This predicate returns "true" if the condition is satisfied.

Fig. 1. Permission integration

3.2   Prohibition Integration

This process of the algorithm begins by seeking for transitions with a prohibition rule to integrate. Once this transition is found, the algorithm can either create a new predicate or strengthen an existing predicate depending on the existence or the absence of a predicate in that transition. The strengthening or creation of a predicate is done by adding the opposite of each condition in the XACML security rule. This algorithm is described below.

Algorithm 2. Prohibition integration

Require: The transition Tr that maps the prohibitions.
1: if ($\exists$ associated predicate P) then
2:      $P := P \wedge (\vee_i (\neg condition_i))$
3: else
4:      create predicate $P := \vee_i (\neg condition_i)$
5: end if

An example is shown in the Fig. 2. In the left transition, the system can pass from S1 to S2 when it receives input A. If the rule specifies that the system is prohibited from sending output X in condition C, the transition is modified by the creation of a corresponding predicate, as in the left transition.

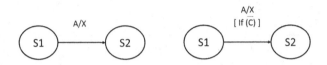

Fig. 2. Prohibition integration

4   Case Study

4.1   DRP Description

In order to demonstrate the reliability of our approach, we conduct a case study. Supported by the INTER-TRUST project, this case study is an application to a service called Dynamic Route Planning (DRP). The user (driver) wants to reach his destination by the optimal route. Therefore, he must activate the service through his client interface. Then, he must activate only the DRP service. Once the service is activated, the infrastructure (modeled as the control center) must check if the user is authorized to access the service. Here we consider at first a simple service with various features, such as those commonly used in GPS devices. First of all, the service is open to anyone. Without using the security policy, any user can access the service with premium-user privileges. Such access causes different security problems, such as denial of service and malicious use of shared data.

To tackle this problem, we specify a security rule that protects information within the organization by preventing illegitimate users from using the DRP service.

We model the specification of this system by the EFSM shown in Fig. 3. This EFSM models the initial system without security properties. This EFSM has three states S1, S2, and S3. S1 presents the initial state of the server before any interaction with the user. S2 shows that the server is connected to the user and waiting for the desired destination from the user. S3 shows that the service is monitoring the navigation of the user, indicating that it already calculated the optimal route and is just waiting for any other request from the user to stop the service or to calculate another route.

The transitions marked t_1, t_2, and t_3 are defined as follows:

- t_1: `ask_access(login, password,GPSposition) / access_authorised`
- t_2: `ask_for_route(destination,class) / response(optimalRoute)`
- t_3: `exit_service / exit_ok`

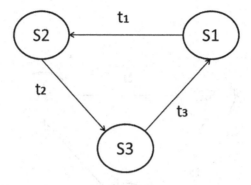

Fig. 3. Initial model of the server

4.2   Security Policy Specification

In this case study, we implement some security properties to get a secure system that considers security issues. In the security policy, services must be accessed only by authorized users. To access the DRP service, the user must introduce a valid login and password and must have a valid GPS position. Once connected to the service, the regular user can use only basic functionalities. For example, the user cannot use international navigation, which is reserved for premium users. This security policy is described in XACML. Each security rule contains one or more conditions. We can summarize the conditions as follows:

- C_1 - *GPS position is in France*
- C_2 - *login and password are valid*
- C_3 - *the user's class is PREMIUM*
- C_4 - *the user's class is REGULAR*
- C_5 - *GPS position is valid*
- C_6 - *GPS position is not in France*
- C_7 - *destination is not in France*
- C_8 - *destination is in France*

Thus, the security policy contains the three following rules:

- **Rule 1:** The server grants access to a user if he has a valid couple (login, password) and a valid GPS position.
- **Rule 2:** The server gives an international optimal route for PREMIUM users.
- **Rule 3:** The server does not give an international optimal route for REGU-LAR users.

4.3   Security Policy Integration

By applying our algorithm to the initial model and the security policy described in Subsect. 4.2 we obtain a secured model of the system that takes into account the security policy. This model is presented by the EFSM shown in Fig. 4.

The final model contains the same states, but some transitions are modified and other transitions are added. We have two new transitions:

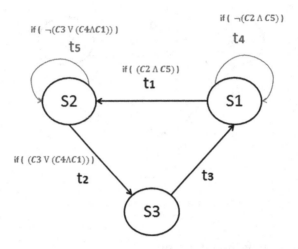

Fig. 4. Final (secure) model of the server

- t_4: ask_access (login, password, GPSposition) / access_denied
- t_5: ask_for_route(destination, class) / need_premium_class

Moreover, two transitions are modified, and two conditions are added to t_1 and t_2. Table 1 compares the model before and after security policy integration.

Table 1. Initial model of the Server

Model	Number of states	Number of transitions	Number of signals
Initial model	3	3	6
Final model	3	5	8

4.4 Experimental Results

Fixing Test Objectives. The test cases are generated by using an automatic test case generation tool, TestGen-IF [10], which is based on the Hit-Or-Jump [11] algorithm. The tool generates a test case guided by predefined test purposes which are sequences of conditions. A test purpose verifies that when the server communicates with its environment and if a security rule is satisfied, the server behaves as specified by the security rule. In order to validate the security between the server and its environment, we define for each security rule the corresponding test purpose and obtain seven test cases that cover all of the security policy. The first step in the experimentation is the specification of the system into an IF code format.

While defining the test purposes, we notice that in some cases, we need more than one condition in a test purpose to verify a security rule. For example, when a user tries to access a DRP service in a foreign country, the server should check if the user's class is premium before granting an access. In this case, we define the test purpose as a sequence of two conditions. The first condition verifies that the user is in a foreign country. The second condition verifies that the user's class is premium.

Test Case Generation. Using the TestGen-IF tool we are able to generate a test sequence that verifies the two conditions. Figure 5 shows the test case generated for Rule 3 (presented in 4.2). Note that the inputs and outputs are applied and observed by the tester.

```
?ask_access{log1,pwd1,GPSin}  !access_autorised{}

?ask_for_route{destinationOut,regular}  !response{optimalRoute}

?ask_for_route{destinationIn,regular}  !response{optimalRoute}

?exit_service{}  !exit_ok{}
```

Fig. 5. Test case related to security rule 3

5   Conclusions

In this paper, we present a formal approach to testing security rules specified in XACML. We propose a method to integrate security rules in a functional model represented by an EFSM. A detailed study is carried out to specify the transitions into which a security rule has to be integrated. The resulting functional model is used to test the security rules. Our method can be used to integrate any security policy specified with the same modality as XACML. A detailed case study is provided along with results. We plan to extend our work to consider timed security policies and to improve our approach to consider interoperability security policies.

References

1. Damianou, N., Dulay, N., Lupu, E.C., Sloman, M.: The ponder policy specification language. In: Sloman, M., Lobo, J., Lupu, E.C. (eds.) POLICY 2001. LNCS, vol. 1995, pp. 18–38. Springer, Heidelberg (2001)
2. Toumi, K., Cavalli, A., El Maarabani, M.: Role based interoperability security policies in collaborative systems. In: 2012 International Conference on Collaboration Technologies and Systems (CTS), pp. 471–477. IEEE (2012)
3. Godik, S., Anderson, A., Parducci, B., Humenn, P., Vajjhala, S.: Oasis extensible access control 2 markup language (XACML) 3, Technical report, OASIS, Technical Report (2002)
4. Bertolino, A., Daoudagh, S., Lonetti, F., Marchetti, E., Schilders, L.: Automated testing of extensible access control markup language-based access control systems. IET Softw. **7**(4), 203–212 (2013)

5. Felderer, M., Agreiter, B., Zech, P., Breu, R.: A classification for model-based security testing. In: The Third International Conference on Advances in System Testing and Validation Lifecycle, VALID 2011, pp. 109–114 (2011)
6. Li, K., Mounier, L., Groz, R., Test generation from security policies specified in or-bac. In: 31st Annual International Computer Software and Applications Conference, COMPSAC 2007, vol. 2. IEEE, pp. 255–260 (2007)
7. Senn, D., Basin, D., Caronni, G.: Firewall conformance testing. In: Khendek, F., Dssouli, R. (eds.) TestCom 2005. LNCS, vol. 3502, pp. 226–241. Springer, Heidelberg (2005)
8. Mallouli, W., Orset, J.-M., Cavalli, A., Cuppens, N., Cuppens, F.: A formal approach for testing security rules. In: Proceedings of the 12th ACM symposium on Access control models and technologies, pp. 127–132. ACM (2007)
9. El Maarabani, M., Hwang, I., Cavalli, A.: A formal approach for interoperability testing of security rules. In: 2010 Sixth International Conference on Signal-Image Technology and Internet-Based Systems (SITIS), pp. 277–284. IEEE (2010)
10. Hwang, I., Lallali, M., Cavalli, A., Verchere, D.: Modeling, validation, and verification of PCEP using the IF language. In: Lee, D., Lopes, A., Poetzsch-Heffter, A. (eds.) FMOODS 2009. LNCS, vol. 5522, pp. 122–136. Springer, Heidelberg (2009)
11. Cavalli, A., Lee, D., Rinderknecht, C., Zaïdi, F.: Hit-or-jump: An algorithm for embedded testing with applications to in services. In: Wu, J., Chanson, S.T., Gao, Q. (eds.) Formal Methods for Protocol Engineering And Distributed Systems, pp. 41–56. Springer, Ney York (1999)

Author Index

Printed in the United States
By Bookmasters